Essential Interviewing and Counseling Skills

Tracy A. Prout, PhD, is assistant professor of psychology at the Ferkauf Graduate School of Psychology. She is a licensed psychologist and has a clinical practice in New York City, where she sees children, adolescents, and adults and provides psychological testing. Dr. Prout also has a master's degree in mental health counseling. She has provided training on psychodynamic psychotherapy techniques and integrating spirituality into clinical practice for clinical professionals from many disciplines, including psychiatry residents, psychology interns, and practicing psychiatrists, psychologists, and social workers. Her research focuses on psychotherapy process within psychodynamic treatment models and the role of religion and spirituality in mental health and recovery. Dr. Prout has published peer-reviewed articles on the role of religion and spirituality in the lives of those with mental illness and the role of spirituality in pedagogy. She is a former fellow of the American Psychoanalytic Association and has completed advanced research training with the International Psychoanalytic Association at the Anna Freud Centre in London, England and at the Yale University Child Study Center. Dr. Prout is the recipient of the Dennis J. Enright Award for Excellence in Teaching and grant funding from the Psychoanalysis and the Academy Committee of the American Psychoanalytic Association.

Melanie J. Wadkins, PhD, is a clinical psychologist and assistant professor of psychology at the Ferkauf Graduate School of Psychology. She is on the faculty of the combined School-Clinical Child Psychology program and provides training to doctoral students in evidence-based interventions for youth and cognitive assessment. In addition, Dr. Wadkins is senior psychologist at the Institute for Cognitive Behavior Therapy and Research in White Plains, New York. She has expertise in psychoeducational assessment and consultation, as well as in treating individuals with anxiety and mood disorders. Dr. Wadkins's research focuses primarily on anxiety and related disorders. Specifically, she is interested in the basic emotion of disgust and its relationship to the maintenance and development of anxiety disorders, as well as the treatment of anxiety. Dr. Wadkins has presented her research at national and international conferences, and her work has been published in a range of books and peer-reviewed journals. Dr. Wadkins is a faculty delegate of the National Council of Schools of Professional Psychology (NCSPP) on behalf of Ferkauf Graduate School. She is also an active member of the Association for Behavioral and Cognitive Therapies (ABCT) where she serves on the Academic Training Committee.

Essential Interviewing and Counseling Skills

An Integrated Approach to Practice

Tracy A. Prout, PhD
Melanie J. Wadkins, PhD

SPRINGER PUBLISHING COMPANY
NEW YORK

Springer Publishing Company, LLC
11 West 42nd Street
New York, NY 10036
www.springerpub.com

Acquisitions Editor: Sheri W. Sussman
Composition: Exeter Premedia Services Private Ltd.

ISBN: 978-0-8261-9915-7
e-book ISBN: 978-0-8261-9916-4
Instructor's Manual ISBN: 978-0-8261-9912-6
Instructor's PowerPoint Slides ISBN: 978-0-8261-9911-9

Instructor's Materials: Instructors may request supplements by emailing textbook@springerpub.com

14 15 16 17 / 5 4 3 2 1

The author and the publisher of this Work have made every effort to use sources believed to be reliable to provide information that is accurate and compatible with the standards generally accepted at the time of publication. The author and publisher shall not be liable for any special, consequential, or exemplary damages resulting, in whole or in part, from the readers' use of, or reliance on, the information contained in this book. The publisher has no responsibility for the persistence or accuracy of URLs for external or third-party Internet websites referred to in this publication and does not guarantee that any content on such websites is, or will remain, accurate or appropriate.

Library of Congress Cataloging-in-Publication Data
Prout, Tracy A.
Essential interviewing and counseling skills : an integrated approach to practice / Tracy A. Prout, PhD, Melanie J. Wadkins, PhD, Springer Publishing Company, LLC.
    p. ; cm.
  ISBN 978-0-8261-9915-7
1. Interviewing.   2. Counseling.   I. Title.
  BF637.I5.P76 2014
  158.3–dc23

                                                                                          2013047755

Printed in the United States of America by Bradford & Bigelow.

To my husband, Bernard F. Bunye, for his unflagging support and encouragement and incredible ability to provide comic relief.

—T.A.P.

To my wife, Evelyn Farny Wadkins, without whom this book would have been completed more quickly, but far less joyfully and with many more typographical errors.

—M.J.W.

Contents

PART II: GETTING STARTED—INTERVIEWING AND DEVELOPING A RELATIONSHIP

Foreword

Counseling and psychotherapy are dominated by theories, and with these theories there are professionals who hold strong opinions about the suitability of the theory they use for their everyday practice. These opinions have, in some cases, blinded practitioners to the value that may be present in perspectives embraced in other theoretical approaches. This is especially true among clinicians who function primarily in research settings. To illustrate, psychodynamic researchers have long held that therapeutic alliance is a centrally important feature of any successful treatment. For years, cognitive behavioral therapists seemed to deliberately ignore therapeutic alliance in their research, instead focusing on protocols and procedures that showed efficacy for different psychological disorders. When faced with the problems of treatment nonresponse or ambivalence, cognitive behavioral therapy (CBT) researchers focused largely on identifying prognostic indicators of illness, such as chronicity and specific complicating client aspects. In a telling illustration of how diligently CBT-oriented researchers avoided the concept of therapeutic alliance, Foa and Emmelkamp (1982), in their visionary book on treatment failures, only alluded to therapeutic alliance in a single chapter depicting poor treatment response in clients with obsessive compulsive disorder (OCD). This allusion came when describing how one therapist on their treatment team had a generally negative tone with clients. This seeming allergy to the concept of therapeutic alliance only recently appeared to improve, with some investigators now acknowledging the role of alliance in producing better treatment outcome (i.e., Chu et al., 2004). This is only one example, but there is evidence from both major schools of therapy that this kind of aversion to concepts from the other theory exists. This divide may be narrowing, and in *Essential Interviewing and Counseling Skills: An Integrated Approach to Practice,* Tracy A. Prout and Melanie J. Wadkins illustrate clearly how this gap between the theories and the practitioners who espouse them may be closed. For example, many practitioners of CBT do not associate psychodynamic approaches with empirical support. And yet, that is a narrow-minded assumption. Prout and Wadkins help early developing practitioners gain a full appreciation for scientific approaches from both major schools of therapy (see, for example, Chapters 3 and 7).

One could (and should) reasonably ask, "Why has this divide persisted?" There are some reasonable answers, and some that can be best addressed from a social psychological standpoint. Let us start with the social psychological perspectives. Therapists as a group self-identify as caring and empathic individuals. This is self-evident since these are people who have dedicated their professional life to helping others through emotional tumult and difficult psychological and behavioral problems. This professional identity in turn gets bound up with the manner of professional conduct. Here is where the differing theories of practice come into play. The two most dominant schools of psychological thought, psychodynamic and cognitive behavioral, appear at least superficially to be at diametrically opposite poles. One embraces discovery of inner processes (i.e., unlocking the unconscious; Davenloo, 1995) to alleviate emotional suffering, while the other emphasizes collaborative self-directed scientific inquiry to be used in the service of alleviating distress (i.e., Beck, Rush, Shaw, & Emery, 1979). These two perspectives are very different in guiding philosophy, therapeutic techniques, and means of evaluating satisfactory outcome. And yet, despite these seeming differences, there are a number of important points of intersection. These begin with the act of initiating a therapeutic contact and the manner of listening to clients, an approach adopted in a similar style regardless of theoretical orientation. Typically, introductory counseling texts take a decidedly specific theoretical stance on the point of listening strategy. Refreshingly, Prout and Wadkins intermingle listening skills that are informed from psychodynamic theory (such as content and process of information conveyance) with concepts derived from cognitive science (such as top-down and bottom-up processing; see Chapter 6).

Here is exactly where social psychological processes come into play in explaining the strong and enduring divide between theoretical approaches. First, attitude formation helps explain how these theoretical approaches become entrenched. When attitudes are held strongly, countervailing information generally only serves to strengthen the already held belief (Ajzen & Fishbein, 1977). This means that when cognitive behaviorally oriented therapists present their data supporting the efficacy of their approach, the strongly psychodynamically oriented therapists are unlikely to lend credence to these findings simply because it is counter to their already firmly held beliefs about the therapeutic process and the mechanisms of treatment effectiveness. The same is true from the other side. For example, recent research has supported a variety of so-called experiential approaches to treatment that resemble implicitly or explicitly psychodynamic approaches. One prominent example is process-experiential therapy (Elliot & Greenberg, 2007). This approach may have garnered some empirical support, but given that the form and style are so unlike that practiced by cognitive behavioral therapists it would be difficult for many in that theoretical circle to take it seriously.

Attitude explains only the resistance to incorporating different theoretical approaches into one's treatment repertoire. However, spend any time with therapists who hold one or the other theoretical approach as a strong attitude, and one finds that it is not mere rejection of the other theory that comes up in discussion. Imply in any way to a firm cognitive behavioral therapist that you are persuaded by the recent research by Meyer's group (Mihura et al., 2013) regarding the validity of specific scores of the Rorschach projective test, and the response could range from anger to rejection of any other therapeutic concepts you offer as totally invalid. Terror management theory (TMT; Pyszczynski, Greenberg, & Solomon, 1999), which also comes from the social psychology subdiscipline of psychology, helps to explain this reaction. Briefly, TMT suggests that when confronted with information that challenges one's identity, it is also construed as a threat to one's life. When confronted with this threat, even something as remote from mortality as a threat to one's personal identity (referred to as a distal threat), the reaction is often a mix of anger and revulsion. We (McKay & Ojserkis, in press) recently extended the TMT model to apply to therapists who show a strong aversion to conducting exposure therapy, with several clinical supervision examples demonstrating how strong the reaction is when practitioners are faced with circumstances that clearly call for conducting this form of CBT although it flies in the face of their theoretical orientation. Our discussion of this reaction was consistent with that described in TMT (Greenberg, personal communication).

These two social psychological perspectives help explain the behavior of therapists who hold strong attitudes and strongly identify with one or the other major theoretical school of therapy. I have deliberately listed the social psychological perspectives as other than reasonable in explaining these differences. That is because these approaches are not subject to what we would ordinarily refer to as reasonable discourse. Presented with countervailing information, one who holds a strong opinion is driven to hold that opinion more firmly. Continue to present the countervailing information, and TMT suggests you will be firmly rejected and incur a fair bit of ire. These are unreasonable responses, yet they are completely predictable.

So what are the reasonable explanations? First, many clinicians are pragmatic. That is, market forces may drive their decisions. "Give the people what they want" is in some ways the mantra of practitioners. Many clients come to therapy with expectations, and to the extent these expectations match those of the clinician, then treatment may be partially guided accordingly. If you doubt this, try convincing clients that exposure therapy is right for them when they instead feel that they need play therapy. Good luck with that. Second, many clinicians practice therapies that are widely accepted in the public eye. Further, it has long been held that therapy in general produces some beneficial outcome. The recent resolution of psychotherapy effectiveness (Campbell, Norcross, Vasquez, & Kaslow, 2013) published by Division 29 (Psychotherapy) of the American Psychological Association suggests that empirical evidence supports the use of psychotherapy, broadly defined. This would suggest that clinicians may stick to their theoretically preferred approach to treatment, safe in the knowledge that they are performing an efficacious procedure. Finally, the vast majority of practitioners do not really have the time for or interest in settling scores between the theoretical approaches. They are too pragmatic for all that, instead focusing on "what works right now with this person."

The academic world has been trying to move in some new directions to promote scientific practice by therapists, regardless of theoretical orientation. This has led to the development of clinical practice guidelines (Areán et al., in press) that emphasize empirically supported methods but do not endorse any single theoretical approach. This may help to bridge the divide that separates different theoretical approaches by conferring status to each with clear guidelines for ensuring that consumers are protected, not theoretical turf.

Counseling texts that introduce aspiring clinicians to the methods inherent in the process are, in general, clearly slanted toward one theoretical approach. This leads inexorably to a narrowing of focus and it limits beginning clinicians in how they understand the therapeutic relationship. I am delighted that Prout and Wadkins have come together in an effort to bridge this divide at an early point in the careers of practitioners. This is an extremely rare thing. Others have tried to close the gap between the theoretical perspectives only by appealing directly to established clinicians (i.e., Wachtel, 1997). By offering balance in a text for professionals just starting in their careers, they contribute a significant good to the profession; they are providing developing clinicians with more balanced attitudes and an opportunity to form professional identities that support the full corpus of effective therapeutic methods.

Dean McKay, PhD, ABPP
Fordham University

REFERENCES

Ajzen, I., & Fishbein, M. (1977). Attitude-behavior relations: A theoretical analysis. *Psychological Bulletin, 84,* 888–918.

Areán, P. A., Craske, M. G., Crawford, K. A., Hollon, S., Kivlahan, D. R., Magnavita, J. J., … Spring, B. (in press). Development of clinical practice guidelines. *Annual Review of Clinical Psychology.*

Beck, A. T., Rush, A. J., Shaw, B. F., & Emery, G. (1979). *Cognitive therapy of depression.* New York, NY: Guilford Press.

Campbell, L. F., Norcross, J. C., Vasquez, M. J. T., & Kaslow, N. J. (2013). Recognition of psychotherapy effectiveness: The APA resolution. *Psychotherapy, 50,* 98–101.

Chu, B. C., Choudhury, M. S., Shortt, A. L., Pincus, D. B., Creed, T. A., & Kendall, P. C. (2004). Alliance, technology, and outcome in anxious youth. *Cognitive and Behavioral Practice, 11,* 44–55.

Davenloo, H. (1995). *Unlocking the unconscious.* New York, NY: Wiley.

Elliot, R., & Greenberg, L. S. (2007). The essence of process-experiential/emotion-focused therapy. *American Journal of Psychotherapy, 61,* 241–254.

Foa, E. B., & Emmelkamp, P. M. G. (1982). *Failures in behavior therapy.* New York, NY: Wiley.

McKay, D., & Ojserkis, R. (in press). Exposure in experiential context: Imaginal and in vivo approaches. In N. Thoma & D. McKay (Eds.), *Engaging emotion in cognitive-behavior therapy: Experiential techniques for promoting lasting change.* New York, NY: Guilford.

Mihura, J. L., Meyer, G. J., Dumitrascu, N., & Bombel, G. (2013). The validity of individual Rorschach variables: Systematic reviews and meta-analyses of the comprehensive system. *Psychological Bulletin, 139*(3), 548–605. doi: 10.1037/a0029406

Pyszczynski, T., Greenberg, J., & Solomon, S. (1999). A dual-process model of defense against conscious and unconscious death-related thoughts: An extension of terror management theory. *Psychological Review, 106,* 835–845.

Wachtel, P. L. (1997). *Psychoanalysis, behavior therapy, and the relational world.* Washington, DC: American Psychological Association.

Preface

Essential Interviewing and Counseling Skills: An Integrated Approach to Practice is written for students from a wide range of helping professions—counseling, psychology, psychiatry, social work, mental health advocacy, and creative arts therapy. These disciplines are as varied as the clients who serve them. What they share in common are the foundations of listening, observation, assessment, empathy, and skills to help individuals change and heal. The purpose of this introductory counseling text is to teach students the fundamental skills of interviewing, empathy, active listening, treatment planning, promoting change, and developing a strong therapeutic alliance.

This text stands apart from other introductory counseling textbooks because it provides a balanced and theoretically integrative approach to counseling. We came together to write this book largely because we approach psychotherapy from two different paradigms. Dr. Wadkins has extensive training in cognitive behavioral approaches and provided the cognitive behavioral therapy (CBT) foundation for this text. Dr. Prout's contributions are grounded in her training in psychodynamic psychotherapy. It was our hope that these two theoretical approaches—the dominant perspectives used in clinical practice today—could be presented as complementary and with an emphasis on integration. This textbook is also intended for students just learning the art and science of counseling. Each chapter of *Essential Interviewing and Counseling Skills: An Integrated Approach to Practice* is deliberately written to be accessible to a beginning audience. Those seeking more advanced reading, particularly on a specific topic, will find the Further Reading section of each chapter helpful.

Our work with a diverse population of clients in New York City and our own backgrounds have consistently taught us the importance of recognizing the multicultural facets of interviewing and counseling. Throughout the text you will find case examples and sections titled "Spotlight on Culture" that emphasize the many ways difference and diversity inform our work. We believe multicultural competence is vital to training effective and sensitive clinicians. This includes the many forms diversity can take, including ethnicity, immigration, country of origin, age, gender, sexual orientation, religion, language, and physical and cognitive abilities. Finally, and related to multicultural competence, this book is designed to challenge students to examine their own backgrounds and biases as they develop as professionals. You will see the call for trainees to pursue their own therapy throughout the book, and we have provided numerous exercises to help you begin to consider your own blind spots.

An Instructor's Manual and PowerPoint slides to accompany each chapter are also available to supplement the text. **To obtain an electronic copy of these materials, faculty should contact Springer Publishing Company at textbook@ springerpub.com.**

Writing this book has been a labor of love. We are both incredibly passionate about teaching and want to formalize what we do in the classroom and share it with others. The genesis for this book came from our own search for an introductory counseling skills textbook and the challenges we faced having to pull together multiple sources to create a whole. It is our hope that we have created something that integrates the many facets of learning counseling skills into a single source that will benefit instructors and students alike.

Tracy A. Prout, PhD
Melanie J. Wadkins, PhD

Acknowledgments

We are grateful to our students, who have raised so many important questions and challenged us to think critically about how to teach counseling skills. Several students in particular deserve special recognition because they have provided invaluable support to this project. Batya Bronstein was tireless and meticulous in her work on permissions and copyright issues and contributed to the instructor's manual for this text. Amanda Boris, Leore Faber, Amy Fox, Katrina Garland, and Lourdes Lazo also made significant contributions to the instructor's manual. We also want to thank our clients, both past and present, for sharing their lives with us and instructing us in the art and intensely personal nature of psycho-therapy. To our professors, professional mentors, and supervisors, we are grateful for the education they have given us in the science and practice of clinical work. A special thank you to Dean McKay, who has seen us grow into the clinicians we are today and who was gracious in lending support to this project. Sheri W. Sussman and Kathryn Moyer at Springer Publishing Company have been the absolute best publishing and editing team. We could not have asked for more. The speed and quality of their work is unmatched and was always accompanied by genuine warmth and encouragement, especially when we needed it most. Finally, we are especially thankful for our partners, whose love and support has buoyed us throughout this entire process. Evelyn's amazing work as our at-home editor also deserves special mention. Thank you!

Introduction to Counseling and Interviewing

We do not need magic to transform our world. We carry all of the power we need inside ourselves already.—Rowling (2008)

LEARNING OBJECTIVES

- Define the following terms: counseling, psychotherapy, therapeutic experience
- Identify the importance of establishing a counseling relationship
- Identify the specific skills that are essential for counseling
- Describe the importance of a therapeutic alliance
- Discuss how ideas of counseling have changed over time
- Identify and describe different career options in the field of counseling
- Describe the concept of clinical interview and identify various types
- Describe multicultural competence
- Explain the importance of a counselor knowing oneself well

WHAT IS COUNSELING?

Counseling is helping another person to make sense of what seems senseless. It is a process of empowerment that allows people to connect with the power they have within themselves—power they may never have been aware they possessed. The process of counseling may employ many methods, techniques, and interventions, but its end goals are almost always the same—to alleviate distress and to promote change. As mental health professionals we are often faced with individuals who are desperately searching for answers and a way out of what feels like an endless maze. The purpose of this book is to help you develop the skills you will need to help others navigate the challenges of life and find answers to the questions that trouble them.

Counseling is a profession that endeavors to assist individuals, couples, families, and groups to deal with a wide range of problems. Counseling may focus on emotional problems such as depression and anxiety; relationship issues such as divorce or infidelity; vocational difficulties like procrastination or performance problems; social issues like homelessness and prejudice; environmental issues such as coping with a natural disaster; or biological problems like chronic illness or infertility. Counseling is a relatively new resource available to individuals who are struggling to cope effectively. Only in the past century has counseling become a primary intervention for individuals experiencing psychological distress.

A considerable amount of time and energy has been devoted to distinguishing between counseling and **psychotherapy** (Adler, 1958; Corsini & Wedding, 2000; Patterson, 1973). We believe there are more similarities than differences between the two practices. As a result, we will use the terms *counseling* and *psychotherapy* interchangeably throughout this book. A therapeutic experience is an encounter that results in a desirable or beneficial effect. Whether you have been in formal therapy or not, you have probably had a therapeutic experience with a friend, family member, physician, massage or physical therapist, or through individual practices like journaling, meditation, or prayer. All of us have experienced the alleviation of distress through some type of therapeutic experience; however, these may not have been psychotherapy or counseling per se.

Counseling involves a professional relationship; it is therefore distinguished from the relationships we have with family or friends. Mental health professionals do not usually assess or treat people they know in other settings or capacities for ethical reasons (see Chapter 2). Typically, the counseling relationship is established for a specific reason—the reduction of symptoms, to effect change in a person's life, or to develop a deeper understanding of the self. It is a relationship that is bound by clear ethical guidelines for conduct. These standards of practice (described in detail in Chapter 2) create a framework for the counselor and the client and are intended to protect the rights of the client. Each discipline within the field of mental health has its own unique code of ethics, but most principles of ethical practice are universal across disciplines.

The practice of counseling also employs a unique set of skills that are not utilized in other helping professions. Students often tell us that they have chosen counseling as a profession because they are "good at giving advice" or because people regularly turn to them for guidance. Although advice-giving is certainly a skill and one that may add value to others' lives, it is not the hallmark of most counseling relationships. Rather, counseling is an endeavor that requires very particular types of listening, questioning, interpretation, and, at times, confrontation. The counselor and the client are on a journey together—a journey toward self-understanding and change. If you are to become a counselor who truly connects with clients and is effective, you must put aside your reliance on advice-giving. This textbook and the learning experiences you have at your internship or practicum site will provide you with an entirely new repertoire of skills for helping.

BOX 1.1

Putting It Into Practice

Choose a partner. Each of you will take a turn as the "counselor" and "client." First, the client should describe a problem to the counselor. This should be a "moderately sized" problem like procrastination, difficulty communicating with your partner effectively, or roommate conflicts, for example. Once the client has described the problem, the counselor should attempt to learn more about the problem and help the client discover ways to move forward *without* giving advice. Instead, the counselor should try asking for elaboration, paraphrasing what the client has said, and being curious about how this problem fits into the context of the client's social environment, culture, and personal history. Do this for 7 to 10 minutes and give each other feedback on how you did.

There are many ways to interact with clients during treatment. Certainly, there are times in which advice or praise will be helpful to clients, but these modes of intervention are not the primary ways we help. One useful way to think about interventions with clients is to consider the **expressive–supportive continuum** (see Figure 1.1), first described by the Menninger Clinic Treatment Interventions Project spearheaded by Jon Allen, PhD, and elaborated by Gabbard (2000).

Many of these interventions will be discussed in much greater detail in Chapter 7. As you can see now, advice is only one of many options on the expressive-supportive continuum. Within each of the interventions listed in Figure 1.1 there are numerous subcategories of intervention. For example, empathic validation might include things like reframing the client's perspective or normalizing his or her subjective experience as understandable and reasonable given the circumstances. The degree to which you will use more supportive or expressive techniques will vary based on the needs of your clients. You may even use all of these interventions within one session with the same client! We will discuss indications and contraindications for these skills later.

What continues to astound us as we work with clients every day is the incredible power of psychotherapy. To witness another individual's pain and to then accompany him or her on a journey of self-discovering and healing is truly

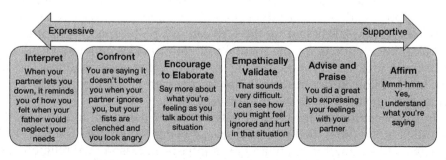

FIGURE 1.1 The expressive–supportive continuum.
Based on Gabbard (2000).

a privilege. Elyn Saks's description of therapy in her riveting memoir, *The Center Cannot Hold*, says it best,

> Medication has no doubt played a central role in helping me manage my psychosis, but what has allowed me to see the meaning in my struggles—to make sense of everything that happened before and during the course of my illness, and to mobilize what strengths I may possess into a rich and productive life—is talk therapy… [Therapy] is, at the heart of things, a *relationship,* and for me it has been the key to every other relationship I hold precious. (2007, p. 331)

This relationship between therapist and client is something to be cultivated, fostered, and built upon so that your clients will experience the relief they seek. Even as we discuss the skills, methods, goals, and theoretical underpinnings of counseling, we will return again and again to the fundamental importance of the relationship between therapist and client. This collaborative bond between therapist and client is often referred to as the **therapeutic alliance**. Research has consistently demonstrated that therapeutic alliance is an essential ingredient in the effectiveness of psychotherapy and even in medication management (Horvath & Luborsky, 1993; Horvath & Symonds, 1991; Krupnick et al., 1996). As master therapist Irvin Yalom has said, "It's the relationship that heals, it's the relationship that heals, it's the relationship that heals" (Yalom, 1989, p. 98).

Evolution and Professionalization of Counseling

Written accounts of mental illness and psychological distress date back to ancient Egypt (Nasser, 1987), and the treatments provided to sufferers have varied widely throughout history. Early historians report that the treatment of mental disorders was provided by sorcerers, shamans, and other religious figures. Ancient people typically attributed emotional problems to forces outside of themselves, like spells, animistic spirits, and supernatural forces (Millon, 2004). As Christianity spread through the Western world, religious interventions for mental illness became the norm. Psychological distress was understood as a type of estrangement from God, and the prescription for this kind of alienation was often fasting, prayer, confession, and bloodletting (Laffey, 2003). Prior to the Enlightenment, those with psychological problems were not treated but were kept chained in secure settings. The primary goal of mental health care prior to the Enlightenment was to suppress bad behavior rather than understand the subjective experience of sufferers (Laffey, 2003). During the 17th century, philosophers also attempted to develop interventions for the mentally ill. John Locke understood madness as an error in logic and proposed using reason to argue away madness (Suzuki, 1995). In the 18th century, responsibility for the care of the mentally ill shifted from religious institutions to medical professionals.

In some institutions for the mentally ill, nearly half of all inmates (as they were called at the time) died within a year of being sequestered (Weiner, 1992). The arrival of the Enlightenment and its emphasis on reason over religious faith shifted power from the realm of the church to that of the state in an effort to create a new society that valued the welfare of the individual and the protection of human rights. This period of history ushered in a new age in the treatment of psychological disorders. A new paradigm in this advancement of psychological treatment was introduced by Phillipe Pinel, a French physician entrusted with the care of the mentally ill at two Parisian hospitals in the late 18th century. He introduced what he referred to as **moral treatment**. This treatment approach was revolutionary because it focused on offering patients kindness and empathy rather than an authoritarian presence intended to control the mentally ill. Pinel was the first to see insanity as a mental condition that could be addressed with psychological rather than religious, philosophical, or medical treatment (Bynum, 1964). Pinel also encouraged interaction between patients and the workers in asylums. Additionally, in an early foreshadowing of the peer-to-peer recovery movement (for more on the peer-to-peer recovery movement see Davidson et al., 1999), Pinel advocated the hiring of recovered patients as attendants because they were the most likely to refrain from inhumane treatment.

Over time, humans began to connect their feelings, thoughts, and actions to internal forces. Along with more sophisticated explanations of psychological suffering came more nuanced and appropriate treatments. We have also moved beyond treating only acute and chronic mental illness—referred to as insanity or madness in the early years of counseling—to developing treatment approaches for a broader range of people. As counselors, we have moved outside the walls of the inpatient institution to work with people in clinics, day treatment programs, group residences, schools, nursing homes, medical units, private practices, religious institutions, and the community at large.

Today's counseling practice has been shaped by influential figures like Sigmund and Anna Freud, Carl Rogers, Aaron and Judith Beck, Jay Haley, Jean Baker Miller, Karen Horney, Albert Ellis, Irvin Yalom, Otto Kernberg, Marsha Linehan, and many others. Sigmund Freud was the first to outline a comprehensive theory of psychotherapy, something his patient Bertha Pappenheim referred to as "the talking cure" (Freud, 1910/1989). Many therapists point to this historical moment as the genesis of talk therapy. Since Freud first posited his theories, numerous therapists have built upon and transformed talk therapy. Whereas this book will address certain aspects of theory and the contributions of these giants of psychotherapy, a comprehensive review of theories of psychotherapy is beyond the scope of this book. We encourage you to learn more about personality theory and systems of psychotherapy (Corsini & Wedding, 2000) and to seek out additional information from your mentors' and supervisors' approach to counseling. Your own style and method of counseling will emerge out of the theoretical foundations that ground you and your ongoing clinical experience and engagement with empirical research.

Career Options

There are many different paths you can take toward becoming a mental health professional. Several of these paths are detailed below, and each varies in terms of how much education is required, what the licensing requirements are, the types of settings in which you might work, and the focus each profession emphasizes. We encourage you to explore several career options through internships, interviewing and shadowing professionals in the field, and speaking with your mentors. Choosing a vocation involves finding a career that fits your personality, interests, skills, and values. Each of these variables can be assessed in a variety of ways. Personality and interests are typically assessed using self-report inventories that can be obtained from your college or university career office. Grades in your courses and feedback from your internship supervisors are often the best way to evaluate your skills. Finally, values cover a wide range of domains and can be best understood through a process of careful self-exploration. Is it important for you to be financially successful? Would you prefer a job that would allow you to spend more time with family? Do you prefer a work environment that is fast-paced and sometimes chaotic? By carefully assessing these four areas— personality, interests, skills, and values—you will be able to better ascertain what type of career path is best for you.

Mental Health Counseling and Marriage and Family Therapy

The field of counseling includes master's and doctoral degree counselors who receive training in counseling programs that are licensed by the Council on Counseling and Related Educational Programs (CACREP). All 50 states, the District of Columbia, Puerto Rico, and Guam currently provide licensure for mental health professionals under the title licensed professional counselor (LPC) or **licensed mental health counselor** (LMHC). Licensure requirements vary by state, but most require: (a) a master's degree in counseling or a related field; (b) specific academic coursework on normal human development, counseling theories, and counseling methods; (c) supervised practicum experience; (d) successful completion of a licensing exam; and (e) a significant amount of postgraduate supervised work. LMHCs work in a wide variety of settings, including hospitals, clinics, day treatment programs, group homes, and private practice.

Marriage and family therapists (MFTs) have similar training and licensure requirements but their education and professional practice are focused on matters of the family. They have specialized training in couples counseling and how to work within a family system. Some have argued that master's level clinicians, like LMHCs and MFTs, are the future of the delivery of mental health services (Lawless, Ginter, & Kelly, 1999). In the 1990s and 2000s there was rapid growth in the number of LMHCs in our midst, and there continues to be high employment demand for these types of clinicians.

Clinical and Counseling Psychology

Historically, there were significant differences between clinical and counseling psychology. Counseling psychologists were more likely to take a strengths-based approach to clients rather than focusing on deficits or impairment. Counseling psychologists were also trained to address more moderate difficulties rather than the severe psychopathology that clinical psychologists tended to focus on. These historical differences have lessened over time. Today, there is considerable overlap between clinical and counseling psychology, and the training and practice of **psychologists** with these degrees tend to be very similar. Both types of psychologists also assess intellectual and personality functioning through various types of testing. Assessment is an area of practice that is unique to psychologists; no other counseling professional is trained extensively in this area. The field of clinical and counseling psychology includes individuals who have doctoral degrees (which typically take 5–7 years to complete) and have earned state licensure as psychologists. Psychologists differ from psychiatrists in several ways. Psychiatrists have completed medical school and often prescribe medication for individuals with emotional problems. An increase in the complexity and reliance on pharmacotherapy has led to a decline in the number of psychiatrists specializing in psychotherapy (Harris, 2011; Mojtabai & Olfson, 2008). Additionally, until 2001, there was a steady decline in the emphasis on psychotherapy training in residency programs. The relative absence of therapy training was remedied in 2001 when the Residency Review Committee mandated psychotherapy training (Tucker, Garton, Foote, & Candler, 2009). That said, the primary emphasis within psychiatry training remains on medication management rather than developing expertise in psychotherapy. More recently, some states (e.g., New Mexico and Louisiana) have granted prescription privileges for psychologists with advanced post-doctoral training. Within hospital settings, psychologists and psychiatrists are typically the professionals that lead the treatment team.

Social Work
Social work is a profession that has many different faces. Historically, the field of social work has emphasized understanding the client in the context of his or her environment and community, that is, the social context of individual experience. Advocacy remains a cornerstone of social work practice, and most training programs emphasize the importance of championing individual rights through an ongoing process of direct intervention and empowerment. The field of social work has also become more clinically focused, with many social workers providing therapy more often than concrete social services. **Social workers** are often the link between the larger institution (e.g., the hospital or clinic) and the broader social milieu. Today, there are many social work graduate programs that focus more heavily on the practice of counseling and train social workers to be clinically focused psychotherapists. Graduate school in social work typically takes 2 to 3 years to complete, and most states require some period of supervised work after graduation to achieve licensure. Clinical social workers have a wide variety of career options, including working in public mental health as disposition coordinators and in private practice.

Creative Arts Therapies
Those who practice creative arts therapies, sometimes referred to as *expressive therapies*, emphasize the creative process as a way to express feelings, emotions, and thoughts that are difficult to express in words. Expressive therapies include art therapy, dance and music therapy, drama therapy, and writing therapy. The International Expressive Arts Therapy Association (IEATA) explains that the creative arts therapies enable people to gain access to their inner resources to experience healing and clarity (IEATA, 2012). Creative arts therapy may be provided to clients as a stand-alone treatment but is often incorporated as an adjunctive treatment. One of the unique contributions of creative arts therapy is its ability to give voice to emotional and physical states that the client simply cannot put into words.

Many states do not currently have a licensure program for creative arts therapists, although some states include **creative arts therapists** under licensure programs for counselors. Those who practice in the creative arts typically attend graduate school for 2 to 3 years and obtain a master's degree. Creative arts therapists work in a variety of settings, including medical units, rehabilitation, inpatient psychiatry, private practice, and schools.

Psychiatric/Mental Health Nurse Practitioner
Psychiatric nurse practitioners represent a unique crossroads of mental health counseling. They work in multiple settings and occupy a variety of roles.

For example, nurse practitioners often prescribe medication and conduct psychotherapy with clients. Nurse practitioners have post-secondary education that typically includes a bachelor's degree in nursing and a master's in the science of nursing with extensive clinical training. Psychiatric nurse practitioners may serve as the medical link between the institution and the individual in the community, often visiting clients in their homes and therefore providing an essential continuum of care. Many nurse practitioners seek post-graduate training in psychotherapy because their nursing training is largely focused on biological aspects of treatment (e.g., psychotropic medication) and providing psycho-education to patients. The certification requirements for these types of advance practice nurses are complex and vary by state (APRN Consensus Work Group, 2008).

Pastoral Counseling

Pastoral counselors serve clients at the intersection of emotional distress and faith. They often work in collaboration with other counseling professionals and have specialized training that allows them to address psychospiritual issues and to provide a holistic approach to caring for persons. The tradition of pastoral counseling extends from the long history of religious communities caring for those who suffer with mental and emotional distress. Within psychology, theorists and practitioners like William James, Carl Jung, Karl Menninger, and M. Scott Peck have emphasized the interrelationships between psychology and spirituality. Training programs in pastoral counseling typically last four years, and students participate in several community ministry placements. Pastoral counselors work in a variety of institutional and private settings.

THE CLINICAL INTERVIEW

Before you begin working with a client, you need to have detailed information about why she or he is seeking your services. Thus, the beginning of your work with a client will typically include a clinical interview. The term **clinical interviewing** may be off-putting to some as it suggests a kind of businesslike interaction with a clear power dynamic. In fact, a better term for the clinical interview would be something like "intentional" or "directed conversation." This conversation, which is often led by the therapist, should be characterized by respect, empathy, active listening, and continuous attention to shifts in affect and tone. You will learn about many of the skills and personal characteristics that make for a successful interview later in this book.

Interviewing is a skill that can be taught didactically but is best learned experientially. Trainees in psychotherapy should take every opportunity to observe colleagues and supervisors conducting interviews. It is important to ask questions about why interviews are conducted in a particular way. If you have the opportunity, watching videos of other professionals conducting interviews can also be very helpful. These may be available in your university library or through online databases, such as PsycTherapy (American Psychological Association). Many counseling programs provide trainees with the opportunity to be videotaped while conducting intake or diagnostic interviews. Watching one's self interact with a client provides invaluable information about tone, speech patterns, body language, and facial expressions. The information gleaned from the video is incredibly rich and unparalleled compared to most other types of feedback experiences.

There are many different types of clinical interviews, including intake interviews, mental status exams, safety assessment for suicidal or homicidal potential, and diagnostic interviews, among others. Each type of interview and each type of client will require adjustments on the part of the interviewer. The way you interview in the psychiatric emergency room will be vastly different from how you operate during a consultation in your private practice. Your skills in this area will grow over time as you develop your professional identity, theoretical orientation, and understanding of persons.

Why Do We Interview?

The primary reason we conduct interviews with clients is quite simple—we want to learn more about them. Additionally, we also want to build rapport with the client and develop a shared understanding of the client's experience. You might think of the interview as a view of the world that is shared between counselor and client—an "inter view" or a shared worldview. The questions we have with each individual client may be different, but there are some overarching goals that seem to apply to all interviewing situations. We typically want to know what is troubling the person, when these problems began, and how the client has managed to cope thus far. More specifically, we may want to ask about the symptoms of the problem and social supports in the person's life. Most interviewers are especially interested in aspects of the person's functioning that may represent some degree of risk; these things include substance abuse and suicidal or homicidal ideation. In addition to assessing deficits and areas to address in treatment, we recommend evaluating the client's strengths, character strengths, and positive coping mechanisms (Duckworth, Steen, & Seligman, 2005). We will discuss how to evaluate all of these areas of functioning in Chapter 5.

It is likely that all mental health professionals will engage in clinical interviewing frequently throughout their careers. The tone, format, and direction of the interview will vary with each individual client and as a result of the setting in which you work. When working in an acute care setting, interviews tend to be more focused and directive. There is more emphasis placed on obtaining certain information efficiently: for example, if you are working in a psychiatric emergency room, you will want to know what has brought the person in and whether he or she is presenting for treatment voluntarily or involuntarily. You also want to ask about the intensity, frequency, and duration of symptoms, and any history of substance abuse or suicidal or homicidal ideation. The ease of gathering this information will vary depending upon the level of cooperation you have from the client, the degree to which the client is impaired (either by symptoms, cognitive limitations, or intoxication), and the amount of time you have. In a private practice setting, you will likely have more freedom in terms of how you interview; you may not have to be as focused and narrow in your scope of inquiry. Typically, interviews conducted outside of the public mental health system and research settings are less structured and more amenable to meeting the immediate needs of the client.

All clinical interviews are purposeful. When a therapist conducts an interview with a client, he or she is not simply having a friendly conversation or just trying to "get to know" the client; the clinician is trying to form a picture of the individual's distress. What does life look like for the client and does it work well?

How have his or her symptoms become so salient? What has he or she already tried to alleviate suffering? What has brought the client to seek treatment *now*? Are there significant social supports in his or her life? Are there roadblocks in place that will make treatment difficult? These questions are not asked directly in each and every interview, but they are part of a mental framework we refer to as we learn about our clients. We are also trying to determine whether we can help this person. Sometimes it is very obvious that we are not the right person to help.

BOX 1.2

Case Example

A client came to his first session and indicated he wanted to improve his relationship with his parents. During the initial interview, this client mentioned that he drank "a bit." When the therapist heard that phrase, "a bit," she wanted to know more. It turns out he was drinking 7 to 10 drinks a night and using a significant amount of powder cocaine, marijuana, ecstasy, and benzodiazepines. The clinician knew immediately that she would not be able to provide the level of care that this person needed given his level of drug and alcohol use and the safety risks it posed. She referred him to a colleague who specialized in substance abuse and could also address the parental relationship concerns the client had.

Evaluating our ability to help a particular client is not always as clear as it was for the counseling professional in this instance. Part of the job of the interviewer is to constantly integrate new information to develop a richer understanding of the person and their environment. As a new counselor, you may find that it is difficult to balance all of the different tasks of interviewing in the beginning. After participating in an experiential learning activity where she was a peer counselor, one student recently said, "I couldn't do everything all at once! I was trying to listen, take notes, keep track of my facial expressions and body language, think about what to say in response, and what to ask next. It was so difficult!" Her experience is similar to learning to drive a car. Although driving a car eventually becomes a relatively automated task, the first 6 months or so requires a great deal of thinking about all the individual steps involved in driving. Over time, balancing all of the different aspects of psychotherapy becomes easier and you will be able to direct your energies toward higher-level goals, like building empathy, using your own reactions to inform treatment, and attending to the client's subjective experience.

As you begin interviewing, we encourage you to return to this question of *why* we interview. The questions we ask our clients are not out of sheer curiosity; we are not voyeurs. We interview to learn important information about the client that will ultimately inform our ability to help. During a clinical interview, one attends to many different sources of input. The content of what the person is saying is obviously very important. Why has the client come for treatment? Most people come to a counseling professional because they have some type of emotional distress that is affecting their ability to function socially, academically, and/or occupationally. Some may present for treatment at the recommendation of another interested party, such as a spouse or a parent. Similarly, some individuals may be mandated for treatment by their parole officer, the courts, or their employer. Individuals who are seeking treatment at someone else's request are often the most difficult to engage in the process of counseling. We will address this specific challenge in Chapter 7, when we cover the topic of therapeutic alliance. Finally, some clients may come for treatment to engage in a process of self-discovery that is relatively nonspecific; this is more common among mental health professionals and those in training who seek treatment as part of their professional and personal growth and development.

Most clients are able to identify particular symptoms that cause them distress: loneliness, anxiety, sadness, tendency to procrastination, hearing voices, and so on. As an interviewer, your job is to help the client talk about these symptoms in a way that may be entirely new to them. In addition to learning about the inception, duration, and frequency of the symptoms, you will want to explore what they mean to this particular client. For example, if a client expresses that they have difficulty building friendships, this could have myriad causes and meanings. You should be curious about what makes it difficult for the client to make friendships. What gets in the way? Additionally, you may want to understand what friendship means to the client. Clients may have radically different ideas about what it means to build better friendships. Here are two exchanges that illustrate these potential differences:

BOX 1.3

Case Example: Exploring the Meaning of Symptoms

Exchange 1

Client 1: I try really hard to be friendly, but it seems like nobody wants to reciprocate!

Therapist: Do you have ideas about why you think that happens? Is there some way you explain it to yourself?

Client 1: Yeah, I think it must be the way I talk or look. [breaks eye contact] People see me and they have a low opinion of me, and then they think I'm just trying too hard or am desperate or whatever. I wouldn't want to be friends with me either, I guess.

Exchange 2

Client 2: I try really hard to be friendly, but it seems like nobody wants to reciprocate!

Therapist: Do you have ideas about why you think that happens? Is there some way you explain it to yourself?

Client 2: Yeah, I think it must be the way I talk or look. [sits up straighter] People see me and maybe they get intimidated. They just shrink away because they don't want to put in the work it takes to have a meaningful friendship with someone like me.

In the first example, the client seems to have a low opinion of himself or herself, which may be evidence of self-esteem problems, depression, anxiety, or something like body dysmorphic disorder. The second client appears to have a high opinion of himself or herself, which may be evidence of a healthy self-esteem, a narcissistic personality style, or even a delusional disorder. The work you would do with each of these clients would be quite different. Only with more questioning would you be able to learn about the causes, meanings, and implications of these two unique perspectives. Although the skills you would use might be quite similar (e.g., empathy, support, and active listening), the content and underlying goals for treatment would be tailored to meet the needs of the individual.

BOX 1.4

Putting It Into Practice

Consider the following statements and develop a wide-ranging list of possible explanations as to why the client is experiencing the described symptoms. You should be able to come up with at least five or six explanations for each statement.

- "I can't stop fidgeting."
- "Every time I ride the subway I get so nervous."
- "I've lost my appetite. I barely eat."
- "There's no way I can go to my cousin's wedding."

How Do We Interview?

There are many ways to approach clinical interviewing (see Chapter 5 for detailed information on this topic). In this introductory chapter, we will focus on some of the central components of clinical interviewing that are universal. As an interviewer you will wear many hats simultaneously. The initial interview is an opportunity to build rapport with the client, to apply your assessment and diagnosis skills, to expand your understanding of persons, and to develop new skills that will enhance your future practice.

Building rapport is a complex and mutual process that begins with you. Clients will come to you in a range of emotional states, with infinitely different personality traits, and varied attitudes toward you and the process of counseling. Additionally, your clients will come from different cultures, ethnicities, socioeconomic backgrounds, and religious traditions; will be of different genders, sexual orientations, ages, professions, physical abilities; and will bring different sexual experiences, values, interests, and worldviews. How will you attempt to build rapport with so many different types of people? Can you be all things to all people? The truth is that you can't. But you can know yourself. By becoming increasingly aware of your own biases, blind spots, implicit values, and personality traits you will increase your ability to build therapeutic relationships that are built on trust and mutual respect.

To do this well, to be able to connect with another person, you need to adopt a personal style that is nondefensive. You must be willing to stretch yourself, to consider your shortcomings, and to recognize how your personal background has shaped your worldview and how it will affect others with whom you interact. One of the most helpful things I learned during graduate school is something that a supervisor reminded me of time and time again: "The client is the expert on her own experience. You are there to learn." This is especially true during the interviewing process. Assume you know nothing about the individual's experience and open yourself up to seeing the world in a completely different way.

Multicultural competence is a fundamental component of counseling. Sue (2001) outlines the beliefs and attitudes that are central to developing cultural competence. His multidimensional model of cultural competence (MDCC) will be explored in greater detail in Chapter 4, but we will highlight some of its essential elements here. Sue explains that culturally competent counselors must be aware of their own heritage and how they influence psychological processes. They must be comfortable with the differences that exist between themselves and their clients and be able to connect with the negative reactions and stereotypes they have about other racial and ethnic groups. If you believe that you are "colorblind" or that other factors that make us different from one another have no impact on you, it's likely that you are missing something. Colorblindness has been described as another form of racism (Carr, 1997) because it ignores the fact that different groups have received unequal treatment. Additionally, our prejudices are not limited to those outside of our own group. Bias and prejudice exist both between and *within* groups. Although you may be working with someone of your same religion, ethnicity, or sexual orientation, you are still likely to hold implicit attitudes that may inadvertently interfere with your ability to understand the client.

BOX 1.5

Spotlight on Culture

To learn more about thoughts and feelings you may have that exist outside of your conscious awareness or control, we encourage you to visit Harvard University's Implicit Association Test (IAT) website at https://implicit.harvard.edu/implicit. The IAT is an empirically-derived assessment tool that will give you feedback about attitudes you have but that are likely outside of your awareness. The demonstrations on the website look at implicit associations regarding gender, age, sexuality, race, disability, religion, weight, and many other categories.

Sue (2001) also suggests that counselors should be respectful of other religious and spiritual practices and the helping practices of other cultures. Perhaps the most interesting and important element of Sue's model is his recommendation that the culturally competent counselor recognize the limits of his or her competencies and expertise. For some this is a radically different way of approaching competence. It is antithetical to how we have operated in our social, academic, and familial spheres until this point. The suggestion here is that by acknowledging our shortcomings, we are actually *more* competent than someone who is unable to recognize his or her limits.

These two issues—**rapport** building and multicultural competence—are critical for establishing a foundation on which successful clinical interviewing and counseling can take place. (Note: We use the term multicultural competence as broadly as possible to include countless types of diversity.) If you can focus on these two core competencies, the actual task of interviewing will flow much more smoothly. The bread and butter of clinical interviewing is questioning and asking for elaboration. You may develop a directive or nondirective interviewing style, and this will influence the types of questions you ask in a clinical interview. A directive style of interviewing may provide a more expedient path toward understanding the problems and can be very helpful when time is of the essence or the goal of the interview is to arrive at a diagnosis or disposition plan for the client. This type of interviewing style may be too structured for some clients. A nondirective interviewing style provides less structure and may allow the interviewer to understand more of the complexities and ambiguities of the individual's experience. This style of interviewing may also help the client feel more empowered but may also leave the client feeling directionless or unmoored. Both types of interviewing styles have strengths and weaknesses.

If you favor a directive style of interviewing, you are likely to ask more questions, and these questions will probably be focused and narrower in scope. If you prefer a less directive style, the questions you ask will tend to be more open-ended, with the goal of following the client's lead. Regardless of the approach you take and the types of questions you ask, there is information that must be gathered. Understanding the client's current functioning and the history of his or her current difficulties is essential. This is often referred to as the **presenting problem**. You will also want to know something about the client's family and relationship history, educational background, occupational functioning, and medical history, including any medications he or she is currently taking. It is also useful to ask about the client's strengths and current coping mechanisms. You should also inquire about any treatment he or she may have received, including psychotherapy, medication, and hospitalization.

As clients answer questions and speak about their lives, you will be listening on multiple levels. There are many analogies that can help illuminate what it means to listen to the multifaceted layers of what the person is saying. You might think of it as looking for the forest *and* the trees. The trees are the basic content of what the person is saying (e.g., his or her symptoms, experiences, and history). The forest is the bigger picture. What is the context within which all of this has taken place? Are there overarching themes that seem to appear repeatedly? What is the lens through which this person sees the world? We also think about what our clients say as a kind of narrative that is more poetry than prose. Poetry does not have to be linear or even logical and it can have multiple meanings simultaneously. The same is true for what you might hear in a clinical interview. Poet and psychoanalyst Forrest Hamer has written about his efforts to "hear better" (Hamer, 2008, p. 86), and he highlights the issue of multiple levels of meaning that can be found in poetry and in the therapeutic space. He explains that the speaker, the spoken, and the spoken-to affect one another in ways that are not always observable. For this reason, the experience of interviewing can sometimes be disorienting as you try to locate the client within a broader matrix of relationships and life events. As we said in the beginning of this chapter, counseling is a process that helps people make sense of the senseless.

BECOMING A COUNSELING PROFESSIONAL

Imagine your first day at your internship or practicum site. You walk into the waiting room to greet your very first client. What is going through your mind as you sit down with this person? What anxieties do you have about this meeting? How will you handle questions about your experience, level of training, marital status, ethnicity, or sexual orientation, if they arise? Will you take notes? What types of interventions will you use? How will you begin and end the session? These are just some of the questions that we will help you explore as you read this book. As you consider what it means to become a counseling professional, we would like to highlight several issues. Specifically, we want to: (a) describe how to learn from the mistakes that we all make as mental health professionals; (b) explore some of the practical aspects of counseling in an era of managed care; and (c) describe how theory and research come together to inform the practice of counseling.

Mistakes

The old adage, "Practice makes perfect," does not apply to the life of the counseling professional. A more accurate statement might be, "Practice makes better." Although you will continue to learn and grow as a counseling professional, you will never be perfect. We continue to make mistakes with our clients. On good days, we are able to learn from these mistakes in a nondefensive way and integrate those lessons into our work. On other days, we are unaware that we have even made a mistake! Mistakes in psychotherapy are inevitable, but sensitive handling of our mistakes can make all the difference. In fact, the errors we make within the therapeutic relationship can present an enormous opportunity for growth—both for therapist and client (Cook, 2012; Mazzetti, 2012).

Both of us have distinct memories of the many mistakes we have made throughout our careers. Early on, Dr. Prout worked as a mental health worker in an inpatient unit for women with a history of trauma. Several of the patients in this unit had severe personality disorders, a cluster of disorders she knew very little about at the time. Dr. Prout was young, eager to please, and believed that if she was nice to the patients, they would feel better. She had very little supervision at the time, and when, during her first week on the unit, several of the patients expressed their appreciation for her work, she was flattered. They told Dr. Prout she was the "best" mental health worker they had ever seen in the unit and shared their deep sense of relief that she had finally arrived to help them. In her naiveté, Dr. Prout thought she must be doing a *great* job. It did not take long for the tide to turn. This idealization quickly turned into devaluation, and the patients began complaining bitterly to the nursing staff, physicians, and supervisor that Dr. Prout was "inept," "clueless," and should be fired immediately. This type of hot-and-cold behavior is not uncommon among individuals with borderline personality disorder, but the concept was entirely new to Dr. Prout. There were many mistakes in this situation, including her assumption that being nice was the most helpful thing she could do. Since then, after extensive training from multiple theoretical perspectives and the opportunity to work with many clients with borderline personality disorder, Dr. Prout has developed a greater degree of competency with this particular diagnosis. Her understanding of what it means to be helpful to clients has also been redefined and has matured significantly.

Yet another mistake came much more recently. A client with a particularly harsh view of herself told Dr. Prout, with some trepidation, that she had spent her day cooking a pot of stew. She indicated that others, including her therapist, might think this was a poor use of her time and probably thought she had wasted her day. In a poorly executed effort to introduce other possible cognitions about her day of cooking and to insert some humor Dr. Prout said, "Maybe they were wondering, 'Where's my stew?'" It seemed at the time that she was able to understand that there were many possible responses people could have to her cooking other than judgment, and we moved on to another topic. Several weeks later the client brought Dr. Prout a tin of cookies. When she inquired about what had prompted her to make them she said, "When you asked me where your stew was, I felt so guilty. Like, who is taking care of you? I wanted to share my cooking with you, so you wouldn't be hungry." This was the moment Dr. Prout realized her mistake. With an offhand comment, Dr. Prout had communicated to the client that she needed to take care of her therapist and that Dr. Prout somehow wanted something from her. In retrospect and with the help of individual and group supervision on this case, Dr. Prout gained insight into her own motivations and was able to think carefully about what she had learned about her client through this exchange. Dr. Prout had learned firsthand how the client's own judgments of herself affected her relationships with others. Dr. Prout's understanding of this interaction also enhanced the work they did together going forward.

In the first example, Dr. Prout's mistake was largely a result of lack of training and knowledge about a particular disorder. From it she learned that she was truly a beginner in this field and began to challenge her own assumptions about what it means to be a helping professional. The second example demonstrates a mistake that was the result of carelessness and a lack of active thinking about the client's needs and personality style. Thankfully, this mistake did minimal harm and, in fact, the client and therapist both learned a bit about some patterns of interacting that had been problematic for the client outside of the consulting room. Dr. Prout came to see that the client often felt she was letting people down and would then go to great lengths to gain their approval and meet their needs, just as she had with the tin of cookies. In their work together they returned to this example several times and shared their experience of it with one another in a way that helped the client be more true to herself and her own needs.

We regularly reflect on our own mistakes and have found them to be wonderful teachers. Mistakes are always a part of the learning process, and we predict that each of you will make numerous mistakes in your counseling practice. You and your clients will be best served if you can be open and honest about the mistakes you do make. There is no need to be embarrassed. Sharing your mistakes with your peers, supervisors, and other trusted professionals will provide a great sense of relief and improve the work that you do as a therapist.

Managed Care

Many students of psychotherapy today have never known an era without managed care. It may be such a given that a discussion of its impact on the practice of counseling may seem curious. However, managed care is actually a relatively new force that has shaped contemporary psychotherapy in powerful ways. The rapid growth of managed care began with the Health Maintenance Organization Act of 1973. The term **managed care** refers to a variety of techniques and organizations that are intended to provide Americans with health benefits and to improve the quality and cost of health care. Managed care includes organizations like health maintenance organizations (HMOs), preferred provider organizations (PPOs), and, less frequently, flexible indemnity plans. The overarching goals of managed care organizations (MCOs) are to control the cost of health care delivery and to increase cost sharing. The impact of managed care has been hotly debated since its inception, and the quantity and intensity of discussion has increased exponentially with the introduction of the *Patient Protection and Affordable Care Act* (2010), otherwise known as the federal health care law or Obamacare.

In addition to managed care, the mental health parity law has shaped the way we practice today. The 2010 Wellstone-Domenici Mental Health Parity and Addiction Equity Act (MHPAEA) was intended to create parity between medical and mental health services. This means that "coverage for mental health and substance abuse benefits must be at least equal to coverage for medical health benefits" (American Psychological Association, 2010). This means that if a client's insurer does not impose session limits for medical services, they cannot limit the number of counseling sessions. The caveat to mental health parity is "medical necessity." MCOs must provide coverage for services that are deemed medically necessary. If the client does not meet criteria for a clinical diagnosis or if the clinician cannot make a convincing case for the necessity of care, the treatment may not be covered by insurance and benefits may be denied.

Every mental health care setting is influenced by managed care and mental health parity. Even private practice offices that do not accept insurance are affected by these federal mandates. Some have argued that managed care, often referred to as third-party payers, is a third party that is always in the consulting room, asserting its influence (Calmar, 1985). Despite the ubiquity of managed care, graduate programs are still learning how to include information about it in training (Daniels, Alva, & Olivares, 2002; Smith, 1999). Anderson (2000) offers several suggestions for practitioners regarding how to work in a managed care environment. It is important for the clinician to be able to communicate effectively with the case manager about the client. When called upon to do a clinical case review with the MCO, it is the counseling professional's job to distill all that has transpired in the sessions or during the hospitalization into a succinct summary. MCOs value measurable and achievable goals. These are usually presented in a comprehensive treatment plan that includes specific and concrete goals, objectives, and interventions. The treatment plan should also incorporate measurable criteria that will be used to evaluate whether the treatment goals have been achieved. In addition, the counselor must have expertise in diagnosis using the *Diagnostic and Statistical Manual of Mental Disorders* (5th ed., *DSM-5*; American Psychiatric Association, 2013) criteria. Clinical diagnosis will often determine whether mental health services will be covered by the insurer.

Psychotherapists often express resentment about having to answer to MCOs (Cantor & Fuentes, 2008; Schreter, Sharfstein, & Schreter, 1994), and we are certainly sympathetic to those feelings. Despite that, managed care is a reality that all counseling professionals will face, and your clients will be better served if you can develop strategies for meeting the requirements of managed care without sacrificing quality of care. It is important to learn the language of mental health treatment from the perspective of MCOs. For example, you cannot use global, nonspecific treatment goals such as, "help the client feel less depressed." Treatment goals for depression might include things like, "Client will report no suicidal ideation for three consecutive weeks," or, "Client will engage in physical activity such as walking or running for 30 minutes, twice a week, for four consecutive weeks." Additionally, when participating in a clinical case review with an MCO, we recommend asking the case worker what information they need and requesting a second phone appointment to provide the information. This will allow you the time you need to review the case and develop a summary of the case that is accurate, specific, and succinct. Learning effective and culturally sensitive diagnostic and treatment planning skills has always been important for the counseling professional. In the new age of managed care they are essential.

Integrating Theory and Research Into Practice

When students hear us talk about theory or empirical research sometimes their eyes glaze over. In the absence of any *in vivo* opportunities to apply it to practice, theory and research can feel abstract and difficult to understand, even irrelevant. As you grow and develop as a counselor, your theoretical orientation will become a critical part of your professional identity. It is important to begin building that foundation now. You can begin learning about counseling theories by taking a *systems of psychotherapy* course and a *personality theory* course. The predominant theories in practice today are cognitive behavioral, psychodynamic, family systems, and humanistic, also referred to as client-centered theory. In addition to these major theoretical approaches, we recommend learning about interpersonal psychotherapy, existential and evolutionary theories, dialectical behavior therapy, biological approaches, motivational interviewing, and phenomenological or postmodern theory. There are many other approaches that are not listed here that you may also encounter and become curious about. We suggest critically evaluating the peer-reviewed research on these new and innovative therapies before adopting them yourself.

You may be wondering how you can learn about so many different approaches. There are several ways. You will encounter professors and supervisors throughout your training with different theoretical orientations, and these people will be your greatest resource. Ask questions about how and why they conceptualize emotional distress the way they do. Be curious about how they arrived at their particular viewpoints. We have also learned a great deal from our colleagues. You can attend conferences and strike up conversations with your peers who are drawn to perspectives different from your own. Finally— read, read, read! There are an infinite number of articles and books that describe theoretical perspectives and their application to counseling practice. Do not be dismayed by the sometimes dogmatic nature of the discussion about theoretical orientation. Although the divide between cognitive behavioral and psychodynamic approaches sometimes resembles the partisan battles of our political parties, most people integrate multiple perspectives in their daily practice. When what you have learned comes alive in an inpatient unit or at a day treatment program, your appetite for learning about theory will grow.

Reading and integrating empirical research is essential if you want to maintain an ethical counseling practice. The American Mental Health Counselors Association's (AMHCA) professional standards require mental health counselors to participate in continuing education and to stay apprised of the latest developments in counseling. The American Psychological Association and most other professional practice organizations require that counseling professionals maintain a high level of competence throughout their careers. Even if you do not have a deep understanding of statistics or research methods, you can still consume and digest research in a way that will enrich your clinical work.

There are several ways to expose yourself to research. As you maintain your membership in professional organizations, you will likely receive peer-reviewed journals. This will give you access to the most recent research in your area of interest. If you are affiliated with a medical institution, you should attend grand rounds, journal clubs, and any other presentations that offer new research findings. Professional meetings and scientific poster sessions at these gatherings also provide opportunities to learn about empirical research.

Integrating theory and research into your work with clients is more art than science. You will learn from experience what works for you and what helps the clients you serve. We recommend considering what you read and learn from others carefully before making any radical changes to the way you work. You should also be flexible enough to take in new findings with an open-minded attitude. You will learn much more about being a savvy consumer of empirical research and the importance of developing a practice based on empirical evidence (see Chapter 14). In the past several years, both of us have gone to seminars and read many books and articles on several treatment approaches that are new to us. Dr. Prout recently began learning about acceptance and commitment therapy (ACT; Hayes, Strosahl, & Wilson, 2012), which is derived from cognitive behavioral models and affect phobia therapy (McCullough et al., 2003). ACT combines short-term psychodynamic approaches with cognitive-behavioral therapy and experiential learning. One of the things we love about the profession of counseling is that we will always have opportunities to learn something new.

Know Thyself

Earlier we discussed the importance of developing multicultural competence and being aware of how your individual background will affect your work with clients. You will be best equipped to be an effective counselor if you know yourself well. This includes understanding how your personal background and identity impact the work you do and also developing insight into your personality characteristics, values, and personal history. There are many ways to get to know yourself. Personal reflection, being truly present in your interpersonal relationships, and feedback from supervisors are all tools that can illuminate parts of the self that might otherwise remain obscured.

Personal therapy can be one of the most helpful experiences in the shaping and preparation of a new therapist (Bike, Norcross, & Schatz, 2009). A personal experience of psychotherapy serves many purposes. It can help the neophyte therapist learn what it means to be in the client role (McWilliams, 2004), and this can be incredibly helpful in terms of identifying and empathizing with those you seek to help. As Alice Miller (1997) points out, many of us become psychotherapists because we came into the world with an emotional giftedness and found ourselves in the service of others for most of our childhood. There is a particular shared history among many psychotherapists that is important to understand prior to moving into the role of helper. Even if Miller's argument (which she outlines in her classic book, *The Drama of the Gifted Child*) does not resonate with you, it is indisputable that we all have our own neurotic tendencies, complex histories and relationships, unmet expectations, and emotional disappointments that we are likely to carry with us into the consulting room. Personal therapy is a place to work out some of those issues so that you can be less affected by these factors and more equipped to help. A former professor of mine, for whom English was a second language, often remarked in his translation of the old phrase, "We all have luggage." And it is true that we all come to this profession and to our clients with some degree of baggage...or luggage. Building on my mentor's observation, I often tell my students that they have to do everything in their power to check their baggage at the door so they do not burden their clients with it.

CHAPTER REVIEW

Counseling and psychotherapy involve methods that are distinct from other modes of social interaction. Individuals may receive support from family, friends, and a wide variety of professionals including medical doctors, life coaches, acupuncturists, and spiritual directors. The healing that is afforded them within the confines of a counseling relationship is distinct from those other helping relationships. It is based on assisting clients in finding solutions to problems they have been unable to solve using other means. Psychotherapy may employ many types of interventions, but the *relationship* between client and therapist is the cornerstone of change.

Since the beginning of recorded history, people have suffered from emotional and psychological distress. Despite this, psychotherapy proper did not begin until recently, at the beginning of the twentieth century, with the introduction of "the talking cure." Since its origination, many professions have emerged within the field of counseling. These include mental health counseling and marriage and family therapy, among others. The educational trajectories, licensing requirements, and professional settings of each profession differ. Considering your personality, interests, skills, and personal values will assist you in discovering the career that is right for you.

This book will teach you many interviewing and counseling skills. Clinical interviewing is a very particular way of interacting with a client. We conduct interviews to learn more about the client and to develop a course of action for treatment. The best interviews are based on a feeling of trust and mutual respect; clients should have the sense that you understand their vantage points and have a sincere commitment to helping them. Part of developing rapport involves being aware of and sensitive to the differences that exist between you and your clients. You and your clients may differ in terms of ethnicity, sexual orientation, religion, physical ability, or any other myriad characteristics. Many of our biases are implicit in nature. By acknowledging our limited ability to truly know all of our prejudices, we can take a step forward in being more culturally competent.

To become a counseling professional, it is important to be honest about the mistakes we make and be open to learning from them. In addition to learning from mistakes, all professional counselors must learn how to work effectively in an era of managed care. Developing expertise in diagnosis, effective treatment planning, and communicating with MCOs are all tools that will enhance your practice and further aid your clients. We have also discussed the complex interplay of theory and research and how to integrate these elements into your clinical practice. By learning about multiple theoretical orientations and reading peer-reviewed research, you will enhance the work you do and become a more sophisticated and mature clinician. Perhaps the most important job of the counselor is to know oneself. Self-reflection, personal therapy, and being open to constructive criticism and feedback will enrich you both personally and professionally in ways that are unmatched by any type of didactic learning.

PERSONAL REFLECTION ESSAY QUESTIONS

1. What are three personal qualities or strengths that led you to pursue a career in counseling? What personal limitations do you have that will challenge you as a professional?
2. After taking the Implicit Association Test (https://implicit.harvard.edu /implicit), discuss what surprised you about your results. Do you believe in the concept of implicit attitudes? Why or why not? What implications does your belief have for your work with clients?
3. Consider a recent mistake you made that resulted in someone's feelings being hurt. How did you respond to this situation? If they were to confront you about the mistake, what would you say and/or do in response?
4. Many students reading this book will have health insurance. What experiences, if any, have you or your family had with your own MCO? Has it been a positive or negative experience? Why? How might your own feelings about managed care be communicated to your clients?
5. Imagine you were to pursue personal therapy. What would you want to work on or discuss with your therapist? Identify three ways that personal therapy could help make you a more effective counselor.

KEYWORDS

clinical interviewing	marriage and family therapist	psychologist
counseling	moral treatment	psychotherapy
creative arts therapist	multicultural competence	rapport
expressive-supportive continuum	pastoral counselor	social worker
licensed mental health counselor	presenting problem	therapeutic alliance
managed care	psychiatric nurse practitioner	

FURTHER READING

For more information about creative arts therapies:

- Wiener, D. J. (1999). *Beyond talk therapy: Using movement and expressive techniques in clinical practice.* Washington, DC: American Psychological Association.

Paul L. Wachtel's book, *Inside the session: What really happens in psychotherapy* (2011; Washington, DC: American Psychological Association), is a wonderful resource to see word-for-word what happens during a counseling session. In addition to verbatim text, he also discusses his motivations, insights, hindsight, and critiques of his own work with the client.

- Wachtel, P. L. (2011). *Inside the session: What really happens in psychotherapy.* Washington, DC: American Psychological Association.

To learn more about how coming from a place of privilege can impact the practice of counseling, we recommend:

- Fine, M. (1984). Coping with rape: Critical perspectives on consciousness. *Imagination, Cognition, and Personality, 3*(3), 249–267.
- McIntosh, P. (1988). White privilege: Unpacking the invisible knapsack. Working paper 189—White privilege and male privilege: A personal account of coming to see correspondences through work in women's studies. Wellesley, MA: Wellesley College Center for Research on Women. Retrieved from http://www.nymbp.org/reference/WhitePrivilege.pdf

One of the most comprehensive overviews of multicultural competence is Derald Wing Sue's 2001 article in *The Counseling Psychologist* entitled "Multidimensional Facets of Cultural Competence." His colleagues also present thoughtful critiques of his MDCC model in that same issue.

- Sue, D. W. (2001). Multidimensional facets of cultural competence. *The Counseling Psychologist, 29*(6), 790–821.

For an excellent pocket-sized guide to diagnostic interviews based on the *DSM-5* criteria:

- Zimmerman, M. (2013). *Interview guide for evaluating DSM-5 psychiatric disorders and the mental status examination* (2nd ed.). East Greenwich, RI: Psych Products Press.

Several resources on the privileges and responsibilities that come with being a therapist:

- Kottler, J. A. (2010). *On being a therapist* (4th ed.). San Francisco, CA: Jossey-Bass.
- Yalom, I. (2003). *The gift of therapy: An open letter to a new generation of therapists and their patients.* New York, NY: Harper Perennial.

Doing Our Best—Ethics and Professional Responsibility

*Ethics is a state of mind that abstains from engaging in any
situation or event that would prove harmful to others. The
perfection of ethics is accomplished when you have developed
to the ultimate point the conviction not to harm others....
The pure observance of ethics is like a beautiful jewel that suits
everyone, irrespective of height, weight, age, and nationality.
Material ornaments may look beautiful on one person but not
on another, whereas the ornament of ethics looks beautiful on all
practitioners irrespective of their physical appearance. With the
pure observance of ethics you will naturally command respect
within the human community.*—Dalai Lama (1994, p. 161)

*Becoming an ethical psychotherapist or counselor is
more than memorization of rules—it is a journey.*
—Anderson and Handelsman (2010, p. vii)

LEARNING OBJECTIVES

- Define the following terms: ethics, confidentiality, subpoena, privilege, dual relationship
- Identify and describe the five aspirational principles of APA's *Ethical Principles of Psychologists and Code of Conduct*
- Discuss the importance of confidentiality to the therapeutic relationship
- Identify examples of situations in which it is acceptable to breach confidentiality
- Identify and discuss the relevant court cases that set precedents for the acceptability of breaching confidentiality
- Discuss the purpose of The Health Insurance Portability and Accountability Act of 1996 (HIPAA)

(continued)

(continued)

- Discuss the limits of confidentiality in terms of working with children and adolescents or adults under guardianship
- Identify and describe several examples of dual relationships
- Discuss the meaning of multicultural incompetence and why it is unethical
- Identify and describe the different models for ethical decision making
- Identify several tools professionals have for making ethical decisions and dealing with ethical dilemmas
- Describe the importance of the core value of humility for a mental health professional

UNDERSTANDING ETHICS

Imagine that you are meeting someone for the first time. Some people are quite comfortable making new acquaintances and easily approach strangers with a sense of curiosity and openness, whereas others are nervous at the idea of meeting someone new and feel a sense of apprehension and guardedness in this situation. Think about where you fall on this continuum from comfort to discomfort in the presence of someone new. Now imagine that you are expected to divulge personal information to this stranger. In fact, you are expected to tell this person about your thoughts, feelings, and behavior in great detail and, perhaps, to the extent that you have not previously shared with anyone else. Would you still feel as comfortable as you typically do in the presence of someone new? What assurances would you want to have about the other person's intentions and motives to feel confident that you could safely share this information?

When clients approach their first therapy appointment, they may feel anxious and vulnerable because they are faced with the daunting dual tasks of meeting a new person and discussing very personal issues. Clients are able to disclose information to therapists because they believe that it will be kept private and used only to benefit them. This task of revealing private material often becomes easier in subsequent therapeutic encounters. The client comes to know the therapist as a responsible professional who is committed to behaving ethically, which includes maintaining confidentiality and promoting the client's well-being. This trust in the therapist subsequently leads to the development and strengthening of the therapeutic relationship, which enhances treatment outcomes (see Chapter 7). Therefore, an essential and important task of developing as a mental health professional is becoming familiar with the foundations of ethics as they apply to counseling situations and reflecting on how to adopt a professional identity that reflects one's commitment to enacting these principles to protect and promote the welfare of clients.

Guiding Principles

Each person has a unique set of values that serves as a guide in daily decision making and for interactions with others. As mental health professionals, we strive to share a common set of values and aim to use them as our guide when we interact with our clients, act on their behalf as professionals, and make decisions regarding their care. **Ethics** are guidelines and principles that inform moral judgment and professional conduct. The American Psychological Association (APA) has outlined five aspirational ethical principles in its *Ethical Principles of Psychologists and Code of Conduct* (2002, amended 2010) that should guide the behavior of all mental health professionals in practice.

Beneficence and Nonmaleficence

This principle suggests that mental health professionals should not only seek to benefit their clients in practice (i.e., do good), but they should also strive to prevent hurting them (i.e., do no harm). Adherence to this principle means that when conflicts arise, the mental health professional aims to find a resolution that avoids or reduces harm to their clients and others (APA, 2002, amended 2010). In addition, mental health professionals should remain aware of their ability to help those who seek their services and how their ability to benefit their clients may be compromised by their own physical or mental health concerns. When mental health professionals are experiencing personal or professional stressors, the risk of potential harm to their clients is increased (Celenza & Gabbard, 2003). Making the decision to seek personal therapy, professional consultation, or to refrain from providing services when one's ability is impaired by personal issues is one important way to uphold the principles of **beneficence** and **nonmaleficence**.

Fidelity and Responsibility

This principle refers to the ideal of developing a faithful and trusting relationship with one's clients through ethical actions and, furthermore, behaving in a manner that promotes the public's trust of mental health professionals as a whole. This principle also highlights the responsibility of mental health professionals to conduct themselves in a professional manner and to clarify their role as necessary to minimize conflicts of interest that might harm others (APA, 2002, amended 2010). One important way that mental health professionals show **fidelity** and **responsibility** to their clients is by maintaining the confidentiality of the information revealed in a session, within legal limits (see section on Confidentiality and Its Limits later in this chapter). Furthermore, mental health professionals should inform their clients if and when the limits of confidentiality have been reached and disclosure of confidential information must be made to another individual or group.

Integrity

When acting with **integrity**, mental health professionals seek to be accurate, honest, and truthful with their clients and with others. This means that one should keep promises and avoid making commitments that are unclear or impossible to maintain (APA, 2002, amended 2010). Mental health professionals act with integrity when they practice within the bounds of their competence. In practice, this means that when a client is seeking services for a particular issue that exceeds the limits of the therapist's expertise, the professional should either obtain the education and supervision necessary to provide effective care or refer the client to another qualified professional.

Justice

This principle recognizes the value of **justice** or fairness in terms of access to mental health services for all people and also in working to ensure the equal quality of services offered to all people (APA, 2002, amended 2010). For example, a therapist should not refuse to provide therapy to a client based solely on demographic characteristics. There are times when a mental health professional may decide to refer a potential client to another practitioner because she is not competent to treat the presenting problem. However, the decision to refer should not be based on the personal attributes or economic status of the client. Furthermore, clinicians should remain aware of the effects of oppression based on ethnicity, sexual orientation, gender, age, and/or ability in the clients with whom they work. Mental health professionals must strive to meet the needs of clients who seek help and recognize when social and economic inequities necessitate different but comparable professional services (Fisher, 2003).

Respect for People's Rights and Dignity

This ethical principle guides mental health professionals to examine and eliminate the possible effects of biases on their work. These biases may be based on age, gender, gender identity, race, ethnicity, culture, national origin, religion, sexual orientation, disability, language, and socioeconomic status (APA, 2002, amended 2010). In addition to exploring personal biases, mental health professionals should seek to be familiar with knowledge relevant to working with individuals with diverse backgrounds and strive to become competent in providing appropriate and effective services to these clients.

An important part of respecting the dignity of each person is to recognize their **autonomy** and responsibility for making their own decisions. An ethical mental health professional believes that his or her clients are capable of directing their own lives and making choices about their futures. In an informative study, Jennings, Sovereign, Bottorff, Mussell, and Vye (2005) interviewed "master therapists" to elicit information about their core ethical values. One participant remarked, "I mean, we really know what's best for ourselves and what the truth is about ourselves and our own direction. I think that a big part of our job as therapists is to help get all the other voices out of the way for the clients, so they can hear their own and begin to have some faith in it" (Jennings et al., 2005, p. 38). Ethical mental health professionals not only recognize and respect the autonomy of their clients but foster the growth of their clients' independent decision-making.

THE ETHICS CODE AND PROFESSIONAL STANDARDS

In addition to the recognition of general ethical principles that guide the behavior and decisions of mental health professionals, many professional organizations have also adopted a set of enforceable ethical **standards** based on these general **principles**. These ethics codes are vital to safeguard the welfare of clients and others who work with mental health professionals, in addition to protecting professionals who are accused of ethical violations. Without an ethics code or an agreement of what professional behaviors are acceptable in a range of situations, mental health professionals might be held to standards imposed by those outside of their field (e.g., state licensing boards or courts; Fisher, 2003). Additionally, the existence of an ethics code increases the general public's trust in the profession by demonstrating the field's commitment to providing services responsibly and with integrity. People may trust that mental health professionals are trained in and committed to upholding high professional standards and conduct because there is an ethics code (Fisher, 2003).

The APA Ethics Code

The APA is a professional organization for psychologists, and membership in the APA requires adherence to its ethics code. The APA's *Ethical Principles of Psychologists and Code of Conduct* (2002, amended 2010) contains ethical standards relevant to 10 areas of professional practice (see Table 2.1). Each area contains 6 to 15 specific standards intended to assist psychologists in making decisions regarding their professional behavior in addition to consideration of relevant laws and other regulations imposed by psychology licensing boards (APA, 2002, amended 2010).

The American Counseling Association (ACA) Ethics Code

The ACA is an organization made up of professional counselors such as licensed professional counselors (LPCs) or school counselors. The *ACA Code of Ethics* (ACA, 2005) contains eight sections relevant to professional practice (see Table 2.1). As you can see, there is extensive overlap between these two sets of standards, which highlight the universal importance of particular aspects of mental health practice. A discussion about the specifics of any ethics code is beyond the scope of this chapter, and we encourage you to locate and obtain the ethics code for your particular field. (See the Further Reading section at the end of the chapter for information regarding locating professional codes of ethics for a variety of disciplines.)

We will describe two important topics in detail here: (a) confidentiality and its limits and (b) dual relationships. These two areas will be covered in depth because they present complex issues for mental health providers and are universally relevant to all mental health disciplines. Confidentiality is a vital characteristic of the therapeutic relationship, but it must at times be broken for ethical or legal

TABLE 2.1 A Comparison of Categories of Ethical Standards in the APA Ethics Code (2002, Amended 2010) and the *ACA Code of Ethics* (2005)

THE APA ETHICS CODE (2002, AMENDED 2010)	ACA CODE OF ETHICS (2005)
1. Resolving ethical issues	H. Resolving ethical issues
2. Competence	C. Professional responsibility
3. Human relations	A. The counseling relationship; D. Relationships with other professionals
4. Privacy and confidentiality	B. Confidentiality, privileged communication, and privacy
5. Advertising and other public statements	C. Professional responsibility
6. Record keeping and fees	A. The counseling relationship
7. Education and training	F. Supervision, training, and teaching
8. Research and publication	G. Research and publication
9. Assessment	E. Evaluation, assessment, and interpretation
10. Therapy	A. The counseling relationship

ACA, American Counseling Association; APA, American Psychological Association.

reasons. The decision to breach confidentiality is not easily made by mental health professionals because of the negative impact it may have on the therapeutic relationship. The second topic, forming dual relationships with clients, is another area that may negatively affect the therapeutic relationship. Dual relationships are associated with the greatest number of complaints of ethical violations against mental health practitioners (Boland-Prom, 2009; Neukrug, Milliken, & Walden, 2001), which indicates the importance of being aware of potential difficulties that may arise when therapists have contact with clients outside of treatment.

CONFIDENTIALITY AND ITS LIMITS

Confidentiality is a standard of professional behavior that requires mental health professionals to not reveal or discuss information about their clients without the clients' authorization. As was discussed at the beginning of the chapter, it is difficult to imagine forming a trusting therapeutic relationship without assuring clients that you will protect their personal information to the greatest extent possible. Privacy is a basic right for all people, and mental health professionals respect the dignity of their clients by keeping their personal information private. This standard applies to information discussed in session or in other communication with the client, as well as information that the mental health professional has written about the client in files, documents, or notes. Furthermore, maintaining clients' confidentiality is an extended commitment lasting forever. The *ACA Code of Ethics* (2005) explicitly states that counselors are required to protect the confidentiality of deceased clients.

Because mental health professionals aim to practice with fidelity and integrity, they should discuss confidentiality and its limits carefully and clearly as soon as possible with clients. It is recommended that this conversation happen during the initial session with a new client, if not sooner. Written information about confidentiality and its limits may be provided to clients electronically on a practitioner's website or via e-mail before their first session. The discussion of confidentiality and its limits prior to or within the first session not only helps clients to feel comfortable sharing private information with mental health professionals, but it also helps to clarify for the client instances in which the therapist may be obligated to breach confidentiality *before* the potential situation has arisen. It is much more difficult to explain to a client that you are not able to keep what they have just revealed to you confidential than it is to outline the limits from the beginning of the professional relationship.

BOX 2.1

Social Networking and Client Privacy: Should You Search?

The popularity of social networking websites has made it easier than ever to gain personal information about individuals. It is becoming widely accepted to connect with new acquaintances via social networking sites such as Facebook, Instagram, and Twitter. There are even professional networking sites, such as LinkedIn, that provide virtual spaces for people to interact and share information about themselves. In a recent study, 77.3% of early

(continued)

(continued)

career psychologists and graduate students reported that they use social networking sites to communicate with family and friends (Taylor, McMinn, Bufford, & Chang, 2010). The ubiquity of social networking has led some to explore the ethical issues surrounding professionals' ability to access private information shared in these public spaces by people with whom they have professional relationships.

For example, imagine you are a graduate student seeing clients in a university-based clinic. It is likely that you might have a connection to a client on Facebook. Your client might be the "friend of a friend," and depending on the privacy settings that the client has selected, you could potentially have access to information that the client has posted on Facebook that is not available to the general public. Search engines, such as Google, also make it incredibly easy to discover personal information about individuals, and the recent popularity of publishing blogs online also enables mental health professionals to find and read private information about clients. Seeking out and obtaining personal information about clients on the internet, whether publicly available or not, may put a strain on the therapeutic relationship.

If you were to discover something online that the client has not directly revealed to you that you want to discuss in the session (e.g., something you think is important or something that is discrepant from what the client has revealed to you), you are in the position of having to acknowledge that you searched for information about him or her and deal with your client's reaction to discovering that you have invaded his or her privacy. This course of action is at odds with upholding the ethical principles of fidelity and responsibility as well as beneficence and nonmaleficence in your professional relationships. On the other hand, you may discover personal information but decide not to disclose that you sought out information or bring it up in session, which also impacts the honesty and genuineness of the therapeutic relationship and is at odds with the ethical principle of integrity in professional relationships. Although there are times that mental health professionals discover information about their clients without seeking it out (see subsection Ethical Dilemma at the end of the chapter for an example of this), the opportunity (or temptation) to use social networking to learn more about clients presents a new kind of ethical dilemma. Recent surveys of mental health professionals indicated that 27% to 32% of respondents have searched for client information online; a majority did so out of curiosity or therapeutic concern (Lehavot, Barnett, & Powers, 2010; Tunick, Mednick, & Conroy, 2011).

When deciding whether or not to search for clients on the internet, it is important to keep in mind that the ethical standards regarding safeguarding clients' privacy typically refer to seeking out personal information in the session only when it is necessary and not just to satisfy curiosity. When searching for personal information outside of the consulting room, there may be potential benefits to the well-being and safety of clients or there may be potential risks of harm to the client and the relationship. Consider all potential outcomes and how you would handle each one before you decide to click on the search button.

Most ethics codes for mental health professionals include specific standards for maintaining confidentiality. The APA Ethics Code (2002, amended 2010) indicates that psychologists have the obligation to "take reasonable precautions to protect confidential information obtained through or stored in any medium" (Standard 4.01). The remaining standards pertaining to confidentiality highlight discussing the limits of confidentiality at the "outset of the relationship" (Standard 4.02), obtaining permission before making audio or video recordings of clients (Standard 4.03), communicating only the minimum amount of information "germane to the purpose" when providing written or oral reports about clients (Standard 4.04), obtaining appropriate consent from the client to disclose confidential information when it is requested (Standard 4.05), protecting the identity of clients discussed with colleagues in consultation such that the client cannot be identified (Standard 4.06), and protecting the identity of clients in professional writings, lectures, or public media appearances (Standard 4.07).

BOX 2.2

Standard 4.06 Illustrated

The importance of protecting the identity of clients discussed in consultation with colleagues was recently illustrated for Dr. Prout. She was attending a case conference with professional colleagues and listened to a peer present information about a client for approximately 20 minutes. The colleague revealed some very personal details about the client's sexual abuse history, current sexual performance issues, and current risky behaviors. Eventually, she revealed enough detail for Dr. Prout to realize that this client was someone she knew. Upon this realization, Dr. Prout immediately informed the group that she knew the client and offered to leave the room. The group chose to discontinue the presentation, and Dr. Prout discussed her ethical concerns with the clinician afterwards.

The *ACA Code of Ethics* (2005) includes several standards related to confidentiality that are similar to those in the APA Ethics Code. These include avoiding disclosure of confidential information without consent, legal justification, or ethical justification (Standard B.1.c), explaining the limits of confidentiality "at initiation and throughout the counseling process" (Standard B.1.d), and revealing only the essential information when disclosure is appropriate (Standard B.2.d). In addition, the *ACA Code of Ethics* stresses having "awareness and sensitivity regarding cultural meanings of confidentiality and privacy" (Standard B.1.a), which alerts counselors to be attentive to the potential that clients may have different views of how and when information may be shared with others based on their cultural norms. The *ACA Code of Ethics* also includes a standard for respecting the privacy of clients by seeking private information from clients only when it is beneficial to the counseling process (Standard B.1.b).

Koocher and Keith-Spiegel (1998) recommend three steps for mental health professionals to use to manage risk and make ethical decisions regarding breaking confidentiality. First, they recommend that mental health professionals review relevant ethical standards and legal obligations to determine the specific circumstances under which they would breach confidentiality in the course of practice. Second, mental health professionals should make these limits known to each of their clients. Finally, when a situation arises that seems to warrant disclosure of confidential information, Koocher and Keith-Spiegel encourage mental health professionals to consult with colleagues to see if there is an appropriate alternative to disclosure.

The following section highlights some of the situations that may occur in mental health practice that typically lead to disclosure of confidential information. This list is not exhaustive, and you must be familiar with your professional ethics code as well as state and local laws applicable to confidentiality in mental health settings. The following sections will help you begin to develop your personal policy regarding maintaining confidentiality and its limits.

Safety of Patient and Others

Mental health professionals are not required to keep information confidential when they are compelled by ethical or legal standards to act to protect individuals (i.e., clients or potential victims identified by clients) from serious harm. Mental health professionals may have a **duty to warn** and protect third parties against danger posed by patients (for more information see Box 2.3). Mental health professionals also have an ethical obligation to protect clients when they are at risk of seriously harming themselves. Another specific situation in which mental health professionals are required to disclose confidential information is to report abuse of children or the elderly. In many states, mental health professionals (along with other professionals such as teachers and clergy) are mandated reporters, which means they are obligated to protect vulnerable populations (i.e., children and the elderly) by reporting suspected cases of abuse.

What situations may arise in therapy to signal that there is clear and present danger? Clients may express explicit suicidal ideation and intent in session (see Chapter 13 for more information on suicide assessment), or they may make specific homicidal threats with intent toward a specific victim. However, there are other more complex situations for which there is no established or agreed-upon precedent for breaching or maintaining confidentiality.

The duty of mental health professionals to warn or protect third parties from risk of acquiring HIV through risky sexual contact with HIV-positive clients is an example of an ethical dilemma on which professional standards and expert opinions differ (Huprich, Fuller, & Schneider, 2003). The American Psychiatric Association and the American Medical Association both require professionals to discuss the limits of confidentiality with patients with HIV and to take steps to disclose HIV status to unknowing sexual partners (American Medical Association Council on Ethical and Judicial Affairs, 1988; American Psychiatric Association Ad Hoc Committee on AIDS Policy, 1988). The APA (1991), on the other hand, has concluded that there is no legal duty to warn in this situation. Furthermore, if legislation is imposed that requires psychologists to disclose clients' HIV status, the psychologist should only do so when a known partner, who is unaware of the risk, is identified, and the client is unwilling to tell that individual directly. As with many other ethical issues, the law varies from state to state, and mental health professionals have a duty to be informed about the legal mandates within the jurisdiction in which they practice.

BOX 2.3

Is There a Duty to Warn and Protect?

In 1969, Prosenjit Poddar, a graduate student at the University of California, Berkeley, murdered Tatiana Tarasoff. Prior to the homicide, Poddar had been in therapy with a psychologist at the university's student health center. During the course of therapy, Poddar discussed his strong feelings toward Ms. Tarasoff as well as his feelings of depression because she did not feel the same way about him. Poddar reported fantasies of killing Tarasoff to his therapist in session, and outside of their sessions, the therapist learned from a third party that Poddar intended to buy a gun. The psychologist consulted with his colleagues and decided to inform the police that he thought Poddar was dangerous, given his obsession with Tarasoff and his intent to purchase a gun. The police followed up on the therapist's report and ultimately determined that Poddar did not pose a serious threat and released him based on his promise that he would stay away from Ms. Tarasoff. Poddar did not return to therapy after this experience with the police, and killed Ms. Tarasoff soon after (Stone, 1976). Ms. Tarasoff's parents brought a lawsuit because they felt that the university had failed to protect their daughter. This landmark case established the duty of mental health professionals to warn potential victims of threatened harm by their clients and to protect those not specifically named by taking steps to use civil commitment procedures for potentially dangerous clients as allowable by existing mental health legislation (Young, 2011).

However, a more recent ruling by the Texas Supreme Court is at odds with *Tarasoff* (1976). In *Thapar v. Zezulka* (1999) the court decided not to mandate a duty to protect third parties upon considering the case of a client who informed his psychiatrist that he was considering killing his stepfather and killed him weeks later. The psychiatrist did not contact police or try to warn the client's stepfather about these threats. The court concluded that they would not adopt a duty to warn because of the confidentiality statute governing mental health professionals in Texas. They also went further to state that mental health professionals "make disclosures at their own peril" when they warn third parties about threats made by clients because violations of the state's confidentiality statute leave them vulnerable to civil liability (994 S. W2d 635).

As you can see, it is important to be aware of the state legislation and common laws pertaining to mental health where you practice because it is likely to have a significant impact on whether you choose to maintain or break confidentiality in situations involving threats made by clients toward identifiable third parties. Although many jurisdictions have followed California's lead and adopted a duty to warn and protect, this is not the case in all states. Accordingly, if you breach confidentiality in good faith to warn a potential victim in a jurisdiction without an established duty to warn and protect, you may be at risk of a potential lawsuit (Younggren & Harris, 2008). Making the decision to reveal confidential information may feel stressful to all mental health professionals, and it is recommended that you seek supervision, consultation, and other resources, such as colleagues from your professional organization, for support in making this big decision.

Tarasoff v. Regents of the University of California (1976);
Thapar v. Zezulka (1999)

Court Requests

In the course of mental health practice, there are times when professionals are issued a request from a court or litigant to provide confidential information about a client. There are two types of requests that may be encountered: a subpoena or a court order. A **subpoena** is a request that may not come directly from a judge, and, accordingly, the professional may not be required to provide the information that has been requested if the client has not given consent for disclosure and it is privileged communication. **Privilege** is a legal term that refers to particular relationships that are protected from disclosure during legal proceedings (e.g., attorney-client or spousal privilege). In 1996, the Supreme Court wrote a decision granting clients of licensed psychotherapists privilege under Federal Rules of Evidence (*Jaffe v. Redmond*, 1996, pp. 4492–4493). Privilege belongs to the client, and, therefore, the client must grant permission for the mental health professional to disclose privileged communication.

To fulfill your ethical obligation to keep client information confidential, the first step to take when issued a subpoena is to seek legal advice. An attorney can help you to clarify the source of the request and your resulting obligations. If the subpoena is issued by a judge (and, hence, is a **court order**), you may be compelled to release the information even without the consent of your client. Before you do, you should seek legal counsel and try to take all reasonable steps to avoid disclosing the confidential information before making the decision to do so. When compelled by law to perform an action that violates ethical standards, mental health professionals may choose civil disobedience and face legal repercussions. Likewise, mental health professionals who choose to knowingly violate ethical standards to fulfill a legal obligation are rarely sanctioned for this ethical violation by their professional organization (Koocher & Keith-Spiegel, 1998).

If the subpoena is not a court order, it may have been issued by your client's attorney or an attorney representing someone else. If the request comes from your client's attorney, you should seek the consent of your client to release the information. If the request has come from another party's attorney, you may contact that attorney and explain that you cannot disclose whether or not the person listed on the subpoena is or was your client. You should also assert that if the person was your client, you could not ethically disclose confidential information without the client's signed consent or a valid court order. Once you have responded to the attorney requesting the subpoena, you may contact your client and request authorization to contact the client's attorney to discuss how to respond to the subpoena or possibly move to quash the subpoena. If you do disclose information to the court, it is wise to offer a notarized copy rather than the original because there is a risk these documents could be lost. In addition, mental health professionals should release the minimum amount of information necessary to fulfill the request to protect their clients' privacy (Koocher & Keith-Spiegel, 1998).

The Health Insurance Portability and Accountability Act of 1996 (HIPAA)

The HIPAA Privacy Rule pertains to the protection and release of health care information (i.e., PHI or patient health information) that is electronically transmitted or maintained (45 C.F.R. Pts. 160 and 164; U.S. Department of Health and Human Services, 2002). Mental health care providers who submit information electronically related to managed care claims or several other types of specific transactions related to health care must comply with mandated standards for protecting PHI. This includes obtaining a written release from the client to disclose PHI, which includes a detailed description of exactly what will be disclosed, to whom it will be disclosed, the purpose of the disclosure, an expiration date, and a signature (45 CFR 164.508[c]). The HIPAA Privacy Rule also authorizes disclosure of PHI without client consent in a variety of situations, such as when required by law; to report suspected abuse, neglect, or domestic violence; or for law enforcement purposes.

Under HIPAA, psychotherapy notes are protected in a special way compared to other health care information. Mental health professionals are allowed to keep psychotherapy notes that are separate from the client's health record.

Psychotherapy notes mean notes recorded (in any medium) by a health care provider who is a mental health professional documenting or analyzing the contents of conversation during private, one-to-one counseling or group, joint, or family counseling session; such notes are separated from the rest of the individual's medical record. Psychotherapy notes exclude medication prescription and monitoring, counseling session start and stop times, the modalities and frequencies of treatment furnished, results of clinical tests, and any summary of the following items: diagnosis, functional status, the treatment plan, symptoms, prognosis, and progress to date (U.S. Department of Health and Human Services, 2000, p. 82805).

The ability to keep this separate set of notes helps to safeguard client privacy by protecting sensitive information from disclosure to managed care companies

ILLUSTRATION 2.1 Remember to keep your psychotherapy notes in a separate physical location. This way clients or courts are not privy to them if the records are reviewed or subpoenaed.

Courtesy of Kathleen Franklin.

or others requesting PHI. Mental health professionals must keep these notes in a separate physical location from the rest of the record for them to be protected. Furthermore, HIPAA regulations mandate that clients must make an additional consent for the psychotherapy notes to be disclosed, but mental health professionals should ultimately make the decision as to whether to release the psychotherapy notes—even in cases when the client has given consent.

Special Cases

The previous discussion has focused on ethical behavior related to maintaining confidentiality when working with adults who have the ability to consent to treatment and are typically able to understand the limits of confidentiality when they are informed by mental health professionals. However, there are two special populations that require additional consideration: minors and adults under guardianship. All healthy therapeutic relationships are built on the trust that results from the promise of confidentiality. When mental health professionals are working with these particular populations, additional considerations must be made to ensure that clients and other involved parties understand the importance of confidentiality to mental health treatment. Mental health professionals should work with legal guardians to agree upon set limits to that confidentiality.

Working With Children and Adolescents

Mental health professionals who work with minors need to be aware not only of the rights afforded to children and adolescents regarding confidentiality in therapy but also of the ability for minors to consent to mental health treatment without their parents' knowledge. There is an inherent conflict between the right of minors to confidentiality in therapy and the right of their parents to gain information about their health care information (Younggren & Harris, 2008). The law typically grants parents access to their child's health care information because it is assumed that children may not be competent to understand and make decisions about it. However, in some areas there are exceptions to the rule. Currently, Ohio and California both have laws concerning the right of adolescents to consent to mental health treatment without parental involvement in specific circumstances (Younggren & Harris, 2008).

Although parents generally have rights to information about their children, mental health professionals should discuss the importance of confidentiality to the therapeutic relationship with parents. Most parents will understand the importance for their child to have a safe space to open up and share private information without fear that it will be revealed to others. It is important to speak to parents about your intention to use professional judgment to determine when sharing or not sharing information with them is in their child's best interest. It is also recommended that you discuss the limits of confidentiality with parents and their children regarding your obligation to protect your client and others from harm.

Professional standards have addressed this problem. The *ACA Code of Ethics* (2005) suggests that counselors should take steps to "clearly define who is considered 'the client' and to discuss expectations and limitations of confidentiality" (Standard B.4.b). This refers to making it clear who is receiving treatment (i.e., the client) and who is assisting in treatment (i.e., collaterals, meaning family members or friends who may be involved in therapy sessions but are not considered to be in treatment themselves). This is especially relevant when working with a teen, because revealing personal information could potentially damage the therapeutic relationship if parents assert their right to information about their child's treatment. It is recommended that mental health professionals not only discuss their preferences with parents about maintaining confidentiality of private information shared by children and adolescents but also to create a contract, a written and signed agreement between all the involved parties—therapist, parents, and the minor client (ACA, 2005; Younggren & Harris, 2008).

Working With Adults Under Guardianship

Many of the same principles apply when working with adults who have a legal guardian because of their diminished capacity to live independently or make autonomous decisions about their health care. Mental health professionals must discuss the limits of confidentiality with these individuals, including specific details about how and when information may be shared with their guardian. If the client is cognitively impaired, the mental health professional must inform the client to the extent possible in a way that is understandable and in addition discuss the limits of confidentiality with the legal guardian. Adults under guardianship are a vulnerable population, and mental health professionals should be well acquainted with the laws regarding reporting suspected cases of abuse to protect the well-being of their clients.

DUAL RELATIONSHIPS

An examination of the types of complaints filed against LPCs revealed that the most common complaint to state licensing boards was to report inappropriate dual relationships (24%; Neukrug et al., 2001). The pattern is the same for social workers, with 12.2% of sanctions issued against professionals between 1999 and 2004 pertaining to sexual and romantic dual relationships and 11.2% pertaining to nonsexual or unspecified dual relationships (Boland-Prom, 2009). Dual relationships are one of the most common reasons for clients to feel that their therapist has acted in an unprofessional or unethical manner. Because of the harm that can be caused by a dual relationship, it is vitally important that mental health professionals be familiar with the ethical standards and principles that apply to developing appropriate relationships with clients outside of the therapeutic relationship.

Definition and Examples

Multiple role relationships, or **dual relationships**, are defined as those situations in which the mental health professional is either (a) in more than one professional relationship with an individual or (b) in another "definitive and intended role" in addition to the professional relationship (Sonne, 1994, p. 336). This definition does not include chance encounters with clients at the grocery store or the gym, although those limited encounters can also affect the therapeutic relationship. Dual relationships are those in which the mental health professional is intentionally entering into an additional professional or personal relationship with a client.

Dual relationships can be concurrent or consecutive (i.e., prior to initiation of treatment or subsequent to termination) with the therapy relationship (Koocher & Keith-Spiegel, 1998). A dual relationship can include situations in which the mental health professional seeks professional services from the client, concurrently or consecutively. For example, Dr. Wadkins once briefly considered seeking services from the parent of a teenage client who was a professional piano tuner but decided not to because it was easy to find another piano tuner in the area. A dual relationship may also arise if the mental health professional has another professional identity and the client seeks a different type of service with the therapist, either simultaneously or sequentially. For example, a counselor may also provide services as a personal trainer at a local gym and a client may seek personal training with his or her counselor.

In addition to professional dual relationships, there may also be multiple relationships that are personal in nature. A mental health professional may consider entering into a friendship or romantic relationship with a current or former client. A mental health professional may also choose to enter into a personal relationship with a client by signing up her child on the same community soccer team as her client's child.

Most professional codes of ethics contain standards relevant to avoiding dual relationships (Gottlieb, 1993). Sexual relationships with clients are *always* unethical and are frequently illegal. However, it is not always the case that dual relationships are unethical. Realistically, multiple relationships are at times unavoidable. In fact, the *ACA Code of Ethics* (2005) was revised to acknowledge that not all types of dual relationships may be harmful (Kocet, 2006). A famous example of a dual relationship between therapist and client is the collaboration of Irvin Yalom and his client "Ginny Elkin." The pair wrote a book together, *Every Day Gets A Little Closer: A Twice-Told Therapy* (1974), about their experiences during her treatment. There are, however, a variety of other types of relationships that mental health professionals may contemplate engaging in with their clients and may do so ethically.

In general, concurrent dual relationships with clients have the highest potential of harm and conflicts of interest (Sonne, 1994), but mental health professionals may choose to enter into dual relationships with clients, simultaneously or sequentially with treatment, after careful analysis of the risks and benefits along with the weighing of ethical standards and principles. The APA Ethics Code (2002, amended 2010) states that psychologists may enter into dual relationships with clients if the relationship is not likely "to impair the psychologist's objectivity, competence, or effectiveness in performing his or her function as a psychologist or otherwise risks exploitation or harm to the person with whom the professional relationship exists" (Standard 3.05).

Avoiding Exploitative Multiple Relationships

Gottlieb (1993) developed a model for mental health professionals to use when contemplating entering into a dual relationship with a client. The model includes analyzing three dimensions of both the current and contemplated relationships: power, duration, and clarity of termination. Each dimension includes three levels, and when professionals find that the current or proposed relationship falls in

POWER		
Low	**Mid-Range**	**High**
Little or no personal relationship or Persons consider each other peers (may include elements of influence)	Clear power differential present but relationship is circumscribed	Clear power differential with profound personal influence possible
DURATION		
Brief	**Intermediate**	**Long**
Single or few conflicts over short period of time	Regular contact over a limited period of time	Continuous or episodic contact over a long period of time
TERMINATION		
Specific	**Uncertain**	**Indefinite**
Relationship is limited by time externally imposed or by prior agreement of parties who are unlikely to see each other again	Professional function is completed but further contact is not ruled out	No agreement regarding when or if termination is to take place

FIGURE 2.1 Dimensions of ethical decision making.

Reprinted from Gottlieb (1993).

the "high" range on one or more of these dimensions (i.e., higher power differential, longer duration of the professional relationship, and less clear and definite termination), there is a risk of harm or exploitation, and the dual relationship should not be pursued (see Figure 2.1). In relationships where all dimensions fall in the mid or low range, professionals should evaluate whether the roles are incompatible and obtain consultation to determine whether the relationship is likely to be nonexploitive. Gottlieb further urges professionals to discuss these dimensions and considerations with the client as a matter of informed consent before engaging in the dual relationships.

Younggren and Gottlieb (2004) have further elaborated on the process for a mental health professional to determine the nature of dual relationship they are considering pursuing with a client. They have outlined a series of questions for professionals to ask themselves about the particular situation: (a) "Is entering into a relationship in addition to the professional one necessary, or should I avoid it?"; (b) "Can the dual relationship potentially cause harm to the patient?"; (c) "If harm seems unlikely or avoidable, would the additional relationship prove beneficial?"; (d) "Is there a risk that the dual relationship could disrupt the therapeutic relationship?"; (e) "Can I evaluate this matter objectively?" (pp. 256–257). Avoiding multiple relationships is difficult for all professionals and nearly impossible for some (e.g., mental health professionals in rural locations). When deciding what to do, an ethical therapist examines both the potential for harm or exploitation (nonmaleficence) but also the likelihood that the multiple relationship may be beneficial to the client (beneficence).

BOX 2.4

Spotlight on Culture: Multicultural Incompetence Is Unethical

Brown and Pomerantz (2011) examined how nonprofessionals viewed cultural and noncultural ethical violations, and the results highlighted the importance of cultural competence in mental health treatment. Undergraduate students were presented with 12 short vignettes about a psychologist who committed an ethical violation. Half of the vignettes included culturally based unethical behavior (i.e., a prejudicial or insensitive response to a client's race gender, religion, socioeconomic status, age, or sexual orientation), and half of the vignettes illustrated a noncultural ethical violation (i.e., a sexual multiple relationship, a nonsexual multiple relationship, breaching confidentiality, practicing outside the bounds of competence, practicing while impaired, and mishandling and interruption of services while on vacation).

The results indicated that the students felt that both cultural and noncultural ethical violations would have equally negative effects on the professional relationship and the client's progress. However, as compared to a noncultural ethical violation, students viewed the culturally based violations in a significantly more negative light. They reported higher agreement that the culturally insensitive therapists had indeed committed an unethical act, would be less desirable as therapists, and were more deserving of being reported to a supervisor or the state licensing board for their behavior (Brown & Pomerantz, 2011).

This study illustrates the importance that the general public places on multicultural competence in mental health treatment. In fact, these results imply that clients may view cultural insensitivity as more egregious than other ethical violations, and mental health professionals should seek training and experiences, which increase their multicultural sensitivity to practice ethically and to benefit their clients.

MAKING ETHICAL DECISIONS

Although it is extremely important for mental health professionals to be familiar with the ethics code for their specific field and its enforceable standards, we prefaced this chapter with an acknowledgement that there is more to becoming an ethical professional than the memorization of principles and standards. As part of their training and formation, mental health professionals must also be taught how to make decisions about their conduct in situations in which several (sometimes opposing) ethical principles may be relevant. Ethics have traditionally been taught by presenting students with ethical predicaments and discussing how to apply universal ethical principles in a responsible manner (Beauchamp & Childress, 1983). Whereas this is a valuable teaching tool (and we will present our own ethical dilemma at the end of this chapter for you to consider), there are also several formal methods of ethical decision making that have been proposed and adopted by mental health professionals.

The Philosophical Approach to Decision Making

Rest (1984) proposed a philosophical model that focuses on the processes of moral reasoning for mental health professionals to use when making ethical decisions. It is comprised of four steps: (a) to interpret the situation by considering how one's actions affect the welfare of clients, (b) to decide what a moral action would be by recognizing the moral ideal for the specific situation, (c) to select the one to act upon, deciding whether or not to try to fulfill their moral ideal, and (d) to implement what one intends to do (Rest, 1984). He later conceptualized these four components as (a) "moral sensitivity"; (b) "moral judgment"; (c) "moral motivation"; and (d) "moral character" (Rest, 1984, pp. 23–24). There may be difficulties for the mental health professional at each step of the process, including failing to see an ethical quandary (i.e., not seeing how one's professional actions are negatively affecting client well-being) or being unable to make a decision about a course of action or even being unable to act on a chosen resolution. This model stresses a rational cognitive approach to recognizing a problem, identifying alternative courses of action, and summoning the motivation and determination to carry out the chosen ethical behavior.

Practice-Based Decision Making

Tarvydas (1998) developed an alternative model that highlights not only the cognitive aspects of ethical decision making, but also the emotional and contextual aspects of the process. Her model emphasizes the professional's self-awareness, paying attention to the context of the ethical dilemma, and collaboration of the involved parties (Cottone & Claus, 2000). Tarvydas' model is comprised of: (a) interpreting the situation, (b) reviewing the dilemma, (c) determining the professional ethical standards that apply to the dilemma, (d) formulating possible and probable courses of action, (e) considering the consequences for each possible course of action, (f) consulting with other professionals about the dilemma, (g) selecting an action by weighing competing values given in the context, (h) planning and implementing the action, and (i) evaluating the outcome. The strength of this model is the recommendation that the professional think back on the action taken and evaluate the results in terms of how well one balanced or fulfilled competing moral principles. This model provides more structure and how-to than Rest's philosophical model.

Virtue Ethics

Virtue ethics is an approach to ethical decision making that emphasizes the virtues of the mental health professional and is an alternative to **principle ethics**, which focuses on the rational selection and application of universal ethical principles to resolve a dilemma. Jordan and Meara (1990) suggested that principle ethics approaches professional behavior by posing the question, "What shall I do?" while virtue ethics focuses on the professional and poses the question, "Who shall I be?" It is important to note that principle and virtue ethics are not mutually exclusive systems for approaching ethical behavior, but they differ in terms of focus on *doing* good versus *being* good. Specifically, when considering what course of action to take in a situation, there may be times when multiple actions could all be seen as ethically sound, but Jordan and Meara encourage professionals to go beyond what is merely acceptable and "emphasize not so much what is permitted as what is preferred" (p. 112).

Jordan and Meara (1990) encourage mental health professionals to reflect on the virtues outlined by May (1984) to assist them in becoming ethical by developing their personal character. According to May, these virtues represent ideals for the professional that go beyond following rules or principles and include fidelity, prudence, discretion, perseverance, courage, integrity, public spiritedness, benevolence, humility, and hope. May further states that professionals are obligated to approximate the ideal. It is his hope that professionals do not merely hold themselves to the rules of ethical behavior when faced with quandaries, but strive further to reflect on their identity as virtuous professionals in choosing their actions and meeting professional responsibilities. Accordingly, virtue ethics in practice assumes that virtuous professionals *are* ethical professionals and does not provide a formula for ethical decision making.

BOX 2.5

Thinking About Humility

> One of the things that I tell people when they are looking for
> a therapist is to really ask them the question about what can't
> they do. And boy, if they don't have something they can't do,
> get out.—Jennings et al. (2005, p. 40)

May (1984) suggested that humility is one of the core professional ethical values, and Jennings and colleagues (2005) found that master therapists indicated that an ethical mental health professional should approach his or her work with a sense of humility. Ideally, a person's awareness of the limits of her competence and skill acts as a catalyst to seek out further professional growth. Formal and informal educational experiences, such as attending workshops and conferences to hear about the latest developments in treatment and seeking peer consultation with colleagues, contribute to expanding competence and supporting ethical professional conduct. The dark side of a lack of humility is the development of grandiosity, which may increase the risk of failing to carefully consider one's actions and increase the potential risk of harm to clients.

CONSIDERING SPECIFIC ETHICAL DILEMMAS

When graduate students in mental health professions were presented with an ethical dilemma about having knowledge that a peer was abusing alcohol and that this drinking problem was negatively affecting the student's clinical work, results from three independent research studies indicated that these students "would" do less than they reported they "should" do concerning their colleague's drinking problem (Bernard & Jara, 1986; Betan, 1996; Linstrum, 2009). In Linstrum's study, 67.2% of the sample reported that they knew they "should" tell the clinical director about their peer's drinking problem, but only 29.9% reported that they "would" perform this action. Why do graduate students have difficulty imagining themselves acting according to the ethical principles and standards they are taught in their training? Although more research is necessary to answer this question, it seems that the social context of the ethical dilemma is important. Please read and consider the following ethical dilemma while imagining yourself in the shoes of the professional. Ethical decisions are best understood by considering the range of emotions and competing values that the professional is faced with during decision making.

Ethical Dilemma

Imagine you are working in a university counseling center and one of your clients talks about her romantic feelings for a graduate student who is teaching one of her courses. The graduate student who is the object of the client's affections is one of your close friends. Suppose the client began to speak in great detail about her thoughts and fantasies about this graduate student. How would you handle this situation? Would you disclose the existence of your friendship to the client? Why or why not? Let's imagine you did not disclose this information and the client saw you on campus eating lunch and laughing with her instructor? How would you handle that situation in the moment and after the fact, at your next counseling session?

There are times when professional ethical standards are unclear, and research has indicated that mental health professionals tend to operate based on their own individual value systems and personal interpretation of the ethics code in these situations in which there are competing ethical values (Bersoff & Koeppl, 1993; Eberlein, 1987). Considering ethical dilemmas before being confronted with one in practice may help to shape your professional ethical identity and build your confidence in terms of facing real-world dilemmas.

Seeking out consultation has been mentioned throughout the chapter as a tool to maintain ethical professional practice. Continuing education is also vitally important. Many mental health practitioners continue to seek training in ethics after licensure. In fact, among psychologists, ethics training is the most commonly completed topic of continuing education. A majority of licensed psychologists (60%) reported that they completed at least one course in ethics during the previous year (Niemeyer, Taylor, & Wear, 2010).

CHAPTER REVIEW

Ethics are guidelines and principles that inform moral judgment and professional conduct. There are five ethical principles that guide mental health professionals in their practice: beneficence and nonmaleficence, fidelity and responsibility, integrity, justice, and respect for people's rights and dignity.

Professional organizations adopt a set of enforceable ethical standards, also known as an ethics code. These ethics codes are vital to safeguard the welfare of clients and others who work with mental health professionals in addition to protecting professionals who are accused of ethical violations.

Confidentiality is a standard of professional behavior that requires mental health professionals to not reveal or discuss information about their clients without the clients' authorization. Privacy is a basic right for all people, and mental health professionals respect the dignity of their clients by keeping their personal information private. This standard applies to information discussed in the session or in other communication with the client as well as information that the mental health professional has written about the client in files, documents, or notes.

Mental health professionals must discuss the limits of confidentiality as soon as possible with clients. This is particularly important when working with children and adolescents or adults under guardianship because their guardians have a right to information about their mental health. Mental health professionals are not required to keep information confidential when they are compelled by ethical or legal standards to act to protect individuals (i.e., clients or potential victims identified by clients) from serious harm (i.e., duty to warn or protect). Mental health professionals may also be required to release confidential information about a client in response to a court order.

Dual relationships are those in which the mental health professional is intentionally entering into an additional professional or personal relationship with a client. Dual relationships can be concurrent or consecutive (i.e., prior to initiation or subsequent to termination) with the therapy relationship. Mental health professionals may choose to enter into some types of dual relationships with clients after careful analysis of the risks and benefits. Sexual relationships with clients are *always* unethical and frequently are illegal.

Several formal methods of ethical decision making have been proposed and adopted by mental health professionals. Rest (1984) proposed a philosophical model for mental health professionals to use when making ethical decisions; this model is a rational approach to recognizing a problem, identifying alternative courses of action, and summoning the motivation and determination to carry out the ethical behavior chosen. Tarvydas (1998) developed an alternative model, practice-based decision making, which highlights not only the cognitive aspects of ethical decision making but also the emotional and contextual aspects of the process. The strength of her model is the recommendation that the professional thinks back on the action taken and evaluates the results in terms of how well one balanced or fulfilled competing moral principles.

Virtue ethics is an approach to ethical decision making that emphasizes the virtues of the mental health professional and is an alternative to principle ethics, which focuses on the rational selection and application of universal ethical principles to resolve a dilemma. Jordan and Meara (1990) encourage mental health professionals to reflect on virtues, such as fidelity, prudence, discretion, perseverance, courage, integrity, public spiritedness, benevolence, humility, and hope, to assist them in becoming ethical by developing their personal character.

PERSONAL REFLECTION ESSAY QUESTIONS

1. Confidentiality is essential to therapy. Although there are times when mental health professionals are faced with decisions about revealing confidential information to protect clients and others from harm, there are other times when confidentiality becomes a challenge for professionals. As a therapist, you may struggle with keeping secrets. For example, imagine that you are seeing a client for treatment. She ends therapy because she is going to be spending a semester studying abroad. After termination with that client, you begin seeing another client. It becomes apparent that these two clients are acquaintances, and your new client frequently brings up negative things

about your first client in session. At the end of the semester, the second client leaves to study abroad, and your first client calls you and asks to resume therapy. Think about how you might feel and act in this situation. Write about possible and probable courses of action in this situation.

2. Dual relationships with clients can occur prior to, during, or subsequent to treatment. Write about what types of dual relationships have a low potential for harm at each of these three stages, keeping Gottlieb's three dimensions in mind. (When thinking about dual relationships prior to therapy, you will have to think about an existing personal or professional relationship in which you would feel comfortable agreeing to treat the potential client.) Are there other dimensions that you would personally consider when contemplating the dual relationship (e.g., type of presenting problem)? Are there types of dual relationships that can be beneficial to clients? Do you agree with Sonne that dual relationships that are simultaneous with therapy have the highest potential for harm?

3. Think about your own moral values and how they have been shaped by your cultural background, family influences, and personal experiences. Reflect particularly on those professional virtues named by May (1984): fidelity, prudence, discretion, perseverance, courage, integrity, public spiritedness, benevolence, humility, and hope. Which do you hold most strongly? Which would you like to develop more fully as you begin your work as a mental health professional? (If you want help thinking about your values, visit www.yourmorals.org to take a survey to find out more about your personal ethics.)

KEYWORDS

autonomy	ethical principles	principle ethics
beneficence	ethical standards	privilege
confidentiality	ethics	responsibility
court order	fidelity	subpoena
dual relationship	integrity	virtue ethics
duty to warn	nonmaleficence	

FURTHER READING

- Brown, C., & Transgrud, H. B. (2008). Factors association with acceptance and decline of client gift giving. *Professional Psychology: Research and Practice, 39,* 505–511. doi:10.1037/0735-7028.39.5.505

  Clients sometimes give gifts to their therapists, and navigating this situation can be tricky for mental health professionals. There are ethical justifications to accept or decline gifts in particular situations or with certain clients. Brown and Transgrud examine the factors that may contribute to a therapist's decision about how to respond when a client offers a gift.

- Celenza, A., & Gabbard, G. (2003). Analysts who commit sexual boundary violations: A lost cause? *Journal of the American Psychoanalytic Association, 51*(2), 617–636. doi:10.1177/00030651030510020201

Whereas it is easy to demonize those who commit sexual boundary violations, the truth is that the therapist who engages in sexual misconduct is usually motivated by a variety of factors that most of us can understand and perhaps even relate to. This article reviews data from over 200 cases of sexual misconduct and describes typical characteristics of transgressors. Celenza and Gabbard also describe the viability of rehabilitation for those that violate these foundational aspects of our shared codes of ethics.

- Clark, C. D., & Gordon, M. C. (2003). Acknowledging the inevitable: Understanding multiple relationships in rural practice. *Professional Psychology: Research and Practice, 34,* 430–434. doi:10.1037/0735-7028.34.4.430

Although it is easy to make conscious choices about entering into dual relationships with clients in urban or suburban settings, it is much more difficult for mental health professionals in rural settings. In New York City, where we both live and work, it is easy to find another piano tuner if you are treating one, but in some areas, there may be only one. If you are also one of the few mental health professionals in town, it is likely that you may have to enter into a dual relationship if your piano goes out of tune. In this article, Clark and Gordon outline strategies for evaluating, preventing, and managing dual relationships in rural locations.

- Cottone, R. R., & Claus, R. E. (2000). Ethical decision-making models: A review of the literature. *Journal of Counseling and Development, 78,* 275–283. doi:10.1002/j.1556-6676.2000.tb01908.x

This review article is a comprehensive description and comparison of the multiple ethical decision-making models that have been proposed, including more in-depth coverage of Rest's (1984) and Tarvydas' (1998) models.

- Gottlieb, M. C. (2006). A template for peer ethics consultation. *Ethics & Behavior, 16,* 151–162. doi:10.1207/s15327019eb1602_5

Throughout this chapter, we have recommended consulting with a colleague when you find yourself in an ethical dilemma. This article by Gottlieb delineates a comprehensive list of questions to address when engaged in peer ethics consultation, in addition to a section about whether to accept the request of others to consult on a particular ethical issue.

The ethics codes for the following professional organizations may be found online:

- American Psychological Association (2002, amended 2010):
  www.apa.org/ethics/code/principles.pdf
- American Counseling Association (2005):
  www.counseling.org/ethics
- National Association of Social Workers (2008):
  www.socialworkers.org/pubs/code/code.asp
- American Association of Marriage and Family Therapy (2012):
  www.aamft.org/imis15/Content/Legal_Ethics/Code_of_Ethics.aspx
- American Psychiatric Association (2010):
  www.psychiatry.org/practice/ethics/resources-standards

Understanding Your Clients: Case Conceptualization and Selection of Counseling Interventions

Psychological health is not merely the absence of symptoms;
it is the positive presence of inner capacities and resources
that allow people to live life with a greater sense of freedom
and possibility.—Shedler (2010, p. 105)

LEARNING OBJECTIVES

- Describe historical influences on the major schools of thought regarding psychological treatment
- Identify the major mechanisms of change utilized by psychodynamic psychotherapists
- Explain possible obstacles to successful treatment of psychological distress
- Describe the major components of ego psychology, object relations theory, self-psychology, humanistic and existential psychology, family systems theory, and biological approaches to psychology
- Identify the essentials of a case formulation from the psychodynamic perspective
- Identify and explain the main components of cognitive behavioral theory
- Explain the interconnectedness of emotions, thoughts, and behavior according to cognitive behavioral theory
- Identify the necessary components of a thorough case formulation from the cognitive behavioral perspective
- Describe evidence-based treatments from both psychodynamic and cognitive behavioral perspectives
- Explain how to integrate components of various theoretical orientations to meet the needs of a client

To determine how best to help the clients with whom you work, it is important to have a firm grasp of the theories that form the foundation of your practice. A **theory** is a set of basic assumptions and principles that help explain a particular phenomenon. Within counseling practice, a theory should help explain the etiology of a client's distress and offer a set of strategies or principles for helping alleviate these problems. Theory is likely to help predict which interventions you will use, how long therapy is expected to last, and what type of change you expect to see. Without theory to guide us, we may simply be "vulnerable, directionless creatures bombarded with literally hundreds of impressions and pieces of information in a single session" (Prochaska & Norcross, 2003, p. 5). On the other hand, theory may also lead to overly reductionistic explanations for complex human experiences and distress. We believe theory is the cornerstone of counseling practice but should always be amenable to modification in the light of new information, either from the client or from empirical research. As with any theory-driven science, no one theory fits all. Every person is a unique product of cultural influences, individual experiences, historical events, as well as biological and genetic variability. This chapter will provide you with an introduction to the predominant theories within the practice of counseling. We strongly encourage you to pursue learning about these theoretical perspectives and others in depth as you continue to grow as a professional. Your theoretical perspective will develop over time and should be informed by clinical practice and available empirical evidence.

Psychotherapy, as we know it today, has its roots in **psychoanalysis**, a treatment that was first developed by Sigmund Freud in the late 19th century. Freud was an Austrian neurologist who became increasingly interested in psychological processes through his work with the renowned French physician, Jean-Martin Charcot. Freud and Charcot collaborated in the treatment of **hysteria**, a type of psychological distress that is now referred to as somatization disorder or conversion disorder. During the late 19th century, hysteria was a problem that most often afflicted women. These patients presented with an unusual array of symptoms including partial paralysis, fainting, nervousness, difficulty swallowing and speaking, irritability, and loss of appetite. Initially, Freud and his colleague, Josef Breuer, used hypnosis as their primary treatment intervention. While Freud was treating a young woman known as Anna O., he invited her to talk about her symptoms while under hypnosis. He eventually abandoned hypnosis altogether and focused on enabling Anna O. and his other patients to speak freely about what troubled them; he referred to this process of speaking in an unstructured and reflective way as **free association**. Anna O. was the first to coin the term "the talking cure" in reference to her treatment.

Nearly all treatment approaches in contemporary psychotherapy stem from the basic premise, first identified by Freud's work, that talking about one's problems with a professionally trained counselor can result in symptom reduction, subjective well-being, and an improvement in overall functioning. We will focus primarily on psychodynamic and cognitive behavioral psychotherapy, as most psychotherapies being practiced today flow out of these two predominant schools of thought. In addition to these two, we also recognize the contributions of developmental, interpersonal, systemic, supportive, and group psychotherapies, as well as the recent impact of cognitive neuroscience. Each orientation has its own unique view of human behavior that includes a way of explaining how

people think, act, and relate to one anoth[...]
some time to develop a sense of their own[...]
you to be open-minded and to continual[...]
experience. It is important to always be e[...]
ferent treatment modalities and interven[...]
the client.

PSYCHODYNA[...]

A Brief Overview of [...]

Freud is often identified as the father o[...]
human mind and how to treat psycho[...]
evolved throughout his life. Although [...]
unified system of thinking, his writings reflect a constantly develop[...]g
in progress. Freud's theoretical perspective was largely shaped by his one-
on-one work with individual patients, rather than empirical research with
clearly stated hypotheses. This method of developing treatment interventions
has led to many critiques of psychodynamic treatment. More recently, psychodynamic researchers have sought to evaluate the major assumptions of
the theory and to develop empirically supported psychodynamic treatments
(Kernberg, 2006).

Despite the many forces that have modified and shaped Freud's initial
ideas, a brief overview of the primary components of psychoanalytic theory is
important. Freud postulated that all human beings are motivated, at least in part,
by wishes, fears, desires, and conflicts that are outside of their conscious awareness. His work with his patients led him to believe that becoming aware of these
unconscious motives would increase an individual's choices (Safran, 2012). Freud
outlined three hierarchical layers of the mind—the conscious, pre-conscious, and
unconscious—and this became known as the **topographic model** of the mind,
referencing a topographic map that shows different elevations (Freud, 1915). An
iceberg metaphor is often used to illustrate this point, with the majority of the
structure being submerged under water, out of view (Figure 3.1).

This emphasis on the role of the unconscious—that which exists outside
of one's awareness—has played a central role in the development of psychodynamic theory and the practice of psychodynamic psychotherapy. Freud suggested that thoughts, wishes, and desires may remain inaccessible to a person
because their content is simply too distressing or anxiety-provoking. As a result,
the psychodynamic perspective emphasizes the fact that we often behave in
certain ways for reasons that are unknown to us at the time. For example, an
individual may habitually arrive late to work and attribute this to traffic or over-
sleeping. Psychodynamic theory would postulate that this tardiness could be
motivated by the individual's anger at her boss, insecurity about her ability to
perform at work, or a desire to sabotage an upcoming promotion. These are all
examples of possible unconscious motivations that may be driving the behavior,
and they highlight Freud's assertion that we are not always masters of our own
house (Freud, 1917).

In addition to the topographic model, Freud suggested a **structural model**
of the mind (Freud, 1923/1961). The structural model focuses on the three

FIGURE 3.1 Topographic model of the mind: The unconscious is like the massive portion of an iceberg, submerged underwater, unseen, and difficult to access.

mental agencies of the mind: the id, ego, and superego. The **id** is the most primitive structure and is present at birth. The id is driven by instinctual needs without any regard for realistic concerns or others' needs; it operates on a pleasure-seeking principle. The **ego** is a mediator of sorts and allows the individual to adapt to the demands of reality. The ego is often challenged with the role of forming compromises between the id and the superego. By using **defense mechanisms**, the ego allows for a delay of gratification and the channeling of aggressive and sexual impulses into more socially acceptable responses (see Figure 3.2).

The **superego** is a mental structure that arises out of societal norms and expectations. It can at times be overly harsh and punitive and is largely shaped by the influences of parental figures, religious institutions, and peers.

BOX 3.1

Learning Exercise

Take a moment to think about times in the past few weeks when you have felt an uncomfortable but familiar feeling. Perhaps you were late (again) for class, found yourself procrastinating despite promises to yourself to do otherwise, or felt attracted to someone with all the same qualities of a previous partner whom you swore off. Can you identify defenses you may have utilized in an instance like this? Perhaps during the past week you have explained some behavior away by intellectualizing or rationalizing. Think about what might have happened if you had confronted the underlying reasons for your behavior. What unwelcome feelings might have arisen without your strategy for avoiding them?

Defense	Description
Denial	One of the few defenses that is often consciously employed. Refusal to admit or acknowledge reality or an obvious truth.
Displacement	Taking out frustrations, feelings, and impulses on a less threatening person or object. Instead of yelling at your boss, you go home and yell at your spouse.
Dissociation	Mental detachment from your immediate surroundings. Can range from zoning out to more severe forms such as dissociative fugue.
Fantasy	Tendency to retreat into one's imagination in order to resolve or avoid psychic conflict.
Humor	A mature defense. Making a joke about things that would otherwise be too difficult to speak of.
Identification	Joining with another person or modeling your behavior, ideals, or beliefs based on theirs. Sometimes employed to escape feelings of envy.
Intellectualization	Using abstraction or scientific reasoning to avoid direct experience of difficult feelings.
Isolation of affect	Creating a gap between an emotion and the experience of that emotion. For example, talking about a violent incident with little to no expression of fear, anxiety, or sadness.
Projection	Accusing another person of having the feeling that is difficult for you to express yourself.
Rationalization	Using logic or rational explanation to make certain behaviors and feelings tolerable. Sometimes described as "making excuses."
Reaction formation	Unacceptable feelings or impulses are channeled into the exact opposite. For example, showering an enemy with gifts and praise.
Regression	Moving to an earlier developmental time. Often seen in children experiencing the birth of a younger sibling or students going off to college.
Repression	The exclusion of unacceptable impulses or experiences from conscious awareness. In its most extreme form, this can manifest as psychogenic amnesia.
Somatization	Expression of negative emotion or psychic conflict through the body via physical symptoms that have no medical cause.
Splitting	Black and white thinking. The inability to integrate good and bad aspects of the self or others.
Sublimation	Channeling of unacceptable impulses into socially acceptable behavior. For example, aggression channeled into contact sports or depressive feelings expressed through creative writing.
Undoing	Attempting to take back some behavior or action that is seen by the self as unacceptable.

FIGURE 3.2 Defense mechanisms.

Freud's methods of providing symptom relief focused on the use of **free association** as a tool. Free association involved saying whatever came to mind without any censorship. It did not take long, however, for Freud to recognize that many of his patients could not follow these directions. They exhibited what Freud referred to as **resistance**, the reluctance or inability to cooperate with the therapist. The exploration of resistance was and continues to be understood as central to the therapeutic process. Resistance may be evident when a client misses sessions or is silent for long periods of time. Finally, Freud discovered that patients often interacted with him in ways that were reminiscent of their relational patterns with early childhood caregivers. He hypothesized that they were "transferring" onto him certain dynamics and expectations from the past, and he called this phenomenon **transference**. Transference might be evident when a client withholds information from the therapist in fear that she will be judged or shamed by the therapist, just as her mother frequently judged or shamed her. Although this holding back may be in response to the therapist's own critical nature, at times it is more representative of the clients' expectations of how others will respond to them. Freud initially saw transference as an impediment to therapy, but he later came to see it as a central component of the therapeutic process. Freud also acknowledged his growing awareness of **countertransference**, the therapist's reaction to the client that arose out of the therapist's own unresolved unconscious conflicts. For example, a therapist whose father was emotionally unavailable might experience anger toward a client who has great difficulty talking freely and openly about his own feelings.

Saying psychodynamic theory is all about Freud is like saying rock and roll is all about Elvis. A lot has happened since then. As a result, we will provide a whirlwind tour of post-Freudian influences on psychoanalytic theory here. Freud's daughter, Anna Freud, elaborated on the importance of defense mechanisms and the central role of the ego (Freud, A., 1937). This school of thought is referred to as **ego psychology** and was further elaborated by American psychoanalysts like Jacob Arlow and Charles Brenner (Arlow & Brenner, 1964; Brenner, 1994), who largely dismissed the structural model of the mind in favor of a model that focuses less on the actual structure of the mind and more on the role of compromise formation. Another post-Freudian development was the emergence of Kleinian and British **object relations theory**. Melanie Klein focused on the earliest interactions between mother and child and the development of primitive mental representations of the maternal figure. Klein was one of the first theorists to highlight the critical importance of splitting as a defense. **Splitting** is a defense that occurs when the mind attempts to protect positive mental representations of other individuals from being contaminated by negative ideas. According to Klein, this defense is important for infants, who rely on an image of the primary caregiver as "all good" and cannot tolerate the integration of ideas related to the caregiver's physical unavailability or unresponsiveness. Klein understood integration of the good and bad representations as a developmental achievement (Klein, 1958). This emphasis on internalized mental representations was the central focus of object relations and attachment theorists such as Winnicott, Fairbairn, and Bowlby. Winnicott (1958) and Fairbairn (1952) added a great deal to psychodynamic thought with their exploration of the role of fantasy and the need for the therapist to be flexible, creative, and authentic. Bowlby's work focused on the basic human need to maintain physical proximity to a primary attachment figure and the complexity of the parent-child relationship. Bowlby suggested that the parent-child relationship leads to the development of representations that help the individual predict how others will behave in close interpersonal relationships (see Bowlby, 1969, 1973, 1980).

American relational theorists, such as Harry Stack Sullivan (1953), also stressed the importance of significant interpersonal relationships by focusing on the bi-directional transmission of relational dynamics between client and therapist. Sullivan and his protégés have also highlighted the fundamental human striving for relatedness as a primary motive for human behavior, rather than focusing on the discharge of sexual and aggressive drives.

Yet another contemporary psychoanalytic school of thought is **self-psychology**. This perspective was developed by Heinz Kohut (1984) and emphasized the importance of empathy in the development of healthy self-esteem and an integrated sense of the self. Finally, no discussion of contemporary psychodynamic thought would be complete without highlighting the work of Otto Kernberg. He has focused on integrating several of the aforementioned paradigms within psychodynamic theory, specifically ego psychology and object relations perspectives.

Basic Tenets of Psychodynamic Psychotherapy

Given the diversity of psychodynamic theories, it is useful to have a sense of what unifies these theories and distinguishes them from other predominant perspectives, such as cognitive behavioral approaches. Blagys and Hilsenroth (2006) outlined seven features that they argue reliably distinguish psychodynamic therapy from cognitive behavioral and interpersonal approaches:

1. *Focus on affect and expression of emotion.* Psychodynamic therapy encourages the expression of a full range of emotions, particularly those that are contradictory, threatening, or difficult to initially understand. This focus is in contrast to other therapies that may emphasize elaboration of thoughts and beliefs over feelings (Hill, O'Grady, & Elkin, 1992; Startup & Shapiro, 1993).
2. *Exploration of attempts to avoid distressing thoughts and feelings.* This criterion is a reference to Freud's initial discussion of the importance of defense mechanisms and resistance to the therapeutic process. These attempts at avoidance may take many forms, including what are referred to in other treatment modalities as "treatment-interfering behaviors." These may include missing sessions, arriving late, or being unwilling to consider certain aspects of functioning. Defensive functioning and resistance may be more subtle. For example, a client may speak about angry feelings she has toward her husband and then quickly cover them by describing his many positive attributes. A psychodynamic therapist might wonder aloud what was so distressing about those angry feelings that they needed to be counteracted with such statements. Similarly, psychodynamic approaches are more focused on examining behaviors that may impede the progress of treatment such as missing sessions. The psychodynamic psychotherapist is likely to ascribe these types of resistances to unconscious motivations.
3. *Identification of themes and patterns.* Clients may or may not be consciously aware of themes and patterns that arise repeatedly throughout their lives. The psychodynamic therapist must work to highlight these themes and, along with the client, construct a coherent narrative. For example, a client with a sexual abuse history may consistently find herself in relationships in which she gets some of her needs met—such as intimacy and companionship—while feeling severely deprived and abused by the other person. Although cognitive behavioral approaches seek to identify patterns in thinking and behavior, psychodynamic therapists are more likely to focus on patterns of interpersonal functioning (Goldfried, Castonguay, Hayes, Drozd, & Shapiro, 1997).

4. *Developmental focus.* Psychodynamic theory is inherently based on developmental science that emphasizes the many social and systemic influences on individual maturation. Psychodynamic psychotherapy is careful to connect the elements of earlier years that live on in the client's life today. The practice of connecting the experiences of childhood and adolescence to an individual's current functioning originated in the psychoanalytic paradigm but has certainly been integrated into contemporary cognitive behavioral approaches (Beck, 1991; Robins & Hayes, 1993). The goals of highlighting these connections are to enable the client to write new endings to her own stories, and not to repeat the patterns established earlier in the development.

5. *Interpersonal relationships.* There is a focus on current and past interpersonal relationships in psychodynamic psychotherapy. Whereas other treatment approaches may focus on the impact specific symptoms have on interpersonal relationships, psychodynamic approaches recognize that different aspects of an individual's personality—separate from any specific psychiatric symptoms—greatly impact interpersonal functioning. These relational dynamics are seen as reflective of the personality style of the individual and can provide important information about both adaptive and nonadaptive aspects of the client's functioning.

6. *Focus on therapeutic relationship.* The repetitive themes that are seen in the client's interpersonal relationships are likely to be recapitulated within the therapeutic relationship. Whereas both psychodynamic and cognitive behavioral approaches emphasize the centrality of the therapeutic alliance, psychodynamic psychotherapy differs in its reliance on the therapeutic relationship as a medium for the process of change. This is the transference that Freud described in his writings. Within psychodynamic psychotherapy, the therapist is likely to make connections between the therapeutic relationship and other relationships. For example, a client who often avoids conflict with his friends and family may also have difficulty expressing dissatisfaction with the therapist when she is late, suggests something that does not resonate with the client, or makes a mistake in billing. This type of avoidance within the therapeutic relationship presents an opportunity to examine the client's difficulties in the here and now.

7. *Exploration of fantasy life.* Psychodynamic theory proposes that dreams, fantasies, and seemingly irrational ideas provide important information about the unconscious processes that may be motivating the client's behavior. This aspect of psychodynamic theory is closely linked with the emphasis on speaking as freely as possible within the session. Allowing and even encouraging the exploration of a more primitive thought process often provides insight into how certain psychic functions such as defense mechanisms help the individual maintain self-esteem, regulate affect, and cope with stress and trauma. A client struggling with anger management in his relationship with his wife related a lifelong recurring dream in which he violently attacked his mother. The client's first memory of this dream was shortly after his mother removed him from public school in favor of home schooling. Over time, the client was able to connect his sense of losing autonomy and friendships

because of the restrictions placed on him by his mother with his current anger issues; these feelings had been unconsciously transferred onto his wife, someone who actually encouraged her husband's independence.

BOX 3.2

Learning Exercise

Take a moment to think about several of your favorite fairy tales, such as *The Emperor's New Clothes, Rapunzel, The Ugly Duckling,* or *Little Red Riding Hood.* Each of these stories uses fantasy to explore and address more primitive aspects of mental functioning. Can you identify some of the wishes and fears of some of the main characters? For example, the emperor is very preoccupied with appearing "dumb" in front of his subjects. In some ways this fear protects him from certain types of interpersonal interactions; it also leads him to realize his fears in the most transparent way. Can you think about this story and others from a psychodynamic perspective? How does fantasy help the main characters master and work out their fears? Are there ways in which fantasy is helpful to their functioning? Harmful?

Case Formulation From a Psychodynamic Perspective

Case formulation involves developing a working hypothesis about the causes, precipitating factors, development, and maintenance of your client's distress (Eells, 2010; Ivey, 2006). A good case formulation is concise and includes all essential information. It should focus on specific details of the client's symptoms, history, and current functioning. The case formulation should account for any predisposing and precipitating factors that are related to the client's current difficulties. The information included in the case formulation should be jargon-free and should provide a satisfying sense of understanding of the client's difficulties. Finally, all case formulations should include an overview of how treatment will proceed based on the clinician's hypotheses.

According to Ivey (2006), psychodynamic case formulation should identify the relationship between conscious and unconscious feelings, mental representations and motives, and the primary conflicts between these feelings. Special attention should be paid to the individual's interpersonal functioning, especially to competing motives between dependency and attachment. A working model of the client's attempts to manage anxiety-provoking and unpleasant affects should be presented in order to identify which strategies are adaptive and which represent functional deficits. These may take the form of multiple defenses, resistances, or fantasies. Any psychodynamic case formulation will focus on the client's interpersonal functioning, and the ways in which her primary symptoms have negatively impacted her close relationships with family, friends, and significant others. Finally, case formulation from a psychodynamic perspective will outline patterns that have emerged out of the client's developmental experiences.

Although case formulation is based on hypotheses, it is important to keep inferences closely tied to what the client has actually expressed during the evaluation process. As much as possible the case formulation should anticipate possible ruptures that may arise in the therapeutic alliance (Safran, Muran, Samstag, & Stevens, 2002). For example, a client might say of her interpersonal relationships, "Once people cross a certain line with me, I cut them out of my life." A psychodynamic case formulation would identify this type of acting out behavior as something that is likely to reoccur within the therapeutic relationship and as an element that should be attended to by the therapist. Most psychodynamic case formulations will increase the therapist's sense of empathy for the client insomuch as they offer explanations for the client's behavior, which might otherwise be off-putting or difficult to tolerate (Ivey, 2006; McWilliams, 1999).

BOX 3.3

Does Psychotherapy Work?

As you read through this chapter and begin to consider a variety of theoretical perspectives, you might be asking yourself whether psychotherapy even works. Given that we have at our disposal so many interventions—medication, acupuncture, meditation, prayer, social support from friends and families—to treat medical and psychological problems, why should anyone bother with therapy? The short answer to that question is, "It works!"

Without going into great detail about statistical principles, it is important to know how the effectiveness of psychotherapy is evaluated. One of the primary methods is to gather multiple studies and evaluate their collective effectiveness for a particular disorder or type of client. This method is referred to as **meta-analysis**. A meta-analysis typically uses **effect sizes** as the unit of measurement for assessing whether change has occurred among the participants in the study. One can think of an effect size of 1.0 as equivalent to one standard deviation of change. This represents a huge change. If there was an intervention that could reliably increase income with an effect size of 1.0, the average American's income would go up by nearly $34,000. Everyone would sign up for that intervention. In research, an effect size of 0.8 is considered to be large, 0.5 medium, and 0.2 relatively small (Cohen, 1969).

Numerous meta-analyses have been conducted to examine the efficacy of psychotherapy. In their landmark paper, Smith, Glass, and Miller (1980) examined 475 studies of psychotherapy and found an overall effect size of 0.85 for all types of psychotherapy combined. By comparison, Aspirin as an intervention for preventing heart attack has an effect size of 0.034 (Rosnow & Rosenthal, 1989). In one of the most rigorous studies of the effectiveness of antidepressant medication versus placebo, the combined effect size for the impact of antidepressants was 0.17 (Moncrieff, Wessely, & Hardy, 2011). The use of prophylactic aspirin to prevent heart attack is a widely used intervention, as are antidepressants. Despite this, the effect sizes for these types of psychopharmacological treatments do not even approach those for psychotherapy across all theoretical approaches (Butler, Chapman, Forman, & Beck, 2006; Cuijpers et al., 2011; Driessen et al., 2010). For an extensive review of psychological, educational, and behavioral interventions, we recommend reading Lipsey and Wilson's (1993) paper.

Selection of Counseling Interventions

Although the psychodynamic approach began as a relatively brief and focused therapeutic approach, it soon evolved into a long-term treatment aimed at restructuring the entire personality, rather than reducing specific symptoms (Roth & Fonagy, 2005). Psychodynamic psychotherapy has become more focused, but clinicians with this perspective remain interested in exploration of unconscious conflicts in order to reduce symptoms, *and* effect transformation of dysfunctional personality and interpersonal patterns. In order to help the many theoretical components of psychodynamic theory come to life, here we offer several examples of empirically supported psychodynamic psychotherapies.

Evidence-Based Treatments

Transference-Focused Psychotherapy for Borderline Personality Disorder

Transference-focused psychotherapy (TFP) is a structured treatment approach that is closely linked with object relations theory and is used to treat borderline personality disorder. TFP has the unusual designation of having strong but controversial research support because of mixed findings (Clarkin, Levy, Lenzenweger, & Kernberg, 2007; Giesen-Bloo et al., 2006). Developed by Otto Kernberg and his colleagues (Clarkin, Yeomans, & Kernberg, 1999; Kernberg, Selzer, Koenigsberg, Carr, & Appelbaum, 1989; Yeomans, Clarkin, & Kernberg, 2002), TFP integrates object relations theories with contemporary attachment research to promote change in behaviors and mental structures among individuals with borderline personality disorder (Clarkin & Levy, 2003). The basic assumption of TFP is that the early caregiver relationships are internalized in order to shape mental representations of the self and others. Among individuals with borderline personality disorder, these representations and personality organization in general are severely disturbed and result in the use of more primitive defenses and substantial impairment in reality testing.

TFP typically begins with a formal contract between patient and therapist that outlines the conditions of treatment and the roles of the client and the therapist. The treatment focuses on themes connected to intense expression of affect, and the here-and-now relationship between the client and the therapist often referred to as transference. Practitioners of TFP emphasize the reduction of identity diffusion within the client and the development of an increased capacity for reflective functioning. In the beginning, special attention is paid to suicidal and self-injurious behaviors, attempts to sabotage the treatment, and the predominant relational patterns that are expressed within the transference. The therapeutic relationship is seen as a laboratory in which relational patterns will be played out and can be understood and restructured. This here-and-now emphasis is what allows client and therapist to carefully examine parts of the client's self-representations that were previously split off and disavowed.

Evaluation of TFP has demonstrated that a majority of clients who remained in treatment for an average of 1.3 years no longer met diagnostic criteria for borderline personality disorder (Perry, Banon, & Ianni, 1999). Clients receiving TFP also experienced a significant reduction in emergency room visits (55% reduction), psychiatric hospitalizations (67%), and days of inpatient hospitalization (89% reduction; 39.2 vs. 4.5 days; Clarkin & Levy, 2003) as well as positive changes in the structure of attachment style (Diamond et al., 1999; Diamond, Stovall-McClough, Clarkin, & Levy, 2003).

Mentalization-Based Therapy for Borderline Personality Disorder

Mentalization-based therapy (MBT) is another psychoanalytic psychotherapy treatment for borderline personality that has demonstrated effectiveness in day hospital settings (Bateman & Fonagy, 2001, 2009). This psychodynamic treatment approach focuses on improving the client's ability to mentalize, that is, to recognize and identify mental states in oneself and others. The emphasis in MBT is to increase the client's capacity for self-reflection in ways that will enhance functioning and reduce symptomatology. MBT differs from TFP in its assumption that early interpretation is potentially damaging to the treatment because it does not mirror the client's current mental states (Kernberg, Yeomans, Clarkin, & Levy, 2008). MBT's emphasis on mentalization overlaps a great deal with the concept of mindfulness in dialectical behavior therapy (DBT; Bateman, 2010; see Chapter 10 for more on DBT).

Empirically Supported Psychodynamic Treatments for Panic and Depression

In addition to the aforementioned treatments, psychoanalytic psychotherapy for panic disorder (Milrod, Busch, Cooper, & Shapiro, 1997; Milrod et al., 2007) focuses on psychodynamic conflicts that include the tension between separation and autonomy as well as difficulties with the expression and management of anger. It is described by the American Psychological Association's Division 12 as "probably efficacious," which means it has one well-designed study or two or more adequately designed studies that support this treatment's efficacy. This treatment for panic disorder also utilizes transference to work through unconscious conflicts. Another empirically supported psychodynamic treatment is short-term psychodynamic therapy for depression (Hilsenroth, Ackerman, Blagys, Baity, & Mooney, 2003; Luborsky et al., 1995), which is conducted in 16 to 20 sessions. This treatment approach focuses on many of the components described earlier in this chapter, such as a focus on affect and the expression of emotion, the identification of themes and patterns, examination of attempts to avoid distressing thoughts and feelings, and an emphasis on panic within a developmental context (see Blagys & Hilsenroth, 2006).

Summary

The psychodynamic perspective provides several ways to conceptualize clients' distress. It emphasizes the important role of the unconscious in shaping behavior, the contributions of the past to an individual's current distress, and the way emotional suffering can affect interpersonal relationships. Early in the development of the psychodynamic paradigm, it faced criticism for its lack of empirical rigor and reliance on case studies as evidence of effectiveness. A new approach to psychotherapy arose in response and focused on thoughts, feelings, and behaviors—variables that are more easily measured than more amorphous concepts like the unconscious. This perspective, cognitive behavioral therapy (CBT), has also made a point of empirically testing and measuring effectiveness since its inception. The advent of a new approach to psychotherapy, one that goes in an entirely new direction rather than simply building on earlier perspectives, reflects a long tradition of paradigm shifts within the development of science (Kuhn, 1996).

COGNITIVE BEHAVIORAL THEORY

CBT is an approach to treatment that focuses on alleviating symptoms and improving mood through helping clients change behaviors and modify patterns of thinking. CBT was designed to be a short-term treatment that primarily focuses on the client's current daily functioning. It is based on enduring theories of the connection between our thoughts, feelings, and actions. The Greek Stoic philosophers wrote about the interplay of cognition and emotion. Epictetus posited, "Men are disturbed not by the things which happen, but by the opinions about the things" (1991, p. 14). CBT is focused on promoting adaptive thinking and behavior that lead to diminished negative mood and emotion. "If we can reorient our thoughts and emotions, and reorder our behavior, not only can we learn to cope with suffering more easily, but we can prevent a great deal of it from starting in the first place" (Dalai Lama, 1999, p. xii). There is wide acceptance of the basic theoretical underpinnings of CBT; the way we think and act impacts our feelings and vice versa.

Overview of CBT

CBT is based on information processing theory and stipulates that it is often not the events around us that trigger emotional distress, but our interpretation and assessment of those events that lead us to experience painful emotions, and trigger maladaptive behavioral responses. For instance, imagine that you are walking down the street and approach a woman who is walking her small dog on a leash. This may seem like a non-threatening event to you. You may think to yourself, "What a cute dog," smile briefly at the puppy, and keep walking down the sidewalk. Another person, that is, a person with a specific phobia of dogs, is more likely to think "That dog could bite me." Her heart may start racing, and she may feel frightened and quickly cross the street to avoid coming close to the dog. The same event (or external stimuli) may trigger quite different emotional and behavioral reactions in two different people. According to cognitive behavioral theory, the difference lies in the thoughts that individuals have when encountering situations and objects in the world around them.

The Interconnectedness of Emotions, Thoughts, and Behavior

CBT is based on the theory that our thoughts and perceptions, and feelings and behavior are all connected. Mental health professionals use the cognitive model to understand how symptoms and emotional distress are manifested and maintained in the daily lives of their clients (see Figure 3.3). Specifically, when we encounter events and situations in our environment, we tend to make quick judgments. These are called **automatic thoughts**. Because our thoughts, feelings, and behaviors are connected, those snap judgments (i.e., automatic thoughts) have the power to change our mood, alter our physiological sensations, and determine our behavioral reactions. These automatic thoughts happen instantaneously, and

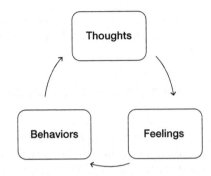

FIGURE 3.3 The basic cognitive behavioral model.

we may not always be aware of them. Although we may not notice them unless we intentionally draw our attention to them, these automatic cognitions have an effect on us.

BOX 3.4

Learning Exercise

Think about a time during the past week when you had a strong or sudden shift in your mood. Identify what you were doing at the time and what you were feeling. A quick change in emotion is a reliable indicator that you have just experienced a significant amount of automatic thoughts. Put yourself back in that situation in your imagination. Try to remember your automatic thoughts. Think about how a different automatic thought might have led to a different feeling in the moment.

Historical Influences

CBT is a relatively young approach to psychotherapy. As the name suggests, CBT is a blending of cognitive and behavioral theories and techniques (Meichenbaum, 1977). The behavioral aspects of CBT were introduced first by clinicians, such as Wolpe (1958) and Eysenck (1966), who applied the findings from experimental behaviorists, including Pavlov and Skinner. The cognitive theory and techniques were formally developed by Albert Ellis and Aaron Beck in the early 1960s. Each represented a departure from the prevailing psychoanalytic theories of mental health treatment.

Behaviorism

Behaviorism began in the animal laboratory, and yet has become the basis of an enduring theory of human behavior modification. Ivan Pavlov was the first to identify the phenomenon of **classical conditioning** through his classic experiments with salivating dogs. Pavlov discovered that he could make dogs respond to a novel cue (i.e., a ringing bell) by pairing that **conditioned stimulus** with something that naturally evokes the response that he wanted (i.e., an **unconditioned**

ILLUSTRATION 3.1 Classical conditioning from the subject's point of view.

stimulus). Pavlov presented meat powder (i.e., the unconditioned stimulus) to hungry dogs, which stimulated the dogs to salivate (i.e., the **unconditioned response**). He paired a ringing bell (i.e., the conditioned stimulus) with the meat powder, which continued to make the dogs slobber (i.e., the **conditioned response**). After a few pairings of meat and bell, Pavlov was able to make the dogs salivate with the ringing bell alone.

Classical conditioning is not only for the dogs! It has also been used to explain the development of anxiety disorders. Specifically, when a person experiences a sudden frightening event, the event (i.e., the unconditioned stimulus) may be paired with another cue in the environment (i.e., the conditioned stimulus) to produce the unconditioned response (i.e., fear). Accordingly, a person who is involved in a car accident may develop a fear of driving or riding in a car. Although the car was previously a neutral stimulus that did not produce fear, after being paired with the fear naturally evoked by being involved in an accident, it continues to produce the fear response in isolation.

This conditioning of fear response was demonstrated by John B. Watson and his colleagues. In their famous experiments with Little Albert, Watson and Rosalie Rayner demonstrated that fear and phobias could be learned through classical conditioning. They exposed the baby to a variety of objects and animals, and he showed little or no fear of these items prior to the experiment. To condition the fear, Watson and Rayner (1920) introduced a sudden loud noise when Albert came into contact with these previously neutral stimuli, including a white rat and a white rabbit. After several pairings, Little Albert became distressed in the presence of white furry objects in the absence of the startling loud noise. Joseph Wolpe (1958) translated this research into a clinical intervention with his process of **systematic desensitization**. Wolpe attempted to countercondition fear by pairing relaxation with frightening stimuli.

B. F. Skinner (1938) outlined the principles of **operant conditioning**, which also made a significant contribution to the development of behavioral theory. Operant conditioning describes the situations in which behaviors may be increased or decreased. Specifically, behaviors that are reinforced are likely to be repeated. To increase behaviors, one may either provide a reward, or **positive reinforcement**, or remove an aversive stimulus, known as **negative reinforcement**. For example, to increase the likelihood that individuals will buckle their seatbelts while driving, cars are designed to emit an annoying buzz until the seatbelt is fastened. When the buckle is clicked, the aversive noise is silenced. This makes it more likely that the driver and passengers will buckle their seatbelts in the future to avoid the noise.

Skinner also described the way in which behaviors may be decreased. **Positive punishment** is adding something aversive, whereas **negative punishment** is removing something desired (or potentially reinforcing) from the person. Negative punishment can also be understood as a penalty. When you receive a speeding ticket, you are frequently required to pay a fine, which is the removal of something you treasure—your hard-earned money. These concepts might sound like those your parents used to encourage your good behavior. In fact, the principles of operant conditioning form the backbone of Parent Management Training, an effective treatment for oppositional, aggressive, and antisocial behavior in children and adolescents (Kazdin, 1997).

Cognitive Theories of Psychological Problems

Parallel to the development of behavioral treatments based on classical and operant conditioning, Albert Ellis and Aaron Beck were formulating cognitive theories to explain the emotional distress experienced by their clients. Both men were practicing psychoanalysts who grew dissatisfied with that method and developed a new understanding of psychological distress—and its relief—based on the notion that the client's thinking plays a pivotal role in determining her emotional experience.

Albert Ellis: Rational Emotive Behavior Therapy

Albert Ellis (1962) created the ABC model to explain how people develop maladaptive emotional and behavioral responses (see Figure 3.4). In this model, A represents an activating event, B represents the person's beliefs about the event, and C represents the emotional and behavioral consequences. This understanding that the individual's beliefs about the event, which are often irrational, cause painful, emotional, and behavioral consequences was quite different

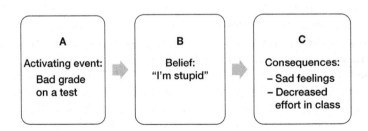

FIGURE 3.4 The ABC model.

Source: Ellis (1962).

from the prevailing theory that the events themselves directly cause a person's reactions. Therefore, the focus of Ellis' rational emotive therapy, which was later named rational emotive behavior therapy, is helping clients to "dispute and surrender these basic irrationalities" (Ellis, 1980, p. 331). He further hypothesized that people hold these irrational or anti-empirical perceptions because of underlying "musts," and he encourages clients to dispute these "*must*urbatory premises" (Ellis, 1980, p. 329). For example, a person is participating in what Ellis provocatively calls *must*urbation when she thinks to herself, "I must get an A on this test, or everyone will think that I am stupid."

In addition to confronting the irrational thinking of clients, Ellis also included behavioral techniques in his treatment. He particularly recommended experiential learning to help individuals explore the validity of their irrational beliefs. "The therapist encourages, persuades, cajoles, and occasionally even insists that the patient engage in some activity (such as doing something he is afraid of doing) which itself will serve as a forceful counter-propaganda agency against the nonsense he believes" (Ellis, 1962, p. 95).

Aaron Beck: The Negative Cognitive Triad

Aaron Beck was treating depressed patients with traditional psychoanalysis when he developed his cognitive theory of depression. He noticed that his depressed patients seemed to have an additional self-critical stream of thought during free association (Beck, 2011). This realization that clients have automatic negative thoughts evolved into a cognitive conceptualization of depression that described depressive symptoms as arising from negative thinking in three main areas: self, world, and future, which is known as the **negative cognitive triad** (Beck, 1963, 1964; Figure 3.5). He theorized that these thoughts arise from **schema**, which are cognitive structures similar to a lens through which an individual views the world. Beck suggested that schema develop based on early life experiences and events such as loss and rejection.

Beck designed therapy interventions focused on identifying and modifying these negative thoughts and theorized that there were specific types of **cognitive errors** that characterize the thinking of people experiencing emotional distress. Beck (1976) described the most commonly occurring cognitive errors. For example, **selective abstraction**, which is also known as mental filter, is focusing only on one negative detail or aspect of the situation and ignoring the bigger picture.

Negative beliefs

Situation	Self	World	Future
Bad grade on a test	"I am not very smart"	"This class is stupid and a waste of my time"	"I will never do well in school"

FIGURE 3.5 The negative cognitive triad.
Source: Beck (1963, 1964).

Another cognitive error is **catastrophizing**, also called fortune telling, and is characterized by predicting a negative outcome without considering other more probable outcomes. Remember the person, we described earlier, who dashed across the street when encountering a dog on the sidewalk? That individual was catastrophizing by predicting that the dog would bite her instead of considering the more likely scenario that the dog would not pay any attention to her.

Cognitive Behavioral Case Formulation

A mental health professional must come to an understanding of her client's problems, strengths, and current situation in order to develop a plan for treatment. As we explained earlier in this chapter, the process of **case formulation** helps the clinician form a comprehensive hypothesis for how the client's current symptoms and difficulties began and how they are being maintained. Once a clear understanding of the client's situation is developed, the keys to helping the client improve her mood and her daily life begin to emerge. Cognitive behavioral case formulation combines information learned about the client through assessment with the base of empirical knowledge about the development, maintenance, and treatment of particular psychological disorder. It is a work in progress. The mental health professional crafts a formulation based on initial assessment of the client and refines the formulation throughout the intervention as new information becomes available.

Persons and Tompkins (1997) described three characteristics of a good cognitive behavioral case formulation. They suggest that it should have strong treatment utility (i.e., increase the effectiveness of treatment), be parsimonious (i.e., simple, including only the necessary information to guide effective treatment), and be supported by evidence. They encourage mental health professionals to seek evidence from the research literature regarding the way symptoms and disorders may present in a typical case, as well as what conditions are likely to be comorbid and what treatments are effective. In addition, Persons and Tompkins advise clinicians to collect data (i.e., evidence) from their clients using objective measures of symptoms and distress to monitor and guide treatment. For example, when treating a client with depressive symptoms, a clinician might administer the second edition of the Beck Depression Inventory (BDI-II; Beck, Steer, & Brown, 1996) weekly to check on the client's symptoms.

A thorough cognitive behavioral formulation includes information about the problems, mechanisms, origins of the mechanisms, and precipitants of the current problems in a way that is comprehensive and cohesive (Persons & Tompkins, 1997). Dudley and Kuyken (2006) refer to these elements of a cognitive behavioral formulation as the five Ps: **presenting issues, precipitating factors, perpetuating factors, predisposing factors**, and **protective factors**. The mental health professional begins by creating a full list of the current problems the client is experiencing. Once all of the presenting issues have been discussed, the clinician may assign a diagnosis and turn to the research literature to learn more about the development, characteristics, and treatment of that primary diagnosis. After learning more about the current scientific knowledge of the client's problems, the mental health professional begins to individualize the formulation: he or she makes hypotheses about what mechanisms are maintaining the problems (or keeping the problems from becoming worse); given the information obtained about current thoughts, behaviors, and emotions (i.e., perpetuating and protective factors); and about how the difficulties have arisen for this particular client by considering plausible psychological, biological, and social explanations given the family and social history and details of the client's upbringing and development (i.e., predisposing factors). Finally, the mental health professional considers what brought the client to treatment at this point in time (i.e., precipitating factors). There are typically major life events or stressful situations that drive a client to seek treatment for a problem. Once all of these factors—predisposing, precipitating, perpetuating, and protective—are carefully considered, the mental health professional may develop a clearer picture of a way to alleviate the problems. Formulation can be essential to prioritizing the client's problems to guide treatment. A good cognitive behavioral formulation is done collaboratively with the client and remains open to revision as the treatment progresses.

Selection of Counseling Interventions

Once a mental health professional has developed an understanding of her client's problems and needs, it is time to think about the intervention. As previously discussed, a good case formulation will point the way to effective treatment. Chances are that the clinician has already encountered a description of the empirically supported techniques of CBT for the client's presenting issues during the process of creating the case formulation. In this section, we will briefly describe the plethora of counseling situations in which CBT may be effectively implemented. We will also take a more in-depth view of two frequently used CBT interventions, and how each is directly related to the cognitive behavioral formulation of the client's distress.

Evidence-Based Treatments

CBT has been tested extensively and has been shown to be an effective treatment for many different psychological disorders, including depression (Hollon & Ponniah, 2010), anxiety disorders (Stewart & Chambless, 2009), substance abuse (Carroll et al., 2008), and psychosis (Lincoln et al., 2012). Furthermore, CBT is an effective approach to treatment for a variety of types of clients, spanning from the very young (e.g., Scheeringa, Weems, Cohen, Amaya-Jackson, & Guthrie, 2011) to the elderly (e.g., Gould, Coulson, & Howard, 2012). CBT has also been demonstrated to work for culturally diverse clients living in the United States (Horrell, 2008) and in other countries (e.g., Pakistan; Naeem, Waheed, Gobbi, Ayub, & Kingdon, 2011).

CBT may be delivered in several different formats, including individual, family-based (Ginsburg & Schlossberg, 2002), and group therapy (Khoo, Dent, & Oei, 2011). Furthermore, CBT is currently being used in a variety of different types of settings, including private practice, psychiatric hospitals, primary care settings (Craske et al., 2009), schools, and correctional facilities (Hollin & Palmer, 2009). Recent research has indicated that CBT can be effectively delivered by students in psychology training programs (Öst, Karlstedt, & Widen, 2012). These students were treating primarily depressed or anxious clients and receiving supervision in CBT. The rates of improvement in their client's symptoms and quality of life were comparable to those of more experienced clinicians. CBT is a goal-oriented approach to counseling that may be used with clients experiencing psychological distress. CBT utilizes a number of approaches to guide clients to identify, examine, and change their dysfunctional thoughts and beliefs.

Exposure Therapy for Anxiety Disorders

Exposure therapy involves asking clients to gradually confront the things that make them feel afraid, but are objectively safe, without escaping or avoiding the fear until their anxiety gradually decreases. Treatment begins by creating a list of feared objects and situations collaboratively with the client and organizing these items into a hierarchy ranging from the least to the most anxiety-provoking. Once the hierarchy is developed, the therapist and client begin to conduct exposures. Exposure involves coming into contact with the object or situation and experiencing the feelings of fear without escape, such as fleeing or looking away from the focus of the exposure, or mental avoidance, such as distraction, until the fear naturally decreases. As clients master items in the hierarchy, they move up to the next item on the list. Depending on the type of fear, exposure therapy can produce relief quickly, sometimes in just one session (Zlomke & Davis, 2008). Exposure is an evidence-based treatment for specific phobias, panic disorder with agoraphobia, agoraphobia without history of panic disorder, social anxiety disorder, obsessive compulsive disorder, and posttraumatic stress disorder (Hazlett-Stevens & Craske, 2008).

Exposure therapy is the treatment suggested by the cognitive behavioral conceptualization of anxiety as arising from the pairing of a previously neutral object with a strong emotional response of fear or anxiety. Let's consider the case of arachnophobia, or fear of spiders. In terms of predisposing factors, the client and therapist might identify multiple pathways by which the fear developed, including a significant negative experience with spiders or, perhaps, observing a parent or peer react fearfully in the presence of spiders. The therapist and client are also likely to hypothesize that the fear is perpetuated or maintained by avoidance of situations in which the client may come into contact with a spider (e.g., camping or visiting the zoo), and extreme distress when unexpectedly encountering a spider. A typical precipitating factor in this case might be that the client is now motivated to seek treatment to prepare for travel to an exotic location where she might encounter a large and fuzzy eight-legged creature. Because the mental health professional hypothesizes that the fear is being maintained by avoidance, exposure is well-suited as a CBT intervention because it specifically targets and eliminates avoidance by asking clients to confront their fears. Furthermore, exposure provides an opportunity for the client to reconsider her beliefs about the danger associated with the feared stimulus. Clients learn during repeated exposure to feared items that they are not as dangerous as they previously estimated and that they can tolerate being in contact with those stimuli.

Cognitive Restructuring for Depression

Cognitive restructuring is an empirically supported intervention suggested by the conceptualization of depression as arising from negative thinking (i.e., schema and automatic negative thoughts). When working with clients who present with symptoms of depression that are being maintained by negative thinking, teaching them to dispute their irrational or dysfunctional beliefs is very effective at improving mood. Treatment should begin by presenting the formulation to the client to illustrate how her thoughts, feelings, and behaviors are connected. When clients are able to see the connection between thinking and feeling, they are motivated to evaluate their beliefs to obtain a more healthy philosophy and be less prone to psychological disturbance (Ellis, 1980). One technique that is used during cognitive restructuring is **Socratic questioning**. Socratic questioning is a way to guide clients to be curious about their beliefs rather than simply believing them to be true. It assists them to consider alternative thoughts, reflect on the source of their beliefs, and to examine evidence for and against their beliefs. The beauty of Socratic questioning is that it can be empowering to clients to uncover a new belief rather than to be told an alternative belief by their therapist.

INTEGRATING OTHER PERSPECTIVES

Humanistic and Existential Psychology

During the 1950s and 1960s, when cognitive and behavioral theories were emerging, there was a parallel movement away from the prevailing psychoanalytic theory toward a different psychological theory that sought to recognize the innate ability of individuals to grow and solve their own psychological problems. Existential psychology is based on the premise that humans are faced with certain inescapable conditions (i.e., death, freedom, isolation, and meaninglessness), which can stir up anxiety when confronted (Yalom, 1980). The psychologists, who played key roles in shaping humanistic psychology—Abraham Maslow and Carl Rogers, and Rollo May, who brought existential psychology from Europe to join humanistic psychology in America—stressed in their work that the client is capable of guiding therapy by engaging in self-exploration and self-discovery in the context of a healthy client-therapist relationship (see Chapter 7 for more information about the characteristics of a good therapeutic relationship). In essence, humanistic psychology turned away from the deterministic, mechanistic, and pathologizing views of mainstream psychology and its endorsement of the medical model, which is the view that psychotherapy is a treatment for mental illness (Elkins, 2009). Humanistic and existential therapies help clients to understand their own experiences and recognize their freedom and ability to choose their own path. Vontress described existential therapists as "philosophical companions, not as people who repair psyches" (2013, p. 161).

Because humanistic psychology does not support traditional psychiatric diagnosis and, instead, relies on the client to identify the areas for self-exploration and growth, the case formulation process is highly collaborative. The mental health professional uses **phenomenological inquiry** to elicit a comprehensive description of the client's current psychological experience, including emotional, cognitive, behavioral, and somatic components (Cooper, 2007). Through this process, the therapist seeks to support the client's curiosity about the characteristics and meaning of her difficulties and experiences that might generate a path for personal growth by asking questions such as, "What was that experience like for you?" or, "How did that feel in the moment?" From a humanistic standpoint, the mental health professional is encouraged to leave behind her own assumptions, theories, prejudices, and needs and truly engage with the client's narrative to see the client as a whole person, rather than focus on developing and thinking about her own theories as to why the client is currently experiencing distress (Cooper, 2007). Through phenomenological inquiry and engaging in a genuine relationship with clients, therapists assist clients to see the reasons they are feeling or behaving in particular ways, develop an understanding of their choices, and decide to modify aspects of their experience to reach optimal personal growth.

Family Systems

Family therapy emerged in the 1950s as an alternative way of understanding psychological difficulties as arising within the context of the family unit. The clients' problems were viewed as existing within the family, typically as a result of problematic communication and interaction, rather than being within the individual. Accordingly, just as the family became the focus of treatment, the understanding of psychological problems shifted to include factors such as family development, family structure, family culture, and family functioning (Rigazio-DiGilio & McDowell, 2013). In systems theory, the formulation of the problem is highly collaborative and consists of the mental health professional working with the family to identify problematic situations and interactions and how they developed. A **genogram**, or illustration of the family tree, including multiple generations, is typically used in systems formulation to examine family patterns and structure (see McGoldrick & Gerson, 1985).

One way of understanding how problems have emerged in a family is to consider that they may be attempted solutions to regain stability (or **homeostasis**) in a family when there has been a change in the system (Dallos & Stedmon, 2006). Specifically, family systems theory suggests that a family will typically seek treatment for one member, the **identified patient,** while it is the whole unit that requires treatment. The identified patient has been selected by the family to be blamed for the problems, whereas it is more likely the case that each is contributing to the distress in the family. For example, in a systems conceptualization of a family in which a child is showing oppositional behavior, the identified problem might include hypotheses about the child's behavior serving the purpose of relieving the anxiety of conflict between the parents. This is the concept of **triangulation,** described by Murray Bowen (1972). In triangulation, an unstable two-person system attempts to regain balance by including another person. In this case, the couple is focusing their attention (e.g., through worry or criticism) on the disobedient child rather than on the tension in their own relationship. A formulation of oppositional conduct in a child from another perspective might not include such a heavy emphasis on the parents' relationship, whereas it will be one of the primary areas of focus in family systems theory and therapy.

Biological Approaches

The biological approach to psychological distress highlights the medicalization of the mind. From a biomedical perspective, the experience of depression, anxiety, or any other emotion is a result of polygenetic influences, the actions of the central and peripheral nervous system, brain structure, and/or the behavior and availability of **neurons** and **neurotransmitters**. The psychological problem is understood to have a biological cause; therefore, the solution to the problem is a medical intervention. This may involve electroconvulsive therapy (ECT), deep brain stimulation, or pharmacological solutions. Underlying vulnerability to mental illness is often a result of the genetic transmission of risk factors.

Researchers often learn about the role of genetics by comparing the development of psychiatric disorders among monozygotic (identical) and dizygotic (fraternal) twins. Genetic research can equip counseling professionals with information that can lead to the development of early intervention and prevention programs for at-risk individuals.

The primary area of research within the biological framework involves understanding the mechanisms of action between neurons and nerve cells in the brain. Neurotransmitters, including dopamine, serotonin, norepinephrine, and glutamate, are the chemicals in the brain that allow neurons to communicate with one another. Nearly all psychiatric medications are designed to affect the availability of neurotransmitters. In order to illustrate this point, we will focus specifically on selective serotonin reuptake inhibitors (SSRIs) like fluoxetine (Prozac), paroxetine (Paxil), and sertraline (Zoloft), which are often prescribed for depression and anxiety disorders. This class of medications works by inhibiting the reabsorption of the neurotransmitter, serotonin, by the presynaptic neuron. In order to understand what this means, one needs to understand how neurons work.

Neurons communicate with each other by sending neurotransmitters across a gap between them called a synapse or synaptic cleft. Neurotransmitters leave the sending (presynaptic) neuron and are released into the synapse. Before they reach the receiving (postsynaptic) neuron, the presynaptic neuron goes through a process of **reuptake** or reabsorption of some of the neurotransmitters. The basic assumption behind the use of SSRIs is that the presynaptic neurons are reabsorbing too much serotonin, thus creating a depletion of serotonin in the synapse, which can lead to feelings of depression and anxiety. SSRIs inhibit this process of reuptake, which, theoretically, should reduce the subjective experience of distress. Recent research suggests that, at least for depression, antidepressants are most effective for those with severe depressive symptoms (Fournier et al., 2010). We agree that biology plays a critical role in the development of psychiatric illness, and we often work in collaboration with psychiatrists and psychiatric nurse practitioners. As with all theoretical perspectives, the biological approach is most useful when understood within context and in conjunction with the many other paradigms discussed in this chapter.

Integration of Perspectives

In this chapter we have discussed different approaches that may be used to care for clients. For the sake of clarity, we have presented each perspective as a separate entity, clearly distinguished from the others. A great deal of energy has been devoted historically to staking out positions within the counseling professions, and some proponents of different theoretical camps have approached others with a somewhat hostile attitude. Wachtel (2010) has argued that theoretical orientations are similar to ethnicity in that differences are magnified, and caricatures and stereotypes about the outgroup predominate. Goldfried (1991) has referred to a process of desegregation that has begun to emerge. Desegregation is the breaking down of barriers between different factions within psychotherapy theory and practice, in order to look with sincere interest and seriousness at neighboring approaches. Organizations like the Society for the Exploration of Psychotherapy Integration (SEPI) and the *Journal of Psychotherapy*

Integration have made theoretical integration their primary focus. In practice, most clinicians—even those with a strong affiliation to one theory or another—integrate techniques and conceptual frameworks from a variety of traditions. The ability to blend multiple theoretical approaches is a skill that requires deep knowledge of the similarities and differences between paradigms.

Some attempts have been made to deliberately integrate components from different theoretical schools. In the United Kingdom, cognitive analytic therapy (CAT; Ryle, 1995) integrates psychodynamic approaches with CBT that emphasizes reflecting on personal constructs. Similarly, Young and Lindemann (1992) have proposed schema-focused psychotherapy, which expands the traditional cognitive framework to include psychodynamic therapeutic approaches in order to treat personality disorders. Most cross-fertilization of perspectives happens more organically. In the daily practice of counseling, most clinicians borrow from multiple perspectives in an effort to best meet the needs of their clients. In fact, some clinicians resist pressures to choose a singular theoretical orientation (Ingram, 2009). We encourage you to consider multiple perspectives and to adopt theories, interventions, strategies, and conceptualizations that are appropriate for the individual client.

AN INTEGRATED CASE FORMULATION EXAMPLE

We acknowledge that reading about theories can be difficult in the absence of any real clinical data. In order to demonstrate how theoretical perspectives can be applied to a clinical scenario, we will now present a case formulation of a client that integrates several perspectives into a comprehensive treatment approach. There are several ways to approach the information the client has shared with the therapist. We will consider psychodynamic and cognitive behavioral aspects of the client's functioning as well as some of the humanistic/existential, systems, and biological aspects of the client's experience of distress. At the conclusion of this section you will find an integrated case formulation with some suggestions for therapeutic interventions.

Alyssa

Alyssa was 25 years old when she presented for individual psychotherapy. She explained during the initial appointment that she had experienced depression and anxiety for much of her life and that these symptoms had frequently interfered with her ability to succeed in school and maintain close interpersonal relationships. Alyssa had never been in therapy, despite asking her parents to take her at around age 16. According to Alyssa, her mother had told her at that time, "The problem is that you are lazy and lack motivation," and left it at that. Alyssa managed to graduate from high school with mediocre grades and few friends. Since graduating she worked as an office assistant, in food service, and as a nanny, but she was never able to maintain employment for more than 6 months because of missing work and an inability to manage tasks that she found "overwhelming." Alyssa described her employers as "demanding" and "unsympathetic" to her problems and expressed a sense of relief at each firing, when she could receive unemployment benefits and have "a break." Her reason for seeking therapy now is her desire to feel less hopeless, less socially anxious, and to be able to have more meaningful friendships and possibly a romantic relationship. At the end of the initial evaluation, Alyssa stated to the therapist, "I'm really just hoping you can give me a magic pill to fix all of this."

Psychodynamic Case Formulation

From a psychodynamic perspective Alyssa seems to have a mother who was ineffectual in meeting her emotional and psychological needs. She has internalized aspects of herself that are (a) in need of caretaking (as evidenced by her sense that her employers are unsympathetic to her suffering); and (b) ineffectual, undeserving, and destined to repeat the mediocrity of the past. Alyssa even seems to undermine her ability to use therapy effectively, instead seeing the therapist as the one who holds the answers. Alyssa's feelings of sadness and anxiety are likely because of the way she has internalized her mother's assessment of her. These negative self-evaluations are likely to come up frequently within the therapeutic relationship. It may be that Alyssa's self-defeating behaviors are ways to defend against more positive feelings about herself; these feelings, that she is capable and worthy of a better life, are threatening because they are in conflict with her mother's appraisal of her.

Cognitive Behavioral Formulation

Alyssa's feelings of hopelessness are likely the result of negative schema and automatic thoughts regarding her abilities. When faced with work-related tasks, she thinks, "I can't do this," and, "This is too much for me to handle." These thoughts lead to negative emotional and behavioral consequences, including feelings of sadness and worry, and social isolation and absenteeism from work. This passive coping, through withdrawal from the world, further triggers negative thinking about her lack of social success and work-related abilities.

Alyssa's automatic negative thoughts may have arisen from a schema regarding her ineffectiveness. She may have developed this schema as a result of her mother's denial of Alyssa's request for treatment to alleviate her emotional distress as a teenager and subsequent messages that Alyssa should overcome these perceived difficulties on her own. Her inability to shake her negative emotions may have reinforced her belief that "There's something wrong with me." Alyssa reports negative thinking about herself as ineffective and damaged, the world as "demanding" and "unsympathetic," and sees her future as hopeless (see Figure 3.5).

Other Components

Alyssa also seems to be confronting important questions about the purpose and meaning of her life. As a young adult her identity should be increasingly distinct from her parents as she defines her own wants and needs. This seems to be an area in which Alyssa faces many challenges. It may be that distinguishing herself from her family of origin, by highlighting her own unique needs, may threaten the family's homeostasis. From a biological perspective, Alyssa's experience of depression and anxiety may be because of genetic influences and/or neurotransmitter deficits. Treatment from this perspective might include pharmacological intervention.

An Integrated Treatment Approach

A therapist working with Alyssa might focus on the negative automatic thoughts she has regarding her ability to be occupationally and socially effective. We expect that Alyssa's negative self-schema will arise repeatedly throughout treatment and will be a continual focus. It may also be useful, as treatment proceeds and the therapeutic alliance deepens, to consider some of the larger existential and humanistic issues that Alyssa highlights regarding her purpose and sense of self. Alyssa would also likely benefit from a discussion of how she perceives her relationship with the therapist; examination of issues that arise between the two of them may be very informative and helpful in getting a better understanding of Alyssa's interpersonal functioning. A psychiatric evaluation might also be helpful in order to consider whether medication might help alleviate some of her depressive symptoms. Finally, any therapist would be wise to consider how Alyssa's current relationship with her family (which we currently know little about) is affecting her functioning. There may be elements of the family system that would need to change in order to allow Alyssa to experience herself differently.

CONCLUSION

As you can see, the major theoretical perspectives approach psychological distress from slightly different angles. As a result of the differences inherent in each paradigm, their approach to treatment varies accordingly. Although we have highlighted the differences between theories, there are also many points of connection. Both psychodynamic and cognitive behavioral approaches focus on underlying causes for psychological distress—CBT on schemas and automatic thoughts; psychodynamic therapy on unconscious feelings and interpersonal patterns—but the techniques of each differ. CBT is more likely to emphasize the identification of schemas, the use of exposure, problem solving, developing skills, and evaluating evidence for beliefs; whereas psychodynamic therapy focuses on interpreting defenses, resistances, and transferences in order to identify repetitive patterns and encourage working through in order to effect change. Developing deep understanding of the various theories that are used in counseling will enrich your practice and help you be a more effective therapist.

CHAPTER REVIEW

Psychodynamic psychotherapy is an approach to treatment that emphasizes the role of the unconscious in motivating behavior and addresses problems in interpersonal functioning. Psychodynamic theory began with the work of Sigmund Freud but has been expanded and revised by many theorists who have come after him.

CBT is an approach to treatment that focuses on alleviating symptoms and improving mood through helping clients change behaviors and modify patterns of thinking. CBT is based on information processing theory, and stipulates that it is often not the events around us that trigger emotional distress, but our interpretation and assessment of those events that may lead us to experience painful emotions and trigger maladaptive behavioral responses.

The process of **case formulation** helps the clinician form a comprehensive hypothesis for how the client's current symptoms and difficulties began and how they are being maintained. All case formulations should include an overview of how treatment will proceed based on the clinician's hypotheses. The mental health professional crafts a formulation based on initial assessment of the client, and refines the formulation throughout the intervention as new information becomes available.

Although the varying theoretical approaches to counseling have arisen in response to one another, there are moves to build bridges between the different approaches. A case study is presented in order to demonstrate the ways in which differing theoretical paradigms can work together to provide the most comprehensive care for those experiencing emotional turmoil.

PERSONAL REFLECTION ESSAY QUESTIONS

1. As you consider the major theoretical perspectives, is there one (or more) that appeals to you or seems to make the most sense when you think about how people function? Why or why not?
2. Choose one of the theoretical perspectives (or focus on integration) and identify three professional organizations that serve to further teaching, research, and dissemination of information. How do the organizations differ in terms of their mission, membership, and/or publications?
3. Although psychodynamic and cognitive behavioral theories have often been conceptualized as distinct from one another, they have many points of overlap. Can you identify some of the common principles or points of contact between these two perspectives?
4. If you are involved in an externship or practicum experience this semester, think about one of your clients. Write up a concise and parsimonious case summary (typically one to two paragraphs) and present several different case conceptualizations, utilizing a variety of perspectives and attempting to integrate them.
   a. If you are not currently seeing clients, consider the following case summary and follow the instructions listed in #4 (above).
   b. Jonathan's parents divorced when he was 12 years old. It was a bitter and angry divorce and Jonathan moved back and forth between his parents' separate homes each week until he left for college. This was a very difficult time for him and he has difficulty even talking about it. He is now 32 years old and seeking individual psychotherapy because of several problems. He and his partner, Greg, have noticed that Jonathan cannot leave the house without checking three or seven times to see if the lights, stove, and water supply are off. Jonathan has also struggled with telling his friends, sister, and parents that he is gay and believes that they will not approve.

KEYWORDS

automatic thoughts	id	resistance
case formulation	mentalization	reuptake
catastrophizing	meta-analysis	topographic model
classical conditioning	mindfulness	schema
cognitive errors	negative cognitive triad	selective abstraction
cognitive restructuring	negative punishment	self-psychology
conditioned response	negative reinforcement	Socratic questioning
conditioned stimulus	neurons	structural model
defense mechanisms	neurotransmitters	superego
dialectical behavior therapy	object relations theory	theory
effect size	operant conditioning	topographic model
ego	perpetuating factors	transference
ego psychology	phenomenological inquiry	transference-focused
empirically supported	positive punishment	psychotherapy
treatments	positive reinforcement	triangulation
exposure therapy	precipitating factors	unconditioned response
free association	predisposing factors	unconditioned stimulus
genogram	protective factors	unconscious
hysteria	psychoanalysis	

FURTHER READING

- Division 12 of the American Psychological Association (The Society of Clinical Psychology) keeps an updated list of treatments with modest or strong research support (www.PsychologicalTreatments.org). There is a companion website maintained by Division 53 (The Society of Clinical Child and Adolescent Psychology) that lists the current treatments for youth with research support (http://effectivechildtherapy.com).

- Johnstone, L. & Dallos, R. (Eds.). (2006). *Formulation in psychology and psychotherapy: Making sense of peoples problems.* New York, NY: Routledge.

  This is an excellent text, which offers an in-depth discussion of several different theoretical approaches to case formulation with illustrative examples for each approach.

- Craske, M. G., Antony, M. M., & Barlow, D. H. (2006). *Mastering your fears and phobias: Therapist guide* (4th ed.). New York, NY: Oxford University Press.

  This is a treatment manual for mental health professionals, which includes step-by-step procedures for conducting exposure therapy for specific phobias. There is also a companion workbook for clients to use during treatment.

- McWilliams, N. (1999). *Psychoanalytic case formulation.* New York, NY: Guilford Press; McWilliams, N. (2004). *Psychoanalytic psychotherapy: A practitioner's guide.* New York, NY: Guilford Press.

Both of these texts by Nancy McWilliams outline the principal components of psychodynamic psychotherapy and case formulation. There are numerous case examples that help illuminate how theory can guide the interventions used in psychodynamic treatment.

Introduction to Issues of Diversity

*Although all of us are racial, ethnic, and cultural beings,
belonging to a particular group does not endow a person with
the competencies and skills necessary to be a culturally skilled
counselor. After all, does a person who is born and raised in a
family make that individual a competent family counselor?*
—Sue, Arredondo, and McDavis (1992)

*There is increasing recognition that we have failed to see others
clearly but have instead treated their cultural worlds like
funhouse mirrors that hold up distorted reflections of our own
cultural preoccupations.*—Kirmayer and Minas (2000, p. 438)

LEARNING OBJECTIVES

- Recognize skills that are relevant to serving well the diverse range of clients seeking counseling
- Discuss multiculturalism in counseling and what it represents
- Recognize the importance that multiculturalism has had in shaping the counseling profession
- Identify the specific characteristics that counselors need to develop in order to demonstrate multicultural competency
- Identify all the different types of diversity: race, ethnicity, gender, physical ability and disability, spoken language, religion, sexual orientation, and cognitive ability and disability
- Understand what cultural responsiveness means and what it entails as part of therapy
- Understand the meaning of "White privilege" and "cultural mistrust" and the effect these may have in therapy
- Recognize the importance of addressing multicultural issues in therapy in order to build a better therapeutic alliance
- Understand the meaning of "racial identity development" and "acculturation," and the role they play in the process of understanding clients

INTERVIEWING AND COUNSELING FROM
A MULTICULTURAL PERSPECTIVE

During the past 30 years, mental health professionals have become increasingly aware of the need to develop a particular set of knowledge and skills relevant to serving well the diverse range of clients seeking counseling. Traditionally, psychology has taken an **etic** view of individuals. That is, a view that there are universal principles of healthy personality development and all people should achieve the same optimal outcome (i.e., one definition of mental health), regardless of culture. On the other hand, an **emic** perspective states that every culture has its own norms and values and no one model of mental health can be applied to all individuals. The traits of individuals who function well within their own cultural groups may be considered unhealthy or undesirable characteristics in another culture. For example, an individualistic independent thinker may rise to great success as the leader of a company in the United States, but that same independent streak would not be valued in certain Asian cultures that value community and interdependence more highly.

Multiculturalism in counseling represents an emic perspective and aims to meet clients where they are in terms of their unique cultural worldview and the recognition of the historical stressors and experiences that led to their development. As an acknowledgement of the important role multiculturalism has had in shaping the counseling profession, Pedersen (1990) called it the "fourth force" in counseling and psychology. He described multiculturalism as referring to "a wide range of multiple groups without grading, comparing, or ranking them as better or worse than one another and without denying the very distinct and complementary or even contradictory perspectives that each group brings with it" (p. 4).

BOX 4.1

Which Came First?

The first three forces in counseling are: (a) psychodynamic; (b) cognitive behavioral; and (c) existential humanistic theories of psychology, which were each covered in the previous chapter. Multiculturalism has been described as the fourth force. Be on the lookout for a proposed "fifth force" later in this chapter.

The idea that a counselor should demonstrate specific multicultural competencies to work with clients was first proposed by Sue and colleagues (1982). Sue and colleagues (1992) elaborated on this concept and proposed that counselors should develop three characteristics (i.e., attitudes and beliefs, knowledge, and skills) within three domains. Specifically, counselors with cross-cultural competence should increase their awareness of their own values and biases, gain knowledge about the worldviews and experiences of individuals from other cultural backgrounds, and learn strategies and techniques to effectively work with clients from diverse cultural backgrounds. For example, a mental health professional should continually seek to understand how his or her cultural background influences the way he or she perceives information about other cultures. And, in so doing, he or she strives to compare the way he or she views an issue to his or her clients' perspectives nonjudgmentally.

The importance of multicultural competence among mental health professionals has been posited to increase the effectiveness of services provided to clients. Specifically, research has shown poorer treatment outcome and higher treatment dropout for ethnic minority clients, and the development of multicultural competence is an attempt to improve the effectiveness of services provided to people from diverse racial and ethnic groups (Sue, Fujino, Hu, Takeuchi, & Zane, 1991). Accordingly, accrediting bodies have mandated the inclusion of courses that address multicultural issues in the curriculum of graduate training in mental health because of its vital importance to being an effective counselor. Worthington, Soth-McNett, and Moreno (2007) have found that positive therapy outcomes are associated with multicultural competence, including increased therapist credibility, therapist effectiveness, client self-disclosure, client satisfaction, and reduced attrition. The goal of this chapter is to introduce you to the concept of multiculturalism and urge you to reflect on your knowledge about other cultures and attitudes toward individuals from diverse cultural backgrounds.

BOX 4.2

Learning Exercise

The Miville-Guzman Universality-Diversity Scale—Short Form (MGUDS-S; Miville et al., 1999; Fuertes, Miville, Mohr, Sedlacek, & Gretchen, 2000) measures **universal-diverse orientation** (UDO), which is "an attitude toward all other persons that is inclusive yet differentiating in that similarities and differences are both recognized and accepted; the shared experience of being human results in a sense of connectedness with people and is associated with a plurality or diversity of interactions with others" (Miville et al., 1999, p. 292). Research has found that counselors' scores on the three factors of the MGUDS (i.e., Diversity of Contact, Relativistic Appreciation, and Sense of Connection) are related to both multicultural knowledge and awareness (Constantine et al., 2001) and the ability to empathize with culturally different clients (Miville, Carlozzi, Gushue, Schara, & Ueda, 2006), thus making UDO an important personal quality among counselors related to working more effectively with diverse clients.

How do you measure up? The MGUDS-S is found in the appendix to this chapter. Answer the 15 questions and calculate your score based on the instructions provided there. You do not have to share your scores with anyone, but we believe it is valuable to gauge your personal level of UDO in preparation for reading the rest of this chapter. To give you an idea of a typical score for a counseling graduate student, Miville and colleagues (2006) found that the average total score was 71.84 (with a standard deviation of 7.26) among 211 students enrolled in five different academic programs in the United States. Reflect on your scores and how each of the factor scores compare to one another. Factor scores range from 5 to 30 in each of the following areas:

- Higher scores on Diversity of Contact indicate an interest in learning about other cultures, countries, and ethnicities.

(*continued*)

(continued)

- Higher scores on Relativistic Appreciation indicate an appreciation of similarities and differences among people and recognition of the usefulness of acknowledging similarities and differences in understanding others.
- Higher scores on Discomfort with Differences (originally labeled Sense of Connection) indicate discomfort relating to people of different ethnicities.

Which area is the best developed at this point in your training? Which area is the least developed?

TYPES OF DIVERSITY

The majority of mental health professionals agree that all clinical encounters are cultural in some way (Sue, 1998). People quickly identify racial and ethnic variables as important types of diversity, but there are many more types of differences to consider. Some are highly visible, such as gender, physical ability and disability, and spoken language, whereas others are less apparent on the surface, such as religion, sexual orientation, and cognitive ability and disability. In the following section, we will discuss several types of diversity and the ways in which you may attend to these aspects of your clients' experiences when providing mental health services.

While you are reading the following sections, we encourage you to take the perspective of each group to the extent that you can and reflect on how certain individuals may view their experience differently than mental health professionals. For instance, clients may interpret certain kinds of symptoms differently than therapists seeking to make a psychiatric diagnosis. Furthermore, some people may have sought help for the symptoms from other culturally acceptable sources before turning to mental health treatment. These clients have likely not received a formal diagnosis and may have a strong reaction to a description of the problem that is outside of their cultural lexicon, particularly if it deviates from the understanding provided by the first helper they approached for the problem. A third consideration is that symptoms may present differently among various cultures.

How exactly do mental health professionals respond to diversity in session? In Chapter 3 we described the process of case formulation as integrating various types of information about the client to form a good understanding of the client's current problems and how they developed. To do this well, a mental health professional must acknowledge the role of culture in the development or exacerbation of the presenting problems by seeking the client's perspective. Other examples include demonstrating culturally sensitive knowledge, showing appropriate empathy, and expressing interest in cultural values and experiences. All of these behaviors are a part of **cultural responsiveness**. Cultural responsiveness entails responding to the cultural content that is present in a therapy session. Atkinson and Lowe (1995) describe culturally responsive counselors as those who "acknowledge the existence of, show interest in, demonstrate knowledge of, and express appreciation for the client's ethnicity and culture...[and]...place the client's problem in a cultural context" (p. 402). This section highlights some of the important factors of diversity to consider when working with clients.

Race, Ethnicity, Country of Origin, and Language

Robert Carter (1995) argued that the mental health literature is characterized by assumptions that "reflect a profound denial of the reality of race" (p. 16). Carter is referring to the long history of research on human development that has ignored race as a contributing factor to personality development. **Race** and **ethnicity** shape our identity and make a significant contribution to who we are. Accordingly, Carter advocated for mental health professionals to bring up issues of race in therapy as opposed to simply ignoring them. That is, mental health professionals cannot adopt a color-blind stance, but instead should actively engage issues and experiences related to the client's race. In fact, Knox and colleagues found that when they compared a small group of African American and European American psychologists, the African American psychologists reported that they typically address race with clients of color, whereas the European American therapists reported that they did not normally address race with racially different clients unless the topic was raised by the client (Knox, Burkard, Johnson, Suzuki, & Ponterotto, 2003). Some of the European American psychologists also acknowledged that they would not address race even if the topic was raised by the client.

BOX 4.3

Learning Exercise

Knox and colleagues (2003) examined the experience of therapists working with clients of a different race. Take a moment now to ponder how you might decide whether to address race in therapy with a client of a different race from your own. Brainstorm with a partner about situations that might arise in therapy that might encourage you to start a conversation about race. When would you do this? How would you bring up the topic of race? Practice role-playing with your partner to find out what it might be like to discuss race with a client. After the role play, take a moment to discuss what it felt like for the two of you. Was it awkward? Or did you feel comfortable? Lastly, discuss the likely results of having a conversation about race in therapy. Contrast that with the potential effects of deciding not to discuss race in therapy.

Discussing race seems to help to engage clients in treatment. Thompson, Worthington, and Atkinson (1994) found that African American college students tended to self-disclose more intimately and indicated more willingness to return to therapy when counselors asked directly about their experience of being Black. Specifically, the therapists in the study were instructed to make three cultural content statements during an intake session (e.g., "Tell me about how your feelings of loneliness reflect your experiences as a Black student on this campus") or three universal content statements (e.g., "As a student here, you've encountered some difficulties in your effort to make friends," p. 157). Results indicated that direct discussions about race encouraged a stronger therapeutic alliance. It seems that what you say about race and how you say it may be as important as what you don't say about race in session.

Furthermore, addressing race early in treatment may be better than later. Fuertes, Mueller, Chauhan, Walker, and Ladany (2002) found that European American therapists who directly addressed racial issues within the first two sessions with African American clients created an environment more conducive to establishing a strong therapeutic relationship and reported significant progress in treatment after 12 sessions. Although there is much evidence that addressing issues of race directly in therapy is likely to have a positive impact, this may be something that is easier said than done. Constantine and Sue (2007) hypothesized that discussions of race may be difficult for White Americans for several reasons, including fear of appearing racist, difficulty realizing and acknowledging their own racism and unconscious prejudices, difficulty confronting **White privilege**, and feeling responsible for taking steps to end racism. (See Box 4.6 for more information about White privilege.) These factors may lead some mental health professionals to avoid topics of race in session through avoidance or attention to other cultural variables instead. Carter (1995) stressed that mental health professionals should remain aware that focusing on the client's culture as it is broadly defined may divert attention away from the specific issues of race and ethnicity. Focusing on other cultural variables to the exclusion of race and ethnicity may be seen as minimizing the impact of racism that clients may have experienced.

BOX 4.4

Spotlight on Culture

A striking example of how culture may impact mental health treatment has been highlighted by several studies that identified the tendency for African American clients to be perceived by non-African American clinicians as demonstrating clinical symptoms of paranoia, which subsequently leads to psychiatric misdiagnosis of severe mental illness. For example, Trierweiler and colleagues (2006) found that non-African American clinicians were more likely than African American clinicians to identify paranoid symptoms in African American psychiatric patients and diagnose them with schizophrenia. This phenomenon, where African American clients appear guarded to clinicians, has been attributed to **cultural mistrust**, or healthy cultural paranoia (Whaley, 2001). This cultural mistrust is likely to have developed as a result of the individual's experiences with racism and oppression. This history of coming into contact with prejudice is likely to contribute to efforts at self-protection, which may be interpreted as paranoia or the negative symptoms of schizophrenia (e.g., flat affect and poverty of speech).

Thus, Whaley (2001) urged clinicians to carefully consider cultural aspects of paranoia from true pathology in diagnosis and assessment and initiate discussions of racism with African American clients, including those with serious mental illness. Clinicians may increase cultural mistrust in clients if they dismiss complaints of racism without listening, exploring, and validating them when appropriate.

Cardemil and Battle (2003) outlined practical recommendations for mental health professionals to assist in addressing issues of race and ethnicity in therapy. These authors recommend that counselors directly ask clients early in the therapy process how they identify their race and ethnicity. This is particularly important because not all individuals within a racial or ethnic group prefer to use the same label to describe their identity (e.g., some people may prefer the term African American, whereas others prefer Black); and furthermore, a well-meaning therapist may make assumptions about a client's racial and ethnic background based on skin color (e.g., assuming someone is African American when, in fact, they are Caribbean American), particularly when the client is multiracial. Therefore, Cardemil and Battle encourage therapists to initiate an open conversation with clients about how they identify their racial and ethnic background. The second suggestion offered by Cardemil and Battle is that mental health professionals recognize the heterogeneity within racial and ethnic groups and avoid relying on stereotypes to understand a client's personal experience. They suggest assessing two key processes to better understand clients, **racial identity development** and **acculturation**, because members of the same racial or ethnic group may have disparate experiences and stressors depending upon their identity development and acculturation.

Cardemil and Battle (2003) also encourage mental health professionals to consider how racial and ethnic differences between therapist and client might affect therapy, including differences in conceptualizing mental health and mental illness and different communication styles. Particularly, mental health professionals should consider the different types of nonverbal communication that might be typical in different cultures. For example, Japanese clients may avoid direct eye contact as a sign of respect, but this may be misinterpreted by a European American therapist as an indication of shyness or shame. Cardemil and Battle next recommend that counselors acknowledge that power, privilege, and racism might affect interactions with clients. They suggest that mental health professionals in doubt about the importance of race and ethnicity in treatment err on the side of bringing it up when it seems to be relevant to the client's problems. The final recommendation Cardemil and Battle make to mental health professionals is to continue learning as much as possible about issues relating to race and ethnicity.

BOX 4.5

The Minority Identity Development Model

Research indicates that all individuals go through racial identity development, a process of growth and maturation related to one's own culture. The model proposed by Atkinson, Morten, and Sue (1998) is the most widely accepted and proposes that individuals from minority groups in the United States progress through five stages.

- **Stage 1 (Conformity):** Individuals in this stage reject and devalue characteristics of their own culture while embracing the dominant culture's beliefs and customs. People who are in the Conformity stage are likely to experience low self-esteem because they view themselves and their culture as inferior to the dominant group.

(continued)

(continued)

- **Stage 2 (Dissonance):** In this stage, dissonance arises as a result of beginning to value aspects of one's own culture and beginning to question the values and customs of the dominant culture. In this stage, the individual is developing more positive views of herself that are in conflict with previously held negative attitudes.
- **Stage 3 (Resistance; also called Immersion):** In this stage, the individual moves to the other extreme, feels a strong sense of identification with her own cultural group, and rejects the dominant values of society and culture. The individual sees her culture as superior and develops ethnocentrism and racial pride.
- **Stage 4 (Introspection):** During Introspection, the person begins to analyze her attitudes and feelings in a more nuanced way and recognizes that there are elements of the dominant culture that are desirable. The individual begins to intentionally integrate the views of her culture with the dominant culture's outlook.
- **Stage 5 (Integrative Awareness):** This final stage marks the person's ability to acknowledge the positive and negative aspects of her own culture as well as that of the dominant culture and other minority cultures.

Acculturation

Acculturation describes the extent to which members of one culture adopt the views and practices of the dominant culture. Berry (1990, 1997) proposed a model of acculturation that focuses on two main factors: *cultural maintenance*, which refers to the extent to which individuals value and strive to maintain their own cultural heritage, and *contact and participation*, which describes the extent to which individuals attempt to interact with and adopt the values and

Cultural maintenance

	Yes	No
Yes	Integration	Assimilation
No	Separation	Marginalization

(left axis: Contact and participation)

FIGURE 4.1 Berry's acculturation strategies.

behaviors of the dominant culture. If the individual considers it to be of value to maintain his or her cultural heritage, he or she endorses cultural maintenance. If the individual considers it to be of value to develop relationships with the larger society, he or she endorses contact and participation. Each of these two dimensions may vary independently, and the combination describes a person's acculturation strategy. As shown in Figure 4.1, an individual who endorses both cultural maintenance and contact and participation can be described as using the integration strategy, whereas an individual who values cultural maintenance but does not value contact and participation is using the separation/segregation strategy.

BOX 4.6

White Privilege: Unpacking the Invisible Knapsack

In 1988, feminist and anti-racist activist Peggy McIntosh wrote about the invisible knapsack that Whites carry. "White privilege is like an invisible weightless knapsack of special provisions, maps, passports, codebooks, visas, clothes, tools and blank checks" (McIntosh, 1988, pp. 1–2). She then listed privileges she felt that she had because of her light skin. Some examples are:

- "I can turn on the television or open to the front page of the paper and see people of my race widely represented" (p. 5).
- "I can go into a music shop and count on finding the music of my race represented, into a supermarket and find the staple foods that fit with my cultural traditions, into a hairdresser's shop and find someone who can deal with my hair" (p. 6).
- "I can do well in a challenging situation without being called a credit to my race" (p. 7).
- "I can go home from most meetings of organizations I belong to feeling somewhat tied in, rather than isolated, out-of-place, outnumbered, unheard, held at a distance, or feared" (p. 7).

Depending on your skin color, you may be surprised to realize that your knapsack contains statements beginning with "I can," similar to McIntosh, or those that begin with "I can't." You may want to further reflect on this and come up with your own list of things in your knapsack.

As part of any conversation about race and ethnicity, clinicians should inquire about country of origin. National identity is another important cultural variable that should be considered when working with clients. For instance, **nationality** is very important to anyone of Latino origin, as there are many differences among individuals from different countries in Latin America. Along with discussions of race and ethnicity, asking clients about nationality should be a standard practice in order to avoid invalidating their identity and unique experience.

Language can be an obvious barrier to effective counseling when the client and mental health professional do not speak the same language. However, language can also be problematic in situations where the client is fluent in English but may be more comfortable speaking her native language, particularly because conversation in therapy may be more personal and laden with emotion than other interactions. Javier, Barroso, and Muqoz (1993) found that bilingual adult Latino clients, who spoke Spanish in childhood and learned English later in life, provided more details in Spanish when describing their childhood experiences.

Although it is certainly ideal for bilingual mental health professionals to work with bilingual clients when possible, there are ways for monolingual therapists to enhance their work with bilingual clients. Jeanette Altarriba (2003) recommended that counselors who are not bilingual allow clients to switch between their native language and English to provide clients with the opportunity to tap into their emotions, which may be more easily done when they are speaking their first language. Although the counselor may not be able to fully understand the content of the client's communication, it is likely that he or she will be able to gather useful information about the emotions summoned by the content in addition to facilitating emotional expression in the client.

In situations when you are not capable of conducting assessment or treatment in the client's dominant language, you may consider using a translator or interpreter to conduct a brief assessment and collaborate with the client to locate another more appropriate mental health professional. It may be difficult to immediately discern whether you and a bilingual client are able to communicate effectively. It may be helpful to consider the client's level of acculturation and his or her use of language with family and friends to determine fluency and whether it is a good idea to proceed with therapy in the shared language.

BOX 4.7

Family Matters

The definition of family and the emphasis on the importance of family are likely to vary among different ethnic and cultural groups. Thus, it is important to directly ask clients to define their family and describe how they are connected to their family. A **genogram** (McGoldrick & Gerson, 1985) or drawing of the client's family tree can be a useful tool in working with clients to outline the various family members with whom they are connected and can open up a way to discuss the importance and impact of their relationships with different relatives. Mental health professionals should remain aware that certain cultural groups, including Native Americans, African Americans, Asian Americans, and Latinos, typically place a high value on family and have a definition of family that goes beyond the traditional American nuclear family to include extended family members as well as non-biologically related community members and close friends in family roles (Jones & Lindahl, 2011). This concept is known as **familism**, which is a multicultural value that describes the central role of family bonds and the presence of extended kinship systems in some people's lives (Comas-Díaz, 2012). For some clients who endorse familism, it may be important to include family in treatment sessions because of their closeness to each other.

Immigration

The 2010 U.S. Census data indicated that approximately 13% of the U.S. population was born in another country. The states with the largest immigrant populations are California, New York, Texas, and Florida. Nearly 35% of the immigrant population recently moved to the United States, arriving between 2000 and 2010. Most immigrants to the United States were born in Latin America or the Caribbean (53%), followed by Asia (28%), Europe (12%), and Africa (4%). Approximately 55% of Latin American immigrants were born in Mexico.

For immigrants, Phinney and colleagues (2001) found that positive psychological outcomes are related to having an integrated acculturation strategy as described in Berry's model. Other factors that contribute to an individual being able to integrate her cultural heritage with a new culture include gender (women may have a more difficult time during acculturation if there is a large difference in the status and role of women in the two cultures), age at the time of immigration (it is typically easier to migrate earlier in life), generation of immigration (first, second, or third), and education (Berry, 1997).

Whereas most **immigrants** voluntarily move to the United States for varied reasons, there is a subset of individuals who are **refugees**, individuals forced to leave their countries involuntarily as a result of war, political persecution, or disaster. Immigrants tend to be better prepared to establish themselves in the new country, whereas refugees may have little or no familiarity with the new culture or language (Chung & Bemak, 2007). Thus, mental health professionals should assess the reason for relocation as well as the circumstances surrounding the move to the United States with clients who were not born in the United States. In addition, it is important to develop a good understanding of the client's pre-migration and post-migration experiences when establishing therapeutic alliance. It is important to note that typically an immigrant's "departure status" was higher than his or her "entry status," which can lead to negative experiences during acculturation (Berry, 1997, p. 22).

Sexual Orientation

Herek, Norton, Allen, and Sims (2010) recently conducted a survey to gather more demographic information about self-identified gay, lesbian, and bisexual U.S. residents. The probability sample of 662 respondents was selected from English-speaking U.S. households with a landline telephone; this included about equal numbers of men and women. Specifically, the sample comprised gay men (34.8%), lesbians (14.6%), bisexual males (26.9%), and bisexual females (23.7%). Herek and colleagues found that the typical age of self-identification was reported to be in the late teen years (i.e., 15.1 years old for gay men, 17.5 years old for bisexual men, 18.0 years old for lesbians, and 19.9 years old for bisexual women). In contrast, the mean age for the first disclosure of sexual minority status was reported to be several years later on average (i.e., 20.2 years old for gay men, 21.0 years old for bisexual women, 21.1 years old for lesbians, and 21.5 years old for bisexual men). Accordingly, when working with adolescent or young adult clients, it may be the case that they are not currently identifying as gay, lesbian, or bisexual to themselves. Furthermore, if an individual has identified himself or herself as homosexual or bisexual, he or she may not have made the disclosure to

anyone else. Because the majority of individuals responding to the survey indicated that they felt they had little or no choice about their sexual orientation, you
may also encounter clients who are struggling to accept an identity they feel they
did not choose in the midst of messages from others that sexual orientation is a
choice to follow a sinful path (Herman, 1997).

The results of Herek and colleagues' research (2010) also highlight another
important issue, which is that there are differences between gay, lesbian, and bisexual individuals in terms of sexual minority identity and level of "outness" (i.e.,
out of the closet). In contrast to bisexual men and women, a significantly higher
number of gay men and lesbians were out to their parents and siblings. The same
pattern was apparent with regard to being out to friends and coworkers. Bisexual
individuals, particularly men, are less likely to disclose their sexual orientation
to friends and coworkers. Gay men and lesbians reported that they were more
strongly committed to a minority sexual identity than bisexual men and women
in the sample. These findings may be due to the marginalization of bisexual
individuals in established gay and lesbian communities in the United States.
Furthermore, most of the bisexual respondents who reported being in a committed
relationship stated that they were in a relationship with an opposite sex partner.

Coming out is one of the most important life experiences in terms of identity development for gay men and lesbian women, and it is important to be sensitive to a client's stage in that process. Cass (1979) identified six major stages in the
coming out process for gay men and lesbians. When working with clients who
disclose sexual minority status, you should assess whether they are experiencing: (a) identity confusion, in which they are questioning whether or not they are
homosexual; (b) identity comparison, in which they accept the possibility that
they may be homosexual but continue to experience conflict about their identity;
(c) identity tolerance, in which they have come out to themselves as gay or lesbian; (d) identity acceptance, in which they have increased self-acceptance and
more contact with gay and lesbian culture; (e) identity pride, in which they prefer
immersion in gay and lesbian culture and are rejecting of heterosexual norms; or
(f) identity synthesis, in which they appreciate and maintain heterosexual allies
and have integrated their sexuality into their identity.

When working with any client, it is best practice not to assume they are
attracted to the opposite sex. For example, when working with a teen girl, you
may consider asking whether she has any romantic relationships rather than asking whether she has a boyfriend. Additionally, you cannot assume that a person
in a relationship with a member of the opposite sex identifies as heterosexual. It
is important to ask clients how they label themselves and use that term in your
work with them. For sexual minorities, there are myriad possibilities including:
gay, lesbian, homosexual, and queer. Herek and colleagues (2010) found that a
majority of homosexual men in their sample preferred the term gay to describe
themselves (93.0%). Among homosexual women, there were large numbers who
reported using the term lesbian (73.4%) and gay (75.9%) to describe themselves.

Issues of Gender and Gender Identity

Gender roles and expectations may impact the experiences of clients seeking
treatment as well as impact the counseling relationship. For instance, men in the
United States who conform to dominant masculine norms are reticent to seek

help from mental health professionals due to self-stigma about failing to live up to masculine ideals of stoicism and self-reliance. Recent research has indicated that this finding appears to be consistent for European American heterosexual men as well as men from minority racial and ethnic groups and with minority sexual orientation (Vogel, Heimerdinger-Edwards, Hammer, & Hubbard, 2011). Thus, mental health professionals may specifically explore men's beliefs regarding what it means to be in therapy as early in treatment as possible in order to reduce the stigma of seeking help and encourage men to remain in counseling. Vogel and colleagues recommend that seeking therapy may be reframed to be considered a sign of strength and courage rather than weakness for men who express self-stigmatizing beliefs about counseling.

Rigid gender-role attitudes of mental health counselors may interfere with therapy and prevent a professional from responding in a sensitive way to clients who do not conform to gender stereotypes. You can imagine the family's reaction to the news that Greg Focker is a male nurse in the movie, *Meet the Parents*, for a good example of rigid gender roles at play. Flexible gender-role attitudes, on the other hand, emphasize personal choice rather than adherence to cultural norms or stereotypes. Gender-role attitudes of clients may also affect the therapeutic relationship. Research has shown that men and women tend to view female therapists as more capable of forming effective therapeutic relationships with clients than males because they are seen as more caring and emotionally supportive, consistent with the female nurturing stereotype, whereas male therapists are seen as being more focused on problem solving (Gehart & Lyle, 2004). Knudson-Martin and Mahoney (1999) identified four common "gender traps" for clinicians to avoid falling into during interactions with clients: (a) assuming that differences among men and women are "natural"; (b) unconsciously acting out gender scripts such as "women should seek relationships and men should be independent"; (c) ignoring gender power differences in the therapeutic relationship; and (d) concluding that gender inequality is no longer an issue. Gehart and Lyle (2004) recommend clinicians ask themselves the following questions to consider how their gender-role attitudes might impact their practice: "How do I connect with male versus female clients? ... Do I have different expectations about the level of emotional expression for men and women? Do I interpret tears and anger the same across genders? Should I?" (p. 456).

Mental health professionals should also be prepared to work with clients with a gender identity that does not align with their physical sexual characteristics. Riley, Wong, and Sitharthan (2011) discussed the need for counselors to be aware that individuals with gender variance who self-identify with a gender on the spectrum between male and female do not always seek to change their physical sexual characteristics. The broadest classification of individuals with gender variance is **transgender**, whereas **transsexual** refers to those people who are seeking sexual reassignment surgery. As was previously discussed, a direct conversation with clients about how they self-identify is important in addition to inquiring about their desire to seek surgery. Riley and colleagues urge therapists to take a "trans-positive approach," which affirms the individual's preferred gender (2011, p. 397). Two key methods for providing care to transgender clients are for mental health professionals to take a nonpathologizing approach by recognizing the individual's right to his or her own gender expression and to recognize and validate the oppression and constraints imposed by society on transgender people. Carroll, Gilroy, and Ryan (2002) point out the negative effects of the "gender privilege" that nontransgender people experience in society (p. 137). Most nontransgender people are unaware of gender privilege, but it affects everyday activities such as using a public restroom and choosing clothes to wear.

Religion and Spirituality in Context

According to a 1996 Gallup Poll, 96% of Americans believe in God, more than 90% pray, nearly 70% are members of a church or community of faith, and over 40% have attended a religious service within the past week. Additionally, nearly one in five Americans describes themselves as "spiritual but not religious." These data suggest that the majority of individuals seeking psychotherapy will be involved in religious activities or have spiritual beliefs that are important to them. Religion and spirituality are important aspects of individual experience and are included under the broader umbrella of multicultural competence.

As with other aspects of culture, spiritual and religious aspects of the individual may be an important variable in how a person understands and copes with personal struggles. Culture, and specifically spirituality and religion, can: (a) create sources of distress; (b) shape the individual's experience of an illness; (c) influence the symptomatology of general distress or specific syndromes; (d) determine how an individual interprets symptoms; (e) provide specific ways of coping with distress; (f) guide the process of help-seeking and response to treatment; and (g) govern how an individual responds to distress and disability (Alarcon et al., 2005; Huguelet, Borras, Gillieron, Brandt, & Mohr, 2009). In addition to the important overlaps between religion, spirituality, and care of the psyche, sensitivity to spiritual and religious issues is important because this is an area in which many individuals have experienced discrimination.

Religion is sometimes a lightning rod for prejudice, and in the United States, there is a long history of religious discrimination. This includes federal policies that infringe on Native American religious practices, state laws that exclude atheists, agnostics, and New Age practitioners from running for office, and hate crimes against Sikhs and Muslims in the aftermath of 9/11. In addition to these discriminatory forces coming from outside of the communities of faith, marginalization of those with mental illness has sometimes come from within churches, synagogues, temples, and mosques. Take this case example drawn from Dr. Prout's work with individuals with serious and persistent mental illness:

> Joan is a 45-year-old woman with bipolar disorder and a long history of psychiatric hospitalizations. Every time she is hospitalized, her pastor comes to visit, bringing with him food, crossword puzzles, and other comforts of home. These visits are a source of support for Joan, but every time her pastor ends the visit he tells her, "So good to see you. Don't worry. If anyone asks I won't tell them what you're in the hospital for." This message—that mental illness is a secret—has added to Joan's feelings of shame and alienation.

It is important to remember that clients are likely to find their religious and spiritual communities to be both supportive and a source of stress. The beliefs, practices, and socialization aspects of faith are complex and hold multiple meanings for clients. Additionally, unlike other forms of diversity, religion and spirituality are aspects of the self that are changed and refashioned throughout the life span. For example, a client who talks at length about astrological beliefs and the ways in which these guide her life and provide her with comfort may have been raised as a strict Roman Catholic, having since rejected that belief system. Given the mutability and complexity of individual belief systems and their relevance to clients' daily lives and recovery, learning to conduct a thorough spiritual assessment is an important component of multicultural competence.

Spiritual assessment can follow many paths, and several systems of assessment have been proposed. Koenig and Prichett (1998) have suggested the mnemonic device FICA to refer to questions that should be asked:

- Faith: "Is religious faith an important part of your life?"
- Influence: "How has faith influenced your life (past and present)?"
- Community: "Are you currently a part of a religious or spiritual community?"
- (**A**) Needs: "Are there any spiritual needs that you would like me to address?"

Similarly, Anandarajah and Hight (2001) proposed the HOPE questions for use in medical settings that can be easily adapted to mental health care; this set of questions addresses several domains of spiritual and religious experience.

- Hope: What are your sources of hope, strength, comfort, meaning, peace, love, and connection? What do you hold on to during difficult times? What sustains you and keeps you going?
- Organized Religion: Do you consider yourself part of an organized religion? How important is this to you? What aspects of your religion are helpful and not so helpful to you?
- Personal Spirituality: Can you tell me something about your private spirituality and practices? Do you have personal spiritual beliefs that are independent of organized religion? Do you believe in God? What kind of relationship do you have with God?
- Effects of Spirituality on Care: Has your current situation affected your ability to do the things that usually help you spiritually? Are you worried about any conflicts between your beliefs and the care you will receive here? What effects does your religious/spiritual faith have on the care you will receive here? Would it be helpful to speak to a clinical chaplain/ community spiritual leader?

It is nearly impossible to know all there is to know about every religion. For this reason, we encourage you to settle into the position that the client is the expert on his or her own experience. This approach to cultural issues will be discussed in greater detail later in the chapter. For a detailed list of spiritual assessment questions, see Figure 4.2.

Physical and Cognitive Abilities

The Americans with Disabilities Act of 1990 is a civil rights law that prohibits discrimination based on physical or mental disability. It was enacted over 25 years after the Civil Rights Act of 1964, which made discrimination based on

---

Religious/spiritual history
Family background
- What were your father's religious or spiritual beliefs and practices?
- What were your mother's religious or spiritual beliefs and practices?

Childhood/adolescence
- In which religious tradition were you raised?
- When you were a child, what kind of religious practices were you involved in? How often?
- When you were a teenager, did you experience changes in your religious beliefs or religious practices? Which ones?

Adulthood
- In your adult life, have you experienced changes in your religious beliefs or practices? Which ones?

Effect of distress upon spirituality/religiousness
- Since you have been [depressed, anxious, etc.], have you experienced changes in your religious beliefs and practices? Which ones?

Current spiritual/religious beliefs and practices
- At the present time, what is your religious preference?
- What are your spiritual or religious beliefs today?
- Do you have private religious or spiritual practices? Which ones? How often?
- Do you engage in religious or spiritual practices with other people? Which ones? How often?
- To what extent do people in your religious community help you cope? In which ways? Are there ways in which they are not supportive?

Subjective importance of religion in life
- In general, how important are your religious or spiritual beliefs in your day-to-day life? In which ways?
- To what extent do your religious or spiritual beliefs give meaning to your life? How?

Subjective importance of religion to cope with illness
- To what extent do your religious or spiritual beliefs give meaning to your [depression, anxiety, etc.]? In which ways?
- To what extent do your religious or spiritual beliefs help you to cope with your [depression, anxiety, etc.]? In which ways?
- To what extent do your religious or spiritual beliefs help you gain control over your [depression, anxiety, etc.]? In which ways?
- To what extent are your religious or spiritual beliefs a source of strength and comfort for you? In which ways?

Synergy of religion with psychotherapy and psychiatry
- To what extent are your religious and spiritual beliefs in conflict with receiving psychotherapy and/or medication? In which ways?
- How does it make you feel talking about your religious or spiritual beliefs with me?

FIGURE 4.2 Spiritual and religious assessment questions.

race, religion, sex, and national origin illegal. Individuals with disabilities have only relatively recently been offered legal protection from discrimination and continue to experience prejudice and oppression in their daily lives. Just as we have discussed previously with other aspects of multiculturalism, mental health professionals need to confront their biases and attitudes about **people with disabilities** (PWDs) in order to be culturally responsive in therapy.

Artman and Daniels (2010) urge mental health professionals to increase their awareness of the language and attitudes they have about PWDs. They encourage clinicians to be mindful of the words they use to describe PWDs, such as indicating that an individual *uses* a wheelchair rather than is *confined* to a wheelchair or is *wheelchair bound*. Additionally, as has been previously discussed with other forms of multiculturalism, direct discussion with the client is warranted to ensure that you understand the impact his or her disability has on daily life. Artman and Daniels recommend that clinicians ask about the nature of the disability or condition if the client mentions it in session. However, if the client does not mention the disability, the therapist may bring it up, asking if the client feels his or her disability affects the presenting problem. Be mindful not to ask intrusive questions to satisfy your own curiosity, but consider whether the question will further your understanding of the client's current mental health concerns. Two common mistakes that mental health professionals make with PWDs is either completely ignoring the disability or assuming that the disability is central to the client's problems.

Working with clients with **intellectual disability** (ID) should incorporate increasing knowledge about ID with a personal examination of biases. ID is generally defined as having an IQ below 70. The American Academy of Child and Adolescent Psychiatry published practice guidelines for working with individuals with ID, which include many suggestions for how to interview in a sensitive manner (Szymanski & King, 1999). The guidelines offer practical recommendations, including allowing sufficient time to put the client at ease before initiating assessment and adapting verbal communication so that it is clear and understandable to the client. In addition, it is advised that clinicians begin the interview with a discussion of the patient's strengths and interests and later focus on the patient's understanding of disability, limitations, and reason for referral.

Social Class and Socioeconomic Status—Crossing the Divide

Social class has been identified as one of the three most important cultural cornerstones in multicultural theory, alongside race and gender (Pope-Davis & Coleman, 2001). Accordingly, mental health professionals should develop a clear understanding of how they perceive their own class membership as well as how others may perceive them. Liu, Ali, Soleck, Hopps, and Pickett (2004a) defined social class as "an individual's position within an economic hierarchy that is determined by his or her income, education level, and occupation; the individual is also aware of his or her place in the economic hierarchy and of others who may share a similar position" (p. 8). Furthermore, **classism** results when people in one social class hold prejudice against individuals from another social class. Classism can be illustrated by having negative feelings toward individuals in higher social classes, who are perceived as "snobs," or negative feelings against others, who are perceived as worse off or "trash." **Socioeconomic status** (SES) is a similar concept that refers to an individual's perceived place in an economic hierarchy based on subjective indicators such as prestige, lifestyle, and control of resources (Liu et al., 2004a).

Practical barriers to seeking treatment and maintaining regular treatment attendance are clearly linked to SES. For instance, research has shown that underutilization of mental health services by Latinos is a function of both cultural barriers, including language, and socioeconomic factors such as lack of health insurance, child care, and transportation (Kouyoumdjian, Zamboanga, & Hansen, 2003). Low SES has also been linked to premature termination of therapy (Wierzbicki & Pekarik, 1993). Mental health professionals should engage in dialogue with clients facing economic difficulties to avoid dropping out of treatment.

The importance of social class and SES for mental health professionals is that they contribute to an individual's worldview. Not only does consideration of social class and SES help clinicians to understand how a client's attitudes, feelings, and behaviors may have developed as a means of coping with economic realities or dealing with classism, but a consideration of class and SES may also urge counselors to monitor their own reactions to others based on social class. Liu, Soleck, Hopps, Dunston, and Pickett (2004b) encourage mental health professionals to reflect on their biases related to social class. They suggest that a common way to identify classist biases is to think about what social behaviors you find inappropriate or off-putting, including use of nonstandard English or slang, thick Southern accents, or trendy or nontrendy dress. Negative reactions to these social behaviors may indicate underlying classist attitudes. Liu and colleagues (2004b) also recommend that counselors directly ask clients about how money and finance issues were discussed in their family and their feelings about money to better understand their social class concerns.

KNOWING YOURSELF

Now that you have read about the impact various cultural factors may have on the experience of clients seeking mental health treatment, we would like you to turn your attention to your own cultural identity. It is likely that you may have had an emotional reaction to some of the material presented above. Perhaps you had a positive or negative reaction to the material? Maybe you identify with some of the groups described and evaluated the material to determine whether it rings true to your experience?

The importance of knowing yourself and the lens through which you see the world cannot be overstated. Our cultural identity shapes our beliefs, attitudes, and assumptions. If unexamined, we are unaware of its potential effects. As we seek to understand the history, conditions, and social reality of multiple groups in our society, we must also be willing to acknowledge the positive and negative aspects of our own groups' expectations and perspectives.

BOX 4.8

Learning Exercise

Consider your own values. Begin by completing the following to create value statements:

a. Life is _____
b. The purpose of work is _____
c. Marriage should be _____
d. Homosexuality is _____

What types of clients would you have difficulty working with? Are there particular values that clients might present that could create conflict for you as a therapist? How would you handle these value conflicts?

Working With Clients Who Share Your Cultural Background

It is important to recognize that sharing common cultural elements with a client (e.g., gender, ethnicity, or sexual orientation) may not be sufficient evidence from which to assume that you share the same cultural background. Sue (1998) suggested that although ethnicity is a salient demographic variable, the psychological variables associated with culture (e.g., identity, attitudes, beliefs, and personality) are likely more important in terms of a cultural match with a client. You may observe when working with a client who shares some important aspects of cultural identity that assumptions about her experiences may jeopardize your therapeutic alliance. For example, when Dr. Wadkins works with clients who also identify as Mexican-American, she has learned to ask just as many questions about the meaning or significance of family traditions as she does with clients from other ethnic groups. Although at times there is significant overlap with her own perspective and understanding, there have also been surprising moments. Maintaining a stance of curiosity about your clients' experiences can enhance your ability to build a strong therapeutic alliance and maintain a multicultural perspective.

Furthermore, is cultural match important for effective therapy? Some have argued that this is no longer a question worth asking. Berg-Cross and So (2011) wrote, "It no longer makes sense to ask how important is it to match clients with therapists who are similar to them because the number of cultural traits, attitudes, and behaviors on which matching can take place is too large" (p. 12). Berg-Cross and So recommend asking clients directly what characteristics they are looking for in a therapist, what type of therapist would help them to be open about their struggles, and whether they believe their therapist needs to be similar to them on some important characteristics such as ethnicity, gender, or sexual orientation.

Potential Challenges to Helping

The largest challenge to helping multicultural clients is **ethnocentrism**. That is, the tendency to view the world from a fixed cultural perspective. If you are behaving in an ethnocentric manner, you are unlikely to be able to help all people who come to you for counseling because your work may be geared toward helping clients to function according to your idea of optimal mental health and functioning (Comas-Díaz, 2012). This will mean that if you see clients from different cultures, you may encourage them to adopt new ways of living that are out of sync with their cultural norms. As discussed in Chapter 2, it is the ethical duty of mental health professionals to respect the rights and dignity of the persons they serve. An important way of doing this is to avoid ethnocentrism.

Lillian Comas-Díaz (2012) views unawareness as the foundation of ethnocentrism. Accordingly, we hope that this chapter has encouraged you to reflect on your cultural identity and how that heritage has shaped the way you view the world. Not only should you think about your own culture but you should also consider how this personal exploration assists you in terms of the development of multicultural sensitivity. To do this, examine your own biases. Recent research with graduate students indicated that most expressed racial tolerance and gender equality after completing a course on cultural diversity, but some indicated they were not accepting of gay men and lesbians (Mcauliffe, Grothaus, Jensen, & Michel, 2012). Do you anticipate that you will have difficulty counseling others from particular cultural groups?

THE CLIENT AS EXPERT

Tervalon and Murray-García (1998) urged physicians in training to adopt a stance of **cultural humility** in their interactions with clients. They described cultural humility as an ongoing focus on self-evaluation, critique, and attention to redressing the power imbalances present in the doctor-patient relationships. Cultural humility is in opposition to the traditional approach of achieving cultural competence, or the mastery or a set of skills. "Humility is a prerequisite in this process as the physician relinquishes the role of *expert* to the patient, becoming the *student* of the patient with a conviction and explicit expression of the patient's potential to be a capable and full partner in the therapeutic alliance" (p. 121).

Working collaboratively with your client to develop a case formulation is an important skill for a culturally sensitive clinician. If you and your client can come to an agreement about the most important problems, how these problems interfere with daily functioning, and how these problems might have developed, you have created a culturally sensitive case formulation. In the process, you have probably deferred to the client as the expert of his or her experience in several areas.

DEVELOPING CROSS-CULTURAL COMPETENCE

A developmental model for becoming culturally sensitive has been proposed (López et al., 1989). In the first stage, mental health professionals are initially unaware of cultural issues in their work. Next, clinicians develop a heightened awareness of their client's culture, which leads to the next stage of feeling burdened by the demands of incorporating cultural variables. In the final stage of this developmental model, clinicians adopt cultural sensitivity. You are on this journey.

Campinha-Bacote (2003) created a mnemonic for combining the important aspects of multicultural competence. Awareness, skill, knowledge, encounters, and desire (ASKED) are depicted as the components of a volcano, with the *desire* to be culturally competent erupting into the process of becoming culturally competent via seeking out opportunities to gain cultural *awareness* (including awareness of personal biases), acquiring *skills* in multicultural assessment, gaining cultural *knowledge*, and engaging in face-to-face *encounters* with multicultural people. The ASKED method may be useful to you to gauge your multicultural development.

Experiences in Community

Research has found that people's attitudes and stereotypes change as a result of making connections with people that belong to diverse groups (e.g., Allport, 1954). Television shows and movies frequently portray this phenomenon in a simplistic and humorous way. Specifically, when a character, who is a member of the majority group, makes a slip and says something insensitive that reveals a cultural stereotype about the minority group, the character attempts to recover by remarking that he or she did not mean it and has many (insert name of minority group here) friends.

Whereas multiculturalism was called the fourth force in counseling (Pedersen, 1990), there is a more current movement toward **social justice**. Ratts, D'Andrea, and Arredondo (2004) urged counselors to focus on social justice advocacy as the fifth force to shape counseling. Goodman and colleagues (2004) defined social justice as "the scholarship and professional action designed to change societal values, structures, policies, and practices, such that disadvantaged or marginalized groups gain increased access to these tools of self-determination" (p. 795).

Thus, a powerful way to increase your effectiveness as a multicultural counselor is to get involved in your community. Make contact with individuals from diverse backgrounds when possible, and work as an advocate and ally for those who are disenfranchised by working toward social justice. A professional ethic of care for the broader community is an important aspect of taking a social justice perspective toward our work as mental health professionals (Swenson, 1998). Dr. Prout has worked as a volunteer clinician for HealthRight International's Human Rights Clinic (www.healthright.org). She provides psychological assessments for survivors of human rights abuses who are seeking asylum in the United States. As a result of her work with HealthRight, she has become more informed about global social justice and the long-term effects of trauma. This has increased her competence as a multicultural counselor and has provided invaluable support to individuals seeking refuge in the aftermath of torture, persecution, and trafficking. This type of community engagement is one way to work toward alleviating the effects of oppression and degradation worldwide.

Continuing Education

There is no denying the major impact that awareness of multiculturalism has had on changing and molding the counseling profession to strengthen its effectiveness in serving all people seeking services. Knox and colleagues (2003), in an extremely small sample, found that all African American psychologists surveyed ($n = 5$) reported attending multicultural workshops or conferences, whereas European American psychologists surveyed ($n = 7$) reported minimal or no postgraduate experiences focused on race. Although it cannot be assumed that these results generalize to all counselors, Knox and colleagues found in their study that the European American therapists reported greater discomfort than the African American counselors addressing race in cross-racial dyads. It seems that lack of ongoing training and educational experiences may contribute to greater discomfort with and lack of knowledge about addressing race and diversity in session.

In addition to formal continuing education experiences, Berg-Cross and So (2011) suggest seeking out culture consultations. These authors recommend contacting your professional organization or other local resources (e.g., a religious organization or immigrant services) to locate a colleague that shares the cultural heritage that seems salient to your client's distress. During consultation, discuss the presenting problem, the client's important cultural subgroups, and ask questions to place the problem in a salient cultural context. The American Psychological Association also maintains several electronic mailing lists that can be a helpful resource.

CHAPTER REVIEW

Traditionally, psychology has taken an etic view of individuals. That is, a view that there are universal principles of healthy personality development and all people should achieve the same optimal outcome (i.e., one definition of mental health) regardless of culture. On the other hand, an emic perspective states that every culture has its own norms and values and no one model of mental health can be applied to all individuals. Multiculturalism in counseling represents an emic perspective and aims to meet clients where they are in terms of their unique cultural worldview and recognizes the historical stressors and experiences that led to their development.

Counselors with multicultural competence should increase their awareness of their own values and biases, gain knowledge about the worldviews and experiences of individuals from other cultural backgrounds, and learn strategies and techniques to effectively work with clients from diverse cultural backgrounds. Cultural responsiveness entails responding to the cultural content that is present in a therapy session. Atkinson and Lowe (1995) describe culturally responsive counselors as those who "acknowledge the existence of, show interest in, demonstrate knowledge of, and express appreciation for the client's ethnicity and culture…[and]…place the client's problem in a cultural context" (p. 402).

Studies have shown that it is best for mental health professionals to not adopt a color-blind stance, but instead to actively engage issues and experiences related to the client's race. Cardemil and Battle (2003) encourage therapists to initiate an open conversation with clients about how they identify their racial and ethnic background. The second suggestion offered by Cardemil and Battle is that mental health professionals recognize the heterogeneity within racial and ethnic groups and avoid relying on stereotypes to understand a client's personal experience.

Along with discussions of race and ethnicity, asking clients about nationality should be a standard practice in order to avoid invalidating their identity and unique experience. It is important to directly ask clients to define their family and describe how they are connected to their family. When working with immigrants, mental health professionals should assess the reason for relocation as well as the circumstances surrounding the move to the United States. In addition, it is important to develop a good understanding of the client's pre-migration and post-migration experiences when establishing therapeutic alliance.

Coming out is one of the most important life experiences in terms of identity development for gay men and lesbian women, and it is important to be sensitive to a client's stage in that process. It is important to ask clients how they label themselves and use that term in your work with them. Gender roles may affect clients' experiences in treatment. Knudson-Martin and Mahoney (1999) identified four common "gender traps" for clinicians to avoid when working with male versus female clients. Two key methods for providing care to transgender clients are for mental health professionals to take a nonpathologizing approach by recognizing the individual's right to his or her own gender expression and to recognize and validate the oppression and constraints imposed by society on transgender people. Finally, classism results when people in one social class hold prejudice against individuals from another social class.

Berg-Cross and So (2011) recommend asking clients directly what characteristics they are looking for in a therapist, what type of therapist would help them to be open about their struggles, and whether they believe their therapist needs to be similar to them on some important characteristics, such as ethnicity, gender, or sexual orientation. It is also important to adopt a stance of cultural humility and allow yourself to learn about a different culture through your client. The largest challenge to helping multicultural clients is ethnocentrism, which is the tendency to view the world from a fixed cultural perspective. To avoid ethnocentrism, examine your own biases, seek out encounters with multicultural individuals, and take advantage of educational opportunities to increase your multicultural knowledge.

PERSONAL REFLECTION ESSAY QUESTIONS

1. Write your cultural autobiography by reflecting on your childhood and later life experiences as an individual who can be described in all the different ways we have explored in this chapter: race, ethnicity, nationality, language, immigration status, sexual orientation, gender, religion, ability, social class, and SES. Reflect on how your cultural background and experiences have shaped what you value and how you evaluate the world around you, as well as how culture has shaped your thinking and your behavior. For an excellent example of a cultural autobiography of one of our colleagues, see Silverstein, L. B. (2010). French, Catholic, Jewish. Outsider within. *Women & Therapy*, *33*(3–4), 275–280.
2. Write about an event when you met someone from a different culture. What did you ask that person to better understand his or her background and perspective? Reflecting on the experience with a multicultural lens, would you approach that social encounter in a different way in the future?
3. Reflect on your UDO score, which you completed as part of the Learning Exercise in Box 4.2. As you were completing it, you were probably thinking about different cultures. Although it may be the case that you are comfortable and interested in learning about different cultures, are there cultures from which you feel more distant? Think about the personal connections and groups that you encounter on a daily basis.

KEYWORDS

acculturation	familism	refugees
classism	gender role	sexual orientation
coming out	immigrants	social class
cultural humility	intellectual disability	social justice
cultural mistrust	language	socioeconomic status (SES)
cultural responsiveness	multiculturalism	transgender
emic	nationality	transsexual
ethnicity	people with disabilities (PWDs)	universal-diverse orientation
ethnocentrism	race	
etic	racial identity development	

FURTHER READING

For more information about developing multicultural competence, we suggest the following resources with excellent case examples. *Whistling Vivaldi* is a wonderful work to stimulate your thinking about how stereotypes affect all of us.

- Comas-Díaz, L. (2012). *Multicultural care: A clinician's guide to cultural competence*. Washington, DC: American Psychological Association.
- Hansen, N., Pepitone-Arreola-Rockwell, F., & Greene, A. F. (2000). Multicultural competence: Criteria and case examples. *Professional Psychology: Research and Practice, 31*(6), 652–660. doi:10.1037/0735-7028.31.6.652
- Steele, C. M. (2010). *Whistling Vivaldi: How stereotypes affect us and what we can do*. New York, NY: W. W. Norton & Company.

We also encourage you to watch films and read novels and autobiographies written from the experience and perspectives of individuals from the cultural groups we discussed in this chapter and that you may encounter in therapy. Here are some of our suggestions:

Race

- Larsen, N. (2004). *Passing*. Mineola, NY: Dover.
- Morrison, T. (2007). *The bluest eye*. New York, NY: Vintage Books.
- Ragusa, K. (2006). *The skin between us: A memoir of race, beauty, and belonging*. New York, NY: W. W. Norton & Company, Inc.

Language/Immigration

- Weitz, C. (Director). (2011). *A better life*. USA: Summit Entertainment.
- Dumas, F. (2004). *Funny in Farsi: A memoir of growing up Iranian in America*. New York, NY: Random House.
- Fadiman, A. (1997). *The spirit catches you and you fall down*. New York, NY: Farrar, Straus & Giroux.
- Shadid, A. (2012). *House of stone*. New York, NY: Houghton Mifflin.
- Tan, A. (1989). *The joy luck club*. Raleigh, NC: Ivy Books.

Disability

- Connolly, K. M. (2010). *Double take: A memoir*. New York, NY: Harper Perennial.
- Rapp, E. (2007). *Poster child*. New York, NY: Bloomsbury.
- Silver, R. (2012). *Invisible: My journey through vision and hearing loss*. Bloomington, IN: iUniverse.

Sexual Orientation and Gender Issues

- Bechdel, A. (2007). *Fun home: A family tragicomic*. New York, NY: Mariner Books.
- Dubowski, S. S. (Director). (2009). *Trembling before G-d*. USA: Pretty Pictures.
- Feinberg, L. (1993). *Stone butch blues*. New York, NY: Firebrand Books.
- Krieger, N. (2011). *Nina here nor there: My journey beyond gender*. Boston, MA: Beacon Press.

Religion

- Brooks, J. (2012). *The book of Mormon girl: A memoir of an American faith.* New York, NY: Free Press.
- Huguelet, P., & Koenig, H. G. (2009). *Religion and spirituality in psychiatry.* New York, NY: Cambridge University Press.
- Kehoe, N. (2009). *Wrestling with our inner angels: Faith, mental illness, and the journey to wholeness.* Hoboken, NJ: Jossey-Bass.

Class Issues

- Dubus, A., III. (2012). *Townie: A memoir.* New York, NY: W. W. Norton & Company, Inc.
- Kotlowitz, A. (1992). *There are no children here: The story of two boys growing up in the other America.* New York, NY: Anchor Books.
- Fine, M. (1984). Coping with rape: Critical perspectives on consciousness. *Imagination, Cognition, and Personality, 3*(3), 249–267.

APPENDIX

Miville-Guzman Universality-Diversity Scale—Short Form (MGUDS-S)

The following statements define several terms. Please refer to these definitions throughout the rest of the questionnaire:

Culture refers to the beliefs, values, traditions, ways of behaving, and language of any social group. A social group may be racial, ethnic, religious, etc.

Race or racial background refers to a sub-group of people possessing common physical or genetic characteristics. Examples include White, Black, American Indian, etc.

Ethnicity or ethnic group refers to a specific social group sharing a unique cultural heritage (e.g., customs, beliefs, language). Two people can be of the same race (i.e., White), but from different ethnic groups (e.g., Irish-American, Italian-American).

Country refers to groups that have been politically defined; people from these groups belong to the same government (e.g., France, Ethiopia, United States). People of different races (White, Black, Asian) or ethnicities (Italian, Japanese) can be from the same country (United States).

Instructions: Please indicate how descriptive of you each statement is by circling the number corresponding to your response. This is not a test, so there are no right or wrong, good or bad answers.

INDICATE HOW DESCRIPTIVE OF YOU EACH STATEMENT IS BY CIRCLING THE NUMBER CORRESPONDING TO YOUR RESPONSE	STRONGLY DISAGREE	DISAGREE	DISAGREE A LITTLE BIT	AGREE A LITTLE BIT	AGREE	STRONGLY AGREE
1. I would like to join an organization that emphasizes getting to know people from different countries.	1	2	3	4	5	6
2. Persons with disabilities can teach me things I cannot learn elsewhere.	1	2	3	4	5	6
3. Getting to know someone of another race is generally an uncomfortable experience for me.	1	2	3	4	5	6
4. I would like to go to dances that feature music from other countries.	1	2	3	4	5	6
5. I can best understand someone after I get to know how he or she is both similar to and different from me.	1	2	3	4	5	6
6. I am only at ease with people of my race.	1	2	3	4	5	6
7. I often listen to music of other cultures.	1	2	3	4	5	6
8. Knowing how a person differs from me greatly enhances our friendship.	1	2	3	4	5	6
9. It's really hard for me to feel close to a person from another race.	1	2	3	4	5	6
10. I am interested in learning about the many cultures that have existed in this world.	1	2	3	4	5	6
11. In getting to know someone, I like knowing both how he or she differs from me and is similar to me.	1	2	3	4	5	6
12. It is very important that a friend agrees with me on most issues.	1	2	3	4	5	6
13. I attend events where I might get to know people from different racial backgrounds.	1	2	3	4	5	6
14. Knowing about the different experiences of other people helps me understand my own problems better.	1	2	3	4	5	6
15. I often feel irritated by persons of a different race.	1	2	3	4	5	6

*Items 3, 6, 9, 12, and 15 above are reverse scored.

Below are the items listed by subscale:

Diversity of Contact: Students' interest in participating in diverse social and cultural activities

1. I would like to join an organization that emphasizes getting to know people from different countries.
2. I would like to go to dances that feature music from other countries.
3. I often listen to music from other cultures.
4. I am interested in learning about the many cultures that have existed in this world.
5. I attend events where I might get to know people from different racial backgrounds.

Relativistic Appreciation: The extent to which students value the impact of diversity on self-understanding and personal growth.

1. Persons with disabilities can teach me things I cannot learn elsewhere.
2. I can best understand someone after I get to know how he or she is both similar to and different from me.
3. Knowing how a person differs from me greatly enhances our friendship.
4. In getting to know someone, I like knowing both how he or she differs from me and is similar to me.
5. Knowing about the different experiences of other people helps me understand my own problems better.

Comfort With Differences: Students' degree of comfort with diverse individuals (all of these items are reverse scored).

1. Getting to know someone of another race is generally an uncomfortable experience for me.
2. I am only at ease with people of my race.
3. It's really hard for me to feel close to a person of another race.
4. It is very important that a friend agrees with me on most issues.
5. I often feel irritated with persons of a different race.

Beginnings: The Initial Interview

One very important way to befriend your sorrow is to take
it out of its isolation, and share it with someone who can
receive it.—Nouwen (2006, p. 45)

LEARNING OBJECTIVES

- Understand the goals of the initial clinical interview
- Describe the necessary components of a therapist's office environment and the impact that a therapist's office has on clients
- Understand the importance of privacy within the therapeutic relationship
- Recognize the importance of keeping interruptions to a minimum during sessions
- Discuss safety and the critical incident review process as they relate to mental health settings
- Understand the effects of first impressions, personal appearance, and presentation
- Describe effective ways for therapists to mentally prepare for the first interview (including meditation and mindfulness exercises)
- Explain the process of initially contacting/greeting the client and discussing confidentiality with the client
- Describe the importance of keeping clients' cultural differences in mind (facial expressions, eye contact, physical contact) during the first interview
- Understand the meaning of therapeutic alliance, warmth, genuineness, and empathy within the context of the initial interview and further therapy
- Describe the different types of clinical interviews (unstructured, semi-structured, structured)
- Explain the importance of documentation throughout the therapeutic process

The initial interview with a new client often provokes anxiety in new therapists. It can be challenging to engage a client in the first meeting, and there are many factors that contribute to the building of sufficient rapport and trust between therapist and client. Generally speaking, the purpose of the initial interview is to hear, elaborate, and discuss with clients the problems they are having and how they generally experience these problems (Eisenthal & Lazare, 1976). Clinicians are also expected to help clients feel comfortable sharing intimate details of their lives with a perfect stranger. Additionally, the therapist is likely interested in gathering information about certain elements of the client's functioning, such as substance abuse and mental health history. In addition to the functional aspects of the interview—for example, information gathering, comfort and privacy of the office, and rapport building—both client and therapist bring to the interview their own expectations and anxieties. Although these often go unspoken, they also have an impact on what transpires between the two parties. This chapter will address both the practical aspects of the initial interview and the latent variables that may shape this first in-person contact with the client.

Generally speaking, it is widely assumed that in the initial consultation the client will talk about personal matters, whereas the therapist will remain attentive and communicate very little about herself (Pope, Siegman, Blass, & Cheek, 1972). **Clinical interviewing** is an essential skill for all mental health professionals, and it requires an extraordinary set of complex skills. The adept clinical interviewer will have a deep understanding of psychopathology, be highly skilled in interpersonal communication, and have an appreciation for the rich and multilayered interaction between the interviewer and the interviewee (Turner, Hersen, & Heiser, 2003). The clinical interview is also the starting point for diagnosis, treatment planning, and goal setting, and sets the foundation for the therapeutic relationship. These challenges are amplified when there are cultural, socio-economic, religious, or other unspoken differences between the interviewer and the client (Vasquez, 2007). This first encounter with the client is one that will provide the clinician with a wealth of information based on the content and process of the interview and nonverbal cues. The type of information you can obtain will vary based on how comfortable and safe the client feels with you and in the interviewing room.

THE OFFICE

The environment in which the interview is conducted can greatly affect the client and influence the process of interaction between client and therapist. Although there are exceptions to the traditional clinical interview (e.g., therapists who work in the aftermath of a disaster like Hurricane Katrina or at Ground Zero), most clinical work is conducted in a room that is private and free from distractions. The room in which you conduct interviews and counseling sessions can say a lot about you as a professional. It is useful to think of the room as a representation of you as therapist. An overly formal setting may suggest to the client that you are unapproachable or cold. A cluttered office may be distracting and communicate that you are disorganized or do not have enough mental space to hear and contain the client's troubles. Even seemingly innocuous items in the office can serve as distractions for clients. A student once told Dr. Prout that she saw a gift bag sitting on her therapist's desk throughout their last session. Too apprehensive to ask about it, she spent the whole session wondering about the present and left disappointed and wondering if another client would receive the gift (see Chapter 9 for a more detailed discussion of gifts). Your office should be a place where clients can feel at ease and welcomed without being burdened with elements of space, décor, and clutter that take away from the purposes of psychotherapy.

Privacy suggests that what is said is confined to and intended only for the therapist; the content of the session should not be shared with others and should not be overheard by passersby or individuals in the waiting room. One way to protect the privacy of what clients share within a session is to ensure that the office is soundproof. It is unusual to find an office space that is entirely soundproofed—this particular feature seems to be reserved for recording studios rather than therapists' offices. In order to compensate for the lack of total soundproofing in offices, most clinicians use a white noise machine to mask the sound of conversation between client and therapist. This type of device provides an additional layer of privacy around the consulting room. Even with the white noise machine, sometimes noises and voices can be heard between offices. One evening, Dr. Wadkins and her client clearly heard a very distressed individual expressing suicidal ideation during his session with the psychologist in the neighboring office. Think about how you would handle a situation like that. She and the client discussed the other client's right to privacy and moved down the hall to finish the session in an unoccupied office.

In a perfect world, all mental health facilities would provide easy access for all clients, including those with physical disabilities. In accordance with the **Architectural Barriers Act** (ABA, 1968), all buildings that are designed, constructed, or altered with federal funds must comply with federal standards for physical accessibility. As a result, most facilities devoted solely to providing medical or mental health care are fully accessible to clients with a wide variety of physical disabilities. Private offices are sometimes located within buildings that do not meet the federal standards for disability access. If you find yourself in a situation where your office is not fully accessible, it is important to acknowledge this with clients and, if you are unable to accommodate them, to provide an adequate referral.

Your office should also be designed with your specific population in mind. If you plan to do individual psychotherapy with adults, consider your seating arrangement. Will you have a comfortable couch or armchair for clients to sit in? Will both client and therapist sit in identical chairs, which often communicates that both parties are of equal status? When clients enter the room, will they choose where they sit or will the seating arrangement be pre-determined? It is important that both client and therapist feel relatively comfortable and at ease. You might try sitting with a classmate in different arrangements to see how it feels to sit at 90-, 120-, and 150-degree angles from one another. There are a wide variety of seating arrangements that may work and different set-ups work better for various clients. Most clinicians avoid having a table or other furniture between themselves and the client. This type of obstruction can create distance or distraction and may communicate a less than ideal level of intimacy.

If your work is with couples, families, or children your office should accommodate several people comfortably. The same is true for clinicians who work with interpreters; all three parties—clinician, client, and interpreter—should be able to arrange themselves easily in the space. Working with children often involves sitting on the floor or playing games that may require a table. Similarly, certain types of therapy such as art and dance therapy will be more effective with a flat workspace or ample space for movement. Therapists who conduct groups will need a large enough office or room to comfortably seat several individuals (typically sitting in a circle) with enough personal space for each client. Similarly, clinicians who provide specialized services such as evaluations for clients seeking bariatric surgery will need to have furniture that can accommodate individuals who may not fit comfortably in a traditional chair with arms on either side.

At some points in your training and throughout your career, you may have to work in offices or rooms that are less than ideal. This is especially true in clinics and hospital settings where resources are scarce and space is in high demand. In order to foster a more welcoming environment in her rather austere hospital office, Dr. Prout brought in a throw rug, wall art, and several table lamps. She was soon informed that such items were in breach of the hospital's fire code and would need to be put away in a closet at the end of each work day. In order to create a more personalized office and simultaneously follow the hospital regulations, Dr. Prout complied with the request. It seemed preferable to seeing clients in a room that was otherwise devoid of any warmth. Dr. Wadkins works mainly with children and adolescents and began traveling with a mobile toy box when working in a hospital setting. Although it was not ideal, her sessions were often conducted in different locations. Thus, it was helpful to have an unchanging set of games, activities, and supplies present in each session.

The clinical interview and all subsequent sessions are conducted in a place and a time that are set aside for that specific purpose. This means that **interruptions** to the session should be avoided at all costs. In most therapeutic settings, there is widespread understanding that when therapists are "in session" they should not be disturbed. You might consider placing a *Do Not Disturb* or *Therapy Session in Progress* sign on your door to let others know you are not available for consultation or conversation. In addition, the session should not be interrupted by cell phones (ringing or vibrating), incoming faxes, loud noises, or personal business. Although you will want to take many precautions to ensure that your space is safe, protected, and private, we advise you to *not* lock the door to the office. A locked door can convey many things. It can be frightening to some clients, making them feel trapped. For others, it can suggest a level of intimacy that borders on inappropriate.

Despite making every effort to avoid interruptions, they do happen. The adage *"expect the unexpected"* is a good rule of thumb for the experience of interruptions in the clinical interview. Clinicians are sometimes interrupted by brief and unexpected intrusions. For example, someone may knock at the door or there may be excessive noise in the hallway or waiting room. When this happens, we suggest the interviewer quickly and gently deal with the disruption and then resume the client meeting. Although often unwelcome, intrusions into the therapeutic space are not always counterproductive.

BOX 5.1

Case Example

In one instance, Dr. Prout was seeing a client in her private practice office in New York City. As the client began speaking about experiencing discrimination (due to her immigration status) in the workplace, loud chanting and police sirens began filling the street below the office window. The noise became so overpowering that they were unable to hear each other, and the client asked if they could look out the window together to see what the fuss was about. Both client and therapist stood at the window and watched as thousands of people wearing hoodies marched down the street chanting and carrying signs in support of Trayvon Martin, an African American teenager who had recently been shot and killed in Florida (see Times Topics, 2012, information page for Trayvon Martin). Dr. Prout and her client watched the march for about 10 minutes and then resumed the session. The client was tearful as she expressed how supported and connected she felt both to the people on the street and her therapist during this interruption.

Other interruptions may be personal or professional emergencies. Personal emergencies—a sick child or parent, for example—do arise and should be handled as quickly and efficiently as possible, with respect for the client's time. If the emergency requires an interruption in the session you should apologize and offer to make up the time that has been lost. You might ask the client, "Can we make up these 5 minutes at the end of today's session?" or, if you have to end the session prematurely, you might offer to make up the time in the next scheduled appointment.

Professional emergencies certainly arise in this field. Your session may be interrupted by a colleague or secretary letting you know that something requires your immediate attention. Or a client you are seeing may disclose something that requires you make a report to protective services or hospitalize them. This type of disclosure will inevitably interfere with your ability to meet with the next client on time. In either case, these types of professional emergencies may require you to reschedule with the client who has been displaced. We recommend that the therapist offer a sincere apology and a convenient time to reschedule as soon as possible. You should expect that the client may have questions in the subsequent session about what transpired. It is important that you try to deal with all types of interruptions with a calm demeanor, a non-defensive style, and with an eye toward problem solving. All of us struggle to do these things well when we are under pressure and especially when we are being observed by another party. With time and practice, your ability to manage interruptions should become more natural and effortless.

SAFETY

Safety in mental health settings is an issue of increasing importance due to more frequent reports of violence against practitioners (Newhill, 1995; Nolan, Dallender, Soares, Thomsen, & Arnetz, 1999). The Occupational Safety and

Health Administration (OSHA, 2004) reports that compared to other professions, mental health professionals experience some of the highest rates of nonfatal violence within the workplace. Safety risks are certainly greater within an inpatient hospital setting than in outpatient settings. Some surveys have demonstrated that nearly 75% of therapists have been assaulted at some time in their career (Erdos & Hughes, 2001). As a result of these data, we recommend taking several precautions whenever meeting with a new client, regardless of the setting.

With higher-risk populations, we recommend that therapists sit near the door in the unlikely event there is a need for rapid exit. This is especially important in psychiatric emergency rooms and forensic settings. In these settings, we also suggest wearing identification badges either on a waistband clip or, if you must wear the badge around your neck, on a **breakaway lanyard**. Many health care facilities provide these lanyards with breakaway clasps for the safety of their employees. If these are not available, you can buy one online for just a few dollars. With all clients, it is important to do adequate screening before the first meeting. This may involve speaking with collateral contacts (e.g., the client's previous providers, staff at the day treatment program) or simply reading the client's chart. If there is a client with a history of violence, you may request that security officers be available during the meeting or meet with the client in a nontraditional setting such as the dining room or a windowed meeting room in view of the nurses' station. It is important to keep in mind that intoxication, acute psychosis, and certain personality disorders may increase the likelihood of client violence. In hospital settings, nearly two-thirds of assaults take place during an attempt to contain a patient and the other third were random (Carmel & Hunter, 1989).

Outside of the hospital setting, safety precautions should still be seriously considered. Many clinicians in private practice work in a suite of offices where other clinicians are also working. Often, the initial phone call provides important information that may allow you to screen out clients. Although there is little research evidence to support this, we recommend that you listen to your instincts. If a client is making you feel uneasy in some way, you need to act, either by not agreeing to see them or by removing yourself from the situation. Dr. Prout once received a phone call from a prospective client who said he wanted to work on his anger management issues and thought Dr. Prout would be the perfect person with whom to work. She asked why he thought that and the client responded, "You're a woman and that's who I tend to get angry and out of control with." Needless to say, Dr. Prout did not agree to meet the client and instead recommended a local anger management group run at a mental health clinic.

It is best to err on the side of asking explicitly about safety concerns if you are wondering about the possibility of violence or danger. Dr. Wadkins conducts sessions at the homes of some of her clients because of her specialty in exposure treatment for anxiety and related disorders. As she was arranging to meet a new client with a specific phobia of driving for the first time in her home, the client casually mentioned that she wanted Dr. Wadkins to know that she had "a lot of stuff piled up around her apartment" because she had difficulty discarding certain items. Dr. Wadkins asked about the extent of the clutter and whether the client felt that her apartment was a comfortable and safe space to meet. The client reported that she felt it would be fine. Several days later, when Dr. Wadkins arrived at the appointment, the client was extremely agitated and angry about being questioned about the "safety" of her apartment. She reported that she would not be able to work with Dr. Wadkins because of the assumption she had made that there were "rats" in the client's apartment. Although the client's interpretation of the inquiry about safety was extreme and unsupported, Dr. Wadkins felt that it was better to get as much information as possible about the environment she would be entering alone.

Most health care facilities conduct a **critical incident review** process in the aftermath of an assault, death or attempted suicide of patient, or other safety problems. Participating in such a review can be especially helpful in learning about what factors contribute to critical incidents. The review process typically involves examining factors related to the patient, task, individual staff, team, work environment, organization management, and institutional context. A violent incident is most often caused by multiple factors. For example, a patient-on-staff assault may be due to language barriers, the physical health and skills of the staff, lack of supervision within the team, understaffing on the unit, and lack of financial resources in the organization (Woloshynowych, Rogers, Taylor-Adams, & Vincent, 2005). Close examination and investigation of a critical incident and debriefing of all those involved (including the patient) are designed to improve conditions and reduce the likelihood of future events. Although this type of review may provoke anxiety among those being scrutinized, it can be especially helpful in cases where emotions run high (Kendall & Wiles, 2010). By participating in this type of review, trainees have the benefit of seeing the process played out from start to finish. Critical incident review can be very helpful to trainees as they begin to develop strategies and policies for their own professional practice.

PERSONAL APPEARANCE AND PRESENTATION

First impressions are powerful and can leave a lasting impression (Bar, Neta, & Linz, 2006; Willis & Todorov, 2006). Clients form attitudes and evaluations of therapists often based on limited information. Similar to the self-presentation conveyed through your office, personal appearance communicates information to clients that can help shape these lasting evaluations. Therapist attire has consistently been shown to influence clients' perceptions of the therapist's expertise, trustworthiness, and helpfulness (Dacy & Brodsky, 1992; Hubble & Gelso, 1978). When comparing informal (jeans or sweatpants), business casual (slacks and a dress shirt), or formal attire (suit), therapists in business casual or formal attire were perceived to be more skilled, knowledgeable, and trustworthy (Dacy & Brodsky, 1992). Some clients experienced increased anxiety when faced with a therapist in very informal dress (Hubble & Gelso, 1978).

You will find that clients respond to your style of dress in one way or another. Everyone has a personal style. Without completely sacrificing your own taste, it is important to dress appropriately. Many students dress for class in clothing that would not be appropriate in a therapeutic setting, because it is too revealing, has commercial slogans or embellishments, or is too casual. Although it is unfortunate that first impressions can be formed so quickly, you must be aware of their relevance in this field. Consider some of the following issues:

- How low of a neckline is appropriate? How will you respond if a client is overtly gazing at your chest?
- Are shorts ever appropriate? What skirt length is appropriate for women?

- Is it a problem to have visible tattoos? How will you respond to client questions about them?
- Is it acceptable for therapists to have multiple piercings or facial piercings?

In addition to your style of dress, we recommend that you consider things like how much perfume, cologne, or makeup to wear, type of hairstyle, the scent of cigarette smoke, and jewelry. These are all aspects of self-presentation. Your goal should be to make clients feel as comfortable as possible. You can still maintain aspects of your individuality, but these should not be obtrusive or overpowering. Take a quick look at what you are wearing now or think about what you wore to class this week. What would you change or modify to be more appropriately dressed for a clinical setting? Keep in mind that you provide clients with a wealth of information simply through your appearance and how you carry yourself.

HOW TO PREPARE MENTALLY

It is expected that most novice therapists will have several anxieties about the first interview. Although we expect that you will become more comfortable with interviewing over time, it is still absolutely essential that you take time to mentally prepare before each client contact. This is one of the reasons most therapists have a 45- or 50-minute hour. We typically use those 10 or 15 minutes between sessions to do brief documentation, stretch, and ready ourselves for the next client contact. Whether it is your first or your 500th client contact, preparing mentally is an essential step in readying yourself to be available and helpful to your clients.

One method of preparing mentally is to engage in your own treatment. Individual psychotherapy for therapists is highly recommended. It is critical that you take care of yourself before you attempt to care for others. Many psychotherapists have written about the importance of personal therapy for the therapist (Kottler, 2010; McWilliams, 2004; Weiner & Bornstein, 2009; Yalom, 2002). Nancy McWilliams offers a great summary of why individual therapy for the therapist is essential. As she says,

> the best chance we have for increasing our capacity to understand, and thus our therapeutic range, is to know and accept ourselves as deeply as possible. Personal treatment may not inoculate us with "objectivity," but it can vastly increase our capacity to observe and make good use of the dynamics that inevitably get stirred up in our work. With all its hazards and limitations, personal treatment seems to me the best route to mature, empathic listening. (2004, p. 63)

This summary of the reasons for the clinician's treatment highlights the intensely personal nature of interviewing and counseling.

You are not simply an objective observer; all therapists will have emotional, behavioral, and affective responses to what clients share with them. The most important thing is how you handle these reactions. Engaging in your own personal treatment is an important aspect of the long-term preparation to be an effective psychotherapist, and it should enhance your ability to understand and empathize with another person. We suggest that you begin your own treatment as soon as possible. We are constantly surprised by the reluctance exhibited by students of psychotherapy in pursuing their own treatment. Not only does individual treatment help you experience what it is like to be in the hot seat as a client; it will also enable you to address your own limitations before they get inadvertently expressed in your work.

In addition to personal treatment, there are many other things you can do to mentally prepare for your work with clients. Taking steps to still your mind and alleviate your own stress will enable you to maintain greater focus. You might consider **meditation** or **mindfulness** exercises that can be done anywhere and at minimal cost. Simply focusing on your own breathing for 2 or 3 minutes before meeting with a client can slow central nervous system activity and allow you to be more mentally present with clients. There are many CDs and MP3 files available for purchase that can guide you through similar exercises.

Overall, providing ongoing care for yourself will allow you to be more mentally prepared and emotionally present for your clients. **Self-care** for psychotherapists is an area that has been widely studied. There are several ways to take care of oneself in order to be a more competent and engaged clinician. Engaging in regular physical activity is closely linked with a general sense of well-being and an ability to cope effectively with stress (Anderson, King, Stewart, & Camacho, 2005). Additionally, creating ample time and space to manage one's personal affairs is one way to ensure that you are able to be mentally present for your clients. Although no clinician is able to be focused on an individual client 100% of the time (Kottler, 2010), reducing unnecessary distractions (such as worrying about when you will do the laundry or who will pick up the kids from school) is one way to improve your ability to be mentally prepared. Receiving emotional support from friends and family and being involved in ongoing supervision, consultation, and other connections with professional colleagues will further enable you to be at your best when you meet with clients.

OPENING COMMUNICATION

Contact with a client often begins before the first face-to-face meeting. If you receive a referral or a client is transferred from another program, unit, or the emergency room, you may have the opportunity to review a case summary or other clinical data related to the client. Different clinicians treat this opportunity in a variety of ways. Some therapists prefer to have very little information about the client prior to the initial interview; this allows the therapist to get to know the patient without the noise of another person's perspective. There is ample evidence that even the best clinicians can have their judgment clouded by information that is provided prior to actually meeting the client (Gauron & Dickinson, 1966; Srivastava & Grube, 2009).

In a hospital setting, you may receive information about the client from the emergency room, the nursing staff on the unit, or other members of the treatment team before you meet the client. When working in a hospital-based setting, Dr. Prout would often hear off-the-cuff remarks about clients before meeting them. For example, a nurse on the unit might say, "Oh, she's an adorable young woman. You're going to love her!" or "You're going to have your hands full with that one!" Both of these comments convey quite a bit of loaded information. They take into account the nursing staff's interaction with the client during the weekend or overnight and also consider certain aspects of Dr. Prout's personality as perceived by the staff. It is sometimes difficult to enter into the initial interview with a truly open mind with these comments in the background.

In a clinic or private practice setting, you will likely have some phone contact with the client prior to the initial meeting. These pre-interview data points are likely to give you information that can inform you (or mislead you) about the patient's general level of functioning ahead of time. Dr. Prout recently received three voicemail messages within a day from a prospective client. The caller spoke very rapidly and expressed numerous worries in the voicemail. From this data, Dr. Prout assumed that she would be meeting with a very anxious individual. As it turned out, the client was extremely disorganized and had marked impairment in basic social interaction, both things he wanted to work on in therapy. Whether you have access to years of medical records or no information at all, it is important that you remain aware of how outside information can affect your perceptions and lead to the development of preconceived notions about the client.

In some settings you may find that you work with clients who are not proficient in English. It is important to work with a trained interpreter who will, as much as possible, remain a neutral presence in the therapeutic interaction. Dr. Wadkins once worked with an American Sign Language (ASL) interpreter while conducting an assessment of a woman with hearing impairment. It was an eye-opening experience to focus on speaking to the client and to avoid only interacting with the interpreter who could hear and respond verbally to her questions. Many problems can arise when mental health providers rely on family members or other untrained individuals to provide interpretation services. Many health care organizations use a team of professional in-person interpreters that can be requested on demand. For less common languages or in smaller treatment settings, institutions may rely on a Language Line (www.languageline.com), which offers instant access to translators by phone for most languages. Working with an **interpreter** or **translator** requires special knowledge of interpersonal dynamics (Freed, 1988) and the unique complexities of having a third person in the room (see Chapter 6).

How to Begin

The question of how to begin an initial interview will depend on many factors, including the setting, the client's presentation, the therapist's expectations and goals for the meeting, and many other unpredictable variables. As you consider your current practicum setting or where you see yourself working down the road, think about how you might begin your initial interview with a client. What thoughts will run through your mind as you prepare? How will you greet them in the waiting room? Where will each of you sit in the consulting room? What questions will you ask or not ask?

BOX 5.2

Learning Exercise

Pair up with a classmate, preferably someone you do not know very well, and pretend you are greeting them for an initial psychotherapy session. You will each take turns playing the role of the therapist. Before you begin, share with each other the fears and concerns you have about this exercise. How will you begin and what question or statement will you start with? Spend about 2 minutes each playing the role of the therapist and attempting to find out more about them. Once you have both finished, give each other feedback about how you did. Provide constructive feedback to each other about your body language, style of speech, eye contact, choice of words, physical presence, and any other notable aspects of the interaction.

Greetings and Initial Contact

Depending on the setting in which you will be working, your first meeting with the client may be part of a scheduled intake interview or occur in the midst of an acute crisis. Regardless of the circumstances, it is useful to consider how you will greet a client at the beginning of the first meeting. Students sometimes have concerns about presenting their credentials, often feeling the need to compensate for feelings of inexperience or inadequacy. We encourage our trainees to present themselves calmly, confidently, and accurately. Never misrepresent or overstate your credentials. If clients have questions about your qualifications or concerns about your ability to interview or counsel them, they can ask. You should also share with clients that you are being supervised and that the goal of supervision is to ensure that clients are receiving the best care possible. Examples of opening lines include:

- "Good afternoon, Mr. Corcoran. My name is Samantha Robins, and I am a mental health counselor in training here at the clinic."
- "I understand you've come to the emergency room to talk about some troubles you have been experiencing. I am a social work intern here, and my name is Jonathan Meyer."
- "Welcome to our office. I am April Garcia, the psychology extern you spoke with on the phone."

It is helpful to introduce yourself by name and to discuss with the client how he or she would like to be addressed. You should also explain the purpose of the meeting and the time available. For example, "The purpose of this meeting is for me to learn a bit about what's been troubling you lately and for us to see how we might be able to work together. We will meet for 45 minutes and can meet again on Wednesday." We also recommend affording clients the opportunity to ask questions about the process of the interview or other related matters. Many counselors are overly focused on the content and accuracy of what is being said during counseling rather than the process of the communication (Sue, 1990). The way in which communication flows within the session is sometimes more important than what is actually said by either party.

BOX 5.3

Spotlight on Culture

Many of the nonverbal and paralinguistic types of communication that occur within the counseling relationship are loaded with meanings that are firmly embedded in culture. Here are some examples of these **nonverbal cues** that may communicate more than you intend.

- *Physical Distance:* In traditional European American culture, there are several interpersonal zones that identify distance between two parties (Sue, 1990). For intimate interactions, individuals are expected to make direct contact or be up to 18 inches apart. For personal interactions (like psychotherapy), distance is usually from 1.5 to 4 feet. For public interactions such as lectures and speeches, distance is expected to be greater than 12 feet. Within the United States, discomfort seems to increase when strangers are closer together, and this may lead to a feeling that one's personal space is being violated. These unspoken rules for interpersonal distance vary across culture. In many cultures—including Latin Americans, Africans, Black Americans, Arabs, and South Americans—normal conversation with another person requires a much closer stance than is typically comfortable for Northwest Europeans. These differences in need for personal space are sometimes described as a divide between southern, "contact cultures" and northern "low-contact cultures" (Høgh-Olesen, 2008). If you create more distance between yourself and the other party, you may unwittingly be communicating an attitude of aloofness, coldness, or superiority. These differences may also inform where seats in the room are located and how far the counselor sits from the client. When there are cultural differences between the counselor and the client, it may be useful to acknowledge them and discuss them explicitly.
- *Facial Expressions*—Although smiling often communicates positive affect, joy, or happiness, it may have other meanings to particular cultures. Among the Japanese, smiling may instead convey embarrassment, shyness, or discomfort with the situation (Sue, 1990). Japanese also tend to smile less when they perceive the status of the other person to be much higher than their own (Nagashima & Schellenberg, 1997). Women also tend to smile more than men (Szarota, 2010). Ekman (1992) has highlighted a wide variety of smiles, including one that reflects true enjoyment, the social smile, and smiles that mask other emotions. As you monitor clients' affect, exercise caution and consider all expressions of emotion within their appropriate cultural context.
- *Eye Contact and Physical Contact*—Eye contact has similar differences across culture. Mexican Americans and Japanese may avoid eye contact as a sign of respect or deference. When considering the answer to a question, Japanese clients are likely to break eye contact and look downward (McCarthy, Lee, Itakura, & Muir, 2006). Among African

(continued)

(*continued*)

> Americans, eye contact is not seen as a necessary component of interpersonal communication. Additionally, physical contact may be prohibited for individuals from certain religious faiths or even for those experiencing certain symptoms. When working with Orthodox Jewish clients of the opposite sex, it is important to be mindful of the prohibitions against touching. Although not a cultural issue, it is also important to remember that individuals with contamination-based obsessive compulsive disorder may be very uncomfortable with close interpersonal contact such as shaking hands.

Once you have oriented the client to the interviewing process, you may begin gathering information. If you are using a semi-structured or structured interview, you will simply follow the outline of the proscribed interview. In many cases, you will be conducting an unstructured interview that will take its shape around what the client discusses. One challenge faced by beginning interviewers is how to encourage clients to speak freely and productively. Too often interviewers who become overly inquisitive can create an uneven power dynamic in which they ask questions and the client's job is simply to answer them. In order to avoid this type of "tennis match" style of interviewing and to encourage clients to elaborate and spontaneously volunteer information, we recommend a different approach. As you follow the client's lead we recommend phrasing your questions as statements (Weiner & Bornstein, 2009). For example, "What did you think when that happened?" can be phrased, "I wonder what thoughts came into your mind at that time"; "What was that treatment like?" can be phrased, "You've been talking about how much you disliked that hospital; I'm interested in hearing about other types of treatment you've received as well." Rather than simply directing and questioning clients, you are sharing your thoughts with the client without demanding a specific response.

Depending on what you know about the client prior to the interview and the setting in which the interview is being conducted, you may have specific bits of information that you want to obtain. It may be helpful to jot down a few notes ahead of time about elements of the interview that your supervisor wants to hear about or that the treatment facility requires. Often, these facts center on mental health history, suicidal or homicidal behavior, substance abuse, and any history of sexual or physical abuse. We highly recommend practicing pursuing these areas of inquiry with a classmate. See Figure 5.1 for examples of how to ask about each of these potentially difficult subjects.

Within certain diagnostic categories, you may want to pursue particular lines of questioning. You will inevitably develop skills for specific types of interviews as a result of the setting you work in and the types of clients you see. Some therapists develop specialization in interviewing children, working with individuals with eating disorders or psychosomatic symptoms, or other unique areas. Aside from your direct clinical experience you can further your education about interview strategies by reviewing peer-reviewed and empirical literature relevant to a particular area.

Mental health history	1. Have you ever been in therapy before? 2. Have you ever taken psychiatric medication? 3. Have you ever been hospitalized psychiatrically? 4. Have you ever visited the emergency room for an emotional or psychological problem? 5. Have you ever used herbs or alternative therapies to help control your mood, anxiety, or thinking?
Suicidal or homicidal behavior	1. Have things ever gotten so bad that you thought about taking your own life? 2. Have you ever hurt yourself either by cutting, burning, branding, or another type of self-injury? 3. Have you ever attempted suicide? 4. Have you ever been hospitalized for a suicide attempt? 5. Have you ever been so angry that you threatened another person's life? 6. Is there anyone that you wish you could kill or that they would simply just die?
Substance abuse	1. How often do you drink? How much? 2. Do you ever have a hangover the next day? 3. Have you ever lost consciousness or blacked out when using substances? 4. Have you ever become ill (e.g., vomiting) when using? 5. Have your friends or family ever said they were concerned about your use of alcohol/drugs? 6. Have you ever been involved in a 12-step group like AA or NA? 7. Have you ever felt you should cut down on your substance use? 8. How do you cope with stress? What do you do to relax after a long day? 9. Have you ever had legal problems because of your substance use? (includes DUI, DWI, possession, etc.) 10. What prescription medications do you use? Do you ever "borrow" medications from friends or family members? 11. Have you ever tried to quit or cut down on your substance use? Why?
Sexual or physical abuse, neglect, and bullying	1. Tell me a bit about your childhood. 2. What is your best childhood memory? Worst? 3. How did you get along with your parents? Extended family members? 4. How were you disciplined? 5. Were you ever hit or slapped? 6. Were you ever punished with a belt, board, or cord? 7. Did these injuries ever require a visit to the hospital? 8. Did anyone ever touch you inappropriately, in a sexual way? 9. Did anyone ever force you to touch them or ask you to watch pornography with them? 10. How did you get along with your peers? 11. Were you ever teased or bullied by your peers or siblings? 12. Did anyone in your family ever call you names, insult you, or threaten you? 13. Was Children's Services ever involved with your family? Were you ever placed in foster care?

FIGURE 5.1 How to ask difficult questions.

AA, Alcoholics Anonymous; DUI, driving under the influence; DWI, driving while intoxicated; NA, Narcotics Anonymous.

Confidentiality

Discussing **confidentiality** at the outset of a therapeutic relationship is essential. The limits of confidentiality are discussed elsewhere in this book (see Chapter 2); however, they are worth revisiting and elaborating on how to communicate with clients about confidentiality. It is important that clients have a clear understanding of how protected they will be as they talk about their concerns. Generally speaking, most clients have a right to blanket confidentiality with just a few exceptions. Therapists should discuss issues of confidentiality with clients at the outset of treatment and may also provide information about the limits of confidentiality in writing. To see one option for communicating about these issues in writing, see the Appendix at the end of this chapter. With a typical client in individual outpatient treatment, it is useful to say something like, "Everything you say here is confidential. You have the utmost right to privacy. There are just a few exceptions to this, such as if I believe you are a danger to yourself or others. If that ever becomes an issue I will discuss it with you directly."

In a hospital setting it is important to let clients know with whom you will share information about the interview. Often, information from the initial interview is shared with other members of the treatment team or with staff on an inpatient unit or clinic where the client is being referred. When clients present to the hospital due to police involvement, information about the client's status is sometimes shared with law enforcement or involved family members. These types of disclosures of protected health information (**PHI**) are typically covered by the Health Insurance Portability and Accountability Act (**HIPAA**). Mental health professionals working in hospital settings are encouraged to be as upfront as possible with clients prior to sharing information about the interview with other parties.

When beginning a clinical interview, it is important to remember that this first face-to-face interaction will set the tone for future clinical contacts. Part of your job is to educate the client about the therapy process or the process of hospitalization or day treatment. It can be especially helpful to give the client some idea of what to expect from the treatment. This education process should include some information about the challenges of psychotherapy, such as the difficulty of sharing things that are intensely personal and the expectation that painful or uncomfortable feelings will arise. Many therapists use a variety of metaphors to describe the process of therapy. Dr. Prout sometimes likens therapy to the process of cleaning out a closet or a garage. First, the contents need to be unpacked and reorganized, while some things are discarded. During this part of the process, most people are hopeful that no one comes over to see what a mess has been created; it is difficult to hide this comprehensive type of cleaning from friends and family. In the end, the closet (or the mind) is much more manageable and organized. This analogy is not unlike the quote from one of Freud's earliest clients who describe their work together as "chimney sweeping." Dr. Wadkins uses the metaphor of the client and therapist acting as detectives in identifying the things that are leading to the client's challenges and piecing this evidence together to discover ways to overcome these challenges. The therapist-client pair then act like scientists to test the hypotheses about the causes of those challenges as well as potential ways of easing those challenges through experiments. You may find your own **analogies** that you feel work well.

One of your tasks as a therapist is to also provide an environment that encourages the client to open up, speak freely, and feel safe. You can establish this type of atmosphere by carefully monitoring your tone, body language, eye contact, and the types of questions you ask and the responses you provide. The best way to develop a personal style of interviewing that fosters the development of a **therapeutic alliance** is to participate in supervision and constant review of your work. During our years in training, we both had our therapeutic work audio and video recorded so we could review aspects of personal style that are difficult to self-monitor. Once you get over the discomfort of hearing your own voice on a recording, it provides invaluable data about your verbal and nonverbal communication.

Psychotherapy is inherently an intensely interpersonal process. There are certain personality characteristics that seem to allow for greater sensitivity and effectiveness in working with clients. According to Weiner and Bornstein (2009), "Successful therapists create a climate in which their patients feel safe, secure, accepted, and understood" (p. 27). Much of the research on what makes a successful therapist has focused on three attributes—warmth, genuineness, and empathy.

Warmth

Warmth refers to the therapist's ability to accept patients for who they are, even if they are not attempting to please the therapist. Rogers (1951) referred to this as unconditional positive regard or the ability to accept uncritically everything the client might say, do, or think. A therapist who exhibits warmth will demonstrate unconditional positive regard and see all aspects of the client as being worthy of understanding. Warm therapists respond to a client's suffering with compassion and by acknowledging the client's experience as primary. This means that if the therapist perceives a client's behavior as self-destructive and the client describes it as soothing and comforting, the therapist must first begin to understand the meaning this behavior has for the client. The therapist's interpretation and experience must be secondary and introduced gently. This type of warmth can be difficult to convey with certain client populations. For example, could you imagine sustaining warmth with a sex-offending client or a parent involved with the legal system for abusing his or her child?

Genuineness

It is important that the therapist respond to clients in a truthful, open, and nondefensive way; these are the key components of **genuineness**. Another way to think about genuineness is to remember that you should say what you mean and mean what you say. Clients are amazingly perceptive and will quickly detect discrepancies between what you are saying and what you are actually thinking. A therapist who lies, omits, or otherwise hides information is unlikely to be trusted by his clients. There is a difference, however, between genuineness and expressing every thought that comes into your mind. Over time you will develop a balance between being genuine and protecting your clients from feelings and thoughts you have that may be counterproductive to the therapy process. This edict to maintain a genuine and authentic presence can sometimes be in conflict with warmth and empathy. What if your genuine reaction to a particular client is anger, jealousy, or frustration? We will discuss this particular problem in greater detail later in the text (see Chapter 9). In the meantime, you should keep in mind that there are ways to be genuine without revealing everything.

Empathy

Empathy is the ability to take on another individual's perspective and understand the world from his or her point of view. Empathy differs from sympathy in several ways. Empathy involves understanding what another person is thinking and feeling because you are able to metaphorically put yourself in his or her shoes. Sympathy is acknowledging another person's suffering or hardship and providing comfort. To clarify this, when a friend tells you her troubles and you say, "I'm so sorry that happened to you," you are expressing sympathy. An empathic response would be something like, "This sounds so painful. Do you want to talk more about what's been going on?" Empathy may involve reflecting the content of what the client is saying or the affect he or she is expressing either explicitly or implicitly. Empathy is being willing to enter into suffering with another person, to join them in the journey. As a therapist, you will maintain a reasonable emotional distance so that you can be most helpful to your clients, but you will continually strive to accurately perceive your clients' concerns and express your awareness of their experience in words.

There is research that suggests that novice therapists experience greater anxiety than experienced professional interviewers; however, there are few differences between level of warmth, genuineness, and empathy between these two groups (Pope, Nudler, Vonkorff, & McGhee, 1974). These interpersonal variables are more closely linked with individual differences in personality than level of training. Similarly, research suggests that in therapeutic relationships where there is a discrepancy between client and therapist in terms of ethnicity or other cultural variables, misunderstandings can arise (Aklin & Turner, 2006); however, it appears that when there is interpersonal harmony between therapist and client on relational variables like warmth and friendliness, they are able to work effectively across social identities. Recognition of the therapeutic relationship as a dynamic process, influenced by both members of the dyad, is an important aspect of its functioning.

BOX 5.4

Learning Exercise—Practicing Empathy

Consider the following client profiles and imagine how you might empathize with each. What would you say or ask? To which clients would you have the most difficulty showing empathy?

- Max is a 30-year-old man who is deeply troubled over an extramarital affair but is not willing to give it up.
- Jennifer is a very dogmatic individual who is convinced that all of her problems will be solved if she does God's will and makes God the center of her life.

(continued)

(continued)

- Paul is an Iraq war veteran who wants to process the violent acts he engaged in while at war, including killing civilians.
- Anjali is an 18-year-old who has tested HIV-positive and has no intention of informing her partner.
- Frank wants to leave his family so he can be "free from the burdens of responsibility."
- Joe is a depressed young man who expresses a desire to talk about persistent thoughts of ending his life because he sees little hope for his future.
- Sylvia is seeking treatment because she physically and psychologically abuses her husband.

You may notice that some clients are easier to identify with than others. This is because our **personal values** and beliefs often get activated by the work we do with clients. Some theorists have recommended that therapists defer to clients' values and explore how values inform client goals *unless* the client's values are impeding the therapeutic process (Williams & Levitt, 2007). This fine line between respecting the client's **autonomy** and providing competent care that may sometimes involve confronting client values can be a difficult one to negotiate. Being a competent psychotherapist sometimes requires one to safeguard the client's freedom to make choices in keeping with his or her own values. This balance is described very clearly in a seminal article on clinicians' private thoughts about values related to freedom, love, identity, truth, symptom management, and work.

> We have to be patient while people struggle with their choices and may have to watch them make bad decisions without interference, but it is irresponsible to fail to inform them of our educated opinions about the alternatives…We need to be honest and open about our views, collaborate with the client in setting goals that fit his or her needs, then step aside and allow the person to exercise autonomy and face consequences. Our expertise should help shape the goals of treatment according to our best judgment of how the disorder can most effectively be modified and how the change can best be maintained. To do less than this is to pretend we do not care about the outcome or to expend effort on behalf of goals we do not value, which is self-defeating. (Bergin, 1984, p. 107)

As Bergin suggests, mental health professionals must continually seek equilibrium between their clinical expertise and the client's need to be self-sufficient and to develop a great sense of agency within his or her own value-laden context.

Types of Interviews

The clinical interview is the cornerstone of our clinical work and our efforts to understand the clients we see. Although interviewing occurs in the context of a two-way interpersonal relationship, the majority of the interview is focused on the client revealing pertinent information to the interviewer. Clients rarely present for treatment with one simple problem. It is more likely that the interviewer will be sitting with a very complex individual, who is experiencing multiple symptoms that stem from an intricate array of causes. The goal of the interview process is to carefully unpack what the client has been experiencing and understand it in the context of his or her social and developmental history and culture. In order to do this, mental health professionals use several interview methods and techniques. Interview style will vary depending on the clinician's setting, the purpose and goals of the interview, and the information the clinician wants to obtain. The three types of interviews are unstructured, semi-structured, and structured. Each type of interview has its own strengths and weaknesses.

An unstructured or open clinical interview allows clinicians to rely on their instincts and to closely follow the client's train of thought. However, the clinician may have a general idea of what she wants to accomplish during an **unstructured interview**. For example, you might think to yourself, "I want to be sure to cover the problems the client has been having recently, any mental health or substance abuse history, and any current risk factors such as suicidal or homicidal ideation." In an unstructured interview, the questions can take any form and can be brought up at any time, allowing the interviewer a great deal of flexibility. This type of interview is generally informed by the therapist's own clinical judgment. The unstructured interview is widely used today and is especially useful in its ability to capture the uniqueness of each individual client.

There are several potential problems associated with the use of unstructured clinical interviews. Research demonstrated that ethnic minorities are far more likely than Caucasians to be misdiagnosed when assessed using an unstructured interview (Aklin & Turner, 2006). There are a number of other problems associated with unstructured clinical interviewing. The questions asked may reflect the clinician's own bias or theoretical perspective, rather than being concordant with the client's experience of distress. Similarly, there is ample evidence that unstructured clinical interviewing may, in some cases, lead to poor test-retest and inter-rater reliability and misdiagnosis (Gauron & Dickinson, 1969; Trierweiler et al., 2000).

Semi-structured interviews provide flexible guidelines for clinicians that allow them to tailor the interview to a specific client's needs. This allows for a more spontaneous interaction than a highly structured interview would. There are many semi-structured interviews available for use today. Some are focused on a particular population or diagnostic profile, whereas others cover a broad range of symptoms. Semi-structured interviews can be especially useful because they reduce the likelihood that topics will be inadvertently left out. They also increase the validity and reliability of diagnosis that arises out of the interview. Errors in diagnosis are often linked to cultural and ethnic variables (Adebimpe, 2004; Paniagua, 2001; Trierweiler et al., 2000); however, semi-structured interviews greatly enhance the reliability and validity of assessment of ethnic minorities (Aklin & Turner, 2006; Widiger, 1997).

Highly **structured interviews** are used in research settings, for diagnostic purposes, or when the treatment being offered is for individuals with a specific diagnostic profile. The structured interview is highly systematized and provides very clear guidelines for each step of the evaluation. Structured interviews can often be administered by laypeople, as they do not require or allow for clinical judgment (Figure 5.2).

Interview Type	Children	Adults
Structured	• Diagnostic Interview Schedule for Children (DISC; Shaffer, Fisher, Lucas, Dulcan, & Schwab-Stone, 2000) • Children's Interview for Psychiatric Syndromes (ChIPS; Weller, Weller, Fristad, Rooney, & Schecter, 2000)	• Current and Past Psychopathology Scales (CAPPS; Endicott & Spitzer, 1972) • Mental Status Exam (Spitzer, 1961) • Structured Clinical Interview for *DSM-IV* (SCID; First, Spitzer, Gibbon, & Williams, 1997) • Structured Clinical Interview for *DSM-IV* Axis II disorders (SCID-II; First, Spitzer, Gibbon, Williams, & Benjamin, 1994) • Structured Clinical Interview for *DSM-5* (SCID-5-RV; in development)
Semi-Structured	• Schedule for Affective Disorders and Schizophrenia for School-Age Children (K-SADS-PL; Kaufman et al., 1997) • Diagnostic Interview for Children and Adolescents (DICA; Welner, Reich, Herjanic, Jung, & Amado, 1987) • Child and Adolescent Psychiatric Assessment (CAPA; Angold & Costello, 2000) • Interview Schedule for Children and Adolescents (ISCA; Sherrill & Kovacs, 2000)	• Eating Disorder Examination (EDE; Cooper & Fairburn, 1987) • Mood and Anxiety Semi-Structured Interview (MASS; Interview for individuals with intellectual disabilities; Charlot, Deutsch, Hunt, Fletcher, & McLivane, 2007)

FIGURE 5.2 Commonly used structured and semi-structured interviews for children and adults.

Documentation

Upon conclusion of the intake interview you will need to summarize the content and interview process for the client's chart and for other possible audiences. The report may be used to inform your supervisor, relevant agencies, professional colleagues, the client's insurance company, the legal system, or may be used in the event of a referral. The nature of the report will vary slightly based on the audience, but here is an overview of information that is likely to be included in the report.

Your report will begin with basic demographic information about the client, including his or her name, address, telephone number, emergency contact, age, sex, ethnicity, marital status, sexual orientation, housing status (e.g., lives with roommates, homeless), family makeup, referral source, reason for referral, and presenting problem. This brief overview of identifying characteristics should be followed by some of the following information:

1. Behavioral Observations
   a. Appearance, including grooming, hygiene, eye contact, affect
   b. Level of cooperation with the interview, including level of responsiveness to questions
   c. Estimate of the accuracy and reliability of the information obtained

2. History of Presenting Problem
   a. Current level of functioning and brief history of current distress, including the course of the problem and relevant symptoms

    b. History of psychiatric treatment, including therapy, medication, hospitalizations, case management, and substance abuse treatment, and a brief description of relationship with previous service providers

    c. Family history of mental illness and/or substance abuse, with an emphasis on first-degree relatives but including extended family members of note

3. Medical History
    a. List and brief description of major medical illnesses and history of related treatments
    b. Description of client's current health status, including subjective experience of the illness(es)
    c. Current medications and dosages
    d. Contact information for all medical providers

4. Developmental History (especially important for child, adolescent, and young adult clients)

5. Social and Family History
    a. Early losses
    b. History of physical, sexual, and emotional abuse and neglect, including any children's services involvement with the family
    c. Educational history, including estimate of intellectual functioning, highest level of education attained, and current educational goals
    d. Employment history, including type of work, reasons for job changes, and overall satisfaction with current workplace environment (include military service here)
    e. Close relationships, including romantic relationships, friendships, and groups with which the client is affiliated (e.g., clubs, organizations, parenting groups, etc.)
    f. Sexual history, including history of risky sex practices, sexually transmitted diseases, pregnancies, abortions, and miscarriages
    g. Legal history, including current probation status, pending charges, and financial problems
    h. Recreational history with focus on client strengths and interests
    i. Spiritual/religious history, including any conversion or change in affiliation, including loss of faith; overview of role of current faith community if applicable (e.g., supportive, judgmental, etc.)

6. Overview of Current Functioning
    a. Brief description of current interpersonal, psychological, social, and occupational functioning
    b. Client's self-reported strengths and weaknesses
    c. Ability to perform tasks of daily living

7. Diagnostic Impression
    a. *DSM-5* diagnosis with supporting evidence, including duration and frequency of specific symptoms (see Chapter 8 for details)

8. Case Formulation and Recommendations
   a. Description of the presenting problems
   b. Factors that have created vulnerability or precipitated the problems
   c. Factors that may not have been present at the beginning of the client's experience of distress but that are helping to maintain the problem
   d. Factors that may aid in coping or act as resources for the client
   e. Specific recommendation for type of treatment indicated

9. Basic Treatment Plan and Goals
   a. Immediate recommendations related to current crisis or action that must be taken now
   b. Short- and long-term treatment goals with specific, measurable outcomes

This type of thorough written assessment can be fundamental to helping the clinician to form a comprehensive understanding of the client's problems and the expected course of treatment (consider reviewing the case formulation in Chapter 3). When writing and preparing an intake report, always consider your audience, the structure of the report, maintaining a clear writing style, and issues of confidentiality.

CHAPTER REVIEW

Conducting an initial intake interview can provoke anxiety in new therapists and clients. For mental health professionals, the tasks are many. You will be gathering a great deal of sensitive information while managing complex interpersonal interactions. Simultaneously, clients are being asked to reveal a great deal to a perfect stranger. This communication will likely occur across several cultural, ethnic, and identity fault lines. There are several layers of communication contained within the interview, and both parties will be influenced by environmental factors of the interview setting.

The clinician's office should be comfortable and afford the client a high level of privacy. Offices should be accessible to multiple populations, including individuals with disabilities. Additionally, the office may need to be designed to accommodate a range of counseling situations, including couples, groups, families, or others. The initial interview and subsequent counseling sessions should be as free from interruptions as possible; when interruptions do occur, clinicians should deal with the intrusion with a calm demeanor and a nondefensive attitude. Given that assaults are more common in mental health settings than other professional workplaces, issues of safety must be considered. There are several key steps new clinicians can take to enhance safety. Participating in a critical incident review process is one type of experience that may improve an individual's ability to identify triggers and factors that contribute to unsafe working conditions.

When meeting a client for the first time, first impressions can be very powerful. Your appearance can make a significant impact on the person you are interviewing. It is important that you maintain a professional appearance and presence that is not overbearing or distracting. Another factor that can detract from the counseling situation is lack of mental preparation. There are several ways to mentally prepare for contact with clients, including ongoing personal treatment, meditation, mindfulness exercises, regular physical exercise, and other aspects of self-care.

You should begin the clinical interview with as little distracting "noise" as possible. If you have been provided with information about the client ahead of time, be aware that this may cloud your judgment and perception of the person with whom you are meeting. As you greet your client and inquire into his or her current experiences, keep in mind that cultural differences and individual personality styles may influence the process of communication. Attending to nonverbal and paralinguistic cues is as important as following the content of the session. You will want to remind your clients of their rights to privacy and prepare them for the process of treatment. As you open up communication, it is your genuineness, warmth, and ability to be empathetic that will have the greatest influence on the development of a therapeutic alliance. Over time you may experience conflict between your personal values and those of your clients. Supervision and consultation can be very helpful in resolving value conflicts.

Most trainees learn how to conduct unstructured interviews; however, semistructured and structured interviews can be useful in diagnosis and evaluating specific types of psychopathology or functioning. Semi-structured interviews may reduce the reliability and validity of problems associated with assessment of ethnic minorities. Upon conclusion of the interview, you will likely be asked to document the findings of your evaluation. Report writing is a specific skill that can help you formulate your findings and communicate them to professional colleagues.

PERSONAL REFLECTION ESSAY QUESTIONS

1. Think about friends and family members that you consider to be either too intrusive or too distant/cold. What behaviors, speech patterns, or facial expressions convey their over-involvement or their lack of involvement and connection? How do you respond to these styles of interacting? Imagine yourself meeting with a new client with one of these styles? What do you imagine would happen? How would the client respond?
2. Are there certain verbal or behavioral habits or tics that you exhibit when you are anxious, bored, or angry? Do you say "um" repeatedly, twirl your hair, jiggle your foot, tap your pen, or just zone out, losing track of what is being said? You may want to ask your friends, family, or your instructor if they have noticed these types of habits. Locate several mindfulness exercises (many mindfulness activities can be found online at sites like: www .the-guided-meditation-site.com). Do several brief exercises (usually less than 2 minutes) and describe the effect they have on your overall sense of well-being. What effect might these exercises have on the habits you identified at the beginning?
3. What is meant by nonverbal and paralinguistic cues? What are some nonverbal signals you expect you will send to particular clients? How will you handle this if you become aware of something you may have inadvertently communicated?
4. Imagine that a client is silent for much of the initial interview. How might you understand this silence? What empirical research has been done on the topic of the meaning of silence across cultures? How does this research affect your understanding of the multiple meanings of silence?

KEYWORDS

analogies	genuineness	privacy
Architectural Barriers Act	HIPAA	safety
autonomy	interpreter	self-care
breakaway lanyard	interruptions	therapeutic alliance
clinical interviewing	Language Line	translator
confidentiality	meditation	warmth
critical incident review	mindfulness	watchwords
empathy	nonverbal cues	
first impressions	PHI	

FURTHER READING

- Fadiman, A. (1997). *The spirit catches you and you fall down.* New York, NY: Farrar, Straus, & Giroux.

  This novel details a Hmong refugee family's experience with Western doctors as they seek treatment for their daughter who has epilepsy. This book provides great insight into the communication difficulties that can arise between patients and doctors who come from different cultures.

- Southwell, P. (2005). Vision impaired. *Counselling & Psychotherapy Journal, 16*(5), 34–37.

  This article provides a good overview of working with clients who have acquired sight loss later in life. The author argues that working with clients experiencing acquired sight loss involves helping them to grieve, reconstruct meaning in their lives, and redefine their identity in the face of vision loss.

- Weiner, I. B., & Bornstein, R. F. (2009). *Principles of psychotherapy: Promoting evidence-based psychodynamic practice* (3rd ed.). Hoboken, NJ: Wiley & Sons.

  The first three chapters of this book offer a great overview of patient and therapist factors that contribute to successful psychotherapy. It is an introductory text that is easy to read and relevant to all types of psychotherapy.

- Zeer, D. (2000). *Office yoga: Simple stretches for busy people.* San Francisco, CA: Chronicle Books.

  This is an accessible guide to basic stretches and relaxation strategies that can be done in any office, including exercises for while you are on the phone or standing at the copy machine.

- Zimmerman, M. (2013). *Interview guide for evaluating DSM-5 psychiatric disorders and the mental status examination.* East Greenwich, RI: Psych Products Press.

  This pocket guide to interviewing organizes questions according to *DSM-5* diagnostic criteria. It is a handy and affordable guide for clinical interviewers at any career stage.

APPENDIX

Disclosure Statement & Confidentiality Agreement
Tracy A. Prout, PhD - Licensed Clinical Psychologist (License #018680)

Confidentiality

With the exception of a few limited circumstances, you have the absolute right to confidentiality of your therapy. I cannot and will not disclose to anyone what we discuss in therapy or in outside phone contacts, or even that you are in therapy without your express written permission.

The following are the exceptions to your right to confidentiality. I would inform you any time when I think I will have to put these into effect.

1. If I have good reason to believe you will harm another person, I am obligated to inform that person of your intentions and contact the local police.
2. If I have good reason to believe you are abusing or neglecting a child or vulnerable adult, or if you give me information about someone else who is doing this, I must inform the Administration for Children's Services or Adult Protective Services.
3. If I believe you are in imminent danger of harming yourself, I may legally break confidentiality in order to call the police or local crisis team. I would explore all other options with you before I take this step. If you were unable to take steps to guarantee you safety, I would have to take steps to insure your safety.

Your Rights as a Client

1. You are entitled to information about my methods of therapy, techniques I use, and the duration of therapy (if it can be determined), as well as my fees. Please feel free to ask if you would like to receive this information or have additional questions.
2. You are entitled to terminate therapy at any time.
3. You are entitled to confidentiality (see description above).

Your Responsibilities as a Client

1. You are responsible for arriving at the time we have scheduled.
2. If you need to cancel a session, please allow 72 hours notice. Fees will be charged for missed appointments without 72 hours notice.
3. You are responsible for on-time payment for services. Payment by cash or personal check is expected at the time of the appointment. Returned checks that are not honored by your bank will incur a returned check fee of $40.

Contact Information & Emergencies

If you need to contact me regarding appointments, cancellations, or any other non-emergency matter, please call (XXX) 555-5555. This is a confidential voice-mail and will be checked only by me once or twice a day. I will typically return calls within 24 to 48 hours, although it may take me longer during a weekend. If you are having a psychiatric emergency please call 911 or go to your nearest emergency room.

    I have read the preceding information and understand my rights and responsibilities as a client. I accept the conditions of psychotherapy.

Client Signature _____ Date_____

Therapist Signature _____ Date_____

Interviewing and Counseling Skills: Modes of Listening

In English you have this wonderful difference between listening
and hearing, and that you can hear without listening, and
you can listen and not hear. Not every language has that.
—Barenboim (2006)

LEARNING OBJECTIVES

- Identify and describe the different types of listening that are employed in psychotherapy
- Evaluate your own listening skills
- Describe the importance of reflecting affect and how to utilize this skill
- Explain how paraphrasing, reflection, and summarization are used in counseling
- Identify different types of nonverbal communication
- Describe how interpreters can both aid and hinder effective therapeutic communication

If you were to make a list of all the skills and qualities of top-notch mental health professionals, "a good listener" may be one that you will add to the list, and immediately identify as a personal quality that needs no further development as you work toward becoming a counselor. Most students come to this field of study because their friends and loved ones have told them they are good people to talk to about their problems. Some may be tempted to skip this chapter all together because they listen to others every day.

The quotation above is from Daniel Barenboim, a celebrated pianist and conductor, who has lived and worked all over the world. He made this observation about the distinction between hearing and listening when he was invited to deliver the Reith Lecture, which is broadcast annually on BBC Radio.

Barenboim (2006) described that he believes our ears have been "anaesthetized" to classical music because of its prevalence: we hear it piped into elevators and department stores on a daily basis (p. 11). He was lamenting the brain's ability to accept information from our ears while avoiding processing it with attention (which would result in listening to the music). Perhaps because of its vague familiarity we feel we can understand it, digest it, and move on without paying too much attention to it.

How many times each day do you really listen to others? A quick reflective experiment might tell you the answer. Think about the last person you spoke to today. Maybe this was a serious emotional conversation, or perhaps it was a banal exchange about what to buy at the grocery store. What was that person saying to you? What did that person *not* say to you? Could you tell if you were being listened to by the other person? Did you have to repeat yourself or clarify what you said or meant during the conversation? Were there unnamed emotions behind what you and the other person were saying? Could you identify all of those feelings? Did you end the conversation feeling as though you had accurately communicated with that person?

This chapter will help you to engage your ears (and eyes) in order to be aware of and attentive to what your clients are communicating to you in a session. Just as Barenboim reflected on his disappointment that many audience members at performances may not really listen to the music because they have heard it before, we aim to help you listen each time, even though you may have some familiarity with what is being said. Maybe you heard it from a similar client. Maybe it is resonating with your own experience, so you are mentally filling in the blanks without eliciting more detail. Maybe you are worried and anxious as a new counselor and are desperately searching your mind for the next therapeutic thing to say. In these situations and others, listening well is of the utmost importance.

A DIFFERENT TYPE OF LISTENING

The International Listening Association defines listening as "the attending, receiving, interpreting, and responding to messages presented aurally" (Bodie, Janusik, & Valikoski, 2008, p. 7). This is a good basic definition to build upon, but the way that a mental health professional must listen to her clients is a unique form of listening that goes beyond basic hearing to simple comprehension of the words being said and onward to deeper processing of the meaning of those words. Moreover, the therapist must knit together what is being said with how it is being delivered and what is being left out. Not to mention that the counselor must also be communicating to the client that she is attentive and empathic while listening! All of this happens simultaneously in conjunction with creating a mental representation of the client's problems (i.e., a case formulation) while planning and tailoring an effective intervention (i.e., treatment planning). The type of listening that takes place in counseling is often referred to as **therapeutic listening**. It is a unique way of connecting with another person and has been compared to becoming completely absorbed in a musical performance or a book (Jones & Cutcliffe, 2009). This may seem like a daunting task, but we will begin by discussing the foundation. Listening to our clients helps build a strong therapeutic relationship.

A Different Type of Relationship

Who do you listen to in your daily life? We speak to many people on a daily basis, but upon closer examination, you may find that you are listening most closely to the people with whom you have the closest personal relationships. Listening with full attention communicates respect, admiration, and care, and thereby fosters close connections with others. A focus on listening enables counselors to be human with their clients while maintaining appropriate professional boundaries. This is achieved not by hiding behind a role but by connecting with clients through listening, noticing their behavior and emotion, and being with them while they speak (Stickley & Freshwater, 2006). The therapeutic relationship will be discussed in more detail in Chapter 7, but we want you to read this chapter while thinking about developing your listening skills in the context of forming a strong professional relationship with your clients.

Arnold Lazarus has written about the need for counselors to vary their interpersonal style when working with different clients. He refers to this as being an "authentic chameleon" (Lazarus, 1993, p. 406). Lazarus believes that although there are basic components of one's therapeutic stance that are universal, including respecting client dignity and autonomy, different styles of interaction will be better suited to different types of clients. Specifically, the level of warmth and empathy expressed by a therapist will be different for clients who are anxious and timid than for those who are energetic and seeking directive coaching from their therapist. The client's expectations will often determine which therapeutic stance makes them feel most comfortable sharing and participating in therapy. Thus, as you read, recognize that the components of listening (and communicating verbally and nonverbally that you are listening) will have slightly different variations depending on the client. Furthermore, Lazarus warns that there are limits to the flexibility we each have: "The authentic chameleon changes colors and blends in quite naturally in various settings, but no creature has an infinite range of different shades, hues, tints, and tones" (Lazarus, 1993). Accordingly, it is helpful to recognize that your skills have limits, and that this is natural.

Active Listening

Researchers have described three different levels of listening (Comer & Drollinger, 1999). During **marginal listening**, individuals are hearing but not paying attention to the other person. The listener may be distracted or involved in formulating the next response, and this inattention is likely to lead to a less than ideal interaction because the listener is not accurately processing all the material. **Evaluative listening** involves concentrating intently on what is being said, but this type of listener focuses only on the literal meaning of words and does not acknowledge subtle verbal cues or nonverbal communication that may be conflicting with the overt verbal message. **Active listening** entails receiving verbal and nonverbal messages from others, processing them, and responding in a way that encourages further discussion. Gordon (2008) was the first to use the term *active listening*, and he developed this concept as an important component of effective parent-child communication. Comer and Drollinger recently expanded upon the concept of active listening to incorporate empathy. They wrote, "for communication to be effective, genuine concern is requisite" (Comer & Drollinger, 1999, p. 19).

In the spirit of full disclosure, Comer and Drollinger (1999) were writing about listening as it pertains to making sales. However, the inclusion of empathy in their discussion of active listening makes it just as relevant to mental health professionals. For instance, does the phrase "genuine concern" sound familiar to you? Genuineness, unconditional positive regard, and empathy are the key components of Carl Rogers' (1980) humanistic psychology (see Chapter 5). Rogers called these three qualities the facilitative conditions of therapy, which create an environment that allows clients to grow and change. When engaged in active-empathic listening with clients, counselors must pay full attention to the other and suspend their own attitudes and judgment in an attempt to understand the client's experience without bias. In order to receive verbal and nonverbal communication accurately, listeners must not only attend to the meaning of words and body language, but must also put themselves into the shoes of the other person in order to intuit the meaning and importance of what is being communicated.

For example, when listening to an adult client discuss a recent incident with his parents that led to distress, a therapist who is not close with her own parents might have a difficult time understanding the emotional impact of this situation if she were to use her own experience as a guide for the client's experience. The therapist is likely to underestimate the importance and emotion associated with the verbal messages from the client. What is even more problematic is for a therapist to use her own understanding not just as a guide for what the client might be experiencing but as a standard of "normal" that she feels the client *should* be experiencing. Personal differences that might be associated with culture or other life experiences may be integral to understanding others. It is typical, and not pathological, for certain adults to remain closely connected to their parents. It would be inappropriate and lead to a rupture in the therapeutic alliance for a clinician to impose her views on the experiences of her clients. To avoid pitfalls associated with misunderstanding clients, active listening works; no matter whether you are trying to sell a car or understand more about a counseling client's distress, it leads to people feeling as if they have been truly heard and understood.

Bodie (2011) defined **active-empathic listening** as the "active and emotional involvement of a listener during a given interaction—an involvement that is conscious on the part of the listener but is also perceived by the speaker" (p. 278). He further described how listening can be broken down into three stages of *sensing*, *processing*, and *responding*, and the listener should strive to demonstrate active-empathic listening during each part. Different types of behavior and cognitions are taking place during these stages to communicate active involvement.

When sensing, listeners must receive all verbal and nonverbal cues given by the speaker. The listener must register not just the **content** of the message, but also the **process** of delivery. The listener strives to incorporate the words with the speaker's voice inflection and rate of speaking to get a sense of the tone of the communication. The listener should also sense the nonverbal cues, which include body language and facial expressions. During this stage of listening, the counselor is allowing the client space to talk, and using verbal and nonverbal cues to indicate that they are absorbing all the relevant details as well as the emotional content of the message.

During processing, listeners must remember what was said, obtain clarification when necessary, and integrate the messages received into a whole.

There are two types of processing that occur simultaneously when listening. **Top-down processing** describes the way in which the listener uses existing cognitive frameworks, including prior knowledge and expectations, to interpret the meaning of the communication; whereas **bottom-up processing** starts with the specific behaviors and the meaning of the words used in the interaction (Edwards, 2011). When the two types of mental processing lead to a compatible interpretation, processing is easy and fast. However, consider the example of a close friend telling you to "be careful" after you have tripped and nearly fallen. If you consider that friend to be critical, the message might be interpreted as a personal attack on your clumsiness during top-down processing. The bottom-up processing of the same utterance might be interpreted as well-meaning concern for your safety. Of course, tone and body language are also considerations during both forms of processing. In summary, bottom-up processing begins by taking words at their face value, whereas top-down processing looks for meaning behind the words.

Finally, when responding, listeners show active-empathic listening both verbally and nonverbally. The listener may ask questions or paraphrase the material to communicate that she has heard the client and to encourage ongoing communication. The listener may mimic the speaker's body language and vocal volume to indicate that she has picked up on the emotion behind a message. The listener may also use the same vocabulary to let clients know that she is listening and understanding from the client's perspective.

BOX 6.1

Self-Assessment With the Active-Empathic Listening Scale

To gauge your current active-empathic listening skills, rate how frequently you perceive each of the following 11 statements to be true of you on a 7-point scale ranging from 1 (*never or almost never true*) to 7 (*always or almost always true*) with a midpoint of 4 (*occasionally true*).

1. I am sensitive to what others are not saying.
2. I am aware of what others imply but do not say.
3. I understand how others feel.
4. I listen for more than just the spoken words.
5. I assure others that I will remember what they say.
6. I summarize points of agreement and disagreement when appropriate.
7. I keep track of points others make.
8. I assure others that I am listening by making verbal acknowledgements.
9. I assure others that I am receptive to their ideas.
10. I ask questions that show my understanding of others' positions.
11. I show others that I am listening by my body language (e.g., head nods).

To total your AELS score, add all 11 ratings. To examine your sensing score, add items 1–4; the processing score is the total for items 5–7, and the responding score is the sum of items 8–11.

(continued)

(continued)

Bodie (2011) found in a sample of undergraduate students that listeners who were rated by others as "good" listeners were given an average score of 4.91 on sensing, while those who were identified as "bad" listeners were given an average rating of 3.05 on sensing. Other analyses found that "good" listeners were rated as scoring 5.05 and 5.29 on average for processing and responding respectively, while "bad" listeners were rated as scoring 3.26 and 3.31 on average for processing and responding. How do you measure up? Does your score exceed these average levels? Would another person who knows you well also rate you the same way on your active-empathic listening skills in these three domains? Can you identify ways you might develop and improve these active-empathic listening skills?

Drollinger, Comer, and Warrington (2006)

Paying Attention

The behavioral skills that counselors may use to outwardly indicate to clients that they are actively and empathically listening in responding will be discussed later in this chapter, but the crux of active listening involves the counselor's internal attention and being able to cognitively focus and concentrate on the client. Greason and Cashwell (2009) noted that trainees are often not explicitly taught how to increase their core attention capacities. Additionally, although we have discussed the value of identifying and validating the client's feelings, empathy also has an internal component. Counselors must be able to hear, and perhaps tolerate vicariously experiencing distressing emotions that may occur during counseling. When you are listening empathically to a client describe strong emotions of sadness, this may also stir up feelings of sadness in you. Thus, a mental health professional must develop **affect tolerance** to respond empathically to client's experience of distress without overly identifying with it or avoiding it. Affect tolerance has been described as being willing and open to experiencing feelings (Fulton, 2005). Stickley and Freshwater (2006) urged mental health nurses to focus on "not being engulfed" when listening to patients (p. 13). It is important for mental health professionals, while listening, to be able to differentiate between the feelings of the client and the feelings that are stirred up within themselves to be able to accurately understand the client's perspective.

   Mindfulness has been suggested as a practice that can help counselors train their minds to attend fully to their clients and tolerate affect. Jon Kabat-Zinn defined mindfulness as "paying attention in a particular way: on purpose, in the present moment, and nonjudgmentally" (1995, p. 4). Given this definition, mindfulness emerges as an excellent stance for counselors working with clients. Listening mindfully to clients is remarkably similar to Freud's instructions to the analyst. He wrote that the analyst should "suspend...judgment and give... impartial attention to everything there is to observe" (Freud, 1909, p. 23). He described this stance as "evenly suspended attention" (Freud, 1912a, p. 111), and he was advocating this approach because he believed analysts should keep their unconscious minds available to interpret the material produced during free association to the clients. Current theories of listening also support that active-empathic listening requires being able to quiet one's mind to focus intentionally and fully on the client. Nobody is perfect. This can a difficult task, but therapists should strive for practicing an approach of mindfulness in session.

Trainees who are mindful in their everyday lives also report higher levels of self-efficacy, and that ability to strategically control attention appears to mediate the relationship between mindfulness and self-efficacy (Greason & Cashwell, 2009). In other words, mindfulness significantly influences one's ability to control attention, which leads to higher self-efficacy among new counselors. The authors hypothesized that individuals who are more mindful can "sustain nonjudgmental attention on the client's narrative as well as divide attention to observe such things as client nonverbals without getting lost in their own inner dialogue" (p. 10). Mindfulness has been used widely as an intervention for many forms of psychological distress (Baer, 2003), and it appears that mental health professionals benefit from cultivating their own mindfulness practice in terms of being able to attend to their clients.

There are five core mindfulness skills: observing, describing, nonjudging, nonreacting, and acting with awareness (Baer, Smith, Hopkins, Krietemeyer, & Toney, 2006). Mindfulness is learned and practiced by meditation exercises involving nonjudgmental observation of one's internal and external states (Baer, 2003). Individuals are taught to focus attention on a particular target, such as walking or breathing, and to observe the mind and body as feelings, thoughts and sensations arise. When engaged in mindfulness, you might notice that your mind has wandered from the target of your attention. At that point, the content of your thoughts is noted, and then attention can be gently returned to the target in a nonjudgmental fashion.

BOX 6.2

Learning Exercise—Practice Mindfulness: Exploring an Object

You have probably eaten many raisins in your lifetime, but have you ever done so mindfully? Find a raisin and use the following prompts adapted from Jon Kabat-Zinn (2005) to guide you through mindful eating. Kabat-Zinn teaches this raisin exercise to people who are trying mindfulness meditation for the first time. You might feel silly, but remember that practicing nonjudgment is a core mindfulness skill. Sit comfortably, and give it a try.

- *Holding*: Take the raisin into your hand and hold it. Imagine that you have never encountered an object like this in your entire life.
- *Seeing*: Examine the raisin. Think about its size, weight, shape, texture, color. Is it firm or squishy? Does it have deep grooves? Shallow grooves? A mixture of both? Think about its journey from being a plump grape out in the sun to its current state.

(continued)

(continued)

- *Smelling*: Lift the raisin to your nose and smell it. Inhale its scent deeply and notice anything that might be happening in your mouth or stomach when you do this. Does the smell awaken sensations in your body?
- *Placing*: Put the raisin in your mouth without chewing it. Let it rest on your tongue and think about its size, weight, shape, and texture as your tongue experiences it. Move it around in your mouth with your tongue to create other sensations that you may observe and describe.
- *Tasting*: The moment has arrived! Bite into the raisin slowly. Take only three bites and stop. What is its flavor? What is its texture? How is your body reacting as you taste the raisin?
- *Swallowing*: Finish chewing slowly and swallow the raisin. Can you feel it traveling from your mouth, down your throat, and deeper into your body?
- *Following*: Continue to think about your current state as you rest for a few moments after swallowing the raisin. Be aware of your breathing and other sensations you are noticing, like a breeze on your skin or warmth in your stomach.

Research has indicated that a focus on active listening early in the training of mental health counselors increases students' confidence and ability to effectively use counseling skills in working with clients (Levitt, 2002). It is necessary to listen and understand the client before any other counseling skill can be effectively utilized. However, people who are new to counseling are frequently preoccupied with learning *what to do* to help clients, instead of focusing on *how to be*—the facilitative condition for being able to enact those specific counseling strategies. Levitt noted in her study that students experienced steady increases in active listening and self-efficacy (i.e., belief that one has the knowledge and ability to be a good counselor) over 10 weeks in a counseling practicum course, but both ratings took a sharp decline when students switched to a new client after working for 5 weeks with one client. Interestingly, these ratings rebounded after that initial session with the new client to be just as high or exceeding the listening and self-efficacy ratings with the first client. Therefore, it may be typical for new counselors to have a setback in active listening and self-efficacy when faced with a new client, but this perhaps represents a brief crisis of confidence. It is possible that during an initial session, performance anxiety generated by wanting to make a good impression as a counselor interferes with the expression of the basic and important skill. Keep in mind that Rogers (1980) felt that therapy would be successful when the therapist provided the basic facilitative conditions and nothing more, so a focus on active listening is an important component of being an effective counselor.

REFLECTIVE LISTENING

Once you have focused on developing skills for attention and empathy as part of effective listening, you can begin developing advanced listening skills. When listening to others, making reflective statements indicates to speakers that you are sensing, processing, and understanding what they are communicating. Reflective listening is an important skill in all relationships. In fact, it is one of the core skills taught to parents for use with their children with disruptive behavior problems in parent-child interaction therapy (Querido, Bearss, & Eyberg, 2002).

Reflective listening is a core component of a therapeutic approach called motivational interviewing (Miller & Rollnick, 2002). Motivational interviewing will be described in depth in Chapter 10 of this text, but for now, we would like to introduce the way that reflective listening is described and utilized in that approach. There are two types of reflective statements. **Simple reflections** are made by repeating or rephrasing the client's statements. With a simple reflection, you are capturing the client's perspective and presenting it back to that client in a manner that indicates you understand their perspective. A **complex reflection** goes further. When making a complex reflection, a mental health professional is making an interpretation of a client's statement by substituting a new word or making a guess at unspoken meaning (Miller & Rollnick, 2002). Complex reflections allow counselors to test hypotheses about the meaning of clients' statements.

For example, imagine listening to a depressed client describing her perspective on her friendships with the words "I am so tired of my friends constantly bugging me to spend time with them. They are so pathetic." A simple reflection might be, "So, your friends are frequently asking you to go out with them, and you think this is annoying." A complex reflection might be, "You seem angry that your friends are asking you to spend time with them when you would rather just be alone." The simple reflection captures the emotions and content of the message, while the complex reflection suggests that her friend's behavior is making her upset because she would rather spend time alone because of her depression symptoms.

BOX 6.3

Reflections With Inflection

When making reflective statements, think about the pitch and inflection in your voice. When speaking, if your pitch rises slightly on the last word, it makes the statement sound like a question. You will want to use that vocal inflection when you are more tentative about your interpretation of the client's words. However, it is also a great technique for drawing more information out of your client. Try it today! Reflect a statement back to a friend or family member with the last word at a slightly higher pitch. Raise your eyebrows while doing this to provide another cue that you are looking for the other person to respond.

BOX 6.4

Learning Exercise—Reflective Listening

Pair up with two classmates to practice making reflective statements. In fact, use ONLY reflective statements during a brief 3- to 5-minute exchange with one of your classmates (i.e., the *speaker*) while the other (i.e., the *observer*) keeps track of the types of utterances you make as the *listener*. A tip for making sure that your statements are reflective is to avoid asking any questions during the conversation. The observer should tally how many simple reflections, complex reflections, questions, and expressions of empathy the listener gives during the exchange. Don't forget to use good nonverbal listening skills. The observer should also make notes about the listener's use of nonverbal communication. After the exchange, spend some time debriefing before switching roles. Were you able to use only reflective statements? Did the speaker feel that you heard and understood? What were your strengths and weaknesses during this exercise?

Mirroring Affect

When engaged in reflective listening, it is important to not just focus on the content of the message to summarize or interpret it in a reflective statement, but to also incorporate all the other relevant aspects of the communication that indicate the affect, or feelings, being expressed by the client. Counselors should be reflecting the emotional state of the client, which is likely to be communicated by the content of the verbal message as well as the tone of voice, and by other nonverbal cues. This will be natural when the client's affect and words are congruent. That is, it is easy to recognize a client's depressed affect when she is tearful, speaking quietly, gazing at the floor and reporting that she sometimes thinks about killing herself. The counselor is able to mirror the client's affect and also speak in a softer voice while reflecting that the client seems to feel very hopeless about her future. On the other hand, imagine the case where the verbal content is the same, but the client is speaking rapidly, making direct eye contact, and smiling while she shares that she has thought about suicide. In that situation, the counselor has a more difficult job of deciding how to reflect the incongruence between the content and process of the communication. What would you do in this situation? One approach would be to notice the incongruence and gently inquire about it or comment on your confusion.

Snow White's wicked stepmother asked her magical mirror who was the fairest one of all, and, if you recall the events that transpired afterward, you know that she wasn't too happy with the answer she received. While the mirror was telling her the truth about Snow White's exceptional beauty, she preferred to see what she thought and felt about her own beauty. We expect our mirrors to reflect back what we see accurately and not to speak their minds or offer their own opinions. There is a place in counseling for challenging the statements clients make and offering advice, but when listening to clients, it is our goal to reflect clearly and accurately what the client is communicating.

Following the Client's Words

Just as a listener may mimic the speaker's body language and vocal volume to indicate that she is picking up on the emotion behind a message, a mental health professional may use the same vocabulary to let clients know that she is listening and understanding the client's perspective. It may be tempting to correct clients or challenge their thinking at times during therapeutic encounters, but using the client's own words is a powerful way to indicate that you are listening and withholding judgment. For example, if a depressed client describes that he felt "glum" most of the time since the last session, you may wish to echo his term for his sadness when discussing it with him. Furthermore, you may be making the assumption that he is using the word "glum" to mean sad, but he may actually be referring to feelings of guilt. Also consider the word "upset." Clients and counselors are likely to use this vague word frequently when describing negative emotions, but it has a unique meaning to each person. Following and reflecting the client's words is likely to help you listen mindfully and become absorbed in the client's world, seeing it from his perspective. Keep in mind that a powerful way to indicate that you are listening attentively is to provide short vocalizations, such as "hmmm" and "uh-huh."

Avoiding Digression

Counselors should strive to follow clients' words with active-empathic listening by responding to clients' specific points and not digressing to other topics or material. There are some topics or material that might cause you to become uncomfortable when listening that may motivate you to change the subject. There might also be times in which the client momentarily strays from the main topic when speaking. Just as mental health professionals may seek to move away from painful emotional material, clients may depart from distressing topics with or without full awareness of their motives or method.

When listening, if you note that the client has suddenly changed topics, you should take a moment to analyze whether there has also been a change in the client's affect or nonverbal cues, including eye contact or shifts in body position. A client may adopt a more closed physical stance (e.g., with arms crossed), drop eye contact, or slightly turn away if disconnecting from the interaction or attempting to withdraw his words. If you suspect that a client may be digressing because of the emotions stirred up by the material being discussed, gently report what you are noticing about the shift in his affect. You might say, "I notice that you stopped talking about your mother suddenly and crossed your arms before mentioning your new car." The client may continue to pursue the new topic and, as the listener, you should continue to follow the client's lead as a way to respect his dignity and autonomy. However, good counselors remember this material that has led to a digression and are alert to the possibility that the client will bring it up again in the same or a later session. At that time, the counselor can integrate the new information about the client's affect and nonverbal behavior from each of the presentations in her mental representation of the client to achieve a more complex and nuanced understanding.

Another potential occurrence in a clinical encounter is when a client's digression, or aside, raises new material. For example, a teenage girl reveals in session that she dislikes another girl in her social circle. As she describes this other girl, she mentions several past incidents of "annoying" behavior, along with the statement that the girl is "homophobic." The therapist reflects back, "She's homophobic?" and the client replies that she knew that this was the case because this girl had reacted with disgust when the client revealed that she sometimes finds herself attracted to other girls. She quickly adds, "Well, I hope I don't see her at this party." This therapist faces a difficult decision about how to respond because there are multiple options. She could try to encourage the client to elaborate about other potential negative feelings or incidents she has experienced because of same-sex attraction, or she could pursue elaboration about the client's worries about the upcoming party. Furthermore, the therapist knows the client is in a relationship with a member of the opposite sex and this was the first disclosure of any same-sex attraction. In this case, the departure from the client's main point has presented new information, but she did not stay with that topic long enough for the therapist to respond. At times, the therapist must be careful to follow the client's words when tempted to back-track to a digression.

Listening for Themes

When listening to clients, mental health professionals must be attentive to recurring topics or themes in the client's presentation. Some issues may be brought up by clients that seem peripheral or tangential to their main problem or complaint, but these motifs may represent patterns in their everyday lives. As previously discussed, mental health professionals must listen carefully to clients in addition to remembering what is said in sessions and being able to integrate new information into memory as therapy progresses and more is revealed by the client. To facilitate congruity across sessions it is important to take careful notes and to remember the client's life history and current stressors. It is typically very meaningful to clients when counselors remember the names of their friends and family members or important events that happened in their lives.

People are sometimes unaware of patterns in their life, or have limited insight as to how different traits and behaviors are connected. For example, a client seeking counseling about her failing relationship proudly described her devotion to her immediate family. When asked about her relationship, she failed to mention herself or her feelings at all—only details about her partner and her partner's family. The therapist observed this and responded that he noticed the client likes to "flex her caretaking muscle." A part of the client's identity that she valued, her role as a strong caretaker for her family, had been "turned upside down" when it was placed in the context of her romantic relationship.

Another theme that might arise in therapy is lack of self-care, which might be mentioned as difficulty finding time to eat regular meals or getting too little sleep. The client may not be integrating all these seemingly harmless, isolated behaviors into the whole concept of neglecting herself. Although the clients are the experts when it comes to their thoughts, feelings, and behaviors, many benefit from having their attention drawn to disparate parts of their experience that may be knit together.

There is a Hindu tale that describes blind men trying to determine what an elephant is by touching it (Rumi, 2001). One feels the feet, one the trunk, and so on. When they attempt to describe the elephant to each other, they disagree. It's a different animal to each because they have access to limited information. Everyone has a different piece of the truth. Just as an elephant isn't only a tusk, sometimes you may see aspects of the clients in a different light. Putting all these pieces together is a collaborative and healing process.

Listening for Cues

Peter Drucker, a pioneer in business management, said "the most important thing in communication is to hear what isn't being said" (Moyers, 1990, p. 408). Paying attention to body language and cadence of speech will provide information about when to respond and when to allow for a pause in the conversation. There may be instances when you want to encourage the client to elaborate further because she has stopped speaking and appears to be lost in her thoughts. A client who has paused to think will show physical signs of mental processing (see Box 6.8). For example, when people are remembering things or searching their memory bank, they often look up and away from the listener. It is prudent to give space to ensure that the client has stopped speaking before responding.

At times, clients will provide direct cues that they desire you to respond by asking a question or looking at you expectantly. As you get to know your clients, you will begin to recognize each individual's unique style of letting you know that she is seeking a response or prefers more time to think before continuing. Sharing talking time is important to communicating that you are willing and available to listen (Andersen & Andersen, 2005).

Getting the Whole Picture

Therapeutic listening is a complex process. The mental health professional must knit together disparate yet connected information to create a whole understanding of the client and the client's perspective. It is like completing a jigsaw puzzle. You will connect more pieces during each clinical encounter, but you start with the edge pieces to create an outline. Although one feels satisfaction when the corner pieces have been found and the frame completed, you really begin to visualize the whole picture as you match up pieces, organize them into like groupings, and begin to fill in the middle. The picture on the box can be a guide for completing a puzzle, but in therapeutic encounters, the full image is not available and comes into focus only after careful listening and collaboration with the client.

BOX 6.5

Learning Exercise—Practice Listening

StoryCorps is an organization whose mission is to record and preserve stories told by Americans. To participate in this large-scale oral history project, you can make an appointment at a recording booth or make a Do-It-Yourself recording at home to submit to StoryCorps. The process entails enlisting someone important in your life to interview, and the conversation is recorded and archived at the American Folklife Center at the Library of Congress. The interviews are also available online at http://storycorps.org and aired regularly on National Public Radio. Many of the stories are moving and entertaining.

For this exercise, visit the StoryCorps website and click the link to "Listen to Stories." Pick a story to practice listening to a conversation attentively, following the speaker's words, managing your affect, and remembering details. You may search for stories by topic, and you may want to select a story in the category of "Discovery," "Identity," or "Struggle." Reflect on what it was like to listen to these personal stories of strangers. You may find that it is addicting to listen to these stories, and you may want to consider taking someone you care about to record a story yourself.

FOUR LISTENING RESPONSES

Verbal person centeredness (VPC) has been described as a key component of supportive therapeutic listening (Bodie & Jones, 2012), and focuses on the last stage described by Bodie (2011): responding. In conversation with others, our comments can demonstrate low, moderate, or high person centeredness. One strives to give highly person-centered communication, which is characterized by explicit recognition of the other person's feelings and encouragement to elaborate and contextualize those feelings according to the perspective of the other. On the other hand, messages that are low in person-centeredness criticize or challenge the other person's feelings or perspectives and may even consist of telling the other person how she ought to feel in that situation. Moderately person-centered responses include an implicit recognition of the other's feelings, but may consist of expressions of sympathy or attempts at distraction, steering away from the distressing situation instead of directly exploring the person's feelings in context (e.g., "I'm sorry to hear that. At least you have a lot of other things going for you."). Highly person-centered communication validates the other person's feelings and is a powerful component of active listening. VPC requires skill. Burleson (2011) found that people with higher levels of **interpersonal cognitive complexity**, which is the ability to obtain information about people and social situations, are better at producing highly person-centered communication. Individuals with high interpersonal cognitive complexity have a good understanding of other peoples' thoughts, behaviors, and traits. This allows them to respond in a way that is highly person-centered when listening. Research has also shown that high interpersonal cognitive complexity facilitates deep processing of communication and the ability to remember the details of conversations (Burleson, 2011).

BOX 6.6

Assessing Interpersonal Cognitive Complexity With Crockett's (1965) Role Category Questionnaire (RCQ)

To gauge your level of interpersonal cognitive complexity, think about a person your age that you know very well and like. Take 5 minutes to write down as many of this person's characteristics as you can. Think about the person's habits, beliefs, and ways of treating others. Think of another person you know well, but this time a person whom you dislike. Spend 5 minutes making a list of this person's characteristics. Once your lists are complete, inspect them and count how many unique personality constructs you listed. Don't count physical descriptions, demographics, or specific behaviors. Samter (2002) found that among college students, women on average listed approximately 23 personality characteristics while men had a mean RCQ score of about 16. How do you measure up?

Burleson and Waltman (1988); O'Keefe and Sypher (1981)

Clarification

There may be times during clinical encounters that you are unable to fully (or even partially) understand what a client is saying. Perhaps the client is using a term with which you are unfamiliar. Perhaps the client is speaking quickly or mumbling. Perhaps the client has just made successive contradictory statements. When you cannot follow the client, you should respond by asking for **clarification** unless it seems to be tangential or a minor unimportant detail. There are also times you may want to seek clarification when you think you have correctly understood the client, but you want to make it clear and succinct for the client, who seems to not know exactly what she is saying.

To seek clarification, you may simply restate what you think you heard and ask the client if you got it right. For example, "I think that I am hearing you say that you wish you could make friends more easily at school. Is that right?" You may also seek clarification by offering a forced choice to the client: "Are you saying that you have a hard time making friends at school, or is it that you are unhappy with your current friendships?" When you are unable to provide a restatement because you have not understood enough to make an informed attempt, you should acknowledge your confusion and simply ask for the client to repeat what she said. Over time you may notice that patterns of communication emerge. For example, if a client begins to trail off and say "I don't know" repeatedly when talking about her spouse, you might carefully recognize that with her. A therapist in this situation might say, "You are most often very articulate and clear but I've noticed that when you begin talking about your spouse, it becomes harder to communicate what you're thinking and feeling."

Paraphrase

Another specific response is **paraphrasing**. During paraphrasing, individuals restate in their own words what they think the other person is trying to communicate, including both the verbal and emotional content (Weger, Castle, & Emmett, 2010). Not only does paraphrasing indicate clearly that the listener has received the message accurately, but trust is fostered when the message is reflected without judgment. It can also be beneficial for clients to hear their messages reflected to gain a better understanding of their own feelings in that context. Weger and colleagues (2010) found that people reported liking individuals who paraphrased their messages during a mock interview. As a counselor, while it is not necessary to be likeable, it is beneficial: people tend to disclose more information to those they like than to people they dislike in first encounters. This is helpful during an intake interview, when clients are expected to reveal a great deal of personal information (Collins & Miller, 1994). Thus, paraphrasing as part of active listening may be an effective way to increase your likeability and the amount of client self-disclosure in initial and all sessions.

BOX 6.7

Likeability and Self-Disclosure

Now that you know initial likeability is significantly related to self-disclosure, it has given you impetus to develop your active listening skills and boost your likeability; you should also know that evidence suggests that making self-disclosures to another person tends to influence how much we like that person (Collins & Miller, 1994). So, even if you are not initially likeable to your client for some reason, chances are his or her esteem for you will be strengthened during the course of treatment as your client makes more personal disclosures to you.

Reflection

As discussed previously, when reflecting, a counselor should focus on simple reflections of content, reflections of process, as well as more complex reflections to test hypotheses about the meaning of the client's words and help generate a new way for the client to view her situation. Therapists also strive to reflect the client's mood, which is communicated through nonverbal cues. Consider the following interaction between a client and therapist.

Client: I feel so uncomfortable when I'm at work. (pause) Well, I know why I'm uncomfortable there.

Therapist: You know why you are uncomfortable at work?

Client: Yes. But I don't want to talk about it.

Therapist: So, you know what it is. And it seems like you are not hopeful about whatever it is, changing.

Client: It's my behavior.

Therapist: Knowing what leads you to feel uncomfortable at work might mean that you can do something to feel more comfortable there.

Client: I know I can. But I also just want to leave and stop working there.

Therapist: It seems as if you not only want to avoid talking about work but also to avoid going to work.

The reflections in this brief vignette illustrate moving from simple reflection of content to more complex reflections of process and emotion. This type of reflection is a foundational component of active listening. We will explore how to use reflection skills to move from content to process in greater detail in Chapter 11.

Summarization

Summarizing what the client has said is different from paraphrasing the message. When you are ready to summarize you have arrived at a succinct and clear understanding of the client's perspective. You are encapsulating not only what the client said but also adding and integrating the material that was generated by your responses to the client. Because many topics may be covered in a single session, it may be necessary to take the time to summarize multiple times during the session. It is also important to bear in mind that you need not take sole responsibility for summarizing session content, but you may try a collaborative approach with your client and sum up the session together. Summarization is facilitated if you are working from an agenda that was generated with the client at the beginning of the session. Working from an agenda allows you to know more clearly when topics are shifting in session and signal a natural space in the session to summarize content before moving on.

NONVERBAL COMMUNICATION

Nonverbal immediacy describes the group of behaviors that reflect to listeners the degree of distance or closeness between themselves and another person (Andersen & Andersen, 2005). Nonverbal immediacy communicates how tuned-in the listener is during an interaction and consists of head nods, a forward body lean, smiling, and eye contact. In general, these immediacy behaviors indicate to others that you are available for interaction and are approachable.

Body Language

To indicate that you are listening, you should physically align yourself to face your client. Body angle and orientation are important, and face-to-face and eye-to-eye positions communicate warmth and availability (Andersen & Andersen, 2005). Some therapeutic manuals suggest arranging chairs at a 45-degree angle as it allows clients to more naturally break eye contact when they feel overwhelmed or embarrassed (Gabbard, 2010). This may require you to intentionally set up the room you will be using to conduct therapy to allow a comfortable distance between you and the client, where you may be seated directly facing one another or just slightly angled. You should take care to sit in a manner so that you are not towering or looming over the client. You may want to sit in a lower chair or kneel or sit on the floor when interacting with children or in a regular desk chair when working with adults.

The physical proximity between you and the client also communicates how attuned you are to the client. While you do not want to invade your client's personal space, you also do not want to be so far away that you may actually have difficulty hearing what is said. Leaning forward slightly communicates interest when listening to clients (Andersen & Andersen, 2005). Imagine what your body would physically do while metaphorically hanging onto the client's every word. You would be inclined to lean forward to draw the words out.

A variety of other body movements communicate warmth and interest, including smiling, nodding, use of gestures, and interactional synchrony (Andersen & Andersen, 2005). Smiles are not always appropriate to the content of the session, but increased facial expressiveness during times when smiling might feel inappropriate may also be read by others as a sign of nonverbal immediacy.

Eye Contact

Looking at your client while she is speaking is the most direct way to communicate that you are listening. While maintaining eye contact is recommended with most clients, too much eye contact may be distracting or unnerving to clients. Eye contact habits are quite individual and are developed according to cultural norms (see Box 6.8). You are likely to find that clients will intermittently make and break eye contact during sessions. It is important to keep your gaze directed at the client, to be there when the client is seeking eye contact or checking in to see if you are listening. Remember that this may be the first time that a person is divulging personal information to another person and that, in the beginning, you are a relative stranger. They may be surprised by the feelings of vulnerability that may arise when having a "one-sided" conversation with a counselor. We are used to reciprocity in most of our interactions with other people, and some clients may have a difficult time maintaining eye contact while feeling vulnerable. Some clients may also have difficulty maintaining eye contact when experiencing depressed mood. Research has shown that people who feel sad are less likely to make eye contact, while happier people typically seek out eye contact from others (Hills & Lewis, 2011).

BOX 6.8

Spotlight on Culture

The preference to seek eye contact is related to culture. Research has demonstrated that cultural difference becomes apparent when individuals are asked to answer questions in an interview format. McCarthy, Lee, Itakura, and Muir (2006) found that when answering questions that did not require thinking, participants from Trinidad and Canada maintain more eye contact (88% and 64% of the time, respectively) than Japanese participants (54% of the time). When looking away, the participants from Trinidad and Canada did not show a trend in gaze direction, but Japanese participants typically looked downward. Notably, these cultural differences in maintaining eye contact disappeared when participants were asked questions that required thinking, which suggests the universal need to avert one's gaze when thinking.

(continued)

(continued)

> However, the tendency for Japanese participants to look down and for the other participants to look up remained. Thus, gaze aversion and eye contact is likely to vary according to culturally prescribed norms during clinical encounters.
>
> In another recent experiment, Senju and colleagues (2013) recruited British and Japanese volunteers to study potential differences in eye gaze while viewing computer avatars with faces turned slightly to the side. This experiment was less realistic because it measured individuals' eye gaze while passively viewing a computer-generated face, but the value is that the use of the computer allowed the researchers to determine exactly where on the face and on which eye people are focusing. The results indicated that British participants gazed longer at the avatar's mouth than Japanese participants, and found that both cultural groups looked for an equally long amount of time at the eyes. Notably, when the avatar was programmed to suddenly shift eye positions toward or away from the participant, Japanese participants immediately shifted their gaze to the same direction as the avatar (i.e., the "front" eye when looking forward or the "back" eye while looking away), whereas British participants maintained eye contact with the avatar (i.e., looking at the "front" eye) even when the avatar was looking away. Thus, there may be a cultural preference among some Asian people to match the gaze of others, which supersedes the desire to avert one's gaze periodically, whereas others prefer to maintain eye contact even when they are interacting with someone whose gaze has shifted. Senju and colleagues also found that this effect was most robust for men in their study.

What to Avoid

To pay attention fully, it is best to minimize potential distractions in the space. When you are setting up an office, think about where the windows are with regard to where you and your client will be sitting. Will you be tempted to glance out of the window at passersby while your client is speaking? Might a window be distracting for your patients, who may feel insecure about maintaining anonymity? If the window is large and on street-level, the use of curtains or blinds might provide a sense of security while letting in light and making the room feel welcoming. You should also take care to avoid placing a large barrier (e.g., a desk or table) between you and the client; such barriers can communicate distance instead of connection.

Once you have set up the physical space, think about what you are doing with your hands and feet during session. Will you be holding a pad of paper and a pen to take notes while the client is speaking? How might your client view that? Will you be fidgeting with the pen when not writing? Are you aware of any body movements that you make when you are sitting, such as tapping your foot or drumming your fingers on a nearby surface? You may not be fully aware of all the physical movements that you make when focused on other matters, but your client will observe and make judgments about what they might mean with regard to your attention.

Take care to silence all devices that may unexpectedly interrupt your client while speaking. In addition to silencing your phone and computer notifications, you should monitor your habits for checking your devices. You may not be aware how frequently you look at your cell phone to check for incoming messages and updates even when the sound is turned off. Many people no longer wear wrist watches but instead rely on their mobile phone to tell the time. Think about your habits, and plan ahead for making your clients more comfortable while they are in your office. Place a clock in an unobtrusive position so that you may monitor the time during a session without looking away from your client or turning your body, which may be distracting. You may also consider keeping a clock positioned behind you so that clients can easily notice the time elapsed and remaining in session.

THE USE OF INTERPRETERS

This discussion of listening has been based upon the assumption that you are capable of processing the verbal content of the speaker's statements. This might not always be the case during your career because you may at times have clinical encounters with individuals who speak a different language. You may work with a bilingual client who switches between languages while speaking, or you may work with an individual who has recently immigrated and is developing his English language skills. Your client may be a child who speaks fluent English, but her parents do not, which means you will have a challenge listening to her parents' concerns.

When there are language differences, listening skills become even more important. Nonverbal immediacy and using reflective listening to confirm what you believe you have heard are useful with bilingual clients with limited English proficiency. Empathy and mirroring affect are also important because clients may feel and communicate frustration about the difficulties that language differences present when trying to get their points across in counseling. Expressing genuine concern for the client and reflecting and validating those frustrated feelings may help to ease the discomfort of clients. Showing that you are interested in listening to the best of your abilities despite these difficulties to work toward greater understanding or a more appropriate solution is also important.

An **interpreter**, someone who is trained to translate spoken language, may be used when working with clients or important collateral contacts who are not proficient in English. Research has found that having an interpreter present in sessions leads to many desirable outcomes, including helping clients feel a sense of belonging during sessions and increasing clients' trust in the counselor and counseling itself (Paone & Malott, 2008). The interpreter may also serve as a source of information and insight about the client's culture (Raval, 1996).

It is important to use only trained professionals as interpreters. At times, counselors may be tempted to use family members or other bilingual individuals to translate for them. However, there are ethical and professional concerns with relying on untrained individuals, including the potential to violate confidentiality or for the family member to withhold or alter information that is sensitive (Amodeo, Grigg-Saito, & Robb, 1997). Another important reason to use trained professionals that have experience with working with counselors is that the interpreter should also have the knowledge and skills to attend to the client in a professional and empathic manner. Miller, Martell, Pazdirek, Caruth, and

Lopez (2005) found that some interpreters used in their study reacted to session content with distress because they lacked training in coping with the disturbing emotional content that some counseling sessions may contain. The authors recommend working with interpreters in a collaborative fashion and making sure to debrief after sessions with the interpreter. This can be a great time for the interpreter to share her insights about the impact of culture on the client's presentation and for the counselor to make sure that the interpreter is managing any emotional impact of the session.

On the other hand, having another person present in session presents some unique challenges, particularly in attending and listening. Now that you have become more aware of the nonverbal communication involved in showing that you are attending to clients, imagine how difficult this will become when you have to attend to both the client and the interpreter and vice versa. It is not uncommon for counselors to feel detached from the session when not directly engaged in communication (Raval, 1996), and counselors may also feel excluded from the interpreter-client relationship when a positive and supportive relationship forms because of the direct communication flowing between them (Miller et al., 2005). It is important to be aware that nonverbal communication norms may vary across different cultures. When working with an interpreter, the counselor may focus on the client's nonverbal communication because she cannot understand what is being said. It is best practice to remain aware of potential differences in what comprises typical nonverbal communication to avoid making an inappropriate interpretation of the client's nonverbal behaviors (Cushing, 2003). Remember that the interpreter is likely to be an invaluable source of cultural information about the client and can assist you in understanding the client's verbal and nonverbal communication.

CHAPTER REVIEW

Counselors strive to listen to clients in a way that goes beyond basic hearing to simple comprehension of the words being said and onward to deeper processing of the meaning of those words. They must be attentive and empathic to clients, and this can be accomplished through active-empathic listening. When engaged in active-empathic listening with clients, counselors must pay full attention to the other and suspend their own attitudes and judgment in an attempt to understand the client's experience without bias. To receive verbal and nonverbal communication accurately, listeners must not only attend to the meaning of words and body language, but must also put themselves into the shoes of the other person to intuit the meaning and importance of what is being communicated. Counselors must be able to tolerate the feelings produced when listening to clients in distress and to attend fully to clients' words, perhaps by using mindfulness.

When listening to others, making reflective statements indicates to speakers that you are sensing, processing, and understanding what they are communicating. There are two types of reflective statements. Simple reflections are made by repeating or rephrasing the client's statements. A complex reflection involves making an interpretation of a client's statement by substituting a new word or making a guess at unspoken meaning. Complex reflections allow counselors to test hypotheses about the meaning of clients' statements. In addition to reflecting the content of client communication, counselors should also reflect the affect being expressed by the client.

In addition to reflection, there are three other types of responses that a counselor may make while listening to clients. The first is seeking clarification when you cannot follow what the client is saying if it seems important. The second is paraphrasing, which involves stating in your own words what you think the other person is trying to communicate, including both the verbal content and emotions. The third is summarizing what the client has said by producing a succinct and clear understanding of the client's perspective.

Nonverbal communication is important during therapeutic listening. It is important for the counselor to indicate attentiveness through body language and eye contact. It is equally important for the counselor to be tuned in to the client's body language to understand her feelings.

There may be times when it is necessary to use an interpreter when working with clients or their families. Nonverbal immediacy and using reflective listening to confirm what you believe you have heard are useful with bilingual clients with limited English proficiency. Empathy and mirroring affect are also important because clients may feel and communicate frustration about the difficulties that language differences present when trying to get their points across in counseling. It is important to use only trained professionals as interpreters when necessary. It is best to work with interpreters in a collaborative fashion, debrief after sessions with the interpreter, and manage your feelings about being excluded from the interpreter-client relationship because of their ability to communicate directly in sessions.

PERSONAL REFLECTION ESSAY QUESTIONS

1. Think of a time when you felt truly *heard*. What did the other person do (or not do) that allowed you to feel that way? Are these skills you can apply to your own practice?
2. Think about how your anxiety might interfere with your ability to listen to new clients you are meeting for the first time. Have you had an experience in your personal life when a strong emotion, like anxiety, interfered with your ability to listen to others? Reflect on how you can best prepare to enter into clinical situations confidently.
3. How prepared do you feel to tolerate negative affect in your future clients? Think about the types of situations or feelings that may be the most difficult for you to tolerate as a clinician, and discuss self-care and other strategies that you could employ to manage your emotions and listen to your clients without "being engulfed."

KEYWORDS

active-empathic listening	evaluative listening	process
active listening	interpersonal cognitive complexity	simple reflection
affect tolerance	interpreter	summarizing
bottom-up processing	marginal listening	therapeutic listening
clarification	mindfulness	top-down processing
complex reflection	nonverbal immediacy	verbal person
content	paraphrasing	centeredness

FURTHER READING

- Nichols, M. P. (2009). *The lost art of listening: How learning to listen can improve relationships.* New York, NY: Guilford Press.

  This book is an excellent guide to improving your listening skills. The tips provided by Nichols are written for strengthening your interpersonal relationships but are just as easily applied to developing therapeutic listening skills to improve your therapeutic relationships with clients.

- Flickinger, A. (1992). Therapeutic listening. *Phenomenology Pedagogy, 10,* 186–193.

  This article is a compelling personal account of how listening to another can create strong emotions in the listener.

- Fulton, P. R. (2005). Mindfulness as clinical training. In C. K. Germer, R. D. Siegel, & P. R. Fulton (Eds.), *Mindfulness and psychotherapy* (pp. 55–72). New York, NY: Guilford Press.

  If you are interested in more information about how cultivating your own mindfulness practice may enhance your skills as a therapist, this chapter is an excellent guide to how mindfulness is a positive adjunct to clinical training.

- Bays, J. C. (2011). *How to train a wild elephant: And other adventures in mindfulness.* Boston, MA: Shambhala Publications.

  If you have decided to take on mindfulness practice, this book, written by a woman who is both a Zen master and a pediatrician, offers many suggestions for ways to be mindful in your daily life.

Counseling Skills: Empathy and the Therapeutic Alliance

The essential elements appear to be not technical knowledge nor
ideological sophistication, but personal human
qualities—something the therapist experiences, not something
he knows.—Rogers (1965, p. 107)

LEARNING OBJECTIVES

- Identify the nonspecific factors that are closely associated with psychotherapy outcomes
- Understand what makes the therapeutic relationship unique
- Recognize what factors are linked to the relationship between client and therapist: working alliance/therapeutic alliance
- Identify the most important factors for the development of the therapeutic alliance: empathy, emotional attunement, and unconditional positive regard
- Recognize the different ways in which therapists and clients work together to build a strong working alliance
- Identify and name the different modes of therapeutic action in the expressive-supportive continuum
- Understand the meaning of "frame" and its factors within the context of the therapeutic relationship
- Understand the pros and cons of self-disclosure and empathy
- Identify Carl Roger's core necessary conditions for psychotherapy: congruence (genuineness), unconditional positive regard, and accurate empathy
- Understand what can lead to the rupture of the therapeutic alliance
- Explain the different rupture-repair interventions that play an important role in restoring the therapeutic alliance

Research has focused on what factors within therapy are the most relevant to outcomes. Grencavage and Norcross (1990) identified four broad categories of nonspecific factors that are closely associated with psychotherapy outcomes: (a) client characteristics such as hope and faith, or eagerness to seek help; (b) therapist qualities such as warmth, positive regard, being nonjudgmental; (c) change processes like insight, provision of information; and (d) methods of treatment, including specific techniques and procedures. This chapter focuses on the second category of nonspecific factors, those relating to qualities of the therapist.

Because psychotherapy is inherently based on an interpersonal relationship, possessing strong interpersonal skills and being able to demonstrate these skills with clients is central to being a good therapist. Consider novelists and playwrights: these professionals often have a deep understanding of personality development, hidden motivations, the etiology of personal distress, and methods for resolving personal crises and conflicts. Despite this wealth of knowledge, these artists create characters in a bit of a vacuum. Effective counselors are expected to have a similar wealth of understanding *and* be able to communicate and interact with these complex characters in real time.

Among the many therapist–client variables highlighted as being central across diverse types of psychotherapy, the **working alliance** or **therapeutic alliance** is the one with the most research support and endorsement from practitioners (Baldwin, Wampold, & Imel, 2007; Dinger, Strack, Leichsenring, Wilmers, & Schauenberg, 2008; Greencavage & Norcross, 1990; Horvath & Bedi, 2002). The therapeutic alliance refers to the relationship between the client and the therapist and is influenced by a number of interpersonal factors such as empathy, emotional attunement, and unconditional positive regard. In this chapter, we will explore several of the variables that contribute to the building of a strong therapeutic alliance and how to understand and respond to ruptures in the alliance.

UNIQUENESS OF THE THERAPEUTIC RELATIONSHIP

In previous chapters we have focused on the foundations of the therapeutic relationship. With a basic understanding of the theoretical and empirical underpinnings of psychotherapy, we can now move forward to understand what makes the therapeutic relationship unique. Research has consistently demonstrated that factors linked to the *relationship* between client and therapist (rather than specific therapy technique, length of treatment, etc.) are most strongly tied to a positive outcome for the client (Castonguay, Goldfried, Wiser, Raue, & Hayes, 1996; Lambert & Barley, 2001; Orlinsky, Grawe, & Parks, 1994). In this chapter, we will explore some of those factors and discuss how to develop strong connections between client and therapist.

> *It's the relationship that heals, it's the relationship that heals, it's the relationship that heals—my professional rosary.*—Yalom (1989, p. 98)

As students begin to think about careers in the helping professions during their undergraduate years, they often say to their instructors, "I think I would make a good therapist because I'm the person everyone comes to for advice." The idea that therapists are trained to give advice is one of the biggest misconceptions about the process of psychotherapy. Anyone can give advice; therapy, however, is an entirely different process. The relationship between therapist and client is exceptionally unique. It is distinct from the relationships clients have with their friends, family members, clergy, physicians, and other professionals. Although therapists offer a supportive presence to their clients, therapists do not only provide support. Ultimately, the goals of therapy are to help clients discover solutions to the problems that trouble them and keep them from functioning at school, home, or work. Therapy also equips clients to maintain and build upon the gains they have achieved through the therapeutic process.

There are many modes of therapeutic action. You may recall the expressive-supportive continuum in Figure 1.1 in Chapter 1. At the expressive end of the continuum, therapists use interpretation, confrontation, and encouragement to elaborate. On the supportive end of the continuum are empathic validation, advice and praise, and affirmation. Traditionally, interventions on the expressive end of the continuum have been less focused on specific symptoms such as the alleviation of acute anxiety or panic; rather, the emphasis is on increasing the client's level of insight and providing the individual with a greater sense of freedom in his or her daily life. Strategies on the supportive end of the continuum tended to be more focused on relief for specific symptoms. Within more contemporary and integrative approaches to psychotherapy, expert therapists will move back and forth along the expressive-supportive continuum, providing what is needed for the client at different moments and in various stages of life.

Interpretation is the most expressive type of intervention, and it involves helping clients identify aspects of themselves of which they were previously unaware. Interpretative comments are often statements that help the client make new links between thoughts, feelings, behaviors, and relational dynamics. For example, a client began experiencing acute social anxiety, specifically fears of judgment and humiliation, in situations where he was with certain co-workers or acquaintances. The client became so preoccupied that he was unable to speak in these situations. In this case, the client also spoke at length about undesirable personality characteristics of these individuals and his sense that he should like them. He felt that he was a terrible person because he did not like these individuals who were rude, selfish, or narcissistic. An interpretation that was highly effective with this client went something like this: "Perhaps your anxiety around these people is connected to your sense that you don't really like them?" Once the client was able to acknowledge and accept the negative feelings he had about these individuals, he felt significantly less anxious. He experienced a newfound freedom in his social interactions with them and was able to speak up whenever he found himself in similar situations.

Although the term **confrontation** suggests an aggressive or blunt approach, most confrontation in psychotherapy is done gently. The purpose of confrontation is to help the client identify or address thoughts and feelings that they have a tendency to minimize. A client struggling with long-term fertility issues was facing a great deal of pressure from unknowing family members pressuring her to have children. She described her experience of these comments by saying, "It's fine. I really don't mind." The therapist used confrontation by saying, "I think it's easier to say it doesn't bother you than to face the feelings you might have about infertility and this unrelenting pressure you're getting from your family."

Clarification strives to aid the client in articulating something that is difficult to say or pulling together thoughts and feelings that might otherwise seem disparate. This is similar to rephrasing but requires more active participation on the part of the therapist. For example, if a client contradicts himself or backtracks on something he has said, it might be helpful to clarify by stating, "It sounds like you're not quite sure how you feel about all of this. What I'm hearing is that you have some mixed feelings about it." This type of clarification can open the door for the client to explore in greater depth what he is experiencing.

Encouragement to elaborate is a tool that is often used during the interviewing process or when clients are sharing new information during the process of therapy. This is one of the most commonly used interventions by therapists of all theoretical orientations. Open-ended questions (as opposed to questions that can be answered with a simple "yes" or "no") are particularly helpful when encouraging a client to elaborate. The therapist might simply say, "Can you tell me more about that?" or, "You mentioned that you were feeling depressed yesterday. What was happening before you noticed that feeling?" Therapy is unique from other interpersonal interactions in that the focus is primarily on the client's experience. Many clients do not have the opportunity in their day-to-day lives to speak at length about their thoughts and feelings with an attentive listener. By providing clients with the time and space to speak at length about themselves, the therapist is expressing genuine curiosity and creating a therapeutic environment for the client.

This chapter is centered on the importance of empathy in psychotherapy. Empathy can be expressed in many different ways. **Empathic validation** is when the therapist's empathic attunement is verbalized. Many theorists (Kohut, 1971, 1984; Ornstein, 1996; Rogers, 1951, 1961) have argued that empathy is the central element of psychotherapy and produces change in clients' lives. Sometimes, simply sitting with clients through their suffering is a form of empathic validation. The therapist's presence and ability to contain overwhelming emotions often communicates empathy. Empathic validation is often communicated with statements such as, "It sounds like that was very difficult for you," or, "I imagine that it felt like such a relief to say that to your husband." Later in this chapter, we will address the importance of *accurate* empathy and the importance of truly understanding what the client is feeling before making a validating statement.

Advice and **praise** are often linked together and they are used to suggest or reinforce certain behaviors or activities. Historically, these two interventions have been more closely aligned with cognitive behavioral interventions in psychotherapy. They were less likely to be associated with psychodynamic approaches because they depart from that theoretical perspective's emphasis on the neutrality of the therapist. This dichotomy—between cognitive behavioral and psychodynamic approaches—is one that is becoming less well-defined. With practice, therapists can move fluidly between offering advice and praise and using interventions closer to the expressive end of the continuum.

Advice and praise should always be used with the client's autonomy in mind. Therapists often suggest certain behaviors, assign homework to clients, and make recommendations about next steps. When clients engage effectively in treatment and take risks (e.g., confronting a previously feared situation or having a difficult conversation with a family member), therapists may offer positive feedback about these behaviors in order to reinforce them. These interventions can be very supportive and helpful, but they should never supersede the client's sense of personal agency. Later in the text, we will discuss issues of resistance and ambivalence (see Chapter 10) that may need to be addressed prior to offering advice and/or praise.

Perhaps the simplest form of therapeutic intervention is **affirmation**, which is defined as brief comments that are offered in support of what the client is saying. This includes nonverbal responses such as nodding and empathic affect as well as comments like, "I see," "Uh-huh," and, "Yes, I understand." Many beginning therapists have a tendency to overuse affirmation in an attempt to connect with clients. These responses can be used judiciously and still have a great impact, letting the client know that the therapist is listening and following what the client is saying.

BOX 7.1

What Really Happens in Therapy?

Although the purpose of this book is to describe the basic skills, interventions, and attitudes that make for a successful counseling relationship, we acknowledge that much of what we do is more art than science. There are many good resources available that may enrich your understanding of what actually happens within the therapeutic situation. Here are several recommendations:

- *Every Day Gets a Little Closer: A Twice-Told Therapy* (1974) is a legendary text written by Irvin D. Yalom and his client, Ginny Elkin. As the subtitle of the book suggests, Dr. Yalom and his client tell the story of their ongoing therapy from their own perspective. The book offers reflections from both therapist and client on each session as well as their reactions to each other's writing.
- Paul Wachtel's *Inside the Session: What Really Happens in Psychotherapy* (2011) provides verbatim transcripts of several sessions of psychodynamic psychotherapy, along with Wachtel's reflections and critiques of his own interventions.
- Finally, The Moth is a nonprofit organization dedicated to the art and craft of storytelling. They often broadcast stories relevant to the practice of psychotherapy. One story in particular allows listeners to go inside the world of a therapist working with a client who is dying of cancer. You can hear this story and many others by visiting www.prx .org/themoth and looking for episode 1,304, which aired on January 22, 2012. In this episode, Dr. Martha Manning shares her experience working with a terminally ill client.

Defining the Therapeutic Relationship

Unlike relationships with family and friends, a client's interactions with his or her therapist are typically characterized by certain "ground rules." These ground rules allow patients to feel safe and secure as they go through the process of therapeutic discovery. In addition to the basic policies and procedures that create a framework for the therapeutic relationship, there is a certain therapeutic stance that includes a particular type of listening, warmth, and empathy. Each of these aspects helps define the therapeutic relationship and make it distinct from other interpersonal relationships.

The Frame

Some clinicians refer to the ground rules for therapy as the **frame**. In essence, adherence to a basic system of providing therapy creates a framework of safety and security for the client. The term "frame" is frequently used within a psycho-dynamic orientation; however, there is general agreement among therapists of all theoretical perspectives that having a framework that remains constant is a requirement for ethical practice. Maintaining the frame—in terms of fees, time, confidentiality, and a safe environment—protects the therapeutic process and creates an environment in which the therapist can truly act in the best interest of the client. If there were no guiding principles for therapy or these were not clearly stated at the outset, it would be difficult for both parties to know what to expect.

This includes aspects of the relationship such as the time and length of the meeting, the fee structure, and the way in which the two parties interact. Most therapists make a concerted effort to begin and end sessions on time. There is an agreed-upon fee paid by the client. This fee is the only aspect of the relationship in which the client "cares for" the therapist. Otherwise, it is primarily the therapist's job to serve as caretaker. Whereas we expect reciprocity in our relationships with friends and family in terms of sharing problems and stories with one another, this is not the case in clinical work. Additionally, we maintain certain boundaries with our clients that might seem artificial if they were in place in a friendship. Although some therapists may choose to hug patients at the end of treatment or under other special circumstances, there is usually a minimal degree of physical touch. If a therapist is behaving ethically, he or she will not be physically intimate with patients or fall in love with a patient (see Chapter 2).

A balance must be struck between flexibility and maintaining appropriate boundaries. Some theorists (Eeissler, 1953; Langs, 1977) have taken an extreme stance on the ground rules for psychotherapy, suggesting that modifications should be made only in extreme emergencies. It is important that therapists maintain flexibility in the frame and be amenable to requests from clients to make modifications when necessary (Gold & Cherry, 1997), without being overly accommodating. All counselors will eventually be asked by a client to adjust their fees, extend the length of the session, or be asked questions that may feel intrusive. It is essential that counselors be clear about what they are willing and able to alter and what policies and practices they will consistently follow. This reflects the ongoing tension in the therapeutic relationship: the necessity to be responsive to the client's needs and circumstances while being respectful of one's own needs for autonomy and professionalism.

Often times, clients seeking therapy for the first time or clients with cultural backgrounds that differ from the therapist's may respond negatively to the ground rules of this unique relationship. Consistently starting and ending the session on time may be interpreted by some clients as unnecessarily rigid or unwelcoming. It is often necessary to explicitly discuss the need for a framework and the ways in which this structure is intended to protect the rights and interests of the client. Similarly, therapists should carefully consider ways in which certain policies may be counter-therapeutic. For example, rigid adherence to fee structures may exclude economically disadvantaged clients or prevent clients experiencing financial hardship from continuing in psychotherapy.

Although counseling is intended to serve the client's needs, it is also important that the therapist have some basic needs met. The therapist should be paid adequately for the services provided, though the definition of "adequately" varies widely. There are myriad intricacies of setting fees and collecting payment. For example, a client called her therapist the day before their weekly session (which happened to fall on the client's birthday) and said she did not have the money to pay for the upcoming session. Both client and therapist had agreed at the outset of treatment that the client would pay at each meeting rather than at the end of the month. The client asked the therapist to see her "just this week" without payment, insisting that if she could not see the therapist on her birthday she would "lose it." The client suggested she could pay five dollars additional for each subsequent week until the cost of this birthday session had been fulfilled. The therapist sought consultation with a colleague and discussed her desire to care for the client, who was experiencing financial hardship and strong feelings around her birthday. She also discussed her feelings of being taken advantage of and her fears that this would become a pattern in which the client would ask more and more of her. How would you handle this situation?

Therapists must feel safe from harm and be equipped to protect themselves from emotional or psychological intrusions on the part of clients. The need for safety may trump typical aspects of the frame, which require a quiet and private meeting place free from distraction. When working on an acute inpatient unit, therapists may meet with their clients in the day room or another public space in order to insure their safety. Although certainly less dangerous, questions about the therapist's personal life may also threaten the traditional stance that therapists remain largely anonymous and neutral. These questions may be posed by clients for many reasons. It may be an attempt to identify with the therapist or assess the therapist's ability to understand the client's experience.

Personal questions may be a way to avoid confronting one's own issues or may be a way to challenge the therapist. These aspects of practice are highly individual, and novice therapists should consider carefully what type of information they feel comfortable sharing if asked. Clients might ask about the therapist's sexual orientation, religion, marital status, age, or hobbies. Whether to answer such questions depends on the situation, the therapist's comfort level, the possible therapeutic or counter-therapeutic effects of answers, what the therapist knows of the client's history and motivations for asking, as well as other factors. Consider the following questions that therapists have been asked and evaluate the possible motivations behind the question and the potential consequences of answering or not answering them.

- Where do you get your hair done?
- How long have you been at this office?
- Where are you going on vacation?

- Did you watch the Super Bowl?
- Have you read the book *50 Shades of Grey*?
- Have you ever been depressed?
- Do you know what it feels like to have one of your parents die?
- Are you in a relationship?

Each of these questions is presented without any context in order to help you consider the many possible motivations and situations in which they may have been asked. Although it may be difficult to anticipate how one would respond to each question, it is important to reflect on what it might feel like to be asked.

There may also be situations in which the therapist identifies with the client's experience or, for some other reason, wants to share something personal. This type of sharing, often referred to as **self-disclosure**, should be done carefully and sparingly. When the therapist feels compelled to volunteer information, she must first consider her own motivations. Disclosing personal information may be a way to genuinely connect with the client, but it may have undesired effects. When the content of therapy moves away from the client's own experience and becomes about the therapist, it may threaten the therapeutic alliance. On the other hand, there are times when this type of spontaneity and transparency can be respectful and empathic.

Listening and Attending to Clients

Our interactions with clergy, physicians, and other professionals are usually built around seeking direction or guidance from someone with specialized knowledge. Although therapists do have advanced training in how to conduct psychotherapy, it is clients themselves that are truly the experts on their own experiences. The task of the therapist is to guide clients to identify for themselves what has been hindering their ability to change and to collaborate with clients to discover mechanisms for change. This process of discovery is one of the most complex and nuanced within clinical work. It requires active listening and attending to the client's experience, a profound degree of trust, and an unusual level of empathy.

As discussed in detail in Chapter 6, the type of listening that takes place in clinical work is often referred to as "**therapeutic listening**." It is a unique way of connecting with another person and has been likened to the process of becoming completely absorbed in a musical performance or a book (Jones & Cutcliffe, 2009). It requires a certain degree of dissociation from your everyday worries and concerns so that you can be totally transported into the client's life and experiences. Maintaining this purposeful and highly attentive type of listening is often an enormous challenge for newcomers to clinical work. If you are listening well, it is not uncommon to hear clients say something like, "I talk to people all week, but this is the only place I actually feel *heard*."

In our daily lives, we frequently listen with one ear and are already formulating what we might say in response; or we let our minds wander to our own concerns or wild associations to what the person is saying. Additionally, in our relationships outside of the consultation room, we tend to focus primarily on the content of what the person is saying rather than the process. Attending to the client's experience involves being keenly aware of both content *and* process.

While we are listening, we are also paying attention to how things are being said and what is being left out or avoided and looking for body language or expressions of affect that may be incongruous with what the person is saying.

Trust and Empathy

Trust and empathy are also aspects of the therapeutic relationship that make it distinct from other types of relationships. Although we have other people in our lives that we trust and connect with, the work of therapy involves being profoundly vulnerable in a way that is unusual in our day-to-day interactions with others. Clients come to therapy because they have a problem they have been unable to solve and are often unable to share with another person. Therapists are the keepers of many, many secrets. But how do clients know they can trust their therapist?

The relationship between client and therapist is afforded a very high degree of confidentiality, more protected than most other professional relationships. But simply telling clients, "Everything you say here is confidential," is not enough to earn their trust. As a therapist, you must say what you mean and mean what you say. The expectation is that you will truly enter into the client's world as a companion through his or her struggles. It is not enough to convey sympathy, as we do in most of our relationships. Rather, we must have an empathic attitude toward the patient. Kohut (1984, p. 82) defined empathy as "the capacity to think and feel oneself into the inner life of another person." It is an orientation toward the other that moves far beyond sympathy. Similarly, Atticus Finch, a central character in *To Kill a Mockingbird*, says to his daughter, "You never really understand a person until you consider things from his point of view—until you climb into his skin and walk around in it" (Lee, 1960, p. 30). To truly provide a safe and empathic environment to the client, the therapist must put aside her own assumptions, beliefs, and biases in favor of the client's emotional world.

Carl Rogers pioneered the person-centered or client-centered approach, and therapists from nearly all theoretical perspectives have integrated many of Rogers' core concepts into their work. Rogers (1961) wrote about the importance of the three core conditions necessary for psychotherapy: congruence (or genuineness), unconditional positive regard, and accurate empathy. These components of the therapeutic relationship are central to the development of trust within the therapist–client dyad.

Congruence or **genuineness** refers to consistency in a person's thoughts, feelings, and behavior. Wilkins (2000) has described it as "openness towards one's self" (p. 30). Congruent therapists behave in a way that is consistent and integrated. They are often described by clients and supervisors as genuine, authentic, and comfortable with their clients. Practicing genuineness requires awareness and acceptance of feelings and attitudes that exist within yourself (Rogers, 1961). Lietaer (1984, p. 44) describes it this way:

> The more I accept myself and am able to be present in a comfortable way with everything that bubbles up in me, without fear or defense, the more I can be receptive to everything that lives in my client. Without this openness, without this acceptance, it is not possible to let the experience of my client unfold, to let it come to life fully.

Effective congruence requires the therapist to temper the need for authenticity and transparency with caring for the client's welfare. Congruence does not mean that the therapist should engage in excessive self-disclosure or say things that will detract from the therapeutic focus of the relationship. Rogers's approach to psychotherapy is aptly called "client-centered" or "person-centered," emphasizing that all interventions and interactions should center on the well-being, growth, and development of the client.

Being genuine should serve the needs of the client rather than the needs of the therapist. Gazda, Asbury, Balzer, Childers, and Walters (1984) suggest several questions that clinicians can ask themselves before disclosing their genuine reactions and feelings in the moment with a client: "Who is it for? Am I doing this for me, the other person, or to impress those who observe?" (p. 111). Congruence requires that the clinician consider her own motives before, during, and after spontaneously expressing her own internal experience. The goal is for the clinician to be as transparent and honest as possible and to avoid deceiving the client or being inauthentic. For example, if a client speaks in a rapid and somewhat disorganized manner for several minutes and then pauses briefly to say, "Do you think this sounds crazy?" how might you respond? An incongruent response would be something like, "No, not at all. You're making perfect sense." Alternatively, you might say, "I get the sense that what you're sharing with me is very overwhelming and may be difficult to organize in your mind. Maybe we can go back to the beginning so we can both be on the same page with what is going on."

Unconditional positive regard is a concept that has been written about extensively but can be difficult to understand and fully integrate into the therapeutic situation. Rogers (1951) has described unconditional positive regard as an attitude that allows the client to think, "I can be the real me, no pretenses" (pp. 208–209). A counselor who is able to demonstrate unconditional positive regard deeply values her clients' humanity and is able to accept them fully, without judgment. This means that the therapist sees the client as an autonomous individual with his or her own feelings and experiences. When the therapist is able to provide this type of therapeutic environment, she wholly values the client, and conditions are not placed on the client in order to earn or achieve self-worth. Whereas the concept of unconditional positive regard makes sense at the outset, and we can all agree that therapists should not be judgmental, putting it into practice can be challenging at times. Imagine you are working with a client who relapses after 10 months of sobriety. You are likely to feel disappointed, frustrated that all the work you have done together has been undone, and perhaps even angry. How will you demonstrate unconditional positive regard to this type of client?

In contrast, Wilkins (2000) describes **conditional positive regard** as "the offering of warmth, respect, acceptance, etc. only when the other fulfils some particular expectation, desire or requirement" (p. 25). Rogers posited that many children experienced this type of regard from their parents and thus grew up to have many conditions built up around their self-worth.

Wilkins also describes his work with a client who challenged his liberal sensibilities by speaking at length about his love of the military and his hatred of women and African Americans. Through much self-reflection and reading of professional resources, Wilkins found himself being more able to adopt an attitude of unconditional positive regard. As he writes,

> Part of my change lay in the realisation that "acceptance," *unconditional* positive regard was exactly that—the issue of my approval or disapproval, my judgment of the views and way of being of another, was impertinent and immaterial...he had racist and misogynist views, but these were essential to his way of being in the world. He was doing the best he could, given his antecedents and the way he perceived the world to be. (2000, p. 28)

In addition to confronting beliefs and values that clients possess that are in contrast to the counselor's own, therapists often encounter clients who are described by others as "attention seeking" or "manipulative." These commonly used terms and the underlying attitudes they reveal can impede the therapist's ability to experience unconditional positive regard. Behaviors that are sometimes described as "attention seeking," in fact, reveal the client's unrecognized need for support. For example, a client came in each week and, without fail, described in detail a different way she was considering committing suicide. She would then conclude the session with all the reasons she would never carry out this very detailed plan. After several months of this, and once she had a thorough understanding of the client's developmental history, the therapist asked, "I wonder if there is something that makes you feel you have to talk about plans for suicide each week." Weeping, the client said, "I'm just afraid that if I don't have a crisis you won't see me anymore." This intervention exemplifies accurate empathy and also helped the therapy progress significantly.

Earlier in this chapter, we described how the use of empathic validation can be helpful in the therapeutic situation. Rogers' third core condition, the concept of **accurate empathy**, highlights the importance of the therapist accurately and sensitively understanding the client's experience and his or her feelings. This means that the therapist must understand the client on the client's own terms. Empathy is closely related to unconditional positive regard, but the two constructs differ. Accurate empathy refers to the therapist's ability to listen sensitively and to accurately *experience* the client's feelings in the here-and-now. Unconditional positive regard does not require the therapist to feel the same feelings or to even identify with the client's experience. Rather, unconditional positive regard is a therapeutic stance based on acceptance of the client, regardless of what they think, feel, or do. Kohut (1978) described empathy as "a fundamental mode of human relatedness, the recognition of the self in the other; it is the accepting, confirming and understanding human echo" (pp. 704–705). Although it is human nature to view others through one's own lens, in therapy, the idea is to truly enter into the client's worldview and experience of life. Empathic understanding involves entering into the private perceptual world of another person and being able to sense the meaning of what the client is saying and feeling. Empirical research on this construct suggests that empathy accounts for as much (and probably more) of the variance in outcomes in psychotherapy than does the specific interventions the therapist uses (Greenberg, Watson, Elliot, & Bohart, 2001).

Consider the following scenarios and talk them over with a classmate or your instructor to see if you can ascertain what the client may be feeling and experiencing.

Client 1: I love that I can figure out what people want from me and I'm able to contort myself to meet their expectations. It's like I don't even know who I really am anymore.

Client 2: Your confidentiality policy is terrible. You told me that if I'm suicidal you might have to tell someone about it so I guess that means I can never talk about those things here.

Client 3: My daughter finally left for college. It's a huge change. I feel like I have to get to know my wife all over again.

Some of these comments may reflect conflicted feelings or an experience that is very different from your own. Is there additional information you would need before knowing how to experience accurate empathy?

Developing Empathy

There is no easy path or clear prescription for developing empathy. Contemporary neuroscience research suggests that empathy is mediated by the human mirror neuron system (MNS). The MNS is thought to allow primates and humans to imitate one another and to mediate the ability to feel empathy for another's experience (Jabbi, Swart, & Keysers, 2007; Kaplan & Iacoboni, 2006; Pfeifer, Iacoboni, Mazziotta, & Dapretto, 2007). There is evidence that the MNS is inhibited in individuals with autism spectrum disorders, thus limiting their capacity for imitation and empathy (Dapretto et al., 2006; Shamay-Tsory, Tomer, Yaniv, & Aharon-Peretz, 2002). The research base for neurochemical correlates of empathy is still in its infancy and in no way forecloses the possibility for further growth and development of one's own empathic abilities. In fact, the current research suggests that we are hard-wired for empathic understanding.

There are many ways to increase one's own ability to empathize with others. All the paths to empathy development are experiential. Engaging in service learning or volunteer activities is one way to enter into someone else's world. By coming into contact with individuals whose life experiences are different from one's own, it may be possible to appreciate alternative ways of being. Although it can be difficult to identify with and feel compassion for individuals who are angry, harsh, or withholding, it is possible to develop an empathic response. One way to develop this skill is to do so internally when you encounter such a person in your daily activities. Although you are not in a therapeutic role, it is a useful exercise to attempt to empathize with those you might otherwise dismiss or find annoying. Empathy is not simply an intellectual exercise; it is a complex response to suffering that has cognitive, affective, and motor components (Baird, Scheffer, & Wilson, 2011). Cognitive aspects of empathy are related to Theory of Mind or the ability to think about another person's thinking. This is also referred to as metacognition. Affective components of empathy are often measured as heart rate and arousal; however, these are signals that point to an unobservable experience of emotion. Motor empathy is usually measured as facial mimicry, the ability to frown or smile in congruence with another person. This type of empathy is typically impaired in individuals with autism spectrum disorders and conduct disorder (Bons et al., 2013).

BOX 7.2

Empathy

Much of the research on empathy has been done with primates and other animals. For a great introduction to this research, watch Frans de Waal's TED talk on Moral Behavior in Animals (www.youtube.com /watch?v=GcJxRqTs5nk). Sam Richards also has a TED talk where he challenges viewers to put themselves in the shoes of an Iraqi insurgent (www .ted.com/talks/sam_richards_a_radical_experiment_in_empathy.html), a great exercise in building empathy.

When Empathy Is Not Optimal

There has been much written about the importance of empathy in psychotherapy and its role in producing change in clients. A great deal of emphasis has been placed on the development of empathy within the therapist (see previous section). There is a sense that empathic understanding is the only optimal response to the client's experience. Less has been written about the inherent conflict that may arise between congruence and accurate empathy. The issue of remaining authentic in the therapeutic situation is a complex one. As we discussed earlier in this chapter, Rogers uses the term "congruence" to describe a type of authenticity and consistency within the therapist. One of the reasons this can be difficult, particularly for novice therapists or for clinicians working with challenging clients, is that congruence and empathy may conflict with one another.

If one is to be truly authentic and genuine, it seems unlikely that she will always experience empathy for the other. Bacal (1998) has written about and questioned whether empathic attunement is always the optimal response. He explains that although the optimal therapeutic situation may involve empathy and acceptance, it is not synonymous with them. In fact, it can sometimes be a powerful and therapeutic experience when a therapist shares her own subjective and divergent experience with the client (Bacal & Carlton, 2010). This type of self-disclosure should be done carefully and with great respect for the client's own worldview.

While maintaining beneficence toward the client and upholding one's obligations to professional ethics, the therapist can share her own perspective. This may allow the client to consider an alternative way of thinking and reframe his or her understanding of a particular situation or interaction. For example, a client continually experienced others—her neighbors, co-workers, store clerks, and the like—as hostile and aggressive and was asked by the therapist to provide more detail about these interactions by giving specific examples (e.g., encouragement to elaborate). As the therapist listened to the examples, she began to wonder if the client was misinterpreting these individuals' words and actions and shared this divergent perspective while acknowledging the client's subjective experience. Here is a sample of the exchange during a session:

Client: Well, every time I go to the deli, the guy at the counter barely makes eye contact. It's like he can't wait to be rid of me. And the woman in the elevator the other day didn't even say "hello." She just nodded like you would nod to a police officer or a stranger on the street. I see her all the time in the building. She definitely has something against me. She can't even muster up a one-word greeting.

Therapist: It seems like everywhere you go, you feel like you're unwanted and unacknowledged.

Client: Yes. Exactly. No one wants me around.

Therapist: One of the tricky things about these interactions is that it's hard for us to really know what these people were thinking. We just have their behavior to go on. And with such limited information, it occurs to me that there might be other ways to interpret the lack of eye contact or restrained greeting that you experienced.

Client: Really? I don't think so…it's hard to imagine. Can you give me an example?

Therapist: Well, I wonder if perhaps there were a lot of people in line with you at the deli counter, and the staff was trying to work as quickly as possible without getting caught up in the niceties. Not the best customer service, perhaps, but maybe it was more reflective of what was going on with him and less about how he felt about you.

Client: It was Saturday afternoon, right before the storm. The place was a zoo. Hmmm…I never thought about it that way.

This interaction between client and therapist highlights the importance of balancing authenticity with empathy. By gently reflecting on her own interpretation of the events, the therapist was able to introduce a new perspective to the client. This type of intervention may be helpful in increasing the client's capacity for cognitive flexibility and perspective-taking. Accurate empathy requires that the therapist express empathy whenever possible; however, if the therapist's subjective experience of the material significantly diverges from the client's, there are therapeutic ways to share this perspective. Later in this chapter, we will present several clinical cases that further elucidate how to remain client-centered while maintaining a high degree of authenticity.

The Therapeutic Alliance

Being an effective therapist requires more than in-depth knowledge of strategies aimed at facilitating change for the client. Experienced clinicians know that proficiency in therapeutic techniques is a necessary, but not sufficient, condition for successful treatment. The work of therapy takes place within the context of the interpersonal relationship between the therapist and the client, and learning how to develop a strong relationship with clients is a critical aspect of becoming a skilled clinician. It is difficult, if not impossible, to untangle the technical interventions from the relationship factors that contribute to the alliance because all procedures delivered take place in the context of a real interpersonal relationship.

The **therapeutic alliance**, sometimes referred to as the *working alliance*, spans theoretical orientations and treatment modalities, and there is a body of empirical research that supports the notion that it is significantly responsible for positive outcome. Lambert and Barley (2001) conducted a meta-analysis of psychotherapy outcome research across a wide range of theoretical orientations, disorders, and methods of measuring client and therapist characteristics, and found that the client–therapist relationship factors (or *common factors*) contribute the most to positive outcome. Common factors include many of the client–therapist relationship constructs discussed in this chapter, such as empathy, warmth, congruence, and therapeutic alliance. Lambert and Barley (2001) found that specific therapeutic techniques only accounted for 15% of the variance in outcome, whereas common factors accounted for approximately 30% of the improvement in psychotherapy. It is clear that the therapeutic relationship and the therapist's characteristics, which foster and maintain this alliance with the client, are vital to the success of psychotherapy.

What Is Therapeutic Alliance and Why Does It Matter?

Therapeutic alliance is a trans-theoretical construct that has been examined by therapists and researchers across theoretical orientations, including psychodynamic, cognitive behavioral, interpersonal, family systems, and supportive (Arnow et al., 2013; Crits-Christoph, Barber, & Kurcias, 1993; Gaston, Thompson, Gallagher, Cournoyer, & Gagnon, 1998; Isserlin & Couturier, 2012; Krupnick et al., 1996; Samstag et al., 2008; Strauss et al., 2006). It has also been evaluated across a variety of therapeutic modalities, including psychotherapy, pharmacotherapy, case management, and primary care behavioral health settings (Corso et al., 2012). The relationship between therapist and client has been characterized in several different ways. Carl Rogers (1957) emphasized the role of the therapeutic relationship as the major vehicle of change, and he specified the active components of the therapeutic relationship as congruence, unconditional positive regard, and empathy. Whereas Rogers felt that therapy would be successful when the therapist provided these necessary conditions and nothing more, most other definitions of therapeutic alliance describe it as the context for effectively delivering specific counseling strategies.

Therapeutic alliance has been conceptualized as the collaborative working relationship between the therapist and client and the interpersonal bond that develops due to working together to meet therapy goals (Dufi & Bedi, 2010). Bordin (1976) developed a comprehensive definition of the therapeutic alliance that breaks the concept into three different parts: agreement between the therapist and the patient on the *tasks* of therapy, agreement on the *goals*, and the strength of the *bond* between the therapist and the client. Specifically, a good therapeutic alliance includes agreement between therapist and client on the relevance and effectiveness of therapy tasks, agreement on the goals of the intervention, and a positive personal attachment. Similarly, Luborsky (1984) defined therapeutic alliance as "the degree to which the patient experiences the relationship with the therapist as helpful in achieving his or her goals" (p. 6). Other theorists have diverged from this consensus on the meaning of therapeutic alliance to focus on more fundamental aspects of human interaction, such as **complementarity** and **intersubjectivity** (Henry & Strupp, 1994; Safran & Muran, 2006). Complementarity refers to the tendency of one person's actions to evoke corresponding reactions from another person, essentially cause and effect. When someone behaves in a hostile manner, the person on the receiving end is likely to feel defensive. Intersubjectivity emphasizes the co-construction of emotional experience. Both therapist and client bring individual histories, perceptual styles, emotions, and interpersonal dynamics to their interactions. Each one is dependent upon the other and their subjective experiences inform and help create a particular dynamic.

Not only is therapeutic alliance important in terms of predicting positive treatment outcomes, but it is also strongly related to the likelihood that clients will remain in therapy. A recent meta-analysis of 11 empirical studies indicated that there is a moderately strong relationship between psychotherapy dropout and therapeutic alliance (Sharf, Primavera, & Diener, 2010). Specifically, clients who have a poorer sense of therapeutic alliance are more likely to drop out of therapy prematurely.

How to Build Therapeutic Alliance

There are several important therapist behaviors that have been identified by clients as particularly helpful in establishing a good therapeutic relationship. Duff and Bedi (2010) found that behaviors in two major categories were strongly related to clients and therapists experiencing a good therapeutic alliance. The first major category is *validation behaviors* and includes asking questions, making encouraging comments, identifying and reflecting back the client's feelings, making positive comments about the client, and validating the client's experience. The next category is *physical attending skills* and includes verbal and nonverbal communication or attention to the client such as making eye contact, greeting the client with a smile, referring to details discussed in previous sessions, being honest, sitting still without fidgeting, and facing the client.

Clinical reports have suggested that the therapeutic alliance in the early phases of treatment, before the client truly has a sense of the therapist, may be determined by what the client brings to therapy. These have been referred to in the literature as "expectancy effects" (Lambert & Barley, 2001). Therapeutic alliance is a wholly interpersonal variable that is influenced by the client's expectations, previous relationships, prior experiences of therapy, and a myriad of other variables. The client enters the therapeutic situation with these things in tow, and the therapist responds to them. The importance of client factors in determining the quality of the therapeutic alliance suggests that therapeutic alliance is heavily dependent on how the therapist responds to the client as the treatment progresses (Crits-Cristoph, Barber, & Kurcias, 1993).

A client may be predisposed to a good or poor therapeutic alliance due to his or her own attachment status. Attachment style is an enduring interpersonal style developed in early childhood through the relationship with the primary caregiver (e.g., mother or father) and elaborated across the life span. There are four primary attachment styles—secure, avoidant, ambivalent/anxious, and disorganized—as described by Ainsworth Blehar, Waters, and Wall (1978). In a meta-analytic review, Diener and Monroe (2011) found that a more positive therapeutic alliance was associated with secure attachment style, and poorer alliance with avoidant and ambivalent styles.

Attachment style helps determine how an individual will relate to others in a vast array of domains. Secure and insecure attachment styles are developed early in life and are relatively consistent across different interpersonal arenas. As a result, we would expect that a client's attachment style would greatly influence the evolution and nature of the therapeutic relationship. Therefore, it is important to attend to attachment-related patterns and develop an understanding about how different attachment styles may enhance or detract from the therapeutic process. A client reported that his parents left him with his grandmother at 2 weeks of age so his parents could travel the globe for 6 months. Although he had no memory of this time period, he believed that it affected his relationships with others, especially because he had never been able to sustain a romantic relationship for more than a few weeks. In order to bolster the alliance, the therapist was careful to monitor the client's thoughts and feelings throughout treatment, especially after the client had been particularly vulnerable or there had been a shared experience of interpersonal closeness between the two. This conscious attunement allowed the client to speak about his fears of loss and to work through problems that often emerged in his romantic relationships as well.

Similarly, the therapist's attachment style may also influence the development of therapeutic alliance. Research in this area suggests that therapists with more anxious and preoccupied attachment styles tend to have poorer therapeutic alliance with their clients (Dinger Strack, Sachsse, & Schauenburg, 2009; Sauer, Lopez, & Gormley, 2003). Those therapists with attachment anxiety are more likely to talk frequently, be overly deferential and supportive of the client, and to seek out validation of their own performance as a therapist. Although this overattending to the client may initially produce positive feelings in clients for whom the attention is welcome, over time, it may become infantilizing or patronizing. Therapists with secure attachment styles are more equipped to endure the natural ebb and flow of the therapeutic relationship and are better able to respond nondefensively to clients' questions and concerns.

Ruptures and Repair of the Therapeutic Alliance

Building a strong therapeutic alliance is integral to counseling, but there are times when the alliance changes during treatment. Although we hope that the alliance becomes stronger during the course of counseling, there are times when the alliance is ruptured. An alliance rupture is a rift between the therapist and client that momentarily or permanently prevents true encounters from taking place in therapy. Anything from a subtle, fleeting miscommunication between therapist and client or some major barrier to the initial establishment of the alliance can be considered a rupture in the therapeutic alliance. Ruptures vary in intensity and duration and, if not addressed, can lead to treatment failure or early termination of treatment.

Safran, Muran, and Eubanks-Carter (2011) conceptualize ruptures in the therapeutic alliance as consisting of disagreements about the tasks of therapy, the goals of treatment, or nonspecific strains in the client–therapist relationship. These types of ruptures may happen concurrently and may have effects on both the client and the therapist. Clients may feel misunderstood or criticized by the therapist in a particular moment. Simultaneously, therapists may feel frustrated or misunderstood themselves. In a small qualitative study, clients and therapists were individually interviewed 1 week after experiencing a rupture in the therapeutic alliance (Coutinho, Ribeiro, Hill, & Safran, 2011). Most reported that the rupture was a repetition of a previous problem in the client–therapist relationship and often emerged when the client was not ready to respond to the therapist's intervention. The authors provide several examples of this type of precipitant. One therapist in the study explained, "For the first time I confronted the client with the possibility of changing her needs instead of expecting others to change their behaviors" (Coutinho et al., 2011, p. 532). Both members of the dyad interviewed reported feeling confused and ambivalent and experiencing intense negative emotions. If there are strains like this on the client–therapist alliance, it may be difficult for the client and therapist to come to agreement on the goals or tasks of therapy.

Cultural incongruence between the therapist and client may also lead to problems within the therapeutic alliance (Gaztambide, 2012). For example, a Caucasian American therapist who values autonomy and independence may have difficulties with a client of a different cultural and ethnic background who values interdependence, familial piety, or communal affiliation. This discrepancy in worldviews may be a source of incongruence resulting in a rupture in the therapeutic alliance. The complex power dynamic that is inherent in the client–therapist relationship may also implicitly lead to a rupture. This may manifest itself in clients who are overly deferential, disengaged, or withdrawn. Close attunement to the process of psychotherapy and the relational aspects of treatment can assist therapists in identifying and repairing breakdowns in the therapeutic relationship.

BOX 7.3

Spotlight on Culture

Ruptures in the therapeutic relationship happen for many reasons, often because there is incongruence between therapist and client. The discontinuity that leads to rupture may be because of differing views on the goals of treatment, the pace of change, personal values, or interpersonal styles. At times these differences can feel very personal and may trigger strong countertransference reactions (see Chapter 9) in the clinician.

George is a therapist who self-identifies as Muslim and Iranian. This identity is not clearly evident to clients or acquaintances, as he does not have an obviously Middle Eastern last name, is light-skinned, and speaks English fluently and without an accent. A client of his spoke negatively about African Americans, and George made a mental note of these statements but did not comment on them. Several weeks later, the same client began expressing anti-Muslim sentiments, and this provoked a very strong and negative reaction in George. He found himself unable to continue listening to the client, as

(continued)

(continued)

he felt attacked and became preoccupied with feelings of anger. The client's comments had stopped George in his tracks. He felt paralyzed, unable to move on. He and the client were experiencing a rupture, although the client was unaware of the impact his comments were having on George.

After consultation with a trusted colleague, George was able to bring up this incident with the client and utilize it for the client's benefit. George disclosed his ethnic identity to the client and revealed that these comments had affected him in a negative way. Because there was a strong therapeutic bond, therapist and client were able to talk about this exchange as an example of how the client may inadvertently alienate people around him. One of the client's primary interpersonal problems was difficulty maintaining satisfying friendships. Now they had a prime opportunity to think together about how the client's values and discriminatory attitudes might create barriers to forming closer relationships. Outside of this therapeutic moment, George also took time to consider his reticence about the client's earlier comments about African Americans. For George, when the comments became more personal and were targeted at his own ethnic group, he became activated to address them. In retrospect he was able to consider how, if he were White or Asian, he might not have addressed this obviously problematic style of interaction so directly with the client.

In this example, there are several critical elements that made the interaction ultimately therapeutic. This counselor and his client had a strong therapeutic bond that allowed them to speak openly about a rupture. The therapist was able to be thoughtful and measured in his response to the client and did not react in anger or with accusation. He also sought consultation with a trusted colleague in order to help him manage the situation and his feelings about it. The rupture also offered a clear parallel to the struggles the client was facing in his interpersonal relationships.

Whereas ruptures in the therapeutic alliance may represent a challenge to the progression of therapy, it is also possible that these difficulties may represent an opportunity for growth. Safran (1998) views the alliance rupture as an important therapeutic juncture for three reasons. First and foremost, this is a point at which a rupture must be repaired to help clients continue with therapy and avoid risk for poor outcome. A second reason that rupture should be considered an important therapeutic event is that investigating the factors underlying the negative interaction may reveal important information about the client's interactions with other important individuals in his or her life. Safran's final reason is that the exploration and resolution of the rupture can provide an important corrective emotional experience for the client. He argues that the experience of working through an alliance rupture may play a role in aiding clients to view themselves as capable of attaining relatedness in the face of conflict and see others as emotionally available. Thus it seems that this "rupture-repair cycle" (Asay & Lambert, 2002) of psychotherapy is perhaps as critical to the therapeutic progress as the initial development of alliance because of its impact on accessing and addressing interpersonal issues.

Safran and colleagues (2011) have outlined six rupture-repair interventions that can play an important role in restoring the therapeutic alliance.

1. Reiterating the therapeutic rationale: Restating the reasons for treatment and the agreed-upon methods of treatment can be helpful in order to repair a strained therapeutic relationship. This intervention is yet another reason to have clearly stated treatment goals at the outset. Whether the rationale for therapy is written in a treatment plan or agreed upon verbally between client and therapist, it can be an excellent starting point for repair. It can help the client realign with her own reasons for pursuing treatment. Therapy is often an uncomfortable process that is easier to adhere to and persist in when the client revisits the reasons for beginning it in the first place.

2. Changing tasks or goals: This type of response to a perceived rupture requires the therapist to be flexible and highly attuned to the client's emotional needs. Clients may become frustrated, angry, or submissive if the therapist is too confrontational. If the therapist picks up on this, she should address the client's discomfort and consider taking another approach. There may be times when a client needs increased guidance or support but is unable to ask for it. The client may feel abandoned or unsupported by the therapist. Often times, changing tasks or goals involves being able to move fluidly along the expressive-supportive continuum in response to the client's needs.

3. Clarifying misunderstandings: As in any interpersonal relationship, misunderstandings are bound to arise between client and therapist. These may be simple or complex miscommunications that, in a different type of relationship, might go unaddressed. For example, a normally fluent client spent the first few minutes of a session noticeably withdrawn and glancing repeatedly at the door to the office. The therapist inquired about this change in the client's behavior. After a long pause, the client explained, "You didn't turn on the white noise machine in the hallway. It's like you don't think what I have to say is really important enough to protect." The key to responding to this type of misunderstanding is for the therapist to take a nondefensive stance and to empathize with the client's experience. Although later it may be useful to relate this interaction to ways the client experiences others in her life, the primary job of the therapist is to protect the working alliance.

4. Exploring relational themes: An analysis of the factors that led to the rupture may help both client and therapist identify important underlying causes of the breakdown. In the example provided earlier, a later exploration of how the client felt entering the office revealed that the absence of the white noise machine made her feel unsafe and unsupported, in effect silencing her. She felt that she could not speak up at the outset and asked that the machine be turned on. Perhaps a more common scenario is when clients assigned homework or behavioral tasks to complete outside of therapy fail to do so. This type of behavior interferes with the progress of therapy and can bring up feelings of frustration for the therapist and guilt on the part of the client. It may suggest a rupture in the alliance but can be repaired with exploration of the meaning and nature of the behavior.

5. Linking the alliance rupture to patterns in the client's life: Often the relationship between client and therapist reflects relational patterns in the client's life outside of the consulting room. The rupture may be resolved by connecting the session material with situations in the client's life. For example, an adolescent client engaged in ongoing power struggles with parents and teachers may similarly experience the therapist as a domineering and controlling force. Making this connection explicit may help the client consider the therapist in a different way and can be instructive for the therapist regarding behaviors that might be perceived as authoritarian.
6. Offering a new relational experience: Therapy has been described as offering a corrective emotional experience (Alexander & French, 1980). There are times in which the therapist can offer a new relational experience to the client without explicitly exploring the underlying meaning of the interaction. For example, a client may express dissatisfaction or disappointment with the therapist. By responding simply and nondefensively, the therapist can demonstrate that old relational patterns do not have to be repeated.

A small meta-analysis of studies that examine similar principles of rupture-repair intervention (Safran et al., 2011) demonstrated that the presence of rupture-repair episodes was associated with positive outcomes for clients. Whereas it is nearly impossible to avoid ruptures and impasses—they are a normal and expected part of interpersonal relationships—the way the clinician handles these challenges is crucial to the success and progress of treatment.

CHAPTER REVIEW

A successful therapeutic relationship is one that produces change that the client desires and respects the autonomy of both parties involved. The therapeutic dyad is distinguished from other relationships, even those that are naturally therapeutic. There are several things that make the therapeutic relationship distinct from those one has with friends, family, clergy, medical professionals, and other helpers. Although the therapist's skills are an important part of the healing process, much of the available research suggests that the relationship between therapist and client is what is most predictive of positive outcome. Other helping professionals such as instructors, massage therapists, and medical doctors can provide healing and relief even if their bedside manner is lacking, whereas counseling is more dependent on a high-quality interpersonal relationship. There is something special about the relationship between client and counselor, and there are specific aspects of interpersonal relations that can enhance interactions between these two parties.

One important aspect of the therapeutic alliance is being emotionally attuned to the client's needs. This will require the therapist to move flexibly along the expressive-supportive continuum and to use a variety of different interventions with each session. At the expressive end of the continuum, therapists are likely to utilize interpretation, confrontation, and clarification. A more neutral position—in the middle of the continuum—is encouragement to elaborate. Toward the supportive end of the continuum, therapists may provide empathic validation, advice, praise, and affirmation.

All of these interventions occur within an existing framework that outlines the process and ground rules for therapy. Often referred to as the *frame*, this structure includes clear expectations for fees, the timing of sessions, prohibitions against inappropriate physical contact, the setting of the office (e.g., free from intrusion), and the client's right to confidentiality. Maintaining structure is important because it creates a safe and predictable environment for the client and protects the therapist. All counselors must strike a balance between being flexible in order to respond to the client's changing needs and maintaining a consistent and reliable approach to the treatment that respects the client's autonomy. This type of modulation protects both the client and the therapist.

Part of the frame involves one's own therapeutic stance. There are common factors that most therapists aspire to possess and communicate to their clients. These include therapeutic listening, trust, accurate empathy, unconditional positive regard, and congruence. Counseling professionals will encounter situations in which some of these constructs are in conflict with one another. For example, there may be times in which it is impossible to be both congruent (e.g., authentic) and empathic. Similarly, offering accurate empathy may not always be optimal and may conflict with our commitment to promote the health and welfare of our clients.

Each of these components contributes to the development of therapeutic alliance, or the collaborative working relationship between the therapist and the client. Therapeutic alliance is an important variable in predicting outcomes in psychotherapy and a strong therapeutic alliance is associated with persistence in psychotherapy. Therapeutic alliance can be built through concrete attending behaviors and the development of the aforementioned constructs—empathy, unconditional positive regard, and so on. Therapeutic alliance is determined by both therapist and client variables. There is some evidence that clients' expectations about therapy and their own attachment styles influence the development and quality of the therapeutic alliance. It is essential to keep in mind that therapeutic alliance is a highly interpersonal and co-constructed concept.

Most therapeutic relationships will encounter at least minor ruptures in the therapeutic alliance; these bumps in the road may sometimes, if left unresolved, develop into impasses. Ruptures in the alliance are bound to affect both client and therapist and may occur due to miscommunications that are culturally bound. The emergence of a rupture in the relationship does not have to be a setback in the process of psychotherapy. These types of breakdowns may represent opportunities for growth and change for both parties and the relationship overall. There are several rupture-repair interventions that therapists can consider using. The overarching purpose of this chapter is to highlight the importance of developing and maintaining a therapeutic alliance with the client and to outline the challenges that may arise in this intensely interpersonal relationship.

PERSONAL REFLECTION ESSAY QUESTIONS

1. Consider the Golden Rule, which says, "Do unto others as you would have done unto you." How might this ideological position interfere with your ability to be empathic? How does the Golden Rule limit our ability to develop multicultural sensitivity and understanding?

2. What are the potential advantages and disadvantages of always maintaining an empathic stance as a therapist?
3. Can you think of a time in your life in which your desire to be authentic conflicted with your ability to demonstrate unconditional positive regard or empathy? How did you handle this situation? How might you have handled it differently if it had been a therapeutic relationship?

KEYWORDS

accurate empathy	congruence	praise
advice	empathic validation	self-disclosure
affirmation	encouragement to elaborate	therapeutic alliance
clarification	frame	therapeutic listening
complementarity	genuineness	unconditional positive regard
conditional positive regard	interpretation	working alliance
confrontation	intersubjectivity	

FURTHER READING

For a great insider's view of how therapeutic alliance develops:

- Yalom, I. D. (1974). *Every day gets a little closer: A twice-told therapy.* USA: Basic Books.

For more on mirror neurons and neuroscience developments in empathy research:

- Iacoboni, M. (2008). *Mirroring people.* New York, NY: Picador.
- Watch the RSA Animate—The Empathic Civilization video at www.youtube .com/watch?v=l7AWnfFRc7g

Several resources about different perspectives on therapeutic alliance and the role of alliance with specific populations:

- Muran, C. J., & Barber, J. (2010). *The therapeutic alliance: An evidence-based guide to practice.* New York, NY: The Guilford Press.
- Safran, J. D., & Muran, J. C. (2003). *Negotiating the therapeutic alliance: A relational treatment guide.* New York, NY: The Guilford Press.
- Meissner, W. W. (2007). Therapeutic alliance: Theme and variations. *Psychoanalytic Psychology, 24*(2), 231–254. doi:10.1037/0736-9735.24.2.231
- Michel, K., & Jobes, D. A. (2010). *Building a therapeutic alliance with the suicidal patient.* Washington, DC: American Psychological Association.
- Friedlander, M. L., Escudero, V., & Heatherinton, L. (2006). *Therapeutic alliances in couple and family therapy: An empirically informed guide to practice.* Washington, DC: American Psychological Association.
- Donnelly, V., Lynch, A., Mohan, D., & Kennedy, H. G. (2011). Working alliance, interpersonal trust and perceived coercion in mental health review hearings. *International Journal of Mental Health Systems, 5.* doi:10.1186/1752-4458-5-29

Counseling Skills: Assessment, Diagnosis, and Treatment Planning

*The only true voyage of discovery ... would be not to visit
strange lands but to possess other eyes, to behold the universe
through the eyes of another, of a hundred others, to behold
the hundred universes that each of them beholds, that each of
them is.*—Proust (1923)

LEARNING OBJECTIVES

- Understand the purpose of assessment (specifically behavioral assessments and functional behavioral assessments)
- Explain the necessity of gathering collateral data during assessment
- Describe the value of testing (including self-report measures) during assessment
- Understand the process and purpose of diagnosis
- Describe the general organization of the *DSM-5* and some of its advantages/disadvantages
- Explain the *Psychodynamic Diagnostic Manual* and how it differs from the *DSM-5*
- Explain the *DSM-5* Cultural Formulation
- Describe the various steps in goal setting and treatment plans
- Explain the importance of continuous goal assessment
- Understand the necessity of communicating with clients about treatment recommendations
- Discuss the Evidence-Based Model of Wellness
- Explain the various levels of prevention services

Most people would agree that counseling involves discovery. Individuals often enter counseling because they are interested in discovering ways to alleviate distress, solve problems, or otherwise improve their lives. The art of therapy lies in helping clients to see their worlds with new eyes and lead satisfying lives equipped with new skills and perspectives. Thus far, we have discussed the important components of active–empathic listening coupled with reflective listening as a way to help clients see and hear themselves in counseling. We have also discussed developing a therapeutic relationship and forging a working alliance with clients to move toward discovery and change. This chapter focuses on the methods mental health professionals use to discover and understand the client's world, including assessment and diagnosis. This discovery is a collaborative process that aids in creating an effective individualized treatment plan. Each of the skills previously covered (i.e., active listening, empathy, and relationship-building) are necessary but not sufficient to developing a whole understanding of the client to effect change.

ASSESSMENT

Assessment in counseling is the process of gathering data about individuals to understand characteristics such as treatment needs, risk level, and current functioning. It is a way to understand the client's strengths and weaknesses, including current distress, coping skills, and risk of self-harm (Carlson, 2013). Assessment is not just reserved for the beginning of treatment. It may be conducted repeatedly throughout the course of therapy in order to monitor progress. Given the impact of managed care on the provision of mental health services, ongoing assessment is an important tool to track progress and demonstrate the potential need for ongoing treatment.

Assessment is a broad term used to encompass all methods that a mental health professional may use to collect information about the individuals or groups (e.g., couples or families) that present for treatment. Thus, assessment is likely to include interviewing the client and other important persons, observing the client's behavior, formal testing, and reviewing relevant records (Carlson, 2013). Although assessment is a formal process in therapy, each of us engages in informal assessment each time we encounter a new person. When you attend a social function and make a new acquaintance, you are unlikely to perform diagnostic tests or review the person's medical record; however, you will engage them in conversation, listen to what they say and how they say it, and observe how they interact with others. In some ways, everyone has experience with assessment. The type of assessment we conduct in a counseling situation is more formalized and should be less subjective in nature.

Behavioral Assessment

Behavioral assessment is an important component of understanding the way clients respond to different situations in everyday life. Behavioral assessment is any method of observing clients or families in a naturalistic or analog (i.e., simulated) setting to gain information about their behavior. You might be interested in observing a problematic behavior that the client wishes to decrease or a positive behavior that the client wishes to increase. An important aspect of behavioral assessment is measuring the behavior, perhaps by counting the frequency of occurrence during a given period of time, the duration of the behavior, or quantifying the intensity of the behavior.

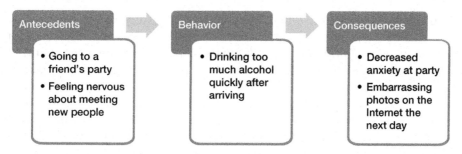

FIGURE 8.1 Functional behavioral assessment.

For children, behavioral assessment might include observing a child in his classroom to identify how frequently he raises his hand, speaks out of turn, or leaves his seat. Behavioral assessment of a family might include observing a parent and child playing together and noting what happens during interactions before and after a child is defiant or aggressive. A frequently used behavioral assessment technique for phobias and other anxiety disorders is to set up a behavioral avoidance task (BAT), in which the client is observed while attempting to approach and interact with a feared object (such as a harmless snake in a terrarium) or engage in some other feared task (such as approaching a stranger and asking for the time).

Functional behavior assessment (FBA) is a specific type of behavioral assessment that entails observing an individual to determine the factors that lead up to a particular behavior (i.e., the antecedents) and what occurs immediately afterwards (i.e., the motivating factors) that may be maintaining this behavior (Figure 8.1). Haynes and O'Brien (1990) defined FBA as "the identification of important, controllable, causal functional relationships applicable to a specified set of target behaviors for an individual client" (p. 654). This conceptualization focuses on identifying variables that meet three criteria (i.e., important, controllable, and causal), and one can accordingly target these variables for treatment. Although there may be many variables associated with a target behavior, not all will be clinically useful. For instance, there may be important variables that are causal but not controllable (e.g., exposure to a traumatic event leading to the development of posttraumatic stress disorder).

The goal of FBA is to develop a hypothesis about why the particular behavior is occurring and why it persists time and again by piecing together the circumstances that trigger the behavior and the consequences. Typically, behaviors may function to help individuals obtain something that they desire (i.e., positive reinforcement) or to help individuals avoid something they find aversive (i.e., negative reinforcement). For example, a young boy who tantrums loudly and disrupts the entire classroom each day may be observed to begin his tantrums when the teacher transitions to math instruction with the result that he is removed from the classroom because of his disruption and hence does not have to complete the math assignment. Being removed from the classroom negatively reinforces his temper tantrums, causing them to persist. Understanding what triggers and motivates behavior leads to a better understanding of the client and points toward an effective treatment plan to reduce distress and maladaptive behaviors by adapting one's response to antecedents or altering consequences.

FBA may be initiated when treatment is not progressing adequately. It may be that the selected treatment is not effectively addressing the antecedents and consequences maintaining a problematic behavior. On the other hand, it is recommended that FBA be implemented at the outset of treatment to make sure that the relevant environmental contexts are taken into account during treatment planning. Based on the data gathered during FBA, treatment components may be altered or entirely omitted depending on the particular functions that the behavior is serving. This ensures that the intervention will focus on the idiosyncratic variables that have been maintaining behavior problems for the individual. Despite the strong connection between conducting a thorough FBA and identifying the most important targets for treatment, evidence suggests that this is an under-utilized approach to treatment planning (Ortega & Haynes, 2005). Perhaps it is not often included in assessment because it takes more time and effort than diagnosis.

BOX 8.1

Functional Behavioral Analysis

Review Figure 8.1. Pick a behavior that you do several times each day without thinking about it. Maybe it is a habit you would like to decrease. Think back to the last time that you did this behavior. Think about the antecedents and the consequences. What triggers this behavior? It might be something in the environment or an internal sensation or emotion. What motivates you to perform this behavior? What keeps it going? With all of that in mind, what purpose does this behavior serve for you?

It is not always possible to observe the client in a particular setting to conduct a live behavioral assessment, so mental health professionals may conduct a "postmortem" of a recent event with the client in a session. Counselors should guide clients through remembering all the details of a recent behavior of interest to gather data about the circumstances and consequences. A disadvantage of this type of functional assessment is that the clinician is unable to identify aspects of the behavioral sequence (i.e., antecedent conditions and consequences) that are currently outside the awareness of the individual and those interacting with him or her.

Chain analysis, an integral part of dialectical behavior therapy (DBT; Linehan, 1993), is a specific application of FBA after the fact. DBT is an evidence-based treatment for reducing self-harm in clients diagnosed with borderline personality disorder, and its first stage is focused on reducing life-threatening behaviors, including deliberate self-injury or suicidal behaviors. In DBT, therapists and clients conduct chain analyses to identify the links in the chain that led up to the harmful behavior, including biological vulnerability factors such as missing a dose of medication and environmental factors, such as getting into a fight with one's partner or being fired from a job.

In addition to these structured methods of behavioral assessment, counselors are constantly assessing client behavior. A client may report calling in sick to work after giving a presentation the previous day and a history of pulling away from romantic relationships after getting too close. The therapist may notice that this same client cancels an appointment after revealing something very personal in the prior session. This type of pattern may be evidence of the client's tendency to withdraw from interaction when he or she feels too exposed or vulnerable. Repeated behavioral patterns like this are worthy of exploration with the client, either through interpretation of the behavior or through FBA.

When counselors work on inpatient units or within group or residential programs, they may have a unique opportunity to observe client behavior. Inpatient staff—including social workers, licensed mental health counselors, occupational and creative arts therapists, and psychologists—often document behavioral observations. They may note that clients have a tendency to isolate themselves from the rest of the milieu, appear more irritable around mealtimes, or become agitated just after change of shift. Some inpatient units use formalized behavioral assessment tools that have reliability and validity estimates that are comparable to written measures (LePage & Mogge, 2001). Interestingly, some children's inpatient units offer 24-hour visiting hours. This type of policy allows families to be more incorporated into the treatment plan and also affords staff ample opportunity to observe and address factors within the family system that may be contributing to the child's distress (see Regan, 2006, for a first-hand account of a unit with this policy).

Collateral Data

In addition to interview and behavioral assessment conducted with the client, it is important to include information from other available sources. **Collateral data** is additional information relevant to the client's current mental health needs that may be obtained from sources such as past psychiatric records, medical records, or educational records. Mental health professionals should determine what information might be pertinent to better understand the client after initial interviews and obtain signed authorization from the client to obtain and review those records. You may wish to discuss with the client during intake if there is any information you should seek out to more fully understand the presenting problem.

Collateral interviews can also be valuable during assessment. Interviews with important people in the client's life, including parents, children, spouses, partners, teachers, or other providers are often critical to understanding the context of the client's behavior. For example, if you are working with an adult client who lives with his parents and reports explosive fights with them, it may be helpful to interview his parents to discover their views on the triggers and consequences of these fights. As with obtaining written records, you will need the client's permission to interview collateral contacts and be careful to keep the client's private information confidential.

BOX 8.2

Sample Consent Form for Collateral Contact

JANE SMITH, LMHC

Licensed Mental Health Counselor
100 Main Street ♦ Springfield, IL ♦ Phone number ♦ e-mail address

CONSENT TO DISCLOSURE OF CLIENT RECORDS/INFORMATION

I, the undersigned, hereby consent to, direct, and authorize Jane Smith to (initial all that apply)

_____ provide

_____ obtain

_____ exchange

information with _____ concerning my psychological or medical history and treatment.

The information or records to be released or disclosed include only the following (initial all that apply):

_____ Therapy Notes

_____ Summary of Treatment

_____ Billing Records

_____ Transfer/Termination Summary

_____ Tests Taken and Testing Scores

_____ Other (specify): _____

_____ Any and all records/information

I acknowledge and understand that I am waiving my right to confidentiality with respect to the records and information released pursuant to this consent and hereby release Jane Smith from any and all liability arising from release and disclosure of the information and records to the above-named person.

_____   _____   _____

Client Name (printed)   Client Signature   Date

_____   _____

Client Telephone Number   Client Address

Witnessed by:

Jane Smith, LMHC   _____   _____
License # xxxxxx   Signature   Date

Before conducting a collateral interview, it is good practice to discuss with the client ahead of time that you plan to share the minimal amount of information necessary with the collateral contact to obtain the relevant data. For example, you may tell the client that you plan to tell his parents that the client has reported that there are frequent fights and you are seeking their side of the story but will not share what the client has told you. You may also decide to interview the other person(s) with the client in the room so that the client knows that you have respected his privacy and also knows what the collateral contact has told you. This is a good way to maintain a trusting relationship with the client and to further develop the therapeutic alliance.

Testing

Psychologists and counselors often use tests to measure symptoms, determine diagnosis, and aid in selecting the most appropriate treatment plan. **Self-report measures** are frequently used by mental health professionals in assessment. A clinician may administer a self-report measure of symptoms in the first session as a broad screening for areas of distress, which may indicate where to focus in subsequent sessions. Some clinicians prefer to use a secure website to administer screening measures before the first appointment as well as regularly throughout the course of treatment to gauge symptom domains and levels. Research has shown that self-report data collected via the Internet is typically equivalent to data collected in person via paper and pencil (Weigold, Weigold, & Russell, 2013).

BOX 8.3

Learning Exercise

The majority of assessment tools that are used for clinical diagnosis are not available for purchase or use by the general public. Companies that publish these tests indicate in their catalogs the types of qualifications that are necessary to buy and administer particular tests.

In some cases, licensure or certification to practice in your state in a field related to the purchase is necessary. Visit the websites for the specific tests mentioned in this chapter to see what requirements are mandatory for use of each of the instruments. For example, the Beck Depression Inventory (BDI) can be purchased from Pearson Assessment (http://pearsonassess .ca/haiweb/cultures/en-ca/ordering/qualification-levels.htm).

There are myriad types of tests available to mental health professionals to assist in understanding clients. Tests range from comprehensive and focused symptom checklists (e.g., BDI, Brief Symptom Inventory) to personality tests (e.g., Minnesota Multiphasic Personality Inventory, Sixteen Personality Factor Questionnaire, Rorschach) to vocational assessments (e.g., Campbell Interest and Skill Inventory, Strong Interest Inventory). Often, professionals calculate scores and then apply clinical judgment to the interpretation of those scores. Many of the tests used are **norm-referenced** tests. This means that scores obtained on these tests are reported in terms of the frequency of the score in a normative sample (Carlson, 2013; McGrath, 2011). For example, if you knew that a person achieved an intelligence quotient (IQ) score of 100, without knowledge of how other people score on the test, you cannot interpret the score. In fact, you may think that a score of 100 is the highest possible IQ score because you assume that means the person answered 100% of the items correctly. However, IQ is measured with a norm-referenced test, and IQ scores have an average of 100 and a standard deviation of 15. With that knowledge, you have a better understanding that this individual has an IQ that is typical in comparison to his or her same-aged peers. Norm-referenced tests help one understand how unusual a score is and can help the therapist and client identify specific treatment goals. Clients may be motivated to work toward achieving goals that move scores out of the extremes and into the normal range.

A popular broad screening tool is the Symptom Checklist-90-Revised (SCL-90-R; Derogatis, 1983), which measures nine domains of symptoms, including somatization, obsessive compulsive, interpersonal sensitivity, depression, anxiety, hostility, phobic anxiety, paranoid ideation, and psychoticism. It is important to remember that screening tools like the SCL-90-R, which will be discussed more fully in the next section of the chapter, are not meant to be diagnostic tools. Rather, it is intended to screen for problem areas that may need further attention. The BDI-II (Beck et al., 1996) is a narrowly focused assessment that is often used to measure presence and severity of depression symptoms. There are 21 questions, and these items closely follow the diagnostic criteria outlined in the *Diagnostic and Statistical Manual of Mental Disorders* (5th ed.; *DSM-5*; American Psychiatric Association, 2013). The manual for the BDI-II provides **cutoff scores,** which reliably distinguish individuals with minimal, mild, moderate, and severe depression. In other words, if an individual's score exceeds a given cutoff score, it is probable that he or she will fall into a certain category. For example, on the BDI-II, scores falling between 14 and 19 (inclusive) indicate mild depression.

BOX 8.4

Ethical Selection and Use of Tests

The American Psychological Association's *Ethical Principles of Psychologists and Code of Conduct* (2002, amended 2010) contains ethical standards relevant to 10 areas of professional practice. Standard 9 specifically addresses issues related to the use of tests, including choosing tests with good reliability and validity, obtaining informed consent for testing, appropriate test interpretation, and ethical reporting of test results. An important aspect of this standard is that psychologists are required to select tests that are designed to measure the domain of interest and have been proven to be good tools. This means that the tests provide consistent scores (i.e., are reliable) and measure what they purport to measure (i.e., are valid). Practitioners must also be mindful to administer tests to individuals in the intended population. Issues such as age, culture, or language may prohibit the valid use and interpretation of tests for certain people. There are resources available to guide practitioners in test selection. For example, *Tests* (Maddox, 2008) and *Test Critiques* (Keyser, 2005) are a companion set of reference books that include information on thousands of psychological tests searchable by subject area. In *Test Critiques*, in particular, you will find valuable information about test uses and administration.

The *Standards for Educational and Psychological Testing* (American Educational Research Association, American Psychological Association, & National Council on Measurement in Education, 1999) assert that "a test taker's score should not be interpreted in isolation; collateral information that may lead to alternative explanations for the examinee's test performance should be considered" (p. 117). In other words, a counselor should not assume that a single test score is a perfectly accurate depiction of the client's symptoms, distress, or abilities. For example, a client may endorse items on a comprehensive symptom measure like the SCL-90-R that leads to highly elevated scores on almost all of the clinical scales. Taken at face value, it would seem that the client suffers with clinical levels of anxiety, depression, thought disorder, and many other symptoms. However, when combined with the results of a more focused self-report measure of depression like the BDI-II and information from a clinical interview, it may become clear that the client has significant depression symptoms that cause him or her much distress. This high level of distress may then lead to endorsement of a broad range of symptoms in addition to the depression symptoms; the endorsement may be a way of communicating distress to the clinician but not an indication that he or she is likely to meet diagnostic criteria for those other disorders. In rare circumstances, clients in forensic settings may also endorse most items in order to appear more distressed. The purpose of this type of "faking bad" is often to obtain some type of secondary gain such as benefits or avoiding penalty for a crime. Accordingly, test data is information that should be thoughtfully incorporated with information that the client and others who know the client well have shared with the clinician. It is of the utmost importance to remember that the client is the expert on her own experience, and thus her perspective should be considered when interpreting test scores.

BOX 8.5

More Resources for Test Selection

Whereas some tests must be purchased from publishers, there are many good assessments available for clinicians (and graduate students) on a budget. These measures are in the public domain, which means they are free for use. Check out this website, which is a collection of many public domain screening measures: www.bhevolution.org/public/screening_tools.page.

DIAGNOSIS

Assessment is conducted with the goal of gaining a better understanding of the client, which includes but is not limited to identifying current symptoms. **Diagnosis** is the process of classifying an individual's symptoms. A diagnosis is a label that describes the type of problems the client is experiencing and provides a way for clinicians to communicate efficiently with each other and managed health care companies. Imagine, if each time you needed to describe a client's problems to another professional (or an insurance company), you had to list the primary five or six symptoms that the client reports (e.g., insomnia, irritability, sadness,

ILLUSTRATION 8.1 Frog or prince charming? As with any other construct, diagnostic categories have many meanings depending on the person using the term.

Photo by Jonathan Choe. Retrieved from http://www.flickr.com/photos/crazyegg95/10831761/

lack of energy, poor concentration, and decreased appetite) instead of being able to succinctly describe the client as "depressed." In other words, diagnosis helps professionals and clients quickly understand common mental problems, but the diagnostic categories are broad. For example, picture a frog. Chances are the frog you are currently imagining is not the same as another person's mental frog. Maybe you are thinking about a large dark green toad, but someone else is thinking about a tiny brightly colored poison dart frog or even Kermit. So it is with diagnostic labels. A diagnosis cannot stand on its own to fully describe an individual's unique state of mental health.

Overview of *DSM-5* Diagnosis

The *DSM-5* is the reference used by mental health professionals to make clinical diagnosis. It is based on a medical model of classification, which means that the client's symptoms are assessed and must meet a certain number of equally weighted criteria to meet diagnostic criteria for a particular disorder. A client is either in or out of discrete diagnostic categories. The bulk of the manual contains descriptions and the criteria for each of the mental health disorders. Each diagnosis is grouped within a chapter with similar disorders, including:

- Neurodevelopmental disorders (e.g., intellectual disability, autism spectrum disorder, and specific learning disorder)
- Schizophrenia spectrum and other psychotic disorders (e.g., schizoaffective disorder)
- Bipolar and related disorders. (e.g., cyclothymic disorder)
- Depressive disorders (e.g., major depressive disorder)
- Anxiety disorders (e.g., generalized anxiety disorder)
- Obsessive-compulsive and related disorders (e.g., body dysmorphic disorder)
- Trauma- and stressor-related disorders (e.g., posttraumatic stress disorder)

- Dissociative disorders (e.g., dissociative identity disorder)
- Somatic symptom and related disorders (e.g., conversion disorder)
- Feeding and eating disorders (e.g., pica and anorexia nervosa)
- Elimination disorders (e.g., enuresis and encopresis)
- Sleep-wake disorders (e.g., insomnia disorder and narcolepsy)
- Sexual dysfunctions (e.g., erectile disorder)
- Gender dysphoria
- Disruptive, impulse-control, and conduct disorders (e.g., oppositional defiant disorder)
- Substance-related and addictive disorders (e.g., alcohol use disorder and caffeine intoxication)
- Neurocognitive disorders (e.g., major or mild neurocognitive disorder due to Alzheimer's disease)
- Personality disorders (e.g., paranoid personality disorder and borderline personality disorder)
- Paraphilic disorders (e.g., voyeuristic disorder and pedophilic disorder)
- Other mental disorders (e.g., unspecified mental disorder)

The criteria listed in the *DSM-5* are intended to be guidelines that mental health professionals use to make diagnoses using their clinical judgment. Because physical health can affect mental health (and vice versa), the client's current or chronic medical diagnoses or injuries are listed as well. For example, thyroid disease may be associated with increased anxiety or depression if it is unmanaged. If a client's mental health symptoms are unresponsive or worsen during treatment, the client may need to see her physician for a thyroid check. The inclusion of medical problems as part of *DSM* diagnosis is a helpful reminder to her clinician to think of the client holistically.

The previous version of the *DSM* (4th ed., text rev.; *DSM-IV-TR*; American Psychiatric Association, 2000) presented a five-axis system of diagnosis, in which state and trait (i.e., personality disorders) mental disorders were listed on the first two axes, medical diagnoses were listed on the third axis, psychosocial stressors were specified on the fourth axis, and a rating of the client's functioning was made on the fifth axis. In *DSM-5*, there is no longer a multiaxial diagnostic system, but clinicians are instructed to list all mental disorders and general medical conditions together (formerly Axes I, II, and III) with additional information about important life circumstances (formerly Axis IV) and disability (formerly Axis V) included. The stressors are reported using a list of "V Code diagnoses" (or "Z Code diagnoses") that are listed as additional diagnoses rather than contextual factors influencing the target disorder (Wakefield, 2013). Some of the stressors or environmental factors that might be listed are homelessness, unemployment, or recent loss of a loved one. Disability may be rated using the World Health Organization Disability Assessment Schedule (Üstün, Kostanjsek, Chatterji, & Rehm, 2010) found in Section III of the *DSM-5*.

When more than one diagnosis is appropriate for a client, the mental health professional should indicate the principal diagnosis is by listing it first. The principal diagnosis may be difficult to identify, but it should be determined by evaluating the main reason for the current visit or the condition that is the primary focus of treatment. The other diagnosis (or diagnoses, if there is more than one additional diagnosis) should be listed in the order of focus in treatment. When a client meets criteria for more than one disorder, the two problems are said to be **comorbid**, meaning they exist simultaneously. There may be times when it is unclear whether the client meets diagnostic criteria for a disorder because there is not enough known about the client's symptoms or history. If the clinician presumes that full criteria will be met when additional information is available, is it appropriate to label a diagnosis as "provisional" in that case. At other times, a client may not meet full criteria for a diagnosis, and a designation of "other specified" or "unspecified" may be made. For example, if a client does not meet full criteria for a major depressive disorder (i.e., having five out of nine symptoms), the diagnosis of "other specified depressive disorder, depressive episode with insufficient symptoms" should be made. The clinician may also choose not to specify why the diagnosis is being qualified and make a diagnosis of "unspecified depressive disorder" instead. Some *DSM-5* diagnoses may be accompanied by an additional designation of a subtype or a specifier, which further describes the features, course, or severity of the disorder. For example, obsessive-compulsive disorder may be specified "with poor insight" if the client does not recognize that the content of her obsessions is irrational.

BOX 8.6

Spotlight on Culture—*DSM-5* Cultural Formulation

The *DSM-5* includes a section on Cultural Formulation that includes recommendations for accounting for the impact of culture on the client's experience of mental illness. The *DSM* distinguishes between culture, race, and ethnicity. **Culture** is defined broadly as systems of knowledge and attitudes that are passed down across generations and includes morals, language, religion and spirituality, family structures, life-cycle stages, ceremonial rituals, and customs. The *DSM* describes **race** as "a culturally constructed category of identity that divides humanity into groups based on a variety of superficial physical traits attributed to some hypothetical intrinsic, biological characteristics" (Cultural Formulation, paragraph 2). **Ethnicity** is defined as "a culturally constructed group identity used to identify peoples and communities ... [that] ... may be rooted in a common history, geography, language, religion, or other shared characteristics of a group, which distinguish that group from others" (Cultural Formulation, paragraph 3). One's identity is comprised of thoughts and feelings related to each of these three concepts, and mental health professionals must be aware of the potential impact these have on a client's distress, coping, and support.

The authors of the *DSM-5* have created a semi-structured interview called the Cultural Formulation Interview (CFI) that may be used to elicit information from clients during assessment about their cultural background. The CFI contains questions in four domains: cultural definition of the problem; cultural perceptions of cause, context, and support; cultural factors affecting self-coping and past help seeking; and cultural factors affecting current help seeking. This interview, as well as an alternative version appropriate for use in interviewing collateral contacts, can be found in their entirety in Section III of the *DSM-5*.

Advantages and Disadvantages to Classification

Since its inception, classification of mental disorder has been murky territory. Kraeplin (1917) is credited with creating the first taxonomy of mental disorders, and he wrote, "wherever we try to mark out the frontier between mental health and disease, we find a neutral territory, in which the imperceptible change from the realm of normal life to that of obvious derangement takes place" (p. 295). The idea that one must meet a certain threshold (i.e., number of symptoms) to be diagnosed with a mental disorder implies that there is a firm difference between normal and pathological functioning. At times, not meeting diagnostic criteria might be due to the lack of one additional symptom. There is no guarantee that a person with four symptoms that cause significant distress is less "ill" (or in any less need of treatment) than another individual with five symptoms. However, insurance companies frequently make decisions about the necessity of treatment based on exceeding the given threshold to meet *DSM* diagnostic criteria. *DSM* diagnosis is controversial because it implies discrete classification into separate categories of disorder. Many advocate doing away with diagnostic categories based on symptom criteria and recommend the use of dimensional diagnosis, which describes the level of symptoms and functioning on a continuum from normal to impaired (Widiger & Samuel, 2005).

One major critique of the *DSM* categories of disorder is that there is widespread co-occurrence (or comorbidity) of disorders (Widiger & Samuel, 2005). That is, the disorders do not appear to be distinct because there is so much overlap, which suggests that some disorders share something in common and furthermore that a firm boundary between them is inappropriate. There are blurred lines between anxiety and depression, for example. Rivas-Vazquez, Saffa-Biller, Ruiz, Blais, and Rivas-Vazquez (2004) described anxiety and mood disorder comorbidity as "more the rule rather than the exception" (p. 74). Recent research indicates that the onset of anxiety disorders typically precedes the onset of depression, and, furthermore, an anxiety diagnosis increases the risk of later depression at a 5-year follow-up (Wittchen, Beesdo, Bittner, & Goodwin, 2003). With that much overlap, are these really distinct disorders? Or is it one disorder that manifests differently in each individual—sometimes with more anxiety than depression or vice versa? It has been proposed that negative affect is an underlying shared mechanism, which contributes to both disorders (Clark & Watson, 1991). Perhaps it is more useful to recognize the elevated negative affect, which shows itself in two symptom domains (i.e., anxiety and depression), rather than treat depression and anxiety as separate disorders. In fact, medications used to treat anxiety, such as selective serotonin reuptake inhibitors, like Prozac, are the same ones used to treat depression. With dimensional diagnosis, clinicians may be better able to recognize and target core dysfunctional processes rather than try to fit clients into discrete and pre-determined categories. Dimensional diagnosis may lead to more specific treatment recommendations (Widiger & Samuel, 2005). Additionally, because it is more specific and individualized, dimensional classification is more likely to appropriately account for cultural differences in behavior and mood. Categorization according to *DSM* criteria is based on descriptions of behavior and emotion that may change over the course of illness (e.g., from having sadness most days to being irritable without sadness most days during a depressive episode).

Despite these critiques, the *DSM-5* is the tool that is most widely used by mental health professionals to communicate with each other, managed care companies, and the public about mental illness. It is intended to be atheoretical, which means that it is used as a common language by all clinicians regardless of theoretical orientation. It provides a means for making clinical decisions, which are by nature categorical (e.g., to hospitalize or not), and this clinical utility is the reason that it prevails as a necessary tool for clinicians (First, 2005).

Psychodynamic Diagnostic Manual

The *Psychodynamic Diagnostic Manual* (PDM Task Force, 2006) is an alternative diagnostic system developed by a group of psychoanalytic clinicians for adults, adolescents, children, and infants. It was created as a reaction to the "shift from inferential to descriptive psychiatry" (McWilliams, 2011) that was apparent in the diagnostic criteria included in the third edition of the *DSM* (*DSM-III*; American Psychiatric Association, 1980). The goal of the *PDM* was to turn away from *DSM* categorical diagnosis based on observable symptoms to provide a framework for diagnosing people in a more rich and individualized manner by describing inferred internal dynamics with the goal of lending itself to comprehensive case formulation and highlighting treatment targets. Wallerstein (2011, p. 156) wrote,

> *DSM* categorizes what people have in *common*, the distinctive symptom clusters that assign them to a particular diagnostic box, whereas *PDM* is designed to describe what makes each individual under scrutiny idiosyncratically *unique*, different from every other person in the world, thus restoring a balance of individual and universal perspectives.

The *PDM* has several levels of classification. First, an individual's personality pattern (or disorder) is described as falling along a continuum from healthy to borderline to neurotic according to the summaries of the typical temperament, defense mechanisms, affect, implicit beliefs about self and others, and transference-countertransference patterns observed in each type (P axis). Next, mental functioning (or severity of dysfunction; M axis), and finally the subjective experience of symptoms (S axis) is described. Although it is called the *Psychodynamic Diagnostic Manual*, there is some evidence that psychodynamic and cognitive behavioral therapy psychologists, alike, rate the *PDM* positively in terms of its helpfulness in conceptualizing the different levels of personality organization (i.e., healthy, borderline, or neurotic) and the benefits of understanding "borderline" as a personality organization rather than a personality disorder (Gordon, 2009).

GOAL SETTING

When a client presents for treatment, he or she may or may not have a well-articulated therapy goal in mind. The process of assessment and diagnosis helps the mental health professional and the client to focus on difficulties in daily life that will ultimately become treatment goals. The Bern Inventory of Treatment Goals (Grosse & Grawe, 2002) is a taxonomy that identifies five goal types, 27 nested goal categories, and 52 nested subcategories and can be used for goal set-ting in clinical practice (see Box 8.7). This taxonomy is a valuable tool because it serves as an important reminder that therapy goals often go beyond symptom relief to other areas of life improvement, including interpersonal relationships and personal growth. For instance, in an inpatient setting, most clients listed two to three treatment goals, and when those goals were analyzed using the Bern Inventory of Treatment Goals, it was found that whereas most client goals were related to specific problems or symptoms (P; 77.3%), there were many interper-sonal goals (I; 36%), personal growth goals (G; 26.1%), goals concerning well-being (W; 18.8%), as well as existential issue goals (E; 6.2%) identified by clients (Holtforth, Reubi, Ruckstuhl, Berking, & Grawe, 2004). In an outpatient sample, the pattern of treatment goals was slightly different. Most clients listed their primary treatment goal as an interpersonal goal (I; 74.5%), followed by symp-tom-related goals (P; 60.5%), personal growth goals (G; 45.9%), well-being goals (W; 13.4%), and existential goals (11.1%; Grosse & Grawe, 2002). This diversity of treatment goals suggests that clinicians should have conversations with clients about their goals throughout treatment rather than to plow forward with their own plan or priorities.

A checklist version of the Bern Inventory of Treatment Goals has been developed, which may be quite useful in collaborative goal-setting with cli-ents (Grosse Holtforth, 2001). Whereas assessment and diagnosis often point the way to therapy goals, mental health professionals may be surprised at times by the goals clients present. When the therapy goals of a sample of out-patients with non-comorbid anxiety and depression were compared, the anx-ious clients most frequently named treatment goals related to symptom relief, whereas depressed clients most frequently listed interpersonal goals rather than symptom-related goals (Holtforth, Wyss, Schulte, Trachsel, & Michalak, 2009). Furthermore, the treatment goals identified by clients diagnosed with depression were varied, which indicates that even individuals who fall in the same diagnostic categories based on symptom presentation may have diverse individualized treatment goals.

BOX 8.7

The Taxonomy of Treatment Goal Themes of the Bern Inventory of Treatment Goals

Coping with specific problems and symptoms (P)
- Depressive symptoms
- Suicidality and self-injury
- Fears or anxiety
- Obsessive thoughts and compulsive behaviors
- Coping with trauma
- Substance use and addiction
- Eating behaviors

(continued)

(continued)

- Sleep
- Sexuality
- Coping with somatic problems
- Difficulties in specific life domains/stress
- Medication

Interpersonal goals (I)

- Current relationship
- Current family
- Other specific relationships
- Loneliness and grief
- Assertiveness and boundary issues
- Connectedness and intimacy

Well-being and functioning (W)

- Exercise and activity
- Relaxation and composure
- Well-being

Existential issues (O)

- Past, present, and future
- Meaning of life

Personal growth (G)

- Attitude toward self
- Desires and wishes
- Responsibility and self-control
- Emotion regulation

Only the first two levels of abstraction are shown (goal type and goal category).

The complete Bern Inventory of Treatment Goals checklist is available in English at http://www.psychologie.uzh.ch/fachrichtungen/kliptaf/forschung/downloads/BIT_CP_US.pdf

(v. 3.3l; Holtforth et al., 2004)

Once you have determined the treatment goals with the client, you and the client should agree upon the order in which they will be addressed. You may not necessarily work on therapy goals in the order of importance. It may be wise to begin treatment with a goal that will make a big impact on the client's daily functioning, or you may decide to tackle a smaller, quickly achievable goal to increase the client's hope and motivation to achieve those major goals on the list. Most clinicians collaborate with clients to identify both short-term and long-term goals, in an effort to triage problems and develop a concrete plan of action. Knowing the client's level of motivation and likely success in doing the tasks necessary to achieve objectives and goals will also help you to determine an agreeable order of treatment.

Treatment Plans

*What treatment, by whom, is most effective for this individual
with that specific problem, under which set of circumstances?*
—Paul (1967, p. 111)

A comprehensive case formulation should contain all the information necessary to craft a treatment plan that addresses the client's presenting problems. As you may recall from Chapter 3, developing a case formulation involves creating a working hypothesis about the causes, precipitating factors, development, and maintenance of the client's problems and distress (Eells, 2010; Ivey, 2006). All the data collected during assessment must be integrated by the mental health professional to create a cohesive explanation for the client's current thoughts, feelings, and behaviors in the light of development, past experiences, and environmental influences. By illuminating the factors that seem to have created the distress (e.g., biological mechanisms, past learning, or trauma history) as well as the factors that seem to be keeping the client in distress (e.g., poor coping strategies, maladaptive behaviors, or dysfunctional relationships), the clinician is also identifying the targets of treatment. A good formulation has been described as one that provides a "rationale, conceptual scheme, or myth that provides a plausible explanation for the patient's symptoms and prescribes a ritual or procedure for resolving them" (Frank & Frank, 1991, p. 42). If you have developed an understanding of how the problems came to be, you will also have a good understanding of how to ameliorate them. It is also likely that you will have greater empathy for your clients when you come to understand the development of their problems as well as the context of their distress through case formulation (Eells, 1997).

A better formulation leads to a stronger treatment plan. When novice, experienced, and expert therapists were asked to complete "think-aloud" case formulations to patient vignettes, experts were significantly better at creating comprehensive and complex formulations. The treatment plans of experts were not only more closely linked to the formulation, but the treatment plans were also more elaborate, which indicates that better formulations lead to more sophisticated treatment plans (Eells, Lombart, Kendjelic, Turner, & Lucas, 2005). Interestingly, the treatment plans of novices were of higher quality than the treatment plans of experienced therapists who were not experts. Perhaps just as experts' formulations and treatment plans benefit from intentional focus and training on the task, experienced clinicians drift from the models they learned during training and the quality of their work diminishes. This is a compelling reason to seek continuing education throughout your career.

Clinicians use various methods to develop their treatment plans, and the cognitive processes involved in deriving a treatment plan have not been adequately studied. Decision making is likely based on a clinician's preferred methods of intervention. Witteman and Kunst (1997) asked psychologists to read a case vignette and then think aloud about how and what treatment they would plan for the hypothetical client if he came in for treatment. The researchers found that therapists often first made an interpretation of the client's problem, suggested an intervention, and discussed supporting evidence without considering any alternative treatments.

A treatment plan contains **goals** for the client to achieve as well as specific **objectives** and **interventions** to help realize those goals. Developing a treatment plan should be a collaborative process between client and clinician. Both parties should initially agree on the goals for treatment, and there should be a clear path to achieving those goals through measurable objectives. For instance, a therapy goal might be to reduce feelings of depression. The objectives for achieving that goal might be to increase socialization on a weekly basis and identify and challenge negative thoughts about self-worth. Depending on the theoretical orientation of the treatment, the focus may also be on implicit schemas that are contributing to depressive affect, improving interpersonal relationship dynamics, and resolving earlier losses that may be a predisposing factor for depression.

Continuous Goal Assessment

In order to maintain momentum in treatment, mental health professionals should continually assess progress toward goals as well as recognize the need to add or delete goals.

Witteman and Kunst (1997) urge clinicians to be aware of the client's progress instead of moving forward with an unwavering plan. They wrote that once clinicians develop a formulation of a particular case, "they may too easily judge all information about the patient and her or his complaint to accord with it; and with this judgment, they will, in turn, have found confirmation of the appropriateness of the interpretation" (p. 158). In other words, therapists can become fixated on one particular approach without taking in all the appropriate information about the client's response to the intervention and other possible avenues for intervention given other plausible formulations of the client's problems.

COMMUNICATING WITH CLIENTS ABOUT TREATMENT RECOMMENDATIONS

Once you have conducted a thorough initial assessment of the client's current functioning and symptoms and created a case formulation and treatment plan, you must communicate your findings and conceptualization to the client as well as how you plan to go about helping the client through treatment. This can be a challenge for clinicians because it is necessary to discuss diagnosis and prognosis with the client. It can be difficult to predict how the client will react when receiving assessment feedback and discussing the treatment plan. Some people will feel relief to know that the therapist has a good understanding of the problems faced in their daily life. Others may react negatively to a diagnostic label or feel unheard. It may also be overwhelming to some clients to discuss the work that will be required to reduce symptoms and improve functioning. The key to making this a positive encounter is to maintain a collaborative approach by balancing delivery of feedback with active-empathic listening (see Chapter 6).

Careful Communication

When discussing the treatment plan with clients, it is important to ensure that the client fully understands and consents to the plan. Not only is it ethical to ensure that they are willing participants in the treatment plan, but also the client's motivation to work toward treatment goals is likely to be higher if he or she is in agreement about how to achieve treatment goals.

The way that mental health professionals approach assessment, formulation, and treatment planning develops with experience. For example, in a recent qualitative study of how experienced therapists assess and understand their clients and how they make decisions about the treatment plan in early sessions, several themes, which indicate that clinical judgment is typically based on internal standards (e.g., reactions to the client) rather than external standards such as assessment tools or diagnostic criteria (Oddli & Halvorsen, 2012), emerged. Specifically, Oddli and Halvorsen noted that many therapists discussed using their own emotional reactions to the client (and the emotional climate of the therapeutic encounter) as a tool to understand the client's worldview and life circumstances. This type of reflective process will be discussed in further detail in Chapter 9.

Another study found that therapists do not necessarily practice what they preach. In a large survey of psychologists, half of the respondents were asked which parts of diagnostic assessment were necessary to best understand clients and plan treatment, and the other half were asked which types of diagnostic assessment they regularly use in their clinical practice. In general, many psychologists judged most areas of assessment to be necessary, including identifying and describing the client's complaint, listing problem behaviors, and identifying appropriate treatment goals. However, for each of those activities, there were fewer psychologists who reported doing them in practice. In terms of formulation, psychologists were least likely to see providing an explanation or hypothesis for the client's problems as necessary, and, accordingly, they indicated that they were not very likely to do so in clinical practice (Groenier, Pieters, Hulshof, Wilhelm, & Witteman, 2008).

Therapeutic assessment is an evidence-based approach to assessment and delivering feedback to clients about assessment findings (Finn & Martin, 2013). Therapeutic assessment is a collaborative approach to discovery, which stresses that both client and counselor are active parties in seeking data about the client's current state as a way of capitalizing upon strengths and highlighting areas for growth and improvement. In therapeutic assessment, clinicians involve clients in setting goals by eliciting the questions they have about themselves to guide the assessment process.

There is evidence that therapeutic assessment is an effective intervention on its own (Poston & Hanson, 2010), and these authors concluded that "those who engage in assessment and testing as usual may miss out, it seems, on a golden opportunity to effect client change and enhance clinical important treatment processes" (p. 210). Finn and Martin (2013) outlined the main components of therapeutic assessment that are integral to its powerful effects. The first is that therapeutic assessment may change the narrative the client has developed about himself or herself. People who have always seen themselves in particular ways may be enlightened by assessment findings and develop a new perspective about themselves and their struggles and strengths. Finn and Martin also describe effective clinicians as "walking the line between self-verification and disintegration" during therapeutic assessment (p. 455). That is, clinicians strive through empathic listening to balance correcting client views about self without overwhelming the client to facilitate change. In fact, Finn and Martin describe tests as "empathy magnifiers" in the context of therapeutic assessment, in that clients are likely to feel deeply understood by the process of gathering detailed information about their inner experience (p. 456).

Who's Driving the Bus?

As the saying goes, it takes two to tango. The client has likely been unsuccessful in prior independent attempts to achieve therapy goals, and without a client, you as a clinician are unable to help anyone achieve therapy goals. This is a collaborative process, but one in which the client must always give informed consent. There may be times when you are in the driver's seat and directing the client on the path to better health, and there may be other times when you let the client take the wheel. Remember that it is ethical to respect the client's autonomy, which at times will mean respecting the client's decision to focus on different goals. That is not to say that you allow the client to dictate treatment. You, as a mental health professional, are responsible for identifying goals appropriate for intervention and the methods to achieve those goals.

Tryon and Winograd (2011) investigated the importance of **goal consensus** in positive outcomes in therapy. They defined goal consensus as having five major parts: (a) the client and therapist agree on goals; (b) the therapist provides a clear explanation of the nature of and expectations for therapy that the client understands; (c) the goals are discussed and the client believes the goals are clearly specified; (d) the client is committed to the established goals; and (e) the client and therapist are in agreement about the origin of the client's problems as well as about who or what is responsible for the problem's solution. Each of these components is an integral part of best practice in communicating clearly with clients about therapy. Striving for goal consensus with each of your clients is valuable because it is linked to better outcomes in therapy.

WELLNESS AND PREVENTION APPROACHES

Although the bulk of this chapter has focused on assessment and diagnosis of mental disorders, not every client who seeks counseling will meet diagnostic criteria for a disorder. Some individuals seek treatment to improve their lives—not because they are currently struggling with dysfunctional thoughts, feelings, or behaviors. Furthermore, as was highlighted in the previous section, clients who present with a primary problem may wish to remain in treatment after those symptom-related goals are met in order to achieve goals related to wellness, personal growth, or existential issues. In fact, mental health has been conceptualized as a continuum that spans from illness at one extreme to health and onward to wellness at the highest level. Thus, health is seen as a neutral state that indicates lack of symptoms but not necessarily optimal or high-level functioning (Myers & Sweeney, 2008). Accordingly, healthy individuals may not be satisfied with their personal growth and life circumstances and may seek counseling to improve well-being. This section will review one well-established theory of counseling that deals specifically with enhancing wellness in clients in addition to reviewing the methods used by mental health professionals to promote health in communities through prevention.

An Evidence-Based Model of Wellness

The Wheel of Wellness (Myers, Sweeney, & Witmer, 2000; Sweeney & Witmer, 1991; Witmer & Sweeney, 1992) was developed as an evidence-based model of wellness, which was later refined and conceptualized as the Indivisible Self (Myers & Sweeney, 2004). This model of wellness was based upon Adler's theory of Individual Psychology (1927/1954). Specifically, the authors reviewed the psychological research literature to compile a list of characteristics that are related to healthy living, high quality of life, and longevity. They organized these characteristics according to Alfred Adler's three major life tasks (i.e., work, friendship, and love) and two additional tasks (i.e., self-direction and spirit). These characteristics were included in the model as 12 tasks of self-direction that were seen as spokes in a wheel of wellness. Specifically, in this model, wellness is conceptualized as having a core of spirituality surrounded by a wheel of self-direction supported by the 12 tasks (e.g., stress management and sense of worth) that leads to well-being in the three major areas of life (i.e., work, friendship, and love) in the context of external forces and events. To assess the applicability of this model, Myers, Sweeney, and Witmer (1996) developed a questionnaire called the Wellness Evaluation of Lifestyle (WEL) to evaluate the 17 areas of wellness that comprise the Wheel of Wellness. After many research studies, the researchers found that the data support an alternative conceptualization of wellness, which they have named the Indivisible Self model of wellness. The Indivisible Self has three layers comprised of the 12 Self-Direction Tasks and 5 life tasks (i.e., work, leisure, friendship, love, and spirit) at the lowest level, which are each uniquely associated with five higher-order factors (i.e., the physical, social, creative, essential, and coping self), which contribute to one overall wellness factor (see Figure 8.2).

Adler's theory was again used to understand each of the five second-order factors that emerged in analyses. The Essential Self is comprised of the four components of spirituality, self-care, gender identity, and cultural identity. The Creative Self includes five areas: thinking, emotions, control, positive humor, and work. There are four domains in the Coping Self: realistic beliefs, stress management, self-worth, and leisure. The Social Self includes friendship and love, and the Physical Self includes exercise and nutrition. As you can see, each area of the Indivisible Self is an important part of personal wellness and fulfillment ranging from basic physical health to daily cognitive and emotional functioning to personal fulfillment and existential issues. Each contributes to individual wellness and is affected by the person's surroundings. There are four contexts noted in the model: local, institutional, global, and chronometrical. Specifically, our wellness is related to our interactions with family and our community (i.e., local context), education and government (i.e., institutional context), and culture and global events, especially through the media (i.e., global context). Chronometrical context refers to the idea that wellness and lifestyle behaviors and choices change over time throughout an individual's life span. Thus, there are myriad forces that impact wellness. Although an individual may have healthy lifestyle choices and behaviors that promote a sense of wellness in general, situational factors may temporarily erode wellness.

The value of this model lies in its utility in helping counselors and clients understand the components of wellness and the interaction of those underlying

CONTEXTS:

Local (safey)
Family
Neighborhood
Community

Institutional (policies and laws)
Education
Religion
Government
Business/Industry

Global (world events)
Politics
Culture
Global events
Environment
Media

Chronometrical (life span)
Perpetual
Positive
Purposeful

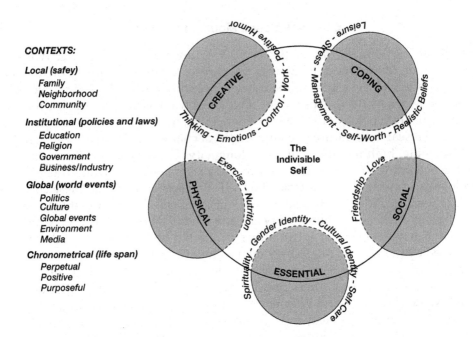

FIGURE 8.2 The indivisible self: An evidence-based model of wellness.
Source: Myers and Sweeney (2004).

components with a person's environment and development over time. There is a new measure of wellness known as the Five Factor WEL (Myers, Luecht, & Sweeney, 2004), developed to assess the domains of the Indivisible Self. This tool may be used by clinicians to assess the client's current strengths. The benefits of using this evidence-based model to help clients achieve wellness include being able to highlight positive characteristics and identify areas for growth. The authors state that this model is ideal because it focuses on characteristics of healthy people and emphasizes personal choice in making intentional strides to wellness.

Helping Groups Avoid Psychological, Educational, and Health Problems

In addition to promoting wellness in individuals through counseling, mental health professionals are also involved in ensuring the wellness of the general public and at-risk groups through prevention. **Prevention** services aim to intervene before the onset of negative outcomes to avoid the development of symptoms or illness. Rather than focus solely on treatment and rehabilitation of individuals who have developed a mental disorder, psychologists recognized the need to focus on prevention of mental illness because of the limited resources available to remediate these problems once they become entrenched; this recognition led to the birth of community psychology in the 1960s (Jason & Glenwick, 2002).

Prevention is about reducing the risk of mental illness. The National Institute of Mental Health has defined risk as "those characteristics, variables, or hazards that, if present for a given individual, make it more likely that this individual, rather than someone selected from the general population, will develop a disorder" (1996, p. 6). Accordingly, prevention researchers are interested in identifying **risk factors** of disorders as well as **protective factors** that may diminish the impact of risk factors.

Prevention interventions have been classified into three categories (Mrazek & Haggerty, 1994). The first are **universal interventions**, which are aimed at the entire population (i.e., the general public). Television public service announcements that warn against the dangers of smoking cigarettes are a familiar universal intervention to prevent lung disease. The next level of prevention interventions includes **selective interventions**, which are aimed at a particular subgroup that is at above-average risk for onset of a disorder. A good example of a selective intervention was conducted by Kennedy, Rapee, and Edwards (2009) in Australia. These researchers identified a high-risk subgroup (i.e., behaviorally inhibited preschool-aged children who also had one parent diagnosed with an anxiety disorder) and offered an eight-session educational group to parents about how to more effectively parent an anxious child, because good parenting is a protective factor against the development of mental disorders. The last level of prevention includes **indicated interventions**, which target individuals who have a predisposition to the disorder and are already showing minimal but detectable signs of the disorder. For example, Gardenswartz and Craske (2001) recruited individuals who had experienced a single panic attack to participate in a one-day cognitive therapy workshop and found that in the following 6 months only 2% developed panic disorder compared to 14% of the control group.

CHAPTER REVIEW

Assessment in counseling is the process of gathering data about individuals to understand characteristics such as treatment needs, risk level, and current functioning. Assessment is conducted throughout of the course of therapy in order to identify treatment goals and monitor progress toward meeting those goals. Assessment is a broad term used to encompass all methods that a mental health professional may use to collect information about the individuals or groups (e.g., couples or families) that present for treatment. Thus, assessment is likely to include interviewing the client and other important persons, observing the client's behavior (i.e., behavioral assessment), formal testing, and reviewing relevant records.

Behavioral assessment consists of observing clients or families in a naturalistic or analog (i.e., simulated) setting to gain information about their behavior. FBA is a specific type of behavioral assessment that entails observing an individual to determine the factors that lead up to a particular behavior (i.e., the antecedents) and what occurs immediately afterwards (i.e., the motivating factors) that may be maintaining this behavior. The goal of FBA is to develop a hypothesis about why the particular behavior is occurring and why it persists time and again by piecing together the circumstances that trigger the behavior and the consequences. Understanding what triggers and motivates behavior leads to a better understanding of the client and points toward an effective treatment plan to reduce distress and maladaptive behaviors by adapting one's response to antecedents or altering consequences.

Collateral data is additional information relevant to the client's current mental health needs; collateral data may be obtained from sources such as past psychiatric records, medical records, or educational records. Interviews with important people in the client's life, including parents, children, spouses, partners, teachers, or other providers are also often critical to understanding the context of the client's behavior. Mental health professionals should determine what information might be pertinent to better understand the client after initial interviews and obtain signed authorization from the client to interview others and/or obtain and review relevant records. You may wish to discuss with the client during intake if there is any information you should seek out to more fully understand the presenting problem.

Psychologists and counselors often use tests to measure symptoms, determine diagnosis, and aid in selecting the most appropriate treatment plan. Tests range from comprehensive and focused symptom checklists to personality tests to vocational assessments. Often, professionals calculate scores and then apply clinical judgment to the interpretation of those scores. Professionals should strive to use valid and reliable tests and not assume that a single test score is a perfectly accurate depiction of the client's symptoms, distress, or abilities.

Diagnosis is the process of classifying an individual's symptoms. A diagnosis is a label that describes the type of problems the client is experiencing and provides a way for clinicians to communicate efficiently with each other and managed health care companies. The *DSM-5* is the reference used by mental health professionals to make clinical diagnosis. It is based on a medical model of classification, which means that the client's symptoms are assessed and must meet a certain number of equally weighted criteria to meet diagnostic criteria for a particular disorder. A client is either in or out of discrete diagnostic categories. The bulk of the manual contains descriptions and the criteria for each of the mental health disorders. Insurance companies frequently make decisions about the necessity of treatment based on exceeding the given threshold to meet *DSM* diagnostic criteria. However, *DSM* diagnosis is controversial because it implies discrete classification into separate categories of disorder. The *PDM* is an alternative diagnostic system developed by a group of psychoanalytic clinicians for adults, adolescents, children, and infants. The goal of the *PDM* was to turn away from *DSM* categorical diagnosis based on observable symptoms to provide a framework for diagnosing people in a more rich and individualized manner by describing inferred internal dynamics with the goal of lending itself to comprehensive case formulation and highlighting treatment targets.

Assessment and diagnosis often point the way to therapy goals. All the data collected during assessment must be integrated by the mental health professional to create a cohesive explanation for the client's current thoughts, feelings, and behaviors in the light of development, past experiences, and environmental influences. By illuminating the factors that seem to have created the distress as well as the factors that seem to be keeping the client in distress, the clinician is also identifying the targets of treatment. However, mental health professionals should collaborate with clients to jointly determine the important goals for treatment. Once you have determined the goals of treatment with the client, you and the client should agree upon the order in which they will be addressed. A treatment plan contains goals for the client to achieve as well as specific objectives and interventions to help realize those goals.

Once you have conducted a thorough initial assessment of the client's current functioning and symptoms and created a case formulation and treatment plan, you must communicate to the client your findings and conceptualization as well as how you plan to go about helping the client through treatment. When discussing the treatment plan with the client, it is important to ensure that the client fully understands and consents to the plan. Therapeutic assessment is a collaborative approach to discovery; the approach stresses that both client and counselor are active parties in seeking data about the client's current state as a way of capitalizing upon strengths and highlighting areas for growth and improvement.

Although the bulk of this chapter focused on assessment and diagnosis of mental disorders, not every client who seeks counseling will meet diagnostic criteria for a disorder. Some individuals seek treatment to improve their lives. The Indivisible Self is an evidence-based model of wellness that can be used to understand the components of wellness and the interaction of those underlying components with a person's environment and development over time. In addition to promoting wellness in individuals through counseling, mental health professionals are also involved in ensuring the wellness of the general public and at-risk groups through prevention.

PERSONAL REFLECTION ESSAY QUESTIONS

1. Throughout the book, we have emphasized the importance of therapy for the therapist. If you are currently in therapy, think about your current treatment goals. If you have not yet pursued counseling, consider what treatment goals you might have. Are your treatment goals specific to a particular problem or diagnosis? Or are they broader, more wellness based? If you prefer not to self-disclose personal information, you may also describe a friend, family member, or even a fictional character and identify his or her current symptoms/level of functioning and several treatment goals.
2. Choose one of the following popular media figures or television show characters: Lindsay Lohan, Snookie (of *Jersey Shore* fame), Dexter Morgan, or Inspector Monk. If you are not familiar with these people, you can find more information about them online. After selecting one person to focus on, consider what diagnostic criteria they might meet and describe several short-term and long-term treatment goals.

KEYWORDS

assessment	functional behavior assessment	race
behavioral assessment	goal consensus	selective interventions
collateral data	goals	self-report measure
comorbid	indicated interventions	therapeutic assessment
culture	interventions	treatment plan
cutoff score	norm-referenced test	universal interventions
diagnosis	objectives	
ethnicity	prevention	

FURTHER READING

- www.apa.org/science/programs/testing/index.aspx

  Please visit this webpage published by the American Psychological Association Science Directorate, which contains resources relevant to testing and assessment, including how to select tests and provide feedback to individuals about test scores.

- Nelson-Gray, R. O., & Farmer, R. F. (1999). Behavioral assessment of personality disorders. *Behaviour Research and Therapy, 37*(4), 347–368. doi:10.1016/S0005 -7967(98)00142-9

  For more information about a unique type of behavioral assessment, this is an excellent article that describes the behavioral assessment of personality disorders, which can be a challenging task.

- *Prevention of Mental Disorders: Effective Interventions and Policy Options*

  For a good list of risk and protective factors for mental illness as well as a listing of universal, selective, and indicated interventions for several mental disorders, see the report published by the World Health Organization: Retrieved from www.who.int/mental_health/evidence/en/prevention_of_mental_disorders _sr.pdf

The Nature of the
Counseling Relationship

*If the only tool you have is a hammer, every problem begins to
resemble a nail.*—Maslow (1966, p. 15)

LEARNING OBJECTIVES

- List the key components of an effective therapeutic alliance
- Define metacognition and explain its importance within the therapeutic
  relationship
- Define transference and countertransference
- Explain ways in which transference can be used as an effective therapeutic tool
- Define and give examples of positive and negative transference
- List and define the different types of transference
- Explain how transference is viewed within two-person psychology
- Explain transference within the framework of various therapeutic orientations
- Explain the difference between subjective and objective countertransference
- Identify the five attributes necessary for the successful management of
  countertransference

Therapy is an intensely personal process. Clients share things with their
therapists that they often do not tell anyone else. Therapy tends to be most
successful when clients are vulnerable and honest about their struggles and
innermost feelings. This therapeutic process is intimate but is distinct from
other types of close interpersonal relationships. The therapeutic relationship
is unique because it is designed to provide care for the client with limited
self-disclosures about the therapist's own private life and personal struggles.

Even though the majority of therapists do not behave like the popular carica-ture of the cold, withholding, blank slate clinician, they still reveal relatively little about themselves to their clients. Overall, therapists use self-disclosure infrequently, ranking it as one of the least-used techniques in psychother-apy (Farber, 2006; Maroda, 2009). This lack of transparency is both necessary and beneficial to the client. Therapists should typically not share their per-sonal problems or details of their private lives with clients; the very nature of the relationship—in which the client is being cared for—suggests that self-disclosure should be used sparingly (see Audet & Everall, 2010, listed in the Further Reading section, for a thoughtful exploration of the reasons for and against therapist self-disclosure).

Despite this lack of concrete information, clients will inevitably develop many ideas about the therapist as a person. Clients may make assumptions about the therapist's personality, sexual orientation, perception of the client, social class, or any number of other factors. These notions about the therapist may be verbalized directly or may be revealed in the client's behavior, body language, or seemingly innocuous omissions. For example, a client may say, "I can tell by how you dress and the jewelry you wear that you are better off than I am." This may be an accurate statement, but perceptions like these are often subjective and are sometimes misinformed. Is this statement evidence of a *real* power differential in the relationship predicated on social class? Or is it sugges-tive of a pervasive sense of inferiority that the client experiences in most of his interpersonal relationships? It could also be that the client is re-experiencing a dynamic that he often felt with his peers in school or a wealthy relative who mocked him for his lower socioeconomic status. There are many possible mean-ings to a statement like this one.

In this chapter we will discuss how early patterns of relating to parents and other important figures may influence the therapeutic relationship. When self-disclosure on one side of a relationship is greater than on the other, as it is in psy-chotherapy, one party is likely to feel much more vulnerable and exposed. The lack of reciprocity in self-disclosure can liberate the client from having to care for another person, as she may have to do in her other close relationships. But it can also instill in the client a profound sense of uncertainty and apprehension. When faced with a constant state of "not knowing" coupled with a feeling of vulner-ability, clients often find themselves filling in the gaps of their knowledge. This "filler" material may resemble ideas and reactions clients have to other important people in their lives.

The nature of these perceptions can have a significant impact on the treat-ment. If the client has positive feelings about the therapist's personality, com-petence, and attentiveness, then they are more likely to persist in treatment. If the client has many negative feelings about the therapist, particularly if those thoughts and feelings remain unexpressed, then they are less likely to continue in treatment. Other types of complicated feelings may also arise; clients may report feelings of attraction toward the therapist, a sense of being in competi-tion, or even a perception that the client and therapist share many of the same personality traits and skills.

Clinicians must respond thoughtfully to these types of reactions and must also carefully monitor their own reactions to each client. Therapists are not immune from having strong emotional and psychological reactions to other people, including their clients. These types of reactions may stem from the therapist's own conflicts, attitudes, and motives. There may also be an expected response to the client's unique type of psychopathology and personality style. Whether the emotional and affective response is coming from the client or the counselor, it is important that these types of interpersonal dynamics be addressed and examined by both members of the dyad.

As in any relationship, the therapeutic bond is influenced by both parties. There will always be complex power dynamics at play and they require ongoing attention. Evaluation of the psychotherapeutic process is as important as the process itself. Clinicians must attend both to what is said and what remains unsaid. **Metacognition**, or thinking about thinking, is an essential skill when it comes to monitoring the interplay of two distinct personalities in the consulting room.

TRANSFERENCE

What are transferences? They are new editions or facsimiles of the impulses and phantasies which are aroused and made conscious during the progress of the analysis; but they have this peculiarity, which is characteristic for their species, that they replace some earlier person by the person of the physician. . . . Some of these transferences have a content which differs from that of their model in no respect whatever except for the substitution. These then— to keep to the same metaphor—are merely new impressions or reprints. [Other transferences] are more ingeniously constructed; their content has been subjected to a moderating influence—to sublimation, as I call it—and they may even become conscious, by cleverly taking advantage of some real peculiarity in the physician's person or circumstances and attaching themselves to that. These, then, will no longer be new impressions, but revised editions.—Freud (1905, p. 116)

Transference is a concept that originated within psychoanalytic theory. Although its definition has evolved over time and across schools of thought, **transference** is generally understood as the client's tendency to view the therapist in ways that are similar to the individual's earlier relationship to primary caregivers. Freud (1949) described transference as a process in which the client views the therapist as a reincarnation of an important figure from childhood. In a more contemporary definition, generally accepted by psychodynamic theorists, Greenson (1965) defines transference as "the experiencing of feelings, drives, attitudes, fantasies, and defenses toward a person in the present, which are inappropriate to the person and are a repetition, a displacement of reactions originating in regard to significant persons of early childhood" (Greenson, 1965, p. 156).

Most psychodynamic psychotherapies encourage the therapist to take a position of neutrality, abstaining from promoting a particular agenda. This approach has been caricatured as a cold and unfeeling psychoanalyst who is disinterested in his or her clients (Figure 9.1).

"I can't get anyone interested in my problems . . . "

FIGURE 9.1 This caricature of a psychoanalyst reflects common misconceptions about psychodynamic treatment. In reality, an effective psychodynamic therapist is highly engaged and attentive to the client's emotional state and the therapeutic relationship.

© Jim Naylor. Retrieved from http://www.cartoonstock.com/cartoonview.asp?catref=jna0751

This is an inaccurate representation of contemporary psychodynamic psychotherapy and, in fact, Freud himself was quite demonstrative and verbose at times with clients, often revealing much more of his personal life and inner reflections to his patients than most therapists do today. The abstinence of the psychodynamic practitioner refers to the fundamental aim to interpret rather than gratify the client's demands or wishes. A client may ask the therapist, "Am I going crazy? I worry so much every day. Maybe this is the beginning of madness." A psychodynamic therapist is unlikely to simply reassure the client by saying, "No, of course not. You're not going crazy." This is a supportive and gratifying response that may be satisfying to the client, but only in the short-term. The psychodynamic approach, along with most psychotherapeutic approaches, recognizes that reassurance is unlikely to provide any long-term remedy to this fear of disintegration. Rather, the clinician would abstain from reassurance and attempt to gain a better understanding of the fear, its origins, and perceived sequelae. The therapist might say, "What do you imagine could happen if you 'went crazy'?" Depending on the client's answer, the therapist might learn that the client has unconscious wishes to abdicate responsibilities, and madness would be, in some ways, a welcome escape from the burdens of everyday life. Or perhaps the client fears he will become like a family member who has a chronic mental illness, that somehow he is predestined to lose control. This type of intervention embraces the unfolding of the transference. The therapist's reluctance to instantly comfort and soothe the client may revive early images from the past that can be transferred onto the therapist. As the client is faced with the task of wrestling with these emotions without blanket reassurance that all will be well, he may be more likely to perceive the therapist in ways that are reminiscent of earlier relationships. This transference can be an effective tool for helping the client to resolve relational wounds from the past.

Clients may react to therapists with anger, love, disappointment, fear, idealization, and affection. Transference is dynamic. It is likely to vacillate widely throughout the relationship and the therapist may come to represent multiple figures from the client's past. A fairly common example of transference is when clients feel criticized or misunderstood by the therapist, when in fact the therapist is being empathic and attuned to the client's experience. For example, a therapist responded to a client's story of being stood up by a date by saying, "It must have hurt to be forgotten like that," in a compassionate tone. To which the client responded, "I can tell you're mocking me when you say that. You probably think it's funny that I was left sitting there all by myself." In this case, it is evident that the client is noticing something that either is not there or, at the very least, was not intended by the clinician. This is evidence of **negative transference**. The client may be expecting the therapist to behave or think in ways that are similar to other important figures in his early life.

Not all transference is negative. There are many varieties of transference, including positive transference, erotic transference, and institutional transference. **Positive transference** involves admiration or appreciation of the therapist and may overlap considerably with **therapeutic alliance**. The close relationship between these two constructs will be discussed in more detail later in this chapter. A positive transference may be beneficial to the therapeutic work and likely feels good to the therapist. Who doesn't like to be appreciated? This type of transference may also perpetuate a myth—that the therapist is healthy, worthy of adoration, skilled, and generous, whereas the client is sick, unworthy, impaired, and selfish in their dependence on the therapist's provision of care. Positive transference may also interfere with the client's ability to develop a deeper understanding of painful affect or to address difficult experiences from earlier in life (Greenson, 1967).

Sometimes what appears to be positive transference may be idealization that is characteristic of a particular personality style in the client. For example, a client reported in the first session, "I've seen eleven therapists in the last three years, and I am so relieved to be here in your office. Even after just a few minutes with you, I know you are the only one who can really help me. I can't believe I wasted all my time with those incompetent counselors." When the therapist inquired about the genesis of this belief, the client became frustrated and was unable to see the therapist as a real person with both strengths and weaknesses. Within a few sessions she became angry with the therapist, saying, "I really thought you could help me. I was obviously wrong. I'm still depressed and you've done nothing to help me." She never returned for the next scheduled appointment and did not return the therapist's follow-up phone call or letter. In this case, what initially appeared to be a positive transference was in fact a pattern of idealization and devaluation that the client had brought to her previous treatments. Therapists who are faced with this type of presentation—which may seem "too good to be true"—should attempt to explore with the client, ahead of time, how they will handle inevitable disappointments when they arise in the therapeutic relationship.

Positive transference is distinguished from therapeutic alliance by the degree to which the client's thoughts and feelings are conscious. Transference is generally an automatic, unconscious process that is a repetition of earlier patterns from the client's life. A working alliance is built around the client's identification with the aims of treatment and her sense that the therapist has an understanding of and is focused on the tasks of therapy. A strong therapeutic alliance is essential to the work of all types of therapy. In a psychodynamic treatment setting, a good working alliance will allow the client to work through all sorts of transference-related issues, including many of those detailed in this chapter.

Erotic transference was originally conceptualized as something that occurs when the client openly declares he or she has fallen in love with the therapist (Freud, 1915). Contemporary writers (e.g., Blum, 1973; Mann, 1995; Stirzaker, 2000) on the subject have offered broader parameters for erotic transference and introduced the term **eroticized transference**. This suggests a more complex transference that is influenced, but not wholly defined, by certain aspects of love or attraction. Most therapists will encounter this type of transference at some point in their professional lives. Given the ethical and legal prohibitions against intimate relationships with clients and the importance of creating a safe space for clients to express a wide range of feelings and emotions, it is important to consider erotic transference carefully.

This type of transference has been evident since the early days of contemporary psychotherapy. Josef Breuer reported to Freud in the 1880s that one of his patients, Anna O., had fallen in love with him. He immediately decided that this type of relationship was unethical for a medical practitioner and left the treatment of the patient to Freud (Jones, 1953).

The concept of **institutional transference** refers to the client's transference to the clinic, hospital, or social service agency rather than directly to a psychotherapist (Reider, 1953). Some clients may find it less distressing to talk about the ways in which the institution is not meeting their needs rather than speaking directly about the therapist's shortcomings (Matarazzo, 2012). This type of transference is seen in individuals who receive treatment from low-cost public mental health clinics, and has been written about extensively with reference to individuals seeking treatment and other services through the Veterans Affairs Administration (Byrne & Valdiserri, 1982; Martin, 1989).

In his book, *The Analyst in the Inner City: Race, Class, and Culture through a Psychoanalytic Lens*, Neil Altman (2010) relates a poignant example of institutional transference in a public mental health clinic. He describes children visiting the clinic who ask the therapist repeatedly for snacks—packets of cookies, apples, juices—to no end. The therapist eventually becomes frustrated because this behavior is subtracting time and energy from the actual therapy session. The therapist engages in a power struggle with the child, saying, "We're not going to have much time left for our session if you keep eating or taking more food" (p. 6). Altman argues that the therapist is serving as a guardian of public resources (the institution) and that the children have significant transference toward the broad social service network upon which they rely. They see agencies as "having enormous resources that they can make available to poor people but that they often withhold" (p. 6). They transfer this unconscious preoccupation with the withholding institution onto the therapist and a re-creation of that same denial of the client's needs follows. The therapist, in an effort to focus the child on the task of therapy, plays into the transference. He begins to see the child as greedy, self-interested, and in need of re-direction. The therapist joins with the institution as guardian and gatekeeper of the coveted resources and becomes the arbiter of how much is enough.

BOX 9.1

Transference in Everyday Life—Learning Exercise 1

Although this chapter is meant to highlight transference and its role in the therapeutic relationship, transference is a ubiquitous construct. It occurs frequently in everyday life. Here are some examples:

- A young woman who grew up with an absent and emotionally distant father complains that her husband is so happy in their current relationship that he never finds fault with her. She says, "I mean, I'm not perfect. He should give me feedback about things he doesn't like so I can grow into a better person. It's as if he doesn't even notice me."
- A middle-aged man seeks treatment to deal with grief and bereavement after the sudden death of his younger sister, the "golden child" of the family. When asked about his work life, he describes his boss, a slightly younger woman, as "perfect." It is as if she can do no wrong. Even when she criticizes and humiliates him in meetings or rejects his ideas, he explains, "She's just trying to sharpen me. She knows so much more than I do and I'm so thankful I can learn from her."
- An introverted woman who grew up in a highly extraverted family received constant messages that she was too shy and quiet. Her parents repeatedly told her, "We worry about you and your ability to succeed because of how shy you are." As an adult she believes that her colleagues and friends think she is "boring" and "stupid" because she is slow to join conversations and bows out of large social events.

Can you think about ways in which transference plays a role in your life? Are there early relationships that may inform how you understand your interactions with friends, partners, colleagues, teachers, and bosses today? Can you identify some aspect of these current relationships that is shaped by those earlier dynamics? If so, how might this new awareness be helpful to you? How might it make things more difficult?

History of Transference

Initially, Freud and Breuer (1895) thought transference was a result of the doctor's influence on the patient or the power of suggestion. Later, Freud (1912b) postulated transference as a type of resistance that distorted the material being addressed within the therapy. In Freud's (1905) famous case study of Dora, he interpreted the maintenance of her physical symptoms as a replication of an unconscious attention-getting strategy that she had enacted with her parents. For Dora, recovery from hysteria would inevitably lead to the loss of an important caregiver. Freud also believed that Dora had an unconscious impulse to exact revenge against certain men in her life and that this manifested itself in her ending the treatment prematurely. Had Freud been further along in the development of his theory, perhaps he could have interpreted Dora's transference and perhaps made their work together more effectual. As he wrote, "I did not succeed in mastering the transference in good time" (Freud, 2001, p. 118).

As psychodynamic theory became increasingly pluralistic, the definitions of transference diversified. British psychoanalyst Melanie Klein (1952) argued that transference may occur as a result of the client's view that the therapist represents part of the self, particularly parts that are disavowed. For example, a client who is very self-critical and self-blaming but unable to acknowledge that tendency may see the analyst as critical and blaming. Whereas Freud had hoped that a successful treatment could lead to the complete resolution of transference, others have suggested different goals. Loewald (1960, 1971) indicated that treatment ought to assist the client in differentiating between interpersonal dynamics of the past and the present. By engaging in a new relationship with the therapist, the client should develop a more mature and realistic view of others.

Kohut's work with narcissistic and relatively fragile clients brought about a new imperative for therapists to immerse themselves empathically in the client's subjective experience. In this way, the therapist could provide clients with attunement and accurate empathy, which may have been missing in their relationships with early caregivers. Whereas others in the client's life may be repelled by certain patterns of transference, the therapist could persist in her attempts to truly understand the client's worldview. This ongoing therapeutic relationship would eventually allow the client to have a new experience of interpersonal relatedness through the development of new mental structures. This would enable the client to find satisfaction and self-worth either from within the self or in the context of healthier interpersonal relationships (Kohut, 1977, 1984).

Many theorists have challenged the position that the therapist is objective and can accurately evaluate the client's responses and perceptions (Racker, 1957; Winnicott, 1949). Because transference is inherently an interpersonal process and each person construes interactions from a subjective perspective, it is almost impossible to be completely objective. This is a radical departure from early ideas that the therapist could be both judge and jury of the client's experience.

Early conceptualizations of transference defined it as a distortion of objective reality based on past experiences. As the relational model of psychodynamic theory has developed over the years, practitioners of psychotherapy have gained appreciation for a **two-person psychology**. This is a departure from Freud's original view of the therapist as a blank slate or an observer who could be wholly objective and neutral. The two-person psychology viewpoint suggests that the therapist and the client are co-participants in a dynamic process. They continually affect each other and exert mutual influence on one another. This constant interplay of two individual psychologies is both a conscious and an unconscious process. Transference, as a result, is a truly interpersonal process (Gill, 1984). It involves displacement of earlier relational dynamics by the current therapeutic relationship and also projections of the self onto the therapist. These unconscious processes are then influenced by the affect and behavior of the therapist.

Contemporary perspectives on transference have begun to incorporate cognitive neuroscience approaches. Transference has been linked with implicit procedural and declarative memory (Gabbard, 2006). Neural networks research has also suggested that patterns of responding develop in response to repeated presentation of complete patterns (Peláez, 1997). For example, if a primary caregiver is consistently unreliable, unavailable, and disinterested, neurological pathways that are then more susceptible to activation develop. When an individual is presented with a vague pattern (e.g., a therapist who is quietly listening and attentive), an automatic associative network may be activated to reduce the ambiguity of the current situation (Diamantaras & Kung, 1996). Although the therapist may be nodding and asking thoughtful questions, the neurological network may see these bits of information as irrelevant and eliminate these components as distractions instead of seeing them as essential to understanding the therapist's attitude.

Adler's Perspective on Transference

Alfred Adler, a Viennese medical doctor, was a student and colleague of Freud who played an active role in the Vienna Psychoanalytic Society. He founded a school of thought he called **individual psychology**, named for its focus on individual personality development from a holistic perspective. His theories focused on concepts such as the **inferiority complex**, an implicit sense of self characterized by lack of self-worth, uncertainty, and a sense that one does not measure up to others' standards. Adler's theories were influential for theorists like Rollo May, Carl Rogers, and Abraham Maslow, so it is not surprising that **humanistic theory** highlights the importance of self-worth and conditions of positive regard.

Freud and Adler spent nearly a decade working together and learning from one another. Their collegial relationship ended with a contentious and well-documented split (Fiebert, 1997), precipitated by Adler's departure from Freud's classical emphasis on sexual and libidinal drives. After a series of debates at the Vienna Psychoanalytic Society in 1911, Adler resigned as president. Going forward, Adler frequently denied that he had been Freud's pupil (Maslow, 1962) and was determined to develop a psychological theory independent of Freud's psychoanalytic perspective.

Adler developed a concept he referred to as "lifestyle," which he understood as personality in action. Lifestyle is evident in how an individual strives to achieve goals (Lombardi, Melchior, Murphy, & Brinkerhoff, 1996). Transference, from an Adlerian perspective, is understood as a lifestyle conviction. This conviction is made up of expectations, hopes, fears, and guidelines that are sometimes childlike. Although some contemporary Adlerians have argued that transference does not actually occur or exist (Mosak & Fasula, 2011), others have described transference as an attempt to exploit the therapist or at the very least a form of dependency. Regardless of the precise definition, the Adlerian approach differs significantly from the psychoanalytic one. Whereas a psychoanalytic approach would likely seek to understand and utilize the transference, Adler saw transference as a phenomenon that should not be encouraged, as it could only lead to a prolonged treatment. Adler's approach highlights problems that can arise as a result of transference. A client's distorted expectations and fears are very likely to add another layer of complexity to the therapeutic process. Differing approaches encourage the therapist to question the transference-based material and either work through it or reduce its impact on the therapeutic relationship.

Transference Within Other Therapeutic Frameworks

The term "transference" is most often used by psychodynamic practitioners, but clinicians and researchers from other theoretical orientations have explored the construct as well. Social cognitive theorists (Berk & Andersen, 2000;

Miranda & Andersen, 2007) have investigated transference in laboratory settings. According to this model, cognitive patterns are activated cues in the social environment that trigger preexisting mental representations. When these memories are activated, the individual views others through the lens of these pre-existing cognitive structures. The model also assumes that representations of others are closely linked with representations of the self. This connection may result in certain interpersonal patterns (*dynamics* in psychodynamic parlance) being re-enacted in these new relationships (Andersen & Berk, 1998).

Paul Wachtel is a well-known psychotherapy integration researcher and author. He conceptualized transference in Piagetian terms, from a largely developmental perspective (Wachtel, 1981). This view of transference focuses on the client's use of assimilation and accommodation. In assimilation, clients perceive new information and incorporate it into a preexisting mental scheme; in accommodation, a preexisting schema is modified or an entirely new schema is created to take in and organize new information that does not fit the schema. According to Wachtel, transference is caused by the predominance of assimilation over accommodation. Rather than create new schemas, which requires a great deal of cognitive effort and complexity, the client may only be able to fit the therapist's behavior into schemas developed earlier in life.

Robert Leahy (2007b, 2008) has explored the therapeutic relationship from a cognitive perspective. He describes transference as consisting of "personal and interpersonal processes that occur between the patient and the therapist" (p. 229). Leahy emphasizes the role of schemas about the self and others in shaping therapeutic relationships. He also highlights the important role emotion plays in therapy (Leahy, 2007a). A client with a borderline personality is likely to express rapidly shifting idealizing and devaluing statements, feel that the therapist is never able to give enough, have inappropriate boundaries, and attempt to attract and repel the therapist to varying degrees. This pattern of behaviors is a result of schemas, conceptual models of interpersonal relatedness that are implemented in the therapist–client dyad. Cognitive behavioral therapists are more likely to describe this phenomenon as a pattern of behavior based on negative attributions, overgeneralization, and a negative view of the self, rather than referring to it as transference.

As cognitive behavioral therapy has begun to address the treatment of personality disorders, clinicians and researchers have also commented on the role of transference responses. Beck, Freeman, and Davis (2004) define transference as the client's emotional response to the therapist. These responses are a result of schemas and core beliefs about the self that underlie various personality disorders. The authors briefly describe the importance of acknowledging these patterns insomuch as they may add to the understanding of the meaning behind a client's behavior. Attachment theorists have also considered transference phenomena as the repetition of internal working models that originate in early childhood relationships and are elaborated across the life span (Levy, 2005).

Regardless of theoretical orientation, most therapists agree that patterns from the client's life outside the consulting room are likely to emerge in therapy. Psychodynamic therapists will most often view transference as a necessary and essential part of the therapy process. Other types of therapists may see transference as a factor that can interfere with achieving positive therapy outcomes.

COUNTERTRANSFERENCE

Countertransference can be the best of servants but is the most awful of masters.—Segal, quoted in Bell (1997, p. 30)

The history of **countertransference** has run parallel to the development of the theory regarding transference. Freud and others became increasingly aware of emotional and cognitive reactions they were having in response to their clients. They found themselves acting on unconscious thoughts and feelings that interfered with their ability to be objective and therapeutic. Many types of reactive feelings can arise in the therapist. For example, a therapist who responds to a client's neediness with inordinate caretaking may foster too much dependency in the client. Similarly, a therapist who feels angry or repulsed by a particular client will also have difficulty providing appropriate care. These types of counterreactions were seen as an impediment to the psychoanalytic process. Freud (1910) understood this type of countertransference, referred to as **classical countertransference**, as unresolved conflicts originating in the therapist's childhood that are triggered by the client's transference. Advocates of this classical conceptualization see no benefit to countertransference and this definition remained predominant until the 1950s.

Countertransference started out as a label for the unconscious limitations on therapists' objectivity. Winnicott (1949) was one of the first to distinguish between subjective and objective countertransference. **Subjective countertransference** refers to ways the therapist may respond as a result of the therapist's own personal issues. The aspects of **objective countertransference** are the therapist's reaction to the client's actual personality or observed behavior. Subjective countertransference, therefore, is more indicative of a process internal to the therapist and may suggest a need for individual treatment, supervision, or consultation. It is akin to the classical definition of countertransference. Objective countertransference is an opportunity for the therapist to learn more about the client's interpersonal dynamics and should be understood as a clinically relevant experience. Objective countertransference is believed to reflect how most therapists would react in a similar situation (Winncott, 1949). A lack of attention to subjective countertransference can lead to blaming clients (Hayes, 2004); however, a failure to attend to objective countertransference or over-attributing countertransference to the therapist's issues can result in a lack of understanding of the client's own personality dynamics that affect the therapeutic relationship (Kiesler, 2001).

Paula Heimann (1950) added to Winnicott's description of objective countertransference with her suggestion that countertransference might not always be a hindrance to treatment. Rather, countertransference began to be seen as a tool that could be utilized by the therapist for the client's benefit. She wrote that "the analyst's immediate emotional response to his patient is a significant pointer to the patient's unconscious processes" (Heimann, 1950, p. 83) and explained that being aware of such reactions could aid the therapist in developing a better understanding of the client. Racker (1957) introduced the idea of **complementary countertransference**. This view suggests that the therapist's reactions are a complement to the client's style of relating. Certain clients may "pull" for certain responses such as care giving, anger, or boredom. Ideally, therapists will notice these reactions rather than acting on them. This restraint will allow the therapist to better understand how and why the client provokes similar reactions in family members and friends.

There has been a great deal of debate about what countertransference includes. Some authors suggest that countertransference consists of *all* the feelings the therapist experiences toward her client (Brenner, 1979; Heimann, 1950). This view of countertransference is referred to as **totalistic countertransference** (Little, 1951). Others have suggested that elements of the therapist's reaction to the client—aspects that contribute to the therapeutic or working alliance—are separate from transference and countertransference reactions (Greenson, 1965). This debate, about what should be included in the overarching term *countertransference*, is ongoing and remains unresolved.

The most contemporary perspective on countertransference, called **relational countertransference,** draws on the relational psychoanalytic perspective. Winnicott's distinction between objective and subjective countertransference has become less rigid as contemporary theorists have come to focus on the intersubjective nature of countertransference (Gabbard, 2001). Intersubjectivity refers to the psychological interplay between two subjects, with one person's emotional and cognitive experience affecting the other's. This growing emphasis on the nonverbal ways client and therapist influence each other is one of the many ways that developments in the theory of countertransference mirror those of transference. As a two-person psychology became predominant within psychodynamic theory, the focus shifted toward examining the ways clients and therapists cocreate certain dynamics. The relational perspective views countertransference as mutually constructed between therapist and client (Mitchell, 1993).

In addition to these perspectives, neuroscience and neuropsychoanalysis has begun to explore pathways that may provoke countertransference reactions. There is some evidence that when individuals are faced with uncertainty, emotions arise to aid in decision making. A network of pathways, including the amygdala, ventromedial, and dorsolateral prefrontal cortices, provide a neuroanatomical basis for this process (Naqvi, Shiv, & Bechara, 2006).

Countertransference in Action

Countertransference manifests itself in a wide variety of ways. The therapist may remember incidents from the therapy inaccurately or may view clients as overly similar or dissimilar to themselves (Cutler, 1958). Therapists may find themselves over involved with the client, perhaps even befriending him or her, or underinvolved, coming across as hostile and distant (Rosenberger & Hayes, 2002a, 2002b). In one of the most frank and vulnerable descriptions of countertransference, Irvin Yalom (1989) describes his countertransference to a client he calls Betty. He writes,

> The day Betty entered my office, the instant I saw her steering her ponderous two-hundred-fifty-pound, five-foot-two-inch frame toward my trim, high-tech office chair, I knew that a great trial of countertransference was in store for me. (p. 93)

He continues later in the chapter with specific reactions he is experiencing, writing, "To be frank, she revolted me" (p. 97). Yalom also reflects on how bored he was in response to the subject matter of the sessions.

> Every one of my notes of these early sessions contains phrases such as: "Another boring session"; "Looked at the clock about every three minutes today"; "The most boring patient I have ever seen"; "Almost fell asleep today—had to sit up in my chair to stay awake"; "Almost fell off my chair today." (p. 99)

Yalom is quite aware of his immediate reactions to Betty. He notices them and begins to embark on a process of self-exploration to better understand how his feelings of repulsion affect the therapy. He writes,

> I have always been repelled by fat women. I find them disgusting: their absurd side-wise waddles, their absence of body contour—breasts, laps, buttocks, shoulders, jaw lines, cheekbones, *everything*, everything I like to see in a woman, obscured in an avalanche of flesh.... (pp. 93–94)

In this passage, Yalom is reflecting on classical countertransference, or what Winnicott referred to as subjective countertransference. Irvin Yalom demonstrates the ability to reflect honestly and authentically on his own biases. Most beginning therapists find Yalom's frank self-disclosure somewhat uncomfortable. He has such strong, negative feelings toward a woman who is seeking help. Therapists aren't *supposed* to feel such powerful and judgmental feelings about their clients. The truth is that all therapists experience potent feelings about their clients, whether they are aware of them or not. Yalom connects his deep-seated feelings to his own history:

> I suppose I could point to the family of fat, controlling women, including—featuring—my mother, who peopled my early life. Obesity, endemic in my family, was a part of what I had to leave behind when I, a driven, ambitious, first-generation American-born, decided to shake forever from my feet the dust of the Russian shtetl. (pp. 93–94)

This countertransference reaction to Betty's appearance and the way she carried herself was clearly connected to Yalom's own familial history. But what about the feelings of boredom that were such a big part of his experience? Yalom writes about his consideration of this reaction in this way:

> I dared not utter the word *boring*—far too vague and too pejorative. I needed to be precise and constructive. I asked myself what, exactly, was boring about Betty, and identified two obvious characteristics. First of all, she never revealed anything intimate about herself. Second, there was her damned giggling, her forced gaiety, her reluctance to be appropriately serious. (p. 102)

In this passage of Yalom's chapter, entitled *The Fat Lady*, he offers insight into how the client's behavior produces a particular reaction within the therapist. This is the complementary countertransference that Racker (1957) described. An individual's personality style and way of being with others has the power to pull specific emotional and cognitive responses in the therapist. Complementary countertransference can be extremely informative for the therapist. In the case of *The Fat Lady*, Yalom was able to notice this reaction within himself and it told him something about how others must be reacting to Betty. She was incredibly isolated and disconnected from friends, family, co-workers, and even those in her psychotherapy group. Over time, and largely in response to the way Yalom worked through his countertransference, Betty was able to engage in therapy and make great strides.

BOX 9.2

Considering Countertransference—Learning Exercise 2

After reading Irvin Yalom's truly transparent description of his own countertransference with Betty, consider what types of thoughts and feelings you would have in response to the following clients:

- A 38-year-old man mandated to treatment after being released from a 10-year prison term, which he served for sexually abusing a 4-year-old girl.
- A college student spends much of the session telling you that your voice is like "nails on a chalkboard" and explains that he enjoys meeting with you because it reminds him that he is more intelligent than most people.
- A 6-year-old boy states, "I want to go home with you. I wish I was your kid."
- An adolescent with encopresis arrives at your office smelling of feces.
- A client shows you bruises on her legs and explains, "I went to a bar last night and met a man. I asked him to rape and beat me. He said, 'Your wish is my command,' and we went home together."
- A young man is raped at a party by another man. He refuses to report the incident or to get tested for sexually transmitted diseases. He states, "I have to trust God on this one. He will take care of me."

As you think about your reactions to these scenarios, try to focus primarily on the feelings you have. Try to distinguish between thoughts (e.g., "I want to run away.") and feelings (e.g., "I feel frightened and repulsed."). How would you manage these feelings? Do they have the potential to interfere with your ability to treat the client? How so?

Working With Transference and Countertransference

The therapeutic relationship between client and therapist has three primary components that shape and inform how the two parties work together. The therapeutic alliance, the transference-countertransference dynamics, and the real or actual relationship all work in tandem and affect the treatment outcome (Cartwright, 2011; Horvath, 2000). The premise behind working with transference is that the feelings, behaviors, and attitudes that emerge in therapy can be utilized to modify the client's way of relating to others in his or her daily life (Mills, Bauer, & Miars, 1989). Therapists are encouraged to utilize the naturally occurring positive transference that may add to the therapeutic alliance. If positive transference begins to look more like idealization or borders on privileging the power of the therapist over that of the client, it should be examined more closely. Although addressing feelings the client may have about the therapist may feel uncomfortable at first, it can also be a foray into important aspects of the client's overall functioning.

In order to begin addressing transference, the therapist must first notice such reactions. Although transference is sometimes overt and clearly stated, most often it is manifested through nonverbal communication such as facial expressions or body language or by behaviors such as habitually arriving late for sessions, delaying payment for treatment, or other forms of acting out. It can be helpful to prepare clients for working with transference as part of the psycho-education that is usually done at the beginning of therapy. The therapist might say,

> I encourage you to be as free as possible in discussing whatever is on your mind. As in any relationship, you may find that you feel annoyed or bothered in some way by something I have said or done. I hope you will feel free to express that when it happens. This relationship can serve as a blueprint for some of the other relationships you want to talk about and improve upon in therapy. Sometimes by exploring together what is happening between the two of us, we can learn something very important and useful about how things unfold between you and your family members (or boss, father, etc.).

Interpreting transference is most useful when the client seems to have some awareness and is in a relatively receptive frame of mind to receive the interpretation (Weiner & Bornstein, 2009). Examining transference phenomena is only indicated when significant and useful information is likely to come from it, when it will facilitate progress in the treatment. For example, suppose a client talks at some length about feeling rejected by others. She then states, "I suppose you're about to tell me I'm a narcissist for thinking I'm the center of everything." The transference here was the client's sense that the therapist was thinking a negative thought about the client, when in fact the therapist in this example was feeling empathically toward the client's sense of alienation. The therapist could have responded at that moment, "I hear you saying you feel rejected by so many people and your next thought is that I must be judging you as well, thinking you are a 'narcissist'." In this case the client was able to digest this interpretation and take it even a step further. She responded, "Yes, I guess on some level I *know* you're not thinking that. You are a supportive person in my life. And actually, so are these friends and co-workers I've been talking about. I wonder if I sometimes feel rejected by them when, in fact, they are trying to embrace me in a way." This reflection by the client opened the door to deeper understanding of the personality dynamics that were being played out in many of her relationships. Over time she developed a greater ability to notice others' warmth and affection for her when, previously, she could see only antipathy.

Although it is impossible to feel the same level of rapport with each and every patient, it is incumbent upon all therapists to effectively monitor, manage, and utilize the relational aspects of treatment to assist the client. Once you are able to notice your reactions toward clients, it will be important to determine how to deal with those responses. The method of handling countertransference depends largely on how it is conceptualized. Therapists who embrace the classical conceptualization of countertransference may argue that therapists should undergo personal psychotherapy or psychoanalysis to reduce manifestations of countertransference. This will allow the therapist to focus exclusively on the client's transference. Therapists who take the view that countertransference is both subjective and objective and is often complementary will likely exploit countertransference reactions in a controlled way for the purposes of therapy. Those who take a relational approach and see *all* reactions as countertransference (e.g., totalistic countertransference) will be guided by it. The relational school sees transference-countertransference reactions as a necessary type of unconscious communication within the therapy. Regardless of one's theoretical orientation, there is widespread agreement that if countertransference is to be a help rather than a hindrance, the therapist must do something to, about, or with his or her countertransference reactions rather than acting thoughtlessly (Hayes, Gelso, & Hummel, 2011).

The effective therapist should work to prevent acting out in response to reactions he or she is having to the client. The trouble is, there is evidence that trainees in psychotherapy actually have difficulty in assessing their own countertransference management abilities accurately (Hofsess & Tracey, 2010). This is one reason supervision is an integral part of training new counselors. It is often useful to share countertransference reactions with a supervisor you trust and to seek peer supervision and consultation throughout your career. Additionally, pursuing your own personal therapy may be very helpful in improving insight into your own personal history and personality style to better manage countertransference reactions. Freud (1937/1964) was the first to suggest personal therapy as an essential component of training new psychoanalysts when he wrote, "But where and how is the poor wretch to acquire the ideal qualification which he will need in this profession? The answer is in an analysis of himself, with which his preparation for his future activity begins" (p. 246). Although few graduate training programs in the United States explicitly require personal therapy for trainees (Norcross, 2005), many therapists pursue psychotherapy before and after entering professional practice (Bike et al., 2009; Guy, Stark, & Poelstra, 1988).

Research on the management of countertransference has almost exclusively used the Countertransference Factors Inventory (CFI; Van Wagoner, Gelso, Hayes, & Diemer, 1991), which is a 50-item measure with five subscales. The subscales of the CFI offer a helpful outline for monitoring and effectively managing countertransference. Developing these skills will also increase a therapist's ability to utilize countertransference as an effective therapeutic tool. The five attributes thought to be important to successful management of countertransference are: self-insight, self-integration, anxiety management, empathy, and conceptualizing ability.

Self-insight refers to the therapist's awareness of, and insight into, his or her own feelings, attitudes, personality, motives, and histories. These represent aspects of subjective countertransference that the therapist brings into the consulting room. It is especially important for therapists to work on their own psychological health and learn how to manage internal reactions to their clients. Self-insight can be pursued in individual psychotherapy and supervision, group supervision, and may be enhanced by other practices such as meditation and journaling.

Self-integration refers to the development of a basically healthy personality structure. Being an integrated individual means being able to recognize the actual boundaries between client and therapist. The ability to differentiate between self and other, particularly the needs of each party, is one aspect of self-integration that protects the client from a variety of boundary violations. The therapist's struggle to gain self-understanding is fundamental to managing and effectively using one's internal reactions. A therapist who has achieved a reasonable degree of self-insight and self-integration is better equipped to attend to client behaviors and to manage internal reactions to these behaviors. These two aspects of countertransference management underscore the importance of the therapist resolving major conflicts to experience better psychological health and to enhance the work he or she does with clients.

Anxiety management refers to therapists' ability to control and understand anxiety so that it does not adversely affect their responses to patients. As the term implies, the ability to manage your own anxiety is a skill that can be developed over time. Being able to control and understand one's own anxiety will help protect the client and allow the therapist to better interpret and respond to counter-transference feelings. For example, a client who speaks explicitly and somewhat sadistically about sex may provoke anxiety in many therapists. The therapist who becomes consumed by this anxiety may find him or herself paralyzed or avoidant of the material. Therapists who have learned to effectively manage their own anxiety will be better equipped to notice the anxious feelings and then consider them as a complementary or objective form of countertransference that needs to be addressed therapeutically. Anxiety management and conceptualizing ability, which is discussed later in this section, have both demonstrated a positive association with trainee and supervisor ratings of client outcomes (Gelso, Latts, Gomez, & Frassinger, 2002).

Empathy, or the ability to partially identify with and put one's self in the other's shoes, permits the therapist to focus on the patient's needs despite difficulties he or she may be experiencing at the moment. Even when clients speak about difficult topics, an empathic therapist will be able to develop an intellectual understanding of the client's experience and be able to respond appropriately. A foundational aspect of managing countertransferential feelings is the ability to focus on the client's needs above and beyond those of the therapist. If the therapeutic alliance is strong, clients are likely to share things that may instinctively repulse or offend the therapist. For example, a client may report a dream he had about harming or humiliating the therapist. A natural countertransference to this type of material would be fear, anxiety, anger, or embarrassment. On the other hand, maintaining an empathic stance might allow the therapist to see ways in which the dream represents a feeling of helplessness or inferiority (or something entirely different) for the client. Without the ability to maintain empathy, this aspect of the client's experience might be overlooked. Although the therapist may face challenges in maintaining an empathic stance, maintaining a genuine sensitivity to the client's experience can prevent acting out of countertransference on the part of the therapist (see Mordecai, 1991).

Finally, the **conceptualizing ability** reflects the therapist's ability to draw on theory and understand the patient's role in the therapeutic relationship. Coursework and supervisory experiences with case conceptualization can greatly improve conceptualizing ability. Theory alone is not enough, but theory in conjunction with the type of personal awareness we have described is a key to the therapeutic use of countertransference. Having a strong theoretical background can help ground therapists so that they are not susceptible to being unnecessarily "carried away" by countertransference reactions.

The most important aspect of countertransference is what the therapist does with his or her internal experience (Gelso & Hayes, 2001). Even when the therapist acts out on countertransference feelings, it is valuable to admit that a mistake was made, particularly when it was the therapist's conflicts that were the source of the mistake (Hill et al., 1996). Increasing self-insight and self-integration is most likely to be achieved through personal therapy and supervision. Empathy and anxiety management are aspects of countertransference management that stem from the ability to be self-reflective and the development of a healthy personality structure. Conceptualizing ability is developed through advanced coursework and ongoing clinical supervision. These five aspects of countertransference management are areas that all therapists, from beginners to the most advanced practitioners, can continue to develop and improve upon.

BOX 9.3

Spotlight on Culture—The Interplay of Transference and Countertransference Dynamics

The French theorist Jacques Lacan has written extensively about the subjectivity of both the therapist and client. In a critique of Freud's work with Dora (Lacan, 1985), he argued that Dora's thinking and behavior, which Freud saw as transference, was in fact a reaction to Freud's own countertransference. Arnd-Caddigan (2013) refers to this interrelationship as **cotransference**. In the spirit of the relational school of psychoanalysis, several therapists have written papers about issues of race (Altman, 2000; Suchet, 2004), disability (Dewald, 1994; Watermeyer, 2012), social class (Javier & Herron, 2002; Ryan, 2006), and gender (Salberg, 2008; Tholfsen, 2000) as they relate to transference and countertransference.

One of the most candid reflections on the interplay of transference and countertransference comes from Neil Altman's (2000) paper "Black and White Thinking: A Psychoanalyst Reconsiders Race." Altman, a middle-class Jewish psychoanalyst, recalls his failed treatment of an upwardly mobile African-American man called Mr. A. According to Altman, Mr. A grew up as a troubled kid in the South Bronx. He was eventually placed in foster care, where he was sexually and physically abused by members of the extended family. At age 12, he was reunited with his parents and vowed to turn over a new leaf. He excelled academically, went to an Ivy League law school, and became a lawyer fighting for social justice. Altman initially felt admiration and solidarity with Mr. A, who sought treatment for panic symptoms and marital difficulties. Mr. A was also preoccupied with and angry about his father's request to repay a large financial loan that he had given him.

Despite his initial positive countertransference toward Mr. A, Altman soon became frustrated with Mr. A as he began to miss sessions and bounce checks. Altman soon recognized that he had a peripheral thought even before the first check had bounced.

(continued)

(*continued*)

> I had the marginal thought that Mr. A would not pay me. I cannot be sure of all the sources of this thought, but I believe my thinking went something like this: I can't believe this man, who has fought his way up from poverty and who still struggles to make ends meet, is going to give substantial sums of money to a privileged person like me. At a somewhat deeper level was a racially prejudiced thought: I thought of him as more likely to stiff me because he was black...I also got caught in a tangled web of guilt, anger, and greed. A complementary anti-Jewish stereotype was activated as well. I began to feel like the stereotypical greedy Jew, like the Jewish landlord feeding off the poverty-stricken residents of the ghetto. (p. 594)

Altman attempted to interpret Mr. A's behavior as a re-enactment of the dynamic that had been created with his father, telling Mr. A:

> You know, the situation that develops when you bounce a check is like that between you and your father. I know that, unlike your father, you eventually pay me. But when you bounce the check, it puts me in your position in relation to your father, having been promised some money, feeling that I got it, and then having it withdrawn. I think you may, without intending it, be letting me know something about how it feels to be you in relation to your father. (p. 595)

Eventually, Mr. A dropped out of treatment, leaving a considerable sum unpaid. Altman speculates that his own shame about his semiconscious racist feelings and internalized anti-Semitism held him back from effectively exploring the situation with Mr. A. This paper is an excellent example of how two individual psychologies can collide in the therapeutic relationship, to poor results.

The Real Relationship

Not all reactions in psychotherapy are transference or counter transference. Some aspects of the relationship contribute to the therapeutic or working alliance, as described earlier in this chapter. Further, there is a distinction between these components of the relationship and the actual or real relationship. The **real relationship** is a separate construct thought to be free of transference/countertransference influences and also separate from the therapeutic alliance. It consists of the experiences of client and therapist that stand apart from the working aspects of the relationship. The real relationship is the personal, nonwork elements of the relationship. Gelso (2011) has defined the real relationship as "the personal relationship existing between two or more people as reflected in the degree to which each is genuine with the other, and perceives and experiences the other in ways that befit the other" (pp. 12–13). The real relationship is thought to contribute to how these other aspects of the relationship—working alliance and transference/countertransference—unfold and develop. For example, clients with avoidant attachment styles in their romantic relationships are also likely to demonstrate avoidance of closeness with their therapist (Marmarosh et al., 2009). This is a real aspect of the therapeutic relationship, undistorted by subjective misperceptions. The question of whether there is any reality in the therapeutic relationship that is *not* subjectively construed remains open for debate (Hatcher, 2009).

Power Dynamics

The therapeutic relationship is bound by certain rules (e.g., the frame) and a level of understanding (e.g., therapist awareness of transference and countertransference dynamics) that make it distinct from other interpersonal relationships. Despite these unique characteristics, there is still a significant power dynamic at work between the therapist and client. When an individual visits his family doctor, he is approaching the meeting with the expectation that the physician is the one who *knows* and will provide answers. The doctor is therefore in the position of power. Many clients present for therapy with a similar perspective; they hope and expect that the therapist will have insights and recommendations that they have been unable to find themselves. There is a prevalent perception that therapists have greater knowledge than clients. In some ways this may be true; therapists have knowledge about mental health and mechanisms for change that their clients may not possess. Some of the work of psychotherapy involves educating clients about these different phenomena to collaborate on the treatment process. This dynamic between the therapist and client automatically puts the therapist in a position of power. Some have even argued that when the therapist takes a neutral stance, this is a powerful position (Cecchin, 1987; Murphy, Cheng, & Werner-Wilson, 2006). Even among master therapists whose theoretical approaches are designed to reduce power dynamics (e.g., feminist, narrative, and collaborative language systems), therapists may still exert power over the client and the situation (Murphy et al., 2006).

When working with any client, issues of power and authority are important. They are especially salient when working with people of color, individuals of lower socioeconomic status or with disabilities, and anyone in an otherwise marginalized group. Cecchin (1987) has suggested that counselors approach clients with a stance of curiosity, suggesting that this approach recognizes and celebrates the complexity of interactions between therapist and client. Certain therapeutic settings, like hospitals and prisons, are inherently structured to afford the therapist a great deal of power. Clinicians in these settings literally hold the keys to the outside world. They determine the client's level of freedom, and they are often involved in approving privileges for the client. The therapist and client are sometimes pitted against each other in forensic settings, as therapists provide testimony for or against the client's release. In these scenarios, it can be difficult to effectively manage power dynamics and maintain a therapeutic alliance with the client.

One of the most effective strategies for managing inherent power dynamics, particularly those associated with ethnic and socioeconomic disadvantages, is to talk about them. Therapists can explicitly discuss with clients the differences between them and develop ways to level the playing field. Clients who have experienced powerlessness in their communities and families may welcome the opportunity to give voice to these experiences and create a new way of relating.

EVALUATING THE PROCESS

Psychotherapy supervision is one of the primary means of growth and development for early career therapists (Watkins & Scaturo, 2013). Some key elements of supervision are evaluation, professional enhancement, quality monitoring, and gatekeeping (Falender & Shafranske, 2012; Watkins, 2012a). Effective clinical supervision is an essential part of protecting client and therapist safety (Kilminster & Jolly, 2000). Supervision for trainees is mandated by all professional licensing bodies and consultation with colleagues continues to be a part of professional development for most practicing clinicians even after licensure. Both authors of this book have participated in a variety of supervision activities, including providing supervision to trainees and colleagues, participation in peer supervision groups, ad-hoc consultation with colleagues who specialize in a particular area, and formalized supervision as part of post-doctoral training in psychotherapy.

Supervision provides the therapist with an opportunity to evaluate both the content and process of psychotherapy with another skilled clinician. The old adage, "Two heads are better than one," is especially applicable to the supervisory process. The best supervisory relationships are ones in which the therapist receiving supervision feels safe and secure (Riggs & Bretz, 2006). The qualities we have described as essential to a strong therapeutic alliance—empathy, attunement, and genuineness—are also important aspects of the supervisory alliance. Supervisees are encouraged to be as vulnerable and forthright as possible in terms of what they are experiencing in the consulting room, but they can only do this if there is a strong **learning alliance**, akin to the working alliance that is foundational to the therapeutic relationship. Much of the learning in supervision flows from supervisor to supervisee, but there is also joint learning that occurs.

One of the key components of effective supervision is the capacity for **self-reflection**. The ability to be psychologically minded, nondefensive, and curious about one's own contributions to the therapy process is a cornerstone of supervision (Watkins, 2012b) for both supervisor and supervisee. If both parties are able to be self-reflective, supervision is more likely to be effective. Supervision can also help clinicians manage countertransference feelings and contend with transference from the client. Additionally, power dynamics can be evaluated in a more objective way within the supervisory situation.

THE ETHICS OF SELF-DISCLOSURE

Earlier in this book (see Chapter 2) we discussed the importance of ethics in avoiding exploitative dual relationships. The principles outlined in professional codes of ethics can be challenging, even within the context of a straightforward professional relationship. Adhering to the principles of beneficence and nonmaleficence become increasingly complex when issues of transference and countertransference arise within the therapeutic relationship. The inherent power dynamics between therapist and client, particularly when they go unacknowledged, can also impede the therapist's ability to act with integrity. Additionally, deciding to share or withhold your observations of the transference and countertransference has ethical implications.

The issue of **self-disclosure** is one that applies to many aspects of psychotherapy. Should the therapist voluntarily reveal contents of his or her own mental life, personal preferences, or other aspects of his or her individuality? Freud alluded to the tendency of new clinicians to feel compelled to reveal aspects of their own psyches: "young and eager psycho-analysts will no doubt be tempted to bring their own individuality freely into the discussion, in order to carry the patient along with them and lift him over the barriers of his own narrow personality" (Freud, 1912/1958, p. 117). Regardless of theoretical orientation, most psychotherapists frequently encounter situations where the question of self-disclosure arises. These questions may range widely in terms of their intrusiveness, scope, and frequency.

BOX 9.4

Questions of Self-Disclosure—Learning Exercise 3

In groups of three or four, consider the following scenarios with your classmates. Notice the different responses each group member has to the questions. Share your reactions with each other and explore the potential consequences of your varying responses.

- A client says she has been watching a new show on a cable network about dating and being single in early adulthood. She says, "I felt so miserable watching last night's episode. Have you seen it?"
- As a client is leaving your office prior to your week-long vacation, he says, "So, where are you going next week?"
- Recall the case of *The Fat Lady* (Yalom, 1989). What if you were Betty's therapist and she had asked, "Am I boring you?"
- Each time a client arrives for his session he starts by asking, "How are you doing today?" Would you answer this question? What if you were having a terrible day? Would you answer honestly? Why or why not? What possible effects could different types of responses have on the work with the client?
- While working as a therapist you experience a pregnancy or an illness that will eventually require some time away from your practice (e.g., maternity or medical leave). At what point will you inform your clients? What will you say?

These overt self-disclosures may raise numerous questions for you. Some of the questions might also provoke a wide variety of countertransference reactions, depending on the individual psychology of the therapist. Discuss the different reactions each group member has to each scenario. Can you identify different personality traits or histories that may explain these differences?

Psychodynamic psychotherapy, which is the approach that has paid the most attention to transference and countertransference dynamics, historically recommended that the therapist remain anonymous and avoid attempts at self-disclosure (Arlow, 1969). This classical injunction follows from Freud's recommendation that "the doctor should be opaque to his patient and, like a mirror, should show nothing but what is shown to him" (Freud, 1912/1958, p. 118). Even therapists who subscribe to this one-person approach acknowledge that all therapists inadvertently convey a great deal of information to their clients. Style of dress, hairstyle, jewelry, timeliness, office furnishings, facial expressions, and apparent age are just some of the things that therapists reveal involuntarily. In an exercise with students, Dr. Prout asked them to verbalize what they felt they knew about her just through their observations on the first day of class. Students reported that Dr. Prout seemed to be "funny," "a little harsh," "stylish," "conservatively dressed," "married," "heterosexual," "lesbian," "young," "too old to relate to me," and so on. As you can see, students differed significantly in their assessment of their professor's personality and private life. Aspects of the self that are disclosed are always seen through the lenses of the observer.

Contemporary perspectives on self-disclosure have focused on what types of self-disclosure are helpful and therapeutic for the client (Cooper, 1998; Renik, 1999). Davies (1994, 1998) and Ehrenberg (1995) have specifically discussed the utility of revealing countertransference reactions insomuch as it facilitates the therapeutic process. It may be helpful to reveal countertransference reactions if, and only if, it is in the best interests of the client. Yalom (2002) has outlined three primary types of self-disclosure: (a) the mechanisms of therapy; (b) here-and-now feelings (e.g., countertransference); and (c) the therapist's personal life. He recommends being totally transparent about the mechanisms of therapy. Yalom suggests therapists be careful about revealing countertransference reactions and use extreme caution when revealing aspects of one's own personal life. In his book, *The Gift of Therapy,* Yalom (2002) relates his experience of revealing his mother's death to members of a psychotherapy group he was co-leading. It is a brief but informative account that demonstrates how self-disclosure, when exercised carefully and judiciously, has the capacity to remove roadblocks in psychotherapy.

In another account of self-disclosure, this time the revelation of countertransference feelings, Marilyn Rifkin (2013) shares a clinical vignette in which she shares her strong negative reactions with a client. At the height of an intense power struggle between therapist and client, the client questions Rifkin's emotional state. Here is the exchange, beginning with the client speaking to the therapist:

> "You hate me," she said, accurately.
> "I guess I do hate you right now," I said. "I don't always hate you, but right now I feel very, very angry and I need to think about why that is—what has happened in here, between us, that created this state…"
> Silence. Suddenly, I recovered some sense of what I wanted to convey. I felt calmer. I had regained my equilibrium. I could breathe. Ms. D, too, seemed calmer. Somehow, by admitting, aloud, that I felt hatred toward Ms. D—and reminding us both that we were in a process that was meant to understand such feelings—helped. It helped a lot. (p. 6)

Rifkin's candid case report is discussed in the same publication by several other clinicians (Ainslie, 2013; Auchincloss, 2013) who take differing perspectives on her frank disclosure. In the case Rifkin presents, this seemingly harsh self-disclosure results in significant leaps forward for the client. The work became more collaborative and the client was much better able to label and discuss her feelings after this exchange. For the first time, the client began to discuss her father's death, a topic she had avoided for several years despite its negative effect on her. This is a particularly useful example because the therapist was able to be aware of her own countertransference reactions and did not attempt to derail the client's perception. A less self-reflective therapist may have attempted to interpret the client's question as a form of transference, which would have likely been quite damaging to the client's sense of reality.

When you consider the power dynamics at play in a particular therapeutic relationship, to what degree should you disclose your observations? Some clients will consistently defer to the therapist's expertise, in effect disavowing their own sense of agency. Other clients may approach psychotherapy as a situation that replicates or repairs certain types of marginalization from the past. Issues of ethnicity, class, disability, sexual orientation, and difference are central to a client's psychic identity. There will always be differences between therapist and client in terms of the level of privilege each has been afforded. Aspects of power in the therapeutic relationship should be explored carefully and consistently within the therapeutic dyad.

CHAPTER REVIEW

The therapeutic relationship is influenced by individual histories and personality structures of both the client and therapist. In order to carefully monitor what is happening between the two parties, therapists must be able to attend to multiple levels of experience. Transference, countertransference, and complex power dynamics are all components of the therapeutic relationship that require ongoing attention and exploration.

Transference is the recapitulation of early childhood dynamics that the client brings to the therapeutic relationship. The client may view the therapist as withholding, overly gratifying, unboundaried, or in some other way that is not necessarily concordant with the actual therapist. The concept of transference has evolved over time from a theoretical construct that was wholly the product of the client's psyche to a complex, multilayered conceptualization that views transference as the result of a two-person psychology. Many theoretical orientations recognize that dynamics of the client's daily life and personality structure emerge within the therapeutic relationship. The therapist's response to transference is largely determined by his or her theoretical orientation. Some practitioners see transference as an interference that needs to be addressed and eliminated, whereas others view transference as a necessary and required part of the therapeutic process.

Countertransference refers to the therapist's own responses to the client. These reactions may be a result of the client's own personality dynamics that "pull" for a particular response. They may also be artifacts of the therapist's own history and personality. Unresolved personal issues within the therapist may emerge within the therapeutic relationship and are best addressed through personal therapy and supervision.

Working effectively with transference and countertransference dynamics requires advanced training in psychotherapy. Transference can be observed and sometimes interpreted by the therapist. It is important that transference interpretations be provided without judgment or admonition; the therapist is encouraged to maintain an empathic stance when attempting to interpret transference phenomena. Countertransference reactions can be managed by the therapist. Self-insight, integrated personality structure, consistent empathy, ability to manage one's own anxiety, and skilled case conceptualization are all important components of countertransference management.

Monitoring power dynamics within the therapeutic relationship is also an important task for the therapist. Power can be exercised by both the therapist and client and is often influenced by variables such as ethnicity, culture, religion, sexual orientation, and other forms of difference. A therapist who is attending to issues of transference, countertransference, and power will likely be forced to consider whether he or she should disclose such information. There has been controversy around self-disclosure throughout the literature; however, most practitioners today agree that carefully considered disclosure can be beneficial to the client.

PERSONAL REFLECTION ESSAY QUESTIONS

1. Consider the major types of transference—positive, negative, erotic, and institutional. Which type of transference would be most difficult for you to tolerate? Why?
2. Has anyone given you feedback about how you present yourself? Perhaps a friend or family member has commented that you giggle a lot or that you seem harsh or withdrawn. Think about a time in which you received a remark about your personality or style of communication that was unwelcome. How did you react? Are there ways in which you might handle it differently in the future?
3. As you think about the five components of countertransference management—self-insight, self-integration, empathy, anxiety management, and case conceptualization—which of these have you developed the most thus far? Which of these will require additional work to achieve to an adequate level? What steps will you take to accomplish that?
4. What types of privilege have you experienced as a result of your gender, ethnicity, sexual orientation, level of ability, religion, or other type of difference? Are there ways in which you have been marginalized during your life due to these types of demographic characteristics? What types of feelings do you have about your experiences? How might these feelings manifest themselves as you begin to work with clients of varying backgrounds?

KEYWORDS

anxiety management	inferiority complex	self-disclosure
classical countertransference	institutional transference	self-insight
conceptualizing ability	learning alliance	self-integration
countertransference	metacognition	self-reflection
empathy	negative transference	subjective countertransference
erotic transference	objective countertransference	therapeutic alliance
humanistic theory		transference
individual psychology	positive transference	two-person psychology

FURTHER READING

- Altman, N. (2000). Black and white thinking: A psychoanalytic reconsiders race. *Psychoanalytic Dialogues, 10,* 589–605.

  This is the article detailed in the Spotlight on Culture and demonstrates how transference and countertransference dynamics can interact across racial and inter-generational social class lines.

- Audet, C. T., & Everall, R. D. (2010). Therapist self-disclosure and the therapeutic relationship: A phenomenological study from the client perspective. *British Journal of Guidance and Counselling, 38*(3), 327–342. doi:10.1080/03069885 .2010.482450

  This article offers a wonderful qualitative study of the effect of therapist self-disclosure on clients. The participants in the study were clients and they reported a number of reactions to therapist self-disclosure, including an enhanced connection with the therapist and feeling overwhelmed by the information.

- Davis, J. (2002). Countertransference temptation and the use of self of self-disclosure by psychotherapists in training: A discussion for beginning psychotherapists and their supervisors. *Psychoanalytic Psychology, 19*(3), 435–454. doi:10.1037/0736-9735.19.3.435

  This article explores management of countertransference with respect to self-disclosure. There is a wide-ranging discussion of perspectives on self-disclosure and two case studies to illustrate the point.

- Gabbard, G. O. (1995). Countertransference: The emerging common ground. *International Journal of Psychoanalysis, 76,* 475–486.

  This classic paper presents a comprehensive overview of countertransference phenomena.

- Mordecai, E. M. (1991). A classification of empathic failures for psychotherapists and supervisors. *Psychoanalytic Psychology, 8*(3), 251–262. doi:10.1037/h0079282

  This article proposes six types of empathic failures that can lead to the therapist acting out. The author also explores ways to avoid these types of errors and how to address and repair failures that have already occurred.

- Winnicott, D. W. (1949). Hate in the counter-transference. *The International Journal of Psychoanalysis, 30,* 69–74.

  Winnicott's classic paper on negative countertransference is a "must read" for all students of psychotherapy.

- Yalom, I. D. (2002). *The gift of therapy: An open letter to a new generation of therapists and their patients.* New York, NY: Harper Perennial.

  A classic in the therapy literature, Yalom provides many of his own thoughts on dealing with transference and countertransference and suggestions for managing the three types of self-disclosure.

Promoting Change: Counseling Skills That Address Thoughts and Behaviors

*However mean your life is, meet it and live it; do not shun it
and call it hard names… Things do not change; we change.*
—Henry David Thoreau, *Walden*

LEARNING OBJECTIVES

- Define ambivalence
- Describe how to address ambivalence that is often experienced by clients
- Outline the Stages of Change model
- Identify how to assess readiness to change
- Describe several cognitive techniques for increasing motivation to change
- Outline social learning theory and describe its relevance to therapeutic work
- Describe the integrated behavior model and explain how it relates to change in psychotherapy
- Define cognitive dissonance and discuss how to increase a client's experience of dissonance
- Describe motivational interviewing and identify how principles of motivational interviewing might be integrated into treatment
- Describe several behavioral techniques for increasing clients' readiness and motivation to change
- Describe several psychodynamic techniques that can aid in addressing ambivalence and resistance to change
- Consider how different theoretical approaches might be integrated to help clients change their thinking and behavior

When people seek counseling, it is typically because they are experiencing some amount of distress in their lives. At times, potential clients may present for treatment because of specific behaviors that they would like to change, such as smoking cessation. Yet another possibility is that individuals are coerced, gently or force-fully, to seek help for a problem or a behavior that is seen as maladaptive by others. Regardless of the client's motivations, the skills in this chapter will help you to work with individuals to achieve cognitive and behavioral change. However, the paths to treatment will take slightly different courses depending on whether and how much the client is motivated to work toward those goals. Accordingly, this chapter will also address how to assess and increase motivation to change in clients.

As previously discussed in Chapter 8, not everyone arrives at their first counseling session with a well-articulated therapy goal in mind, so an important part of the mental health professional's job is to seek to understand the client's distress, and work collaboratively to establish goals that will effect meaningful change in the client's life. In many cases people look for help when they have been overwhelmed by life circumstances, such as a particularly stressful or pain-ful situation like losing a job. Perhaps you can imagine a life stressor that you experienced that led to significant suffering. Was your first instinct to identify personal goals for self-improvement or to bemoan the terrible event?

It is often not easy to guide others (or ourselves) to focus on what is change-able within. In fact, the founder of Alcoholics Anonymous (AA) came across a prayer that speaks to this very issue and adopted it for use in AA groups. The Serenity Prayer states, "God grant me the serenity to accept the things I can-not change, courage to change the things I can, and wisdom to know the differ-ence" (AA General Service Office, 2008). Skillful therapists can balance listening empathically to the client's distress over things that are not likely to change with directing clients toward new ways of thinking and acting that may relieve dis-tress. This chapter will discuss techniques for working with clients to deal with their ambivalence to change before outlining techniques that encourage clients to change their thinking and behavior.

ADDRESSING AMBIVALENCE

Clients who are ambivalent feel *both* ways about changing. That is, they have a contradictory mix of positive and negative feelings about change. Clients may also simultaneously see the need to change and deny that there is a problem. This is a *complex* and yet a *common* state. One moment the client desires change and the next questions the need for change. In clinical work, it is almost certain that you will have to address a client's **ambivalence** toward change at some point in treatment.

Sometimes in sessions ambivalence will present behaviorally or indirectly. Clients may come late or fail to show up for sessions. Clients may also pres-ent practical barriers to treatment when ambivalent, such as reported difficulty affording the fee or scheduling sessions at their convenience. Sometimes pro-longed silences or verbose and overly detailed descriptions of daily events can also be forms of avoidance that suggest ambivalence. It is important to notice and empathically inquire about these types of behaviors in order to better understand their meaning.

Another signal of ambivalence is stagnation. When therapy seems to be going nowhere and is unproductive in terms of meeting treatment goals, it may be that the client is wrestling with ambivalent feelings and waning motivation as well as effort. Ambivalence commonly appears during treatment when the going gets tough, and this creates a problematic feedback loop. Specifically, clients who are ambivalent may put less effort into working on treatment goals. When putting forth less effort, they are less likely to see improvement in their daily lives. Finally, lack of improvement may lead the client to question the efficacy of therapy, which fosters a "why bother?" attitude and in turn feeds ambivalence about the need for therapy and the desire to change at all.

Addressing ambivalence is likely to be an initial treatment target when therapy has been mandated by the court system or insisted upon by another person. Consider a therapist who treated an adult client still living with his parents. The parents insisted upon treatment for increasing their son's socialization and independent living skills and also paid the bill. In the initial session with his parents, the client agreed to work toward these goals. In subsequent sessions, the client discussed his daily life and agreed to try some behavioral changes between sessions; however, he rarely completed these tasks. It became clear during frank conversations about his motivation to change that this young man's treatment goal was simply to keep his parents happy by attending sessions and perhaps making small, easy changes when they increased pressure on him to change. Put simply, he was not motivated to work toward his parents' goals, but he knew that he must appear to be engaged in treatment in order to have a satisfactory home life and thus never missed an appointment.

Working with this young man was an eye-opener to the therapist because once the ambivalence was recognized, sessions consistently focused on addressing ambivalence and negotiating his treatment goals. It initially felt frustrating to the therapist to not be working collaboratively toward treatment goals until those goals were revised to reflect the client's perspective of keeping peace at home by "appearing" to make an effort. Most sessions focused exclusively on assessing and exploring the client's ambivalence about making the changes that his parents saw as necessary, and not resisting his perspective or insisting upon change. The therapist's role was not that of another parent demanding change but that of an advocate to assist the client in taking steps he was prepared to make.

BOX 10.1

Thinking About Your Own Ambivalence

Have you ever attempted to change something about your life? Maybe you wanted to change your behavior to achieve better health or improve your happiness. Reflect on that time. Did you experience both positive and negative feelings about changing? Perhaps there were times that you felt more committed to changing than at other times in your process. Were you successful in that attempt to change?

Transtheoretical Stages of Change Model

The degree of ambivalence may vary dramatically depending upon how ready or open the individual is to change. Prochaska, DiClemente, and Norcross (1992) developed a model, which outlines the pathway to successful change, the transtheoretical **Stages of Change model**. Each stage in the model describes the way

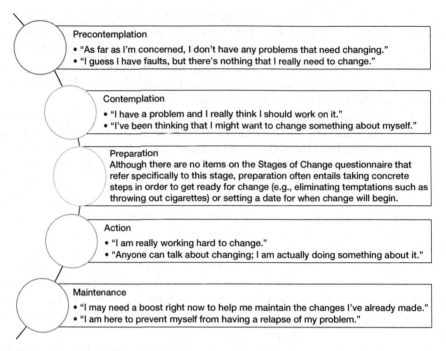

FIGURE 10.1 Prochaska, DiClemente, and Norcross' (1992) Stages of Change with illustrative items from the Stages of Change questionnaire.

Adapted with permission from McConnaughy, Prochaska, and Velicer (1983).

a person thinks about the problem as well as how the person is likely to behave (see Figure 10.1). The first stage is **precontemplation**. As the label implies, a person in the precontemplation stage has not even begun thinking about changing the behavior. In fact, the client may be completely unaware of the problem and has no intention of taking steps to change in the foreseeable future. A person who is abusing alcohol in the precontemplation stage is likely to say, "Why should I quit drinking?"

The next stage is **contemplation**. In this stage, the person has begun to seriously think about overcoming a problem but has not made a firm commitment to take action. A person in contemplation may set a deadline for change but not make a realistic plan to do so. This individual might say, "I can quit any time I want to, but I don't need to now." **Preparation** is the next stage of change. In the preparation stage, individuals intend to take action immediately and are developing a plan to change. This person might locate information about local resources like AA and intend to join straight away. In the next stage, **action**, the person is actively working to overcome the problem. He may be modifying his behavior, experiences, or environment to make changes. The final stage is **maintenance**. That is, the stages of change don't end when the person has successfully made the desired changes, but in this model, there is an ongoing focus on efforts to maintain change. Whether the goal is smoking cessation, weight loss, or reducing depression, it is likely that people will be required to adjust their lifestyle and habits in the long term to continue to enjoy the benefits of change.

Although each stage is presented here in a linear progression toward making change, it is important to note that people don't always travel in a straight line toward change. Individuals may need to return to action if there is a relapse during maintenance, which is considered a normal event in most behavior change. Individuals may also slip from action and making consistent efforts toward change to contemplation when they feel discouraged about the likely success of the plan to change. Prochaska and colleagues (1992) assert that all successful change requires a progression through these five stages, but do not indicate that it is a one-way street to optimal functioning. They described the processes of change as recurring in a spiral.

One strength of this model is that it is trans-theoretical. That is, different systems of psychotherapy can be used in a complementary way when used in different stages of readiness to change. For example, behavioral therapy will be most helpful during the action phase, when clients are focused on taking steps to make change, whereas psychodynamic approaches may be used in earlier stages of change. The Stages of Change model also encourages therapists to approach clients with a high degree of empathy and acceptance for the client's current level of motivation.

Assessing Readiness to Change

In a study of patients who wanted to make changes to their weight, scores on a measure of readiness to change were a better predictor of outcome than many other variables, including the problem's severity and duration, self-efficacy, and social support (Prochaska et al., 1992). Accordingly, assessing a client's readiness to change is an important way to tailor treatment to the individual because stage of change is linked to the type of therapeutic intervention that will be the most helpful to the client. Furthermore, the time that it takes to progress through these stages will vary widely from person to person; thus it is important to regularly assess the client's readiness to change throughout treatment. McConnaughy, Prochaska, and Velicer (1983) developed the Stages of Change questionnaire that can help to identify where clients are in terms of readiness for change (see sample items in Figure 10.1). Prochaska and Norcross (2001) recommend that practitioners should beware of approaching all clients who present for treatment as though they are ready for action. They estimated that approximately 10% to 20% of clients who present for treatment are prepared for action, 30% to 40% are in the contemplation stage, and 50% to 60% are in the pre-contemplation stage. Think about the effect these differing levels of readiness for change might have on treatment when it begins. This is another good reason to listen empathically to clients and understand their readiness to change.

Prochaska and DiClemente (1983) surveyed a large sample of people in each of the different stages of change for smoking cessation. The results indicated that smokers in the various stages emphasize different processes of change. Specifically, individuals in the contemplation stage utilize **consciousness raising** the most. Consciousness raising includes seeking out and being open to information and feedback about smoking. Think about the television advertisements you may have seen for increasing awareness of the negative health effects of smoking. This type of imagery and information may be most effective for people who are contemplating changing their smoking behavior.

Another change strategy, **self-reevaluation,** was emphasized in both the contemplation and action stages of change. This strategy involves re-thinking one's identity as a smoker or "changing responses to consequences without changing contingencies" (Prochaska & DiClemente, 1982, p. 281). That is, although smoking might continue to produce pleasurable effects (i.e., consequences), smokers using self-reevaluation may consider it to be disappointing that they must depend on cigarette smoking to feel good.

Self-liberation, which Prochaska and DiClemente (1982) described as "conscious creation of new alternatives for living" (p. 280), can be understood as a way people purposefully choose to lead different lives. Along with getting support from helping relationships with professionals and peers, self-liberation and reinforcement management are emphasized in the action stage (Prochaska & DiClemente, 1983). Reinforcement management is the process of creating opportunities to receive contingent rewards for successful change behaviors. Counter-conditioning (i.e., changing one's responses to stimuli in the environment) and **stimulus control** (i.e., changing stimuli in the environment to which one is conditioned to respond) are also important change strategies in the action and maintenance stage. To maintain long-term gains requires the use of these methods to resist future temptation to smoke. For instance, if a smoker always enjoys a cigarette while drinking coffee on the drive to work, that smoker might choose to drink coffee before getting in the car as a means of stimulus control, or talk on the phone with a friend while drinking coffee as a means of **counter-conditioning.**

The transtheoretical model of change is a useful tool for understanding clients' motivation to change. Treatment should focus on moving individuals from one stage of change to another to meet treatment goals. Mismatching stages and processes of change can be detrimental to therapeutic change and alliance. Prochaska and Norcross (2001) highlighted two frequently occurring mismatches: relying on consciousness raising and self-reevaluation when clients are in the action stage and using counter-conditioning and stimulus control when clients are in contemplation and preparation stages. Specifically, they suggest that insight alone is not helpful to individuals ready to take action for behavioral change and behavioral techniques are not helpful for clients who do not have awareness of their decision and intent to change.

BOX 10.2

Teens and Readiness to Change

A recent study found that for adolescents increased motivation to change was related to better emotional regulation and better parent–child relationships (Taylor, Zaitsoff, & Paterson, 2012). This is an important finding because it indicates that enhancing parent–child relationships in treatment and teaching emotion regulation skills may help teens to be more motivated to recover.

COGNITIVE TECHNIQUES

In Chapter 3, you learned that cognitive behavioral therapy (CBT) is based on the theory that thoughts, feelings, and behavior are interconnected (see Figure 10.2). The way that you feel may have a strong impact on how you perceive or interpret a situation and also how you act in that setting. Imagine that you are walking into

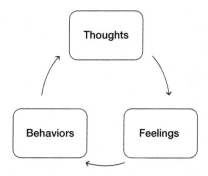

FIGURE 10.2 Cognitive behavioral therapy (CBT) is based on the theory that our thoughts, feelings, and behaviors are interconnected and influence one another.

a classroom, and you see one of your friends select a seat and immediately put some of her belongings on the adjacent desk as if to reserve it for another person. How would you interpret this if you were feeling happy and confident? How would you interpret this if you were feeling sad and insecure? It is likely that you would view her actions as a possible invitation for you to sit next to her if your mood was positive, whereas you would probably assume that she was waiting for someone other than you if your mood was negative. This interpretation, in turn, will affect your decision to walk up and ask your friend if you may take that seat or to walk the other way and sit somewhere else alone.

The Stages of Change model assumes that both cognitive and behavioral components are necessary parts of change (Prochaska & DiClemente, 1982). When people are contemplating and preparing for change, they are likely to benefit from cognitive techniques for increasing their knowledge about the problem, developing a realistic plan to work toward changing the problem, and mustering motivation and effort to tackle the problem. This section will cover cognitive techniques that can be used to help clients change the way they think about changing and feel motivated to do so.

Increasing Self-Efficacy

The strength of people's convictions in their own effectiveness is likely to affect whether they will even try to cope with given situations.—Bandura (1977, p. 193)

In order for a person to do or try something new, she must have some level of confidence in her ability to successfully enact the required behavior. Maybe you have watched a daredevil perform an amazing death-defying feat on a motorcycle. Did seeing this spectacular display inspire you to attempt the same stunt? Perhaps it did, and if you were inspired, did you immediately go out and buy a motorcycle, a bejeweled leather suit, and set out to find the nearest ring of fire to jump through? Although seeing another person perform a highly desired behavior can serve as inspiration for an individual, there must also be a belief that the goal is within one's ability. That is, the likelihood that you would seriously pursue learning motorcycle stunts is related to your desire to perform the behaviors as well as the belief that you can skillfully master motorcycle riding, showmanship, and risk management.

ILLUSTRATION 10.1 Motorcycle daredevils entertain all, but only a few of us will be inspired to take real steps to learn to perform motorcycle stunts ourselves.
Courtesy of Iain Farrell.

Social Learning Theory

Albert Bandura (1971) developed a theory known as **social learning theory** that describes the variables involved in how people decide to act. His theory was written in contrast to the psychodynamic theory, which posits that behavior is driven by unconscious inner forces at one end of the spectrum and strict behaviorism at the other, which suggests that behavior is driven by responses to stimuli in the environment. Bandura believed that behaviorism provided an "incomplete rather than an inaccurate" description of behavior (1971, p. 2). That is, he was critical of behaviorism's total disregard of inner variables, namely cognition and self-direction.

One important component of Bandura's theory is **vicarious learning**. Specifically, he hypothesized that people frequently learn behavioral patterns by watching other people successfully perform them. That is, there is no need to directly experience the consequences of certain actions to either increase or decrease the future performance of that behavior. Watching others can be a powerful learning tool on its own. Remember the motorcycle daredevil? Through vicarious learning, you may have developed the motivation to perform the stunt after watching its successful conclusion and the throng of adoring fans surrounding the brave rider, or you may have decided to cross that off your bucket list after watching him transported away from the scene on a stretcher with multiple injuries and broken bones. A more typical case of vicarious learning is when a child watches her sibling receive praise and attention for brushing her teeth: she may also decide to go and brush her own teeth in an attempt to receive the same desirable praise. Emotional reactions can also be learned vicariously. The same child might see her sibling reacting fearfully to a visit to the doctor and also respond fearfully when it's her turn to visit the pediatrician.

Our capacity to think and anticipate consequences helps us to plan "insightful and foresightful behavior" (Bandura, 1971, p. 3), which is a great benefit when it comes to deciding to act in a certain way. Social learning theory also includes another important component: **observational learning** through **modeling**. Humans learn by example, particularly in situations in which trial-and-error would be costly and when the behavior is complex. Think about learning to ride a bike. It would be much more difficult (and painful) to learn without watching others successfully ride. Bandura wrote, "example is a much better teacher than the consequences of unguided actions" (1971, p. 4). The classic research on learning through modeling was conducted by Miller and Dollard (1941), in which they determined that for observational learning to be successful, the observer must be motivated to perform the behavior, view an example of the behavior, imitate the example, and then receive positive reinforcement for learning to imitate that behavior. Bandura built upon this explanation in social learning theory because he recognized that people modeling for others typically do not immediately mimic and receive a reward or reinforcement for behaviors they see. His theory suggests that observers form symbolic representations (e.g., thoughts) about the modeled behavior, and that observational learning is dependent upon four processes:

- *Attention*: The observer must pay attention to the model, focus on the relevant important components of the action, and perceive the steps accurately. Think back to the motorcycle daredevil. It will be difficult to learn from this model if you are more focused on his outfit than the way that he accelerates the motorcycle and lifts the handlebars. It is also important to note that different people will have access to different types of models from which to learn. Without a television, it is unlikely that many people would have access to observing the motorcycle daredevil.
- *Retention*: The observer must be able to remember the activity that was modeled in the past in order to perform it. Bandura posited that individuals use both visual imagery and verbal descriptions to retain information about modeled behaviors.
- *Motoric reproduction*: In order to successfully perform the behavior, the observer must put the pieces together in terms of the sequence of physical motions required. There are several potential impediments to this part of the process. The person may not have the requisite subskills that need to be strung together or there may be physical limitations that inhibit a person's successful performance. Additionally, the observer may not be able to easily judge whether she is performing the behavior accurately if it is not observable. Imagine learning to play the cello. You may view your teacher holding her bow, but you cannot see your own bow hold to judge if you are making an accurate reproduction of her movements unless you are in front of a mirror.
- *Reinforcement and motivation*: If the observer pays attention, retains, and can accurately reproduce the behavior, it still may not be performed because the observer is not motivated to do so. In observational learning, reinforcement is considered a "facilitative rather than necessary condition" (Bandura, 1971, p. 9) because there are these other factors (e.g., paying attention to a model doing something compelling) that may make the behavior likely to occur in the future. Bandura found that children do not have to be promised a reward for modeling behaviors they see on television.

Bandura (1977) outlined several approaches clinicians can take to increase self-efficacy in their clients based on social learning theory. In fact, Bandura viewed all psychological treatment methods as ways of creating and strengthening a person's perceived self-efficacy. Any method that increases a client's belief that he can successfully perform the required behavioral changes will be an important tool in guiding that client to make changes. Although it matters if a person believes that the particular behavior will produce a desired effect (i.e., outcome expectations), whether a person chooses to try and persist in behavioral change is determined by his efficacy expectations as illustrated by the quotation that began this section.

Specifically, **mastery experiences**, in which the client attempts a task outside of a session that approximates the desired change, will increase self-efficacy and perceived behavioral control. For example, a smoker could eliminate one cigarette a day and feel that he has more control over fighting his urges to smoke than he previously thought. Success is important when assigning a behavioral experiment to a client. Setting up a behavioral task that is too difficult for the client may lead the client to feel more hopeless about change if he fails. Observational learning through modeling is another powerful way to increase self-efficacy. The characteristics of the model are important in terms of helping clients to boost their own self-efficacy. Models should be selected that are similar to the client. Models that are similar to the client are persuasive examples, and the client is more likely to learn by observing this model.

The above two techniques can be successfully combined to help clients achieve increased self-efficacy. Recall the discussion of exposure therapy from Chapter 3. Exposure involves coming into contact with a feared object or situation, and experiencing the feelings of fear without escape, such as fleeing or looking away from the focus of the exposure, or engaging in mental avoidance, such as distraction, until the fear naturally decreases. Skillful implementation of exposure therapy includes two techniques that increase self-efficacy in clients. First, clients typically have a mastery experience by bravely facing and coping with their fears in a step-by-step manner. Throughout treatment, self-efficacy is boosted as clients successfully meet new challenges by confronting successive items on the exposure hierarchy. Second, therapists typically model the exposure task for clients in session, which helps clients learn vicariously how to perform the behavior as well as what the likely consequences of performing the behavior will be. Even when not in the context of exposure therapy, if a task is too frightening or difficult for the client to attempt, the therapist may first model the behavior in session and perform it alongside the client as a way to help the client have a mastery experience.

BOX 10.3

Bandura's Words of Wisdom Regarding Facing Our Fears

Those who persist in mastering subjectively threatening activities that are in fact relatively safe will gain corrective experiences that reinforce their sense of efficacy, thereby eventually eliminating their defensive behavior. Those who cease their coping efforts prematurely will retain their self-debilitating expectations and fears for a long time.

Albert Bandura (1977, p. 194)

Social persuasion is another way that people increase their self-efficacy. Simply discussing the client's capabilities and likelihood to succeed in behavioral change can be a powerful way to enhance self-efficacy. Bandura (1977) acknowledged that people who are verbally persuaded that they are capable tend to show weaker self-efficacy than those who have a behavioral mastery experience, but individuals who are provided with verbal encouragement about their abilities may also expend more effort during attempts than those who are given behavioral instructions only. It is important to keep in mind that conversations about a client's ability should be realistic and not overly optimistic because the boost offered by this conversation may be quickly undermined by a failure to perform the behaviors discussed.

The final route Bandura suggested for boosting self-efficacy is improving mood. Because self-efficacy is enhanced when people are in a good mood, clients should be encouraged to work toward improving mood. Also, individuals may interpret bodily sensations, such as increased heart rate and sweating, as signs of impending danger, which negatively affects self-efficacy. A client may be directed to interpret these benign and typical somatic sensations as arousal that sharpens one's ability to perform to the best of one's ability rather than a sign he is not up to the task. In other words, when it comes to judging anxiety and stress, it is best not to go with one's gut feelings.

BOX 10.4

Learning Exercise

Think about a task that you are afraid to tackle. It may be a new behavior that you are reluctant to start, but one that causes some annoyance or interference with your daily life. Using Bandura's four mechanisms for increasing self-efficacy, think about ways to increase the likelihood that you will make this change.

The Integrated Behavior Model

Fishbein and Ajzen (1975) also developed a comprehensive theory to describe how people act. The theory of planned behavior (TPB) describes the variables that contribute to an individual's motivation to complete a specific behavior (Ajzen, 1985, 1991) that is based on the earlier theory of reasoned action (TRA; Ajzen & Fishbein, 1980; Fishbein & Ajzen, 1975). Both of these theories are explanations of how people take in information around them and use it to form intentions to act. According to the TRA and TPB, **intentions** (i.e., a person's conscious plan to enact a certain behavior) are connected directly to behavior, and there are three other variables that affect a person's behavioral intention. An individual's attitude regarding the behavior and knowledge of **subjective norms** contributes to the likelihood of a person intending to act and are both outlined in the TRA.

A person who believes that performing the behavior will lead to positive consequences and has positive feelings about performing the behavior will have a positive attitude toward the behavior, which increases that person's intention to act and vice versa. Subjective norms refer to what an individual believes others typically do with regard to the behavior as well as others' opinions of the importance of performing the behavior. If a person thinks that other people value the behavior and the person is motivated to please those others, this increases the likelihood of forming an intention to act. Conversely, if a person is not motivated to conform to the behavior norms of those around him and they value the behavior, he is not likely to have a strong intention to act.

For example, imagine that you are working with a client to take medication regularly as prescribed by his physician. To assess the client's attitude, you would explore his thoughts about the outcome of taking his medication regularly and his feelings while taking the medication. If he expects that he will be happier and able to function better, he has a positive attitude toward the behavior. To assess his subjective norm, you would discuss his normative beliefs (i.e., whether his family and friends approve or disapprove of taking medication) as well as his motivation to act according to his loved ones' expectations. If he is motivated to comply with his normative beliefs, he will have a positive or negative subjective norm matching that of the others in his life. If he is not motivated to behave according to normative beliefs, he will have a neutral subjective norm.

The TRA refers only to volitional behaviors because it posits that intention is all that is necessary to enact behaviors. However, ability is also an important piece of the equation. Accordingly, the TPB expands upon the TRA by including a mechanism for explaining complex non-volitional behavior that requires skill. Specifically, the TPB introduced the concept of **perceived control** (Ajzen, 1991). Perceived behavioral control is an individual's perception of whether the behavior will be easy or difficult to perform given the circumstances. Behaviors that one has control over (i.e., that are easily performed) are more likely to be carried out than ones that are difficult to perform. In the above case, the client is likely to take his medication regularly if he has positive attitudes, positive subjective norms, and is also capable of enacting the behavior (e.g., has the resources to fill the prescriptions and accurately time the sequence of doses).

A more recent version of the TRA and TPB is the integrated behavior model (Fishbein, 2000) shown in Figure 10.3. In this theory, one more piece is added

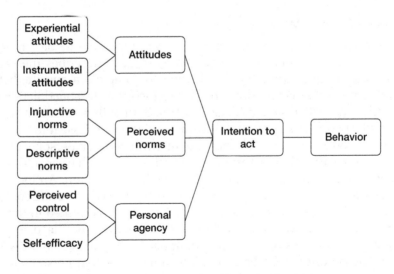

FIGURE 10.3 The integrated behavioral model.
Adapted from Fishbein (2000).

to fully describe how behavioral intentions are likely to form. Attitudes remain important, and the construct is expanded to include both **experiential attitudes** (i.e., related to your emotions about the behavior) and **instrumental attitudes** (i.e., related to the consequences of performing the behavior). Subjective norms, now called **perceived norms**, are also present in this model, but the construct was expanded to include not only **injunctive norms** (i.e., what others feel you should do and your motivation to conform to those expectations) and **descriptive norms** (i.e., what you view others actually doing themselves). **Personal agency** is the third component of the integrated behavior model that is comprised of perceived control and self-efficacy. In this model, it is not only how difficult or easy an individual believes the behavior will be given the circumstances, but also how confident that person feels in performing the behavior given its predicted ease or difficulty. Specifically, some people may be motivated to persist and act in the midst of difficult circumstances because of high self-efficacy.

The integrated behavior model can be helpful when working with clients to identify the beliefs that are the most strongly related to their intention to act. Each client is likely to present a unique constellation of beliefs for each specific behavior, and skillful mental health professionals will work with clients to identify the beliefs that are contributing to (or blocking) the intention to act. Whether the treatment goal is to incorporate a new healthy behavior into a client's lifestyle or decrease a maladaptive behavior, clinicians can work to improve intentions to perform behaviors or highlight beliefs that are sustaining intentions to perform others.

BOX 10.5

Learning Exercise

Recall the same behavioral change that you used for the previous learning exercise. Integrate what you brainstormed about increasing your self-efficacy with the integrated behavior model. Specifically, what are your experiential and instrumental attitudes about this behavior? What are the injunctive and descriptive norms that you perceive from your social network? Because you have already considered your level of self-efficacy, what is your assessment of the expected level of ease or difficulty given your current environmental circumstances?

Increasing Cognitive Dissonance

Helping clients be motivated to make changes to improve their lives is complex. Although using the techniques previously discussed to increase clients' confidence in their ability to act and addressing other attitudes and beliefs that can improve intention to act are powerful treatment techniques, there are times when clients are more resistant to change. Some clients do not see compelling reasons to change their behavior, and thus interventions that are focused on increasing self-efficacy will be less effective.

Cognitive dissonance arises when a person has two thoughts that are inconsistent with one another. Festinger (1957) developed the theory of cognitive dissonance that describes the human tendency to resolve the discomfort that cognitive dissonance causes. Specifically, he theorized that people will alter one or both of the two incompatible cognitions to find relief from cognitive dissonance. Cognitive dissonance is a motivating force that compels people to seek consonance.

The classic example of cognitive dissonance is of a person who smokes cigarettes, yet simultaneously believes that smoking causes cancer. This person is likely to experience cognitive dissonance. One way to resolve the dissonance would be to quit smoking, which is quite difficult, but another would be to alter the other cognition. Smoking is less absurd if the smoker discounts the evidence that smoking is linked to cancer or believes that he does not smoke enough to cause serious harm to himself. Aronson (1969) wrote that "dissonance theory does not rest upon the assumption that man is a *rational* animal; rather it suggests that man is a rational*izing* animal—that he attempts to appear rational, both to himself and others" (p. 3). In other words, people may adopt questionable beliefs in order to resolve cognitive dissonance.

There is evidence that the desire to reduce cognitive dissonance enhances motivation to change. Some empirical studies have shown that when clients are offered a low-effort or high-effort treatment for changing a behavior, even when both treatments are actually placebo conditions unrelated to the purported behavior change, those in the high-effort groups tend to show more successful and lasting changes (Axsom, 1989; Axsom & Cooper, 1985). This has been interpreted as a sign that people increase their motivation to justify the effort being expended on the treatment. That is, individuals who are working hard to change may also alter their cognitions to reflect increased motivation to achieve their desired goal. For example, "If losing weight is going to be this difficult and taxing, I must really *want* to lose weight." Thus, highlighting or intensifying cognitive dissonance in clients can be a tool to increase motivation to change. A systematic approach to this has been developed by William Miller and Stephen Rollnick (2002) and is covered in detail in the next section.

Motivational Interviewing

As discussed at the beginning of this chapter, you are very likely to encounter clients that appear resistant or ambivalent about change. Motivational interviewing (MI) is a treatment method that is used to explore and resolve client ambivalence about change, thus enhancing intrinsic motivation to change (Miller & Rollnick, 2002). It is not a distinct form of psychotherapy, but a method of approaching clients that may be used with many different theoretical approaches to psychotherapy. One of the guiding principles of MI is that most clients are ambivalent about change, and accordingly motivation to change increases and decreases throughout treatment. Miller and Rollnick encourage clinicians to view clients' resistance to change as ambivalence, which is a respectful and a helpful stance. From an MI perspective, clinicians are explicitly focused on ambivalence as a natural part of the change process. When therapists view clients as ambivalent, both sides of the issue (i.e., reasons for changing and reasons for not changing) are examined in session and serve as an important way to increase the client's intrinsic motivation to change.

MI is based on Carl Rogers' client-centered therapy (1951) in that therapists are focused on understanding the client's perspective and values while expressing unconditional positive regard, congruence, and empathy (see Chapter 7 to review these components). Therapists are also focused on highlighting and understanding the discrepancy between a client's behaviors and values. Through the skillful use of the four basic MI principles, the therapist "creates an atmosphere in which the client rather than the therapist becomes the main advocate for change as well as the primary agent of change" (Arkowitz & Miller, 2008, p. 4). The four MI principles, which are easily remembered because they are each alliterative, are:

- **Express Empathy:** See the client's point of view without judgment. Clients must feel safe expressing both sides of their ambivalence.
- **Develop Discrepancy:** Highlight inconsistencies between the client's present behaviors and values.
- **Roll with Resistance:** Respect both sides of ambivalence and accept client arguments for and against change.
- **Support Self-efficacy:** Support the client's beliefs in his or her skills, knowledge, and strength to change. Serve as a consultant when needed.

MI is divided into two phases that roughly correspond to Prochaska and colleagues' (1992) Stages of Change model. In the first phase of MI, clients have strong ambivalence about change and are likely to be in the precontemplation or contemplation stage of change. The goal for this first phase is to resolve this ambivalence and strengthen the client's motivation to change. The second phase begins when clients appear ready to change and are in the preparation stage moving toward action. As a therapist, you will know when your client is ready to change when he begins to talk more about changing, asks more questions about change, and imagines or describes what his future will be like after the changes have been made (Arkowitz & Miller, 2008). In the second phase of MI, the goal is to help the client develop and enact a plan to make change and strengthen his commitment to changing.

In each of the phases of MI, therapists are focused on the four principles and also use the basic skills of MI: asking open-ended questions, listening reflectively, affirming the client, summarizing, and eliciting change talk. The first four skills are fundamental counseling skills that have been covered in previous chapters. For example, reflective listening can be used to clarify ambivalence without provoking the client to defend, which is a way to roll with resistance. Eliciting change talk is unique to MI and consists of using open-ended questions to encourage the client to discuss change without directly advocating for change. When working with a client to elicit change talk, you might proffer, "I wonder how your colleagues might react at work if you didn't have to regularly leave meetings to smoke."

The spirit of MI lies in the therapist's stance as an empathic and nonjudgmental figure that reflects both sides of the client's ambivalence about change back to the client, who uses this to resolve the discrepancy between his actions and values. The therapist does not push change or argue with clients about the need to change. The client's autonomy is respected. The motivation to change comes from the client, facilitated by the therapist's use of the MI skills to elicit change talk.

BEHAVIORAL TECHNIQUES

Although the previous section has discussed several techniques for increasing clients' motivation and readiness for change through cognitive mechanisms, not all therapeutic change requires an explicit cognitive decision. Change can come about as a result of trying new behaviors to see what consequences and effects these behaviors have on one's mood and functioning. Maybe you have experienced this before yourself. Think of a time that someone gave you advice, but you were not convinced that it was a wise opinion. Perhaps you were cooking chili and a friend advised you to add cinnamon to the pot. Cognitively, this might have seemed like a far-fetched idea. However, upon trying it out and tasting the delicious result, you may be convinced to never leave that spice out of your chili again.

Making behavioral changes and responding to the feedback from those experiences can be an effective route to lasting change for clients. Because CBT is based on the premise that thoughts, feelings, and behaviors are all interconnected, behavioral change is likely to lead to cognitive change, including increased self-efficacy and optimism, and emotional change, including improved mood. Behavioral techniques are typically used in CBT to eliminate avoidance, help clients face feared situations and objects, learn positive coping skills, and reduce painful emotions and physiological arousal.

Operant Principles

You may recall from Chapter 3 that operant conditioning describes the manner in which behaviors may be increased or decreased. Specifically, behaviors that are reinforced are likely to be repeated. To increase behaviors, one may either provide a reward, or positive reinforcement, or remove an aversive stimulus, known as negative reinforcement. There are two additional operant principles that serve to decrease behaviors. Positive punishment is adding something aversive, while negative punishment is removing something desired (or potentially reinforcing) from the person. Negative punishment can also be understood as a penalty.

A good example of the way that operant principles work is in the case of anxiety. When a person fears something, such as cats, that person has likely stopped visiting places where he might encounter a cat, or may only do so under duress. This is avoidance behavior that can be reduced behaviorally through exposure therapy. When the client starts gradually confronting his fear, perhaps first by watching videos of cute cats on YouTube and progressing through a hierarchy until he is in the same room as a live cat, he will find that the negative consequences he expects do not happen. He may feel stressed for a short period of time during these exposures, but eventually his arousal will decrease. The relief from anxiety is an example of negative reinforcement that makes it more likely that he will not avoid cats in the future. As discussed previously in the chapter, successful exposure tasks also increase self-efficacy that boosts a person's motivation to continue striving to change patterns of avoidance.

Behavioral Activation for Depression

Behavioral activation is an empirically supported treatment for depression. Just as it sounds, this treatment entails working with clients to increase behavioral activity (Beck, Rush, Shaw, & Emery, 1979). The goal is to create opportunities for the client to be rewarded, internally by pleasant feelings or externally by positive attention from others. From a CBT perspective, depression may develop in part as a result of fewer rewarding interpersonal and behavioral activities. Specifically, negative thoughts about self and the world (part of Beck's negative cognitive triad described in Chapter 3) may cause a person to withdraw from activities (e.g., "No one wants to talk to a loser like me, so I should just stay home."). Thus, one's negative beliefs about self and the world are unchallenged and reinforced because the person has no opportunity to prove them wrong.

There is a strong connection between physical activity and mood. A good slogan for clients engaged in behavioral activation is: Fake it 'til you make it! Although it may be difficult to initiate an activity when feeling depressed, it is likely that starting the activity with false enthusiasm may be replaced with genuine pleasure as time passes and one becomes absorbed in the activity.

BOX 10.6

Behavioral Activation Exercise

Try this experiment to illustrate the connection between activity and mood. First, rate your mood from 1 to 10, with a 10 indicating elated, euphoric bliss. Now stand up and do "the Chicken Dance." That's right. Sing the song and flap your chicken wings. Rate your mood once again. Did it change? This simple experiment can also be used in session with clients to demonstrate the effects of physical activity on mood. Any other playful physical activity can be substituted for the Chicken Dance, such as doing the Hokey Pokey, hula-hooping, or jumping rope.

Components of behavioral activation include monitoring current activity level, collaboratively developing a list of rewarding activities, scheduling those pleasant activities, and rating the pleasure and mastery associated with each activity when it is completed. Mastery is the level of accomplishment the client feels afterwards. Some activities that may be included are moderate exercise, increasing or changing socialization behaviors, and eliminating or curbing avoidance behaviors. It is important to include activities that the patient currently enjoys, has enjoyed in the past, and has considered but never tried. An individual who is depressed may avoid socializing with friends because she thinks they find her repulsive when she is sad and withdrawn. Missing the socialization deprives her of the good feelings she might experience when she is out with her friends, and she stays in her negative mood. An excellent behavior to schedule is calling friends to speak on the phone or meeting a friend for coffee.

If a client feels overwhelmed by the thought of completing the pleasant events scheduled or even developing a list of pleasurable activities, you may consider a **graded task assignment**. A graded task assignment breaks the activity into manageable chunks. For example, the client may not feel prepared to speak to or meet friends, but may be able to make a list of one or two friends that she would consider reaching out to in the future. When using behavioral activation with clients, it is important to remember to respect the client's autonomy in choosing what and how to approach scheduling activities (Leahy, Holland, & McGinn, 2011;

Wright, Basco, & Thase, 2006). Help the client select activities that are manageable to avoid potential setbacks that could arise if the client attempts something that ends up being a disaster. Recall from the earlier discussion of self-efficacy that this can be detrimental to a client's motivation and readiness to change.

PSYCHODYNAMIC TECHNIQUES

Even the normal individual feels, as it were, two souls in his breast; he fears an event and wishes it to come, as in the case of an operation or the acceptance of a new position. Such a double feeling tone exists most frequently and is particularly drastic when it concerns persons whom one hates or fears and at the same time loves.—Bleuler (1951, p. 125)

From a psychodynamic perspective, ambivalence is a normal and expected part of treatment. The behaviors described earlier in this chapter that suggest ambivalence (e.g., arriving late for session, non-payment, prolonged silences) are seen as **resistance** that is indicative of ambivalence. Resistance is any behavior, thought, or feeling that pushes back against the urge to change. As much as a client reports wanting to change, to relinquish old habits or to improve current relationships, there is almost always a conflict with a simultaneous desire to maintain the status quo (Gabbard, 2010). Freud originally viewed ambivalence and resistance as antithetical to the purpose of psychotherapy. The dilemma for Freud was essentially, if a client is arriving late or not fully engaging in the treatment, is there a point to proceeding with them? Over time, however, Freud's understanding evolved and he began to see resistance as an important focus of treatment, something to be understood rather than simply removed.

There are many points of consensus between psychodynamic and cognitive behavioral approaches when it comes to ambivalence and motivational issues. For example, psychodynamic theory acknowledges the important role of secondary gain (what CBT approaches might refer to as positive reinforcement) in maintaining ambivalence. There are certain emotional and tangible benefits that individuals gain by maintaining the status quo. A young woman who is depressed may fear that her friends will abandon her if she gets well. When she is depressed her neighbors and co-workers bring her casseroles and call frequently to check in; when she brightens and is more cheerful, people are less worried about her and tend to pull back. It is therefore understandable that she may be resistant to change and ambivalent about the prospect of being rid of depression. The support of friends and family alone is not enough to maintain depressive affect—there are likely many biological, social, family systems, cognitive, and behavioral aspects of the distress as well—it is one component that may contribute to the client's unacknowledged ambivalence.

Psychic Conflict

The issue of certain aspects of mental life going unacknowledged is central to psychodynamic theory. There are many fears, desires, and motivations that are simply outside of one's conscious awareness; these things reside in the **unconscious** level of awareness. The purpose of the unconscious is to protect the individual from overwhelming anxiety. If we were truly aware of all our motives and could see fully the ways in which we are driven by self-interest or fear of authority, it would be very distressing. Psychodynamic theory posits that the individual is in a state of constant psychic conflict. This type of conflict is most often between the **id** and the **superego.** The id is the most egocentric part of the mind and it is present at birth. It is self-interested and often motivated by primitive drives such as sexual desire and aggression. The superego is the counterpoint to the id and develops several years later. It is the regulatory part of the self that is focused on morality and living up to the expectations of parents and other authority figures. The superego is very focused on what the individual *should* do, whereas the id is committed to what the individual *wants* to do.

BOX 10.7

Learning Exercise

Consider your motives as you read this paragraph. Why are you reading this book? Was it assigned for a class? Are you especially motivated by maintaining your scholarship or proving that you can be academically successful? Is it important to earn your parents' or spouse's approval? Is there an urge to stop reading and to watch television or socialize with your friends instead? If you were to fall asleep and fail to finish reading the chapter, would you beat yourself up about it later? These types of internal motivators emerge from the id and the superego. In essence, this type of unconscious psychic conflict drives every aspect of life. Ambivalence is one of the fundamental characteristics of being human.

Resolving Psychic Conflict

Although psychic conflict is ubiquitous, clients are not often aware of the powerful implicit forces that drive their thinking and their behavior. Instead, these conflicts are managed by **defense mechanisms** that are employed involuntarily and automatically (Freud, A., 1937). Clients are often unaware that they are using a defense and it may take time for the therapist to help the client see the purpose it serves. Defenses serve as a compromise between the needs of the superego and the desires of the id. Their purpose is to mediate between these opposing forces. Defense mechanisms are largely adaptive and their primary goal is to reduce anxiety. They are essentially intrapsychic mechanisms for managing and reducing conflict. This conflict may be a kind of cognitive dissonance or a context-dependent emotional conflict. Unfortunately, using rigid defenses or having access to too few defense mechanisms sometimes causes dysfunction.

Imagine a client who is anxious about public speaking. Here are several defensive strategies that might automatically emerge depending on the client's particular psychological structure and level of functioning:

- *Repression*: The client simply forgets about the presentation and fails to show up. This is sometimes referred to as motivated forgetting. Later in the day the client may suddenly "remember" the presentation and express great distress and consternation about having missed the opportunity.

- *Humor*: As she approaches the podium to begin speaking, she jokingly pretends to trip on the microphone wire and flashes a wide smile at the crowd. She starts her talk by saying, "I was worried all day that I would trip so I thought I'd just get it out of the way. It's great to be here with all of you today."
- *Projection*: The client sits backstage awaiting her turn to speak. Before another speaker goes on, the client turns to him and says, "Whoa. You look really nervous. Are you okay?"

In most cases the client does not make a conscious choice to use one of these strategies over another. Rather, certain defenses come more easily to some individuals than others. A person's defensive style emerges out of a developmental trajectory and is influenced by nature (e.g., temperament) and nurture (e.g., family, friends, peers). Clients may be more motivated to avoid anxiety by maintaining the status quo than by the pursuit of self-fulfillment (Cramer, 2006). Defenses serve many purposes. They may be used to protect the individual's self-esteem, to maintain an interpersonal relationship and therefore avoid loss, or manage anxious or depressive feelings (Brenner, 1982). Often times, defenses serve two opposing purposes simultaneously. They are an attempt to *protect* the individual from a particular thought or feeling while *at the same time* expressing an undesirable impulse (Schafer, 1968).

As the quote at the beginning of this section suggests, ambivalence is particularly intense in the context of interpersonal relationships. The psychodynamic perspective suggests that ambivalence is ubiquitous; it pervades relationships, situations, and thoughts about nearly everything (Brenner, 1994). For example, a man may be unaware of being angry with his wife. They go out to dinner and the man offers his umbrella because it has started raining. The wife declines his offer and the man becomes insistent despite her consistent refusals. An argument ensues. In this example the man is employing a defense mechanism of reaction formation, doing the opposite of what he actually wishes he could do. Kindness replaces hostility but, in the end, his aggressive feelings are expressed through his unrelenting offer and his inattentiveness to his partner's desires. The purpose of the defense (reaction formation) is to avoid unpleasant feelings (e.g., hostility and anger), but ultimately this defense is ineffective and leads to an argument. The hostile feelings are no longer hidden but they emerge in an indirect way, and both the man and his wife are left wondering, "What are we even arguing about?"

Therapeutic change can occur when the client begins to feel a discrepancy between current defensive style and a wish for things to be different. It is often useful to highlight this type of conflict when clients identify it. This can be done by backtracking a bit. The client may report getting into an argument with his wife about the umbrella but fail to mention how angry he was before they even left the house. To get to these feelings, which are likely outside of the client's conscious awareness, the therapist will have to go backwards and ask questions that are thoughtful yet probing. Freud often used the metaphor of an archaeologist on a dig looking for ancient fossils. The therapist must tread lightly, carefully dusting off many layers that keep the material hidden from view and protected. With an empathic approach and maintaining focus on the defensive structure, the therapist can help the client consider his underlying motives. The therapist should inquire about the genesis of the original anger and what made it difficult to speak with his wife directly about his feelings. It is important to understand why the defense was necessary and what purpose it served in the moment. Once the client's current functioning is fully understood, the therapist and the client can begin collaborating to find alternative strategies for managing conflict.

This type of approach can be used for many problems, including those that affect the treatment directly. When clients begin to express ambivalence through resistance, the therapist should address these behaviors in a similar way. Arriving late or maintaining long silences in therapy may be a way to discharge frustration or to avoid painful affect that is bound to arise in a therapeutic setting. By identifying the usefulness of resistance, the therapist may be able to empower the client to find alternative ways of dealing with these unpleasant affective experiences.

Integrating It All

This chapter has presented a variety of approaches that can help clients find more adaptive ways of thinking and behaving. Often times, clients engage in maladaptive cognitive styles and behavioral patterns because of environmental factors. These include patterns of reinforcement, feedback loops, expectations about self-efficacy, and personality factors that lead to the use of maladaptive defenses. The distress clients feel is multiply-determined, meaning that it stems from multiple causes. As a result, it makes sense that therapists should consider an integrative approach that addresses these many predisposing and precipitating factors. Effective integration of differing theoretical approaches takes practice and requires a fluency in each of the theories. The Stages of Change model is one perspective that is atheoretical and relatively easy to combine with cognitive behavioral, family systems, and psychodynamic treatment approaches. For additional information on integrating theoretical perspectives, see the Further Reading section of this chapter.

CHAPTER REVIEW

Clients who are ambivalent about changing have a contradictory mix of positive and negative feelings about change. Sometimes ambivalence will be manifest through behaviors such as being late to session or missing appointments. At other times ambivalence will be manifest as stagnation or failure to make adequate progress toward treatment goals. The changes that one is faced with making are likely to be met with ambivalence at some point in treatment.

Because ambivalence is likely to hinder progress in treatment, it is important to assess a client's motivation. Prochaska and colleagues (1992) developed the transtheoretical Stages of Change model to assist in identifying how ready a client is to change. Furthermore, the stage of change points practitioners to the types of interventions that will be most helpful to that client. There are five stages of change: precontemplation, contemplation, preparation, action, and maintenance. Individuals who are in the earlier stages of change are likely to benefit from therapeutic approaches that emphasize consciousness raising, self-reevaluation, and self-liberation, while individuals in the action and maintenance stages are likely to benefit from behavioral strategies, including counter-conditioning and stimulus control.

An important cognitive component of change is developing self-efficacy. Self-efficacy is confidence in one's ability to successfully perform a particular task in order to achieve desired consequences. Bandura's (1971) social learning theory describes how people develop and strengthen self-efficacy. An important way people develop self-efficacy is through observational learning. People learn by watching others model behaviors. Therapists aim to increase client self-efficacy through treatment. Mastery experiences are a powerful way to increase self-efficacy, while other methods, such as social persuasion and improving mood.

The TRA (Ajzen & Fishbein, 1980; Fishbein & Ajzen, 1975) and TPB (Ajzen, 1985, 1991) are two cognitive models that describe how people form intentions to act. The TPB, which is built upon the TRA, posits that a person's attitudes, knowledge of subjective norms, and perceived behavioral control contribute to a person's intention to perform a certain behavior. That is, a person's attitudes, sense of what other's wish for him to do, and how easy or difficult the behavior will be to complete contribute to intention to act. This model has been recently updated (i.e., the integrated behavior model) to include a more complete set of variables that predict intention, including self-efficacy. The integrated behavior model is useful to clinicians to explore the cognitions that are contributing to (or blocking) the intention to act.

Cognitive dissonance arises when a person has two thoughts that are inconsistent with one another. There is evidence that the desire to reduce cognitive dissonance enhances motivation to change. Thus, highlighting or intensifying cognitive dissonance in clients can be a tool to increase motivation to change. MI is a treatment method that is used to explore and resolve client ambivalence about change, thus enhancing intrinsic motivation to change.

Not all therapeutic change requires an explicit cognitive decision. Change can come about as a result of trying new behaviors to see what consequences and effects these behaviors have on one's mood and functioning. Behavior change occurs via operant principles. Specifically, behaviors that are reinforced are likely to be repeated. To increase behaviors, one may either provide a reward, or positive reinforcement, or remove an aversive stimulus, known as negative reinforcement. Behavioral activation is an empirically supported treatment for depression that entails working with clients to increase behavioral activity. The goal is to create opportunities for the client to be rewarded, internally by pleasant feelings or externally by positive attention from others.

Psychodynamic approaches address ambivalence as a ubiquitous and expected part of life. Clients may demonstrate their ambivalence through resistance within therapy or via other defense mechanisms employed in their interpersonal relationships. Psychodynamic methods involve identifying defensive functioning and helping clients develop insight into how they may seek to avoid conflict. The purpose of a psychodynamic treatment, with respect to thoughts and behaviors, is to help the client develop a more adaptive way of coping with the problems they face. Each of the theoretical approaches has meaningful contributions to make and over time it will become easier to integrate differing perspectives.

PERSONAL REFLECTION ESSAY QUESTIONS

1. Working with clients with low motivation to change can be difficult for many therapists. Think about what types of clients or types of problems may be particularly difficult for you to work with given low motivation. Perhaps seeing a client with a drug or alcohol addiction with low motivation to change would be challenging for you. Reflect on how your personal history and experiences might impact your ability to work with any particular client population or diagnostic group.
2. Given your answer to the first personal reflection, how would you use cognitive and behavioral techniques to increase your client's motivation to change?
3. Think about an argument or conflict you had recently with a close friend. What types of defenses did you use to manage the conflict? You may want to revisit Figure 3.2 for a reminder of the major defenses. Now consider a conflict you had with an authority figure recently—a supervisor at work, a parent, a professor. Which defense(s) did you use in this case? It is likely that you used different defenses in each case. Explain why?

KEYWORDS

action	id	reinforcement management
ambivalence	injunctive norms	resistance
behavioral activation	instrumental attitudes	self-liberation
cognitive dissonance	intentions	self-reevaluation
consciousness raising	maintenance	social learning theory
contemplation	mastery experience	Stages of Change model
counter-conditioning	modeling	stimulus control
defense mechanisms	perceived control	subjective norms
descriptive norms	perceived norms	superego
experiential attitudes	personal agency	unconscious
graded task assignment	precontemplation	vicarious learning
helping relationships	preparation	

FURTHER READING

- May, A. C., Rudy, B. M., Davis, T. E., & Matson, J. L. (2013). Evidence-based behavioral treatment of dog phobia with young children two case examples. *Behavior Modification*, 37(1), 143–160. doi:10.1177/0145445512458524

In this article, two case examples are presented that highlight the efficacy of graduated exposure therapy using reinforcement and participant modeling in treating specific dog phobia. In one of the cases, the child moved up his individualized fear hierarchy by first watching the clinician play with a dog (i.e., modeling) and getting stickers (i.e., reinforcers) on a schedule (every 2 minutes of watching). This positive reinforcement served as motivation for continued participation in increasingly difficult exposure tasks.

- Miller, W. R., & Rollnick, S. (2009). Ten things that motivational interviewing is not. *Behavioural and Cognitive Psychotherapy, 37*, 129–140. doi:10.1017/S13524 65809005128

Miller and Rollnick seek to clarify some of the misconceptions and confusion that have come about in regard to MI. In doing so, the authors chose to discuss 10 things that MI is *not*. Specifically, MI is not a way of tricking people into doing what you want them to do or practice as usual. The authors assert that clarity about what MI is and is not is essential, as it helps to ensure its effectiveness in clinical practice as well as the quality of the research conducted on the effectiveness of MI in clinical practice.

- Martell, C. R., Addis, M. E., & Jacobson, N. S. (2001). *Depression in context: Strategies for guided action.* New York, NY: Norton.

This manual is a great resource for how to use behavioral activation with depressed clients.

- Blackman, J. (2004). *101 defenses: How the mind shields itself.* New York, NY: Brunner-Routledge.

This book offers a wonderfully concise introduction to the many defenses that individuals may employ. Blackman provides many examples of how defenses operate in everyday life and explores several therapeutic techniques for dealing with defenses with clients.

- Norcross, J. C., & Goldfried, M. R. (2005). *Handbook of psychotherapy integration* (2nd ed.). New York, NY: Oxford University Press.

This classic text on psychotherapy integration is a great resource for beginning and experienced clinicians who want to learn more about how to utilize multiple theoretical perspectives simultaneously.

Promoting Change: Counseling Skills That Address Emotions and Relationships

*In the course of a psychoanalytic journey, patient and analyst
... [g]radually mutually regulate each other's behaviors,
enactments, and states of consciousness such that each gets
under the other's skin, each reaches into the other's guts, each is
breathed in and absorbed by the other.*
—Aron and Anderson (1998, pp. 25–26)

LEARNING OBJECTIVES

- Define the following terms: meta-cognition, meta-emotion, emotional intelligence, self-reflection, decentering, mastery, mind-mindedness, ambivalence, scaffolding, alexithymia, emotions, self-awareness, self-management, social awareness, relationship management, double bind, triangulation, differentiation, homeostasis, and ambivalence
- Identify and describe Main, Goldwyn, and Hesse's (2002) and Hesse's (2008) three components of metacognition as they relate to emotional processing
- Identify the different aspects of emotional intelligence
- Discuss some of the deficits that can be consequences of dysfunctional metacognition
- Discuss the importance of early relationships in the successful development of meta-cognition
- Discuss some of the factors/techniques employed in therapy that help alter/increase meta-cognitive capacities
- Discuss the implications of Paul Ekman and colleagues' work concerning nonverbal expression of emotion

(continued)

(continued)

- Discuss some of the research findings related to skills in nonverbal sensitivity and identify the implications this has for trainees
- Describe the four empirically supported principles for enhancing metacognition in Greenberg and Watson's (2006) emotion-focused therapy
- Identify and describe the importance of your own emotions as a mental health professional
- Name and provide examples of the different systems of Bronfenbrenner's (1979) multiple ecological systems model
- Discuss and give examples of theories of relational dynamics, including the double bind, triangulation, differentiation, and homeostasis
- Examine the role of ambivalence in therapy and discuss aspects of Miller and Rollnick's (2002) motivational interviewing (MI) approach to counseling that help to address it

Although this quotation refers specifically to relational psychoanalysis, it has relevance for nearly all clinical and interpersonal experiences. Each interaction with another person involves a complex dance: an interplay of two psyches attempting to connect and communicate with each other. We have an impact on others and they, in turn, have an effect on us. Consider the last time you went to the store and the cashier thanked you for your business in a bored tone, without making eye contact, as she checked her watch. Even in this simple exchange, you probably noticed there was subtext to what she actually said to you. You may have thought she was bored, anxious, hostile, or perhaps not taking her job seriously. Whatever conclusions you drew, you were thinking about another person's mind and how her actions affected you. This chapter elaborates on the ability to understand mental phenomena and explores how it relates to psychotherapy. As a counseling professional, you will encounter a myriad of emotions—your clients' and your own. Learning to understand emotions and how to be attuned to the emotional needs of another person without being consumed by them are some of the primary tasks of becoming an effective counselor.

In addition to understanding emotions, much of what happens in counseling has to do with relationships. In Chapter 9 we explored the therapeutic relationship and the many forces clients and therapists can exert on each other. It is also important to understand how to work with clients with regard to the relationships they have outside of the office. Clients often talk about patterns of relating to others, problems with friends and family they have experienced in the past, and how they manage (or struggle to manage) relationships in their everyday life.

Finally, this chapter explores one of the most common challenges faced by individuals who want to change—conflicting feelings about change. If you reflect on the last time you tried to change something about yourself, you will probably recall that you had mixed feelings about the idea. The same is true for clients who seek professional help to change. There are few things in life that provoke a whole-hearted response that is free of any conflict. Going out for a delicious, gourmet meal also means spending money and perhaps overeating. Having a child or getting married both come with a certain loss of independence. Pursuing a new professional endeavor might mean facing fears of failure by taking a risk. All changes, even the most positive ones, involve positive and negative feelings and thoughts that may be felt simultaneously. Part of the work of psychotherapy will be to notice these mixed feelings and trying to resolve at least some of the conflicts individuals face.

IDENTIFYING AND UNDERSTANDING EMOTIONS

The main character in Mark Haddon's book, *The Curious Incident of the Dog in the Nighttime*, is named Christopher Boone and he has difficulty identifying and understanding other people's emotions. Christopher has an autism spectrum disorder, and he is working with a para-professional named Siobhan to improve his ability to understand others. Haddon relates Christopher's experiences in the first person and demonstrates with great clarity how complicated it can be to accurately perceive the meaning behind what people say and do. Here's how he explains it:

> I find people confusing.
>
> This is for two main reasons.
>
> The first main reason is that people do a lot of talking without using any words. Siobhan says that if you raise one eyebrow it can mean lots of different things. It can mean "I want to do sex with you" and it can also mean "I think that what you just said was very stupid."
>
> Siobhan also says that if you close your mouth and breath out loudly through your nose, it can mean that you are relaxed or that you are bored, or that you are angry, and it all depends on how much air comes out of your nose and how fast and what shape your mouth is in when you do it and how you are sitting and what you said just before and hundreds of other things which are too complicated to work out in a few seconds. (Haddon, 2003, pp. 14–15)

The difficulties Christopher faces are common for individuals on the autistic spectrum, and his description highlights just how complex emotions can be. The manifestation of emotions varies from person to person, both in manner and extent of expression. Each client will present with his own ways of managing emotions.

Metacognition and Meta-Emotion

The capacity to think about mental phenomena and to understand one's own thoughts and the thoughts of others is referred to as **metacognition**. Metacognition is a broad term that is sometimes defined as "thinking about thinking." There are many subdisciplines that study metacognition, including cognitive psychology, neuroscience, and child development (Reder, 1996). Within the field of counseling, the term metacognition is most often applied to understanding thoughts *and* feelings. Main and colleagues (2002) and Hesse (2008) have outlined three components of metacognition as it relates to emotional processing. These include the ability to look beyond the surface, the ability to accept changes in one's own moods, personality, and needs over time, and the ability to recognize and accept differences between the self and others. Others have described metacognition as a process that allows people to create and integrate complex ideas about themselves and others and to respond to those ideas within a social context (Dimaggio & Lysaker, 2010).

Meta-emotion, also referred to as **emotion understanding**, is simply a subcategory of metacognition. It refers to the ability to think specifically about the emotional states of the self and others and to be able to respond to these emotions effectively. Meta-emotion is also closely associated with **emotional intelligence** (EQ), which has to do with awareness of emotions and the ability to use those feeling states effectively. The main components of EQ include being able to identify one's own emotions, self-regulation of those emotions, and being able to use this knowledge in order to successfully manage relationships (e.g., Bar-On, 2000; Goleman, 1998; Salovey & Sluyter, 1997). EQ is separate and apart from the intellect. As the quote from Christopher (in *The Curious Incident of the Dog in the Nighttime*) earlier in this chapter demonstrates, an individual can be highly intelligent but still lack understanding of emotions. Metacognition and meta-emotion are developmental constructs that can be fostered over time. Both are necessary for mature social interactions (LaBounty, Wellman, Olson, Lagattuta, & Liu, 2008).

Dysfunctional metacognition is characterized by deficits in self-reflection, understanding others' minds, and mastery. **Self-reflection** refers to the ability to be aware of one's own emotional life and to distinguish between fantasy and reality. It also involves being able to recognize and tolerate contradictory ideas and thoughts about the self. For example, the ability to generally like oneself but to also be cognizant of feelings of guilt about hurting another person's feelings would require a great deal of self-reflection.

Understanding another person's mind is also referred to as **decentering**. This involves reading behavioral and facial cues to form ideas about what another person is thinking. One of the key components in this aspect of metacognition is being able to recognize that others' perspectives differ from one's own. The type of egocentrism that is often seen in children (e.g., theory of mind) is thought to be due to a variety of neurological, cognitive, developmental, and social-interactional factors. Out of the process of normal development and through interactions in healthy, attuned relationships, children become less focused on themselves and more able to understand another person's mind.

The final element of metacognition involves **mastery,** or the ability to use this knowledge about thoughts and emotions effectively. Once someone has developed the ability to be self-reflective and to accurately understand other people's emotions, he or she must then be able to adapt and respond effectively. Mastery allows an individual to implement effective action strategies and to better cope with mental states that are distressing. In order to achieve mastery, an individual must have the ability to be self-reflective and less egocentric. When all three of these elements—self-reflection, decentering, and mastery—are combined, they enable an individual to engage in metacognition and meta-emotion.

BOX 11.1

Measuring Metacognition

The three components of metacognition—self-reflection, decentering, and mastery—relate primarily to emotional processing and thinking about emotions. Researchers have created a method for researching metacognition in psychotherapy with the development of the Metacognition Assessment Scale (Semerari et al., 2003; Figure 11.1). Explore the items on the scale and think about them as they relate to clients you will see in your field placements. Often times, clients with personality disorders, autism spectrum disorders, substance abuse problems, and psychosis experience impaired metacognition. But each client is different. Certainly, the types of deficits you will see among individuals with autism spectrum disorders will differ from those you notice in clients with psychotic disorders.

This scale may also provide a framework for thinking about your own ability to engage in metacognition. Are there areas where you have more facility with metacognition? Sometimes people are better able to think about the mind of another person but struggle when it comes to reflecting on their own experience. The opposite may also be true for you. Are there aspects of mastery that you find challenging? Think about your own metacognitive skills and consider ways to grow and improve your ability to think about thinking.

Metacognitive abilities are thought to develop out of early interactions with caregivers and other important people. Individuals with secure attachment styles typically have better metacognitive functioning than individuals with insecure attachment styles (MacBeth, Gumley, Schwannauer, & Fisher, 2011). A parent's ability to be attuned to his or her child's thoughts, feelings, and perceptions—what is sometimes referred to as **mind-mindedness** (Lundy, 2013)—is closely tied to the development of metacognition. Clients often speak about ways in which their parents struggled to accurately and empathically respond to what they were experiencing internally. Consider the following statements from clients talking about their parents. Think about how each parent's response may have shaped the client's ability to engage in metacognition.

"When we came home I told my mother I was really upset about my diagnosis. I was crying. She laughed and said so many people have it way worse than I do. I'm not sure what to think. I guess I'm making a big deal out of nothing."

"I remember bringing home a B+ on a math test. I was an A student across the board, except math. I worked so hard for that B+. I showed it to my dad and he said, 'Let's try for an A next time. Okay, sport?'"

"My mother always looked angry or depressed or something. She would never smile. I used to ask her, 'What's wrong?', but she would always say nothing was wrong and would tell me to stop being so sensitive."

Understanding One's Own Mind

Basic Requirements		
1. The subject acknowledges having mental functions	NO	YES
2. The subject represents him or herself as a person with autonomous thoughts and feelings	NO	YES
Identification		
3. The subject is able to define and distinguish his or her own cognitive operations (e.g., remembering, imagining, having fantasies, dreaming, desiring, deciding, foreseeing, and thinking)	NO	YES
4. The subject is able to define and distinguish between his or her own emotional states	NO	YES
Differentiation		
5. The subject recognizes that the representation of the self and/or of the world is subjective and/or fallible and/or that his or her own opinions have changed or are changeable	NO	YES
6. The subject recognizes the representational nature of thoughts and the limited impact that expectations, thoughts, and desires have on reality	NO	YES
Relating Variables		
7. The subject recognizes that his or her behavior may be determined by one specific mode of cognitive and/or emotional functioning and admits he or she is influenced by social and/or interpersonal variables related to the context of his or her cognitive and/or emotional functioning, or related to his or her behavior	NO	YES
Integration		
8. The subject is able to give a complete description of his or her own mental state and/or of the interpersonal processes in which he or she is involved, through his or her perception of cognitive and/or emotional elements	NO	YES
9. The subject is able to integrate his or her different modes of cognitive and/or emotional functioning into a coherent and complex narrative	NO	YES

Understanding Others' Minds

Basic Requirements		
1. The subject recognizes the existence of mental functions in others	NO	YES
2. The subject represents others as persons with autonomous thoughts and feelings	NO	YES
Identification		
3. The subject is able to perceive other individuals' cognitive operations (such as remembering, imagining, having fantasies, dreaming, awaiting, foreseeing, meditating)	NO	YES
4. The subject is able to perceive other individuals' emotional states	NO	YES
Differentiation		
5. The subject considers his or her own representations of other individuals' mental states and functioning as subjective and hypothetical	NO	YES

FIGURE 11.1 The Metacognition Assessment Scale.

Source: Semerari et al. (2003).

(*continued*)

Relating Variables		
6. The subject makes plausible inferences about other individuals' mental states and recognizes the communicative value or signs of attitude or behavior	NO	YES
Integration		
7. The subject is able to give a complete description of other individuals' mental states and/or the interpersonal processes in which they are involved through the perception of cognitive and/or emotional elements	NO	YES
8. The subject is able to integrate other individuals' different modes of cognitive and/or emotional and/or relational functioning into a coherent narrative	NO	YES
Decentration		
9. The subject recognizes that he or she is not necessarily at the center of other individuals' thoughts, feelings, and emotions and/or that their actions stem from goals and reasons mostly independent of the relationships they have with the subject	NO	YES
10. The subject recognizes that other individuals may perceive events in a different way from his or her own and/or interpret them differently	NO	YES
11. The subject recognizes that variables, such as time, individual development, and experiences, determine the modes of the mental functioning of other individuals and/or recognizes that personal and relational events influence their processes and mental states	NO	YES
Mastery		
Basic Requirements		
1. The subject discusses his or her own behavior and psychological processes and relates them not as simple matter-of-fact data but as tasks to be done and problems to be solved	NO	YES
2. The subject is able to define the terms of the problem in a plausible way	NO	YES
First-Level Strategies		
3. The subject tries to act directly on the problem state by modifying the general state of his or her organism	NO	YES
4. The subject avoids the occurrence of problem states and/or uses the relational context as a support	NO	YES
Second-Level Strategies		
5. The subject tackles the problem voluntarily by imposing a certain type of behavior on himself or herself or inhibiting it	NO	YES
6. The subject tackles the problem voluntarily by adjusting his mental order	NO	YES
Third-Level Strategies		
7. The subject tackles the problem by acting upon the evaluations and beliefs that are at the basis of the problem itself and/or by using his or her general knowledge of his or her own mental functioning	NO	YES
8. The subject tackles the interpersonal dimension of the problem by using his or her own general knowledge of other people's mental functioning	NO	YES
9. The subject tackles the problem by accepting his or her own limits in managing his or her own self and influencing events	NO	YES

FIGURE 11.1 (*continued*)

In each of these scenarios the development of metacognition is being challenged. In the first example, the client's thoughts and feelings are disavowed. For the client bringing home a math test, try to imagine what she was feeling when she came home—pride and happiness—and thinking about the approval she was hoping to receive. Her father is unable to respond appropriately, and this interaction has the potential to shape how the client might think about her achievements and the meaning they have for other people in the future. Finally, the last client has a sense that her mother is in distress; she is attempting to use her metacognitive abilities to perceive the mind of another. When she tests out her hypothesis—that her mother is upset—she gets the message that she is doing something wrong. She is discouraged from becoming an empathic person who notices and attempts to address the moods of those around her.

When parents are able to speak openly about conflicting thoughts and feelings, they assist their children in developing social and cognitive understanding (LaBounty et al., 2008). Clients whose parents did not talk about affective perspective taking and the relationships between thoughts, feelings, and actions are likely to have greater impairment in metacognition. Individuals who did not feel physically or emotionally safe as children also have greater difficulty developing the ability to think effectively about thoughts and feelings (Liotti & Gilbert, 2011).

Although difficulty with metacognition has deep roots in early development, it is not immutable. Therapy can help clients develop more accurate and stable mental representations of themselves and others (Dimaggio et al., 2011) and can increase metacognitive abilities (Guastello, Guastello, & Hanson, 2008). By providing a consistent empathic presence and **scaffolding** clients' cognitions, a therapist can help clients improve their ability to understand their own mind and the minds of others. Scaffolding is an educational term that refers to the process of providing supports around a student's (or, in the case of therapy, a client's) learning experience until such supports can be gradually removed. A therapist can provide scaffolding as a client learns to understand his or her own thoughts and feelings. Over time, these functions gradually shift to the client as they become autonomous and begin to pursue their own growth.

Clients who have difficulty with metacognition may also exhibit **alexithymia**, which is an inability to articulate one's own internal emotional life. Alexithymia is often evidence of impairment in metacognition and meta-emotion, and is more common among individuals who come from less expressive families (Kench & Irwin, 2000). This type of difficulty is often seen in clients with psychosomatic problems, substance abuse, and other psychiatric problems (Taylor, Bagby, & Parker, 1997). Clients with alexithymia frequently report a vague and diffuse sense of unease (Stiles, Meshot, Anderson, & Sloan, 1992). They may say, "I just don't feel right. Something feels off," or when asked to elaborate on their emotions may simply say, "I don't know. I can't seem to put it into words." Often, one of the primary tasks of psychotherapy is to help clients develop a richer language and ease of expression around emotional states. To help clients learn how to think about and express emotions appropriately, it is important to be able to have these skills yourself. Much of what you will do as a therapist will revolve around identifying, containing, and acting on emotions. Later in this chapter we discuss therapeutic techniques and interventions that focus on strengthening metacognition and dealing with emotions.

Nonverbal Expression of Emotions

Imagine you come home and your roommate confronts you. She is staring at you, eyebrows raised, one corner of her lip in a slight sneer. She is holding up her favorite sweater for you to see; it has a stain on it. If you carefully consider this scene, can you determine what is she trying to communicate? Are there multiple interpretations?

Psychologist Paul Ekman has dominated the field of understanding facial expressions since the 1960s. The popular show, *Lie to Me*, is loosely based on Ekman's work with the Central Intelligence Agency and Department of Homeland Security trying to develop methods for coding facial expressions that might portend terrorism (Randall, 2011). Ekman and his colleagues argue that facial expressions and other nonverbal markers correspond to basic emotions (Ekman, 2003; Ekman & Rosenberg, 1997). They have developed a complex coding system, the Facial Action Coding System (FACS), which looks at micromovements of the face using video analysis to identify and study the expression of different emotions.

Ekman's work also highlights the physiological and evolutionary underpinnings of nonverbal expressions of emotion. Figure 11.2 demonstrates the different expressions of the FACS. Can you identify each of the emotions shown?

FIGURE 11.2 Paul Ekman's Facial Action Coding System.
Courtesy of Buster Benson.

BOX 11.2

Spotlight on Culture

Nonverbal expressions are not universal across cultures. In some countries, there are striking differences in how emotions and thoughts are expressed nonverbally. Did you know that in some countries—Bulgaria, Macedonia, Albania, and some parts of southern Italy—nodding the head up and down indicates refusal rather than acceptance? A simple "thumbs up"—used in Western cultures to indicate approval—is an obscene or insulting gesture in many Middle Eastern and African cultures (Koerner, 2003). Given that these gestures show variability across cultures and continents, perhaps facial expressions have different meanings among different cultural groups. This is an area of great debate among researchers in the field of expressed emotion.

In their work with the virtually isolated Fore people of Papua New Guinea, Paul Ekman's team of researchers found universality in facial expressions (Ekman & Friesen, 1971). These findings are important because they suggest that commonalities in the expression of emotion through facial expression cannot be attributed to observational learning through social contact. While Ekman's team (Ekman et al., 1987) has found robust agreement across cultures in their interpretation of facial expressions of emotion, other researchers disagree with their findings (Dailey et al., 2010; Stanley, Zhang, Fung, & Isaacowitz, 2013). Those who argue that the expression of emotions is not universal across cultures emphasize the importance of context and the situational factors in the perception of emotions.

These contradictory research findings have important implications for clinical practice. Most counselors will work with a diverse group of clients. Although there may be universality in emotional expression, it is important to attend to the ways in which culture, context, and personal experience may shape both clients' and therapists' interpretation of facial expressions. Consider the multiple meanings a smile may have in various contexts. A smile may be used as a friendly social greeting, but it may also convey appeasement, apology, approval, resignation, solidarity, or sympathy (Fridlund, 1994). This particular expression of emotion may also be a mask, put on to cover up something the client wants to avoid thinking about or feeling. In a therapeutic context, it is essential to inquire about facial expressions to develop an understanding of what they mean for each individual client.

The ability to be sensitive to nonverbal expressions of emotion has important implications for the therapeutic relationship. In a simulated medical doctor–patient scenario, trainees with nonverbal sensitivity were rated as more compassionate and more likeable by patients (Hall, Roter, Blanch, & Frankel, 2009). Clinicians in training with greater nonverbal sensitivity were also more likely to provide patient-centered care. Overall, providers who are sensitive to nonverbal expressions of emotion, particularly negative affect, are described by their patients as warm and as good listeners (Henry, Fuhrel-Forbis, Rogers, & Eggly, 2012); patients tend to be more satisfied with their care than that of providers who pay less attention to nonverbal cues (Gulbrandsen et al., 2012).

Working With Emotions

Ultimately, emotions need to inform our lives and not control them, and in therapy they need to be evoked to promote new experience as well as opportunities for new understanding.
—Greenberg (2012, p. 705)

Emotions are a form of affect, but they are relatively brief and typically in reference to something—a relationship, a situation, a memory—that is externally or internally stimulating (Rottenberg & Gross, 2007). Nearly all types of therapy encourage clients to talk about, identify, experience, and understand their emotions. This includes psychodynamic, (e.g., Gabbard, 2000; Summers & Barber, 2012), humanistic-experiential (e.g., Pascual-Leone & Greenberg, 2007), and cognitive behavioral (e.g., Cristea, Szentagotai Tatar, Nagy & David, 2012; Foa & Kozak, 1986) approaches alike. Counseling is a largely experiential process that helps clients make contact with and begin to manage intense emotions that have long been avoided. There is strong research support for the importance of expressing and engaging with emotions in therapy sessions (Jaycox, Foa & Morral, 1998; Missirlian, Toukmanian, Warwar, & Greenberg, 2005; Stringer, Levitt, Berman, & Mathews, 2010). There is significant and consistent agreement about the importance of working with distressing emotions in psychotherapy. How then do counseling professionals do this type of work?

Greenberg and Watson (2006) developed a treatment for depression called emotion-focused therapy (EFT; www.emotionfocusedclinic.org). This treatment approach has also been used in couples counseling (Greenberg & Johnson, 1988) and with trauma survivors (Johnson, 2002). This therapeutic method is largely based on attachment theory, but also incorporates cognitive, behavioral, motivational, and interactional components for an integrative approach to working with emotions. Clinicians of most theoretical orientations can utilize aspects of EFT to begin working with emotions. Emotion-focused therapy has four empirically supported principles for enhancing metacognition and, specifically, meta-emotion. They are: (a) increasing awareness of emotion, (b) enhancing emotion regulation, (c) reflecting on emotion, and (d) transforming emotion. Regardless of a clinician's theoretical orientation, the foundational aspects of EFT can be applied and utilized in all types of psychotherapy.

Enhancing Awareness

Developing awareness involves cognitive appraisal of emotions and integration of those cognitions with affective experience. Cognitive appraisal involves recognizing and labeling emotions accurately. Once a client is able to do that they can begin to integrate their intellectual understanding of the emotions with their actual experience of the feeling. Emotional awareness cannot be a purely intellectual exercise; the client must also *feel* the feeling while having awareness of it. There are many questions therapists can ask when a client describes an emotional experience:

- What did you feel first in the situation?
- Were there any other feelings underneath?
- Did you have other feelings that you did not show at the time?

- Did other feelings come up later, after the situation was over?
- Were you aware of the feeling at the time? If not, when did you first become aware of it?
- What was this feeling a reaction to?
- What impact did the event first have on you?
- How did it affect you in the moment?
- What did it lead you to want to do?
- Did the feeling serve a purpose? Did it help you in any way?
- Do you have any reactions now as you recall how you felt?
- Can you identify any bodily sensations you had that were associated with the feeling (e.g., racing heart, sweating, shortness of breath, lump in throat)?

These types of questions are intended to help the therapist better understand the client's emotional experience. They are also designed to increase the client's awareness of his or her emotions. By **promoting emotional awareness**, the therapist is also working with the client to increase his or her ability to approach, tolerate, regulate, and transform emotions. Many clients find that they avoid distressing emotions. This has also been conceptualized by McCullough and colleagues (2003) as affect phobia. In behavioral terms, increasing awareness of emotional experience is a process of exposure to distressing affect. The change mechanism by which awareness and tolerance occurs is through desensitization or habituation to the feared stimulus, in this case distressing emotions. One of the mechanisms of change in psychotherapy involves encouraging clients to actually experience their emotions in session. Some clients may find it easier to talk about emotions instead of actually feeling them.

Once a client is more aware of his or her emotional inner life, the next step is to help him or her increase the ability to regulate or manage difficult emotions. For a majority of clients, many emotions are old, familiar feelings that seem to occur repeatedly and without much change. Core feelings like loneliness, sadness, or shame can plague people for many years and rarely lead to productive action in their lives. Instead, they lead to feeling stuck and helpless. These emotions are often accompanied by automatic, negative thoughts such as, "I'm worthless," "I'll never succeed at anything," and "This is all my fault." In order to effect change, clients must be aware of these thoughts and feelings, but they must also be able to regulate and transform them.

Emotional Regulation

Emotional regulation refers to how individuals experience and express difficult emotions. Individuals may over- or under-regulate themselves when it comes to emotions. A client who is overregulated may report being physically abused as a child by her alcoholic father, but when asked how she feels about this experience, emotional expression is absent. She may explain it this way, "I felt nothing. Now, as I'm telling you about it, I'm like a robot. I am simply reporting facts." Clients who under-regulate their emotions are more likely to lash out at others or become overwhelmed and debilitated by emotions. The child client who under-regulates emotions may throw a tantrum to avoid discussing a difficult subject in session. The development of emotional regulation involves coordination of emotional, cognitive, physiological, interpersonal systems. Regulation can only develop after the client has awareness of his or her emotions. This cognitive and affective awareness can be integrated to equip clients to cope with difficult emotions.

One important cognitive intervention for emotional regulation involves psychoeducation about emotions. Clients must develop an intellectual understanding of the power and import of emotional experiences. Therapists can educate clients about how emotions provide information and have value. It is also valuable to help clients think about how to access this information through building better awareness. Pennebaker (1995) suggests that putting feeling states into words can help clients reflect on what they are feeling, evaluate the experience, and begin to create new meaning (e.g., transformation). Thinking about emotions is an essential aspect of emotional regulation. Reappraisal of emotional states has been shown to help regulate emotion better than suppression of emotions (Ochsner, Bunge, Gross, & Gabrieli, 2002). For this to happen, clients also need tools to effectively manage the physiological manifestations of emotions. There are many cognitive and behavioral strategies that can be implemented. Learning to manage distress takes a lot of practice and it is a developmental skill that emerges over the life span.

Try to think back to when you were young and you lost your favorite toy or a classmate called you a name. If you were upset in times like this, what types of things did teachers, parents, or mentors suggest to help you calm down? They may have told you to take deep breaths, to put a cool washcloth on your face, or encouraged you to talk about what you were feeling. Similarly, clients need to learn effective tools to reduce the physiological experience of sadness, shame, anxiety, and other distressing emotions. Although beyond the scope of this text, interventions such as mindfulness, meditative practices, and self-soothing techniques are all helpful tools with which to educate clients. See the Further Reading section of this chapter for suggested readings on this topic and Chapter 6 for more information on mindfulness. In addition to these interventions that address the physiological aspects of overwhelming emotions, there are certain behavioral interventions that may also be helpful. Behavioral recommendations such as exercise, distraction, and sleep hygiene may also help clients build affect tolerance and be better equipped to regulate their emotions.

Finally, working with emotions is a highly interpersonal and intrapersonal endeavor. Counseling can assist individuals in improving their ability to manage emotions in the context of their interpersonal relationships as well as within themselves. By increasing emotional awareness, the therapist can begin to help clients learn how to better regulate their emotions. For example, once a client is fully aware of his anger toward his spouse, he can be primed to consider how to better manage those angry feelings. Simply being deliberate about emotional regulation and addressing the physiological components of emotions (as described earlier) can greatly improve regulation abilities. Other aspects of emotional regulation include increasing positive emotions, allowing and tolerating emotions, and creating a working distance from intense feelings (Greenberg, 2012). Additionally, building a degree of self-compassion can also be helpful in increasing emotional regulation. For example, a client with obsessive and intrusive thoughts about certain ethnic groups may report that he feels terribly guilty and believes that these thoughts are evidence that he is "a bad person." A therapist who can aid the client in having compassion for himself—for example, noticing that he has friends of many different ethnic backgrounds and that these thoughts must be quite difficult to tolerate—will also enable the client to begin taking steps to reduce the frequency and intensity of such thoughts.

BOX 11.3

Case Study in Emotional Awareness and Regulation

It was an oppressively hot summer day and Dr. Hansen's office air conditioner was only working intermittently. The office was a tepid 75 degrees when Michael arrived for his 4:00 appointment. Immediately upon entering, Michael began yelling at Dr. Hansen. "What kind of operation are you running here? Do you know how hot it is in this office? What are you trying to do to me?!"

Dr. Hansen's internal reaction was one of anger and frustration. She wanted to yell back, "Of course I know how hot it is in here! Don't you think I've been sweltering for the last 3 hours? Who do you think you are to yell at me for something that's totally beyond my control?" She was immediately aware of her emotional reaction and began to recognize that Michael was unusually angry—perhaps his anger, which seemed extreme given the circumstances, was about more than just the temperature in the office. She was able to regulate her own emotions and respond therapeutically. Dr. Hansen said, "It is hot in here. I'm having a problem with the air conditioner and will have it fixed tomorrow. It's definitely frustrating. I'm also curious about how intensely it seems to have affected you."

Michael began talking about how the lack of air conditioning made him feel like Dr. Hansen didn't care about his well-being. He was able to connect this to his experience of being abused and neglected by his parents for much of his childhood. Specifically, Michael was reminded of a time when his mother refused to buy him a winter coat and he was forced to walk to school in the cold. That frigid feeling, a physiological sensation of being unable to regulate body temperature, was closely linked with a sense of not being taken care of, not being cared for. Michael explained that it initially felt good to yell at Dr. Hansen because he had never been able to speak up when his mother neglected him. He also reflected that he was a little embarrassed about how he had behaved at the beginning of the session and wanted to think about ways to not "fly off the handle." Michael also noted Dr. Hansen's calm demeanor and her ability to talk about her frustration without yelling, asking if she could help him learn how to do that.

About a month later, after several weeks of working on emotional awareness and regulation, Dr. Hansen was running behind schedule. When they began the session it was 10 minutes after Michael's scheduled appointment time. Michael was now better equipped to notice and name his emotions—anger, rejection, annoyance—and was able to soothe himself using deep breathing and imagery in the waiting room. He was also able to speak frankly to Dr. Hansen about how he felt—this time without yelling or accusing her of not caring about him.

Reflecting on Emotion

> *What we make of our emotional experience makes us who*
> *we are.*—Greenberg (2012, p. 704)

Beyond recognizing and regulating emotions, it is important to help clients make sense of their experiences and assimilate emotions into their ongoing narrative about themselves. Returning to the example from the last section, let us consider differing reflections on intrusive and discriminatory thoughts. These thoughts may be seen as evidence of a personal and moral failing, as symptoms of obsessive compulsive disorder that need to be treated, or as symbolic of anger turned toward an undeserving target. Whichever explanation an individual gives for his or her emotions will in turn lead to a particular emotional state.

Reflecting on emotions and the explanations one gives for different phenomena can help clients develop new narratives, see new patterns, and better understand their own experiences. The type of reflection that happens in psychotherapy can shift cognition, reframe self-schemas, and lead to a more integrated sense of self. Often times, emotions are part of implicit and automatic processes that have been created and elaborated across the life span. Emotions are closely tied to evaluations about the self and others and one's own personal narrative. The process of counseling affords clients the opportunity to carefully consider and reflect on their emotions with a professional. This type of therapeutic reflection can help clients modify their beliefs about themselves, move toward more productive action, and create closer connections with friends and loved ones.

Transforming Emotion

Once clients have awareness of their emotions, can better regulate them, and are able to reflect on them meaningfully, **transformation** can take place. Transformation of emotions may take place through a process of habituation, development of insight, or literal transformation of maladaptive emotions into more adaptive ones. Often times the process of therapy enables clients to transform negative and distressing emotions into more empowering and self-affirming ones. Clients can be activated to experience adaptive emotions such as assertive anger rather than debilitating rage or fear, sadness associated with grief rather than paralyzing sorrow, and compassion for the self rather than self-criticism and shame (Greenberg, 2002a, 2012). By transforming emotion, clients move from a stance of withdrawal and helplessness to a position of empowerment and supportive caring. Therapy in and of itself is sometimes a critical tool in the transformation of emotion. Clients have the opportunity to experience a therapist react differently to them than others have in the past. This interpersonal exchange, sometimes referred to as a **corrective emotional experience**, has the potential to change old feelings into new, more adaptive ones.

Working With Your Own Emotions

The primary tool in the therapeutic process is you, the counseling professional. To be able to work with emotions effectively, there are several proficiencies that therapists must work to develop. These are self-awareness, self-management, social awareness, and relationship management skills (Roberston, 2007). These are the core components of EQ, and together they form the cornerstone of working with emotions in psychotherapy. Before you can assist other people in dealing with their own emotional lives, you must have the understanding and ability to manage your own.

Self-Awareness

Awareness of the self has been hailed as a critical component of skilled clinical practice (Jennings & Skovholt, 1999) and has been defined in several ways. Most theorists agree that there are two types of **self-awareness** (Williams & Fauth, 2005)—reflecting on one's own attitudes, behaviors, and thoughts in retrospect, and "direct awareness of immediate experience or actions rather than retrospective reflection about them" (Safran & Muran, 2000, p. 48). Self-awareness also has a strong cultural component. Constantine, Hage, Kindaichi, and Bryant (2007) have defined self-awareness as being cognizant of one's culturally informed attitudes, beliefs, and values and maintaining awareness of the relevance of cultural privilege, discrimination, and oppression. It is not enough to learn about other cultures and have cross-cultural experiences; therapists must also strive to learn about their own biases and assumptions about cross-cultural clients. Figure 11.3, developed by Roysircar (2004), combines many aspects of cultural self-awareness and may help you evaluate your own degree of self-reflection about the many cultural aspects of counseling.

Being able to reflect on the self and to be aware of potentially distressing emotions can be very helpful in the therapeutic relationship. For example, a therapist who has consistently avoided conflict in other relationships and is not aware of this style of relating may have difficulty dealing with conflict in the therapeutic relationship. There are many distressing emotions that arise on a daily basis in psychotherapy. Consider a therapist whose mother is dying of cancer. This clinician is also seeing a client whose mother is dying of a terminal illness. The therapist's supervisor asks if this client's experience is arousing any reactions in the therapist. Initially, the therapist denied having any feelings about the content of this client's sessions. Over time, however, she began noticing that she was steering the client away from talking about her feelings of grief and anticipatory mourning. The therapist reported to her supervisor that she only became aware of this while she was journaling later that night about the day's events and her own mental state. There is some evidence that practicing mindfulness meditation and other self-reflective practices can lead to greater self-awareness, compassion for others, and awareness of the self in relationships (Boellinghaus, Jones, & Hutton, 2013), as they did in this case.

Self-Management

Self-management is akin to emotional regulation talked about earlier in this chapter. It involves being attuned to one's own emotions and also being able to effectively manage those emotions. Therapists experience an endless array of emotions about their clients and the work of psychotherapy itself. It is not enough to be self-aware; we must also carefully consider whether and how to express the emotions we are experiencing.

The issue of self-management harkens back to our discussion of countertransference in Chapter 9. For example, in a relational psychoanalytic approach, clinicians are more likely to reveal their countertransference reactions to clients when they believe it may be therapeutic. With a client who sits very erect and

Counselor's Awareness of Own Assumptions, Values, and Biases[a]	Development of Self-Awareness Using Internal and External Sources[b]	Ethnocultural Countertransference[c]	Multicultural Counseling Inventory Self-Report Subscales[d]
Beliefs and attitudes 1. Has cultural awareness and sensitivity of own heritage and respects differences 2. Understands influence of own culture on psychological experiences 3. Recognizes own limitations 4. Comfortable with cultural differences **Knowledge** 1. Aware of how own cultural heritage affects definition of normality 2. Acknowledges how cultural/racial discrimination affects own attitudes, beliefs, and feelings 3. Knows about variations in cultural communication styles **Skills** 1. Seeks out educational, consultative, and training experiences; recognizes limitations of competencies 2. Actively seeks understanding of own racial identity and seeks a nonracist identity	**Privilege** 1. Recognizes areas in which one holds privilege 2. Privilege is contextual: It depends on cultural norms 3. The areas in which we hold privilege are those in which we are least aware 4. Psychology is a privileged profession with dominant cultural values **Internal and external feedback** 1. Recognizes important influences in one's own life for the exploration of own culture 2. Personal beliefs often reflect values in therapy 3. Introspection is important, but diversity competence training is also necessary 4. Critical thinking about mainstream cultural information is essential 5. Peer relationships with diverse individuals are a valuable source of enriching diversity competence 6. Humor is invaluable for reducing conflict	**Interethnic countertransference** 1. Denial of ethnocultural differences 2. Clinical anthropologist syndrome 3. Guilt and/or pity 4. Aggression 5. Ambivalence **Intraethnic countertransference** 1. Overidentification 2. Us and them 3. Distancing or ambivalence 4. Cultural myopia 5. Anger 6. Survivor guilt 7. Hope and despair	**Multicultural awareness** 1. Embraces life experiences and professional interactions of a multicultural nature 2. Enjoys multicultural interactions 3. Advocates against barriers to mental health services 4. Has an awareness and understanding of diverse racial, cultural, and ethnic minority groups 5. Is aware of legalities regarding visas, passports, green cards, and naturalization 6. Has knowledge of and tolerance for nonstandard English 7. Draws on multicultural consultation and training resources 8. Solves problems in unfamiliar settings 9. Has increasing multicultural caseload **Multicultural counseling relationship** 1. Comfortable with minority client's differences 2. Confident in facing personal limitations 3. Sensitive to client mistrust 4. Understands countertransference and/or defensive reactions with minority clients 5. Sensitive to difficulties based on cognitive style 6. Strives to avoid stereotyped and biased case conceptualization 7. Understands minority client–majority group comparisons 8. Knows how differences in worldviews affect counseling

FIGURE 11.3 Guidelines for cultural self-awareness assessment.

See [a]Sue, Arredondo, and McDavis (1992); [b]Hays (2001); [c]Comas-Diaz and Jacobsen (1991); [d]Sodowsky, Taffe, Gutkin, and Wise (1994).
Source: Roysircar (2004).

speaks with a clipped, rapid and unemotional pattern and avoids discussing any details of her mental life, a therapist may notice this style of interacting and inquire about it. Expression of the therapist's emotional experience of the client may take one of the following forms:

- In these first few meetings we've had, I have the sense that it is difficult for you to speak openly about more emotionally charged topics. Does that resonate with you?
- I notice that you speak very formally during our sessions. Is that typical or is it something that comes up specifically here in therapy?
- There are times when you're speaking that you begin to speak about something emotional, and I notice that you seem to move away from it quickly. Perhaps there is something uncomfortable about those topics. When that happens it seems to create distance between us.

What do you think about these possible responses? Does one seem more helpful than another? Is it appropriate to share these emotional and cognitive responses with the client at all? Self-management varies widely from clinician to clinician and should always be done in the context of each individual client's needs. In some cases, one or more of these responses would be an appropriate form of self-management that could be very therapeutic. With some clients, these sorts of observations and self-disclosure might come across as punitive, invasive, or too pointed. Effective self-management requires a high degree of social awareness and cultural competence.

Another important type of self-management involves monitoring empathic responses. Clients often cry in therapy as they talk about difficult or painful experiences. Crying is an important part of the therapeutic process for many clients, particularly as they learn to feel their feelings (Mills & Wooster, 1987). If you are someone who cries easily, particularly when someone is crying in front of you, this will be an important area of self-management to consider. Although there are no prohibitions against crying with clients, in most cases it is helpful (and more therapeutic) to be empathic without becoming overwhelmed by the emotion. There will likely be times in your career as a counseling professional in which you will become tearful with a client. In fact, in a nationwide study of psychologists and psychology trainees, 72% of therapists reported crying in the room with clients at some point in their career (Blume-Marcovici, Stolberg, & Khademi, 2013). However, crying in therapy should be the exception rather than the rule. It is important that clients know that the therapist can tolerate a broad range of affective expression without becoming consumed by the tide of emotion.

Social Awareness

Culturally competent counselors are aware that emotions are expressed in many ways across clients and have different cultural meanings for each individual. **Social awareness** involves being able to perceive clients' emotions accurately and understand what they are thinking and feeling (Robertson, 2007). Crying, for example, has a myriad of meanings. It may indicate sadness, joy, grief, anger, relief, or intense nostalgia. Being socially aware can help the therapist build a stronger therapeutic alliance with the client. A new framework of social awareness must be created for each client. To develop this, it is especially helpful to ask clients about the meaning of emotional expressions or lack of expression. Essentially, social awareness involves constant metacognition and the ability to employ meta-emotional awareness.

Relationship Management Skills

In addition to being socially aware of clients' emotions, therapists should also be carefully attuned to the possible meanings of their behavior. **Relationship management** involves consciously employing self-awareness, self-management, and social awareness to communicate effectively and protect the therapeutic relationship. Even trained therapists have difficulty managing relationships, whether they are personal or professional. Interactions with others are greatly influenced by our cultural backgrounds, expectations of others, and our ability to effectively manage distressing emotions.

It is important to recognize that our own values are most often not the values of those with whom we work. A therapist who values punctuality, orderliness, and straightforward communication will likely find it more challenging to work with clients who are often late, disorganized, and speak circuitously. This type of mismatch will require the therapist to have awareness of his or her emotional reactions, take responsibility for managing some aspects of those reactions, *and* be aware of the social, cultural, and personality differences between themselves and the client. This is a hefty and complex responsibility for even the most skilled counselors.

UNDERSTANDING SYSTEMS—CLIENTS IN CONTEXT

Counseling professionals use the term systems or **family systems** to describe the reality that an individual cannot be understood in isolation. Each person is part of a larger system of interconnected and interdependent individuals. If you think about a child's mobile, removing any one piece will cause the other pieces to move in response.

Every system has its own unspoken set of rules. These rules often dictate how decisions are made, how much affect can be expressed, and the degree to which members of the system connect with those outside of the system. The system also dictates rules about the roles each member of the system will have. Think about a client who reports that she could "never, ever" go to college more than an hour away from where her family resides. On the other hand, the client's sister chose to attend school overseas, an 8-hour flight away! How did these two siblings develop such different roles? Why are the rules different for each of them, and what would happen if the client attended school in another state?

Although much of the emphasis in systemic approaches has been on family systems, keep in mind that clients are simultaneously members of multiple systems—schools, peer groups, companies they work for, and beyond. A Russian-American psychologist named Urie Bronfenbrenner (1979) understood that individuals were part of a larger ecological framework of multiple systems. Bronfenbrenner is also well known for having co-founded *Head Start* (www.acf .hhs.gov/programs/ohs), a federally funded preschool program for children of ages birth to 5 years from low-income families. Head Start emphasizes school readiness and works to enhance children's cognitive, social, and emotional development. Bronfenbrenner's ecological framework acknowledges that the

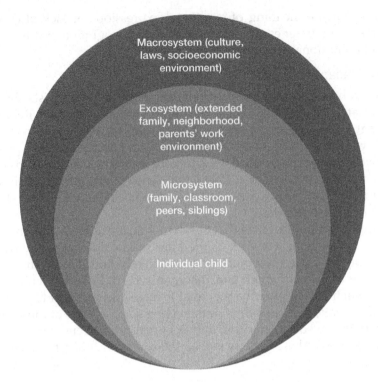

FIGURE 11.4 Bronfenbrenner's ecological model.

individual can only be understood in the context of larger systems. He labeled these the microsystem, mesosystem, exosystem, and macrosystem (Figure 11.4).

The **microsystem** includes the individual's immediate environment—family, schools, neighborhood, peer groups, and religions institutions. The **mesosystem** refers to the natural overflow of one microsystem into another or the relationships between two or more microsystems. For example, children who are bullied at school may come home and be irritable and withdrawn with their parents and siblings; in this scenario the school/peer group microsystem is having an effect on the family microsystem. This interaction is the mesosystem. The **exosystem** involves external environments that have only an indirect effect on the individual. For example, a child and father will be affected by a mother/wife who loses her job. In this scenario, the child and father are experiencing the effects of a system they are not a part of—the mother's workplace. Each of these three system levels are situated within a particular socio-cultural context; this is referred to as the **macrosystem**, and includes things that happen in history as well as the family's own cultural heritage and values. The 2013 Supreme Court decision that struck down the Defense of Marriage Act is an example of a macrosystem event that affected many individuals.

Later in his career, Bronfenbrenner added another layer to the ecological famework. The **chronosystem** reflects the constant evolution of the other four systems over time. For example, moving to another state to pursue new economic opportunities has effects that will change over time. Initially, the system might be a little more chaotic but also hopeful. Over time, as the family settles in and if the new opportunity goes well, the system will become more stable.

Relational Dynamics

Systems theory is primarily a theory about relationships and interdependence. Within interpersonal relationships there are several common patterns that may emerge. You may notice some of these common patterns as you listen to clients provide detail about how they relate to their family members and friends. Many of the relational dynamics we discuss here are explored in greater detail in other family systems textbooks. Each type of relating or communication style is the result of social learning, conditioning, implicit cognitions, attachment styles, and complex interpersonal dynamics. In this way, relational dynamics is a theoretically integrative field that is relevant to nearly all counseling disciplines.

Double Binds

Double bind theory was first described by Bateson, Jackson, Haley, and Weakland (1956) and was later elaborated on by Bowen (1971) and others (Minuchin, Rosman, & Baker, 1978; Palazzoli, Boscolo, Cecchin, & Prata, 1978). A **double bind** is an emotionally distressing dilemma in which an individual feels as though he or she cannot win. There are several features that distinguish a double bind from a standard no-win situation:

1. The individual is involved in an intense relationship (often with a parent or romantic partner) in which it seems very important to discriminate accurately what sort of message is being communicated so as to respond appropriately to it.
2. The other person in the relationship is expressing two types of messages, one of which contradicts or denies the other. The denial is often unspoken—communicated instead with a look, tone of voice, or body language.
3. There is no room for meta-communication. The individual cannot simply inquire, "What is it you're saying?" and therefore cannot precisely describe the exact nature of the paradox he or she is facing.

Double binds are very powerful and often leave the person receiving the double bind communication feeling very anxious. The individual may describe his or her reaction as, "I must do it, but I can't do it." Here are some examples of double bind communication in relationships:

- At a residential treatment center, a resident spoke to his social worker about sexual feelings he was experiencing toward her. The social worker interpreted these feelings as erotic transference, tried to help him understand his feelings, and made the boundaries of their relationship clear. That evening, the social worker was observed at dinner, seated next to the male client and seductively tossing her hair. She spent most of the evening speaking privately with this resident (Markowitz & Nitzberg, 1982).
- A woman met her ex-husband at their son's wedding. It had been a bitter divorce and this was their first in-person meeting in years. The woman extended her hand to her former husband, smiling warmly and saying, "It's so good to see you!" As they shook hands, she winced dramatically and said, "I see you still know how to crush someone's hand."

- A family brings their daughter in to receive treatment for anorexia. As the clinician begins discussing setting a goal weight for the client, the family (who genuinely cares about their daughter) begins arguing that they would feel more comfortable if the goal weight was 120 pounds and not the 135 the therapist is recommending. This double bind conundrum has been succinctly described by Paul Gibney (2006, p. 52)—"We want you better. Grow up. But not too big. Being skinny is good."
- After being publicly humiliated by his mother, Lou tearfully tells her, "I wish you wouldn't say things like that about me in public. It really hurts my feelings." His mother responds, "What do you mean? Oh, honey, you are just so sensitive. I love you so much. I would never do anything to hurt you. You just need to grow a thicker skin. Don't be so touchy."

Each of these case examples should give you an idea of how complicated and, often-times subtle, double bind communication can be. Relationships that are characterized by double binds often create so much distress that other psychological symptoms can arise. Disorientation and difficulty expressing oneself directly, coupled with intense anxiety, has the potential to lead people to find alternative solutions. In a family where one parent encourages emotional expression and the other is repelled by it, the child may find him or herself in an impossible situation. Here is one woman's description of how her eating disorder symptoms arose out of such a double bind:

> I worked out that crying doesn't work. No matter how hard I cried, it never worked. Nothing ever changed and I became very good at just crying on the spot, but it didn't do anything so it (anorexia) is just another way of crying. (Dallos & Vetere, 2012, p. 131)

In this case, family therapy combined with the parents' own couples therapy helped the young woman develop healthy eating habits and develop more adaptive relationships both within and outside of the family.

Triangulation

Triangulation is a pattern of interpersonal relating that is potentially destructive (Bowen, 1985). It occurs when two members of the system align in opposition to another or to otherwise reduce anxiety within the system. For example, parents may focus on their child to distract themselves from a conflictual marital relationship. When there is conflict between the parents, children sense this tension and often respond with distress. The child's emotional expression then becomes the focal point of the parents' attention and allows them to avoid thinking about their own difficulties.

Another triangular process involves cross-generational coalition, in which a parent may try to recruit a child onto their side. A father and child may align in response to an overly harsh mother. These types of triangulations also occur in the workplace and within the therapeutic relationship. For example, a client may go home and report to his or her partner, "The therapist agrees with me. What you did was completely unfair." In this way, the therapist can unwittingly become part of a triangulation with the couple. Triangulation is often evidence of the inability to separate one's own intellectual and emotional functioning from that of the system. This process of separating from the family of origin is referred to as **differentiation** and is discussed later in this chapter.

Triangular relational dynamics can become increasingly complex and confusing, especially when there is no open discussion in the system about what is happening, what people are feeling, and what their intentions are. These types of communication and relational patterns can sometimes be seen in clients with eating disorders. Here is a quote from a young woman named Kate, talking about how her parents have triangulated around her and her eating disorder:

> The only thing I ever hear them talking about is me and if I didn't have this [anorexia] it's kind of like, would everything fall apart, at least it's keeping them talking. And they won't argue while I've got this because it might make me worse. (Dallos & Vetere, 2012, p. 122)

Members of the system often collude to maintain the problem. In this way, symptoms are sometimes an ironic consequence of the ways in which people attempt to maintain family stability and functioning. There is a purpose and function that the symptom serves, and this is closely linked to the importance of maintaining homeostasis in families.

Homeostasis

> A man was sitting on a park bench, continually snapping his fingers. When a passerby asked why he was doing this, he replied that he was chasing away the lions. Said the passerby: "But there are no lions here." To which the man responded: "Shows you it works!" (Fourie, 2003, p. 51)

Homeostasis literally means "standing still." It is a process of maintaining balance and stability. Although the term homeostasis is most often applied to biological mechanisms such as equilibrium inside and outside of a cellular membrane, it also has applications for human behavior and relationships. Within individuals (intrapersonal) and between individuals (interpersonal) there are often opposing forces. Intrapersonal conflict can be seen in the ambivalence many people face when it comes to making meaningful changes in their lives. Interpersonal differences occur frequently when one person's needs or desires do not match those of another person. In relationships, especially within family systems, there is a desire to maintain homeostasis even when it is distressing. There is often a strong pull from within the system to *not* change. The quote at the beginning of this section is one example of how a behavior is maintained because it seems to work—by snapping his fingers repeatedly, the man in the park maintains his sense of safety. Here are some other examples:

- Desiree needs a lot of time to herself. She and Juan have been dating for just over a year, and Desiree's tendency to create distance between the two of them leads Juan to pursue closeness even more. Desiree begins to feel smothered, pulls away, and Juan feels even more abandoned. As a result, he calls more frequently and tries to initiate physical affection more often and the cycle begins again.

- Heather has always been the responsible sibling. She protected her brother, Felix, from their father's alcohol-induced rages throughout childhood. Felix was always more fun-loving, laidback, and spontaneous. Now that they are adults, Heather often bails Felix out of financial jams, covers for him when he fails to meet his responsibilities to his children, and even forged a doctor's note for him when he took a last-minute road trip instead of going to work for several weeks. Felix finds Heather overbearing, controlling, and rigid. He wishes she could just relax.

In both of these scenarios, none of the parties involved is particularly happy. Even though each person wishes things were different, they continue to operate in predictable ways that become more entrenched over time. This type of cycle often persists in order to help the system maintain equilibrium. The desire to maintain homeostasis within the system sometimes overshadows the desire to change. Don Jackson (1957) was the first to offer this counter-intuitive formulation, suggesting that despite system members' protestations that "all would be better if they did not have the problem," they continued to behave in many ways that maintained the problem. In this way, psychopathology and other forms of emotional distress are thought to arise from a relationship process rather than out of some individual etiological deficit (Dallos & Draper, 2005).

Change Within a System

Given all of these entrenched and very complex relational patterns, how can an individual ever begin to effect change within the system? Individuals, couples, and family therapy paradigms can all assist clients as they try to alter these patterns. One important component of change within systems is differentiation. Differentiation is a process that includes both intrapersonal and interpersonal capacities (Bowen, 1978; Kerr & Bowen, 1988). In terms of the intrapersonal capacity, differentiation refers to decreasing one's emotional reactivity and improving the ability to regulate affect (Skowron & Dendy, 2004; Skowron, Holmes, & Sabatelli, 2003). The interpersonal aspect of differentiation involves balancing the forces of separation and togetherness, taking responsibility for one's experience, initiating and receiving intimacy voluntarily, and establishing clear boundaries. It involves finding a balance between independence and togetherness (Kerr & Bowen, 1988). Differentiation often becomes a goal of treatment once the client becomes aware of the way in which anxiety drives the system, including his or her own style of relating. If you recall the example of the children's mobile from the beginning of this section, it will help you envision how one person changing within the system has the power to lead others to change.

AMBIVALENCE AND CONFLICT

Ambivalence involves having conflicting sets of thoughts, wishes, or beliefs (Figure 11.5). These feelings are often incompatible and neither side of the conflict can lay claim to dominance, except temporarily. For example, a goal to quit smoking for health reasons may conflict with a desire to continue smoking for its stress-relieving properties and to avoid withdrawal symptoms. Psychotherapy

FIGURE 11.5 Stop or go? Ambivalence involves having two competing thoughts or feelings simultaneously.
Courtesy of Alex Goldmark.

often aims to understand and reduce ambivalence, or at least the distress caused by the ambivalence. Miller and Rollnick's (2002) MI approach to counseling (see Chapter 10 for more on MI) emphasizes the importance of recognizing and resolving ambivalence in order to change. There is some evidence that for change to occur in therapy, clients need to be able to think about their own ambivalence in productive ways (Kelly, Wood, Shearman, Phillips, & Mansell, 2012).

As a clinician working with clients, you will encounter client ambivalence about all sorts of things. The principles of MI can be very helpful when faced with intense ambivalence, which often expresses itself via resistance to change. MI emphasizes expressing empathy and understanding for the client's position and draws heavily on the work of Carl Rogers (see Chapter 7 for more on unconditional positive regard, congruence, and empathy). Unconditional positive regard is an essential element that will enable clients to openly discuss both sides of their ambivalent feelings. One of the key phrases from MI is *rolling with resistance*. This involves accepting that resistance and ambivalence are natural parts of the change process. Rather than becoming frustrated or trying to convince a client to change, clinicians can use the tools of MI to reflect back the resistance or to highlight areas of concern for the client. Here is an example that illustrates rolling with the resistance and highlighting ambivalence:

> **Client:** I've always been depressed. It's just how I am. I wouldn't know any other way of being. I think I'm done with therapy— I don't really need it.
>
> **Therapist:** Feeling depressed is something that is so familiar to you that it seems to make sense to just continue this way, although you mentioned earlier that being depressed affects your relationships and your ability to keep a job. Can you tell me a little about those concerns?

In this example, the therapist reflects back the client's lack of concern about his depression, but also incorporates material from earlier in the session to shift the focus. The purpose of this type of an intervention is to draw out the client's own arguments for change. Ambivalence is a normal and expected part of the change process. There are many reasons clients seek out counseling and just as many reasons they avoid it or withdraw from treatment. This pursuing and distancing is reflective of an internal experience of ambivalence about change. By speaking about ambivalence and resistance therapeutically, clients may find change easier and more congruent with their own personal goals.

CHAPTER REVIEW

One of the primary tasks of the counseling professional is to understand emotions and help clients improve their relationships. The ability to identify emotions and to effectively manage them is critical to the effectiveness of the therapist. EQ is one of the broad umbrella terms that helps describe this complex skill set. It involves metacognition, which is the ability to think about thinking, and meta-emotion a subcategory of metacognition that involves thinking about emotions. Both skills require an ability to step back and think more objectively about one's own emotional and cognitive experience.

Clients sometimes have difficulties thinking about their own thought processes and identifying specific feelings they experience. One specific deficit therapists might see is alexithymia, or difficulty putting feelings into words. Counselors can provide a framework around the client, a scaffold, to help clients improve their ability to think about their own minds and the minds of others.

Many emotions are expressed nonverbally, either in facial expressions or body language. There is some debate about whether emotions are universal across cultures, but what is clear is that a singular facial expression or gesture can mean many different things. Depending on the context of the expression and the client's own cultural background, a smile or a wink can mean any number of things. Counseling professionals should inquire about the meaning of nonverbal expressions for each individual client.

For those clients who have difficulty acknowledging and managing emotions, there are many options for enhancing emotional regulation skills. These include increasing client awareness of emotions, providing psycho-education and mindfulness training, improving reflective functioning, and, finally, transforming maladaptive emotions into more adaptive ones. To effectively provide these types of therapeutic tools, it is important for therapists to learn to effectively manage their own emotions. This is one of many reasons therapy for the therapist is often highly recommended.

Therapists and clients alike are social beings and have been greatly shaped by their environment. Bronfenbrenner's ecological framework provides a useful outline for understanding the individual in context. The individual is shaped by many different forces, some of which are in opposition to one another. These different contextual levels have the potential to create certain relational dynamics that often persist.

Relational dynamics within systems include double bind communication, triangulation, and homeostasis. Although each of these may appear to be dysfunctional, they are most often activated in an effort to preserve the relationship or system. Change within a system is usually initiated with differentiation, which involves establishing boundaries and effectively separating (without complete withdrawal) from the system. In most therapeutic situations, clients will express or act out ambivalence about change. This may appear in the form of arriving late or missing sessions. Ambivalence may be more directly expressed in words. Although encountering ambivalence may be initially challenging for new therapists, there are many ways to work with ambivalence that incorporate it into the treatment as an expected and valuable part of the process of change.

PERSONAL REFLECTION ESSAY QUESTIONS

1. Reread the passage from Mark Haddon's book, *The Curious Incident of the Dog in the Nighttime*. Imagine you are Siobhan, Christopher's therapist, and try to explain to Christopher what a smile might mean.
2. Do you know anyone with great EQ but lower-than-average intellectual functioning? Or someone with a very strong intellect but below average EQ? Describe this person and consider his or her strengths and/or weaknesses using some of the vocabulary terms in this chapter.
3. Take the Metacognition Assessment Scale. Provide a summary (several paragraphs) of your self-assessment. What areas for growth have you identified? How might you develop these skills going forward?

KEYWORDS

alexithymia

ambivalence

chronosystem

corrective emotional experience

decentering

differentiation

double bind

emotion understanding

emotional regulation

exosystem

family systems

homeostasis

macrosystem

mastery

mesosystem

metacognition

meta-emotion

microsystem

mind-mindedness

promoting emotional awareness

relationship management

scaffolding

self-awareness

self-management

self-reflection

social awareness

transformation

triangulation

FURTHER READING

- Dallos, R., & Vetere, A. (2012). Systems theory, family attachments and processes of triangulation: Does the concept of triangulation offer a useful bridge? *Journal of Family Therapy, 34*(2), 117–137. doi:10.1111/j.1467-6427.2011.00554.x

  Referenced several times within this chapter, this peer-reviewed article provides an excellent overview of how systems theory intersects with attachment theory. The authors provide very cogent and descriptive quotes from their work with one family to illustrate each point.

- Ekman, P. (2003). *Emotions revealed: Recognizing faces and feelings to improve communication and emotional life.* New York, NY: Henry Holt and Company.

  Ekman's book is an accessible and highly readable introduction to the relationship between facial expressions and emotions. There are many photographs throughout the book to help readers think about how to identify emotions in themselves and others.

- Harder, S., & Folke, S. (2012). Affect regulation and metacognition in psychotherapy of psychosis: An integrative approach. *Journal of Psychotherapy Integration, 22*(4), 330–343. doi:10.1037/a0029578

  This article offers an integrative theory of affect regulation, metacognition, and attachment style in psychosis. The authors present a detailed case study in the article that demonstrates how psychotherapy can be beneficial to individuals with psychotic symptoms.

- Randall, K. (2011). Human lie detector Paul Ekman decodes the faces of depression, terrorism, and joy. *Fast Company.*

  Read more about Paul Ekman's Facial Action Coding System in this article from *Fast Company.* http://www.fastcompany.com/1800709/human-lie-detector-paul-ekman-decodes-faces-depression-terrorism-and-joy

- For more on mindfulness, meditation, and self-soothing techniques, consider reading these very accessible and widely available books:

  - Hahn, T. N. (1975). *The miracle of mindfulness: An introduction.* Boston, MA: Beacon Press.
  - McKay, M., Wood, J. C., & Brantley, J. (2007). *The dialectical behavior therapy skills workbook: Practical DBT exercises for learning mindfulness, interpersonal effectiveness, emotion regulation, and distress tolerance.* Oakland, CA: New Harbinger Publications, Inc.
  - Proctor, D. (2013). *Madly chasing peace.* New York, NY: Morgan James Publishing.
  - Salzberg, S. (2010). *Real happiness: The power of meditation.* New York, NY: Workman Publishing Company, Inc.

Endings

*There is no real ending. It's just the place where you stop
the story.*—McNelly, Herbert, and Herbert (1969)

LEARNING OBJECTIVES

- Develop skills to evaluate when treatment should conclude
- Differentiate between evaluating functional impairment and recovery
- Describe the termination phase of therapy
- Define and describe ideal termination
- Identify the differences and reasons for time-limited termination and spaced termination
- Explain why premature termination may occur
- Identify several strategies for reducing premature termination
- Describe the key guidelines for therapist-initiated termination
- Explain the importance of a professional will and an emergency response team
- Develop a personal policy for how to handle post-termination contact

Psychotherapy has both a beginning and an end. Counseling interventions are truly successful when they are no longer necessary. The purpose of therapy is to help clients make sufficient gains in treatment so that they can move on and utilize what they have learned and internalized. This end point in the therapeutic relationship has long been referred to as **termination** (Freud 1937/1953). The word seems to have some negative implication, bringing to mind being terminated from employment or having a terminal illness. Although the end of psychotherapy is in fact the conclusion of a relationship, the end of something, it is also the beginning of a new phase in the client's life. This next chapter is one in which the client begins to cope independently in ways he or she had not been able to previously (Goldfried, 2002). The termination phase of treatment requires a shift in focus as client and therapist begin the process of saying goodbye. Although termination may be represented as a date on the calendar, it is also a transition point between the process of therapy and a new phase of life without therapy.

Different orientations of therapy place varying emphases on the termination phase of treatment (Joyce, Piper, Ogrodniczuk, & Klein, 2007b). In some treatment approaches, termination is actually the central focus (Mann, 1973; Mann & Goldman, 1982). Mann (1973) recommends a "relentless" focus on termination as a way to address separation and ending, which are inevitable in all relationships and in life itself. Others have suggested that the entirety of the work of therapy is a prologue to termination (Hoyt, 1979). Cognitive behavioral approaches view termination as a time of consolidation and preparation for the next phase of independent application, whereas psychodynamic practitioners also incorporate an emphasis on mourning the loss of the therapy. Regardless of therapeutic orientation, all agree that it is important that clients demonstrate the ability to continue the work initiated in psychotherapy on their own. Some therapists will discuss how to manage anticipated future problems and others may help the client make contingency plans for returning to treatment if needed. Termination of therapy gives clients an opportunity to say goodbye in a controlled way, with both parties taking the process seriously. This type of ending is different from many other endings clients may have experienced that were sudden, unexpected, or unreciprocated.

There are different types of termination. Ideally, the decision to terminate will be made mutually, based on the progress the client has made. Termination is sometimes initiated by the client for any number of reasons—including dissatisfaction with the treatment, relocation, or financial pressures. Therapists may also initiate termination because of the end of training, changes in health status, or even death. When termination is unilateral—that is, initiated by only one member of the dyad—many issues may arise. This chapter will begin to explore the many aspects of termination that beginning clinicians should consider before therapy even begins.

TERMINATION ISSUES

There are many things to consider when thinking about termination. There are different reasons for ending therapy and, thus, various types of termination. The end of therapy may be initiated by client or therapist (or both), or it may be brought about by institutional forces or external forces, like finances. Most people—therapists and clients alike—experience a complex array of emotions when it comes to saying goodbye to an important person in their life. Early losses and concerns about being left or leaving others can often affect the process of termination. The ending phase of therapy can be emotionally and cognitively intense. There is a summing up process that involves consolidating and integrating the gains of the therapy. The inherent challenges of termination—which involve embracing independence and leaving a relationship that has been helpful—are a test of the therapy itself, a way to evaluate the stability of the achievements made (Levy, 1986).

When to End Treatment

The question of when a treatment should end is a complicated one. In the first major work ever written about termination, Freud (1937/1953, p. 219) wrote about the requirements that should be fulfilled in order to proceed with termination:

> Two conditions have been approximately fulfilled: first, that the patient shall no longer be suffering from his symptoms and shall have overcome his anxieties and his inhibitions; and secondly, that the [therapist] shall judge that so much repressed material has been made conscious, so much that was unintelligible has been explained, and so much internal resistance conquered, that there is no need to fear a repetition of the pathological processes concerned.

As you begin working with clients, you will become aware that it is deceptively simple to say that therapy ends once the goals of treatment have been achieved, or that the unintelligible has been explained. Therapists of different theoretical orientations may quantify or measure progress in psychotherapy in a variety of ways; however, most agree that termination is ideally a mutually agreed upon decision (between client and therapist) that emerges naturally once the client has achieved relief from distress and mastery of new insight and skills to manage future distress (Jakobsons, Brown, Gordon, & Joiner, 2007; Joyce, Piper, Ogrodniczuk, & Klein, 2007a). There are many things to consider when considering termination. In terms of the appropriate time for termination, clinicians should begin by considering whether the treatment goals have been met and whether the client appears to have achieved some degree of mastery over his or her problems.

Goals Have Been Met—Relief From Distress

The goals of therapy are most often to decrease symptoms or subjective distress. With the exception of therapy that addresses one very specific problem (such as a specific phobia), clients are not expected to reach the farthest extent of their goals. If that were the case, we might be binding clients to lifelong psychotherapy. Rather, counseling professionals help clients make substantial progress on specific treatment goals. Goal-setting in psychotherapy is a critical aspect of measuring progress and outcome. Clients may sometimes have very specific goals that are relatively straightforward to assess, such as, "I want to be able to function at work with less anxiety." Other goals may be more nuanced; clients may want to experience closer and more lasting intimate relationships, or achieve greater independence from their parents. Attainment of goals may be measured in several ways. Many therapists rely on clients' subjective reports coupled with their own clinical assessment. Clients may report fewer depressive symptoms, exhibit a broader range of affect, and demonstrate increased functioning at work and in social relationships. All of these data points suggest that a goal of decreasing depressive symptoms may have been attained.

Alternatively, some clinicians administer self-report measures such as the Beck Depression Inventory (Beck et al., 1996) weekly or by session. This can afford both client and clinician a clear assessment of goal attainment. There are some problems with this type of concrete measurement. First, there is no clear definition of what constitutes a clinically significant reduction of symptoms (Jakobsons et al., 2007). This problem is also inherent in more subjective assessments of symptom reduction. If the goal for the client is to make substantial progress in his or her stated goals, the definition of "substantial progress" is open to interpretation. Second, for clients with comorbid disorders, assessment of multiple domains may be complicated. Finally, there is evidence that as many as 50% of individuals who appear to be asymptomatic on objective symptom measures may not consider themselves to be in remission (Zimmerman et al., 2012). For some clients there appears to be a discrepancy between their scores on self-report measures and their subjective self-assessment of their well-being.

Another aspect of goal attainment is to assess whether additional progress can be made. For many clients, there are periods of life during which therapy may be indicated. A client who comes to therapy to address the death of a parent may make sufficient progress to indicate termination. The client and therapist may decide together that no additional progress can be made. Although the client may return to treatment some years later if another issue arises, for the time being, no additional progress can be made on the goal of overcoming grief. This is also an appropriate juncture to consider termination.

Sustained Remission and Mastery

Symptom reduction is the hallmark of a successful treatment, but the remission of symptoms must be sustained, not simply spontaneous and temporary. For termination to be considered, it must seem likely that symptoms will not reappear in the absence of the therapy. In other words, clients should be able to maintain the gains made during treatment. The goal of psychotherapy is not to create dependence upon the therapist, but rather to foster independence. Some researchers (Bohus et al., 2004) have utilized periodic assessment of symptoms for disorders over the course of several months to assess the sustainability of recovery. This is especially important with clients who experience symptoms, such as those seen in patients with borderline personality disorder, which tend to have great variability across time. Some psychotherapy researchers have recommended that symptom decrease should be maintained for 8 weeks or more (Jakobsons et al., 2007; Keller et al., 1987).

Clients typically learn new skills and coping mechanisms during therapy; they also develop greater insight into the genesis of their distress and acquire an ability to prevent future relapses. Independent implementation of these new skills over time, particularly during times of increased vulnerability, is an important criterion to consider when evaluating readiness for termination. It is often helpful to see carryover of symptom reduction into other areas of the client's life. For example, a client treated for work-related anxiety may report an increased sense of ease in social situations.

During the process of assessment and diagnosis, clinicians typically evaluate **functional impairment**. This refers to the degree to which the client is prevented from operating at full capacity at work or school and in interpersonal relationships. When prolonged symptom remission is coupled with a return to an optimal level of social and vocational functioning, this is referred to as **recovery** (Zanarini, Frankenburg, Reich, & Fitzmaurice, 2010). For some clients with chronic psychiatric problems, the first goal of treatment is not recovery but symptom remission. This conceptualization of healing acknowledges that for some individuals with particular problems, symptoms may return. This is especially true for individuals with substance abuse problems (Walitzer & Dearing, 2006), bipolar disorder (Scott, Colom, & Vieta, 2007), psychotic disorders (Alvarez-Jimenez et al., 2012), and personality disorders (Zanarini et al., 2010). Assessing recovery involves evaluating whether the client has demonstrated improved social and emotional functioning. These aspects of recovery, however, are not required for all types of termination. For example, termination happens within a hospital setting when clinicians deem a client ready for discharge. Although this client has achieved enough symptom relief to recommend a less restrictive level of care, it is not expected that he or she will have returned to a pre-morbid level of social functioning.

Mastery involves resolving many of the problems that gave rise to the symptoms. This includes, but is not limited to, insight and cognitive understanding of the problem. It also suggests an ability to function at a higher capacity if the precipitating problem were to arise again. For psychodynamic clinicians, mastery may include the resolution of certain interpersonal styles that became apparent through the therapeutic relationship. For example, if a client is prone to suspicion and mistrust in relationships and this leads to anxiety and interpersonal dysfunction, termination should be predicated partly on successful resolution of this style of relating. In this case, the transference relationship may be the mechanism that leads to change. As the client has increased opportunity to test his or her hypotheses about other people's motives and intentions, he or she may be able to internalize certain aspects of the therapy and the therapeutic process. Therapist and client can utilize the therapeutic relationship to prepare the client for maintaining a healthier way of interacting with others. Termination is typically recommended when clients report a sense of pride regarding the new skills they have acquired, as opposed to doubt about whether they will be able to function. This type of confidence is often indicative of symptom remission and a significant degree of mastery.

How Treatment Ends

The **termination phase** of therapy is distinct from the initial assessment phase and the working phase (Figure 12.1). It has a tendency to stimulate issues associated with separation and loss and is likely to provoke such feelings in both therapist and client. The salience of the termination phase varies widely with respect to theoretical orientation, duration of treatment, and the quality of the therapeutic relationship. Termination of open-ended psychotherapy is likely to focus more substantially on the loss of the therapeutic relationship and expression of grief over this loss may be encouraged. Within a short-term or problem-focused treatment, termination may emphasize the client's resources and ability to function independently. Therapists who recognize the import of the therapeutic alliance are also more likely to explore all of the feelings—positive and negative—associated with termination.

In most termination processes it is useful to discuss some, if not all, of the following topics with the client:

- Changes in symptoms, problems, and areas of conflict
- Extent of resolution of precipitating stressors or life events
- Improvements in ability to cope with daily hassles and major stressors

FIGURE 12.1 Termination is never truly the end. For many clients it is the beginning of a new way of being in the world.

Courtesy of Jason Scragz.

- Changes in the ability to tolerate a broader range of affect (e.g., feelings of sadness and worry)
- Increased awareness, appreciation, and acceptance of self and others
- Progress that has been made in daily functioning
- Improvements in quality of life, particularly those because of changes in internal capacities to cope
- Capacity to observe oneself and analyze situations (e.g., metacognitive and meta-emotive abilities)

Most therapists approach these topics in a relatively unstructured way. As termination approaches, it can be useful to notice the client's enhanced abilities and skills in self-observation. For example, as a client tells the therapist about a recent event at work, it is therapeutic to use comments such as,

> It's important to notice what happened this time. You experienced a problem that was similar to the ones you faced when we began working together. What is different now is that you were able to think through this challenge without feeling particularly anxious and you resolved it with great skill. Now when you come in to talk about it, there is actually very little to discuss because you've taken care of the problem so effectively.

These types of observations reinforce the client's confidence in his or her own abilities and help the client see concrete evidence that termination is appropriate.

Ideal Termination

Termination can occur in any number of ways. The **ideal termination** situation is one in which the client and therapist mutually agree upon the decision to end treatment and collaborate to develop a process for termination. The intensity and duration of the therapy typically dictate the length of the termination phase. For example, a client receiving six sessions of therapy for a specific phobia will likely require minimal planning for termination. It may be introduced at the end of the fifth session with treatment concluding by the end of the sixth session. At the other end of the spectrum, in a 2-year therapy focused on childhood neglect and long-term sexual abuse, the termination phase of treatment may cover several weeks or months and require extensive preparation. The fact that different clients require different levels of closure may also dictate the length and intensity of the termination phase. Therapists must be sensitive to clients' idiosyncratic reactions to saying goodbye as well as the complex countertransference reactions that may arise.

Clients may come to session with fewer problems to report. There may also be evidence of internalization for the therapist, for example, "I remembered what we talked about last week and it really helped me when I started to argue with my boss." These types of statements may mark the beginning of the termination phase. For some clients, it will be difficult to suggest that termination be considered. In one study of clients' feelings during psychotherapy termination, a participant stated that one of the most positive aspects of termination was the "capacity to end a routine and announce without concern my wish to end and the capacity to cope with the therapist's response" (Roe, Dekel, Harel, Fennig, & Fennig, 2006, p. 75). This comment highlights the importance of the therapeutic relationship, the client's implicit concern about hurting the therapist by leaving, and ultimately the ability to pursue his own goals separate and apart from the therapist.

When therapy ends, the interpersonal connection between therapist and client does not cease to exist. The gains that have been made in therapy should be sustained, and aspects of the therapy (and even the therapist) should have been largely internalized by the patient. Edelson (1963) has said, "what has been happening keeps going on inside the patient" (p. 14). Growth and change continue beyond the bounds of a formal treatment. In an ideal scenario, the termination phase should focus on the gains the client has made, the current strengths, and areas in which he or she is likely to continue growing independently. This is all part of the consolidation process that allows the client to continue in a process of growth and intrapersonal development even after the therapy has ended.

With some clients, particularly children and adolescents, it can be helpful to create a concrete reminder or summary of the work that has been done. Therapist and client may consider creating a **memory book** that describes, visually and in words, how the therapy began, major highlights, and hopes for the future (Elbow, 1987). Another option is to create an award certificate for a child that describes her achievements in therapy (e.g., "This award recognizes Juliet for facing her fears and overcoming them"). This type of ritual is an effective way of providing children with closure and a tangible reminder of this meaningful relationship. Some day-treatment programs or other institutionalized services provide graduation ceremonies or goodbye parties when someone moves on. These types of formal celebrations can also be helpful markers along a person's journey toward mental health.

Even in mutually agreed upon terminations, there is a certain degree of affective turmoil that is expected. Therapists may anticipate clients' reactions to impending termination based on the clients' responses to other separations (e.g., therapist vacations) during the course of therapy and other types of losses the client has experienced (e.g., death of loved one, divorce, children leaving for college). Some clients experience a temporary increase in symptoms as the termination date approaches. This may be a type of resistance to termination, a way to demonstrate the client's need for the therapist. Sometimes it is difficult to discern whether these types of re-emerging symptoms indicate the need for continued psychotherapy or whether they are an expected reaction to the impending loss of the therapist. This can be discussed with the client and an exploration of the meaning of these symptoms may be useful. The experience of sadness or anxiety is a normal part of living. As Greenberg (2002b) has written, "getting depressed, being unsure, or arguing again are all part of a process of living and never go away completely" (p. 359). Difficulty arises when clients become stuck in these old patterns and are unable to effectively manage them. It may be useful to emphasize the client's strengths and to assure them that, should they need further help at a later date, the therapist will be available.

In an ideal termination situation, clients often experience a feeling of pride, a sense of accomplishment, and hope for the independence they are moving toward. Therapists also tend to experience similar emotions toward clients who have successfully utilized the therapy and are ready to conclude. Although saying goodbye is difficult, therapeutic termination has many benefits and rewards. Mutual termination after a successful therapy is an inherently positive step forward. The ending is constructive and serves to consolidate the gains the client has made. Often both therapist and client have the opportunity to make statements about what the therapy has meant (Long, Pendleton, & Winter, 1988).

Time-Limited or Spaced Termination

The termination phase of therapy can be implemented in a variety of ways. In a **time-limited termination**, sessions continue at their usual frequency and then stop abruptly at a pre-determined date. For example, once a termination date is set, the client will be seen in his usual once-weekly manner until the date arrives and then the therapist and client will part ways. In **spaced termination**, sometimes referred to as "fading out," the time between sessions is gradually extended and termination is approached in measured steps. A client in weekly treatment might be seen biweekly for a period of time, then monthly for several months, before treatment finally ends. Spaced termination does not always involve setting a final termination date ahead of time. Client and therapist can take a "wait and see" approach and determine when to conclude treatment spontaneously, based on the client's sense of well-being and subjective readiness for termination.

Traditionally, treatments on the more expressive end of the psychotherapy continuum tend to favor time-limited termination; supportive treatments, on the other hand, are more likely to utilize a spaced termination approach. This is not always the case, and termination plans in any treatment should be developed in accordance with the individual client's needs. Termination plans must be amenable to change. If a client begins bringing up new and unresolved issues, it may be wise to consider extending the timeframe for termination. It is important for the therapist to remain flexible and willing to meet the needs of the client. Later in this chapter, we explore the multiple meanings of symptoms that reappear as termination approaches.

Client-Initiated Premature Termination

Beyond this ideal framework for termination—a mutually agreed upon and purposeful ending to a successful therapy—there are many other scenarios that can unfold (Figure 12.2). **Premature termination** refers to any early ending to the therapy that takes place before it would have ideally ended. It is estimated that between 30% and 60% of clients end therapy prematurely and unilaterally (Reis & Brown, 1999). **Client-initiated premature termination** is when the client decides to end therapy contrary to either the therapist's current recommendation or the originally agreed upon duration of treatment (Ogrodniczuk, Joyce, & Piper, 2005). Premature termination is associated with certain demographic variables. In one meta-analysis of 125 studies of premature termination, increased risk for dropping out of therapy was associated with being non-white, having a lower level of education, and lower socioeconomic status (Wierzbicki & Pekarik, 1993).

Not all premature terminations represent treatment failures. Some clients who discontinue psychotherapy may feel sufficiently helped. Other types of premature terminations may occur because of certain life circumstances such as financial pressures or relocation. These more positive types of premature terminations appear to be the exception rather than the rule. Clients who discontinue psychotherapy early understandably report less therapeutic progress and more psychological distress (Pekarik, 1992). They also have a tendency to overutilize mental health services (Carpenter, Del Gaudio, & Morrow, 1979), by contacting mental health providers at twice the rate of those who complete therapy.

FIGURE 12.2 Parting ways. The decision to end treatment may be mutual or unilateral, on the part of the therapist or client.
Courtesy of Hitesh Shah.

In addition to the effects premature termination may have on clients, it can also impact the therapist. Being left, as it were, can naturally bring up feelings of abandonment and anger. The therapist's own self-esteem may be affected if his or her identity is closely linked with her ability to help others. Treatment failures may have an even greater impact on therapists who strive to demonstrate genuine warmth and empathy with their clients (Piselli, Halgin, & MacEwan, 2011). Premature terminations also have an economic impact on therapists in private practice. For trainees, having a client leave therapy early may cause concern about how their performance will be evaluated by supervisors and colleagues. Counseling professionals should closely monitor the feelings they have in the aftermath of premature termination. Painful reactions such as hurt, rejection, and loss may arise and can potentially affect the therapist's work with other clients.

Given that premature termination appears to be a common problem for therapists, it is important to consider ways to reduce the frequency of therapy dropout. Research has shown that there are three major categories of reasons for leaving therapy prematurely (Pekarik, 1983). These include the aforementioned problem improvement, environmental obstacles, as well as dissatisfaction with treatment. Frequently, clients who choose to terminate prematurely do so without notice. They may tell the therapist, "I will not be coming back next week," or they may simply fail to show up or call, essentially disappearing.

BOX 12.1

Stories We Tell Ourselves

Why do clients leave therapy? When the therapeutic relationship ends abruptly, we are left to consider why a particular client left treatment. It is important to maintain a realistic appraisal of our abilities. Depending on your personality style and general sense of self-efficacy, you may have a tendency to (a) take full responsibility for early terminations in a way that is overly self-punitive or (b) abdicate responsibility and blame the client for the way things ended.

Murdock, Edwards, and Murdock (2010) asked two groups of therapists to read vignettes that described a case of premature termination. In the case presented, the therapeutic alliance was described as strong, and the client had made considerable progress in therapy but had identified remaining issues to be addressed. The vignette then ended with a statement indicating that the client had called and terminated therapy without explanation. The vignettes were identical for both groups of therapists, but differed in one way: The female client in the vignette was either referred to as "your client" or "the client." The therapists who participated in this study were then asked to rate the likelihood that the client, therapist, or other outside factors had caused the treatment to end. The researchers were looking for differences in these ratings based on whether the vignette presented had described the client as "your client" or "the client." Do you have a hypothesis about what differences they may have found?

It turns out that those therapists who read vignettes referring to "your client" were more likely to attribute the cause of termination to the client.

(continued)

(continued)

Therapists presented with vignettes with the term "the client" tended to attribute termination to therapist factors. The researchers concluded that the therapists had engaged in a self-serving bias, which is a tendency to see ourselves in a more positive light than we deserve. Therapists who were primed to see the client as their own were less likely to take responsibility for the termination. This self-serving bias may help protect therapists from threats to their self-esteem and professional identity that arise when clients stop treatment abruptly.

In another study, psychologists were interviewed about a premature termination they had experienced (Piselli et al., 2011). Researchers asked the respondents several questions, including, "What characteristics of this client contributed to his or her premature departure?," "What missteps, if any, do you feel you made in your work with this client?," and "In what way might your actions have contributed to the client's departure?" Psychologists in the study reported that clients found the work of therapy too difficult, became defensive in response to interventions made, or enacted a transference. In addition to these client-related variables, a majority of respondents identified their own mistakes and failures as possible reasons for the termination. These included failing to see or address a problem, using ineffective interventions, and feeling burnt-out, frustrated, or discouraged in their work with the client.

As you move forward with clinical placements, what stories will you tell yourself to fill in the gaps when a client leaves treatment unexpectedly? Are there some explanations for premature termination that are more difficult to consider?

Encouraging Treatment Completion

Ogrodniczuk and colleagues (2005) identified nine strategies for reducing premature termination. They include: (a) pre-therapy preparation, (b) client selection, (c) time-limited treatment, (d) treatment negotiation, (e) case management, (f) appointment reminders, (g) motivation enhancement, (h) facilitation of the therapeutic alliance, and (i) facilitation of affect expression. These strategies are particularly useful in that they balance their focus on both client and therapist factors that may lead to premature termination.

Pre-therapy preparation is one of the most frequently discussed strategies for preventing client-initiated premature termination of psychotherapy. This type of preparation involves teaching the patient about how treatment unfolds, the rationale for treatment, expectations for client and therapist, and identifying the types of difficulties one may face during therapy. The purpose of this type of therapy preparation is to increase psychological mindedness among clients and to reduce incongruence between client and therapist expectations of therapy.

Selection of clients is an important component of beginning psychotherapy. Not all potential clients are suited to all types of therapy. It is important to find a match between the client's capacities and the demands of a specific type of counseling intervention. Some clients are particularly motivated for cognitive behavioral or psychodynamic treatment, whereas others may benefit from supportive psychotherapy or social skills training.

In some cases, **time-limited treatment** or clear consensus between client and therapist about the goals and parameters of therapy—treatment negotiation—are useful tools in facilitating treatment completion. Having a definite time limit for treatment and collaborating with the client to develop a plan of action can be helpful in this regard (see Box 12.4 for a historical example of this). Time-limited treatment offers an explicit and pre-determined ending that can be a helpful boundary for some clients. Additionally, studies have shown that some clients who terminate prematurely do so because they could not come to a common understanding with the therapist about the nature of the client's problem and the methods that should be used to address the issue (Epperson, Bushway, & Warman, 1983; Tracey, 1988).

Particularly for clients from disadvantaged backgrounds or those facing multiple challenges of daily living, case management can be an essential adjunctive treatment. Case managers do not serve as additional therapists; instead they serve as coaches and assistants to help clients maintain basic standards of living. **Case management** can help clients find housing, maintain health insurance coverage, and pursue employment and educational opportunities, as well as provide social support. Maintaining or improving these important aspects of daily living can improve overall mental health. Having fewer daily stressors also allows clients to come to therapy with greater emotional resources and fortitude. Appointment reminders are also a low-cost form of case management. Although eschewed by many practicing clinicians because they tend to deemphasize client responsibility for the treatment, appointment reminders can be helpful for client populations facing multiple stressors. They are often used in day treatment programs for individuals with chronic mental illness and hospital-based outpatient clinics.

Directly out of the motivational interviewing playbook (see Chapter 10; Miller & Rollnick, 2002), motivation enhancement is another tool that can facilitate treatment completion. This strategy involves creating incentives for change, eliciting self-motivational statements about treatment, acknowledging the client's efforts, and reframing problems so they seem less formidable. This type of strategy is particularly relevant for clients who are ambivalent about treatment or exhibit problems (like substance abuse) that are often associated with resistance to change.

The last two strategies for addressing early termination include facilitation of the therapeutic alliance and the expression of affect. As you learned in Chapter 7, therapeutic alliance is one of the essential ingredients of successful therapy. All the components of the alliance—warmth, empathy, genuineness—are factors that will help facilitate communication between therapist and client. Within the context of a strong therapeutic alliance, clients will also have room to express doubts and questions about therapy. A good working relationship between client and therapist will also create space for clients to express a broad range of affect. Exploration of negative affect can help clients resolve emotional problems and will often lead to more frequent expressions of positive affect. Clients who have difficulty expressing their true emotions in therapy are also more likely to terminate prematurely (Oei & Kazmierczak, 1997).

As you can see, there are many ways to foster an environment that leads to treatment completion. Not surprisingly, many of the strategies described here are things you have already learned about—addressing client expectations (see Chapter 5), enhancing motivation (see Chapter 10), building a strong therapeutic alliance (see Chapter 7), and encouraging expression of a broad range of emotions (see Chapter 11). Keep in mind that throughout your career as a counseling professional, clients will leave treatment unexpectedly and sometimes even without notice. It is important to recognize that clients pursue and complete treatment when there is a good working relationship, but also when they are willing and able to engage in the work of psychotherapy.

BOX 12.2

Spotlight on Culture

Surprisingly little research has been done on the role of cultural difference in predicting premature termination of psychotherapy. One study of 527 clients indicated that it was actually the therapist's ethnic identity and gender that predicted premature termination—above and beyond similar client demographic variables (Williams, Ketring, & Salts, 2005). Mental health services are a traditionally European American, middle class institution (Sue & Sue, 1999), and it is possible that the rituals associated with psychotherapy may seem unfamiliar or strange to those of other groups. There may be a mismatch between client and therapist expectations of how therapy should proceed and how the therapeutic relationship will develop. Talking about obvious and also latent differences between client and therapist is one way to address differing expectations before they lead to early termination.

Therapist-Initiated Premature Termination

Therapists, particularly those in training, are frequently forced to terminate therapeutic relationships with clients who have not achieved their treatment goals and, if given the choice, would prefer to continue in treatment. This is referred to as **therapist-initiated premature termination** or **forced termination.** The most common reason for this type of premature termination is the end of the therapist's clinical rotation, signaling that he or she must leave the clinic or hospital. Less frequently, therapists may be forced to terminate care with clients prematurely because of institutional pressures. The agency may be moving to a time-limited treatment model or the service may be closed entirely because of economic realities. Once beyond their training years, therapists may initiate termination before the treatment is complete because of relocation, health reasons such as chronic illness or pregnancy, or retirement.

Whatever the reason for this type of termination, there is a common thread: the therapist is leaving the client. This is an inherently stressful event for both members of the therapeutic dyad. Clients may understandably have negative reactions to therapist-initiated termination. Being forced to accept the departure of a therapist is a loss of control and can trigger feelings of abandonment that may be reminiscent of earlier losses. Some clients may see it as a defection (Siebold, 2007), a kind of switching sides. Clients may give indirect expressions of their disappointment and anger. These can include missed appointments, arriving late, and nonpayment. More direct expressions of frustration are also likely to come. Clients may say things that are difficult for empathic, caring professionals to hear, such as "How can you leave me right after my mother died?" or "If you really cared about me, you would stay."

Therapists are also likely to feel a range of negative emotions surrounding initiating termination. Leaving a job, for any reason, highlights the natural limitations of the therapist. The relationship between therapist and client is limited in time and scope. But when the therapist is the one to discontinue the relationship, she becomes the source of the client's hurt. Therapist-initiated termination often sends a message that is opposite to what the entire therapy has been designed to communicate. Therapists may fear they are communicating to the client, "You are not my first priority," "I have needs and obligations that are more important than your need for me to stay," and, "You have been vulnerable with me and now I will abandon you." As helping professionals whose entire professional identity centers on being a supportive presence, leaving will understandably bring up a complex array of feelings.

Trainees forced to initiate termination because of the end of a clinical placement may feel anxious, depressed, angry, or sad during termination (Baum, 2006; Zuckerman & Mitchell, 2004). Clinicians in training may worry about how much they are harming their clients and feel guilty about leaving (Baum, 2006; Gould, 1978).

Guidelines for Therapist-Initiated Premature Termination

Given the difficulties associated with ending any relationship, particularly a therapeutic one with a strong working alliance, there are several guidelines new therapists should consider as they prepare to say goodbye. It is critical that the therapist allow ample time for the termination phase to unfold (Bostic, Shadid, & Blotcky, 1996). This is especially true for clients who have more substantial difficulties, such as psychosis or personality disorders, as they are likely to have greater difficulty with forced termination (Zuckerman & Mitchell, 2004). You may notice yourself behaving differently with each client, delaying telling certain clients about your upcoming departure. Fair and Bressler (1992) found that trainees had greater difficulty properly attending to termination issues with their more challenging clients.

The length of time required for termination also varies widely, depending on how long and intense the treatment phase has been. It is also highly recommended that students inform clients at the *beginning* of treatment that they will be leaving at the end of their training (Gould, 1978; Mason, Beckerman, & Auerbach, 2002). Natural breaks in the therapy, such as vacations, can also be used as previews for what termination may feel like (Sanville, 1982). This affords both client and therapist the opportunity to discuss the end of treatment multiple times and in advance. The movie *What About Bob?* (Williams & Ziskin, 1991) is a wonderful comic portrayal of the effect a therapist's vacation can have on a client. In the film, Bob follows his new psychiatrist on a family vacation and is relentless in his pursuit of him. Although this type of scenario is (hopefully) unlikely to happen, the characters in the film demonstrate a caricature of the feelings and issues that may come up around temporary terminations.

The therapist who is leaving should also clearly present the reason for the termination. Pumpian-Mindlin (1958) recommended that departing therapists take responsibility for the termination. Although it may be tempting to explain the termination as a result of external institutional forces, this will likely add to the client's sense of loss of control. It suggests that neither party in the dyad has a sense of agency, that they are both simply victims of a system rather than actors creating a situation. If termination is not planned from the beginning (as in the case of a training placement), therapists should announce their decision to leave as soon as possible. It is often useful to let clients know where you are going and why. This should be done with discretion—each client population has different needs and abilities to tolerate this type of self-disclosure.

Clients may react specifically to this type of information. An underachieving adolescent client was informed that his therapist was leaving the clinic to pursue an academic job at a local university. He responded, "Maybe I'll actually stop ditching school. I want to come to that college and learn from you." In another situation, a therapist indicated she would be leaving her private practice in order to spend more time with her family. A client with significant personality disorder symptoms retorted, "Seems kind of selfish to me, but I guess you have to do what you have to do." Another client, with tears in his eyes saying goodbye to his therapist because her training placement had come to an end, told the smiling therapist to "stop crying." It is impossible to prepare for the wide range of reactions departing therapists may get from their clients, but it is helpful to recognize that anything can happen.

Many of the guidelines for reducing client-initiated premature termination carry over to guidelines for managing therapist-initiated termination. It is important to facilitate the expression of the client's feeling about the forced termination. Clients are likely to experience feelings of sadness, frustration, anger, and loss in response to the imminent loss of the therapist (Gelman, Fernandez, Hausman, Miller, & Weiner, 2007). These spontaneous and authentic reactions are an important part of the therapeutic process. Therapists should strive to tolerate these reactions and attempt to process them thoughtfully with clients. This can be challenging when the therapist is facing his or her own feelings about leaving. The therapist must table her own feelings and emotions—to be processed in supervision and individual therapy—and do her best to respond empathically to the client's sense of loss.

Supervision during training is essential and seeking additional assistance around the difficulties associated with forced termination is highly recommended. Given the added responsibility and feelings of guilt that may arise when therapists initiate termination, counselors should seek out supervision specifically focused on managing termination and its related anxieties. Therapists should discuss within themselves the affective factors that may affect the forced termination as well as practical matters of how to talk with clients about termination.

When initiated by the therapist, forced termination often leaves clients with a sense that they have no control over what is happening to them. It is incumbent upon the therapist to encourage clients to make their own decisions when it comes to setting a termination date and considering whether and how to be transferred to another therapist. Transferred clients tend to have much poorer outcomes in psychotherapy, dropping out at nearly twice the rate of non-transferred clients (Wapner, Klein, Friedlander, & Andrasik, 1986; Tantam & Klerman, 1979). Termination plans should be individualized to the unique needs of each client, and departing therapists should work to facilitate the transfer-referral process.

BOX 12.3

Case Study in Termination Transfer

Sarah, a training therapist, was beginning the termination phase with a 6-year-old male client named Josh. Josh asked to meet the therapist to whom he was being transferred (Larry), so Sarah arranged for them to visit Larry's office together. Larry gave Josh a warm welcome and offered him a model airplane kit. He asked if Josh would like to begin the project with Sarah and could then finish it once he and Josh started working together. This gift became a wonderful transitional object for Josh. While building the plane with Sarah, whom he had been seeing for almost a year, he talked about how they had built something together and identified the skills he had gained through their work. When Josh began working with Larry, they resumed work on the model plane, and Josh pointed out how Larry glued parts together in a different way than Sarah had. This comment was a catalyst for a productive discussion about how other things were different—Larry had a slightly different style than Sarah, his office was smaller than hers, and Josh didn't know Larry very well. Larry invited Josh to teach him about some of the things that had been helpful in his work with Sarah and reassured him that they would get to know each other better as time went on.

Self-care is also an important component of successful terminations. Supervision is one avenue for discussing the intense feelings you may experience as you approach this difficult task. Individual therapy, peer supervision, and informal conversations with other trainees and colleagues are also useful ways of finding support. It is also important to maintain your energy level by getting adequate rest, exercise, and maintaining good nutrition.

Other Types of Therapist-Initiated Termination

Counseling professionals may also recommend termination to clients if they believe the client is not making sufficient progress (in which case a referral may be indicated), they feel ill-equipped to treat the client, or if a dual relationship emerges. These are unusual situations that arise infrequently but are important to acknowledge. If a client seems to be stuck and is not improving, it may be because of any number of factors. Clients may be in need of medication in conjunction with therapy, there may be a poor therapist-client match, or the client may be resistant to the interventions being offered. It is important for the therapist to seek consultation and supervision on the case and to explore the lack of progress with the client.

When a therapist recognizes she is not the appropriate clinician to treat the client, she has an ethical duty to consult and refer the client to another professional (Knapp & VandeCreek, 2012). For example, consider a client who comes to treatment for help with sexual performance issues. During the course of treatment, an underlying depressive disorder becomes evident, and the therapist requests a psychopharmacology consultation. The client begins taking medication and focusing on the depressive symptoms in therapy, but the symptoms worsen. The therapist, whose specialty is in sex therapy, pursues supervision on the case and recognizes that she is not the appropriate person to treat this combination of symptoms. In this case, the therapist has an ethical obligation to initiate termination and facilitate a smooth transition to another clinician who can better assist the client.

A conflict of interest or dual relationship may become evident to the therapist during the course of treatment. For example, a therapist may realize after several months that his client has ongoing business dealings with the therapist's spouse. Because the therapist and his spouse do not share the same last name, this conflict was not evident at the beginning of the therapeutic relationship. In most cases, it will likely be appropriate to refer this client to another clinician with whom the client has no overlapping relationships. In both of these situations, the therapist should speak as openly as possible with the client about his assessment of the situation and the recommendation for a referral. Many of the other principles of therapist-initiated termination apply in these types of cases, especially in a discussion of the incompleteness of the therapeutic work.

Untimely Termination

Garcia-Lawson, Lane, and Koetting (2000) found that 90% of therapists who died had no plan in place to safeguard their clients' interests, records, and future treatment. Some authors have recommended that therapists create a professional will and identify several colleagues who can serve as emergency responders in the event of a critical incident such as a catastrophic accident or death (Firestein, 1994; Steiner, 2002, 2011). A professional will should identify other professionals who will notify clients and colleagues in the event of your death or major injury. Your emergency response team and your lawyer should have a copy of your license, liability insurance policy, professional contacts who should be notified if your ability to practice becomes compromised, and contact information for all clients. They should also have access to contact information of former clients who may attempt to contact you for medical records, future appointments, or to simply inquire if they learn of your death or injury. Although it may be existentially difficult to consider your own death or serious injury, it is an important component of being a competent, thoughtful, and helping professional.

BOX 12.4

Freud's Account of a Termination

The first psychotherapist, Sigmund Freud, offered detailed descriptions of his work with clients. One such account, from Freud's "Analysis Terminable and Interminable" (1937/1953), includes this interesting narrative of ending treatment with a long-term patient in psychoanalysis with Freud:

> Before the War, I myself had already tried another way of speeding up analysis. I had undertaken to treat a young Russian, a rich man spoilt by riches, who had come to Vienna in a state of complete helplessness, accompanied by physician and attendant. It was possible in the course of several years to restore to him a considerable measure of independence, and to awaken his interest

(continued)

(continued)

in life, while his relations to the principal people in his life were adjusted. But then we came to a full stop. We made no progress in clearing up his child-hood's neurosis, which was the basis of his later illness, and it was obvious that the patient found his present situation quite comfortable and did not intend to take any step which would bring him nearer to the end of his treat-ment. It was a case of the patient himself obstructing the cure: The analysis was in danger of failing as a result of its—partial—success. In this predica-ment I resorted to the heroic remedy of fixing a date for the conclusion of the analysis. At the beginning of a period of treatment I told the patient that the coming year was to be the last of his analysis, no matter what progress he made or failed to make in the time still left to him. At first he did not believe me, but, once he was convinced that I was in deadly earnest, the change which I had hoped for began to take place. His resistances crumbled away, and in the last months of treatment he was able to produce all the memories and to discover the connecting links which were necessary for the understanding of his early neurosis and his recovery from the illness from which he was then suffering. When he took leave of me at midsummer, 1914, with as little suspi-cion as the rest of us of what lay so shortly ahead, I believed that his cure was complete and permanent.

In a postscript to this patient's case-history I have already reported that I was mistaken. When, towards the end of the War, he returned to Vienna, a refugee and destitute, I had to help him to master a part of the transference which had remained unresolved. Within a few months this was successfully accomplished and I was able to conclude my postscript with the statement that "since then the patient has felt normal and has behaved unexceptionably, in spite of the War having robbed him of his home, his possessions and all his family relationships." Fifteen years have passed since then, without disprov-ing the truth of this verdict. (Freud, 1937/1953, pp. 217–218)

In this vignette we see Freud utilizing termination as a method for "speed-ing up" the process of psychotherapy. He hoped that setting a termina-tion date would actually lead to a greater degree of progress in the patient. Freud referred to the setting of a termination date as a "blackmailing device" (Freud, 1937/1953, p. 218) and recommended complete inflexibility in changing such a date should symptoms reappear. Much has changed in our understanding of termination since Freud's time, but his awareness of the complexities of this unique phase of treatment has informed both the research and practice of psychotherapy endings today.

Issues of Post-Termination Contact

Termination implies a certain degree of finality, the ultimate closure of a relation-ship. Despite this, termination is not always a final conclusion. Post-termination contact should be conditional on the client's need for future help and should rarely be initiated by the therapist—with the exception of billing issues or if the therapist's records are being requested by a third party. Therapists approach the issue of post-termination contact with differing perspectives. Most clinicians will inform clients that they may contact them for future professional services if necessary. Future contact on an as-needed basis is seen as appropriate and important when clients seek it out (Dienes, Torres-Harding, Reinecke, Freeman, & Sauer, 2011). For interns and students, offering clients future treatment may not be possible. Most clinical placements have strict parameters and clients will return to the institution (rather than the individual clinician) for future treatment.

Regardless of the degree of finality of the termination, it is recommended that therapists regard all former clients with professionalism. The APA Code, Standard 10.08(a), states: "Psychologists do not engage in sexual intimacies with *former* clients/patients for at least two years after cessation or termination of therapy." This is often referred to as the 2-year rule. Although there is no prohibition against personal contacts with clients after 2 years have passed, some counseling professionals follow the adage *once a client, always a client*. This is a good rule of thumb to follow.

CHAPTER REVIEW

The end of psychotherapy is often referred to as termination. The term refers not only to the actual endpoint of the treatment, but also the latter phase of the therapeutic process. This is a time when gains are consolidated and the work of psychotherapy is reviewed by client and therapist. Saying goodbye to any meaningful relationship can be difficult, and these challenges can also arise at the end of a therapeutic relationship, for both parties involved.

The decision to end therapy is ideally arrived at by mutual agreement of the client and therapist. Clients should demonstrate a clinically significant reduction in symptoms. Additionally, it is important that clients achieve a substantial portion of the goals they had when treatment began. Perfection or 100% attainment is not the ultimate objective; rather, it is important to make significant progress so that clients can continue the work of therapy on their own. The reduction of symptoms should be sustained over a reasonable amount of time and clients should demonstrate mastery of the issues they identified as distressing at the start. Clients may report less functional impairment. When social and occupational functioning improves and this is paired with symptom reduction, the client is said to have achieved recovery. In an ideal termination situation, recovery will be paired with mastery, which is the client's ability to independently resolve issues that arise in their daily life.

When therapy comes to an end, there will hopefully be a phase of treatment that involves reviewing the progress that has been made and preparing for the future. Although the therapy itself is ending, clients continue to grow and develop as individuals post-termination. Discussion of the areas in which the client has experienced significant growth and change can foster healthy post-termination development. Some clients experience a slight regression, or resurgence of symptoms, as termination approaches. Clinicians should carefully evaluate whether these symptoms suggest the need for more therapy or if they are a normal and expected reaction to termination. The actual process of termination may involve continued sessions leading up to a pre-determined date. In other situations, the therapist and client may agree to "fade out" with a gradual decrease in the frequency of sessions until a final end date is identified.

Outside of the ideal termination scenario, unilateral termination may be initiated by the client or therapist. Client-initiated termination, also referred to as premature termination, is when the client decides to discontinue therapy contrary to the therapist's recommendation. This may occur because of external circumstances such as financial burdens, relocation, or dissatisfaction with the treatment. Premature termination often happens with little or no notice. There are several strategies therapists and clinics can utilize in order to encourage treatment completion. These include preparing clients for the work of therapy, using time-limited treatments, offering case management for disadvantaged clients, facilitating a strong therapeutic alliance, and encouraging the expression of affect, including negative feelings about treatment.

Therapist-initiated termination or forced termination is a common problem for counseling trainees. At every clinical placement, students are forced to leave their clients when they conclude their training at the end of each year. Forced terminations may occur when the therapist retires, relocates, or closes her practice for any reason. This type of termination can be very difficult for client and therapist alike. Therapists are likely to feel guilty and preoccupied with the sense that they are abandoning their clients. Clients will understandably have negative reactions to being left by their therapist. Trainees are strongly encouraged to inform clients of their trainee status and the duration of their internship upfront. Clients may also need to be reminded of the impending termination. They should be given the opportunity to speak openly regarding their feelings about the therapist's departure. There are other types of therapist-initiated termination, most often when a referral is indicated because of the therapist's skill or the emergence of a dual relationship. Therapists should also develop a professional will and emergency response team to manage their affairs, should they experience a life-threatening injury or death.

PERSONAL REFLECTION ESSAY QUESTIONS

1. Think about the endings you have experienced in the past several years—graduations, moving away from home, leaving a job, or another type of goodbye. How did you handle this termination experience? What was difficult about it? How do you think this style of dealing with goodbyes may affect your work with clients?
2. As you prepare for your clinical placements during your training, have you thought about how often you will have to leave your clients? Draft three or four ways that you might discuss termination with a client at the beginning of treatment. Now imagine your client has forgotten that you are a trainee; he or she has no recollection that you will be leaving at the end of the academic year. What will you say to remind him or her? When should this conversation take place?
3. In what ways does the end of a romantic relationship mirror the ending of a therapeutic relationship? In what ways do these two types of endings differ?
4. Elisabeth Kübler-Ross developed the five stages of grief—denial, anger, bargaining, depression, and acceptance—to describe how people cope with significant losses such as the death of a loved one or divorce. How might these different reactions to loss emerge within the therapeutic relationship as it nears its end?

KEYWORDS

case management

client-initiated premature termination

forced termination

functional impairment

ideal termination

mastery

memory book

premature termination

pre-therapy preparation

recovery

spaced termination

termination

termination phase

therapist-initiated premature termination

time-limited termination

time-limited treatment

FURTHER READING

- Joyce, A. S., Piper, W. E., Ogrodniczuk, J. S., & Klein, R. H. (2007). *Termination in psychotherapy: A psychodynamic model of processes and outcomes*. Washington, DC: American Psychological Association.

A comprehensive text on termination from a psychodynamic perspective, this book also includes discussion of cognitive behavioral, supportive, and interpersonal approaches to termination. Many academic libraries have electronic versions of this text available through their online databases.

- Howes, R. (2008). In therapy: A user's guide to psychotherapy. *Psychology Today*. http://www.psychologytoday.com/blog/in-therapy/200809/terminating -therapy-part-i-what-why-how

Ryan Howes, PhD, wrote a great series of posts about termination on his Psychology Today blog. He discusses ideal and less-than-ideal types of termination in an accessible and sometimes humorous way.

Varieties of Counseling Situations

In the wise choice of a vocation there are three broad factors:
(1) a clear understanding of yourself, your aptitudes, abilities,
interests, ambitions, resources, limitations, and their causes;
(2) a knowledge of the requirements and conditions of success,
advantages and disadvantages, compensation, opportunities,
and prospects in different lines of work; (3) true reasoning on
the relations of these two groups of facts.—Parsons (1909, p. 5)

LEARNING OBJECTIVES

- Identify several reasons group counseling might be used
- Explain the differences between process, support, psycho-educational, and skills training groups
- Describe Yalom's therapeutic factors and how they relate to group work
- Outline the role of school counselors and the various ways they work with children, school staff, and parents
- Describe marriage and family counseling
- Identify the major components of family systems theory and apply them to family work
- Identify the major components of structural family therapy and apply them to family work
- Describe the process and goals of career counseling
- Describe John Holland's RIASEC Theory and identify your Holland type
- Outline Super's Life-Career Rainbow theory and its importance across the life span
- Explain the distinction between forensic work and other types of therapeutic intervention
- Define crisis intervention and identify several crisis intervention settings
- Describe the process of suicide assessment and identify several therapeutic interventions used with clients experiencing suicidal ideation

Most people have a stereotypical image of what it means to have a career in counseling. Many imagine a proper professional who sits in a cozy room meeting one-on-one with clients on a daily basis. Although some counselors do structure their careers in this way, mental health professionals can be found in many different roles and in several types of work settings. In 2011, there were an estimated 552,000 mental health professionals practicing in the United States (Grohol, 2011). Among these practitioners, clinical and counseling psychologists comprise the largest group (152,000), followed closely by social workers (138,700) and mental health counselors (113,300). There are smaller numbers of substance abuse counselors (86,100) and marriage and family therapists (27,300). All of these professionals work in a variety of settings, including hospitals, schools, clinics, private practices, and prisons. A master's or doctoral-level degree in psychology, mental health counseling, social work, or marriage and family therapy can open the door to many different work experiences and environments.

This chapter serves as an overview of different work settings and diverse specialty skill areas in which mental health professionals work. Each section describes the duties and attributes of counselors in each particular area. Perhaps you have already imagined yourself as a counselor meeting one-on-one with clients. After reading this chapter, you may be open to exploring new territory in terms of your vocation.

GROUP COUNSELING

Group counseling is an excellent way to reach many people at one time. Although mental health professionals certainly make a positive impact working with clients in individual therapy, group counseling can allow more people access to mental health care. Therapy groups are frequently offered in outpatient clinics, inpatient psychiatric hospitals, residential facilities, and schools. Because clients may benefit from interaction with one or more therapists at a time, group counseling is often a cost-effective intervention. In residential settings as well as day treatment and inpatient hospitals, group counseling is especially prevalent for this reason. Clients are present for care for many hours in residential settings and groups are a helpful way to engage many clients in treatment even when there are few resources.

Group counseling also offers a unique opportunity for clients to interact with others who are experiencing similar issues. Specifically, it provides clients with an environment in which they can benefit from vicarious learning. Recall the discussion of self-efficacy in Chapter 8. Rather than the verbal persuasion that is typically available in individual therapy, group counseling allows clients to hear from others similar to themselves about what behaviors they have tried and what results they experienced. This is a way for clients to learn via modeling. Thus, group therapy not only provides members with a place to experience empathic listening, but also bolsters self-efficacy through modeling and vicarious learning.

For example, Alcoholics Anonymous (AA; www.aa.org) meetings are structured in part to capitalize upon this aspect of group counseling. In meetings, there is a time for individual members to share their stories and experiences. Members may describe recent urges or struggles with abstaining from alcohol. This sharing in the group serves as a way for members to learn through modeling. Clients need not experience hitting rock-bottom to build self-efficacy to change their behavior.

ILLUSTRATION 13.1 Members of Alcoholics Anonymous receive chips or tokens like these to mark the amount of time they have maintained sobriety.
Courtesy of Chris Yarzab.

Group psychotherapy also creates a milieu within which clients can address certain interpersonal problems and personality dynamics that arise when they are in contact with others.

Types of Therapy Groups

There are an infinite number of therapy groups. The sky is the limit when it comes to using your imagination to meet the needs of the population with which you are working. Perhaps you are working in a community mental health clinic and many of the clients you serve have been affected by a local tragedy. You may choose to lead a bereavement group for those who recently lost friends and loved ones. Maybe you are employed at a college counseling center. You may be inspired to begin a group to help young adults sharpen their social skills to improve their dating lives. Although most groups are formed with a specific topic in mind, some groups are more open in terms of content, but are geared to a particular type of person. For example, a counselor at a residential treatment facility may choose to lead a group for male residents aged 15 to 17 but not specify a topic. The content of the group sessions may be determined by the group members and timely needs at each meeting if a group is structured this way.

Although therapy groups are not always defined in terms of their content, they must include rules for the group members to abide by during meetings. You may recall the depth of evidence presented in Chapter 7 that the therapeutic relationship is very important to treatment effectiveness. Accordingly, groups should be organized around rules that foster an environment of respect and safety. Group members should feel comfortable sharing their thoughts and expressing their emotions in meetings. It is a good idea to have group members collaboratively generate their own rules during the first meeting. Important rules to include are to keep information shared within the group confidential and to avoid cross-talk (i.e., interrupting or speaking out of turn). In some groups, particularly with youth, it is good practice to write the rules of the group down and post them during meetings as a reminder to all participants.

As a new counselor, interacting with one client at a time may already provoke some anxiety, so the thought of facing a room full of clients may be overwhelming. An important reason that counseling groups have rules is that this creates a safe atmosphere in which each member can express himself or herself without fear of rebuke or judgment. As the facilitator of group therapy, you will also benefit from this environment of mutual respect and support. Although the leader's role is typically to set the agenda and use counseling skills to encourage discussion among members, the leader may also at times need to enforce rules by gently pointing out violations.

BOX 13.1

Learning Exercise

Think about a group to which you belong. Maybe you are a member of a sports team or club. You may also consider yourself as a member of the group that is made up of the students and instructor of this course. Reflect on the "rules" of this group. They are likely to be unspoken, but you can often recognize these unspoken rules when they are violated. For example, imagine what might happen if a student came to class intoxicated. The behavior of that student might violate the unspoken rules of showing courtesy and respect to other class members. Use these thoughts as a jumping off point to create a list of rules that help groups function well.

Some of the types of counseling groups are discussed in this section. Although not exhaustive, this section aims to acquaint you with the types of groups that are offered by mental health professionals. As you read about each specific group, keep in mind that having read this far in the text, you are already familiar with the requisite skills to be an effective group leader. In therapy groups, the leader uses the same basic counseling skills that are used when conducting individual therapy. The leader uses reflection, clarification, and interpretation to help group members hear, understand, and connect to what they are saying.

Process

Psychotherapy process groups most often adhere to a psychodynamic counseling approach. Process groups do not have a predetermined agenda and may not have a particular focus (e.g., shared diagnosis or symptom). The group is comprised

ILLUSTRATION 13.2 Ideally, a psychotherapy group will have six to eight members. It is important that members attend sessions regularly, as the group dynamic will change when even just one person is missing.
Courtesy of Open Rights Group.

of patients with varying mental health needs and the initial focus of the group is similar to other types of groups—building trust and group cohesion as well as establishing ground rules for how members should interact with one another. Once this groundwork is laid, the actual work of the process group can begin. Members of the group may speak freely about what troubles them, with the group leader or leaders facilitating the discussion. Although group members will provide support, advice, and ask questions of one another, the primary focus of the group is on interpersonal processes. Group members usually re-experience or re-create interpersonal dynamics that brought them to the group in the first place (Rutan, Stone, & Shay, 2007). With guidance from a skilled group therapist, members of the group can point out and reflect on troublesome interpersonal patterns that emerge. The goal is for group members to provide feedback and support and to offer alternative ways of interacting until each group member's interpersonal difficulties are resolved. For process groups to be effective, members must be willing to be honest with one another and potentially hear difficult things about the way they interact with others. The focus of the group is often brought back to the here-and-now of what is transpiring between group members in the moment. For example, one group member may frequently interrupt another member, talking over him and leaving little room for him to speak. The silenced group member may, in turn, respond with withdrawal and accommodation. This type of pattern is likely one that also unfolds outside of the therapy room for each participant. A skilled group therapist will help both members see this pattern and consider the effect it has on others, while developing ways to change.

Support

As the name implies, support groups are appropriate for individuals who are looking to connect with others who are in a similar life situation or experiencing similar issues. In general, support groups are for individuals who do not require mental health services (i.e., are not functionally impaired), but who would bene-fit from sharing with and listening to others in comparable circumstances. A sup-port group is not always led by a mental health professional. AA is one example of a peer-led support group. There is no professional leader, but members take turns leading meetings according to a prescribed format. The National Alliance on Mental Illness (www.nami.org) also offers peer-led support groups for indi-viduals with mental illness and their family members.

There are myriad types of support groups. Support groups may be found in medical settings for people who are experiencing particular medical issues. There are also often support groups for the family members who are struggling to cope with a relative's medical (or psychiatric) diagnosis. In a community setting, there are support groups for parents of all stripes (e.g., single parents, gay parents, parents of children with disabilities). There are also support groups for individuals experienc-ing a difficult life transition (e.g., job loss, bereavement, divorce). There are a grow-ing number of online support groups. For example, the International Obsessive Compulsive Disorder (OCD) Foundation provides an extensive list of online sup-port groups for individuals with OCD (www.ocfoundation.org/yahoo.aspx). A virtual support group is an excellent resource for individuals who live in rural areas or who are seeking to connect with people who are not living in their community.

Psychoeducational

Psychoeducational groups aim to teach group members about various topics related to mental health. They are didactic in nature, and thus they are typically structured and led with a particular curriculum or agenda. In this type of group, members are not as likely to share emotionally laden material but may share personal examples as they ask questions. These educational groups are typically time-limited.

A psychoeducational group may also be blended effectively with a support group. For example, Dr. Thompson led a group for parents of children diagnosed with an autism spectrum disorder (ASD). In fact, the children were simultane-ously meeting in the room next door with a different therapist for group social skills training. In the parent group, Dr. Thompson discussed what skills were being taught to the children and why. This was an excellent way to teach parents more about the typical challenges that individuals with ASD face in daily life. During these discussions, Dr. Thompson also facilitated discussion among the parents about their experiences and stresses raising a child with special needs.

Skills Training

Skills training groups are designed to help clients be more adept in their family, occupational, and social environments. For example, skills training groups are an integral component of dialectical behavior therapy (DBT; Linehan, 1993). In DBT skills training groups, clients learn ways to cope with difficult circumstances and regulate their emotions. Another popular skills training group is social skills groups. Even if a group is not specifically aimed at improving social skills, the social nature of group counseling is a way to help clients improve these skills. Imagine how beneficial it would be to observe clients in their social interactions with other people, particularly when the problem is anger management or lack of assertiveness. The group format allows clinicians to have a sample of a client's real-world behavior and modes of dealing with others.

It is important to facilitate respectful social interaction in the group, and it is equally important to follow the lead of the group. Dr. Thompson's colleague, who led a social skills group for the youngsters diagnosed with ASD, provides a notable example of this. Group members were instructed to take turns starting a conversation for the group by asking a question and eliciting responses by using eye contact and appropriate tone of voice. A list of potential topics of interest to many people was provided to help the group members generate good conversation starters. When it came to a young boy, he looked at his prompting card and asked another child, "What is your favorite vacuum?" At that point the therapist was tempted to re-direct the client to pick a question that was easier to answer, but the child answered using very good nonverbal skills, "The yellow Dyson." Soon thereafter, another child chimed in, "I like the purple one." Although the therapist anticipated that the question might have gone unanswered, the group responded as instructed.

Yalom's Therapeutic Factors

Irvin Yalom (1985), a renowned group therapist, described 11 primary factors that he views as responsible for positive change in group therapy. Some are mechanisms of change but others are conditions for change.

Instillation of hope
Universality
Imparting of information
Altruism
The corrective recapitulation of the primary family group
Development of socializing techniques
Imitative behavior
Interpersonal learning
Group cohesiveness
Catharsis
Existential factors (Yalom, 1985, pp. 3–4)

Instillation of hope is natural in a group therapy setting because members see others in the group who have already benefitted from therapy. Yalom (1985) describes groups as comprised of "individuals who are at different points along a coping-collapse continuum" (p. 6). Thus, group members nearer to "collapse" can benefit in multiple ways from the group members who are "coping," and one important aspect is that they are a source of hope to individuals at the beginning of the process that things will get better. Another important therapeutic factor in group therapy is **universality**, which describes a condition for change. Specifically, in group therapy, members begin to feel they are not alone or unique in their struggles, which allows them to feel accepted and at home in the group. Group therapy is also helpful because the therapist and other members are **imparting information** from time to time. The information may be advice from members or didactic instruction about mental illness from the therapist. Yalom also credits **altrusim** with having a therapeutic impact in group therapy. Altruism is giving without expectation of receiving something in return, and in group-based treatment, members tend to feel the positive effects of having the opportunity to help other group members and subsequently feel an accompanying boost in mood and confidence.

Yalom's theory includes the hypothesis that clients benefit from group therapy because it can be a **corrective recapitulation** of the primary family group. He explains that because most people enter group therapy having had an unsatisfactory experience in their first "group" (i.e., primary family), this therapeutic group experience can help clients to examine their role in the group and work out how to become an effective member of the group instead of rigidly maintaining patterns of relating to others in a group setting that they may have had since childhood. Yalom (1985) wrote, "Working out problems with therapists and other members is also working through unfinished business from long ago" (p. 16). This process of corrective recapitulation allows clients to have a new experience of interaction within a group environment, an experience that can foster hope and more positive expectations for the future. It also enables clients to develop better social skills. Through the **development of socializing techniques**, clients will become more skilled at interacting with others in and out of the group. They are likely to become better at empathic listening and handling conflict, among other important skills. In fact, group members sometimes develop their social skills through direct feedback from others (i.e., imparting information) and sometimes through another mechanism: **imitative behavior.** Not only do clients learn from seeing members model behaviors (see Chapter 10 for a review of Bandura's concept of observational learning), but they may benefit from what Dinkmeyer (1973) called **spectator therapy.** That is, clients learn more about their own situation by hearing other clients discuss and receive feedback on similar topics. Group members profit because they are spectators of others' therapy.

Interpersonal learning is another therapeutic factor identified by Yalom. The value of interpersonal learning in group therapy is that clients have the opportunity to become aware of their interpersonal behavior. In particular, they may develop insight into their maladaptive interpersonal behavior that leads to unwanted responses from others and nongratifying relationships. Experiencing this insight about one's effect on others within the social microcosm of the group and also trying out new behaviors in the groups can generalize to help the client have more rewarding relationships outside of therapy. Interpersonal learning goes beyond development of socializing techniques to include experiencing revelations about one's interpersonal behavior and how to achieve change.

Group cohesiveness is the term Yalom uses to describe what would be called the therapeutic relationship in individual therapy. More specifically, group cohesion encompasses the quality of relationship each member has with the therapist and the quality of the relationship of each member with one another. It is how bonded and connected the group is as a whole and refers to "the attraction that members have for their group and for the other members" (p. 69). Group cohesiveness is important as a therapeutic factor because clients in cohesive groups feel more accepted and thus make more self-disclosure during sessions. Clients are also more likely to attend sessions when they are members of a highly cohesive group. There appears to be an element of not only being attracted to the group, but also a sense that clients do not want to let the group down. Crabtree and Haslam (2010) found that identification with the group predicted increased social support, stereotype rejection, and stigma resistance.

The final two therapeutic factors identified by Yalom are **catharsis**, which is the ventilation or release of strong emotions, and **existential factors**, which include members' struggle with existential givens, such as death and the unfairness of life, as well as learning to accept responsibility for one's life choices. Each of the group members has the opportunity to experience catharsis as well as become a spectator as others experience this emotional release. At some point in group therapy, most members will be confronted with anxiety that arises from existential factors. In treatment, discussing these unchangeable facts of life as a group and ultimately understanding each person's responsibility to make life choices and move forward despite those issues is an important part of group therapy.

Yalom's therapeutic factors are most relevant to psychodynamic groups because he wrote them based on his own practice and research in facilitating those groups, but some of the factors are also present in other types of groups as well. No matter what the setting or type of group, clients are likely to benefit from being accepted by others, learning from others, and having the opportunity to help other people.

WORKING IN SCHOOLS

Chances are that you have had an interaction with a school counselor at some point in your educational career. You may have met with a school counselor during elementary or middle school to help you deal with problems with your peers, or perhaps you had a high school guidance counselor who advised you on your schedule or placement in courses or helped you apply to college. The American School Counseling Association (2013) has defined the role of a school counselor as that of a professional "qualified to address all students' academic, personal/social and career development needs." The focus of a school counselor's duties will vary widely depending on the school, specifically whether it is elementary, middle, or high school. At each developmental stage, students are likely to have different needs.

School counselors are often responsible for a variety of tasks. The role of the school counselor has been broken down into three major components: **counseling**, **consultation**, and **coordination** (Muro & Kottman, 1995). That is, they typically provide individual and group therapy for students in need, in addition to implementing programs that will help to improve emotional and academic outcomes for the entire school population. School counselors are also a resource for the faculty and administration. Because of their specialized knowledge about emotional development, school counselors can provide didactic training to teachers and other staff about students' needs. School counselors are also important personnel because they identify student and school needs and advocate for interventions and solutions to address those problems.

Counseling and consultation are covered in the following sections on Working With Children and Communication With School Staff and Parents. The third task, and the one on which the majority of a school counselor's time is spent, is coordination. Myrick (1993) developed a school guidance program model that outlines the primary components of a school counselor's job and the time that should ideally be allotted to each task. His model does not specify an ideal percentage of time spent on coordination, which includes managing indirect guidance services, including special events and other general school procedures, although he reported that some counselors spend as much as 50% of their time on coordination. **Appraisal** is a time-consuming coordination activity in which counselors are frequently involved at their schools. Appraisal involves duties related to testing in the school. The majority of school counselors surveyed reported that they coordinate school-wide testing programs and provide training to teachers on the assessment procedures and tests (Burnham & Jackson, 2000). This is problematic because being a testing coordinator is a task that does not require any professional counseling skills. School counselors should focus on duties related to addressing students' mental health and optimal social, emotional, and academic development, not administrative tasks that could be assigned to other school personnel.

Working With Children

School counselors spend a majority, but not all of their time, working with children. Accordingly, good school counselors are mental health professionals who enjoy interacting with children and have developed the skills necessary to connect with children. As a school counselor you are likely to provide both individual and group counseling, which requires rapport-building with youth.

Personal and Social Development of Students

School counselors are responsible for helping students as they develop. Myrick's (1993) guidance model specifies that individual counseling should take up approximately 2 to 6 hours each week (i.e., 5%–15% of the counselor's time), small group counseling should take up 10% to 25% of the counselor's time, and classroom large group guidance should take up 7% to 8% of the counselor's time. Altogether, Myrick allots approximately one-third of the school counselor's work week to counseling. In a survey of 80 school counselors, most reported meeting with students on a regular basis for individual counseling, and the majority (i.e., 66 out 80) spend up to 50% of their time meeting individually with students (Burnham & Jackson, 2000). This high frequency of individual counseling in schools has been criticized because meeting one-on-one with students is the least efficient way to reach all students. Small group counseling is a more effective means of providing services to students in schools. Many school counselors offer groups for addressing student needs, such as improving social skills, antibullying, or stress management. Research indicates that children and adolescents benefit from counseling and therapy in schools. Overall, results from a recent meta-analysis indicate that individual and group formats were effective. When conducting group counseling in schools, same-gender groups tended to have better outcomes than co-ed groups (Baskin et al., 2010).

Because school counselors have limited availability to reach all students in need, there are others ways to strengthen the guidance program in addition to group counseling. For example, school counselors may take time to train students to be peer helpers. Although beneficial, peer helpers and other nonprofessional helpers are supplemental. Baskin and colleagues (2010) found that licensed therapists outperformed paraprofessionals, which means that school counselors are invaluable in supporting students' emotional and social needs in school.

Career Development With Students

Although career counseling is covered more in-depth later in this chapter, a brief discussion of the different types of career development services that school counselors provide is helpful to consider here. Although most students will not be seeking employment or starting careers until years later, many school guidance curriculums include activities focused on helping youth understand their skills and interests from an early age. When combined with education about different careers and occupations, students are able to begin career planning and exploration because they have the knowledge about how to achieve different career aspirations and plan for the future. Later, in secondary education, some school counselors will also provide vocational guidance to help students who are unclear about their main interests and skills. In particular settings, school counselors are involved with occupational placement (i.e., helping students obtain a job) and even position coaching (i.e., direct instruction and mentoring to teach and improve students' job skills; Hartung & Niles, 2000).

Academic Achievement of Students

School counselors in elementary, middle, and high schools work to help students succeed academically through individual, small group, and classroom guidance. For example, counselors may offer help in organizational and study skills to help students achieve. School counselors may also work with students to increase motivation and effort. For great examples of interventions school counselors may use to help students improve motivation to succeed academically, see Rowell and Hong (2013). These authors have developed a guidance lesson and suggestions for small group and individual remediation that targets the way students think about how they achieve academic outcomes to improve self-efficacy.

School counselors are often members of the school's multi-disciplinary team that is responsible for meeting and reviewing data to determine whether a student is eligible for an Individualized Educational Program (IEP) or Section 504 Accommodation Plan. Standardized testing is often conducted by a school psychologist, special education instructor, or other professional to determine the student's abilities and current achievement. When there is a significant discrepancy between ability and achievement, which typically indicates a learning disability, the student is likely to qualify for special education or other appropriate academic accommodations. School counselors serve an important role on this team to ensure that there is a plan in place such that not only the student's academic deficits are remediated but that his or her emotional needs are also met. Individual or group counseling is frequently included on IEP or Section 504 accommodation plans to address emotional needs.

Communication With School Staff and Parents

Although school counselors work primarily with youth during the school day, school counselors must often interact in a professional capacity with adults as well. Consultation with parents, teachers, administrators, and specialists is another major task of school counselors. Myrick (1993) suggested that 7% of the counselor's time be spent on consultation. Practicing school counselors reported spending the most time consulting with community agencies (Burnham & Jackson, 2000), but counselors also frequently spend time interpreting test scores for students, parents, and teachers. School counselors may provide didactic training to parents at workshops about special topics, such as test anxiety or college preparation. School counselors are also likely to meet individually with parents and students to interpret test scores, recommend academic courses based on student needs and skills, or advise about alternative educational environments for students with different learning needs.

BOX 13.2

School counselors should spend time developing the skills necessary to work with students from diverse cultural backgrounds. One particularly important group is lesbian, gay, bisexual, transgender, queer, and questioning (LGBTQQ) students, because these youth are likely to reveal their sexual orientation to school counselors more than any other adult at the school (Harris & Bliss, 1997). Self-awareness is an important aspect of working effectively with individuals from minority groups. Specifically, school counselors should be aware of personal biases, beliefs, and attitudes about sexual identity to work effectively with LGBTQQ students. Byrd and Hays (2012) suggested several strategies for school counselors to implement to promote an LGBTQQ affirmative school climate:

FIGURE 13.1 Marking your office as a "safe space" can encourage LGBTQQ students and allies to approach you when they are in need of support. Courtesy of Nazareth College.

- Be visible: To be visible to LGBTQQ students, counselors may display symbols (such as the pink triangle or rainbow flag) to indicate their office or classroom is a safe space. School counselors may also strive to post LGBTQQ information and history alongside other information and history posted in school (Figure 13.1).
- *Spread the word*: School counselors should talk to school faculty and staff about being an ally and their interest in making the school safe for LGBTQQ students.
- *Understand the importance of language*: School counselors should strive to use inclusive language. For example, strive to say "partner" instead of "boyfriend" or "girlfriend."
- *Don't ignore anti-LGBTQQ comments or behavior*: School counselors should conduct research and brainstorm ways to respond appropriately to anti-LGBTQQ comments and behavior. The authors suggest reading Gay, Lesbian, & Straight Education Network's *Safe Space Kit* for ideas (available for download at http://glsen.org/safespace).

MARRIAGE AND FAMILY COUNSELING

Marriage and family therapists (MFTs) have focused their education and professional practice on matters of the family. They have specialized training in couples counseling and how to work within a family system. In addition to those individuals with a specific degree and license to practice marriage and family therapy, many mental health professionals will work with couples and families at some point during their careers. Although couples who are seeking counseling because of marital discord will often seek out a counselor who is specifically trained in marriage counseling, there are times when an individual will present for treatment, but the nature of the issue is complex and requires that the counselor work with additional members of the client's family to adequately resolve the problem. This section describes two major theories of how family systems function and the therapeutic applications of these theories.

Family Systems Theory

Murray Bowen developed his **family systems theory** based on his observations of interactions between mothers and their children with schizophrenia. He noted that these dyads were frequently mutually dependent on one another, a state he called **symbiosis**. Specifically, these mother-child pairs were very intensely and anxiously attached to one another and neither was capable of effectively functioning as an individual. Observing these pairs and their anxious attachment led him to develop the concept of **differentiation**. Differentiation describes the developmental process of gradually gaining autonomy from one's caregivers throughout the life span. In family systems theory, individuals may be described along the continuum from differentiated to emotionally **fused**. When individuals have achieved differentiation of self, they are able to act autonomously rather than respond automatically to emotional pressures, internal or external (Kerr & Bowen, 1988). When people are emotionally fused with family members, they demonstrate clinging behaviors and the inability to separate *or* combative behaviors that lead to fighting and then separation and emotional cutoff. Both of these methods are ways people relieve anxiety related to their fused attachment. Kerr and Bowen described an individual in a fused relationship as a "complete emotional prisoner of the relationship" (p. 69).

Bowen extended his theory to incorporate the whole family and described the ways whole systems can be fused. His concept of **triangles** refers to the theory that relationships with three people involved are more stable than relationships with two people. Thus, when there is anxiety in a relationship, triangulation relieves the tension by spreading it through three relationships. Perhaps the hallmark of Bowen's theory is his focus on **multigenerational transmission process** and **family projection process**. Multigenerational transmission process describes how anxiety is passed from generation to generation. Family projection process describes how parents pass on their lack of differentiation to their children. For example, when there is disagreement between spouses, one spouse might withdraw from focusing on the marital relationships and spend more time with a child (i.e., triangulation). The energy from the conflict is diverted, but, typically, the problem remains in the system and the mother's additional attention to the child is likely to affect his differentiation (i.e., family projection process). In the next generation, this child who was involved in his parent's fusion and subsequently experienced a lower level of differentiation is likely to seek a spouse who also has a low level of differentiation. The pattern of fusion and anxious attachment is likely to continue in the child's marriage and family (i.e., multigenerational transmission process).

A **genogram** (McGoldrick & Gerson, 1985), or drawing of the client's family tree, can be a useful tool in family systems therapy. The diagram includes comprehensive information about three generations in the family, including illnesses, conflicts, and situational stressors. The genogram is used by therapists to develop a treatment plan, to help the client to see how patterns of differentiation and fusion are transmitted in families, and to understand how life events fit together. **Relationship experiments** are also used in family systems therapy. When triangles are identified, experiments can be assigned to help clients connect their internal emotional states to relationship behavior. For example, a mother who anxiously focuses on her children when her husband pulls away from her can be directed to try a new behavior, such as going out with her friends when her husband spends extended time away from home.

BOX 13.3

Learning Exercise

Genograms are not only an important part of family systems therapy, but are helpful to mental health professionals working from a variety of theoretical perspectives. Physicians also work with patients to create genograms to look at the potential risk of disease. Visit www.genopro.com to download free software to help you make your own genogram. Make sure to include three generations as recommended by Bowen.

Structural Family Therapy

Salvador Minuchin's (1974) **structural family therapy** is based on identifying the family structure, specifically **boundaries** and **coalitions** among family members. According to Minuchin's theory, the family structure describes stable patterns of how family members interact. Structure is determined by the expectations of family members, which lead to the development of unspoken rules. The interpersonal boundaries of the individual members lead to different structures. If boundaries are rigid around a person or coalition, there is **disengagement**. If boundaries are too diffuse, there is **enmeshment**. In disengaged families where boundaries are rigid, the family will likely have difficulty adapting to stressful circumstances or normal development. They will have difficulty supporting one another. In enmeshed families with diffuse boundaries, they will likely go overboard in reacting to stressful life events. Children in enmeshed families become dependent and have difficulty independently solving problems (Nichols & Schwartz, 2004).

Structural family therapists use **joining** to become a part of the family. Once they have joined the family, they use **enactment** in sessions to observe and understand the family's structure. During enactment, the therapist prompts the family members to interact with one another while the therapist watches and intervenes in the moment to restructure the family by guiding the interaction. The goal of structural family therapy is not to solve the family's identified problems, but to point the family toward new ways of interacting with one another that change the boundaries and structure to be more adaptive.

These brief descriptions of Bowenian family systems theory and Minuchin's structural family therapy are the tip of the marriage and family therapy iceberg. It is a broad field. The overarching theme in this work is a focus on the family or couple as a unit for treatment rather than a single identified patient. Mental health professionals who are interested in relationships are likely to enjoy this specialty area.

CAREER COUNSELING

Career counseling is a specific type of counseling that involves helping individuals find out more about their own skills and interests and how to use that knowledge to pursue a particular career. Although some mental health professionals choose to work as full-time career counselors, most counselors will encounter a client at some point who is interested in working on career-related goals. We spend most of our waking hours at work, so it makes sense that career choice or career development issues will arise during the course of therapy. As previously discussed, school counselors in high school settings are also frequently responsible for offering career counseling to students. This section will cover two major theories of career choice and career development that career counselors use to assist clients to find and flourish in their occupations.

Aptitude, Interest, Skills Assessment, and Career Matching

You must get to know a client well to guide that client toward a career that will be fulfilling. Important tools that career counselors use to help clients find a satisfying career are aptitude, interest, and skills assessments. These assessments are typically lengthy inventories of knowledge, skills, and interests that can be scored and matched to identify a particular type of career that the test-taker is most suited to pursue. John Holland developed a theory based on his interest in helping people select jobs that are satisfying. Accordingly, he developed interest inventories, including the Vocational Preference Inventory (VPI) and Self-Directed Search (SDS), to find ways to match individuals to work environments. The Strong Interest Inventory (Strong, Donnay, Morris, Schaubhut, & Thompson, 2004) is one of the most frequently used measures for career counselors. The results of the Strong Interest Inventory incorporate Holland's theory, in addition to measuring other areas applicable to career choice.

John Holland's RIASEC Theory

Holland's theory is based on the idea that a people are drawn to particular work and leisure tasks because these environments match their own personality (Holland, 1997). In this theory, personality and environments are described by a unique combination of six types: realistic, investigative, artistic, social, enterprising, and conventional (i.e., **RIASEC**). Once a person has found environments that are of the same type, or similar to one's own personality type, he or she is likely to be satisfied and be interested in contributing to that environment. Therefore, career development according to Holland's theory is based on finding a match between an individual's personality and work tasks and environment. It is a simple idea: different people are suited to different jobs and workplace atmospheres. It's all about person-environment fit.

- *Realistic (R)*: Realistic people are practical and prefer jobs that involve building or repairing things. These individuals may like to work with tools or machines and prefer to develop manual, mechanical, agricultural, or electrical skills.
- *Investigative (I)*: Investigative people are curious and prefer jobs in scientific and medical fields. They tend to develop math and science ability.
- *Artistic (A)*: Artistic individuals are creative and prefer jobs that use their creative talents. These people like to develop their skills in language, art, music, and drama.
- *Social (S)*: Social people are friendly helpers. They prefer careers that involve informing, teaching, and helping others. They enjoy developing their ability to work with people.
- *Enterprising (E)*: Enterprising individuals are ambitious and self-confident, and they enjoy leading and influencing other people. They are likely to develop leadership ability, persuasiveness, and "people" skills. They prefer jobs involving sales or management of people.
- *Conventional (C)*: Conventional people are responsible, dependable, and detail-oriented. They develop organizational and clerical skills. They are likely to enjoy jobs that require record-keeping, computation, typing, or computer operation.

BOX 13.4

Learning Exercise

Think about your own personality. Having read the brief descriptions above, how would you describe yourself according to Holland's (1997) six types? O*NET (www.onetonline.org) is an online resource for career information that is searchable by job name or interest, and each occupation is identified by RIASEC code. According to O*NET, the mental health counseling interest code is SIA (i.e., social, investigative, and artistic) and the clinical psychologist interest code is ISA (i.e., investigative, social, and artistic). Does this match your assessment of your personality type? If you think additional or different types better describe your personality, visit O*NET and search by interest. Once you select the RIASEC type that you think is the best description of your skills, interests, and attitudes, you can input your three Holland types on the following screen to see careers that match those types.

Career counselors may use Holland's theory to help people find a match, but it is unlikely that an assessment and discussion of an individual's Holland code will be the extent of the counseling encounter. There may be times when people score highly on multiple types, such that it is not particularly informative or helpful in narrowing the field of career options. This is known as a profile with little differentiation. Counselors must then work with clients to help understand and apply the client's personal values to making a career choice, including aspirations for income level and ability to balance work life with family life and leisure pursuits. A client may also present with low scores in all six areas, and this client will require help exploring career options because his or her interests and skills are not crystallized. Holland's theory is best applied to career counseling with individuals who are looking to declare a college major or pursue an occupation. It has limited applicability to those who do not have the flexibility to explore their interests and develop a new career path (Amundson, Harris-Bowlsbey, & Niles, 2013).

Career Development

Career counselors do more than simply help clients find a suitable career to pursue. They also offer counseling to individuals who are working in a particular field and seeking to develop their career. For example, career counselors may work with clients who have been steadily employed for a long time but are looking to advance their career or change their work experience in some way because of life dissatisfaction. Donald Super's theory is best applied to career counseling situations with people who have plenty of work experience and are considering or faced with transition related to life events, and it is also applicable to youth who are looking to develop the pre-requisite skills to establish a career trajectory.

Donald Super's Life-Career Rainbow

Super's developmental approach to understanding careers is based on the premise that an individual's **self-concept**, which includes her interests, values, and abilities, strongly influences her career. Because one's self-concept changes throughout one's lifetime, Super's theory describes typical human development and highlights the different values that become more salient at different life stages. Super considers selecting a career to be an implementation of one's self-concept (Super, 1963). Therefore, the job of the career counselor is to help the individual develop a clear self-concept, which leads directly to choosing a complementary career.

According to Super's theory, career development happens throughout five different life stages: **growth** (ages 4–14), **exploration** (ages 15–24), **establishment** (ages 25–44), **maintenance** (ages 45–65), and **disengagement** (ages 60+), which correspond to different life stages. At each of these stages, individuals approach different life roles, including personal and job development. Each of these stages is arranged in an arc, known as the Life-Career Rainbow, and the overlapping life roles and tasks are positioned according to age and stage (see Figure 13.2). Thus, Super's understanding of career is broad and includes not just one's professional occupation but also other aspects of life.

The earliest role is child, which is followed by student and leisurite as a person progresses from growth to exploration and makes more choices about how to spend free time and explore personal interests. When an individual reaches establishment in the mid- to late-20s, the roles of citizen, worker, and eventually homemaker are undertaken in that order. A person continues to balance these roles, putting differing amounts of effort and energy into the various

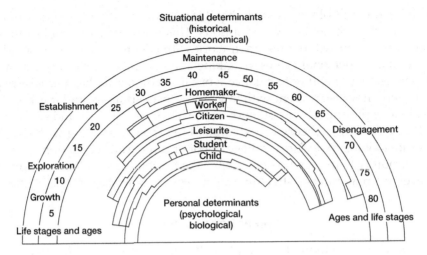

FIGURE 13.2 The Life-Career Rainbow: Six life roles in schematic life space.

Source: Brown and Brooks (1990).

tasks through the maintenance stage. Super hypothesized that the more roles an individual selects and balances successfully, ultimately the more personal satisfaction he or she will experience. In the final stage, disengagement, an individual typically stops working and focuses on the roles of homemaker, citizen, and leisurite during retirement. Although the Life-Career Rainbow clearly progresses from birth through death, a more updated understanding of how individuals work throughout the life span suggests that it is no longer a linear progression from one stage to another, but that people may have to return to establishment after having maintained an occupation for a length of time. Career change is covered in the next section.

The Career Style Interview (CSI; Savickas, 1989, 1998) is an assessment method developed specifically to explore a client's self-concept as described in Super's theory to guide career counseling. The CSI is an assessment that goes beyond the objective measurement that is frequently used in career counseling (e.g., an inventory to determine RIASEC type) to obtain a more contextualized and broader understanding of the client's personality. Specifically, although two people may obtain the same RIASEC type, they are likely to have different values, goals, and experiences that stem from those broad underlying traits (Taber, Hartung, Briddick, Briddick, & Rehfuss, 2011). The CSI is a useful tool to gather that information. In the interview, counselors elicit stories from clients about life roles, motivations, and personality style. The counselor pays attention to the relative balance of work and other life roles. The CSI typically begins with this opening question, "How can I be useful to you in constructing your career?" In addition, there are six domains of questions used to guide clients in constructing their life stories. For example, the questions on the first domain include, "Whom did you admire when you were growing up? Whom would you like to pattern your life after?" (Taber et al., 2011, p. 276). Counselors use the stories clients share when discussing each domain to infer something about the client's self-concept. For example, responses in the first (i.e., Role Model) domain indicate the client's ego ideals, or what the client admires. The CSI is a helpful tool in exploring the context and development of a client's personality traits that can be used to inform career counseling.

Career Change

Career counselors are also responsible for working with clients who are changing careers. For example, counselors may work with clients who have lost their employment after spending many years in a particular field or with a particular company. These clients will require assistance in discerning what options for future employment they should pursue. In the case of career change, Holland's RIASEC theory may be helpful to identify other fields that utilize the same set of skills and interests. For example, an O*NET search reveals that should the authors lose employment as clinical psychologists, they may also be well-suited to pursue careers as homeopathic physicians or political scientists.

Career counseling is frequently offered in educational settings, including high schools and college campuses. Although many students struggle with their plans for future careers, few utilize college career counseling services. There is evidence that the reason individuals are reluctant to pursue voluntary career counseling in college is because of the stigma attached to seeking help for career development (Ludwikowski, Vogel, & Armstrong, 2009). Ludwikowski and colleagues found that college students reported attitudes indicating that society, friends, and family devalue career counseling, thus making them less likely to engage in career-related counseling. Given this knowledge, counselors should be mindful of promoting career counseling as an empowering experience rather than a sign of weakness and utilize group sessions to inform students together about the positive aspects of career counseling. If students are approached together, it may reduce the stigma and generate conversations about the potential value of career counseling in college.

FORENSIC SETTINGS

Some mental health counselors work specifically with individuals who are involved in civil legal disputes or the criminal justice system. The field of forensic mental health includes counselors who work in correctional facilities as well as counselors who work with clients who have been released from prison. Forensic mental health counselors also treat individuals who are compelled to seek mental health services, including counseling and/or skills training, as a condition of a legal decision or sentencing. In addition to providing treatment, many mental health professionals conduct assessments on behalf of the court. As part of legal proceedings, individuals at times require a mental health evaluation to determine whether they have a mental illness diagnosis and how this impacts upon the criminal offense and/or their ability to stand trial. Assessments are also frequently conducted in family court cases involving child custody matters or termination of parental rights.

Forensic Assessment

The majority of forensic assessment is conducted by forensic psychologists, who have specialized training in assessment and law. Varela and Conroy (2012) have developed a list of specific competencies that forensic psychologists should demonstrate to be effective. These include specific knowledge (e.g., case law and governmental rules that impact assessment, unique rights of examinees in forensic contexts), skills (e.g., the ability to integrate data from unique data sources, such as police reports and crime witness statements), and attitudes (e.g., the importance of stating conclusions that are probable as such, despite being pressured by individuals from the justice system to present them as facts).

Forensic assessment is conducted under a variety of circumstances. Specifically, marriage and family conflicts often require assessment when there is a question regarding child custody or termination of parental rights. Assessment is also frequently conducted in workers' compensation, personal injury, and employment cases. Finally, assessment is important in evaluating an individual's competence to stand trial, be sentenced, or waive Miranda rights and in predicting the risk of re-offending in the case of certain individuals (e.g., sex offenders; Packer, 2008).

Forensic Interventions

Although psychologists usually conduct assessment, many different types of mental health professionals are involved in providing treatment services to this population. Varela and Conroy (2012) indicate that the knowledge, skills, and attitudes relevant to forensic intervention include being aware of the rights of treatment recipients (e.g., treatment refusal), treatment planning for legally-relevant goals that may not be client goals (e.g., reducing risk of re-offending), and remaining aware that mental health treatment is sometimes secondary to other goals in legal matters.

Many therapists in forensic settings provide court-ordered counseling and/or skills training. An example is a juvenile offender who set a fire at his school and is likely to have to attend fire safety classes as well as receive individual counseling. Working with clients who are mandated to attend treatment presents unique challenges. The most prominent is the possibility that these clients will have limited motivation to make changes in their lives. To the extent that they are required and supervised, they are likely to attend therapy sessions, but the content of those sessions may be very different from sessions with clients who are voluntarily seeking help.

As discussed in Chapter 10, motivational interviewing (MI; Miller & Rollnick, 2002) is an important tool for counselors to use when working with court-ordered clients who are likely ambivalent about treatment.

CRISIS INTERVENTION AND SUICIDE PREVENTION

Crisis intervention is a special type of counseling situation that may be the focus of a mental health professional's career but is something that every counselor should be prepared to handle, whether or not they are employed specifically to work with clients in crisis. Some examples of settings that provide only crisis intervention are crisis hotlines and psychiatric emergency rooms. A crisis might arise due to a catastrophic life event or intense emotional distress because of symptoms such as anxiety, depression, or hopelessness. Crisis intervention is typically a supportive intervention that provides resources to clients to assist them in coping with the emergency. It is a time-limited intervention with the goal of resolving the crisis to ensure the client's safety and link the client to ongoing

ILLUSTRATION 13.3 Suicide risk assessment is often an important part of crisis counseling.
Photo by Marco Repola.

services to reduce the likelihood of future emergencies. Crisis interventions are also provided in the aftermath of a natural disaster or within a community that has experienced significant loss. This includes international crises, chronic civil conflict, health-related pandemics, school shootings, and acts of terrorism. Counselors who work in crisis intervention provide direct services to populations affected by trauma. In addition, they also provide training and consultation with local agencies and nongovernmental organizations to assist members of the affected communities.

Assessing Risk for Suicide

An important aspect of crisis intervention is assessing the client's risk for suicide. The Substance Abuse Mental Health Services Administration (2011) reported that more than 8 million adults reported having serious suicidal thoughts at some time in the past year, whereas 2.5 million reported making a suicide plan, and 1.1 million reported a suicide attempt. In 2011, suicide was the 10th leading cause of death in the United States, and approximately 38,000 Americans died as a result of suicide (Hoyert & Xu, 2012). In the face of difficult life events and intense distress, risk for suicide is increased. Discussing suicide with clients can be uncomfortable for counselors, but it is a necessary component of ethical and comprehensive mental health treatment. Some counselors fear that inquiring about suicide might lead a client to contemplate suicide. This is a myth. As Pipes and Davenport (1999, p. 113) suggest:

> You can take solace in the fact that there is, as far as we know, consensus among experienced therapists that asking about suicide does not cause suicide. It is entirely possible that by not asking a client about suicidal thoughts you will lose an opportunity to help prevent suicide.

BOX 13.5

Thinking About Suicide

Each of us has a personal reaction to the topic of suicide. Perhaps you know someone who has attempted or committed suicide. Perhaps you previously contemplated suicide. Your previous experiences and attitudes about suicide are likely to impact your comfort when dealing with potentially suicidal clients and even inquiring about suicidal ideation or intent during an intake interview. Reflect on your views, which have been shaped by experience, and imagine what it might be like for you when you encounter clients who express suicidal thinking. How will you react? If this is a difficult topic for you, we recommend reaching out to your instructor about resources for working on how your awareness of this emotional reaction might impact you as a clinician.

The first part of suicide assessment is to ask directly whether the client has experienced any thoughts about suicide (i.e., **suicidal ideation**). If the client endorses ideation, you should determine whether the thoughts are active (e.g., a plan to harm himself) or passive (e.g., wishing he were dead; thinking others would be better off if he were dead). You may choose to ask an open-ended question to elicit the content of the suicidal ideation. If the client has difficulty revealing the thoughts, you may follow up with a direct question, such as, "Have you been thinking about a specific way or method that you might use to end your life?" When interviewing the client about his plan, you want to assess its **specificity,** the **lethality** and **availability** of the method, and **proximity** of help or support (Sommers-Flanagan & Sommers-Flanagan, 2003). You can remember all of these aspects of assessing suicidal ideation by using the acronym: SLAP.

Specificity refers to how thought-out the client's plan seems to be, which may be an indication of how much time the client has spent contemplating suicide. When assessing lethality and availability of the method, you are looking to see how likely the method is to cause death (e.g., overdosing on aspirin versus overdosing on narcotic pain killers) and whether the client has easy access to the materials necessary to implement the plan. Proximity refers to identifying how much social support surrounds the client, because these individuals may be able to intervene and decrease risk of suicide. Individuals who are socially isolated or live alone are at higher risk for suicide.

Once you have inquired about the client's ideation, you should assess **suicidal intent**. Does the client intend to end his life in the near future? You must use your clinical judgment to determine whether the client is likely to follow through on thoughts about killing himself. This determination comes in part from self-report of active suicidal ideation and assessment of the plan. Another important factor is whether the client has previously attempted suicide or if someone close to him has committed suicide in the past. There are a number of characteristics that increase a client's risk for suicide. Along with suicidal ideation and intent, the most robust predictors of suicide are depression and specifically hopelessness (Brown, Beck, Steer, & Grisham, 2000). It is recommended that you ask the client to rate his hopelessness. Each of these factors (and more that are beyond the scope of this brief discussion) increases risk for suicide. In crisis intervention, when a client in crisis does not endorse suicidal ideation or intent, it is good practice to assess for suicide risk factors (see Further Reading).

BOX 13.6

Granello's Twelve Core Principles of Suicide Risk Assessment

Darcy Granello (2010) created a list of philosophical principles that apply to suicide risk assessment. She fully articulates each of these concepts in her article (see Further Reading) and instructs counselors to make a photocopy of the brief list below and keep it on a notecard at their desk to remind them about the process of suicide risk assessment:

> Suicide risk assessment of each person
> is unique.
> is complex and challenging.
> is an ongoing process.
> errs on the side of caution.
> is collaborative.
> relies on clinical judgment.
> takes all threats, warning signs, and risk factors seriously.
> asks the tough questions.
> is treatment.
> tries to uncover the underlying message.
> is done in a cultural context.
> is documented. (Granello, 2010, p. 370)

Therapeutic Interventions

When clients are in crisis or suicidal, therapists should first pay attention to using the foundational skills of active listening and empathy to establish a trusting therapeutic relationship. It may be difficult to listen closely and empathically while the client is expressing the pain he is experiencing, but it is an important way to support the client. You should avoid expressing shock or surprise and try to reassure him that many people contemplate suicide. Sommers-Flanagan and Sommers-Flanagan (2003, p. 363) suggest saying:

> You've told me about some of the difficult experiences you've had recently—losing your wife, your job, and your good health. It's not unusual for you to consider killing yourself. Many people in your situation might think about whether life is still worth living.

When you have established a good rapport with the client, you will want to continue to be empathic to his distress but also become directive about finding alternatives to suicide. If a client is in crisis, it is typically because something has occurred that has exceeded his ability to cope. Helping clients see new alternatives to suicide through boosting coping skills and highlighting reasons to show life is worth living are important aspects of suicide prevention. Shneidman (1984) has described individuals who are considering suicide to have narrowed their focus, which he calls **constriction**. Suicide prevention should be focused on guiding clients to brainstorm alternative options to coping with current life stress and emotional distress, such that their options are not limited to death. Sommers-Flanagan and Sommers-Flanagan (2003) encourage clinicians to ask clients, "Why commit suicide now?" to urge them to explore and try other coping options first before resorting to the permanent choice of suicide. Establishing a positive action plan is important in helping clients see that a better option can be found (and tried) to deal with current distress, no matter how intolerable that distress seems in the current situation.

Referral to Treatment

Once you have conducted a complete assessment of the client's suicidal ideation, plan, and intent in addition to evaluating current support and coping skills, you must decide the best course of treatment. If this is a client that you have been seeing in therapy, you must decide whether to continue to see the client in outpatient treatment or to refer to a higher level of care, such as hospitalization. If you believe the client is at risk for imminent suicide, you should explain your concerns and stay with the patient while you call the police or psychiatric emergency service. As discussed in Chapter 2, if a client is in immediate danger, you are ethically bound to break confidentiality to inform appropriate parties and ensure the client's safety. If the client seems to have mild or moderate suicide risk, you are likely to determine that it is safe to continue seeing the client in outpatient therapy with regular assessment of suicide risk and interventions aimed at increasing coping skills and finding reasons to live. If you find yourself with questions about what to do in a situation with a suicidal patient, you should reach out to supervisors and colleagues. In addition to any professional arrangements you make with your client regarding whether he may contact you in a crisis, you may also like to inform your client about the National Suicide Prevention Lifeline at 1-800-273-TALK (8255), which is a government hotline that connects individuals in suicidal crisis to their nearest suicide prevention and mental health service provider.

CHAPTER REVIEW

This chapter provided an overview of different work settings and diverse specialty skill areas in which mental health professionals work, including group counseling, working in schools, marriage and family counseling, career counseling, working in forensic settings, and crisis intervention and suicide prevention.

Group counseling offers a unique opportunity for clients to interact with others who are experiencing similar issues. This type of psychotherapy also creates a milieu within which clients can address certain interpersonal problems and personality dynamics that arise when they are in contact with others. There are several different types of counseling groups, such as process, support, psychoeducational, and skills training groups. Yalom described 11 primary factors that are responsible for positive change in group therapy, including instillation of hope, corrective recapitulation, and catharsis.

School counselors are professionals who address students' academic, social, emotional, and career development needs. Most school counselors are engaged in counseling students, consultation with parents, school staff, and community agencies, and coordination of special events and general school procedures, including appraisal. Counseling in schools involves individual therapy, small group therapy, and large group or classroom guidance lessons and programs.

MFTs have focused their education and professional practice on matters of the family. They have specialized training in couples counseling and how to work within a family system. Most MFTs utilize Bowen's family systems theory or Minuchin's structural family therapy to understand the relationships among the family members with whom they are working. Genograms, diagrams of family members and their relationships, are important therapeutic tools in family systems therapy.

Career counseling is a specific type of counseling that involves helping individuals explore their skills and interests and learn how to use that knowledge to pursue a particular career. Important tools that career counselors use to help clients find a satisfying career are aptitude, interest, and skills assessments. These assessments are used to match clients with particular types of careers. John Holland developed a theory used in career counseling based on his interest in helping people select jobs that are satisfying. Career counselors do more than simply help clients find a suitable career to pursue. They also offer counseling to individuals who are working in a particular field and seeking to develop their career or who are experiencing a career change. Super's developmental approach to understanding careers is based on the premise that an individual's self-concept, which includes her interests, values, and abilities, strongly influences her career.

The field of forensic mental health includes counselors who work in correctional facilities or work with clients who have been released from prison. Forensic mental health counselors also treat individuals who are compelled to seek mental health services, including counseling and/or skills training as a condition of a legal decision or sentencing. In addition to providing treatment, many mental health professionals conduct assessments on behalf of the court.

Crisis intervention is typically a supportive intervention that provides resources to clients to assist them in coping with the emergency. It is a time-limited intervention with the goal of resolving the crisis to ensure the client's safety and link the client to ongoing services to reduce the likelihood of future emergencies. An important aspect of crisis intervention is assessing the client's risk for suicide. Suicide assessment involves asking directly whether the client has experienced suicidal ideation and/or suicidal intent and making a plan for appropriate intervention.

PERSONAL REFLECTION ESSAY QUESTIONS

1. You probably had contact with a school counselor at some point in your early education. Think about those counselors. What were your perceptions of their duties to you as a student? What would you strive to communicate to your students as a school counselor? If you have children, you might also consider the interactions you have had with a school counselor as a parent.

2. Think about your family or one of your favorite television families. Apply Minuchin's structural family therapy to describe the boundaries and coalitions that exist in that family system. You may want to use the genogram that you created in the Learning Exercise in Box 13.3.
3. Consider the wide variety of services that mental health professionals provide and are involved in. You may already be in a particular degree program for clinical psychology or marriage and family therapy, for example. Consider some of the disciplines outside of your own. Are there some that also appeal to you? Which ones? Is there a way to incorporate some of the work from other disciplines into your own? Does reading about other options help clarify your own career path?
4. Suicide far exceeds homicide as a leading cause of death in the United States. Does this information surprise you? What are some of the sociocultural factors that might cause us to be much more aware of homicides in our community than suicide? How does this skewed awareness affect prevention efforts?

KEYWORDS

altruism
appraisal
availability
boundaries
catharsis
coalitions
constriction
consultation
coordination
corrective recapitulation
counseling
crisis intervention
development of socializing techniques
differentiation
disengagement

enactment
enmeshment
establishment
existential factors
exploration
family projection process
family systems theory
fused
genogram
group cohesiveness
growth
imitative behavior
imparting information
instillation of hope
interpersonal learning
joining

lethality
maintenance
multigenerational transmission process
proximity
relationship experiments
RIASEC
self-concept
specificity
spectator therapy
structural family therapy
suicidal intent
symbiosis
triangles
universality

FURTHER READING

About Group Counseling

- Cappodocia, M. C., & Weiss, J. A. (2011). Review of social skills training groups for youth with Asperger syndrome and high functioning autism. *Research in Autism Spectrum Disorders, 5*, 70–78. doi:10.1016/j.rasd.2010.04.001

  In this paper, the authors compare three types of social skills training groups: traditional, cognitive behavioral, and parent-inclusive.

- Knesek, G., Faircloth, P. K., & Davidson, B. S. (2013). Anecdotal tips and lessons learned while working with men in a group counseling milieu. *National Forum Journal of Counseling and Addiction*, 2(1), 1–5.

This article summarizes and highlights the experiences of the authors while working with men in a support group that dealt with anger, grief, loss of status, loss of job, or notice of termination. The article provides interesting and relevant qualitative tips based on work with the men over several years.

About School Counseling

- Balk, D. E., Zaengle, D., & Corr, C. A. (2011). Strengthening grief support for adolescents coping with a peer's death. *School Psychology International*, 32(2), 144–162. doi:10.1177/0143034311400826

This paper discusses suggestions for strengthening school-based grief support for students following an adolescent's death. The authors explore general themes around adolescent bereavement, mourning, and how these themes can be integrated into counseling within a school setting.

- Perusse, R., & Goodnough, G. E. (2009). Group counseling in the schools. *Psychology in the Schools*, 46(3), 225–231. doi:10.1002/pits.20369

This article outlines various types of groups offered in schools, as well as offers information about group interventions and techniques used in school counseling groups.

- Rowell, L., & Hong, E. (2013). Academic motivation: Concepts, strategies, and counseling approaches. *Professional School Counseling*, 16(3), 158–171.

These authors have developed a guidance lesson and suggestions for small group and individual remediation that target the way students think about how they achieve academic outcomes to improve self-efficacy.

About Marriage and Family Counseling

- Lindbland-Goldberg, M., & Northey, W. F. (2013). Ecosystemic structural family therapy: Theoretical and clinical foundations. *Contemporary Family Therapy*, 35, 147–160. doi:10.1007/s10591-012-9224-4

This article describes Ecosystemic Structural Family Therapy (ESFT), which is a treatment that evolved from Structural Family Therapy and is a strength-based and trauma-informed therapy model. Specifically, ESFT is to be used with families of children with behavioral health problems that are at risk for out-of-home placement.

About Career Counseling

- Taber, B. J., Hartung, P. J., Briddick, H., Briddick, W. C., & Rehfuss, M. C. (2011). Career style interview: A contextualized approach to career counseling. *The Career Development Quarterly*, 59(3), 274–287.

This article offers an in-depth description, including case examples of how to conduct the Career Style Interview with college students.

- Gresham, M. (2010). Vocational counseling. In S. Walfish (Ed.), *Earning a living outside of managed mental health care: 50 ways to expand your practice* (pp. 58–60). Washington, DC: American Psychological Association. doi:10.1037/12138-010

  If career counseling interests you, the best way to get supervised experience is to seek a practicum or job in a college counseling center. This paper offers a good description of how one woman began her career counseling practice.

About Counseling in Forensic Settings

- Benveniste, D. (2012). Relational quandaries in the treatment of forensic clients. *Clinical Social Work Journal, 40*(3), 326–336.

  This article describes how clinicians can deal with their own, sometimes negative, reactions to criminal offenders they work with in treatment. The author includes case examples of how to use countertransference reactions as a mechanism of therapy.

About Suicide Assessment and Prevention

- Bryan, C. J., & Rudd, M. D. (2006). Advances in the assessment of suicide risk. *Journal of Clinical Psychology: In Session, 62*(2), 185–200. doi:10.1002/jclp.20222

  This article describes a number of factors that have been empirically shown to be essential in the risk assessment.

- Granello, D. H. (2010). The process of suicide risk assessment: Twelve core principles. *Journal of Counseling and Development, 88*(3), 363–370. doi:10.1002/j.1556-6678.2010.tb00034.x

  Similar to the previous article in some ways, these authors discuss 12 core process principles that guide suicide risk assessment.

Using Counseling Skills That Work

What we learned in 1950 or 1960 may have served us well,
but if we continue to base our practice on that knowledge and
those skills we may be seriously shortchanging our clients, who
deserve help based on currently available knowledge and on
the latest valid methods our profession has to offer.
—Ross (1974, p. 123)

LEARNING OBJECTIVES

- Describe several reasons clinicians should be familiar with the latest empirical research
- Identify different types of continuing education opportunities
- Explain how to evaluate empirically supported therapies
- Differentiate between well-established, probably efficacious, and experimental treatments
- Identify the key elements of a randomized clinical trial
- Compare and contrast efficacy and effectiveness
- Define evidence-based practice and compare it with practice-based evidence
- Explain the importance of culturally sensitive therapies
- Outline how therapists develop a personal style of psychotherapy practice
- Define and differentiate integrative versus eclectic approaches to psychotherapy

Having read thus far, you have learned the foundations of interviewing and counseling and become familiar with different theoretical perspectives on psychotherapy. You have waded into the water, and you are ready to dive in and swim to deeper waters to gain more knowledge and skills. Equipped with the core skills of counseling, you must now develop a fuller understanding of psychotherapy theory and how to apply that theory in counseling interventions.

Chapter 13 provided a snapshot of the different settings in which you may find yourself working during your career, and this chapter will guide you to think critically about how to approach your clinical practice. In other words, this chapter is about choosing what you will *do* with your clients to help them attain their therapy goals. The first section of this chapter will focus on how to use the latest scientific evidence to inform your clinical practice, and the final section will provide a framework for integrating what you know about effective psychotherapy to fit with your personal style of counseling.

UNDERSTANDING EMPIRICAL RESEARCH

Good counselors are always evolving in some way. It is important to recognize that learning to be an effective counselor is not completed during your graduate training. Your skills will develop throughout your career because you are accumulating experience working with individuals from a variety of backgrounds and issues. Your skills will also develop as a result of continuing education (see Chapter 15). Seeking knowledge to strengthen and sharpen your therapeutic skills is the hallmark of an ethical and smart mental health professional. You should strive to continue to grow and develop as a clinician throughout your career, in step with emerging empirical findings about what helps clients.

For example, imagine how you would feel about receiving treatment from a medical doctor who was not required to maintain current knowledge of advances in medical science. It may be hard to conceive trusting your health to an individual whose only training took place in medical school (and maybe many decades ago) and to follow her treatment recommendations when there may be a more effective option for your problem or, worse, the treatment she recommends has actually been found to be harmful. A recent example is the re-introduction of the drug thalidomide to the market. This medication, called the "most reviled drug of the 20th century," was prescribed by physicians in the late 1950s and early 1960s to treat morning sickness in pregnant women until it was found to cause disfiguring side effects and sometimes death in the unborn children (Schaffer, 2011, p. 1). Recently, the Food and Drug Administration (FDA) has approved clinical trials for thalidomide, not for morning sickness, but to treat some forms of skin disease, including psoriasis, leprosy, and even cancer. In Brazil, the drug is frequently prescribed to treat leprosy, which is a common problem there; however, although there are precautions about the dangerous side effects for fetuses, there are still babies born in Brazil with the typical thalidomide side effects of shortened or missing limbs (Crawford, 2013). Despite the warnings of known side effects, the drug is available on the market and has inadvertently ended up in the hands of women who are pregnant and subsequently give birth to children with a disability that is completely avoidable. It would be devastating to be treated by a physician who was not up to date on the risk factors associated with thalidomide.

Although the consequences of providing an outdated mental health treatment may not seem as dire as the errors that may occur when prescribing medication or conducting an invasive medical procedure, there are a group of psychotherapeutic interventions that have been labeled as "**possibly harmful therapies**" (PHTs; Lilienfeld, 2007). Lilienfeld points out in his article that mental health does not have a governing agency equivalent to the FDA that oversees the safe piloting of new psychotherapies. Instead, practitioners are free to provide the treatment they believe will be the best for resolving the client's problems. However, there is evidence that some treatments may be harmful, which directly violates the ethical mandate to do no harm. Lilienfeld highlights several domains in which psychotherapies may be harmful, including worsening of symptoms following therapy, new symptoms arising during therapy, exacerbation of concern about existing symptoms, excessive dependency on therapists, reluctance to seek more therapy in the future, and physical harm. PHTs may also be associated with premature termination, which was discussed in Chapter 12. If a client senses that things are getting worse instead of better, he might decide to stop treatment. This is potentially harmful if he is then unlikely to seek additional treatment in the future. The list of PHTs includes critical incident stress debriefing (see Litz, Gray, Bryant, & Adler, 2002), Scared Straight interventions for conduct problems (see Petrosino, Turpin-Petrosino, & Buehler, 2003), and attachment therapy (also known as "rebirthing"; see Mercer, 2002), among others.

Whereas mental health professionals should clearly avoid harming clients, it is ideal for counselors to do good. Knowing which treatments may produce negative effects is important, but knowing which treatments are likely to help is the key to being able to provide excellent care to your clients. In his discussion of PHTs, Lilienfeld (2007) identified a second problem, which is that some treatments are "ineffective but innocuous [and] can produce harm indirectly, most notably by exacting opportunity costs such as lost time and the energy and effort expended in seeking out interventions that are not beneficial" (p. 57). Although treatment without strong empirical support may not harm clients, it is possible that clients will lose the chance to find relief and improve their lives more quickly if engaged in ineffective therapy. How can a therapist ensure that she is doing the best for her clients? The best way is to be aware of what the latest scientific research indicates as the most effective treatment for particular psychological problems.

Maintaining Current Knowledge

Mental health practitioners must keep up with the changing times, and it seems they are changing quickly. Neimeyer, Taylor, and Rozensky (2012) recently estimated the "half-life" of knowledge in professional psychology. Half-life, a term first used to describe the timing of the breakdown of radioactive elements, refers to "the time it would take, in the absence of any new learning, for someone to become roughly half as knowledgeable as a function of the development of new knowledge in a given field" (p. 364). The results of their research indicated that clinical psychology currently has a half-life of approximately 8.5 years and counseling psychology's half-life is about 10.4 years. This suggests that within a decade of receiving your degree, your knowledge will already have decayed considerably considering the advances that will have been made in the field. Some specialty areas are estimated to have an even shorter half-life (e.g., clinical neuropsychology and psychopharmacology) and some a slightly longer half-life (e.g., group psychology and psychoanalytic psychology), but no matter what specialty area in mental health you pursue, your knowledge will require updating.

There are several methods for doing this, and it is important to find ways to incorporate learning into your career. If mental health professionals make it a regular practice to stay in touch with the latest advances in their field, they are more likely to keep up their knowledge. The main ways that counselors stay abreast of developments and reinforce their knowledge are by participating in formal continuing education, attending professional conferences and workshops, teaching or taking classes, participating in peer consultation, and conducting self-directed independent learning including reading academic journals and professional publications (Niemeyer, Taylor, & Cox, 2012).

Continuing Education

Continuing education (CE) consists of learning opportunities for mental health professionals to learn new knowledge, refresh their familiarity with particular topics, and learn or further develop therapy skills. CE may be obtained at in-person workshops or seminars at professional conferences or training institutes. There are also online opportunities to participate in CE courses. One novel way to complete CE is to read a required book or article (or even listen to a podcast) and complete a knowledge-based quiz on the content. For an example of this, see the American Counseling Association (ACA) website's "Continuing Education" page (www.counseling.org/continuing-education/overview).

In psychology, CE is mandatory in most states. Psychologists must complete a certain number of hours to renew their professional license to practice. The need for ongoing education to improve skills and knowledge is vital, and CE was designed to protect the public against the "danger of professional obsolescence" (Ross, 1974, p. 122). It has become mandatory in many states and provinces because of the reality that practitioners may become lax in their efforts to seek out regular CE during their careers. The necessity to provide proof of participation in CE to continue legally providing services is the only way that competency to practice is assessed when individuals seek to renew their licenses. Whereas mental health professionals must continually demonstrate their competency in course work and at clinical practicum experiences throughout graduate school to earn their degrees, once an individual passes the licensing examination there is no longer such oversight. Whereas a mental health professional may be investigated if someone files a complaint, there is typically no other reason that one's professional knowledge and skills are evaluated. Thus, requiring completion of CE is an important way that state and provincial licensing boards protect the public. There are also financial incentives to completing CE. Most insurance companies offer a discount on malpractice insurance premiums to therapists who complete a certain amount of CE in a year. In effect, it pays to keep up your skills!

Neimeyer, Taylor, and Wear (2010) conducted a large-scale survey to explore how psychologists choose which types of CE to pursue. Whereas graduate training is full of required courses, most state licensing boards do not dictate the types of courses that should be completed, with one notable exception. Some states explicitly require that each psychologist take at least one ethics course as part of their CE requirement, but otherwise clinicians are free to choose which types of CE to pursue. Neimeyer and colleagues found that the majority of psychologists surveyed (i.e., 55.7%) completed CE in ethics. The next most popular topics were anxiety disorders and assessment, with approximately one-third of respondents reporting they selected programs on each of these topics for CE. Furthermore, the participants indicated that the most important factor for selecting CE programs was their interest in the topic, followed by motivation to choose a particular CE program because of its relevance in their profession.

Being a Savvy Consumer

Not only should mental health professionals participate in CE to learn and practice new skills, but independent learning, which includes reading the scientific literature regarding psychotherapy, is also vitally important. Neimeyer, Taylor, and Cox (2012) found that psychologists spend the most hours each year engaged in self-directed learning, and they also endorse it as the continuing professional development activity that contributes the most to maintaining professional competence. Reading **peer-reviewed** journal articles is an excellent way to learn what is on the cutting-edge of mental health treatment. Research articles that are submitted for peer-review are read and critiqued by leading experts in the field. The reviewers are blind to the identity of the authors, and they make a recommendation to the journal editor about whether the research merits publication. Peer reviewers are typically interested in evaluating whether the authors have designed a valuable study based on a well-supported research question, if the data were appropriately analyzed and interpreted, and whether the conclusions they reached are warranted. Reviewers will often make suggestions for minor revisions that help to make each article published in a peer-reviewed journal stronger, because it is then not only the product of a rigorous vetting process, but also a product potentially influenced by several well-respected researchers and thinkers.

There are numerous peer-reviewed journals in any given field. You may decide to peruse one or two that speak to your main interests on a regular basis, or you may choose to get information about what is new by reading a resource geared to professionals that highlights recent impactful empirical findings. For example, the American Psychological Association (APA) publishes a magazine called *Monitor on Psychology*, which includes news briefs that point out recent empirical articles of note as well as longer articles written in a journalistic style that go more in depth about new research findings. The ACA also publishes a professional magazine entitled *Counseling Today*. This may be a more appealing way to keep up with the latest in your field without wading through several heavy academic journals on a regular basis. When a finding catches your eye, you should always go to the original source to get more information and evaluate the study yourself. Another great way to cover more ground when reading the empirical literature is to start or join a journal club. You could join several colleagues to review and discuss recent empirical studies in an area of mutual interest. The next section will provide you with some tools for evaluating the research articles you read.

How to Evaluate Research

Empirically supported therapies (ESTs) are treatments that have been found to be efficacious for particular disorders. The APA Division 12 Task Force (Chambless et al., 1998; Chambless & Hollon, 1998) led the efforts to develop criteria by which psychotherapy research is evaluated. The criteria were based on the methods used by the FDA to approve medical treatments (Beutler, 1998). They distinguished three levels of empirical support, which correspond to treatments that are **well-established, probably efficacious**, and **experimental.** To be considered a well-established treatment, there must be at least two strong experiments conducted by different research groups that show the treatment as superior to a control condition (e.g., placement on a waiting list for treatment) or **treatment as usual** (TAU; e.g., another *bona fide* treatment). The treatment must be in a standardized format (i.e., clearly described in a **treatment manual**) so that all clinicians participating in the research are providing the treatment in the same manner. The treatment manual is also a beneficial tool because it allows other mental health providers to deliver the treatment similarly to how it was tested in the research study. Well-established treatments may also be shown to be equivalent to an already established treatment in at least two experiments. To be deemed a well-established treatment, 10 or more single case studies are acceptable evidence. To determine if a treatment is probably efficacious, two or more experiments demonstrating the treatment as superior to a control group or one or more studies meeting the criteria for well-established treatment but not conducted by different research groups are required. At least four single-case design experiments are also sufficient to determine that the treatment is probably efficacious. Experimental treatments have not yet been tested in experiments that meet the task force's criteria for methodology.

Understanding Methodology

To establish empirical support for a treatment, the **randomized clinical trial** (RCT) is considered the best way to demonstrate a treatment's efficacy (Chambless & Hollon, 1998). In an RCT, research participants are recruited and then randomly assigned to a treatment condition. They might receive the experimental treatment being tested, be placed in a control condition, or receive an already established treatment or TAU. Whereas the RCT is a carefully controlled experimental design that allows for researchers to determine with a reasonable amount of confidence that the differences between the groups at the end of the study are attributable to the treatment, it does not allow psychotherapy to be tested in a realistic fashion. Seligman (1995) wrote, "the efficacy study is the wrong method for empirically validating psychotherapy as it is actually done because it omits many crucial elements of what is done in the field" (p. 966). In other words, when it comes to psychotherapy research, there is an important difference between demonstrating that a treatment is efficacious versus effective.

Efficacy indicates that the treatment has demonstrated success in treating a particular disorder in closely controlled experimental conditions. **Effectiveness** refers to the finding that a treatment has demonstrated success in treating a particular disorder in usual or community settings. Although one can reasonably expect that an efficacious treatment will also produce positive results while working with individuals outside of the carefully controlled experimental setting, it isn't always the case. Seligman (1995) highlighted five characteristics of typical psychotherapy that efficacy studies do not adequately capture. He argued that most therapies are not scheduled for a fixed duration, whereas efficacy studies frequently limit treatment to a certain number of sessions. He also pointed out that psychotherapy is self-correcting. When one approach is not working, most clinicians naturally switch to another to try to make improvement. In efficacy studies, therapists are not permitted to stray from the standardized protocol for the experimental treatment or the control condition. Seligman also argued that most clients seek a particular therapist and type of therapy through an active search process, rather than passively awaiting assignment to a particular person and treatment as in an RCT. Another major limitation of efficacy studies is that they produce results that do not necessarily apply to people with more than one problem. This is due to the fact that criteria to be eligible to participate in research studies are often very strict, and individuals with comorbid diagnoses or severe symptoms may be excluded. Finally, Seligman pointed out that psychotherapy is typically concerned with general improvement in the client's functioning in addition to symptom reduction, whereas efficacy studies typically have a sole focus on ameliorating symptoms and measure treatment success on specific measures of outcome, which is typically related to symptom severity pre- and post-treatment.

BOX 14.1

Learning Exercise

Division 12 of the APA maintains a list of ESTs, which is searchable by disorder. Visit the Division 12 website at: www.psychologicaltreatments .org. (If you are more interested in working with children, visit effective-childtherapy.org.) Click on any of the disorders listed to find out more about which treatments are empirically supported for that problem. Once you have identified a treatment with strong research support, look at the list of references to find an RCT for this treatment. For example, behavioral activation (discussed in Chapter 10) has strong research support for the treatment of depression. One of the key references is:

Dimidjian, S., Hollon, S. D., Dobson, K. S., Schmaling, K. B., Kohlenberg, R. J., Addis, M. E., . . . Jacobson, N. S. (2006). Randomized trial of behavioral activation, cognitive therapy, and antidepressant medication in the acute treatment of adults with major depression. *Journal of Consulting and Clinical Psychology*, 74(4), 658–670. doi:10.1037/0022-006X.74.4.658

Another treatment with strong research support for depression is Interpersonal Psychotherapy.

Elkin, I., Shea, M. T., Watkins, J. T., Imber, S. D., Sotsky, S. M., Collins, J. F., . . . Parloff, M. B. (1989). National Institute of Mental Health treatment of depression collaborative research program: General effectiveness of treatments. *Archives of General Psychiatry*, 46(11), 971–982. doi:10.1001 /archpsyc.1989.01810110013002

Look at the eligibility criteria listed in the Method section. Think about how these criteria limit the generalizability of the results to a client that you might treat on your practicum. Would some of your clients have been excluded from the study?

Critical Thinking

Each time you read an empirical study, you should do so with a critical eye. Kazdin (1995) outlined three main tasks for authors to complete when writing an article, and these tasks provide a useful framework for individuals reading and evaluating articles as well. The first task is *description*. When reading an article, you should be able to clearly understand all the details about the study, including the characteristics of the participants in the sample and what exactly was done. The next task is *explanation*. Readers should evaluate whether the authors have included sufficient justification for why and how they chose to conduct their study. For example, the researchers should clearly explain their research method (i.e., how they designed their study to attempt to answer their research questions). The final task is *contextualization*. The authors should address how their study fits in with previous findings and the knowledge base. Authors should also explain the limitations of their study.

After you have read an article critically, keeping each of these three components in mind, you should consider the main findings and formulate an idea of how confident you are in the conclusions. When you read an article that carefully describes all aspects of the research, explains why the researcher made each decision in designing the method, and puts the results in context given previous findings and any study limitations, you should reflect on whether you would have made similar decisions. If so, you are likely to be confident in the findings. To further digest empirical research, you may want to consider a few additional questions. Does the research spark an idea for further inquiry? Do you see the importance of the findings, and do you see ways you might apply them to your clinical work? For a more in-depth look at how to review research articles, see Kazdin's (2005) article and Morrow's (2005) article in Further Reading.

Evidence-Based Practice

Whereas the terms **"evidence-based practice"** (EBP), "empirically validated treatments" (EVTs), and ESTs are each used frequently to describe psychotherapy, the first phrase is the most comprehensive and is the most preferred approach to clinical practice (Levant, 2003; Whaley & Davis, 2007). The APA Presidential Task Force on Evidence-Based Practice (2006) developed a definition of EBP in psychology based on the Institute of Medicine's (2001) definition of EBP, which states "evidence-based practice in psychology is the integration of the best available research with clinical expertise in the context of patient characteristics, culture, and preferences" (p. 273). Because EBP includes the combination of these three components—research support, clinical judgment, and client characteristics—it includes and goes beyond a narrow focus on ESTs. It represents the evolution of best practices. When using ESTs the focus is on identifying what treatments work for a particular disorder. With EBP, treatment decisions are made by considering the client's unique constellation of symptoms, characteristics, and context. The APA Presidential Task Force on Evidence-Based Practice (2006) quipped, "It is important to know the person who has the disorder in addition to knowing the disorder the person has" (p. 279). A multifaceted understanding of the client's age, developmental history, culture, family situation, current environment, life stress, and values must be combined with the therapist's clinical experience and understanding of the available treatment outcome evidence to plan effective treatment.

BOX 14.2

Spotlight on Culture

The movement toward ESTs has generated criticism from some psychologists. One of the arguments against listing treatments that are empirically supported is that the bulk of the psychotherapy research conducted to lend support to these treatments was based on "predominantly White, middle-class, English-speaking women" (Bernal & Scharró-del-Río, 2001, p. 329). The authors of the EST list specifically noted the lack of data available on treatment outcome for ethnic minority populations; they nonetheless suggest that clinicians use ESTs when working with ethnic minority clients (Chambless et al., 1996). Because of this startling lack of research on what treatments are effective for ethnic minority clients, the policy statement of the APA Presidential Task Force on Evidence-Based Practice (2006) acknowledged that more types of research evidence need to be integrated to determine what therapies are supported for these diverse populations. Specifically, **qualitative research**, which does not rely on statistical comparison of groups of people but instead strives to explore individuals more in depth through focus groups, open-ended interviews, and field observations, may be particularly well suited to learning more about what types of psychotherapy benefit particular ethnic minority clients (Silverstein, Auerbach, & Levant, 2006). The goal of most qualitative research is to acquire knowledge and develop theories that are **transferable**, as opposed to **generalizable** to other clients. In order to achieve this, qualitative researchers provide detailed information about the researcher, the participants, and the context to allow individuals the opportunity to determine whether the study's findings may or may not transfer to their own context (Silverstein et al., 2006). Alternative research methods, beyond RCTs, need to be utilized to develop support for **culturally sensitive therapies** (CSTs). CSTs are "psychotherapeutic interventions that address the cultural characteristics of diverse patients (e.g., beliefs, customs, attitudes) as well as their socioeconomic and historical context, but also noting the impact the therapist's culture and context can have on the therapeutic relationship" (La Roche & Christopher, 2008, p. 337). The move away from ESTs to EBP is in line with developing more effective treatments for individuals who are dissimilar from the participants studied in most RCTs.

Although EBP requires a complex conceptualization of the client's characteristics and his presenting problems and suggests that research evidence is only one piece of the puzzle, clinicians should avoid "throwing out the baby with the bathwater." Not all therapies are equally beneficial. The **Dodo bird verdict** refers to the finding that most established psychotherapies tend to be effective (Rosenzweig, 1936; Wampold et al., 1997). The name comes from the declaration that the Dodo bird makes in *Alice's Adventures in Wonderland* after the race, which is that "Everybody has won, and all must have prizes" (Carroll, 1865/2000, p. 69). Some theorists suggest that because most meta-analyses show that all *bona fide* therapies are approximately equally effective, it is the **common factors** (e.g., therapist variables, such as warmth and genuineness, or the quality of therapeutic relationship) that contribute to whether therapy is effective. This argument basically asserts that there are no specific therapeutic factors, but that the common factors in psychotherapy are the key components to improvement for clients. There is no doubt that common factors across different types of psychotherapy lead to improvement, but there are some specific therapies that are best for particular problems.

For example, exposure with response prevention has been shown to be more efficacious than nonbehavioral therapies for obsessive-compulsive disorder (OCD), generalized anxiety disorder, and specific phobia (Chambless & Ollendick, 2001). Therefore, when a client presents for treatment with OCD, it is most likely that the appropriate treatment will be exposure with response prevention because of the strong research support for its efficacy. However, there may be compelling reasons to adapt the treatment in response to the client's needs. For example, the client may have religious obsessions and compulsions and have great difficulty completing exposure tasks because they are likely to involve violating moral and religious teaching. As you may recall, exposure therapy involves asking clients to gradually confront the things that make them feel afraid but are objectively safe, without escaping or avoiding the fear, until their anxiety gradually decreases. Thus, a client with religious OCD may have to repeat blasphemous thoughts without praying for forgiveness as an exposure task. If the therapist were to proceed with a standardized treatment protocol without attempting to incorporate specific methods to increase the client's motivation to participate in what might seem like a risky therapy because of the nature of the exposure tasks (and the feared consequence of eternal damnation), it is less likely to be effective because the client may terminate treatment prematurely. Himle, Chatters, Taylor, and Nguyen (2013) provide guidelines for treating religious OCD based on the available research support and their clinical experience. They provide a brief vignette to illustrate how a Socratic dialogue between therapist and client can help to increase motivation and commitment to participate in exposure treatment:

> **Patient:** I am afraid to expose myself to my negative religious thoughts because God might get really offended.
>
> **Therapist:** It sounds like you are concerned that God might not realize that you have OCD and will misinterpret your exposure exercises, is that right?
>
> **Patient:** Yeah, I am worried that he will send me to hell for reciting all those bad thoughts about Jesus.
>
> **Therapist:** Do you think that God is aware of what OCD is?
>
> **Patient:** Sure, He knows everything.
>
> **Therapist:** Do you think He is better than everyone when it comes to diagnosing an illness?
>
> **Patient:** Yes, He is better than everyone at everything.
>
> **Therapist:** Okay, given that this is the case, do you think that God is really likely to misdiagnose you as not having OCD?

Patient: Yeah, I get your point, He knows I have OCD.

Therapist: Okay, since He is the best at diagnosing OCD, do you think He understands that the thoughts are not your fault?

Patient: Okay, that makes sense, but what about all this exposure to negative religious thoughts and cutting way back on my prayers . . . don't you think that will offend him?

Therapist: Do you think God is familiar with exposure and response prevention therapy?

Patient: Sure, He knows of everything.

Therapist: Do you think that God is really good at exposure and response prevention therapy compared to me and any other therapist?

Patient: Sure, He is best at everything.

Therapist: So do you think He understands what we are trying to do?

Patient: Yes, I am sure He does.

Therapist: Do you think he gets angry when people use therapeutic techniques to help themselves?

Patient: No.

Therapist: Given that, do you think that He would be offended by our efforts to do exposure and response prevention?

Patient: I see your point; it really doesn't make sense that He would be offended. (Himle et al., 2013, p. 65)

This specific example of how the client's cultural context (i.e., religious beliefs) impacted his symptoms illustrates how effective EBP must go beyond selecting a treatment from a list to incorporate all the available information to plan effective treatment.

The above example also serves as a reminder of the importance of the therapeutic relationship in psychotherapy. Using your basic counseling skills to forge a strong therapeutic alliance is likely to help your clients improve and remain committed to treatment. The specific interventions that you use in therapy happen in the context of your relationship with the client. Therefore, even if you are using an evidence-based treatment manual, you must also use your basic counseling skills and pay attention to your client's response to treatment.

BOX 14.3

Using Treatment Manuals Wisely

Published treatment manuals are available for most treatments with empirical support. Some clinicians have objections to providing treatment from a manual because following a manual may have a negative effect on

(continued)

(continued)

> the therapeutic relationship or it may diminish the therapist's ability to be creative and authentic in the therapeutic encounter. Whereas it's certainly possible to use a therapy manual in a rigid, inflexible manner, which is likely to have a negative impact on treatment outcome, manuals should be considered a guide—not a script—for the therapist. Being able to use a manual flexibly is predicated upon having a thorough understanding of the theory of treatment instead of viewing the manual as a collection of specific procedures or techniques that must be followed closely. See Kendall, Chu, Gifford, Hayes, and Nauta (1998) for further reading about "breathing life into a manual," (p. 177) including examples of the flexible use of Coping Cat, a cognitive behavioral treatment program for anxious youth (Kendall & Hedtke, 2006).

Although there is empirical support for a growing number of treatments, this does not necessarily mean that the other treatments that are not on the list are not effective. Rather, the efficacy of many treatments has not yet been tested in rigorous RCTs. We are hopeful that many of these treatments will be examined in well-designed research studies. In the meantime, many continue using these treatments despite the lack of empirical support because they find them to benefit their clients.

Practice-Based Evidence

Practice-based evidence (Margison et al., 2000) refers to support for treatments drawn from the clinician's experiences in providing treatment in typical clinical settings. As previously discussed, RCTs provide the careful control necessary to determine that a treatment has efficacy to treat a particular condition. Practice-based research, on the other hand, has the ability to demonstrate a treatment's effectiveness because the clinician is implementing treatment in regular clinical practice. Margison and colleagues suggest that community clinicians collaborate with each other in a **practice research network** (PRN; Zarin, West, Pincus, & McIntyre, 1996) to generate datasets based on their experiences of delivering EBP in the real world. In order to do this, therapists must monitor their client's response to treatment to determine if the treatment is effective.

Assessment in psychotherapy was discussed in depth in Chapter 8; it is the best way to gather feedback about response to treatment and generate practice-based evidence. The main assessment methods include objective measurement of symptom reduction or increase in quality of life. Another important aspect of monitoring progress is eliciting clients' subjective thoughts about how the treatment is helping them meet their treatment goals. Regularly monitoring treatment progress with assessment and reviewing of the results in session is a good segue to initiate a discussion with clients about their subjective views on treatment progress. For example, an assessment might indicate that the client's symptoms have slightly improved, whereas the client subjectively reports that things seem to be about the same. Learning that there has been a slight reduction in symptoms might instill hope in the client and motivate a renewed commitment to therapy to make more noticeable progress. Assessment is a tool that provides both practitioners and clients with feedback about whether treatment is progressing toward a positive outcome. Following the assessment data can assist therapists in making sound clinical decisions about how to adjust the course of treatment.

DEVELOPING A STYLE

As you progress in your training, you will be exposed to varying information about psychotherapy and theory that over time will evolve and coalesce into your personal style. In your coursework, you will likely learn about treatment from instructors who subscribe to differing theoretical orientations. You will be supervised at practicum sites by clinicians who are theoretically diverse as well. This time of development and discernment is where you begin to find your style as a counselor. Integrating what you learn about effective psychotherapy to fit with your personal style of counseling is a process that will ultimately lead you to establish your primary theoretical orientation.

Finding the Theories That Fit

While you will gain knowledge about different theoretical orientations from reading and didactic coursework, a personal approach will likely guide you as well. As an aspiring mental health professional, you will have no shortage of role models in your training. One excellent way to explore how well the different theoretical approaches to providing therapy fit is to seek out varied experiences in your course work and practicum. Don't be afraid to initiate conversations with your instructors and supervisors about their theoretical orientation and what drew them to the theory. Perhaps there is a faculty member who seems to be similar to you in personality. You might want to make special efforts to reach out to that person as a mentor to guide you during your training.

Another excellent way to learn more about how the different theoretical approaches to psychotherapy fit is to watch videos of different practitioners delivering treatment. Watching how others work will give you a good idea about what therapist qualities are complementary to different therapeutic styles. A great resource for finding therapy demonstration videos is APA's PsycTHERAPY database. In addition to using your knowledge of your personality to help refine your counseling style, you are also likely to feel drawn to a theoretical orientation as you gain knowledge of the therapeutic interventions used in each type of psychotherapy.

Buckman and Barker (2010) recently studied the extent to which personality and training factors (i.e., receiving supervision and coursework) predict graduate students' preferences for particular theoretical orientations. Their results indicated that personality factors were more influential for cognitive behavioral therapy (CBT) preference, whereas training factors were more influential for psychodynamic preference. Notably, there were significant differences in personality factors among the students who preferred different theoretical orientations. Psychodynamic preference was associated with high openness to new experience and low conscientiousness, whereas CBT preference was associated with the opposite pattern (i.e., high conscientiousness and low openness to new experience). This research lends support to the idea that theoretical orientation begins to emerge in graduate school as a result of personality factors and personal values as well as exposure to diverse training experiences.

BOX 14.4

Learning Exercise

Visit PsycTHERAPY to search for videos emblematic of different therapy styles (www.apa.org/pubs/databases/psyctherapy). (It is likely that your institution's library has a subscription to this service.) On PsycTHERAPY, over 65 different therapy approaches are represented among over 300 videos. Pick two differing therapeutic approaches (e.g., brief dynamic therapy and CBT) and spend some time watching clips of these different types of sessions. Describe the therapist in each case. Did you notice a difference in style or personality between two therapists working from two different approaches?

Integrative or Eclectic?

Theoretical orientations are not mutually exclusive in psychotherapy. You need not find just one that appeals to you. Clinicians often draw upon theory and techniques from multiple approaches to therapy. Each time an innovative theory or strategy emerges in the field there are pieces of the pre-existing approaches that are maintained, culled, or refined. As the field advances, researchers and practitioners continue to critically examine what works from the new and keep the gems from the old.

Norcross, Karpiak, and Lister (2005) reported on a survey of clinical psychologists who were asked to indicate their primary theoretical orientation, and the largest proportion, 29%, of respondents indicated that it was "eclectic/integrative." Notably, one-half of this group reported having endorsed a different primary theoretical orientation earlier in their careers, with the majority reporting that they identified as psychodynamic/psychoanalytic, before transitioning to integrative. Furthermore, among the psychologists who identified as eclectic/integrative, most reported that they prefer the term *integrative* rather than eclectic.

An **integrative** approach to psychotherapy implies that a mental health professional is using several different theories to inform treatment and case conceptualization, whereas an **eclectic** approach (sometimes called technical eclecticism) refers to using treatment strategies from multiple approaches without regard to the theory from which they were developed. Relatively few psychologists in Norcross and colleagues' (2005) study reported technical eclecticism (19%), but more endorsed theoretical integration (27.5%) and/or a focus on the common factors across different types of psychotherapy (27.5%).

BOX 14.5

Learning Exercise

Dr. Daniel Coleman (2007) developed the Theoretical Evaluation Self Test (TEST), which includes the major psychotherapy theories: cognitive behavioral, family, humanistic, psychodynamic, biological, and ecosystems/cultural orientations. It is meant to be used as a self-scoring tool that allows students to explore their theoretical preferences. Visit web.pdx .edu/~dcoleman/test.html#TEST to take the interactive test on the web for immediate feedback. You may also download the paper version. Are you surprised by your TEST results?

The process of developing your personal style as a counselor is long and influenced by many factors. As you garner experience working with diverse clients, you will begin to develop an understanding of how people progress and grow in therapy. In consultation with supervisors and other mentors, you will find yourself drawn to the theory and therapeutic interventions of one or more theoretical orientations to psychotherapy that are complementary to your personality and your understanding of how people change with regard to the available scientific evidence. You will try on many hats, and this exposure to a variety of approaches early in your training will facilitate your progress on the path to developing a theoretical orientation.

CHAPTER REVIEW

This chapter focuses on how to use the latest scientific evidence to inform your clinical practice. Clinicians should be knowledgeable about which treatments may produce negative effects, and also which treatments are likely to benefit clients. The necessity to keep up with the latest advances in the field means that mental health professionals must be lifelong learners. The main ways that counselors stay abreast of developments and reinforce their knowledge are by participating in formal CE, attending professional conferences and workshops, teaching or taking classes, participating in peer consultation, and self-directed independent learning, including reading academic journals and professional publications.

Empirically supported therapies (ESTs) are treatments that have been found to be efficacious for particular disorders. ESTs have been tested in rigorous experimental studies (i.e., RCTs) and are disseminated to practitioners through published treatment manuals for use as treatment guides in usual clinical practice. There is an important distinction in psychotherapy research between efficacy and effectiveness. Efficacy indicates that the treatment has demonstrated success in treating a particular disorder in closely controlled experimental conditions. Effectiveness refers to the finding that a treatment has demonstrated success in treating a particular disorder in usual or community settings. Although one can reasonably expect that an efficacious treatment will also produce positive results while working with individuals outside of the carefully controlled experimental setting, it isn't always the case.

Whereas the terms EBP, ESTs, and empirically validated treatments are each used frequently to describe psychotherapy, EBP is the integration of the best available research with clinical expertise in the context of patient characteristics, culture, and preferences. When using ESTs, the focus is on identifying what treatments work for a particular disorder. With EBP, treatment decisions are made by considering the client's unique constellation of symptoms, characteristics, and context. A multi-faceted understanding of the client's age, developmental history, culture, family situation, current environment, life stress, and values must be combined with the therapist's clinical experience and understanding of the available treatment outcome evidence to plan effective treatment.

The Dodo bird verdict refers to the finding that most established psychotherapies tend to be effective. There is no doubt that common factors across different types of psychotherapy lead to improvement, but there are some specific therapies that are best for particular problems. For example, exposure with response prevention has been shown to be more efficacious than nonbehavioral therapies for OCD, generalized anxiety disorder, and specific phobia. Although there is empirical support for a growing number of treatments, this does not necessarily mean that the other treatments that are not on the list are not effective. Rather, the efficacy of many treatments has not yet been tested in well-designed research studies.

Practice-based evidence is support for treatments drawn from a clinician's experience in providing treatment in typical clinical settings. RCTs provide the careful control necessary to determine whether a treatment has efficacy to treat a particular condition. Practice-based research, on the other hand, has the ability to demonstrate a treatment's effectiveness because the clinician is implementing treatment in regular clinical practice. Regular assessment in therapy is the best way to gather feedback about response to treatment and generate practice-based evidence.

Integrating what you learn about effective psychotherapy to fit with your personal style of counseling is a process that will ultimately lead you to establish your primary theoretical orientation. You will gain knowledge about different theoretical orientations from reading and didactic coursework, and another excellent way to explore how well the different theoretical approaches to providing therapy fit is to seek out varied experiences in your course work and practicum. In addition to using your knowledge of your personality to help refine your counseling style, you are also likely to feel drawn to a theoretical orientation as you gain knowledge of the therapeutic interventions used in each type of psychotherapy. Theoretical orientations are not mutually exclusive in psychotherapy. You need not find just one that appeals to you. Clinicians often draw upon theory and techniques from multiple approaches to therapy.

PERSONAL REFLECTION ESSAY QUESTIONS

1. A recent survey of social workers found that 76% had used at least one "novel unsupported therapy" in the past year, despite reporting positive attitudes for EBP (Pignotti & Thyer, 2009). Why do you think that clinicians who value evidence-based treatment might sometimes try approaches to

therapy that do not have support? Consider the role of clinical intuition in your reflection. How can clinicians listen to their gut feelings in therapy but also view their intuition critically and in the context of all the available information?

2. What major theoretical orientations have you been exposed to thus far? Think about your undergraduate and graduate professors as well as clinicians who have supervised and trained you. Without considering the empirical support for these approaches, is there one (or more) that appeals to you most? Why are you drawn to that particular approach?

KEYWORDS

common factors

continuing education

culturally sensitive therapies (CSTs)

Dodo bird verdict

eclectic

effectiveness

efficacy

empirically supported therapies (ESTs)

evidence-based practice (EBP)

experimental

generalizable

integrative

peer review

possibly harmful therapies (PHTs)

practice research network

practice-based evidence

probably efficacious

qualitative research

randomized clinical trial (RCT)

transferable

treatment as usual (TAU)

treatment manual

well-established

FURTHER READING

- Morrow, S. L. (2005). Quality and trustworthiness in qualitative research in counseling psychology. *Journal of Counseling Psychology, 52,* 250–260. doi:10.1037 /0022-0167.52.2.250

This article sets forth criteria by which qualitative research can be evaluated. See this article for more information about conducting qualitative research and understanding qualitative research reports.

- Kazdin, A. E. (1995). Preparing and evaluating research reports. *Psychological Assessment, 7*(3), 228–237.

Although this article primarily focuses on helping authors to write strong empirical articles, it is also a valuable resource for understanding how to evaluate quantitative research reports.

- Westen, D., Novotny, C. M., & Thompson-Brenner, H. (2004). The empirical status of empirically supported psychotherapies: assumptions, findings, and reporting in controlled clinical trials. *Psychological Bulletin, 130*(4), 631–663.

For a critique of the assumptions and findings of studies used to establish certain therapies as empirically supported, read this article. The authors make a case for something they call "empirically informed psychotherapy."

- Podell, J. L., Mychailyszyn, M., Edmunds, J., Puleo, C. M., & Kendall, P. C. (2010). The Coping Cat Program for anxious youth: The FEAR plan comes to life. *Cognitive and Behavioral Practice, 17*(2), 132–141. doi:10.1016.j.cbpra .2009.11.001

  Check out the online version of this article, which contains video demonstrations of the implementation of the key components of the therapy manual.

- Halbur, D. A., & Halbur, K. V. (2010). *Developing your theoretical orientation in counseling and psychotherapy: A handbook for helping professionals* (2nd ed.). Boston, MA: Allyn & Bacon.

  This text will be helpful to students who are curious to learn more about the major theoretical orientations and/or how to find one that fits. A quiz (i.e., the Selective Theory Sorter) is included to help students find to which theory they may be most drawn, given personal beliefs about people and the therapy process.

Growing as a Counseling Professional

Self-care is not a narcissistic luxury to be fulfilled as time permits; it is a human requisite, a clinical necessity, and an ethical imperative.—Norcross and Guy (2007, p. 14)

LEARNING OBJECTIVES

- Define professional development and describe its importance
- Identify several professional organizations that relate to your counseling discipline
- Describe the various ways counselors pursue professional development
- Define self-care and identify several reasons it is essential for counseling professionals
- Identify multiple strategies for self-care
- Define burnout and compassion fatigue
- Outline multiple strategies for identifying and preventing burnout and compassion fatigue
- Explain the importance of supervision and identify multiple types of supervision
- Distinguish between process and progress notes
- Identify several reasons therapists should also pursue their own treatment

Choosing a career in counseling is not just a professional decision. It is also the beginning of a journey of personal transformation. The effects of psychotherapy are bidirectional. Just as therapists impact the lives of their clients, clients also affect their therapists. You are embarking on a career that will ultimately disrupt and change the way you understand yourself and others. Many of the changes therapists experience as a result of their professional work are welcome and positive; however, the degree of occupational stress that counseling professionals often face is sometimes too much. The work is demanding and can be isolating, as therapists are the keepers of many secrets and frequently manage complex ethical challenges. Social workers, mental health counselors, psychologists, creative arts therapists, and all helping professionals are at risk for burnout and compassion fatigue. This chapter will outline tools and strategies for self-care and address the many avenues to growing as a professional.

PROFESSIONAL DEVELOPMENT

You will never stop learning. Although this may be one of the first courses you are taking toward a career as a psychotherapist, it will likely be the first of many. Most counseling professionals continue to engage in learning opportunities throughout their career. Many advanced learning opportunities address specific topics like conducting group therapy, working with managed care organizations, ethical and multicultural competencies, and working with special populations (Wilcoxon & Puleo, 1992). In a large global study of 3,900 therapists, Orlinsky and colleagues (1999) found that self-perceptions of therapeutic mastery increased gradually over time and that therapists at all levels of experience reported a sense that they were experiencing professional growth. In another study, Kendjelic and Eells (2007) found that clinicians who received a 2-hour training session on case formulation developed more elaborate, comprehensive, complex, and precise formulations compared to clinicians who did not receive the training. Even a 2-hour seminar can make a significant difference in key clinician competencies. Continuing education (CE) was discussed in Chapter 14, and there are many additional ways to pursue professional development, including attending regional, national, and international conferences; participating in workshops; taking post-graduate seminars; obtaining certificates in specialty areas; and networking with colleagues.

Conferences

Membership in professional organizations will give you a bird's eye view of your field and provide countless opportunities for development. Here are just a few of the organizations that may be of interest to beginning counselors:

- American Association for Marriage and Family Therapy (AAMFT; www.aamft.org)—This is the professional organization devoted to marriage and family therapists (MFTs). The AAMFT develops graduate education standards and offers an annual conference and week-long CE institutes. They offer many levels of membership, including those for students, pre-licensure MFTs, and fully credentialed clinical fellows.
- American Counseling Association (ACA; www.counseling.org)—The ACA is a large organization with 20 divisions, including college counseling, social justice, marriage and family, and counselor education and supervision. The ACA includes substance abuse, school, and mental health counselors in its membership. ACA-sponsored conferences focus on client and therapist factors in the therapeutic relationship as well as the latest research in mental health.
- American Mental Health Counselors Association (AMHCA; www.amhca.org)—The AMHCA has many student-focused opportunities, including special memberships and scholarship opportunities. They are active in public policy issues and offer affordable liability insurance for students.

- American Psychological Association (www.apa.org)—The American Psychological Association has memberships specifically designed for high school, college, and graduate students. Within the American Psychological Association, there are currently 56 divisions that focus on special areas of interest. These include Division 29—Psychotherapy, Division 33—Intellectual and Developmental Disabilities, Division 49—Society of Group Psychology and Group Psychotherapy, and Division 53—Society of Clinical Child and Adolescent Psychology. The American Psychological Association offers annual meetings for the entire organization and most divisions, as well as numerous mid-year conferences.
- National Association of Social Workers (NASW; www.naswdc.org)—The NASW is both a professional organization and a powerful advocacy group. It offers many special practice sessions in topics such as administration/supervision, private practice, and social work and the courts. There are memberships for bachelor's and master's degree students and many meetings and events available for networking.
- National Coalition of Creative Arts Therapies Associations (NCCATA; www.nccata.org)—This is an umbrella organization that brings together many different creative arts therapists, including dance, drama, music, and art therapists. They offer several conferences each year as well as job listings and scholarships for higher education.

Each of these national associations offers large-scale annual conferences. Many also provide smaller, regional meetings throughout the year. Attending your first annual meeting can sometimes be a bit daunting, but there are often smaller student and early career professional events within the larger meeting that are more accessible. Prior to the meeting, most organizations provide a comprehensive program that can help attendees tailor their conference experience ahead of time. Conferences are a wonderful opportunity to hear giants in the field speak and to make connections with other students and professionals. In addition to daytime panels, poster sessions, and individual speakers, there are often evening social events that allow attendees to interact more informally. Membership in national organizations also typically involves subscriptions to professional peer-reviewed publications. Keeping up-to-date on the latest research and trends in practice is another important component of professional development.

BOX 15.1

Learning Exercise

Finding a Professional Home

As you begin to think about professional development, think about which organizations you might be interested in joining. This chapter lists some of the major professional organizations for a variety of disciplines. Keep in mind that there are hundreds of other specialty organizations that may also be a good fit. You might consider joining an organization that reflects your theoretical orientation or represents a niche in which you are interested, such as

(*continued*)

(continued)

> disaster relief, religion/spirituality, trauma, or global issues. Additionally, it is important to stay connected to colleagues at a regional level as well as at a national level. Look online for local and state organizations that might also match your professional goals. List at least four organizations—one national association, two specialty organizations, and one local or regional group—that you would consider joining. Describe each organization briefly and explain what makes it unique from the others. What types of benefits are available for student members?

Workshops and Seminars

Beyond conferences, which are often large and cover a wide range of topics, workshops and seminars may be smaller, more personal, and focused on a particular topic. Counseling professionals often hear about these from colleagues, word-of-mouth, institutions they work for, and supervisors. Currently, many organizations are offering workshops on the *Diagnostic and Statistical Manual of Mental Disorders* (5th ed., *DSM-5*; American Psychiatric Association, 2013) to help clinicians become more familiar with the new diagnostic system. You may also see seminars about the Affordable Care Act and its impact on mental health services, dealing with trauma in school settings and how to respond to new gun safety legislation in a clinical setting. Most workshops and seminars focus on contemporary issues of immediate importance to mental health service providers. They are often offered locally and provide a wonderful opportunity for professional development and building professional connections with others in your area.

Certification

Beyond graduate school, there are many additional certification programs that clinicians pursue. This may involve **board certification**, which is a special designation from an accreditation body. The National Board for Certified Counselors (www.nbcc.org/OurCertifications) offers several certification programs for mental health specialists, school counselors, and addiction specialists. The American Board of Professional Psychology (www.abpp.org/i4a/pages/index.cfm?pageid=3285) offers numerous certification programs in areas ranging from couple and family psychology to police and public safety psychology. There are other certification boards for other disciplines in mental health as well. Certification programs help assess the quality of care and multicultural competence and may be required for certain hospital affiliations. In addition to being a quality control mechanism, board certification is an opportunity for professionals to sharpen their skills and deepen their knowledge base within their area of specialization.

Beyond board certification, counseling professionals may pursue other types of post-graduate programs. Many training institutes offer advanced certification in particular therapeutic approaches including cognitive behavioral therapy (CBT) for psychosis or posttraumatic stress disorder (PTSD), psychodynamic psychotherapy, couples therapy, family systems work, and supervision skills. These programs provide ample opportunity to improve clinical skills and to make additional professional connections. Post-graduate certification programs can run from several weeks to several years long and tuition is typically less than the cost of a full-time graduate program. Most certification programs require that students be fully licensed and practicing in their particular discipline. By attending a certification program, clinicians build their skill set while also increasing the size of their referral network and making meaningful relationships with colleagues.

Networking

Networking involves building business and social relationships. It has also been referred to as "schmoozing" or "rubbing elbows." Meeting with other colleagues is a wonderful way to strengthen connections and build a referral network. There is a great deal of networking that takes place at conferences, seminars, and workshops, and these are often the primary venues for making new contacts. Even outside of a national conference, it is important to build strong relationships with local colleagues. This may involve attending social and professional events of local organizations or arranging one-on-one meetings with other professionals. It is also important to be responsive when another clinician contacts you with a question; you never know when you may need him or her to return the favor. Meeting with colleagues for lunch or coffee, particularly when you have a stated goal, can be a valuable way to build meaningful connections. The purpose of such get-togethers may be to learn more about their practice, talk about how they have built their client base, share information about conferences you have both attended, or to exchange practice-related information (e.g., documentation, HIPAA compliance, etc.).

In sum, there are countless venues for building your professional network and skill base. All of the helping professions involve a lifetime of learning and professional growth. Engaging in professional organizations, additional training programs, and one-on-one networking will help add vitality to your professional career and will afford you new opportunities throughout your career.

BOX 15.2

Spotlight on Culture

There are many ways to build multicultural competence and to increase your exposure to diverse client populations as you develop your professional identity. Participating in activities with multicultural communities is one way to diversify your professional activities. Involving yourself in a wide range of professional activities (e.g., research, clinical work, teaching, supervising, taking classes, and volunteering) is one way to further sustain yourself (Norcross, 2000). Therapists often become involved in activism as part of their professional and personal engagement with the community. Therapists are involved in global social issues like prisoner detainment, female genital mutilation, global warming, the rights of women and girls, and literacy. You might consider being involved with a group like *Therapists for Social Responsibility* (www.therapistsforsocialresponsibility.org/site/Home.html),

(continued)

(continued)

which is a liberal organization that advocates for social change related to the Patriot Act, war and terrorism, and privacy concerns.

Therapists also have an invaluable skill set, which affords them the opportunity to serve communities in need across the globe. Why not consider donating your talents in order to serve in a volunteer capacity? Hassan (2007) reports that SalusWorld (http://salusworld.org) and other nongovernmental organizations are eager to have mental health professionals partner with them to provide culturally responsive interventions throughout the world. One of their programs provides mental health volunteers to bring home-based care to individuals too traumatized to leave their homes. Organizations like HealthRight International (www.healthright.org) provide services worldwide and stateside. Licensed mental health professionals in the United States can volunteer with HealthRight's Human Rights Clinic to provide pro-bono clinical evaluations for individuals seeking political asylum. Clinicians in this program conduct an evaluation, write an affidavit for the immigration court, and provide expert testimony on behalf of asylum-seekers.

SELF-CARE

It is difficult, if not impossible, to effectively care for others when you are unable or unwilling to care for yourself. Being a helping professional involves an incredible amount of "pouring out." Counselors spend much of their professional life caring for clients, supervising trainees, and purposely privileging the needs of others over their own. The importance of appropriate **self-care** or personal health maintenance cannot be understated. Self-care does not involve overindulging to make up for feeling deprived and is not about being selfish. Rather, it is a process of establishing personal well-being by making choices that restore one's sense of vitality and purpose. Nearly all of the counseling-related ethics codes outline an imperative for therapist self-care. The ACA (2005) instructs counselors to "engage in self-care activities to maintain and promote their emotional, physical, mental, and spiritual well-being to best meet their professional responsibilities" (p. 9). The ACA Ethics Code also directs counselors to seek treatment and professional assistance when they notice signs of impairment, especially when such deficits may harm a client. In order to maintain care for others, it is critical that therapists maintain their own physical, interpersonal, emotional, and spiritual health.

Caring for the Body

At a recent lunch meeting, Dr. Khan asked a beloved colleague how she managed to keep a full caseload, publish numerous scholarly articles, spend time with her family, and provide such rich and meaningful supervision. The colleague responded with a laugh, "Look at me! You can't do it all." She was referring to the fact that she is overweight, does not give much attention to her appearance, and is in generally poor health. This exchange highlights the choices that some clinicians make in order to pursue their professional goals, sometimes at the expense of their physical health. This anecdote does not seem to be an unusual occurrence.

In a study of 155 therapists, Mahoney (1997) found that physical exhaustion and chronic fatigue were some of the personal problems participants reported most frequently. A smaller but still sizeable percentage also reported gastrointestinal problems and headaches as problems they had faced in the previous year.

Unmanaged stress can have significant negative effects on physical and psychological health. Stress has been identified as a contributing factor to chronic diseases like heart disease, diabetes, cardiovascular disease, obesity, and overall mortality (Angermayr, Melchart, & Linde, 2010). Some researchers have suggested that it is the subjective interpretation of stress that leads to deleterious health effects (Watson & Pennebaker, 1989). Research findings support this connection and suggest that there is a constant interplay of the mind and body when it comes to overall well-being.

Caring for the Mind

Imagine being a therapist in downtown Manhattan on September 11, 2001. It is the morning of the terrorist attacks, and you are just beginning to understand what is happening. You are uncertain about where your friends and family members were when the planes hit the towers, and you cannot reach them by phone. You have a client sitting in your waiting room. Here is how one therapist described this very experience: "I sat in a session at 11:00 that morning and felt shared grief and horror with my client. I did not feel particularly like a therapist. Moments earlier I had been weeping. I struggled to find my familiar place as a therapist; the familiar was gone" (Saakvitne, 2002, p. 444).

Although there may be some comfort in shared experience of trauma and no longer feeling isolated in the suffering, it can be very difficult for the therapist to manage his or her own feelings in order to effectively care for others. It is important to know your own limits and to develop a plan for self-care before disaster strikes. Mental health professionals have an imperative to be vigilant of their own distress and to take concrete steps to address problems as they arise. The therapist in the 9/11 example goes on to write, " 'How am I doing?' needs to be a regular question for each of us to ask ourselves. As we assess our own psychological health and well-being, it is important to emphasize strategies of self-protection and healing that can support us as therapists and diminish the negative impact of our work" (Saakvitne, 2002, p. 447).

Ellen Baker's book, *Caring for Ourselves: A Therapist's Guide to Professional Well-Being* (Baker, 2003), focuses on the ethical imperative therapists have to maintain their own physical and emotional health. She includes a therapist self-care questionnaire that she uses to interview therapists to begin the process of self-reflection about caring for the self.

BOX 15.3

Learning Exercise

Take a look at some of the self-care questions shown in Figure 15.1. After you have spent some time thinking about several of them, write a brief reflection paper (1–2 pages) summarizing what you have noticed about yourself. You may want to discuss your observations with a classmate or your instructor.

General Self-Care
1. What do you do to take care of yourself as a therapist? Be specific and give examples.
2. What has been most helpful in terms of self-care?
3. Does self-care entail more time with others or more time alone?
4. How important is it for you to balance your life between home and work?
5. What do you consider your greatest challenge in self-care?

Professional Self-Care
1. What motivated you to become a psychotherapist?
2. Are there motivations for becoming a therapist that might hinder your ability to be effective? To set appropriate boundaries?
3. Is the work you do different than what you anticipated? If so, how?
4. How would you describe the fit between your personality and your work? Are there ways in which they do not match up?

Emotional Self-Care
1. How does your work as a clinician impact your emotional life and personal relationships?
2. How do your emotional well-being and personal life affect your clinical work?
3. How does stress manifest in your life (e.g., emotionally, behaviorally, physically)?
4. What is your perception of the effect of your stress upon others?
5. What has been your most stressful experience as a therapist so far? How did you manage it? Are there things you might do differently if you had the opportunity?

Self-Care Activities
1. How often do you do the following:
   a. Practice mindfulness meditation, yoga, prayer, or other spiritual/religious practices
   b. Go on vacation
   c. Exercise
   d. Get a full night's sleep (7–8 hours)
   e. Laugh with family and friends
   f. Pursue your hobbies

If you find that you rarely participate in these activities, consider putting these important self-care activities on your calendar. For many therapists it is imperative to set aside time to specifically care for physical, emotional, and spiritual health.

FIGURE 15.1 Self-care questions to consider.

Building Healthy Relationships

In order to provide care for troubled individuals day after day, therapists must also maintain meaningful relationships with friends and family. It is important to have at least a few people who value us separate from our professional skillset (Guy, 2000). This is an important component of thriving and growing as a professional. It is essential for therapists to have a reliable and wide-ranging support system. These relationships should be varied and numerous (Figley, 2002). Therapists who find that they have toxic relationships in their lives, ones that are draining or unnecessarily burdensome, should consider making changes. Therapists must be able to have relationships in which they can shed the therapist persona and simply be human. Inevitably, acquaintances will try to get a free consultation at social gatherings. It can be helpful to say something like, "I'm sorry, the meter is off and I'm off duty. If you have a question about a referral, please feel free to e-mail me or call my office about that." This is one way to set personal boundaries, which will be addressed in the next section.

Setting Personal Boundaries

Much of the literature on boundaries for psychotherapists revolves around sexual boundaries with clients. In this chapter, **personal boundaries** refer to general

ILLUSTRATION 15.1 Setting appropriate personal boundaries is an important part of being an ethical and effective counseling professional.
Courtesy of Will Russell.

guidelines and expectations of how others should behave around the individual. Personal boundaries also dictate how an individual will respond when another person violates these expectations. A therapist with soft boundaries can be easily manipulated but may feel resentful later that he or she has been taken advantage of. Someone with rigid boundaries is likely to keep a significant amount of emotional distance between him or herself and others; he or she may be seen as walled off or distant. Ideally, therapists will develop boundaries that are flexible and well maintained. Having healthy boundaries involves keeping regular hours and sticking to them and setting appropriate limits with clients for between-session contact. In a broader sense, boundaries are what allow therapists to maintain a healthy work-life balance.

BOX 15.4

Work-Life Balance

Consider the following scenario. You go away for the weekend with your spouse to attend a friend's wedding. On your way to the event you receive an e-mail on your smart phone from a particularly anxious client. The client explains that he is desperate for a phone session—something you have done in the past. He writes, "I am afraid I will disintegrate if I can't talk to you tonight." How will you handle this situation? What feelings come up for you as you consider what to do? What types of boundaries might a therapist in this situation put in place ahead of time to avoid such a conflict?

AVOIDING BURNOUT

*Burnout...is taking place when you realize that you neither
know what is going on with your clients, nor really care.*
—Kottler (2011, p. 182)

At the beginning of one's career, everything is new and exciting. The work of psychotherapy is intensely personal, challenging, and rewarding. There is a certain thrill associated with being the keeper of so many secrets as clients share the intimate details of their lives with you. It may be hard to imagine experiencing **burnout** or becoming cynical about this work, but years of seeing clients can take a toll on even the most enthusiastic therapist. In fact, therapists who are younger in age and have fewer years of work experience are more likely to experience burnout than experienced clinicians (Ackerley, Burnell, Holder, & Kurdek, 1988; Deutsch, 1984).

Burnout is often accompanied by **compassion fatigue**—symptoms include depersonalization, emotional numbing, and decreased sense of personal accomplishment—particularly among therapists working with trauma survivors (Craig & Sprang, 2010). In one study of humanitarian aid workers, 100% (N = 76) of the participants reported experiencing compassion fatigue in the aftermath of their work with survivors (Shah, Garland & Katz, 2007). Burnout may be caused by excessive empathy, a stance that may lead the clinician to become overwhelmed with the enormity of her client's problems (Maslach, 1982). Burnout and compassion fatigue are associated with having a large caseload (Angerer, 2003), insufficient resources, lack of social support, and decreased sense of control over one's own work environment (Maslach & Leiter, 1997). Many clinicians who work in institutional settings may face these types of stressors whether they want to or not. Clinicians in private practice may wind up—inadvertently or otherwise—imposing similar types of risk factors on themselves. In spite of the fact that many of these variables may be difficult to control, there are still many strategies that helping professionals can employ to address professional disengagement before it consumes them.

Jeffrey Kottler (2011) has written about the importance of identifying the beginning signs of burnout before it takes hold. In his book, *On Being a Therapist* (2010), Kottler identifies several symptoms of burnout. Therapists may notice reluctance to talk about their work in social situations or to perform the basic tasks of the job. A kind of cynicism may take hold in which the clinician may notice him or herself ridiculing clients or discounting their ability to change. This is often noticeable through the therapist's thoughts about his or her clients. Counselors

ILLUSTRATION 15.2 Therapists who find themselves burning the candle at both ends are more susceptible to burnout and compassion fatigue.

Courtesy of Wes Peck.

who observe themselves thinking, *There's no hope for you* or *Why would anyone stay in a relationship with a person like this?* may be experiencing burnout. When a therapist's enthusiasm for his or her work has waned, clients are likely to pick up on implicit cues. The therapy sessions may become lackluster for both client and therapist; there is likely to be less vitality and strong affect in the room. Additionally, therapists facing burnout may find they need to lose themselves in mindless and passive leisure activities for long periods of time. They may have little energy left over at the end of the day to devote to their own relationships and pastimes.

What can be done to reduce or ameliorate burnout? There are many ways to address burnout before it even begins. Therapists at every level of experience should develop strategies for providing self-care and building a strong social support network. Here are several recommendations for avoiding, reducing, and reversing burnout:

1. Receiving *supervision from a supportive, encouraging, and empathic supervisor* has been shown to reduce the likelihood of burnout (Gibson, Grey, & Hastings, 2009). Depending on the clinical setting, the quality of supervision can vary widely. It may be useful to speak openly with your supervisor to see what can be done to foster a more supportive relationship. Consider seeking out additional supervision, consultation, or peer supervision if you are not receiving adequate support from your assigned supervisor. This should not be a place to gripe about your primary supervisor. Rather, the purpose of seeking out additional supervision is to receive guidance and support for your professional work with clients.

2. Engaging in *leisure activities* can also improve psychotherapists' ability to cope with the many demands of work, particularly if these activities promote meaningful connections with loved ones (Grafanaki et al., 2005). Although the demands of graduate education and clinical placements are many, it is imperative to maintain a work-life balance. Consider which activities restore your sense of well-being. Being physically active, engaging in hobbies or community service with others, or participating in a religious or spiritual community are all examples of communal leisure activities that can help prevent burnout. Additionally, some solitary activities—such as hobbies, reading for pleasure, or exercise—may provide a similar sense of restoration.

3. Maintaining a positivistic *sense of humor* is associated with lower rates of burnout among psychotherapists. In a study of 133 psychotherapists, Malinowski (2013) found that affiliative humor, the kind that helps build group cohesion (e.g., laughing *with* others rather than *at* them), and self-enhancing humor, which helps alleviate distress by lightening the mood or providing distraction (e.g., recalling and sharing a funny memory with a friend when he or she is stressed), were associated with a sense of professional accomplishment. Conversely, aggressive and self-defeating humor were correlated with emotional exhaustion and depersonalization.

4. Develop an extensive and varied *social support network*. The pastimes described in recommendation 2 above are also ways to increase the therapist's social support network, which is a critical component in avoiding burnout (Emery, Wade, & McLean, 2009). Therapist loneliness

is associated with decreased job satisfaction (Melamed, Szor, & Bernstein, 2001). One of the possible benefits of working in an institutional setting—as opposed to private practice—is the multidisciplinary team of professionals that is readily accessible to the therapist. It is also important to have a varied group of friends, those who work in the helping professions and those who do not. Colleagues who are also friends can understand the unique challenges of the profession; friends who have other professions can afford the therapist a broader worldview and new outlets for expression.

SEEKING SUPPORT FROM COLLEAGUES

There are many ways to seek and receive support from other professionals. These include consultation, dyadic and group peer supervision, and supervision from a more experienced colleague. **Consultation** involves meeting with a trusted colleague in order to discuss a particular case or technical issue. This type of professional support is typically sought on an ad-hoc basis when needed. Therapists may encounter a particular clinical problem that leads them to seek advice from a colleague who has more experience with the issue. This is one of the many ways that the profession of counseling is an ongoing process of learning. **Peer supervision** may be an informal form of consultation or may be a sustained relationship between two or more colleagues who meet on a regular basis to discuss their clinical work. Dyadic and group supervision arrangements have been shown to lead to personal growth and skill development among therapists (Borders, 2012). These types of groups take many forms and may involve focusing on the work of one or more members at each meeting. Some peer supervision groups are interdisciplinary with psychologists, mental health counselors, social workers, and psychiatrists working together to assist one another. Other groups may be made up of members from only one discipline. The form and format of the group depends primarily on the preferences of its members. Because supervision is a required part of the training of new counselors, we will focus more on this aspect of professional support.

Supervision

The supervisory relationship is one of the most important in building a new therapist's skills, confidence, and professional identity (Marmarosh et al., 2013). **Supervision** is a legally required part of professional training for all mental health professions. It involves receiving guidance from an experienced counselor in order to develop as a professional. Working with an effective and supportive supervisor can enable the trainee to learn new ways of thinking about mental health and develop competencies in working with clients. Supervisors and supervisees bring their own expectations, personality styles, and personal histories to this important relationship (Marmarosh et al., 2013). Although not every supervisory relationship is effective, clear communication about the needs of the supervisee and the working style of the supervisor can help foster a beneficial and supportive relationship.

Each supervisor has her own personal style that is usually developed as a result of her own previous supervision experiences, her theoretical orientation, and degree of responsiveness to the needs of her supervisees. Some supervisors in institutional settings split their time and attention across multiple domains. Within a hospital or clinic setting, the supervisor may be responsible for overseeing the trainee's completion of daily tasks, such as required paperwork (e.g., daily notes, treatment plans), managing collateral contacts, and fulfilling institutional priorities (e.g., maintaining accreditation, complying with state and federal laws). In addition, the supervisor is tasked with providing support and guidance for the trainee's clinical work with clients. As a result of these multiple demands, the supervisor simultaneously serves as a task-master and supportive mentor. Effective supervisors can typically balance these dual identities well, but it is sometimes difficult. Trainees may find it helpful to speak directly with their supervisors about these different foci in the supervision in order to identify the difference between administrative and therapeutic priorities.

Trainees should always come to supervision prepared. The meaning of preparedness varies across training sites and, in most cases, supervisors will explicitly indicate what is expected. If the expectations are unclear, trainees should ask for clarification. For administrative tasks, it may be helpful to have a spreadsheet or another way of tracking completion of progress notes, treatment plans, and intake forms. This allows the trainee to provide the most up-to-date information in a straightforward and organized fashion. Some supervisors will ask the trainee to provide **process notes** of their sessions. Process notes, also referred to as psychotherapy notes, are written by the therapist in training, typically right after the session concludes. They include the therapist's best recollection of the verbatim transcript of the session along with reflections, questions, and reactions to the clinical material. Process notes differ from **progress notes,** which are the core of most clinical records. Progress notes include basic information about the who, what, why, and when of the session.

BOX 15.4

Sample Progress and Process Notes

The form of progress and process notes differs dramatically depending on the clinical setting. There may be information that is required for certain progress notes that are unique to the placement site. For example, in an eating disorders clinic, it may be critical to include the client's weight, calorie intake, and frequency of binging and purging. Acute inpatient settings typically require information about the client's suicidal and/or homicidal ideation and the presence or absence of psychotic symptoms. Putting aside these special requirements for different sites, here are examples of a progress and process note for the same session.

Progress Note—August 23, 2013
Client returns today reporting moderately elevated anxiety symptoms, including ruminating, physiological symptoms of anxiety (e.g., heart racing), and sleep disturbance with increased nightmares. Client identifies recent cuts at work and children leaving for boarding school last week as precipitating events. Reviewed recently acquired tools including mindfulness practices, deep breathing exercises, and challenging distorted thinking

(continued)

(continued)

with client. Also discussed how the beginning of the school year reactivates prior losses in client's life and helped client think about ways in which children's departure is different from (and similar to) her brother's death and her own divorce several years ago. Client identified plan to utilize anxiety-management tools, increasing frequency of exercise, and using journaling exercises to process feelings of abandonment. Will also seek out additional social support from friends and family. Continues on 175 mg of Effexor qAM.

Process Note—August 23, 2013

She looks different than last week. Less professional, less care with her appearance. Her skin is a little blotchy. She seems tense.

Client: After I dropped the kids off at school on Saturday, I just sat in my car and cried. The whole drive back I kept thinking, "What if they die?" What if it's just like when Robby died or when Bruce left me and I never see them again? I had to pull over a few times and catch my breath. I mean, I was the one driving away from them, but I just felt like they were leaving me, like I was alone all over again.

[Client was tearful during this, and I felt a little frustrated with her. I was thinking, "This is nothing like those other situations. You're going back for family weekend in 2 weeks and your kids adore you." I was very aware of how distorted her thinking was and how powerful these past experiences were in dictating her view of things now. I wondered if I felt irritated because of my own sense of helplessness, concern that I couldn't fill this void for her—she is going to have to do it herself. I couldn't believe how little empathy I felt for her in this moment. I thought about how she was seeing her own situation through a particular lens, and I was seeing her through my own lens.]

Therapist: You see the kids starting school so far away through a particular lens. It brings up all of these old feelings of loss and abandonment that you felt when your brother died and when your husband left. It's hard to notice, at least in the moment, ways in which the situations are different.

Client: It's all about the feeling. Feeling so alone, almost like I am dying alone. I may never see them again or something, even though I know I will.

[I think I felt a little overwhelmed here. When she mentioned dying I thought, "Oh boy. This is intense." Now that I look back on the session, I think my next comment was a reaction to that, wanting to bring her back to something positive, away from such dark thoughts.]

(continued)

(continued)

Therapist: And you did something, once the feeling got so strong, to take care of yourself…by pulling off the road, I mean. You realized you needed to catch your breath, to re-center yourself.
[I wonder what would have happened if I'd just stayed with the darker feeling.]

Client: Yeah, I would have never done that a year ago. I think I would have just pretended everything was fine, but it would have come out in other ways, like yelling at my kids or crawling into bed for 2 days straight. Even though this is hard, it's better than the way it used to be.

Therapist: And yet you said it felt like dying.
[Now I come back to it. It felt safer now, like she was shored up and ready to talk about this without totally falling apart.]

Client: I guess dying in the sense that I felt so alone, alienated. But, I called a friend that night and went out to dinner. And my daughter called the next morning to tell me about her new roommate. Now that I think about it, that phone call was a good reminder that she still needs me and wants me in her life.

This process note excerpt should provide some sense of the type of material that is often included. The level of detail in a process note far exceeds that of a progress note. Process notes should be kept separately from the client's official medical record, which includes progress notes. Process notes are a more protected part of the client's record and may or may not be subject to subpoena, although this is a complicated area of mental health law.

Working with process notes can be helpful in exploring countertransference reactions and developing new ways of responding to clients. However, not all supervision is based on the review of detailed process notes. Many supervisors eschew this practice and the focus is on developing specific skills and reviewing problem areas with specific clients. It is often incumbent upon the supervisee to come prepared with questions and areas of concern. Psychotherapy supervision differs from other professional management styles. Whereas trainees will want to demonstrate their competence, the primary purpose of the relationship is to receive feedback on areas for growth. In this way, the very nature of supervision requires trainees to be vulnerable and honest about both their strengths *and* weaknesses. Supervisors are in an evaluative role, and they often provide feedback to training programs on supervisee performance. These evaluations tend to have an equal emphasis on the trainee's established abilities and their openness to seeking and receiving feedback on new skills. There are times when the line between supervision and personal psychotherapy can seem blurred. A trainee may report difficulty working with a client whose primary concerns mirror his or her own. In such cases it is especially important that supervision be sought in tandem with personal treatment.

THERAPY FOR THE THERAPIST

It cannot be disputed that analysts do not in their own
personalities wholly come up to the standard of psychic
normality which they set for their patients.—S. Freud (1937)

Personal psychotherapy has been discussed in other chapters of this book, but it is worth reiterating its importance. Pursuing individual treatment is commonplace among mental health professionals. Mahoney (1997) found that psychotherapists expressed concern about the financial (41.3%) and emotional (20.6%) investment therapy requires. Despite these concerns, nearly 90% of psychotherapy practitioners in this study reported having been in personal therapy. Therapists may engage in personal treatment in order to grow as a person, alleviate personal distress, as a requirement of training, or to prevent burnout (Daw & Joseph, 2007). For example, one therapist responded,

> I also work with those who have been sexually abused and who inflict significant trauma to others. I find therapy provides a helpful place to ensure that work does not get taken home and prevents me from losing empathy because I have not processed my reaction to such issues. Some of this can be addressed in supervision but when it relates to one's own personal issues then it needs to be reflected on in a therapeutic space. (Daw & Joseph, 2007, p. 230)

This reflection describes perfectly both the personal and professional aspects of individual therapy for the therapist. The therapist also highlights the differences between supervision and therapy.

Personal therapy can help a therapist identify "blind spots" that may impair his or her ability to care effectively for clients. Therapy is not just for the severely disturbed or those with acute problems. Therapy can be helpful for a wide range of problems, including procrastination, anger management, difficulty maintaining romantic relationships, and bereavement, just to name a few. All clinicians fall short of being completely enlightened and evolved as human beings. Irrespective of theoretical orientation, work environment, caseload, or personal history, psychotherapy can help clinicians develop greater self-awareness and self-insight. The development of these qualities, coupled with the resolution of other personal problems, will help each mental health professional be better equipped to serve and care for others.

CHAPTER REVIEW

Becoming a professional counselor is not only a career choice. It will also have lasting effects on your development as a person, your relationships with friends and family, and your overall sense of well-being. In order to manage the many challenges associated with being a helping professional, it is important to be vigilant of your own mental and physical health. There are many proactive steps therapists can take to develop and grow as professionals and as people.

Participating in professional development activities is one way to avoid stagnation and maintain a sense of professional vitality. These include attending regional and national conferences, participating in workshops and seminars, obtaining additional certification, and pursuing informal networking opportunities. All of these avenues enable therapists to be surrounded with like-minded professionals, who understand the unique challenges associated with being a helping professional. Each organization will have its own culture and may provide different types of support.

Self-care is one of the most important things therapists can do to enhance their effectiveness and passion for their chosen career. In fact, therapists have an ethical imperative to care for themselves in order to avoid burnout or other types of impairment. Caring for the mind and the body are especially important. Clinicians should monitor their own mental health and coping resources and seek assistance early and often. Maintaining good physical health is also important. This includes good sleep hygiene, eating a healthy diet, and participating in regular physical activity. Interpersonal health is also important. The support of a strong social network can be one of the buoys that help therapists weather the storms of professional life. Finally, maintaining strong personal boundaries will allow therapists to maintain a healthier work-life balance.

Burnout is one of the common complaints of longtime therapists but can also affect those new to the profession. If you have participated in a practicum or externship experience already, you have probably heard staff at the clinic or hospital talking about feeling burned out. Or perhaps you have seen evidence of another clinician's cynicism and lack of enthusiasm about his or her clients. Burnout is an understandable phenomenon in mental health work and is often accompanied by compassion fatigue. Clinicians can simply run out of steam and can feel defeated by the scope and intensity of the problems their clients face. Institutional and economic pressures can also contribute to burnout and compassion fatigue. There are many ways to prevent these feelings from becoming entrenched. Supervision with a supportive colleague, participating in leisure activities, maintaining a healthy sense of humor, and relying on an extensive support network are all tools that may reduce therapist burnout. Supervision and personal therapy are two of the most important activities in which therapists should engage. Supervision may be in a dyad with an experienced professional or within a group setting. Supervision often involves the review of process notes, which are distinct from progress notes. Personal therapy, as has been emphasized throughout this text, is a profound way for the individual therapist to grow both as a professional and as a person.

PERSONAL REFLECTION ESSAY QUESTIONS

1. What do you do now to care for yourself? Are there ways you could improve your self-care skills? What happens (to your productivity, relationships, stress level, etc.) when you are not adequately caring for yourself?
2. Consider this description of counseling: "Therapy is about mending something that has been broken. In our work we seek to repair confidence, improve quality of life, restore relationships, and heal the wounds of the past. If we can do that for just one person, we have made a difference."

   In what ways does this reflect your view of what it means to be a therapist? Are there certain hazards inherent in this way of approaching clients and yourself? Consider the effect a failed treatment might have on your own self-esteem, self-efficacy, and confidence.

3. What if you found yourself in a difficult supervisory relationship? What would you do? Are there specific qualities you hope you will find in your supervisors? Which qualities would be difficult to contend with?
4. What attitudes and beliefs do you hold about personal therapy? Are there cultural factors or familial variables that contribute to your view of psychotherapy? Under what circumstances would it seem appropriate to seek therapy? How would you go about finding and choosing a therapist? What specific things might you need to address in individual therapy that could help make you a better clinician? (You do not need to provide specifics; a general idea is fine.)

KEYWORDS

board certification	networking	progress notes
burnout	peer supervision	self-care
compassion fatigue	personal boundaries	supervision
consultation	process notes	

FURTHER READING

- Kottler, J. A. (2011). *The therapist's workbook: Self-assessment, self-care, and self-improvement exercises for mental health professionals* (2nd ed.). Hoboken, NJ: John Wiley & Sons, Inc.

This workbook is designed to help therapists consider the doubts they have about their effectiveness, acknowledge their own limitations, and regain a sense of motivation and energy in their professional life. Kottler has written extensively about therapist burnout and offers some great resources for addressing the problem head-on.

- Norcross, J. C., & Guy, J. D., Jr. (2007). *Leaving it at the office: A guide to psychotherapist self-care.* New York, NY: Guilford Press.

This book is a very accessible, honest, and inspiring look at self-care. The authors offer concrete suggestions for therapist self-care that cover a wide range of domains, including physical, mental, and spiritual areas of life.

- Frawley-O'Dea, M. G., & Sarnat, J. E. (2001). *The supervisory relationship: A contemporary psychodynamic approach.* New York, NY: Guilford Press.

This book takes a relational approach to the supervisory relationship and includes many examples and vignettes. Key topics include the role of power and authority in the supervisory relationship, working with group process in case conferences, and the role of the institution in supporting the supervisory relationship.

- Reiser, R. P., & Milne, D. L. (2013). Cognitive behavioral therapy supervision in a university-based training clinic: A case study in bridging the gap between rigor and relevance. *Journal of Cognitive Psychotherapy, 27*(1), 30–41. doi:10.1891/0889-8391.27.1.30

This article highlights the key elements involved in supervision of graduate students from a CBT perspective. The authors focus on the development of students' professional competencies, metacognition, and management of trainee anxiety. Several illustrative case examples are included.

- Wolfe, J. L. (2000). A vacation from musturbation. *Professional Psychology: Research and Practice, 31*(5), 581–583. doi:10.1037/0735-7028.31.5.581

Janet Wolfe is a long-time psychotherapist and colleague of Albert Ellis. This refreshing and inspirational article provides a brief overview of the many things Dr. Wolfe has done to create her own work-life balance.

References

AA General Service Office. (2008). *Origin of the serenity prayer: A brief summary.* Retrieved from http://www.aa.org/en_pdfs/smf-141_en.pdf

Ackerley, G. D., Burnell, J., Holder, D. C., & Kurdek, L. A. (1988). Burnout among licensed psychologists. *Professional Psychology: Research and Practice, 19*(6), 624–631.

Adebimpe, V. R. (2004). A second opinion on the use of white norms in psychiatric diagnosis of black patients. *Psychiatric Annals, 34*(7), 543–551.

Adler, A. (1954). *Understanding human nature* (H. Ansbadur, Trans.). New York, NY: Fawcett. (Original work published 1927).

Adler, A. (1958). *What life should mean to you.* New York, NY: Capricorn.

Ainslie, G. M. (2013). Commentary on toxic impasse: I. *The Round Robin Newsletter of Section I, 28*(1), 8.

Ainsworth, M., Blehar, M., Waters, E., & Wall, S. (1978). *Patterns of attachment.* Hillsdale, NJ: Erlbaum.

Ajzen, I. (1985). From intentions to actions: A theory of planned behavior. In J. Kuhl & J. Beckmann (Eds.), *Action control: From cognitions to behavior* (pp. 11–39). Berlin: Springer Verlag.

Ajzen, I. (1991). The theory of planned behavior. *Organizational Behavior and Human Decision Processes, 50*(2), 179–211.

Ajzen, I., & Fishbein, M. (1980). *Understanding attitudes and predicting social behaviour.* Upper Saddle River, NJ: Prentice-Hall Inc.

Aklin, W. M., & Turner, S. M. (2006). Toward understanding ethnic and cultural factors in the interviewing process. *Psychotherapy: Theory, Research, Practice, Training, 43*(1), 50–64. doi:10.1037/0033-3204.43.1.50

Alarcon, R. D., Alegria, M., Bell, C. C., Boyce, C., Kirmayer, L. J., Lin, K. M, ... Wisner, K. L. (2005). Beyond the funhouse mirrors: Research agenda on culture and psychiatric diagnosis. In D. J. Kupfer, M. B. First, & D. A., Regier (Eds.), *A research agenda for DSM-V* (pp. 219–282). Washington, DC: American Psychiatric Association.

Alexander, F., & French, T. M. (1980). *Psychoanalytic therapy: Principles and application.* Lincoln, NE: University of Nebraska Press.

Allport, G. W. (1954). *The nature of prejudice.* Cambridge, MA: Perseus Books.

Altarriba, J. (2003). Does cariño equal "liking"? A theoretical approach to conceptual nonequivalence between languages. *International Journal of Bilingualism, 7*(3), 305–322.

Altman, N. (2000). Black and white thinking: A psychoanalyst reconsiders race. *Psychoanalytic Dialogues, 10*(4), 589–605. doi:10.1080/10481881009348569

Altman, N. (2010). *The analyst in the inner city: Race, class, and culture through a psychoanalytic lens* (2nd ed.). New York, NY: Routledge.

Alvarez-Jimenez, M. M., Priede, A. A., Hetrick, S. E., Bendall, S. S., Killackey, E. E., Parker, A. G., . . . Gleeson, J. F. (2012). Risk factors for relapse following treatment for first episode psychosis: A systematic review and meta-analysis of longitudinal studies. *Schizophrenia Research, 139* (1–3), 116–128. doi:10.1016/j.schres.2012.05.007

American Counseling Association. (2005). *ACA code of ethics.* Alexandria, VA: Author.

American Educational Research Association, American Psychological Association, & National Council on Measurement in Education. (1999). *Standards for educational and psychological testing.* Washington, DC: American Educational Research Association.

American Medical Association Council on Ethical and Judicial Affairs. (1988). Ethical issues involved in the growing AIDS crisis. *Journal of American Medical Association, 259*(9), 1360–1361.

American Psychiatric Association. (1980). *Diagnostic and statistical manual of mental disorders* (3rd ed.). Washington, DC: Author.

American Psychiatric Association. (2000). *Diagnostic and statistical manual of mental disorders* (4th ed., text rev.). Washington, DC: Author.

American Psychiatric Association. (2013). *Diagnostic and statistical manual of mental disorders* (5th ed.). Arlington, VA: Author.

American Psychiatric Association Ad Hoc Committee on AIDS Policy. (1988). AIDS policy: Confidentiality and disclosure. *American Journal of Psychiatry, 145,* 541–542.

American Psychological Association. (1991). *Legal liability related to confidentiality and the prevention of HIV transmission.* Washington, DC: APA Council of Representatives.

American Psychological Association. (2002, amended 2010). *The ethical principles of psychologists and code of conduct.* Washington, DC: Author. Retrieved September 15, 2012, from http://www .apa.org/ethics/code/index.aspx

American Psychological Association. (2010). *FYI: Mental health insurance under the federal parity law.* Washington, DC: American Psychological Association. Retrieved from http://www .apapracticecentral.org/good-practice/winter11-mhpaea.pdf

American School Counseling Association. (2013). *The role of the professional school counselor.* Retrieved from http://www.schoolcounselor.org/administrators/role-of-the-school-counselor

Amodeo, M., Grigg-Saito, D., & Robb, N. (1997). Working with foreign language interpreters: Guidelines for substance abuse clinicians and human service practitioners. *Alcoholism Treatment Quarterly, 15*(4), 75–87. doi:10.1300/J020v15n04_06

Amundson, N. E., Harris-Bowlsbey, J., & Niles, S. G. (2013). *Essential elements of career counseling* (3rd ed.). Upper Saddle River, NJ: Merrill.

Anandarajah, G., & Hight, E. (2001). Spirituality and medical practice: Using the HOPE questions as a practical tool for spiritual assessment. *American Family Physician, 63*(1), 81–89.

Andersen, P. A., & Andersen, J. F. (2005). Measurements of perceived nonverbal immediacy. In V. Manusov (Ed.), *The sourcebook of nonverbal measures* (pp. 113–126). Mahwah, NJ: Erlbaum.

Anderson, C. E. (2000). Dealing constructively with managed care: Suggestions from an insider. *Journal of Mental Health Counseling, 22*(4), 343–353.

Anderson, S. K., & Handelsman, M. M. (2010). *Ethics for psychotherapists and counselors: A proactive approach.* Malden, MA: Wiley-Blackwell.

Anderson, R. T., King, A., Stewart, A. L., & Camacho, F. (2005). Physical activity counseling in primary care and patient well-being: Do patients benefit? *Annals of Behavioral Medicine, 30*(2), 146–154.

Angerer, J. M. (2003). Job burnout. *Journal of Employment Counseling, 40,* 98–107.

Angermayr, L., Melchart, D., & Linde, K. (2010). Multifactorial lifestyle interventions in the primary and secondary prevention of cardiovascular disease and type 2 diabetes mellitus—A systematic review of randomized controlled trials. *Annals of Behavioral Medicine, 40*(1), 49–64. doi:10.1007/s12160-010-9206-4

Angold, A., & Costello, E. (2000). The Child and Adolescent Psychiatric Assessment (CAPA). *Journal of the American Academy of Child & Adolescent Psychiatry, 39*(1), 39–48. doi:10.1097 /00004583-200001000-00015

APA Presidential Task Force on Evidence-Based Practice. (2006). Evidence-based practice in psychology. *American Psychologist, 61,* 271–285. doi:10.1037/0003-066X.61.4.271

APRN Consensus Work Group. (2008). *Consensus model for APRN regulation: Licensure, accreditation, certification & education.* APRN Joint Dialogue Group Report. Washington, DC: APRN Consensus Work Group.

Architectural Barriers Act of 1968, Pub.L. 90-480, 82 Stat. 718, 42 U.S.C. § 4151 et seq (1968).

Arkowitz, H., & Miller, W. R. (2008). Learning, applying and extending motivational interviewing. In H. Arkowitz, H. A. Westra, & W. R. Miller (Eds.), *Motivational interviewing in the treatment of psychological problems* (pp. 1 – 25). New York, NY: Guilford Press.

Arlow, J. A. (1969). Unconscious fantasy and disturbances of conscious experience. *The Psychoanalytic Quarterly, 38*(1), 1–27.

Arlow, J. A., & Brenner, C. (1964). *Psychoanalytic concepts and the structural theory.* New York, NY: International Universities Press.

Arnd-Caddigan, M. (2013). Imagined conversations and negative countertransference. *Journal of Psychotherapy Integration, 23*(2), 146–157. doi:10.1037/a0031415

Arnow, B. A., Steidtmann, D., Blasey, C., Manber, R., Constantino, M. J., Klein, D. N., . . . Kocsis, J. H. (2013). The relationship between the therapeutic alliance and treatment outcome in two distinct psychotherapies for chronic depression. *Journal of Consulting and Clinical Psychology, 81*(4), 627–638. doi:10.1037/a0031530

Aron, L., & Anderson, F. S. (Eds.). (1998). *Relational perspectives on the body.* Hillsdale, NJ: The Analytic Press.

Aronson, E. (1969). The theory of cognitive dissonance: A current perspective. *Advances in Experimental Social Psychology, 4,* 1–34.

Artman, L. K., & Daniels, J. A. (2010). Disability and psychotherapy practice: Cultural competence and practical tips. *Professional Psychology: Research and Practice, 41*(5), 442–448. doi:10.1037/a0020864

Asay, T. P., & Lambert, M. J. (2002). Therapist relational variables. In D. J. Cain & J. Seeman (Eds.), *Humanistic psychotherapies: Handbook of research and practice* (pp. 531–558). Washington, DC: American Psychological Association.

Atkinson, D. R., & Lowe, S. M. (1995). The role of ethnicity, cultural knowledge, and conventional techniques in counseling and psychotherapy. In J. G. Ponterotto, J. M. Casas, L. A. Suzuki, & C. M. Alexander (Eds.), *Handbook of multicultural counseling* (pp. 387–414). Thousand Oaks, CA: Sage.

Atkinson, D. R., Morten, G., & Sue, D. W. (1998). *Counseling American minorities* (5th ed.). New York, NY: McGraw-Hill.

Auchincloss, E. L. (2013). Commentary on toxic impasse: II. *The Round Robin Newsletter of Section I, 28*(1), 9.

Axsom, D. (1989). Cognitive dissonance and behavior change in psychotherapy. *Journal of Experimental Social Psychology, 25*(3), 234–252.

Axsom, D., & Cooper, J. (1985). Cognitive dissonance and psychotherapy: The role of effort justification in inducing weight loss. *Journal of Experimental Social Psychology, 21*(2), 149–160.

Bacal, H., & Carlton, L. (2010). Who can do what, therapeutically, with whom, in what way? *Journal of Psychotherapy Integration, 20*(1), 46–50. doi:10.1037/a0018817

Bacal, H. A. (1998). Is empathic attunement the only optimal response? In H. A. Bacal (Ed.), *Optimal responsiveness: How therapists heal their patients* (pp. 289–301). Lanham, MD: Jason Aronson.

Baer, R. A. (2003). Mindfulness training as a clinical intervention: A conceptual and empirical review. *Clinical Psychology: Science and Practice, 10*(2), 125–143. doi:10.1093/clipsy.bpg015

Baer, R. A., Smith, G. T., Hopkins, J., Krietemeyer, J., & Toney, L. (2006). Using self-report assessment methods to explore facets of mindfulness. *Assessment, 13*(1), 27–45. doi:10.1177/1073191105283504

Baird, A. D., Scheffer, I. E., & Wilson, S. J. (2011). Mirror neuron system involvement in empathy: A critical look at the evidence. *Social Neuroscience, 6*(4), 327–335. doi:10.1080/17470919.2010.547085

Baker, E. K. (2003). *Caring for ourselves: A therapist's guide to personal and professional well-being.* Washington, DC: American Psychological Association.

Baldwin, S. A., Wampold, B. E., & Imel, Z. E. (2007). Untangling the alliance-outcome correlation: Exploring the relative importance of therapist and patient variability in the alliance. *Journal of Consulting and Clinical Psychology, 75,* 842–852.

Bandura, A. (1971). *Social learning theory*. New York, NY: General Learning Press.

Bandura, A. (1977). Self-efficacy: Toward a unifying theory of behavioral change. *Psychological Review, 84*(2), 191–215.

Bar, M., Neta, M., & Linz, H. (2006). Very first impressions. *Emotion, 6*(2), 269–278. doi:10.1037/1528-3542.6.2.269

Barenboim, D. (2006). *Lecture 1: In the beginning was sound* [Radio Transcript]. Retrieved from http://downloads.bbc.co.uk/rmhttp/radio4/transcripts/20060407_reith.pdf

Bar-On, R. (2000). Emotional and social intelligence: Insights from the emotional quotient. In R. Bar-On & J. D. Parker (Eds.), *The handbook of emotional intelligence: Theory, development, assessment and application at home, school and in the workplace* (pp. 363–368). San Francisco: Jossey-Bass.

Baskin, W. T., Slaten, C. D., Crosby, N. R., Pufahl, T., Schneller, C. L., & Ladell, M. (2010). Efficacy of counseling and psychotherapy in schools: A meta-analytic review of treatment outcome studies. *The Counseling Psychologist, 38*(7), 878–903. doi:10.1177/0011000010369497

Bateman, A. (2010). *Proceedings from 1st international congress on borderline personality disorder*. Berlin, Germany.

Bateman, A., & Fonagy, P. (2001). Treatment of borderline personality disorder with psychoanalytically oriented partial hospitalization: An 18-month follow-up. *American Journal of Psychiatry, 158*(1), 36–42. doi: 10.1176/appi.ajp.158.1.36

Bateman, A., & Fonagy, P. (2009). Randomized controlled trial of outpatient mentalization-based treatment versus structured clinical management for borderline personality disorder. *American Journal of Psychiatry, 166*(12), 1355–1364. doi:10.1176/appi.ajp.2009.09040539

Bateson, G., Jackson, D. D., Haley, J., & Weakland, J. (1956). Toward a theory of schizophrenia. *Behavioral Science, 1251–1264.* doi:10.1002/bs.3830010402

Baum, N. (2006). End-of-year treatment termination: Responses of social work student trainees. *British Journal of Social Work, 36*(4), 639–656. doi:10.1093/bjsw/bch253

Beauchamp T. L., & Childress J. F. (1983). *Principles of biomedical ethics* (2nd ed.). New York, NY: Oxford University Press.

Beck, A. T. (1963). Thinking and depression: I. Idiosyncratic content and cognitive distortions. *Archives of General Psychiatry, 9*(4), 324–333. doi:10.1001/archpsyc.1963.01720160014002

Beck, A. T. (1964). Thinking and depression: II. Theory and therapy. *Archives of General Psychiatry, 10*(6), 561–571. doi:10.1001/archpsyc.1964.01720240015003

Beck, A. T. (1976). *Cognitive therapy and emotional disorders*. New York, NY: International Universities Press.

Beck, A. T. (1991). Cognitive therapy: A 30-year retrospective. *American Psychologist, 46,* 368–375. doi:10.1037/0003-066X.46.4.368

Beck, A. T., Freeman, A., & Davis, D. D. (2004). *Cognitive therapy of personality disorders* (2nd ed.). New York, NY: Guilford Press.

Beck, A. T., Rush, A. J., Shaw, B. F., & Emery, G. (1979). *Cognitive therapy of depression*. New York, NY: Guilford Press.

Beck, A. T., Steer, R. A., & Brown, G. K. (1996). *Manual for the Beck Depression Inventory-II*. San Antonio, TX: Psychological Corporation.

Beck, J. S. (2011). *Cognitive therapy: Basics and beyond* (2nd ed.). New York, NY: Guilford Press.

Bell, D. (Ed.). (1997). *Reason and passion: A celebration of the work of Hanna Segal*. New York, NY: Routledge.

Berg-Cross, L., & So, D. (2011). The start of a new era: Evidence-based multicultural therapies. *The Register Report, 37,* 8–15.

Bergin, A. E. (1984). Proposed values for guiding and evaluating counseling and psychotherapy. *Counseling and Values, 29*(2), 99–116. doi:10.1002/j.2161-007X.1984.tb00441.x

Berk, M. S., & Andersen, S. M. (2000). The impact of past relationships on interpersonal behavior: Behavioral confirmation in the social–cognitive process of transference. *Journal of Personality and Social Psychology, 79*(4), 546–562. doi: 10.1037/0022-3514.79.4.546

Bernal, G., & Scharró-del-Río, M. R. (2001). Are empirically supported treatments valid for ethnic minorities? Toward an alternative approach for treatment research. *Cultural Diversity and Ethnic Minority Psychology, 7*(4), 328–342. doi:10.1037/1099-9809.7.4.328

Bernard, J. L., & Jara, C. S. (1986). The failure of graduate students to apply understood ethical princi-ples. *Professional Psychology: Research and Practice, 17*(4), 313–315. doi:10.1037/0735-7028.17.4.313

Berry, J. W. (1990). Psychology of acculturation. In J. Berman (Ed.), *Cross-cultural perspectives: Nebraska symposium on motivation* (pp. 201–234). Lincoln, NE: University of Nebraska Press.

Berry, J. W. (1997). Immigration, acculturation, and adaptation. *Applied Psychology, 46*(1), 5–34.

Bersoff, D., & Koeppl, P. (1993). The relation between ethical codes and moral principles. *Ethics and Behavior, 3*(3–4), 345–357.

Betan, E. J. (1996). *Understanding the ethical behavior of clinical psychologists: Incorporating affect into the model of ethical decision-making* (Unpublished doctoral dissertation). University of Kansas, Lawrence.

Beutler, L. E. (1998). Identifying empirically supported treatments: What if we didn't? *Journal of Consulting and Clinical Psychology, 66*(1), 113. doi:10.1037/0022-006X.66.1.113

Bike, D. H., Norcross, J. C., & Schatz, D. M. (2009). Processes and outcomes of psychotherapists' personal therapy: Replication and extension 20 years later. *Psychotherapy: Theory, Research, Practice, Training, 46*(1), 19–31. doi:10.1037/a0015139

Blagys, M. D., & Hilsenroth, M. J. (2006). Distinctive figures of short-term psychodynamic-interpersonal psychotherapy: A review of the comparative psychotherapy process literature. *Clinical Psychology: Science and Practice, 7*(2), 167–188. doi:10.1093/clipsy/7.2.167

Bleuler, E. P. (1951). *Textbook of psychiatry.* New York, NY: Dover.

Blum, P. (1973). The concept of erotized transference. *Journal of the American Psychoanalytic Association, 21*, 61–76.

Blume-Marcovici, A. C., Stolberg, R. A., & Khademi, M. (2013). Do therapists cry in therapy? The role of experience and other factors in therapists' tears. *Psychotherapy, 50*(2), 224–234. doi:10.1037/a0031384

Bodie, G. D. (2011). The active-empathic listening scale (AELS): Conceptualization and evidence of validity within the interpersonal domain. *Communication Quarterly, 59*(3), 277–295. doi:10.1080/01463373.2011.583495

Bodie, G. D., & Jones, S. M. (2012). The nature of supportive listening II: The role of verbal per-son centeredness and nonverbal immediacy. *Western Journal of Communication, 76*(3), 250–269. doi:10.1080/10570314.2011.651255

Bodie, G. D., Janusik, L. A., & Valikoski, T. R. (2008). *Priorities of listening research: Four interrelated initiatives.* A white paper sponsored by the Research Committee of the International Listening Association. Retrieved from http://www.listen.org/resources/documents/white_paper_prioritiesresearch.pdf

Boellinghaus, I., Jones, F. W., & Hutton, J. (2013). Cultivating self-care and compassion in psycholog-ical therapists in training: The experience of practicing loving-kindness meditation. *Training and Education in Professional Psychology.* Advance online publication. doi:10.1037/a0033092

Bohus, M., Haaf, B., Simms, T., Limberger, M. F., Schmable, C., Unckel, C., . . . Linehan, M. M. (2004). Effectiveness of inpatient dialectical behavioral therapy for borderline personal-ity disorder: A controlled trial. *Behavior Research and Therapy, 42*(5), 487–499. doi:10.1016/S0005-7967(03)00174-8

Boland-Prom, K. (2009). Results from a national study of social workers sanctioned by state licensing boards. *Social Work, 54*(4), 351–360. doi:10.1093/sw/54.4.351

Bons, D., van den Broek, E., Scheepers, F., Herpers, P., Rommelse, N., & Buitelaaar, J. K. (2013). Motor, emotional, and cognitive empathy in children and adolescents with autism spectrum disorder and conduct disorder. *Journal of Abnormal Child Psychology, 41*(3), 425–443. doi:10.1007/s10802-012-9689-5

Borders, L. D. (2012). Dyadic, triadic, and group models of peer supervision/consultation: What are their components, and is there evidence of their effectiveness? *Clinical Psychologist, 16*(2), 59–71. doi:10.1111/j.1742-9552.2012.00046.x

Bordin, E. S. (1976). The generalizability of the psychoanalytic concept of the working alliance. *Psychotherapy: Theory, Research and Practice, 16*, 252–260. doi:10.1037/h0085885

Bostic, J. Q., Shadid, L. G., & Blotcky, M. J. (1996). Our time is up: Forced terminations during psy-chotherapy training. *American Journal of Psychotherapy, 50*(3), 347–359.

Bowen, M. (1971). The use of family therapy in clinical practice. In J. Haley (Ed.), *Changing families: A family therapy reader* (pp. 159–192). London: Grune and Stratton.

Bowen, M. (1972). On the differentiation of self. In J. Framo (Ed.), *Family interaction: A dialogue between family researchers and family therapists* (pp. 111–173). New York, NY: Springer.

Bowen, M. (1978). *Family therapy in clinical practice.* New York, NY: Jason Aronson.

Bowen, M. (1985). *Family therapy in clinical practice.* Lanham, MD: Rowman & Littlefield Publishing Group.

Bowlby, J. (1969). *Attachment and loss: Vol. 1. Attachment.* New York, NY: Basic Books.

Bowlby, J. (1973). *Attachment and loss: Vol. 2. Separation, anxiety, and anger.* New York, NY: Basic Books.

Bowlby, J. (1980). *Attachment and loss: Vol. 3. Sadness and depression.* New York, NY: Basic Books.

Brenner, C. (1979). Working alliance, therapeutic alliance, and transference. *Journal of the American Psychoanalytic Association, 27*(Suppl.), 137–157.

Brenner, C. (1982). *The mind in conflict.* New York, NY: International Universities Press.

Brenner, C. (1994). The mind as conflict and compromise formation. *Journal of Clinical Psychoanalysis, 3*(4), 473–488.

Bronfenbrenner, U. (1979). *The ecology of human development: Experiments by nature and design.* Cambridge, MA: Harvard University Press.

Brown, D., & Brooks L. (1990). Using career theories to help clients. *Career choice and development* (2nd ed., pp. 9–31). San Francisco, CA: Jossey-Bass.

Brown, D. L., & Pomerantz, A. M. (2011). Multicultural incompetence and other unethical behaviors: Perceptions of therapist practices. *Ethics & Behavior, 21*(6), 498–508. doi:10.1080/10508422.2011.622182

Brown, G. K., Beck, A. T., Steer, R. A., & Grisham, J. R. (2000). Risk factors for suicide in psychiatric outpatients: A 20-year prospective study. *Journal of Consulting and Clinical Psychology, 68*(3), 371–377. doi:10.1037/0022-006X.68.3.371

Buckman, J. R., & Barker, C. (2010). Therapeutic orientation preferences in trainee clinical psychologists: Personality or training? *Psychotherapy Research, 20*(3), 247–258. doi:10.1080/10503300903352693

Burleson, B. R. (2011). A constructivist approach to listening. *The International Journal of Listening, 25*(1–2), 27–46. doi:10.1080/10904018.2011.536470

Burleson, B. R., & Waltman, M. S. (1988). Cognitive complexity: Using the role category questionnaire measure. In C. H. Tardy (Ed.), *A handbook for the study of human communication: Methods and instruments for observing, measuring, and assessing communication processes* (pp. 1–35). Norwood, NJ: Ablex.

Burnham, J. J., & Jackson, C. M. (2000). School counselor roles: Discrepancies between actual practice and existing models. *Professional School Counseling, 4*(1), 41–49.

Butler, A. C., Chapman, J. E., Forman, E. M., & Beck, A. T. (2006). The empirical status of cognitive-behavioral therapy: A review of meta-analyses. *Clinical Psychology Review, 26*(1), 17–31. doi:10.1016/j.cpr.2005.07.003

Bynum, W. F. (1964). Rationales for therapy in British psychiatry: 1780–1835. *Medical History, 18*(4), 317–334.

Byrd, R., & Hays, D. G. (2012). School counselor competency and lesbian, gay, bisexual, transgender, and questioning (LGBTQ) youth. *Journal of School Counseling, 10*(3). Retrieved from http://jsc.montana.edu/articles/v10n3.pdf

Byrne, J. P., & Valdiserri, E. V. (1982). Psychotherapeutic issues in a Veterans Administration outpatient clinic. *American Journal of Psychotherapy, 36*(4), 547–553.

Calmar, A. (1985). Big brother shares the therapist's couch. *Journal of Psychotherapy in Independent Practice, 3*(3), 9–14.

Campinha-Bacote, J. (2003). Many faces: Addressing diversity in health care. *Online Journal of Issues in Nursing, 8*(1), Manuscript 2. Retrieved from www.nursingworld.org/MainMenuCategories/ANAMarketplace/ANAPeriodicals/OJIN/TableofContents/Volume82003/No1Jan2003/AddressingDiversityinHealthCare.aspx

Cantor, D. W., & Fuentes, M. A. (2008). Psychology's response to managed care. *Professional Psychology: Research and Practice, 39*(6), 638–645. doi:10.1037/0735-7028.39.6.638

Cardemil, E. V., & Battle, C. L. (2003). Guess who's coming to therapy? Getting comfortable with conversations about race and ethnicity in psychotherapy. *Professional Psychology: Research and Practice, 34*(3), 278–286. doi:10.1037/0735-7028.34.3.278

Carlson, J. F. (2013). Clinical and counseling testing. In K. F. Geisinger, B. A. Bracken, J. F. Carlson, J. C. Hanson, N. R. Kuncel, S. P. Reise, & M. C. Rodriguez (Eds.), *APA Handbook of testing and assessment in psychology, Vol. 2: Testing and assessment in clinical and counseling psychology* (pp. 3–17). Washington, DC: American Psychological Association.

Carmel, H., & Hunter, M. (1989). Staff injuries from inpatient violence. *Psychiatric Services, 40*(1), 41–46.

Carpenter, P. J., Del Gaudio, A. C., & Morrow, G. R. (1979). Dropouts and terminators from a community mental health center: Their use of other psychiatric services. *Psychiatric Quarterly, 51*(4), 271–279.

Carr, L. G. (1997). *"Color-blind" racism.* Thousand Oaks, CA: Sage Publications.

Carroll, K. M., Ball, S. A., Martino, S., Nich, C., Babuscio, T. A., Nuro, K. F., ... Rounsaville, B. J. (2008). Computer-assisted delivery of cognitive-behavioral therapy for addiction: A randomized trial of CBT4CBT. *The American Journal of Psychiatry, 165*(7), 881–888. doi:10.1176/appi .ajp.2008.07111835

Carroll, L. (2000). *Alice's adventures in wonderland* (R. Kelly, Ed.). Peterborough, ON: Broadview Press. (Original work published 1865)

Carroll, L., Gilroy, P. J., & Ryan, J. (2002). Counseling transgendered, transsexual, and gender-variant clients. *Journal of Counseling & Development, 80*(2), 131–139.

Carter, R. T. (1995). *The influence of race and racial identity in psychotherapy: Toward a racially inclusive model.* Oxford, England: John Wiley & Sons.

Cartwright, C. (2011). Transference, countertransference, and reflective practice in cognitive therapy. *Clinical Psychologist, 15*(3), 112–120. doi:10.1111/j.1742-9552.2011.00030.x

Cass, V. C. (1979). Homosexuality identity formation: A theoretical model. *Journal of Homosexuality, 4*(3), 219–235. doi:10.1300/J082v04n03_01

Castonguay, L. G., Goldfried, M. R., Wiser, S., Raue, P. J., & Hayes, A. M. (1996). Predicting the effect of cognitive therapy for depression: A study of unique and common factors. *Journal of Consulting and Clinical Psychology, 64*(3), 497–504. doi:10.1037/0022-006X.64.3.497

Cecchin, G. (1987). Hypothesizing, circularity and neutrality revisited: An invitation to curiosity. *Family Process, 26*, 405–414.

Celenza, A., & Gabbard, G. O. (2003). Analysts who commit sexual boundary violations: A lost cause? *Journal of the American Psychoanalytic Association, 51*(2), 617–636. doi:10.1177/00030651 030510020201

Chambless, D. L., Baker, M. J., Baucom, D. H., Beutler, L. E., Calhoun, K. S., Crits-Christoph, P., ... Woody, S. R. (1998). Update on empirically validated therapies, II. *Clinical Psychologist, 51*(1), 3–16.

Chambless, D. L., & Hollon, S. (1998). Defining empirically supported therapies. *Journal of Consulting and Clinical Psychology, 66*(1), 7–18. doi:10.1037/0022-006X.66.1.7

Chambless, D. L., & Ollendick, T. H. (2001). Empirically supported psychological interventions: Controversies and evidence. *Annual Review of Psychology, 52*(1), 685–716. doi:10.1146/annurev .psych.52.1.68

Chambless, D. L., Sanderson, W. C., Shoham, V., Johnson, S. B., Pope, K. S., Crits-Christoph, P., ... McCurry, S. (1996). An update on empirically validated therapies. *The Clinical Psychologist, 49*, 5–18.

Charlot, L. L., Deutsch, C. C., Hunt, A. A., Fletcher, K. K., & McLlvane, W. W. (2007). Validation of the Mood and Anxiety Semi-structured (MASS) Interview for patients with intellectual disabilities. *Journal Of Intellectual Disability Research, 51*(10), 821–834. doi:10.1111/j.1365-2788.2007.00972.x

Chung, R. C. Y., & Bemak, F. (2007). Immigrant and refugee populations. In M. G. Constantine (Ed.), *Clinical practice with people of color* (pp. 125–142). New York, NY: Teachers College Press.

Clark, L. A., & Watson, D. (1991). Tripartite model of anxiety and depression: Psychometric evidence and taxonomic implications. *Journal of Abnormal Psychology, 100*(3), 316–336. doi:10 .1037/0021-843X.100.3.316

Clarkin, J. F., & Levy, K. N. (2003). A psychodynamic treatment for severe personality disorders: Issues in treatment development. *Psychoanalytic Inquiry, 23*, 248–267.

Clarkin, J. F., Levy, K. N., Lenzenweger, M. F., & Kenberg, O. F. (2007). Evaluating three treatments for borderline personality disorder: A multiwave study. *The American Journal of Psychiatry, 164*(6), 922–928. doi:10.1176/appi.ajp.164.6.922

Clarkin, J. F., Yeomans, F., & Kernberg, O. (1999). *Psychotherapy of borderline personality*. New York, NY: Wiley.

Cohen, J. (1969) *Statistical power analysis for the behavioral sciences*. New York, NY: Academic Press.

Coleman, D. (2007). Further factorial validity of a scale of therapist theoretical orientation. *Research on Social Work Practice, 17*(4), 474–481. doi:10.1177/1049731506295406

Collins, N. L., & Miller, L. C. (1994). Self-disclosure and liking: A meta-analytic review. *Psychological Bulletin, 116*(3), 457–475. doi:10.1037/0033-2909.116.3.457

Comas-Díaz, L. (2012). *Multicultural care: A clinician's guide to cultural competence*. Washington, DC: American Psychological Association.

Comas-Díaz, L., & Jacobsen, F. M. (1991). Ethnocultural transference and countertransference in the therapeutic dyad. *American Journal of Orthopsychiatry, 61*(3), 392–402.

Comer, L. B., & Drollinger, T. (1999). Active empathetic listening and selling success: A conceptual framework. *The Journal of Personal Selling and Sales Management, 19*(1), 15–29.

Constantine, M. G., Arorash, T. J., Barakett, M. D., Blackmon, S. K. M., Donnelly, P. C., & Edles, P. A. (2001). School counselors' universal–diverse orientation and aspects of their multicultural counseling competence. *Professional School Counseling, 5*(1), 13–18.

Constantine, M. G., & Sue, D. W. (2007). Perceptions of racial microaggressions among black supervisees in cross-racial dyads. *Journal of Counseling Psychology, 54*(2), 142–153. doi:10.1037/0022-0167.54.2.142

Constantine, M. H., Hage, S. M., Kindaichi, M., M., & Bryant, R. M. (2007). Social justice and multicultural issues: Implications for the practice and training of counselors and counseling psychologists. *Journal of Counseling and Development, 85*, 24–29.

Cook, R. (2012). Triumph or disaster?: A relational view of therapeutic mistakes. *Transactional Analysis Journal, 42*(1), 34–42.

Cooper, M. (2007). Humanizing psychotherapy. *Journal of Contemporary Psychotherapy, 37*, 11–16. doi:10.1007/s10879-006-9029-6

Cooper, S. H. (1998). Analyst-subjectivity, analyst-disclosure, and the aims of psychoanalysis. *Psychoanalytic Quarterly, 67*, 379–406.

Cooper, Z., & Fairburn, C. (1987). The eating disorder examination: A semi-structured interview for the assessment of the specific psychopathology of eating disorders. *International Journal of Eating Disorders, 6*(1), 1–8. doi:10.1002/1098-108X(198701)6:1<1::AID-EAT2260060102>3.0.CO;2–9

Corsini, R., & Wedding, D. (Eds.). (2000). *Current psychotherapies* (8th ed.). Belmont, CA: Thomson/Brooks Cole.

Corso, K. A., Bryan, C. J., Corso, M. L., Kanzler, K. E., Houghton, D. C., Ray-Sannerud, B., & Morrow, C. E. (2012). Therapeutic alliance and treatment outcome in the primary care behavioral health model. *Families, Systems, and Health, 30*(2), 87–100. doi:10.1037/a0028632

Cottone, R. R., & Claus, R. E. (2000). Ethical decision-making models: A review of the literature. *Journal of Counseling and Development, 78*(3), 275–283. doi:10.1002/j.1556–6676.2000.tb01908.x

Coutinho, J., Ribeiro, E., Hill, C., & Safran, J. (2011). Therapists' and clients' experiences of alliance ruptures: A qualitative study. *Psychotherapy Research, 21*(5), 525–540. doi:10.1080/10503307.2011.587469

Crabtree, J. W., & Haslam, S. A. (2010). Mental health support groups, stigma, and self-esteem: Positive and negative implications of group identification. *Journal of Social Issues, 66*(3), 553–569. doi:10.1111/j.1540-4560.2010.01662.x

Craig, C. D., & Sprang, G. G. (2010). Compassion satisfaction, compassion fatigue, and burnout in a national sample of trauma treatment therapists. *Anxiety, Stress and Coping: An International Journal, 23*(3), 319–339. doi:10.1080/10615800903085818

Cramer, P. (2006). *Protecting the self: Defense mechanisms in action*. New York, NY: Guildford Press.

Craske, M. G., Rose, R. D., Lang, A., Welch, S. S., Campbell-Sills, L., Sullivan, G., & Roy-Byrne, P. P. (2009). Computer-assisted delivery of cognitive behavioral therapy for anxiety disorders in primary-care settings. *Depression and Anxiety, 26*(3), 235–242. doi:10.1002/da.20542

Crawford, A. (2013, July 23). Brazil's new generation of thalidomide babies. *BBC News Magazine*. Retrieved from http://www.bbc.co.uk/news/magazine-23418102

Cristea, I. A., Szentagotai Tatar, A., Nagy, D., & David, D. (2012). The bottle is half empty and that's bad, but not tragic: Differential effects of negative functional reappraisal. *Motivation and Emotion, 36*(4), 550–563. doi:10.1007/s11031-012-9277-6

Crits-Christoph, P., Barber, J. P., & Kurcias, J. S. (1993). The accuracy of therapists' interpretation and the development of the therapeutic alliance. *Psychotherapy Research, 3*, 25–35. doi:10.1080/10503309312331333639

Crockett, W. H. (1965). Cognitive complexity and impression formation. *Progress in Experimental Personality Research, 2*, 47–90.

Cuijpers, P., Geraedts, A. S., van Oppen, P., Gerhard Andersson, G., Markowitz, J. C., & van Straten, A. (2011). Interpersonal psychotherapy for depression: A meta-analysis *American Journal of Psychiatry, 168*(6), 581–592. doi:10.1176/appi.ajp.2010.10101411

Cushing, A. (2003). Interpreters in medical consultations. In R. Tribe & H. Raval (Eds.), *Working with interpreters in mental health* (pp. 30–53). London: Routledge.

Cutler, R. L. (1958). Countertransference effects in psychotherapy. *Journal of Consulting Psychology, 22*, 349–356.

Dacy, J. M., & Brodsky, S. L. (1992). Effects of therapist attire and gender. *Psychotherapy, 29*(3), 486–490. doi:10.1037/h0088555

Dailey, M. N., Joyce, C., Lyons, M. J., Kamachi, M., Ishi, H., Gyoba, J., & Cottrell, G. W. (2010). Evidence and a computational explanation of cultural differences in facial expression recognition. *Emotion, 10*(6), 874–893. doi:10.1037/a0020019

Dalai Lama. (1994). *The way to freedom.* San Francisco, CA: Harper Collins.

Dalai Lama. (1999). *Ethics for the new millennium.* New York, NY: Riverhead Books.

Dallos, R., & Draper, R. (2005). *An introduction to family therapy.* Maidenhead: Open University Press/McGraw-Hill.

Dallos, R., & Stedmon, J. (2006). Systemic formulation: Mapping the family dance. In L. Johnstone & R. Dallos (Eds.), *Formulation in psychology and psychotherapy: Making sense of people's problems* (pp. 72–97). New York, NY: Routledge.

Dallos, R., & Vetere, A. (2012). Systems theory, family attachments and processes of triangulation: Does the concept of triangulation offer a useful bridge? *Journal of Family Therapy, 34*(2), 117–137. doi:10.1111/j.1467-6427.2011.00554.x

Daniels, J. A., Alva, L. A., & Olivares, S. (2002). Graduate training for managed care: A national survey of psychology and social work programs. *Professional Psychology: Research and Practice, 33*(6), 587–590.

Dapretto, M., Davies, M. S., Pfeifer, J. H., Scott, A. A., Sigman, M., Bookheimer, S. Y., & Iacoboni, M. (2006). Understanding emotions in others: Mirror neuron dysfunction in children with autism spectrum disorders. *Nature Neuroscience, 9*, 28–30.

Davidson, L., Chinman, M., Kloos, B., Weingarten, R., Stayner, D., & Tebes, J. K. (1999). Peer support among individuals with severe mental illness: A review of the evidence. *Clinical Psychology: Science and Practice, 6*(2), 165–187.

Davies, J. M. (1994). Love in the afternoon: A relational consideration of desire and dread in the countertransference. *Psychoanalytic Dialogues, 4*, 153–170.

Davies, J. M. (1998). Between the disclosure and foreclosure of erotic transference–countertransference: Can psychoanalysis find a place for adult sexuality? *Psychoanalytic Dialogues, 8*, 747–766.

Daw, B., & Joseph, S. (2007). Qualified therapists' experience of personal therapy. *Counselling and Psychotherapy Research, 7*(4), 227–232. doi:10.1080/14733140701709064

Derogatis, L. R. (1983). *SCL-90: Administration, scoring and procedures manual-I for the revised version and other instruments of the psychopathology rating scale series.* Baltimore, MD: Johns Hopkins University School of Medicine, Clinical Psychometrics Research Unit.

Deutsch, C. (1984). Self-reported sources of stress among psychotherapists. *Professional Psychology Research and Practice, 15*(6), 833–845.

Dewald, P. A. (1994). Countertransference issues when the therapist is ill or disabled. *American Journal of Psychotherapy, 48*(2), 221–230.

Diamantaras, K. I., & Kung, S. Y. (1996). *Principal component neural networks: Theory and applications.* New York, NY: Wiley.

Diamond, D., Clarkin, J. F., Levine, H., Levy, K., Foelsch, P., & Yeomans, F. (1999). Borderline conditions and attachment: A preliminary report. *Psychoanalytic Inquiry, 19*, 831–884.

Diamond, D., Stovall-McClough, C., Clarkin, J. F., & Levy, K. N. (2003). Parent-therapist attachment in the treatment of borderline personality disorder. *Bulletin of the Menninger Clinic, 67*(3), 227–259.

Diener, M. J., & Monroe, J. M. (2011). The relationship between adult attachment style and therapeutic alliance in individual psychotherapy: A meta-analytic review. *Psychotherapy*, *48*(3), 237–248. doi:10.1037/a0022425

Dienes, K. A., Torres-Harding, S., Reinecke, M. A., Freeman, A., & Sauer, A. (2011). Cognitive therapy. In S. B. Messer & A. S. Gurman (Eds.), *Essential psychotherapies: Theory and practice* (3rd ed., pp. 1–41). New York, NY: Guilford Press.

Dimaggio, G., Carcione, A., Salvatore, G., Nicolò, G., Sisto, A., & Semerari, A. (2011). Progressively promoting metacognition in a case of obsessive-compulsive personality disorder treated with metacognitive interpersonal therapy. *Psychology and Psychotherapy: Theory, Research and Practice*, *84*(1), 70–83.

Dimaggio, G., & Lysaker, P. H. (2010). *Metacognition and severe adult metal disorders*. London: Routledge.

Dinger, U., Strack, M., Leichsenring, F., Wilmers, F., & Schauenburg, H. (2008). Therapist effects on outcome and alliance in inpatient psychotherapy. *Journal of Clinical Psychology*, *46*, 344–354.

Dinger, U., Strack, M., Sachsse, T., & Schauenburg, H. (2009). Therapists' attachment, patients' interpersonal problems and alliance development over time in inpatient psychotherapy. *Psychotherapy: Theory, Research, Practice, Training*, *46*(3), 277–290. doi:10.1037/a0016913

Dinkmeyer, D. C. (1973). The parent "C" group. *The Personnel and Guidance Journal*, *52*(4), 252–256. doi:10.1002/j.2164-4918.1973.tb04018.x

Driessen, E., Cuijpers, P., de Maat, S. C. M., Abbass, A. A., de Jonghe, F., & Dekker, J. J. M. (2010). The efficacy of short-term psychodynamic psychotherapy for depression: A meta-analysis. *Clinical Psychology Review*, *30*(1), 25–36. doi:10.1016/j.cpr.2009.08.010

Drollinger, T., Comer, L. B., & Warrington, P. T. (2006). Development and validation of the active empathetic listening scale. *Psychology & Marketing*, *23*(2), 161–180. doi:10.1002/mar.20105

Duckworth, A. L., Steen, T. A., & Seligman, M. E. P. (2005). Positive psychology in clinical practice. *Annual Review of Clinical Psychology*, *1*, 629–651. doi:10.1146/annurev.clinpsy.1.102803.144154

Dudley, R., & Kuyken, W. (2006). Formulation in cognitive behavioural therapy: 'There is nothing either good or bad, but thinking makes it so.' In L. Johnstone & R. Dallos (Eds.), *Formulation in psychology and psychotherapy: Making sense of people's problems* (pp. 17–46). New York, NY: Routledge.

Duff, C. T., & Bedi, R. P. (2010). Counsellor behaviours that predict therapeutic alliance: From the client's perspective. *Counselling Psychology Quarterly*, *23*(1), 91–110. doi:10.1080/09515 071003688165

Eberlein, L. (1987). Introducing ethics to beginning psychologists: A problem-solving approach. *Professional Psychology: Research and Practice*, *18*(4), 353–359.

Edelson, M. (1963). *The termination of intensive psychotherapy*. Springfield, IL: Charles C. Thomas.

Edwards, R. (2011). Listening and message interpretation. *The International Journal of Listening*, *25*(1–2), 47–65. doi:10.1080/10904018.2011.536471

Eeissler, K. (1953). The effect of the structure of the ego on psychoanalytic technique. *Journal of the American Psychoanalytic Association*, *1*, 104–143.

Eells, T. D. (1997). Psychotherapy case formulation: History and current status. In T. D. Eells (Ed.), *Handbook of psychotherapy case formulation* (pp. 1–25). New York, NY: Guilford Press.

Eells, T. D. (Ed.). (2010). *Handbook of psychotherapy case formulation* (2nd ed.). New York, NY: Guilford Press.

Eells, T. D., Lombart, K. G., Kendjelic, E. M., Turner, L. C., & Lucas, C. P. (2005). The quality of psychotherapy case formulations: A comparison of expert, experienced, and novice cognitive-behavioral and psychodynamic therapists. *Journal of Consulting and Clinical Psychology*, *73*(4), 579–589. doi:10.1037/0022-006X.73.4.579

Ehrenberg, D. B. (1995). Self-disclosure: Therapeutic tool or indulgence? Countertransference disclosure. *Contemporary Psychoanalysis*, *31*, 213–229.

Eisenthal, S., & Lazare, A. (1976). Specificity of patients' requests in the initial interview. *Psychological Reports*, *38*(3), 739–748. doi:10.2466/pr0.1976.38.3.739

Ekman, P. (1992). Facial expressions of emotion: New findings, new questions. *Psychological Science*, *3*(1), 34–38. doi:10.1111/j.1467-9280.1992.tb00253.x

Ekman, P. (2003). *Emotions revealed: Recognizing faces and feelings to improve communication and emotional life*. New York, NY: Henry Holt and Company.

Ekman, P., & Friesen, W. V. (1971). Constants across cultures in the face and emotion. *Journal of Personality and Social Psychology, 17*(2), 124–129. doi:10.1037/h0030377

Ekman, P., Friesen, W. V., O'Sullivan, M., Chan, A., Diacoyanni-Tarlatzis, I., Heider, K., ... Tzavaras, A. (1987). Universals and cultural differences in the judgments of facial expressions of emotion. *Journal of Personality and Social Psychology, 53*(4), 712–717. doi: 10.1037/0022-3514.53.4.712

Ekman, P., & Rosenberg, E. (1997). *What the face reveals.* New York, NY: Oxford University Press.

Elbow, M. (1987). The memory book: Facilitating terminations with children. *Social Casework, 68*(3), 180–183.

Elkins, D. N. (2009). Why humanistic psychology lost its power and influence in American psychology: Implications for advancing humanistic psychology. *Journal of Humanistic Psychology, 49,* 267–291. doi:10.1177/0022167808323575

Ellis, A. (1962). *Reason and emotion in psychotherapy.* Secaucus, NJ: Citadel.

Ellis, A. (1980). Rational-emotive therapy and cognitive behavior therapy: Similarities and differences. *Cognitive Therapy and Research, 4*(4), 325–340. doi:10.1007/BF01178210

Emery, S., Wade, T. D., & McLean, S. (2009). Associations among therapist beliefs, personal resources and burnout in clinical psychologists. *Behaviour Change, 26*(2), 83–96. doi:10.1375/bech.26.2.83

Endicott, J., & Spitzer, R. L. (1972). Current and past psychopathology scales (CAPPS) rationale, reliability, and validity. *Archives of General Psychiatry, 27*(5), 678–687. doi:10.1001/arch psyc.1972.01750290086015

Epictetus. (1991). *Enchiridion* (G. Long, Trans.). Amherst, NY: Prometheus Books.

Epperson, D. L., Bushway, D. J., & Warman, R. E. (1983). Client self-terminations after one counseling session: Effects of problem recognition, counselor gender, and counselor experience. *Journal of Counseling Psychology, 30*(3), 307.

Erdos, B. Z., & Hughes, D. H. (2001). Emergency psychiatry: A review of assaults by patients against staff at psychiatric emergency centers. *Psychiatric Services, 52*(9), 1175–1177. doi:10.1176/appi .ps.52.9.1175

Eysenck, H. J. (1966). *The effects of psychotherapy.* New York, NY: International Science Press.

Fair, S. M., & Bressler, J. M. (1992). Therapist-initiated termination of psychotherapy. *The Clinical Supervisor, 10,* 171–189.

Fairbairn, W. R. D. (1952). *Psychoanalytic studies of the personality.* London: Routledge and Kegan Paul.

Falender, C. A., & Shafranske, E. P. (2012). The importance of competency-based clinical supervision and training in the twenty-first century: Why bother? *Journal of Contemporary Psychotherapy, 42*(3), 129–137. doi:10.1007/s10879-011-9198-9

Farber, B. A. (2006). *Self-disclosure in psychotherapy.* New York, NY: Guilford Press.

Festinger, L. (1957). *A theory of cognitive dissonance.* Evanston, IL: Row, Petersen and Company.

Fiebert, M. S. (1997). In and out of Freud's shadow: A chronology of Adler's relationship with Freud. *Individual Psychology, 53,* 241–269.

Figley, C. R. (2002). Compassion fatigue: Psychotherapists' chronic lack of self care. *Journal of Clinical Psychology, 58*(11), 1433–1441. doi:10.1002/jclp.10090

Finn, S. E., & Martin, H. (2013). Therapeutic assessment: Using psychological testing as brief therapy. In K. F. Geisinger, B. A. Bracken, M. C. Rodriguez (Eds.), *APA handbook of testing and assessment in psychology, Vol. 2: Testing and assessment in clinical and counseling psychology* (pp. 453–465). Washington, DC: American Psychological Association. doi: 10.1037 /14048-026

Firestein, S. K. (1994). On thinking the unthinkable: Making a professional will. *The American Psychoanalyst, 27*(4), 16.

First, M. B. (2005). Clinical utility: A prerequisite for the adoption of a dimensional approach in DSM. *Journal of Abnormal Psychology, 114*(4), 560–564. doi:10.1037/0021-843X.114.4.560

First, M. B., Spitzer, R. L., Gibbon, M., & Williams, J. B. (1997). *Structured clinical interview for DSM-IV axis I disorders, clinician version (SCID-CV).* Washington, DC: American Psychiatric Association.

First, M. B., Spitzer, R. L., Gibbon, M., Williams, J. B. W., & Benjamin, L. (1994). *Structured clinical interview for DSM-IV axis II personality disorders (version 2.0).* New York, NY: New York State Psychiatric Institute.

Fishbein, M. (2000). The role of theory in HIV prevention. *AIDS Care, 12*(3), 273–278.

Fishbein, M., & Ajzen, I. (1975). *Belief, attitude, intention and behavior: An introduction to theory and research.* Reading, MA: Addison-Wesley.

Fisher, C. B. (2003). *Decoding the ethics code: A practical guide for psychologists.* Thousand Oaks, CA: Sage Publications.

Foa, E. B., & Kozak, M. J. (1986). Emotional processing of fear: Exposure to corrective information. *Psychological Bulletin, 99*(1), 20–35. doi:10.1037/0033-2909.99.1.20

Fourie, D. P. (2003). Limited options: Symptoms as expressions of ambivalence. *American Journal of Family Therapy, 31*(1), 51–59. doi:10.1080/01926180301129

Fournier, J. C., DeRubeis, R. J., Hollon, S. D., Dimidjian, S., Amsterdam, J. D., Richard C., . . . Fawcett, J. (2010). Antidepressant drug effects and depression severity. *The Journal of the American Medical Association, 303*(1), 47–53. doi:10.1001/jama.2009.1943

Frank, J. D., & Frank, J. B. (1991). *Persuasion and healing: A comparative study of psychotherapy* (3rd ed.). Baltimore, MD: Johns Hopkins University Press.

Freed, A. O. (1988). Interviewing through an interpreter. *Social Work, 33*(4), 315–319.

Freud, A. (1937). *The ego and the mechanisms of defense.* Honolulu, HI: Hogarth Press.

Freud, S. (1905). *Fragment of an analysis of a case of hysteria.* Standard Edition (Vol. 7, pp. 7–122). London: Hogarth Press.

Freud, S. (1909). *Analysis of a phobia in a five-year-old boy.* London: Hogarth Press.

Freud, S. (1910). Future prospects of psychoanalytic therapy. In J. Strachey (Ed.), *The standard edition of the complete works of Sigmund Freud* (pp. 139–151). London: Hogarth Press.

Freud, S. (1912a). *Recommendations to physicians practicing psychoanalysis.* London: Hogarth Press.

Freud, S. (1912b). The dynamics of transference. In J. Strachey (Ed.), *The standard edition of the complete psychological works of Sigmund Freud, Volume XII (1911–1913): The case of Schreber, papers on technique and other works* (pp. 97–108). London: Hogarth Press.

Freud, S. (1915). The unconscious. In J. Strachey (Ed.), *The standard edition of the complete psychological works of Sigmund Freud, Volume XIV (1914–1916): On the history of the psycho-analytic movement, papers on metapsychology and other works* (pp. 159–215). London: Hogarth Press.

Freud, S. (1917). A difficulty in the path of psycho-analysis. In J. Strachey (Ed.), *The standard edition of the complete psychological works of Sigmund Freud, Volume XVII (1917–1919): An infantile neurosis and other works* (pp. 135–144). London: Hogarth Press.

Freud, S. (1937). Analysis terminable and interminable. In J. Strachey (Ed.), *The standard edition of the complete psychological works of Sigmund Freud* (Vol. 23, pp. 209–253). London: Hogarth Press.

Freud, S. (1949). *An outline of psychoanalysis.* New York, NY: Norton.

Freud, S. (1953). Analysis terminable and interminable. In J. Strachey (Ed.), *Collected papers* (Vol. 5, pp. 316–357). London: Hogarth Press. (Original work published 1937).

Freud, S. (1958). Recommendations to physicians practicing psycho-analysis. In J. Strachey (Ed. & Trans.), *The standard edition of the complete psychological works of Sigmund Freud* (Vol. 12, pp. 109–120). London: Hogarth Press. (Original work published 1912)

Freud, S. (1961). The ego and the id. In J. Strahey (Ed. and Trans.), *The standard edition of the complete psychological works of Sigmund Freud* (Vol. 19, pp. 3–66). London: Hogarth Press. (Original work published in 1923)

Freud, S. (1964). Analysis terminable and interminable. In J. Strachey (Ed. & Trans.), *Complete psychological works of Sigmund Freud.* London: Hogarth Press. (Original work published 1937)

Freud, S. (1989). New introductory lectures on psycho-analysis. In J. Strachey (Ed. and Trans.), *The standard edition of the complete psychological works of Sigmund Freud. Volume XI (1910): Five lectures on psycho-analysis, Leonardo da Vinci and other works.* London: The Hogarth Press and the Institute of Psycho-analysis. (Original work published 1910)

Freud, S., (2001) *The standard edition of the complete psychological works of Sigmund Freud, Volume VII (1901–1905): A case of hysteria, three essays on sexuality and other works* (J. Strachey, Ed.). London: Vintage Books.

Freud, S., & Breuer, J. (1895). Studies on hysteria. In J. Strachey (Ed.), *The standard edition of the complete psychological works of Sigmund Freud, Volume XXIII (1911–1913). The Case of Schreber, papers on technique and other works* (pp. 97–108). London: Hogarth Press.

Fridlund, A. J. (1994). *Human facial expression: An evolutionary view.* San Diego, CA: Academic Press.

Fuertes, J. N., Miville, M. L., Mohr, J. J., Sedlacek, W. E., & Gretchen, D. (2000). Factor structure and short form of the Miville-Guzman Universality-Diversity Scale. *Measurement and Evaluation in Counseling and Development, 33,* 157–169.

Fuertes, J. N., Mueller, L. N., Chauhan, R. V., Walker, J. A., & Ladany, N. (2002). An investigation of European American therapists' approach to counseling African American clients. *The Counseling Psychologist, 30*(5), 763–788. doi:10.1177/0011000002305007

Fulton, P. R. (2005). Mindfulness as clinical training. In C. K. Germer, R. D. Siegel & P. R. Fulton (Eds.), *Mindfulness and psychotherapy* (pp. 55–72). New York, NY: Guilford Press.

Gabbard, G. (2000). *Psychodynamic psychiatry in clinical practice* (4th ed.). Washington, DC: American Psychiatric Association.

Gabbard, G. (2010). *Long-term psychodynamic psychotherapy* (2nd ed.). Arlington, VA: American Psychiatric Publishing.

Gabbard, G. O. (2001). A contemporary psychoanalytic model of countertransference. *Journal of Clinical Psychology, 57*(8), 983–991. doi:10.1002/jclp.1065

Gabbard, G. O. (2006). A neuroscience perspective on transference. *International Congress Series, 1286,* 189–196.

Gallup Poll. (1996). *Religion in America.* Princeton, NJ: Princeton Religion Research Center.

Garcia-Lawson, K. A., Lane, R. C., & Koetting, M. G. (2000). Sudden death of the therapist: The effects on the patient. *Journal of Contemporary Psychotherapy, 30*(1), 85–103.

Gardenswartz, C. A., & Craske, M. G. (2001). Prevention of panic disorder. *Behavior Therapy, 32*(4), 725–737. doi:10.1016/S0005-7894(01)80017-4

Gaston, L., Thompson, L., Gallagher, D., Cournoyer, L., & Gagnon, R. (1998). Alliance, technique, and their interactions in predicting outcome of behavioral, cognitive, and brief dynamic therapy. *Psychotherapy Research, 8,* 190–209. doi:10.1080/10503309812331332307

Gauron, E. F., & Dickinson, J. K. (1966). Diagnostic decision making in psychiatry: I. Information usage. *Archives of General Psychiatry, 14*(3), 225–232. doi:10.1001/archpsyc.1966.01730090001001

Gauron, E. F., & Dickinson, J. K. (1969). The influence of seeing the patient first on diagnostic decision-making in psychiatry. *American Journal of Psychiatry, 126,* 199–205.

Gazda, G. M., Asbury, F. S., Balzer, F. J., Childers, W. C., & Walters, R. P. (1984). *Human relations development: A manual for educators* (3rd ed.). Boston, MA: Allyn & Bacon.

Gaztambide, D. J. (2012). Addressing cultural impasses with rupture resolution strategies: A proposal and recommendations. *Professional Psychology: Research and Practice, 43*(3), 183–189. doi:10.1037/a0026911

Gehart, D. R., & Lyle, R. R. (2004). Client experience of gender in therapeutic relationships: An interpretive ethnography. *Family Process, 40*(4), 443–458. doi:10.1111/j.1545-5300.2001.4040100443.x

Gelman, C., Fernandez, P., Hausman, N., Miller, S., & Weiner, M. (2007). Challenging endings: First year MSW interns' experiences with forced termination and discussion points for supervisory guidance. *Clinical Social Work Journal, 35*(2), 79–90. doi:10.1007/s10615-007-0076-6

Gelso, C. J. (2011). *The real relationship in psychotherapy: The hidden foundation of change.* Washington, DC: American Psychological Association.

Gelso, C. J., & Hayes, J. A. (2001). Countertransference management. *Psychotherapy: Theory, Research, Practice, Training, 38*(4), 418–422. doi:10.1037/0033-3204.38.4.418

Gelso, C. J., Latts, M. G., Gomez, M. J., & Fassinger, R. E. (2002). Countertransference management and therapy outcome: An initial evaluation. *Journal of Clinical Psychology, 58*(7), 861–867. doi:10.1002/jclp.2010

Gibson, J. A., Grey, I. M., & Hastings, R. P. (2009). Supervisor support as a predictor of burnout and therapeutic self-efficacy in therapists working in ABA schools. *Journal of Autism and Developmental Disorders, 39*(7), 1024–1030. doi:10.1007/s10803-009-0709-4

Giesen-Bloo, J., van Dyck, R., Spinhoven, P., van Tilburg, W., Dirksen, C., van Asselt, T., … Arntz, A. (2006). Outpatient psychotherapy for borderline personality disorder: Randomized trial of schema-focused therapy vs. transference-focused psychotherapy. *Archives of General Psychiatry, 63,* 649–658.

Gill, M. M. (1984). Transference: A change in conception or only in emphasis? *Psychoanalytic Inquiry, 4*(3), 489–523.

Ginsburg, G. S., & Schlossberg, M. C. (2002). Family-based treatment of childhood anxiety disorders. *International Review of Psychiatry, 14*(2), 143–154. doi:10.1080/09540260220132662

Gold, S. N., & Cherry, E. F. (1997). The therapeutic frame: On the need for flexibility. *Journal of Contemporary Psychotherapy, 27*(2), 147–155. doi: 10.1023/A:1025664228870

Goldfried, M. R. (1991). Research issues in psychotherapy integration. *Journal of Psychotherapy Integration, 1*(1), 5–25.

Goldfried, M. R. (2002). A cognitive-behavioral perspective on termination. *Journal of Psychotherapy Integration, 12*(3), 364–372. doi:10.1037/1053-0479.12.3.364

Goldfried, M. R., Castonguay, L. G., Hayes, A. H., Drozd, J. F., & Shapiro, D. A. (1997). A comparative analysis of the therapeutic focus in cognitive-behavioral and pychodynamic-interpersonal sessions. *Journal of Consulting and Clinical Psychology, 65*(5), 740–748. doi:10.1037/0022-006X.65.5.740

Goleman, D. (1998). *Working with emotional intelligence.* New York, NY: Bantam Books.

Goodman, L. A., Liang, B., Helms, J. E., Latta, R. E., Sparks, E., & Weintraum, S. R. (2004). Training counseling psychologists as social justice agents: Feminist and multicultural principles in action. *The Counseling Psychologist, 32*, 793–837. doi:10.1177/0011000004268802

Gordon, R. M. (2009). Reactions to the psychodynamic diagnostic manual (PDM) by psychodynamic, CBT and other non-psychodynamic psychologists. *Issues in Psychoanalytic Psychology, 31*(1), 53–59.

Gordon, T. (2008). *Parent effectiveness training: The proven program for raising responsible children.* New York, NY: Three Rivers Press.

Gottlieb, M. C. (1993). Avoiding exploitive dual relationships: A decision-making model. *Psychotherapy, 30*(1), 41–48.

Gould, R. L., Coulson, M. C., & Howard, R. J. (2012). Efficacy of cognitive behavioral therapy for anxiety disorders in older people: A meta-analysis and meta-regression of randomized controlled trials. *Journal of the American Geriatrics Society, 60*(2), 218–229. doi:10.1111/j.1532-5415.2011.03824.x

Gould, R. P. (1978). Students' experience with the termination phase of individual treatment. *Smith College Studies in Social Work, 48*(3), 235–269.

Grafanaki, S., Pearson, D., Cini, F., Godula, D., McKenzie, B., Nason, S., & Anderegg, M. (2005). Sources of renewal: A qualitative study on the experience and role of leisure in the life of counsellors and psychologists. *Counselling Psychology Quarterly, 18*(1), 31–40.

Granello, D. H. (2010). The process of suicide risk assessment: Twelve core principles. *Journal of Counseling and Development, 88*(3), 363–370. doi:10.1002/j.15566678.2010.tb00034.x

Greason, P. B., & Cashwell, C. S. (2009). Mindfulness and counseling self-efficacy: The mediating role of attention and empathy. *Counselor Education and Supervision, 49*(1), 2–19. doi:10.1002/j.1556-6978.2009.tb00083.x

Greenberg, L. S. (2002a). Integrating an emotion-focused approach to treatment into psychotherapy integration. *Journal of Psychotherapy Integration, 12*(2), 154–189. doi:10.1037/1053-0479.12.2.154

Greenberg, L. S. (2002b). Termination of experiential therapy. *Journal of Psychotherapy Integration, 12*(3), 358–363. doi:10.1037/1053-0479.12.3.358

Greenberg, L. S. (2012). Emotions, the great captains of our lives: Their role in the process of change in psychotherapy. *American Psychologist, 67*(8), 697–707. doi:10.1037/a0029858

Greenberg, L. S., & Johnson, S. M. (1988). *Emotionally focused therapy for couples.* New York, NY: Guilford Press.

Greenberg, L. S., & Watson, J. C. (2006). Principles of working with emotion in depression. In *Emotion-focused therapy for depression* (pp. 67–91). Washington, DC: American Psychological Association. doi:10.1037/11286-004

Greenberg, L. S., Watson, J. C., Elliot, R., & Bohart, A. C. (2001). Empathy. *Psychotherapy: Theory, Research, Practice, Training, 38*(4), 380–384.

Greenson, R. (1965). The working alliance and the transference neurosis. *The Psychoanalytic Quarterly, 34*, 155–181.

Greenson, R. R. (1967). *The technique and practice of psychoanalysis* (Vol. 1). New York, NY: International Universities Press.

Grencavage, L. M., & Norcross, J. C. (1990). Where are the commonalities among the therapeutic common factors? *Professional Psychology: Research and Practice, 21*(5), 372–378. doi:10.1037/0735-7028.21.5.372

Groenier, M., Pieters, J. M., Hulshof, C. D., Wilhelm, P., & Witteman, C. L. (2008). Psychologists' judgements of diagnostic activities: Deviations from a theoretical model. *Clinical Psychology and Psychotherapy, 15*(4), 256–265. doi:10.1002/cpp.587

Grohol, J. (2011). *Mental health professionals: US statistics.* Retrieved August 26, 2013, from http://psychcentral.com/lib/mental-health-professionals-us-statistics/0009373

Grosse, M., & Grawe, K. (2002). Bern inventory of treatment goals: Part 1. Development and first application of a taxonomy of treatment goal themes. *Psychotherapy Research, 12*(1), 79–99. doi:10.1080/713869618

Grosse Holtforth, M. (2001). Was möchten patienten in ihrer therapie erreichen?–Die erfassung von therapiezielen mit dem berner inventar für therapieziele (BIT). *Verhaltenstherapie Und Psychosoziale Praxis, 34*(2), 241–258.

Guastello, S. J., Guastello, D. D., & Hanson, C. A. (2008). The potential impact of psychotherapy on emotional intelligence scores: Mood disorders. *Imagination, Cognition and Personality, 27*(3), 259–266. doi:10.2190/IC.27.3.e

Gulbrandsen, P., Benth, J., Dahl, F., Jensen, B., Finset, A., & Hall, J. A. (2012). Specialist physicians' sensitivity to patient affect and satisfaction. *Medical Care, 50*(4), 290–293. doi:10.1097/MLR.0b013e318242313e

Guy, J. D. (2000). Self-care corner: Holding the holding environment together: Self-psychology and psychotherapist care. *Professional Psychology, Research and Practice, 31*(3), 351–352. doi:10.1037/0735-7028.31.3.351

Guy, J. D., Stark, M. J., & Poelstra, P. L. (1988). Personal therapy for psychotherapists before and after entering professional practice. *Professional Psychology: Research and Practice, 19*(4), 474–476. doi:10.1037/0735-7028.19.4.474

Haddon, M. (2003). *The curious incident of the dog in the nighttime.* New York, NY: Random House.

Hall, J. A., Roter, D. L., Blanch, D. C., & Frankel, R. M. (2009). Nonverbal sensitivity in medical students: Implications for clinical interactions. *Journal of General Internal Medicine, 24*(11), 1217–1222. doi:10.1007/s11606-009-1107-5

Hamer, F. (2008). Listening with both ears. *International Journal of Applied Psychoanalytic Studies, 5*(2), 86–88.

Harris, G. (2011, March 6). Talk doesn't pay, so psychiatry turns instead to drug therapy. *New York Times,* pp. A1. Retrieved from http://www.nytimes.com/2011/03/06/health/policy/06doctors.html

Harris, M. B., & Bliss, G. K. (1997). Coming out in the school setting: Former students' experiences and opinions about disclosure. In M. B. Harris (Ed.), *School experiences of gay and lesbian youth* (pp. 85–100). New York, NY: Harrington Park Press.

Hartung, P. J., & Niles, S. G. (2000). Established career theories. In D. A. Luzzo (Ed.), *Career counseling of college students: An empirical guide to strategies that work* (pp. 3–21). Washington, DC: American Psychological Association.

Hassan, A. (2007). Volunteering abroad, NGO style. *Psychology International.* Retrieved from http://www.apa.org/international/pi/2007/03/action.aspx

Hatcher, R. L. (2009). Considering the real relationship: Reaction to Gelso's 'The real relationship in a postmodern world: Theoretical and empirical explorations'. *Psychotherapy Research, 19*(3), 269–272. doi:10.1080/10503300802527189

Hayes, J. A. (2004). The inner world of the psychotherapist: A program of research on countertransference. *Psychotherapy Research, 14,* 21–36.

Hayes, J. A., Gelso, C. J., & Hummel, A. M. (2011). Managing countertransference. *Psychotherapy, 48*(1), 88–97. doi: 10.1037/a0022182

Hayes, S. C., Strosahl, K. D., & Wilson, K. G. (2012). *Acceptance and commitment therapy: The process and practice of mindful change* (2nd ed.). New York, NY: Guilford Press.

Haynes, S. N., & O'Brien, W. H. (1990). Functional analysis in behavior therapy. *Clinical Psychology Review, 10*(6), 649–668. doi:10.1016/0272-7358(90)90074-K

Hays, P. A. (2001). *Addressing cultural complexities in practice: A framework for clinicians and counselors.* Washington, DC: American Psychological Association.

Hazlett-Stevens, H., & Craske, M. G. (2008). Live (in vivo) exposure. In W. T. O'Donohue & J. E. Fisher (Eds.), *Cognitive behavior therapy: Applying empirically supported techniques in your practice* (pp. 407–414). Hoboken, NJ: John Wiley & Sons, Inc.

Heimann, P. (1950). On counter-transference. *The International Journal of Psychoanalysis, 3*, 181–84.

Henry, S. G., Fuhrel-Forbis, A., Rogers, M. M., & Eggly, S. (2012). Association between nonverbal communication during clinical interactions and outcomes: A systematic review and meta-analysis. *Patient Education and Counseling, 86*(3), 297–315. doi:10.1016/j.pec.2011 .07.006

Henry, W. P., & Strupp, H. H. (1994). The therapeutic alliance as interpersonal process. In A. O. Horvath & L. S. Greenberg (Eds.), *The working alliance: Theory, research, and practice* (pp. 51–84). Oxford, England: John Wiley & Sons.

Herek, G. M., Norton, A. T., Allen, T. J., & Sims, C. L. (2010). Demographic, psychological, and social characteristics of self-identified lesbian, gay, and bisexual adults in a US probability sample. *Sexuality Research and Social Policy, 7*(3), 176–200. doi:10.1007/s13178-010-0017-y

Herman, D. (1997). *The antigay agenda: Orthodox vision and the Christian right*. Chicago, IL: University of Chicago Press.

Hesse, E. (2008). The adult attachment interview: Protocol, method of analysis and empirical studies. In J. Cassidy & P. Shaver (Eds.), *Handbook of attachment: Theory, research, clinical applications* (pp. 552–598). New York, NY: Guilford Press.

Hill, C. E., Nutt-Williams, E., Heaton, K. J., Thompson, B. J., & Rhodes, R. H. (1996). Therapist retrospective recall of impassesin long-term psychotherapy: A qualitative analysis. *Journal of Counseling Psychology, 43*, 207–217.

Hill, C. E., O'Grady, K. E., & Elkin, I. (1992). Applying the collaborative study psychotherapy rating scale to rate therapist adherence in cognitive-behavior therapy, interpersonal therapy, and clinical management. *Journal of Consulting and Clinical Psychology, 60*(1), 73–79. doi:10.1037/0022-006X.60.1.73

Hills, P. J., & Lewis, M. B. (2011). Sad people avoid the eyes or happy people focus on the eyes? Mood induction affects facial feature discrimination. *British Journal of Psychology, 102*(2), 260–274. doi:10.1348/000712610X519314

Hilsenroth, M. J., Ackerman, S. J., Blagys, M. D., Baity, M. R., & Mooney, M. A. (2003). Short-term psychodynamic psychotherapy for depression: An examination of statistical, clinically significant, and technique-specific change. *Journal of Nervous and Mental Disease, 191*(6), 349–357. doi:10.1097/00005053-200306000-00001

Himle, J. A., Chatters, L. M., Taylor, R. J., & Nguyen, A. (2013). The relationship between obsessive-compulsive disorder and religious faith: Clinical characteristics and implications for treatment. *Spirituality in Clinical Practice, 1*(Suppl.), 53–70. doi:10.1037/2326-4500.1.S.53

Hofsess, C. D., & Tracey, T. J. (2010). Countertransference as a prototype: The development of a measure. *Journal of Counseling Psychology, 57*(1), 52-67. doi: 10.1037/a0018111

Høgh-Olesen, H. (2008). Human spatial behaviour: The spacing of people, objects, and animals in six cross-cultural samples. *Journal of Cognition and Culture, 8*(3–4), 245–280. doi:10.1163 /156853708X358173

Holland, J. L. (1997). *Making vocational choices* (3rd ed.). Odessa, FL: Psychological Assessment Resources.

Hollin, C. R., & Palmer, E. J. (2009). Cognitive skills programmes for offenders. *Psychology, Crime & Law, 15*(2–3), 147–164. doi:10.1080/10683160802190871

Hollon, S. D., & Ponniah, K. (2010). A review of empirically supported psychological therapies for mood disorders in adults. *Depression and Anxiety, 27*, 891–932. doi:10.1002/da.20741

Holtforth, M. G., Reubi, I., Ruckstuhl, L., Berking, M., & Grawe, K. (2004). The value of treatment-goal themes for treatment planning and outcome evaluation of psychiatric inpatients. *International Journal of Social Psychiatry, 50*(1), 80–91. doi:10.1177/0020764004040955

Holtforth, M. G., Wyss, T., Schulte, D., Trachsel, M., & Michalak, J. (2009). Some like it specific: The difference between treatment goals of anxious and depressed patients. *Psychology and Psychotherapy: Theory, Research and Practice, 82*(3), 279–290. doi:10.1348/147608308X397040

Horrell, S. C. V. (2008). Effectiveness of cognitive-behavioral therapy with adult ethnic minority clients: A review. *Professional Psychology: Research and Practice, 39*(2), 160–168. doi:10.1037 /0735-7028.39.2.160

Horvath, A. O. (2000). The therapeutic relationship: From transference to alliance. *Journal of Clinical Psychology, 56*, 163–173.

Horvath, A. O., & Bedi, R. P. (2002). The alliance. In J. C. Norcross (Ed.), *Psychotherapy relationships that work: Therapist contributions and responsiveness to patients* (pp. 37–69). New York, NY: Oxford University Press.

Horvath, A. O., & Luborsky, L. (1993). The role of therapeutic alliance in psychotherapy. *Journal of Consulting and Clinical Psychology, 61*(4), 561–573.

Horvath, A. O., & Symonds, B. D. (1991). Relation between working alliance and outcome in psychotherapy: A meta-analysis. *Journal of Counseling Psychology, 38*(2), 139–149. doi:10.1037 /0022-0167.38.2.139

Hoyert, D. L., & Xu, J. (2012). Deaths: Preliminary data for 2011. *National Vital Statistics Reports, 61*(6). Hyattsville, MD: National Center for Health Statistics. Retrieved from http://www.cdc.gov /nchs/data/nvsr/nvsr61/nvsr61_06.pdf

Hoyt, M. F. (1979). Aspects of termination in a time-limited brief psychotherapy. *Psychiatry: Journal for the Study of Interpersonal Processes, 42*(3), 208–219.

Hubble, M. A., & Gelso, C. J. (1978). Effect of counselor attire in an initial interview. *Journal of Counseling Psychology, 25*(6), 581–584. doi:10.1037/0022-0167.25.6.581

Huguelet, P., Borras, L., Gillieron, C., Brandt, P. Y., & Mohr, S. (2009). Influence of spirituality and religiousness on substance misuse in patients with schizophrenia or schizo-affective disorder. *Substance Use & Misuse, 44*(4), 502–513. doi:10.1080/10826080802344872

Huprich, S. K., Fuller, K. M., & Schneider, R. B. (2003). Divergent ethical perspectives on the duty-to-warn principle with HIV patients. *Ethics & Behavior, 13*(3), 263–278.

Ingram, B. L. (2009). The case of Ms. Q: A demonstration of integrative psychotherapy. *Pragmatic Case Studies in Psychotherapy, 5*(1), 1–42.

Institute of Medicine. (2001). *Crossing the quality chasm: A new health system for the 21st century.* Washington, DC: National Academies Press.

International Expressive Arts Therapy Association. (2012, September 18). *What are the expressive arts?* Retrieved from http://www.ieata.org/about.html

Isserlin, L., & Couturier, J. (2012). Therapeutic alliance and family-based treatment for adolescents with anorexia nervosa. *Psychotherapy, 49*(1), 46. doi: 10.1037/a0023905

Ivey, G. (2006). A method of teaching psychodynamic case formulation. *Psychotherapy: Theory, Research, Practice, Training, 43*(3), 322.

Jabbi, M., Swart, M., & Keysers, C. (2007). Empathy for positive and negative emotions in the gustatory cortex. *Neuro Image, 34*, 1744–1753.

Jackson, D. (1957). The question of family homeostasis. *Psychiatry Quarterly Supplement, 3*(1), 79–99. doi:10.1007/BF00936266

Jaffe v. Redmond, 116 S.Ct. 95-266, 64L.W. 4490 (June 13, 1996).

Jakobsons, L. J., Brown, J. S., Gordon, K. H., & Joiner, T. E. (2007). When are clients ready to terminate? *Cognitive and Behavioral Practice, 14*(2), 218–230. doi:10.1016/j.cbpra.2006.09.005

Jason, L., & Glenwick, D. (2002). *Innovative strategies for promoting health and mental health across the life span.* New York, NY: Springer Publishing Company.

Javier, R. A., Barroso, F., & Muqoz, M. A. (1993). Autobiographical memories in bilinguals. *Journal of Psycholinguistic Research, 22*(3), 319–338.

Javier, R. T., & Herron, W. G. (2002). Psychoanalysis and the disenfranchised: Countertransference issues. *Psychoanalytic Psychology, 19*(1), 149–166. doi:10.1037/0736-9735.19.1.149

Jaycox, L. H., Foa, E. B., & Morral, A. R. (1998). Influence of emotional engagement and habituation on exposure therapy for PTSD. *Journal of Consulting and Clinical Psychology, 66*(1), 185–192. doi:10.1037/0022-006X.66.1.185

Jennings, L., & Skovholt, T. M. (1999). The cognitive, emotional, and relational characteristics of master therapists. *Journal of Counseling Psychology, 46*(1), 3–11. doi:10.1037/0022-0167.46.1.3

Jennings, L., Sovereign, A., Bottorff, N., Mussell, M. P., & Vye, C. (2005). Nine ethical values of master therapists. *Journal of Mental Health Counseling, 27*(1), 32–47.

Johnson, S. M. (2002). *Emotionally focused couple therapy with trauma survivors: Strengthening attachment bonds.* New York, NY: Guilford Press.

Jones, A. C., & Cutcliffe, J. R. (2009). Listening as a method of addressing psychological distress. *Journal of Nursing Management, 17*(3), 352–358. doi:10.1111/j.1365-2834.2009.00998.x

Jones, D. J., & Lindahl, K. M. (2011). Coparenting in extended kinship systems: African American, Hispanic, Asian heritage, and Native American families. In J. P. McHale & K. M. Lindahl (Eds.), *Coparenting: A conceptual and clinical examination of family systems* (pp. 61–79). Washington, DC: American Psychological Association. doi:10.1037/12328-003

Jones, E. (1953). *The life and work of Sigmund Freud* (Vol. 1). London: Hogarth Press.

Jordan, A. E., & Meara, N. M. (1990). Ethics and the professional practice of psychologists: The role of virtues and principles. *Professional Psychology: Research and Practice, 21*(2), 107–114. doi:10.1037/0735-7028.21.2.107

Joyce, A. S., Piper, W. E., Ogrodniczuk, J. S., & Klein, R. H. (2007a). Therapist-initiated termination. In *Termination in psychotherapy: A psychodynamic model of processes and outcomes* (pp. 157–165). Washington, DC: American Psychological Association. doi:10.1037/11545-008

Joyce, A. S., Piper, W. E., Ogrodniczuk, J. S., & Klein, R. H. (2007b). Orientation of therapy and termination. In *Termination in psychotherapy: A psychodynamic model of processes and outcomes* (pp. 81–96). Washington, DC: American Psychological Association. doi:10.1037/11545-004

Kabat-Zinn, J. (1995). *Wherever you go, there you are: Mindfulness meditation in everyday life.* New York, NY: Hyperion.

Kabat-Zinn, J. (2005). *Coming to our senses: Healing ourselves and our world through mindfulness.* New York, NY: Hyperion.

Kaplan, J. T., & Iacoboni, M. (2006). Getting a grip on other minds: Mirror neurons, intention understanding, and cognitive empathy. *Society for Neuroscience, 1,* 175–183.

Kaufman, J., Birmaher, B., Brent, D., Rao, U., Flynn, C., Moreci, P., . . . Ryan, N. (1997). Schedule for affective disorders and schizophrenia for school-age children-present and lifetime version (K-SADS-PL): Initial reliability and validity data. *Journal of the American Academy of Child and Adolescent Psychiatry, 36*(7), 980–988.

Kazdin, A. E. (1995). Preparing and evaluating research reports. *Psychological Assessment, 7*(3), 228–237.

Kazdin, A. E. (1997). Parent management training: Evidence, outcomes, and issues. *Journal of the American Academy of Child & Adolescent Psychiatry, 36*(10), 1349–1356. doi:10.1097/00004583-199710000-00016

Keller, M. B., Lavori, P. W., Friedman, B., Nielsen, E., Endicott, J., McDonald-Scott, P., & Andreasen, N. C. (1987). The longitudinal interval follow-up evaluation: A comprehensive method for assessing outcome in prospective longitudinal studies. *Archives of General Psychiatry, 44*(6), 540–548.

Kelly, R. E., Wood, A. M., Shearman, K., Phillips, S., & Mansell, W. (2012). Encouraging acceptance of ambivalence using the expressive writing paradigm. *Psychology and Psychotherapy: Theory, Research and Practice, 85*(2), 220–228. doi:10.1111/j.2044-8341.2011.02023.x

Kench, S., & Irwin, H. J. (2000). Alexithymia and childhood family environment. *Journal of Clinical Psychology, 56*(6), 737–745. pii:10.1002/(SICI)1097-4679(200006)56:6<737::AID-JCLP4>3.0.CO;2-U

Kendall, K., & Wiles, R. (2010). Resisting blame and managing emotion in general practice: The case of patient suicide. *Social Science & Medicine, 70*(11), 1714–1720. doi:10.1016/j.socscimed.2010.01.045

Kendall, P. C., Chu, B., Gifford, A., Hayes, C., & Nauta, M. (1998). Breathing life into a manual: Flexibility and creativity with manual-based treatments. *Cognitive and Behavioral Practice, 5*(2), 177–198. doi:10.1016/S1077-7229(98)80004-7

Kendall, P. C., & Hedtke, K. A. (2006). *Cognitive-behavioral therapy for anxious children: Therapist manual* (3rd ed.). Ardmore, PA: Workbook Publishing.

Kendjelic, E. M., & Eells, T. D. (2007). Generic psychotherapy case formulation training improves formulation quality. *Psychotherapy: Theory, Research, Practice, Training, 44*(1), 66–77. doi:10.1037/0033-3204.44.1.66

Kennedy, S. J., Rapee, R. M., & Edwards, S. L. (2009). A selective intervention program for inhibited preschool-aged children of parents with an anxiety disorder: Effects on current anxiety disorders and temperament. *Journal of the American Academy of Child & Adolescent Psychiatry, 48*(6), 602–609. doi:10.1097/CHI.0b013e31819f6fa9

Kernberg, O. (2006). The pressing need to increase research in and on psychoanalysis. *International Journal of Psycho-Analysis, 87*(4), 919–926.

Kernberg, O., Selzer, M., Koenigsberg, H., Carr, A., & Appelbaum, A. (1989). *Psychodynamic psychotherapy of borderline patients*. New York, NY: Basic Books.

Kernberg, O., Yeomans, F. E., Clarkin, J. F., & Levy, K. N. (2008). Transference-focused psychotherapy: Overview and update. *International Journal of Psycho-Analysis, 89*(3), 601–620. doi:10.1111/j.1745-8315.2008.00046.x

Kerr, M. E., & Bowen, M. (1988). *Family evaluation: An approach based on Bowen theory*. New York, NY: W.W. Norton & Company.

Keyser, D. J. (Ed.). (2005). *Test critiques* (Vol. 11). Austin, TX: PRO-ED, Inc.

Khoo, A., Dent, M. T., & Oei, T. P. S. (2011). Group cognitive behaviour therapy for military service-related post-traumatic stress disorder: Effectiveness, sustainability and repeatability. *Australian and New Zealand Journal of Psychiatry, 45*(8), 663–672. doi:10.3109/00048674.2011.590464

Kiesler, D. (2001). Therapist countertransference: In search of common themes and empirical referents. *Psychotherapy in Practice, 57*, 1053–1063.

Kilminster, S. M., & Jolly, B. C. (2000). Effective supervision in clinical practice settings: A literature review. *Medical Education, 34*, 827–840.

Kirmayer, L. J., & Minas, H. (2000). The future of cultural psychiatry: An international perspective. *Canadian Journal of Psychiatry, 45*(5), 438–446.

Klein, M. (1952). The origins of transference. *The International Journal of Psychoanalysis, 33*, 433–438.

Klein, M. (1958). On the development of mental functioning. *The International Journal of Psychoanalysis, 39*(2–4), 84–90.

Knapp, S. J., & VandeCreek, L. D. (2012). *Practical ethics for psychologists: A positive approach* (2nd ed.). Washington, DC: American Psychological Association.

Knox, S., Burkard, A. W., Johnson, A. J., Suzuki, L. A., & Ponterotto, J. G. (2003). African American and European American therapists' experiences of addressing race in cross-racial psychotherapy dyads. *Journal of Counseling Psychology, 50*(4), 466–481. doi:10.1037/0022-0167.50.4.466

Knudson-Martin, C., & Mahoney, A. R. (1999). Beyond different worlds: A "postgender" approach to relational development. *Family Process, 38*(3), 325–340. doi:10.1111/j.1545-5300.1999.00325.x

Kocet, M. M. (2006). Ethical challenges in a complex world: Highlights of the 2005 ACA code of ethics. *Journal of Counseling and Development, 84*(2), 228–234.

Koenig, H. G., & Pritchett, J. (1998). Religion and psychotherapy. In H. G. Koenig (Ed.), *Handbook of religion and mental health* (pp. 323–336). San Diego, CA: Academic Press.

Koerner, B. (2003). What does a "thumbs up" mean in Iraq? *Slate*. Retrieved from http://www.slate .com/articles/news_and_politics.html

Kohut, H. (1971). *The analysis of the self*. New York, NY: International Universities Press.

Kohut, H. (1977). *The restoration of the self*. Chicago, IL: University of Chicago Press.

Kohut, H. (1978). The psychoanalyst in the community of scholars. In P. Ornstein (Ed.), *The search for the self and selected writings of Heinz Kohut*, Vol. 2. New York, NY: International Universities Press.

Kohut, H. (1984). *How does analysis cure?* Chicago, IL: University of Chicago Press.

Koocher, G. P., & Keith-Spiegel, P. (1998). *Ethics in psychology: Professional standards and cases* (2nd ed.). New York, NY: Oxford University Press.

Kottler, J. A. (2010). *On being a therapist* (4th ed.). San Francisco, CA: Jossey-Bass.

Kottler, J. A. (2011). *The therapist's workbook: Self-assessment, self-care, and self-improvement exercises for mental health professionals* (2nd ed.). Hoboken, NJ: John Wiley & Sons, Inc.

Kouyoumdjian, H., Zamboanga, B. L., & Hansen, D. J. (2003). Barriers to community mental health services for Latinos: Treatment considerations. *Clinical Psychology: Science and Practice, 10*(4), 394–422. doi:10.1093/clipsy.bpg041

Kraepelin, E. (1917). *Lectures on clinical psychiatry* (T. Johnston, Ed., Trans.). New York, NY: William Wood & Company.

Krupnick, J. L., Sotsky, S. M., Simmens, S., Moyer, J., Elkin, I., Watkins, J., & Pilkonis, P. A. (1996). The role of the therapeutic alliance in psychotherapy and pharmacotherapy outcome: Findings in the National Institute of Mental Health Treatment of Depression Collaborative Research Program. *Journal of Consulting and Clinical Psychology, 64*(3), 532–539. doi:10. 1037 /0022-006X.64.3.532

Kuhn, T. S. (1996). *The structure of scientific revolutions* (3rd ed.). Chicago, IL: University of Chicago Press.

La Roche, M., & Christopher, M. S. (2008). Culture and empirically supported treatments: On the road to a collision? *Culture and Psychology*, *14*(3), 333–356. doi:10.1177/1354067X08092637

LaBounty, J., Wellman, H. M., Olson, S., Lagattuta, K., & Liu, D. (2008). Mothers' and fathers' use of internal state talk with their young children. *Social Development*, *17*(4), 757–775. doi:10.1111/j.1467-9507.2007.00450.x

Lacan, J. (1985). Intervention on transference. In C. Bernheimer & C. Kahane (Eds.), *In Dora's case: Freud-hysteria-feminism* (Gender & Culture S.) (pp. 92–104). New York, NY: Columbia University Press. (Reprinted from *Intervention on Transference*, pp. 61–73, by J. Mitchell and J. Rose Eds., 1951, London: Macmillan Press)

Laffey, P. (2003). Psychiatric therapy in Georgian Britain. *Psychological Medicine*, *33*(7), 1285–1297.

Lambert, M. J., & Barley, D. E. (2001). Research summary on the therapeutic relationship and psychotherapy outcome. *Psychotherapy: Theory, Research, Practice, Training*, *38*(4), 357–361. doi:10.1037/0033-3204.38.4.357

Langs, R. (1977). *The therapeutic interaction: A synthesis*. New York, NY: Jason Aronson.

Lawless, L. L., Ginter, E. J., & Kelly, K. R. (1999). Managed care: What mental health counselors need to know. *Journal of Mental Health Counseling*, *21*(1), 50–65.

Lazarus, A. A. (1993). Tailoring the therapeutic relationship, or being an authentic chameleon. *Psychotherapy: Theory, Research, Practice, Training*, *30*(3), 404–407. doi:10.1037/0033-3204.30.3.404

Leahy, R. L. (2007a). Emotion and psychotherapy. *Clinical Psychology: Science and Practice*, *14*(4), 353–357. doi:10.1111/j.1468-2850.2007.00095.x

Leahy, R. L. (2007b). Schematic mismatch in the therapeutic relationship: A social cognitive model. In P. Gilbert & R. L. Leahy (Eds.), *The therapeutic relationship in the cognitive behavioral psychotherapies* (pp. 229–254). London: Routledge.

Leahy, R. L. (2008). The therapeutic relationship in cognitive-behavioral therapy. *Behavioral and Cognitive Psychotherapy*, *36*, 769–777.

Leahy, R. L., Holland, S. J., & McGinn, L. K. (2011). *Treatment plans and interventions for depression and anxiety disorders*. New York, NY: Guilford Press.

Lee, H. (1960). *To kill a mockingbird*. New York, NY: Grand Central Publishing.

Lehavot, K., Barnett, J. E., & Powers, D. (2010). Psychotherapy, professional relationships, and ethical considerations in the MySpace generation. *Professional Psychology: Research and Practice*, *41*(2), 160–166. doi:10.1037/a0018709

LePage, J. P., & Mogge, N. L. (2001). The Behavioral Observation System (BOS): A line staff assessment instrument of psychopathology. *Journal of Clinical Psychology*, *57*(12), 1435–1444. doi:10.1002/jclp.1107

Levant, R. F. (2003, October). The empirically-validated treatments movement: A practical perspective. *The Ohio Psychologist-Update*, (2), 2–4.

Levitt, D. H. (2002). Active listening and counselor self-efficacy: Emphasis on one microskill in beginning counselor training. *The Clinical Supervisor*, *20*(2), 101–115. doi:10.1300/J001v20n02_09

Levy, J. (1986). The working through process during the termination of analysis. *Current Issues in Psychoanalytic Practice*, *3*(1), 121–148. doi:10.1300/J256v03n01_11

Levy, K. N. (2005). The implications of attachment theory and research for understanding borderline personality disorder. *Development and Psychopathology*, *17*(4), 959–986. doi: 10.1017/S0954579405050455

Lietaer, G. (1984). Unconditional positive regard: A controversial basic attitude in client-centered therapy. In R. F. Levant & J. M. Shlein (Eds.), *Client-centered therapy and the person-centered approach: New directions in theory, research, and practice*. New York, NY: Praeger.

Lilienfeld, S. O. (2007). Psychological treatments that cause harm. *Perspectives on Psychological Science*, *2*(1), 53–70. doi:10.1111/j.1745-6916.2007.00029.x

Lincoln, T. M., Ziegler, M., Mehl, S., Kesting, M. L., Lüllman, E., Westermann, S., & Rief, W. (2012). Moving from efficacy to effectiveness in cognitive behavioral therapy for psychosis: A randomized clinical practice trial. *Journal of Consulting and Clinical Psychology*, *80*(4), 674–686. doi:10.1037/a0028665

Linehan, M. (1993). *Cognitive behavioral treatment of borderline personality disorder*. New York, NY: Guilford Press.

Linstrum, K. S. (2009). Ethical training, moral development, and ethical decision-making in masters-level counseling students. *Journal of College and Character*, *10*(3), 1–18.

Liotti, G., & Gilbert, P. (2011). Mentalizing, motivation and social mentalities: Theoretical consider-ations and implications for psychotherapy. *Psychology and Psychotherapy: Theory, Research and Practice, 84*(1), 9–25.

Lipsey, M. W., & Wilson, D. B. (1993). The efficacy of psychological, educational, and behavioral treatment: Confirmation from meta-analysis. *American Psychologist, 48*(12), 1181–1209. doi:10.1037/0003-066X.48.12.1181

Little, M. (1951). Countertransference and the patient's response to it. *International Journal of Psychoanalysis, 32*, 32–40.

Litz, B. T., Gray, M. J., Bryant, R. A., & Adler, A. B. (2002). Early intervention for trauma: Current status and future directions. *Clinical Psychology: Science and Practice, 9*, 112–134. doi:10.1093/clipsy.9.2.112

Liu, W. M., Ali, S. R., Soleck, G., Hopps, J., & Pickett, T., Jr. (2004a). Using social class in counsel-ing psychology research. *Journal of Counseling Psychology, 51*(1), 3–18. doi:10.1037/0022-0167.51.1.3

Liu, W. M., Soleck, G., Hopps, J., Dunston, K., & Pickett, T., Jr. (2004b). A new framework to under-stand social class in counseling: The social class worldview model and modern classism theory. *Journal of Multicultural Counseling and Development, 32*(2), 95–122. doi:10.1002/j.2161-1912.2004.tb00364.x

Loewald, H. W. (1960). On the therapeutic action of psychoanalysis. *International Journal of Psycho-analysis, 41*, 16–33.

Loewald, H. W. (1971). The transference neurosis: Comments on the concept and the phenomenon. *Journal of the American Psychoanalytic Association, 19*(1), 54–66.

Lombardi, D. N., Melchior, E. J., Murphy, J. G., & Brinkerhoff, A. L. (1996). The ubiquity of life-style. *Individual Psychology: Journal of Adlerian Theory, Research and Practice, 52*(1), 31–41.

Long, K., Pendleton, L., & Winter, B. (1988). Effects of therapist termination on group process. *International Journal of Group Psychotherapy, 38*(2), 211–222.

López, S. R., Grover, K. P., Holland, D., Johnson, M. J., Kain, C. D., Kanel, K., . . . Rhyne, M. C. (1989). Development of culturally sensitive psychotherapists. *Professional Psychology: Research and Practice, 20*(6), 369–376. doi:10.1037/0735-7028.20.6.369

Luborsky, L. (1984). *Principles of psychoanalytic psychotherapy: A manual for supportive-expressive treatment.* New York, NY: Basic Books.

Luborsky, L., Mark, D., Hole, A. V., Popp, C., Goldsmith, B., & Cacciola, J. (1995) Supportive-expressive dynamic psychotherapy of depression: A time-limited version. In J. Barber & P. Crits-Christoph (Eds.), *Dynamic therapies for the psychiatric disorders: Axis I.* New York, NY: Basic Books.

Ludwikowski, W., Vogel, D., & Armstrong, P. I. (2009). Attitudes toward career counseling: The role of public and self-stigma. *Journal of Counseling Psychology, 56*(3), 408–416. doi: 10.1037/a0016180

Lundy, B. L. (2013). Paternal and maternal mind-mindedness and preschoolers' theory of mind: The mediating role of interactional attunement. *Social Development, 22*(1), 58–74. doi:10.1111/sode.12009

MacBeth, A., Gumley, A., Schwannauer, M., & Fisher, R. (2011). Attachment states of mind, mental-ization, and their correlates in a first-episode psychosis sample. *Psychology and Psychotherapy: Theory, Research and Practice, 84*(1), 42–57.

Maddox, T. (Ed.). (2008). *Tests* (Vol. 6). Austin, TX: Pro-Ed, Inc.

Mahoney, M. J. (1997). Psychotherapists' personal problems and self-care patterns. *Professional Psychology: Research and Practice, 28*(1), 14–16. doi:10.1037/0735-7028.28.1.14

Main, M., Goldwyn, R., & Hesse, E. (2002). *Adult attachment scoring and classification systems.* Berkeley, CA: Regents of the University of California.

Malinowski, A. J. (2013). Characteristics of job burnout and humor among psychotherapists. *Humor: International Journal of Humor Research, 26*(1), 117–133.

Mann, D. (1995). Transference and countertransference issues with sexually abused clients. *Psychodynamic Counselling, 1*(4), 542–559.

Mann, J. (1973). *Time limited psychotherapy.* Cambridge, MA: Harvard University Press.

Mann, J., & Goldman, R. (1982). *A casebook of time limited psychotherapy.* New York, NY: McGraw-Hill.

Margison, F. R., Barkham, M., Evans, C., McGrath, G., Mellor Clark, J., Audin, K., & Connell, J. (2000). Measurement and psychotherapy: Evidence-based practice and practice-based evidence. *The British Journal of Psychiatry, 177*(2), 123–130. doi:10.1192/bjp.177.2.123

Markowitz, M. A., & Nitzberg, M. L. (1982). Communication in the psychiatric halfway house and the double bind. *Clinical Social Work Journal, 10*(3), 176–189. doi:10.1007/BF00756002

Marmarosh, C. L., Gelso, C. J., Markin, R. D., Majors, R., Mallery, C., & Choi, J. (2009). The real relationship in psychotherapy: Relationships to adult attachments, working alliance, transference, and therapy outcome. *Journal of Counseling Psychology, 56*(3), 337–350. doi: 10.1037/a0015169

Marmarosh, C. L., Nikityn, M., Moehringer, J., Ferraioli, L., Kahn, S., Cerkevich, A., . . . Reisch, E. (2013). Adult attachment, attachment to the supervisor, and the supervisory alliance: How they relate to novice therapists' perceived counseling self-efficacy. *Psychotherapy, 50*(2), 178–188. doi:10.1037/a0033028

Maroda, K. J. (2009). Less is more: an argument for the judicious use of self-disclosure. In A. Bloomgarden & R. B. Mennuti (Eds.), *Psychotherapist revealed: Therapists speak about self-disclosure in therapy* (pp. 17–29). New York, NY: Routledge.

Martin, H. P. (1989). Types of institutional transference. *Bulletin of the Menninger Clinic, 53*, 58–62.

Maslach, C. (1982). *Burnout: The cost of caring.* New York, NY: Prentice-Hall, Inc.

Maslach, C., & Leiter, M. P. (1997). *The truth about burnout.* San Francisco, CA: Jossey Bass.

Maslow, A. (1962). Was Adler a disciple of Freud? *Journal of Individual Psychology, 18*, 125.

Maslow, A. (1966). *The psychology of science: A reconnaissance.* Chapel Hill, NC: Maurice Bassett Publishing.

Mason, S. E., Beckerman, N., & Auerbach, C. (2002). Disclosure of student status to clients: Where do MSW program stand? *Journal of Social Work Education, 38*(2), 305–316.

Matarazzo, B. B. (2012). Adaptive institutional transference in the treatment of individuals with borderline personality disorder. *Bulletin of the Menninger Clinic, 76*(4), 297–313. doi:10.1521/bumc.2012.76.4.297

May, W. F. (1984). The virtues in a professional setting. *Soundings, 67*(3), 245–266.

Mazzetti, M. (2012). Teaching trainees to make mistakes. *Transactional Analysis Journal, 42*(1), 43–52.

Mcauliffe, G. J., Grothaus, T., Jensen, M., & Michel, R. (2012). Assessing and promoting cultural relativism in students of counseling. *International Journal for the Advancement of Counselling, 34*(2), 118–135. doi:10.1007/s10447-011-9142-4

McCarthy, A., Lee, K., Itakura, S., & Muir, D. W. (2006). Cultural display rules drive eye gaze during thinking. *Journal of Cross-Cultural Psychology, 37*(6), 717–722. doi:10.1177/0022022106292079

McConnaughy, E. A., Prochaska, J. O., & Velicer, W. F. (1983). Stages of change in psychotherapy: Measurement and sample profiles. *Psychotherapy: Theory, Research & Practice, 20*(3), 368–375.

McCullough, L., Kuhn, N., Andrews, S., Kaplan, A., Wolf, J., & Hurley, C. L. (2003). *Treating affect phobia: A manual for short-term dynamic psychotherapy.* New York, NY: Guilford Press.

McGoldrick, M., & Gerson, R. (1985). *Genograms in family assessment.* New York, NY: Norton.

McGrath, M. C. (2011). Norm-referenced testing. In J. A. Naglieri & S. Goldstein (Eds.), *Encyclopedia of child behavior and development* (pp. 1024–1025). New York, NY: Springer.

McIntosh, P. (1988). *White privilege and male privilege: A personal account of coming to see correspondences through work in women's studies.* Wellesley, MA: Wellesley College Center for Research on Women.

McNelly, W. E. (Interviewer), Herbert, F. (Interviewee), & Herbert, B. (Interviewee). (1969). *Herbert's science fiction novels, "Dune" and "Dune Messiah"* [Interview transcript]. Retrieved from www.sinanvural.com/seksek/inien/tvd/tvd2.htm

McWilliams, N. (1999). *Psychoanalytic case formulation.* New York, NY: Guilford Press.

McWilliams, N. (2004). The therapist's preparation. *In Psychoanalytic psychotherapy* (pp. 46–72). New York, NY: Guilford Press.

McWilliams, N. (2011). The psychodynamic diagnostic manual: An effort to compensate for the limitations of descriptive psychiatric diagnosis. *Journal of Personality Assessment, 93*(2), 112–122. doi:10.1080/00223891.2011.542709

Meichenbaum, D. (1977). *Cognitive behavioral modification: An integrative approach.* New York, NY: Plenum Press.

Melamed, Y., Szor, H., & Bernstein, E. (2001). The loneliness of the therapist in the public outpatient clinic. *Journal of Contemporary Psychotherapy, 31*(2), 103–112. doi:10.1023/A:1010213606443

Mercer, J. (2002). Attachment therapy: A treatment without empirical support. *Scientific Review of Mental Health Practice, 1*, 105–112.

Miller, A. (1997). *The drama of the gifted child: The search for the true self* (3rd ed.). New York, NY: Basic Books.

Miller, K. E., Martell, Z. L., Pazdirek, L., Caruth, M., & Lopez, D. (2005). The role of interpreters in psychotherapy with refugees: An exploratory study. *American Journal of Orthopsychiatry, 75*(1), 27–39. doi:10.1037/0002-9432.75.1.27

Miller, N. E., & Dollard, J. (1941). *Social learning and imitation.* New Haven, CT: Yale University Press.

Miller, W. R., & Rollnick, S. (2002). *Motivational interviewing: Preparing people for change* (2nd ed.). New York, NY: Guilford Press.

Millon, T. (2004). *Masters of the mind: Exploring the story of mental illness from ancient times to the new millennium.* Hoboken, NJ: John Wiley & Sons.

Mills, C. K., & Wooster, A. D. (1987). Crying in the counselling situation. *British Journal of Guidance and Counselling, 15*(2), 125–130.

Mills, J. A., Bauer, G. P., & Miars, R. D. (1989). Use of transference in short-term dynamic psychotherapy. *Psychotherapy: Theory, Research, Practice, Training, 26*(3), 338–343. doi:10.1037/h0085444

Milrod, B., Busch, F., Cooper, A., & Shapiro, T. (1997). *Manual of panic-focused psychodynamic psychotherapy.* Arlington, VA: American Psychiatric Publishing.

Milrod, B., Leon, A., Busch, F., Rudden, M., Schwalberg, M., Clarkin, J., . . . Shear, M. K. (2007). A randomized controlled clinical trial of psychoanalytic psychotherapy for panic disorder. *American Journal of Psychiatry, 164*(2), 265–272. doi: 10.1176/appi.ajp.164.2.265

Minuchin, S. (1974). *Families and family therapy.* Cambridge, MA: Harvard University Press.

Minuchin, S., Rosman, B., & Baker, L. (1978). *Psychosomatic families: Anorexia nervosa in context.* Cambridge, MA: Harvard University Press.

Miranda, R., & Andersen, S. M. (2007). The therapeutic relationship: Implications from social cognition and transference. In P. Gilbert & R. L. Leahy (Eds.), *The therapeutic relationship in the cognitive behavioral psychotherapies* (pp. 63–89). New York, NY: Routledge/Taylor & Francis Group.

Missirlian, T. M., Toukmanian, S. G., Warwar, S. H., & Greenberg, L. S. (2005). Emotional arousal, client perceptual processing, and the working alliance in experiential psychotherapy for depression. *Journal of Consulting and Clinical Psychology, 73*(5), 861–871. doi:10.1037/0022-006X.73.5.861

Mitchell, S. A. (1993). *Hope and dread in psychoanalysis.* New York, NY: Basic Books.

Miville, M. L., Carlozzi, A. F., Gushue, G. V., Schara, S. L., & Ueda, M. (2006). Mental health counselor qualities for a diverse clientele: Linking empathy, universal-diverse orientation, and emotional intelligence. *Journal of Mental Health Counseling, 28*(2), 151–165.

Miville, M. L., Gelso, C. J., Pannu, R., Liu, W., Touradji, P., Holloway, P., & Fuertes, J. (1999). Appreciating similarities and valuing differences: The Miville-Guzman Universality-Diversity Scale. *Journal of Counseling Psychology, 46*(3), 291–307. doi:10.1037/0022-0167.46.3.291

Mojtabai, R., & Olfson, M. (2008). National trends in psychotherapy by office-based psychiatrists. *Archives of General Psychiatry, 65*(8), 962–970.

Moncrieff, J., Wessely, S., & Hardy, R. (2011). Active placebos versus antidepressants for depression. *The Cochrane Library, 7*, 1–29.

Mordecai, E. M. (1991). A classification of empathic failures for psychotherapists and supervisors. *Psychoanalytic Psychology, 8*(3), 251–262. doi:10.1037/h0079282

Mosak, H. H., & Fasula, A. (2011). Transference in the light of Adlerian psychology. *The Journal of Individual Psychology, 67*(4), 343–348.

Moyers, B. (1990). *A World of Ideas.* Garden City, NY: Doubleday.

Murdock, N. L., Edwards, C., & Murdock, T. B. (2010). Therapists' attributions for client premature termination: Are they self-serving? *Psychotherapy: Theory, Research, Practice, Training, 47*(2), 221–234. doi:10.1037/a0019786

Muro, J. J., & Kottman, T. (1995). *Guidance and counseling in the elementary and middle schools: A practical approach.* Madison, WI: Brown & Benchmark.

Murphy, M. J., Cheng, W. J., & Werner-Wilson, R. J. (2006). Exploring master therapists' use of power in conversation. *Contemporary Family Therapy, 28*(4), 475–484.

Myers, J. E., Luecht, R., & Sweeney, T. J. (2004). The factor structure of wellness: Reexamining theoretical and empirical models underlying the Wellness Evaluation of Lifestyle (WEL) and the Five-Factor Wel. *Measurement Science and Technology, 36*(4), 194–208.

Myers, J. E., & Sweeney, T. J. (2004). The indivisible self: An evidence-based model of wellness. *Journal of Individual Psychology, 60*(3), 234–245.

Myers, J. E., & Sweeney, T. J. (2008). Wellness counseling: The evidence base for practice. *Journal of Counseling and Development, 86*(4), 482–493. doi:10.1002/j.1556-6678.2008.tb00536.x

Myers, J. E., Sweeney, T. J., & Witmer, J. M. (1996). *The wellness evaluation of lifestyle.* Palo Alto, CA: Mindgarden.

Myers, J. E., Sweeney, T. J., & Witmer, J. M. (2000). The wheel of wellness counseling for wellness: A holistic model for treatment planning. *Journal of Counseling & Development, 78*(3), 251–266. doi:10.1002/j.1556-6676.2000.tb01906.x

Myrick, R. D. (1993). *Developmental guidance and counseling: A practical approach* (2nd ed.). Minneapolis, MN: Educational Media.

Naeem, F., Waheed, W., Gobbi, M., Ayub, M., & Kingdon, D. (2011). Preliminary evaluation of culturally sensitive CBT for depression in Pakistan: Findings from Developing Culturally-Sensitive CBT Project (DCCP). *Behavioural and Cognitive Psychotherapy, 39*(2), 165–173. doi:10.1017/S1352465810000822

Nagashima, K., & Schellenberg, J. A. (1997). Situational differences in intentional smiling: A cross-cultural exploration. *The Journal of Social Psychology, 137*(3), 297–301. doi:10.1080/00224549709595441

Naqvi, N., Shiv, B., & Bechara, A. (2006). The role of emotions in decision making: A cognitive neuroscience perspective. *Current Directions in Psychological Science, 15*(5), 260–264.

Nasser, M. (1987). Psychiatry in ancient Egypt. *Psychiatric Bulletin, 11,* 420–422. doi:10.192/pb.11.12.420

National Institute of Mental Health (1996). *A plan for prevention research at the National Institute of Mental Health: A report by the National Advisory Mental Health Council* (NIH Publication No. 96-4093). Bethesda, MD: National Institutes of Health.

Neimeyer, G. J., Taylor, J. M., & Cox, D. R. (2012). On hope and possibility: Does continuing professional development contribute to ongoing professional competence? *Professional Psychology: Research and Practice, 43*(5), 476–486. doi:10.1037/a0029613

Neimeyer, G. J., Taylor, J. M., & Rozensky, R. H. (2012). The diminishing durability of knowledge in professional psychology: A Delphi Poll of specialties and proficiencies. *Professional Psychology: Research and Practice, 43*(4), 364–371. doi:10.1037/a0028698

Neimeyer, G. J., Taylor, J. M., & Wear, D. (2010). Continuing education in psychology: Patterns of participation and aspects of selection. *Professional Psychology: Research and Practice, 41*(4), 281–287. doi:10.1037/a0019811

Neukrug, E.S., Milliken, T., & Walden, S. (2001). Ethical complaints made against credentialed counselors: An updated survey of state licensing boards. *Counselor Education and Supervision, 41*(1), 57–70.

Newhill, C. E. (1995). Client violence toward social workers: A practice and policy concern for the 1990s. *Social Work, 40*(5), 631–636. doi:10.1093/sw/40.5.631

Nichols, M. P., & Schwartz, R. C. (2004). *Family therapy: Concepts and methods* (6th ed.). Boston, MA: Allyn & Bacon.

Nolan, P., Dallender, J., Soares, J., Thomsen, S., & Arnetz, B. (1999). Violence in mental health care: The experiences of mental health nurses and psychiatrists. *Journal of Advanced Nursing, 30*(4), 934–941. doi:10.1046/j.1365-2648.1999.01163.x

Norcross, J. C. (2000). Psychotherapist self-care: Practitioner-tested, research-informed strategies. *Professional Psychology, Research and Practice, 31*(6), 710–713. doi:10.1037/0735-7028.31.6.710

Norcross, J. C. (2005). The psychotherapist's own psychotherapy: Educating and developing psychologists. *American Psychologist, 60,* 840–850.

Norcross, J. C., & Guy, J. D., Jr. (2007). *Leaving it at the office: A guide to psychotherapist self-care.* New York, NY: Guilford Press.

Norcross, J. C., Karpiak, C. P., & Lister, K. M. (2005). What is an integrationist? A study of self-identified integrationist and (occasionally) eclectic psychologists. *Journal of Clinical Psychology*, *61*, 1587–1594. doi:10.1002/jclp.20203

Nouwen, H. (2006). *Here and now: Living in the spirit.* New York, NY: The Crossroad Publishing Company.

O'Keefe, D. J., & Sypher, H. E. (1981). Cognitive complexity measures and the relationship of cognitive complexity to communication. *Human Communication Research*, *8*(1), 72–92. doi:10.1111/j.1468-2958.1981.tb00657.x

Occupational Safety and Health Administration. (2004). Guidelines for preventing workplace violence for health care & social service workers. (OSHA 3148-01R 2004). Washington, DC: OSHA. Retrieved from http://www.osha.gov/Publications/OSHA3148/osha3148.html

Ochsner, K. N., Bunge, S. A., Gross, J. J., & Gabrieli, J. E. (2002). Rethinking feelings: An FMRI study of the cognitive regulation of emotion. *Journal of Cognitive Neuroscience*, *14*(8), 1215–1229. doi:10.1162/089892902760807212

Oddli, H. W., & Halvorsen, M. S. (2012). Experienced psychotherapists' reports of their assessments, predictions, and decision making in the early phase of psychotherapy. *Psychotherapy.* Advance online publication. doi:10.1037/a0029843

Oei, T. P., & Kazmierczak, T. (1997). Factors associated with dropout in a group cognitive behavior therapy for mood disorders. *Behavior Research and Therapy*, *35*(11), 1025–1030.

Ogrodniczuk, J. S., Joyce, A. S., & Piper, W. E. (2005). Strategies for reducing patient-initiated premature termination of psychotherapy. *Harvard Review of Psychiatry*, *13*(2), 57–70. doi:10.1080/10673220590956429

Orlinsky, D., Rønnestad, M. H., Ambühl, H., Willutzki, U., Botersman, J. F., Cierpka, M., . . . Davis, M. (1999). Psychotherapists' assessments of their development at different career levels. *Psychotherapy: Theory, Research, Practice, Training*, *36*(3), 203–215. doi:10.1037/h0087772

Orlinsky, D. E., Grawe, K., & Parks, B. K. (1994). Process and outcome in psychotherapy: Noch einmal. In A. Bergin & S. Garfield (Eds.), *Handbook of psychotherapy and behavior change* (4th ed., pp. 270–376). Oxford, England: John Wiley & Sons.

Ornstein, P. H. (1996). Empathy and the therapeutic dialogue: An historical-conceptual overview of self psychology and a brief clinical example. In J. Gurewich, M. Tort, & S. Fairfield (Eds.), *The subject and the self: Lacan and American psychoanalysis* (pp. 77–86). Lanham, MD: Jason Aronson.

Ortega, J. V., & Haynes, S. (2005). Functional analysis in behavior therapy: Behavioral foundations and clinical application. *International Journal of Clinical and Health Psychology*, *5*(3), 567–587.

Öst, L., Karlstedt, A., & Widen, S. (2012). The effects of cognitive behavior therapy delivered by students in a psychologist training program: An effectiveness study. *Behavior Therapy*, *43*(1), 160–173. doi:10/1016/j.beth.2011.05.001

Packer, I. K. (2008). Specialized practice in forensic psychology: Opportunities and obstacles. *Professional Psychology: Research and Practice*, *39*(2), 245–249. doi:10.1037/0735-7028.39.2.245

Palazzoli, M. S., Boscolo, L., Cecchin, G., & Prata, G. (1978). A ritualized prescription in family therapy: Odd days and even days. *Journal of Marital and Family Therapy*, *4*(3), 3–9.

Paniagua, F. A. (2001). Culture-bound syndromes, cultural variations, and psychopathology. In I. Cuellar & F. A. Paniagua (Eds.), *Handbook of multicultural mental health* (pp. 139–169). San Diego, CA: Academic Press.

Paone, T. R., & Malott, K. M. (2008). Using interpreters in mental health counseling: A literature review and recommendations. *Journal of Multicultural Counseling and Development*, *36*(3), 130–142. doi:10.1002/j.2161-1912.2008.tb00077.x

Parsons, F. (1909). *Choosing a vocation.* Boston, MA: Houghton Mifflin.

Pascual-Leone, A., & Greenberg, L. S. (2007). Emotional processing in experiential therapy: Why 'the only way out is through.' *Journal of Consulting and Clinical Psychology*, *75*(6), 875–887. doi:10.1037/0022-006X.75.6.875

Patterson, C. H. (1973). *Theories of counseling and psychotherapy* (2nd ed.). New York, NY: Harper & Row.

Paul, G. L. (1967). Strategy of outcome research in psychotherapy. *Journal of Consulting Psychology*, *31*(2), 109–118.

PDM Task Force (2006). *Psychodynamic Diagnostic Manual (PDM)*. Silver Spring, MD: Alliance of Psychoanalytic Organizations.

Pedersen, P. (1990). The multicultural perspective as a fourth force in counseling. *Journal of Mental Health Counseling, 12*(1), 93–95.

Pekarik, G. (1983). Improvement in clients who have given different reasons for dropping out of treatment. *Journal of Clinical Psychology, 39*(6), 909–913. doi: 10.1002/1097-4679 (198311)39:6<909::AID-JCLP2270390614>3.0.CO;2-4

Pekarik, G. (1992). Relationship of clients' reasons for dropping out of treatment to outcome and satisfaction. *Journal of Clinical Psychology, 48*(1), 91–98.

Peláez, J. R. (1997). Plato's theory of ideas revisited. *Neural Networks, 10*(7), 1269–1288.

Pennebaker, J. W. (1995). Emotion, disclosure, and health: An overview. In J. W. Pennebaker (Ed.), *Emotion, disclosure, and health* (pp. 3–10). Washington, DC: American Psychological Association. doi:10.1037/10182-015

Perry, J. C., Banon, E., & Ianni, F. (1999). Effectiveness of psychotherapy for personality disorders. *American Journal of Psychiatry, 156*, 1312–1321.

Persons, J. B., & Tompkins, M. A. (1997). Cognitive-behavioral case formulation. In T. D. Eells (Ed.), *Handbook of psychotherapy case formulation* (pp. 314–339). New York, NY: Guilford Press.

Petrosino, A., Turpin-Petrosino, C., & Buehler, J. (2003). "Scared Straight" and other juvenile awareness programs for preventing juvenile delinquency. *Annals of the American Academy of Political and Social Science, 589*, 41–62. doi:10.1177/0002716203254693

Pfeifer, J. H., Iacoboni, M., Mazziotta, J. C., & Dapretto, M. (2007). Mirroring others' emotions relates to empathy and interpersonal competence in children. *NeuroImage, 39*, 2076–2085.

Phinney, J. S., Horenczyk, G., Liebkind, K., & Vedder, P. (2001). Ethnic identity, immigration, and well-being: An interactional perspective. *Journal of Social Issues, 57*, 493–510. doi: 10.1111 /0022-4537.00225

Pignotti, M., & Thyer. B. A. (2009). Use of novel unsupported and empirically supported therapies by licensed clinical social workers: An exploratory study. *Social Work Research, 33*(1), 5–17. doi:10.1093/swr/33.1.5

Pipes, R. B., & Davenport, D. S. (1999). *Introduction to psychotherapy: Common clinical wisdom*. Boston, MA: Allyn & Bacon.

Piselli, A., Halgin, R. P., & MacEwan, G. H. (2011). What went wrong? Therapists' reflections on their role in premature termination. *Psychotherapy Research, 21*(4), 400–415. doi:10.1080/10503307 .2011.573819

Pope, B., Nudler, S., Vonkorff, M. R., & McGhee, J. P. (1974). The experienced professional interviewer versus the complete novice. *Journal of Consulting and Clinical Psychology, 42*(5), 680–690. doi:10.1037/h0037090

Pope, B., Siegman, A. W., Blass, T., & Cheek, J. (1972). Some effects of discrepant role expectations on interviewee verbal behavior in the initial interview. *Journal of Consulting and Clinical Psychology, 39*(3), 501–507. doi:10.1037/h0034046

Pope-Davis, D. B., & Coleman, H. L. K. (Eds.). (2001). *The intersection of race, class, and gender in multicultural counseling*. Thousand Oaks, CA: Sage.

Poston, J. M., & Hanson, W. E. (2010). Meta-analysis of psychological assessment as a therapeutic intervention. *Psychological Assessment, 22*(2), 203–212. doi:10.1037/a0018679

Prochaska, J. O., & DiClemente, C. C. (1982). Transtheoretical therapy: Toward a more integrative model of change. *Psychotherapy: Theory, Research & Practice, 19*(3), 276–288.

Prochaska, J. O., & DiClemente, C. C. (1983). Stages and processes of self-change of smoking: Toward an integrative model of change. *Journal of Consulting and Clinical Psychology, 51*(3), 390–395.

Prochaska, J. O., DiClemente, C. C., & Norcross, J. C. (1992). In search of how people change: Applications to addictive behaviors. *American Psychologist, 47*, 1102–1114.

Prochaska, J. O., & Norcross, J. C. (2001). Stages of change. *Psychotherapy: Theory, Research, Practice, Training, 38*(4), 443–448.

Prochaska, J. O., & Norcross, J. C. (2003). *Systems of psychotherapy: A transtheoretical analysis* (5th ed.). Pacific Grove, CA: Brooks/Cole.

Proust, M. (1923). *The captive & the fugitive: In search of lost time, Volume V* (C. K. Scott-Moncrieff & T. Kilmartin, Trans). New York, NY: The Modern Library. (Original work published 1923)

Pumpian-Mindlin, E. E. (1958). Comments on techniques of termination and transfer in a clinic setting. *American Journal of Psychotherapy, 12*, 455–464.

Querido, J. G., Bearss, K., & Eyberg, S. M. (2002). Parent/child interaction therapy. In F. Kaslow & T. Patterson (Eds.), *Comprehensive handbook of psychotherapy. Volume 2: Cognitive-behavioral approaches* (pp. 91–113). New York, NY: John Wiley & Sons.

Racker, H. (1957). The meanings and uses of countertransference. *The Psychoanalytic Quarterly, 26*, 303–357.

Randall, K. (2011). Human lie detector Paul Ekman decodes the faces of depression, terrorism, and joy. *Fast Company*. Retrieved from http://www.fastcompany.com/1800709/human-lie -detector-paul-ekman-decodes-faces-depression-terrorism-and-joy

Ratts, M., D'Andrea, M., & Arredondo, P. (2004). Social justice counseling: "Fifth force" in the field. *Counseling Today, 47*, 28–30.

Raval, H. (1996). A systemic perspective on working with interpreters. *Clinical Child Psychology and Psychiatry, 1*(1), 29–43. doi:10.1177/1359104596011004

Reder, L. M. (1996). Different research programs on metacognition: Are the boundaries imaginary? *Learning and Individual Differences, 8*(4), 383–390. doi:10.1016/S1041-6080(96)90024-2

Regan, K. (2006). *Opening our arms: Helping troubled kids do well.* Boulder, CO: Bull Publishing Company.

Reider, N. (1953). A type of transference to institutions. *Bulletin of the Menninger Clinic, 17*, 58–63.

Reis, B. F., & Brown, L. G. (1999). Reducing psychotherapy dropouts: Maximizing perspective convergence in the psychotherapy dyad. *Psychotherapy: Theory, Research, Practice, Training, 36*(2), 123–136. doi:10.1037/h0087822.

Renik, O. (1999). Playing one's cards face up in analysis: An approach to the problem of self-disclosure. *Psychoanalytic Quarterly, 68*, 521–539.

Rest, J. R. (1984). Research on moral development: Implications for training counseling psychologists. *The Counseling Psychologist, 12*(3), 19–29. doi:10.1177/0011000084123003

Rifkin, M. (2013). Toxic impasse: Loss and recovery of the analyst's mind. *The Round Robin Newsletter of Section I, 28*(1), 1–7.

Rigazio-DiGilio, S. A., & McDowell, T. (2013). Family therapy. In J. Frew & M. D. Spiegler (Eds.), *Contemporary psychotherapies for a diverse world.* New York, NY: Routledge.

Riggs, S. A., & Bretz, K. M. (2006). Attachment processes in the supervisory relationship: An exploratory investigation. *Professional Psychology: Research and Practice, 37*(5), 558–566.

Riley, E. A., Wong, W. T., & Sitharthan, G. (2011). Counseling support for the forgotten transgender community. *Journal of Gay & Lesbian Social Services, 23*(3), 395–410. doi:10.1080/10538720.201 1.590779

Rivas-Vazquez, R., Saffa-Biller, D., Ruiz, I., Blais, M. A., & Rivas-Vazquez, A. (2004). Current issues in anxiety and depression: Comorbid, mixed, and subthreshold disorders. *Professional Psychology: Research and Practice, 35*(1), 74–83. doi:10.1037/0735-7028.35.1.74

Robertson, S. A. (2007). Got EQ? Increasing cultural and clinical competence through emotional intelligence. *Communication Disorders Quarterly, 29*(1), 14–19. doi:10.1177/1525740108314864

Robins, C. J., & Hayes, A. M. (1993). An appraisal of cognitive therapy. *Journal of Consulting and Clinical Psychology, 61*(2), 205–214. doi:10.1037/0022-006X.61.2.205

Roe, D., Dekel, R., Harel, G., Fennig, S., & Fennig, S. (2006). Clients' feelings during termination of psychodynamically oriented psychotherapy. *Bulletin of the Menninger Clinic, 70*(1), 68–81. doi:10.1521/bumc.2006.70.1.68

Rogers, C. R. (1951). *Client-centered therapy: Its current practice, implications, and theory.* Boston, MA: Houghton Mifflin.

Rogers, C. R. (1957). The necessary and sufficient conditions of therapeutic personality change. *Journal of Consulting Psychology, 22*, 95–1103. doi:10.1037/h0045357

Rogers, C. R. (1961). *On becoming a person.* Boston, MA: Houghton Mifflin.

Rogers, C. R. (1965). The therapeutic relationship: Recent theory and research. *Australian Journal of Psychology, 17*(2), 95–108.

Rogers, C. R. (1980). *A way of being.* New York, NY: Houghton Mifflin Company.

Rosenberger, E. W., & Hayes, J. A. (2002a). Therapist as subject: A review of the empirical countertransference literature. *Journal of Counseling and Development, 80*, 264–270.

Rosenberger, E. W., & Hayes, J. A. (2002b). Origins, consequences, and management of countertransference: A case study. *Journal of Counseling Psychology, 49*, 221–232.

Rosenzweig, S. (1936). Some implicit common factors in diverse methods of psychotherapy. *American Journal of Orthopsychiatry, 6*(3), 412–415. doi:10.1111/j.1939-0025.1936.tb05248.x

Rosnow, R. L., & Rosenthal, R. (1989). Statistical procedures and the justification of knowledge in psychological science. *American Psychologist, 44*(10), 1276–1284.

Ross, A. O. (1974). Continuing professional development in psychology. *Professional Psychology, 5*(2), 122–128. doi:10.1037/h0037559

Roth, A., & Fonagy, P. (2005). *What works for whom? A critical review of psychotherapy research* (2nd ed.). New York, NY: Guilford Press.

Rottenberg, J., & Gross, J. J. (2007). Emotion and emotion regulation: A map for psychotherapy researchers. *Clinical Psychology: Science and Practice, 14*(4), 323–328.

Rowell, L., & Hong, E. (2013). Academic motivation: Concepts, strategies, and counseling approaches. *Professional School Counseling, 16*(3), 158–171.

Rowling, J. K. (2008, June 5). *Harvard University commencement address.* Harvard University, Cambridge, MA.

Roysircar, G. (2004). Cultural self-awareness assessment: Practice examples from psychology training. *Professional Psychology: Research and Practice, 35*(6), 658–666. doi:10.1037/0735-7028.35.6.658

Rumi, M. (2001). *Masnavi i Ma'navii* (E. H. Whinfield, Trans.). Ames, IA: Omphaloskepsis.

Rutan, J. S., Stone, W. N., & Shay, J. J. (2007). *Psychodynamic group psychotherapy* (4th ed.). New York, NY: Guilford Press.

Ryan, J. (2006). 'Class is in you': An exploration of some social class issues in psychotherapeutic work. *British Journal of Psychotherapy, 23*(1), 49–62. doi:10.1111/j.1752-0118.2006.00008.x

Ryle, A. (Ed.). (1995). *Cognitive analytic therapy: Developments in theory and practice.* Chichester: Wiley.

Saakvitne, K. W. (2002). Shared trauma: The therapist's increased vulnerability. *Psychoanalytic Dialogues, 12*(3), 443–449.

Safran, J. D. (1998). *Widening the scope of cognitive therapy.* Northvale, NJ: Jason Aronson, Inc.

Safran, J. D. (2012). *Psychoanalysis and psychoanalytic therapies.* Washington, DC: American Psychological Association.

Safran, J. D., & Muran, J. C. (2000). *Negotiating the therapeutic alliance: A relational treatment guide.* New York, NY: Guilford Press.

Safran, J. D., & Muran, J. (2006). Has the concept of the therapeutic alliance outlived its usefulness? *Psychotherapy: Theory, Research, Practice, Training, 43*(3), 286–291. doi:10.1037/0033-3204.43.3.286

Safran, J. D., Muran, J. C., Samstag, L. W., & Stevens, C. (2002). Repairing alliance ruptures. In J. C. Norcross (Ed.), *Psychotherapy relationships that work* (pp. 235–254). New York, NY: Oxford University Press.

Safran, J. D., Muran, J., & Eubanks-Carter, C. (2011). Repairing alliance ruptures. *Psychotherapy, 48*(1), 80–87. doi:10.1037/a0022140

Saks, E. R. (2007). *The center cannot hold: My journey through madness.* New York, NY: Hyperion.

Salberg, J. (2008). 'Who wears the pants here?': Gender as protest. *Studies in Gender and Sexuality, 9*(3), 274–296. doi:10.1080/15240650802117986

Salovey, P., & Sluyter, D. J. (1997). *Emotional development and emotional intelligence: Educational implications.* New York, NY: Basic Books.

Samstag, L., Muran, J., Wachtel, A., Slade, A., Safran, J. D., & Winston, A. (2008). Evaluating negative process: A comparison of working alliance, interpersonal behavior, and narrative coherency among three psychotherapy outcome conditions. *American Journal of Psychotherapy, 62*(2), 165–194.

Samter, W. (2002). How gender and cognitive complexity influence the provision of emotional support: A study of indirect effects. *Communication Reports, 15*(1), 5–16. doi:10.1080/08934210209367748

Sanville, J. (1982). Partings and impartings: Toward a nonmedical approach to interruptions and terminations. *Clinical Social Work Journal, 10*(2), 123–131.

Sauer, E. M., Lopez, F. G., & Gormley, B. (2003). Respective contributions of therapist and client adult attachment orientations to the development of the early working alliance: A preliminary growth modeling study. *Psychotherapy Research, 13*(3), 371–382. doi:10.1093/ptr/kpg027

Savickas, M. L. (1989). Career-style assessment and counseling. In T. J. Sweeney (Ed.), *Adlerian counseling: A practical approach for a new decade* (3rd ed., pp. 289–320). Muncie, IN: Accelerated Development.

Savickas, M. L. (1998). Career style assessment and counseling. In T. Sweeney (Ed.), *Adlerian counseling: A practitioner's approach* (4th ed., pp. 329–359). Philadelphia, PA: Accelerated Development.

Schafer, R. (1968). The mechanisms of defense. *International Journal of Psychoanalysis, 49,* 49–62.

Schaffer, A. (2011, January 10). Thalidomide's comeback. *Slate.* Retrieved from http://www.slate.com/articles/double_x/doublex/2011/01/thalidomides_comeback.html

Scheeringa, M. S., Weems, C. F., Cohen, J. A., Amaya-Jackson, L., & Guthrie, D. (2011). Trauma-focused cognitive-behavioral therapy for posttraumatic stress disorder in three-through six year-old children: A randomized clinical trial. *Journal of Child Psychology and Psychiatry, 52*(8), 853–860. doi:10.1111/j.1469-7610.2010.02354.x

Schreter, R., Sharfstein, S., & Schreter, C. (Eds.). (1994). *Allies and adversaries: The impact of managed care on mental health services.* Washington, DC: American Psychiatric Publication.

Scott, J., Colom, F., & Vieta, E. (2007). A meta-analysis of relapse rates with adjunctive psychological therapies compared to usual psychiatric treatment for bipolar disorders. *International Journal of Neuropsychopharmacology, 10*(1), 123–129. doi:10.1017/S1461145706006900

Seligman, M. E. (1995). The effectiveness of psychotherapy: The Consumer Reports study. *American Psychologist, 50*(12), 965–974. doi:10.1037/0003-066X.50.12.965

Semerari, A., Carcione, A., Dimaggio, G., Falcone, M., Nicolo, G., Procacci, M., & Alleva, G. (2003). How to evaluate metacognitive functioning in psychotherapy? The metacognition assessment scale and its applications. *Clinical Psychology and Psychotherapy, 10*(4), 238–261. doi:10.1002/cpp.362

Senju, A., Vernetti, A., Kikuchi, Y., Akechi, H., Hasegawa, T., & Johnson, M. H. (2013). Cultural background modulates how we look at other persons' gaze. *International Journal of Behavioral Development, 37*(2), 131–136. doi:10.1177/0165025412465360

Shaffer, D., Fisher, P., Lucas, C. P., Dulcan, M. K., & Schwab-Stone, M. E. (2000). NIMH Diagnostic Interview Schedule for Children Version IV (NIMH DISC-IV): Description, differences from previous versions, and reliability of some common diagnoses. *Journal of the American Academy of Child and Adolescent Psychiatry, 39,* 28–38.

Shah, S. A., Garland, E., & Katz, C. (2007). Secondary traumatic stress: Prevalence in humanitarian aid workers in India. *Traumatology, 13,* 59–70.

Shamay-Tsoory, S. G., Tomer, R., Yaniv, S., & Aharon-Peretz, J. (2002). Empathy deficits in Asperger syndrome: A cognitive profile. *Neurocase: Case Studies in Neuropsychology, Neuropsychiatry, and Behavioural Neurology, 8,* 245–252.

Sharf, J., Primavera, L. H., & Diener, M. J. (2010). Dropout and therapeutic alliance: A meta-analysis of adult individual psychotherapy. *Psychotherapy, 47*(4), 637–645. doi:10.1037/a00211

Shedler, J. (2010). The efficacy of psychodynamic psychotherapy. *American Psychologist, 65*(2), 98–109. doi:10.1037/a0018378

Sherrill, J. T., & Kovacs, M. (2000). Interview Schedule for Children and Adolescents (ISCA). *Journal of the American Academy of Child & Adolescent Psychiatry, 39*(1), 67–75. doi:10.1097/00004583-200001000-00018

Shneidman, E. S. (1984). Aphorisms of suicide and some implications for psychotherapy. *American Journal of Psychotherapy, 38,* 319–328.

Siebold, C. (2007). Everytime we say goodbye: Forced termination revisited, a commentary. *Clinical Social Work Journal, 35*(2), 91–95. doi:10.1007/s10615-007-0079-3

Silverstein, L. B., Auerbach, C. F., & Levant, R. F. (2006). Using qualitative research to strengthen clinical practice. *Professional Psychology: Research and Practice, 37*(4), 351–358. doi:10.1037/0735-7028.37.4.351

Skinner, B. F. (1938). *The behavior of organisms: An experimental analysis.* New York, NY: Appleton-Century.

Skowron, E. A., & Dendy, A. K. (2004). Differentiation of self and attachment in adulthood: Relational correlates of effortful control. *Contemporary Family Therapy, 26*(3), 337–357.

Skowron, E. A., Holmes, S. E., & Sabatelli, R. M. (2003). Deconstructing differentiation: Self regulation, interdependent relating, and well-being in adulthood. *Contemporary Family Therapy, 25*(1), 111–129.

Smith, H. B. (1999). Managed care: A survey of counselor educators and counselor practitioners. *Journal of Mental Health Counseling, 21*(3), 270–284.

Smith, M. L., Glass, G. V., & Miller, T. I. (1980). *The benefits of psychotherapy.* Baltimore, MD: Johns Hopkins University Press.

Sodowsky, G. R., Taffe, R. C., Gutkin, T. B., & Wise, S. L. (1994). Development of the Multicultural Counseling Inventory: A self-report measure of multicultural competencies. *Journal of Counseling Psychology, 41*(2), 137–148. doi:10.1037/0022-0167.41.2.137

Sommers-Flanagan, J., & Sommers-Flanagan, R. (2003). *Clinical interviewing* (3rd ed.). Hoboken, NJ: John Wiley & Sons.

Sonne, J. L. (1994). Multiple relationships: Does the new ethics code answer the right questions? *Professional Psychology: Research and Practice, 25*(4), 336–343. doi:10.1037/0735-7028.25.4.336

Srivastava, A., & Grube, M. (2009). Does intuition have a role in psychiatric diagnosis? *Psychiatric Quarterly, 80*(2), 99–106. doi:10.1007/s11126-009-9094-6

Stanley, J., Zhang, X., Fung, H. H., & Isaacowitz, D. M. (2013). Cultural differences in gaze and emotion recognition: Americans contrast more than Chinese. *Emotion, 13*(1), 36–46. doi:10.1037/a0029209

Startup, M., & Shapiro, D. A. (1993). Therapist treatment fidelity in prescriptive vs. exploratory psychotherapy. *British Journal of Clinical Psychology, 32*(4), 443–456.

Steiner, A. (2002, April/May). The emergency response team: A back up plan every clinician needs. *The California Therapist,* 69–77.

Steiner, A. (2011, November/December). Preparing your clients and yourself for the unexpected: Therapist illness, retirement, and death. *The Therapist,* 47–56.

Stewart, R. E., & Chambless, D. L. (2009). Cognitive-behavioral therapy for adult anxiety disorders in clinical practice: A meta-analysis of effectiveness studies. *Journal of Consulting and Clinical Psychology, 77*(4), 595–606. doi:10.1037/a0016032

Stickley, T., & Freshwater, D. (2006). The art of listening in the therapeutic relationship (cover story). *Mental Health Practice, 9*(5), 12–18.

Stiles, W. B., Meshot, C. M., Anderson, T. M., & Sloan, W. W. (1992). Assimilation of problematic experiences: The case of John Jones. *Psychotherapy Research, 2*(2), 81–101. doi:10.1080/10503309212331332874

Stirzaker, A. (2000). 'The taboo which silences': Is erotic transference a help or a hindrance in the counselling relationship? *Psychodynamic Counselling, 6*(2), 197–213. doi:10.1080/135333300407549

Stone, A. A. (1976). The *Tarasoff* decisions: Suing psychotherapists to safeguard society. *Harvard Law Review, 90*(2), 358–378.

Strauss, J. L., Hayes, A. M., Johnson, S. L., Newman, C. F., Brown, G. K., Barber, J. P., & . . . Beck, A. T. (2006). Early alliance, alliance ruptures, and symptom change in a nonrandomized trial of cognitive therapy for avoidant and obsessive-compulsive personality disorders. *Journal of Consulting and Clinical Psychology, 74*(2), 337–345. doi:10.1037/0022-006X.74.2.337

Stringer, J. V., Levitt, H. M., Berman, J. S., & Mathews, S. S. (2010). A study of silent disengagement and distressing emotion in psychotherapy. *Psychotherapy Research, 20*(5), 495–510. doi:10.1080/10503301003754515

Strong, E. K., Jr., Donnay, D. A. C., Morris, M. L., Schaubhut, N. A., & Thompson, R. C. (2004). *Strong Interest Inventory®,* Revised Edition. Mountain View, CA: Consulting Psychologists Press, Inc.

Substance Abuse and Mental Health Services Administration. (2011). Utilization of mental health services by adults with suicidal thoughts and behavior. *The National Survey on Drug Use and Health Report.* Rockville, MD: Author.

Suchet, M. (2004). A relational encounter with race. *Psychoanalytic Dialogues, 14*(4), 423–438. doi:10.1080/10481881409348796

Sue, D. W. (1990). Culture-specific strategies in counseling: A conceptual framework. *Professional Psychology: Research and Practice, 21*(6), 424–433. doi:10.1037/0735-7028.21.6.424

Sue, D. W. (2001). Multi-dimensional facets of cultural competence. *The Counseling Psychologist, 29*(6), 790–821. doi:10.1177/0011000001296002

Sue, D. W., Arredondo, P., & McDavis, R. J. (1992). Multicultural counseling competencies and standards: A call to the profession. *Journal of Counseling & Development, 70,* 477–486. doi:10.1002/j.1556-6676.1992.tb01642.x

Sue, D. W., Bernier, J., Durran, A., Feinberg, L., Pedersen, P. Smith, E., & Vasquez-Nuttall, E. (1982). Position paper: Cross-cultural counseling competencies. *The Counseling Psychologist, 10,* 45–52. doi:10.1177/0011000082102008

Sue, D. W., & Sue, D. (1999). *Counseling the culturally different: Theory and practice* (3rd ed.). New York, NY: John Wiley.

Sue, S. (1998). In search of cultural competence in psychotherapy and counseling. *American Psychologist, 53*(4), 440–448. doi:10.1037/0003-066X.53.4.440

Sue, S., Fujino, D. C., Hu, L. T., Takeuchi, D. T., & Zane, N. W. (1991). Community mental health services for ethnic minority groups: A test of the cultural responsiveness hypothesis. *Journal of Consulting and Clinical Psychology, 59*(4), 533–540. doi:10.1037/0022-006X.59.4.533

Summers, R. F., & Barber, J. P. (2012). *Psychodynamic therapy: A guide to evidence-based practice.* New York, NY: Guilford Press.

Sullivan, H. S. (1953). *The interpersonal theory of psychiatry.* New York, NY: Norton.

Super, D. E. (1963). *Career development: A self-concept theory.* New York, NY: College Entrance Examination Board.

Suzuki, A. (1995). Dualism and the transformation of psychiatric language in the seventeenth and eighteenth centuries. *History of Science, 33,* 417–447.

Sweeney, T. J., & Witmer, J. M. (1991). Beyond social interest: Striving toward optimal health and wellness. *Individual Psychology, 47,* 527–540.

Swenson, C. R. (1998). Clinical social work's contribution to a social justice perspective. *Social Work, 43*(6), 527–537. doi:10.1093/sw/43.6.527

Szarota, P. (2010). The mystery of the European smile: A comparison based on individual photographs provided by Internet users. *Journal of Nonverbal Behavior, 34*(4), 249–256. doi:10.1007/s10919-010-0093-y

Szymanski, L., & King, B. H. (1999). Practice parameters for the assessment and treatment of children, adolescents, and adults with mental retardation and comorbid mental disorders. American Academy of Child and Adolescent Psychiatry Working Group on Quality Issues. *Journal of the American Academy of Child and Adolescent Psychiatry, 38*(12 Suppl.), 5S–31S. doi:10.1016/S0890-8567(99)80002-1

Taber, B. J., Hartung, P. J., Briddick, H., Briddick, W. C., & Rehfuss, M. C. (2011). Career style interview: A contextualized approach to career counseling. *The Career Development Quarterly, 59*(3), 274–287. doi:10.1002/j.2161-0045.2011.tb00069.x

Tantam, D., & Klerman, G. (1979). Patient transfer from one clinician to another and dropping-out of out-patient treatment. *Social Psychiatry, 14*(3), 107–113.

Tarasoff *v.* Regents of the University of California, 131 Cal. Rptr. 14, 551 P.2d 334 (1976).

Tarvydas, V. M. (1998). Ethical decision making processes. In R. R. Cottone & V. M. Tarvydas (Eds.), *Ethical and professional issues in counseling* (pp. 144–155). Upper Saddle River, NJ: Prentice-Hall.

Taylor, A., Zaitsoff, S. L., & Paterson, A. (2012). Factors related to advanced stages of change in a clinical sample of adolescents. *Child and Adolescent Mental Health.* doi:10.1111/camh.12016

Taylor, G. J., Bagby, R. M., & Parker, J. D. A. (1997). Disorders of affect regulation. *Alexithymia in medical and psychiatric illness.* Cambridge, UK: Cambridge University Press.

Taylor, L., McMinn, M. R., Bufford, R. K., & Chang, K. B. T. (2010). Psychologists' attitudes and ethical concerns regarding the use of social networking web sites. *Professional Psychology: Research and Practice, 41*(2), 153–159. doi:10.1037/a0017996

Tervalon, M., & Murray-García, J. (1998). Cultural humility versus cultural competence: A critical distinction in defining physician training outcomes in multicultural education. *Journal of Health Care for the Poor and Underserved, 9*(2), 117–125. doi:10.1353/hpu.2010.0233

Thapar *v.* Zezulka, 994 S.W.2d 635 (Tex. 1999).

Tholfsen, B. (2000). Cross gendered longings and the demand for categorization: Enacting gender within the transference-countertransference relationship. *Journal of Gay and Lesbian Psychotherapy, 4*(2), 27–46. doi:10.1300/J236v04n02_03

Thompson, C. E., Worthington, R., & Atkinson, D. R. (1994). Counselor content orientation, counselor race, and Black women's cultural mistrust and self-disclosures. *Journal of Counseling Psychology, 41*(2), 155–161.

Thoreau, H. D. (2004). *Walden: The 150th anniversary illustrated edition of the American classic.* New York, NY: Houghton Mifflin Company.

Times Topics. (2012, October 30). Trayvon Martin case (George Zimmerman). *The New York Times.* Retrieved from http://topics.nytimes.com/top/reference/timestopics/people/m/trayvon_martin/index.html?8qa

Tracey, T. J. (1988). Relationship of responsibility attribution congruence to psychotherapy outcome. *Journal of Social and Clinical Psychology, 7*(2–3), 131–146.

Trierweiler, S. J., Neighbors, H. W., Munday, C., Thompson, E. E., Binion, V. J., & Gomez, J. P. (2000). Clinician attributions associated with the diagnosis of schizophrenia in African American and non-African American patients. *Journal of Consulting and Clinical Psychology, 68,* 171–175. doi:10.1037/0022-006X.68.1.171

Trierweiler, S. J., Neighbors, H. W., Thompson, E. E., Munday, C., Jackson, J. S., & Binion, V. J. (2006). Differences in patterns of symptom attribution in diagnosing schizophrenia between African American and non-African American clinicians. *American Journal of Orthopsychiatry, 76*(2), 154–160. doi:10.1037/0002-9432.76.2.154

Tryon, G. S., & Winograd, G. (2011). Goal consensus and collaboration. *Psychotherapy, 48*(1), 50–57. doi:10.1037/a0022061

Tucker, P. M., Garton, T. S., Foote, A. L., & Candler, C. (2009). In support of early psychotherapy training. *Psychiatric Times, 26*(12). Retrieved from http://www.psychiatrictimes.com/display/article/10168/1491210

Tunick, R. A., Mednick, L., & Conroy, C. (2011). A snapshot of child psychologists' social media activity: Professional and ethical practice implications and recommendations. *Professional Psychology: Research and Practice, 42*(6), 440–447. doi:10.1037/a0025040

Turner, S. M., Hersen, M., & Heiser, N. (2003). The interviewing process. In M. Hersen & S. M. Turner (Eds.), *Diagnostic interviewing* (3rd ed., pp. 1–20). New York, NY: Wiley and Sons.

U.S. Department of Health and Human Services. (2000, December 28). Standards for Privacy of individually identifiable health information. *Federal Register, 65,* 82462–82829.

U.S. Department of Health and Human Services. (2002). Standards for privacy of individually identifiable health information; final rule (45 C.F.R. Pts. 160 and 164). *Federal Register, 67,* 53181–53273.

Üstün, T. B., Kostanjsek, N., Chatterji, S., & Rehm, J. (Eds.). (2010). *Measuring health and disability: Manual for WHO disability assessment schedule: WHODAS 2.0.* Geneva, Switzerland: World Health Organization Press.

Van Wagoner, S. L., Gelso, C. J., Hayes, J. A., & Diemer, R. A. (1991). Countertransference and the reputedly excellent therapist. *Psychotherapy: Theory, Research, Practice, Training, 28*(3), 411–421. doi:10.1037/0033-3204.28.3.411

Varela, J. G., & Conroy, M. A. (2012). Professional competencies in forensic psychology. *Professional Psychology: Research and Practice, 43*(5), 410–421. doi:10.1037/a0026776

Vasquez, M. (2007). Cultural difference and therapeutic alliance: An evidence-based analysis. *American Psychologist, 62,* 878–885. doi:10.1037/0003-066X.62.8.878

Vogel, D. L., Heimerdinger-Edwards, S. R., Hammer, J. H., & Hubbard, A. (2011). "Boys don't cry": Examination of the links between endorsement of masculine norms, self-stigma, and help-seeking attitudes for men from diverse backgrounds. *Journal of Counseling Psychology, 58*(3), 368–382. doi:10.1037/a0023688

Vontress, C. E. (2013). Existential Therapy. In J. Frew & M. D. Spiegler (Eds.), *Contemporary Psychotherapies for a Diverse World.* New York: Routledge.

Wachtel, P. L. (1981). Transference, schema, and assimilation. The relevance of Piaget to psychoanalysis. *The Annual Review of Psychoanalysis, 8,* 59–76.

Wachtel, P. L. (2010). Psychotherapy integration and integrative psychotherapy: Process or product? *Journal of Psychotherapy Integration, 20*(4), 406–416. doi:10.1037/a0022032

Wakefield, J. C. (2013). DSM-5: An overview of changes and controversies. *Clinical Social Work Journal, 41*(2), 1–16. doi:10.1007/s10615-013-0445-2

Walitzer, K. S., & Dearing, R. L. (2006). Gender differences in alcohol and substance use relapse. *Clinical Psychology Review, 26*(2), 128–148. doi:10.1016/j.cpr.2005.11.003

Wallerstein, R. S. (2011). The psychodynamic diagnostic manual (PDM): Rationale, conception, and structure. *Journal of the American Psychoanalytic Association, 59*(1), 153–164. doi:10.1177/0003065111402330

Wampold, B. E., Mondin, G. W., Moody, M., Stich, F., Benson, K., & Ahn, H. (1997). A meta-analysis of outcome studies comparing bona fide psychotherapies: Empirically, 'All have won and all must have prizes'. *Psychological Bulletin, 122,* 203–215. doi:10.1037/0033-2909.122.3.203

Wapner, J. H., Klein, J. G., Friedlander, M. L., & Andrasik, F. J. (1986). Transferring psychotherapy clients: State of the art. *Professional Psychology: Research and Practice, 17*(6), 492–496. doi:10.1037/0735-7028.17.6.492

Watermeyer, B. (2012). Disability and countertransference in group psychotherapy: Connecting social oppression with the clinical frame. *International Journal of Group Psychotherapy, 62*(3), 392–417. doi:10.1521/ijgp.2012.62.3.392

Watkins, C. R. (2012a). Contemporary visions of psychotherapy supervision: Sharing perspective, identifying need, and charting possibility. *Journal of Contemporary Psychotherapy, 42*(3), 125–127. doi:10.1007/s10879-011-9203-3

Watkins, C. R. (2012b). Psychotherapy supervision in the new millennium: Competency-based, evidence-based, particularized, and energized. *Journal of Contemporary Psychotherapy, 42*(3), 193–203. doi:10.1007/s10879-011-9202-4

Watkins, C. R., & Scaturo, D. J. (2013). Toward an integrative, learning-based model of psychotherapy supervision: Supervisory alliance, educational interventions, and supervisee learning/relearning. *Journal of Psychotherapy Integration, 23*(1), 75–95. doi:10.1037/a0031330

Watson, D., & Pennebaker, J. W. (1989). Health complaints, stress, and distress: Exploring the central role of negative affectivity. *Psychological Review, 96*(2), 234–254. doi:10.1037/0033-295X.96.2.234

Watson, J. B., & Rayner, R. (1920). Conditioned emotional reactions, *Journal of Experimental Psychology, 3,* 1–14.

Weger, Jr., H., Castle, G. R., & Emmett, M. C. (2010). Active listening in peer interviews: The influence of message paraphrasing on perceptions of listening skill. *The International Journal of Listening, 24*(1), 34–49. doi:10.1080/10904010903466311

Weigold, A., Weigold, I. K., & Russell, E. J. (2013). Examination of the equivalence of self-report survey-based paper-and-pencil and internet data collection methods. *Psychological Methods, 18*(1), 53–70. doi:10.1037/a0031607

Weiner, D. B. (1992). Philippe Pinel's "Memoir on Madness" of December 11, 1794: A fundamental text of modern psychiatry. *The American Journal of Psychiatry, 149*(6), 725–732.

Weiner, I. B., & Bornstein, R. F. (2009). *Principles of psychotherapy: Promoting evidence-based psychodynamic practice* (3rd ed.). Hoboken, NJ: Wiley & Sons.

Weller, E. B., Weller, R. A., Fristad, M. A., Rooney, M. T., & Schecter, J. (2000). Children's interview for Psychiatric Symptoms (ChIPS). *Journal of the American Academy of Child and Adolescent Psychiatry, 39*(1), 76–84. doi:10.1097/00004583-200001000-00019

Welner, Z., Reich, W., Herjanic, G., Jung, K. G., & Amado, H. (1987). Reliability, validity, and parent-child agreement studies of the Diagnostic Interview for Children and Adolescents (DICA). *Journal of the American Academy of Child and Adolescent Psychiatry, 26*(5), 649–653. doi:10.1097/00004583-198709000-00007

Whaley, A. L. (2001). Cultural mistrust: An important psychological construct for diagnosis and treatment of African Americans. *Professional Psychology: Research and Practice, 32*(6), 555–562. doi:10.1037/0735-7028.32.6.555

Whaley, A. L., & Davis, K. E. (2007). Cultural competence and evidence-based practice in mental health services: A complementary perspective. *American Psychologist, 62*(6), 563–574. doi:10.1037/0003-066X.62.6.563

Widiger, T. A. (1997). Mental disorders as discrete clinical conditions: Dimensional versus categorical. In S. M. Turner & M. Hersen (Eds.), *Adult psychopathology and diagnosis* (2nd ed., pp. 3–23). New York, NY: Wiley and Sons.

Widiger, T. A., & Samuel, D. B. (2005). Diagnostic categories or dimensions? A question for the diagnostic and statistical manual of mental disorders. *Journal of Abnormal Psychology, 114*(4), 494–504. doi:10.1037/0021-843X.114.4.494

Wierzbicki, M., & Pekarik, G. (1993). A meta-analysis of psychotherapy dropout. *Professional Psychology: Research and Practice, 24*(2), 190–195. doi:10.1037/0735-7028.24.2.190

Wilcoxon, S. A., & Puleo, S. G. (1992). Professional-development needs of mental health counselors: Results of a national survey. *Journal of Mental Health Counseling, 14*(2), 187–195.

Wilkins, P. (2000). Unconditional positive regard reconsidered. *British Journal of Guidance and Counselling, 28*(1), 23–36.

Williams, B. & Ziskin, L. (Producers), & Frank O. (Director). (1991). *What about Bob?* [Motion picture]. United States: Touchstone Pictures.

Williams, D. C., & Levitt, H. M. (2007). A qualitative investigation of eminent therapists' values within psychotherapy: Developing integrative principles for moment-to-moment psychotherapy practice. *Journal of Psychotherapy Integration, 17*(2), 159–184. doi:10.1037/1053-0479.17.2.159

Williams, E., & Fauth, J. (2005). A psychotherapy process study of therapist in session self-awareness. *Psychotherapy Research, 15*(4), 374–381. doi:10.1080/10503300500091355

Williams, S. L., Ketring, S. A., & Salts, C. J. (2005). Premature termination as a function of intake data based on ethnicity, gender, socioeconomic status, and income. *Contemporary Family Therapy: An International Journal, 27*(2), 213–231. doi:10.1007/s10591-005-4040-8

Willis, J., & Todorov, A. (2006). First impressions: Making up your mind after a 100-ms exposure to a face. *Psychological Science, 17*(7), 592–598. doi:10.1111/j.1467-9280.2006.01750.x

Winnicott, D. W. (1949). Hate in the counter-transference. *The International Journal of Psychoanalysis, 30*, 69–74.

Winnicott, D. W. (1958). *Through paediatrics to psycho-analysis: Collected papers.* New York, NY: Basic Books.

Witmer, J. M., & Sweeney, T. J. (1992). A holistic model for wellness and prevention over the lifespan. *Journal of Counseling & Development, 71*, 140–148. doi:10.1002/j.1556-6676.1992.tb02189.x

Wittchen, H., Beesdo, K., Bittner, A., & Goodwin, R. D. (2003). Depressive episodes–evidence for a causal role of primary anxiety disorders? *European Psychiatry, 18*(8), 384–393. doi:10.1016/j.eurpsy.2003.10.001

Witteman, C. L. M., & Kunst, H. (1997). Planning the treatment of a depressed patient. *Clinical Psychology and Psychotherapy, 4*(3), 157–171.

Woloshynowych, M., Rogers, S., Taylor-Adams, S., & Vincent, C. (2005). The investigation and analysis of critical incidents and adverse events in healthcare. *Health Technology Assessment, 9*(19), 1–143, iii.

Wolpe, J. (1958). *Psychotherapy by reciprocal inhibition.* Stanford, CA: Stanford University Press.

Worthington, R. L., Soth-McNett, A. M., & Moreno, M. V. (2007). Multicultural counseling competencies research: A 20-year content analysis. *Journal of Counseling Psychology, 54*(4), 351. doi:10.1037/0022-0167.54.4.351

Wright, J. H., Basco, M. R., & Thase, M. E. (2006). *Learning cognitive-behavioral therapy: An illustrated guide.* Arlington, VA: American Psychiatric Publishing, Inc.

Yalom, I. D. (1980). *Existential psychotherapy.* New York, NY: Basic Books.

Yalom, I. D. (1985). *The theory and practice of group psychotherapy* (3rd ed.). New York, NY: Basic Books.

Yalom, I. D. (1989). *Love's executioner: And other tales of psychotherapy.* New York, NY: Perennial Classics.

Yalom, I. D. (2002). *The gift of therapy: An open letter to a new generation of therapists and their patients.* New York, NY: HarperCollins.

Yalom, I. D., & Elkins, G. (1974). *Every day gets a little closer: A twice-told therapy.* New York, NY: Basic Books.

Yeomans, F., Clarkin, J. F., & Kernberg, O. F. (2002). *A primer on treating the borderline patient.* New York, NY: Aronson.

Young, A. (2011) The arms of the infinite? The liability of mental health professionals for the violent acts of their patient. *Mental Health and Learning Disabilities Research and Practice, 8*(1), 3–13.

Young, J. E., & Lindemann, M. D. (1992). An integrative schema-focused model for personality disorders. *Journal of Cognitive Psychotherapy, 6*(1), 11–23.

Younggren, J. N., & Gottlieb, M. C. (2004). Managing risk when contemplating multiple relationships. *Professional Psychology: Research and Practice, 35*(3), 255–260. doi:10.1037/0735-7028.35.3.255

Younggren, J. N., & Harris, E. A. (2008). Can you keep a secret? Confidentiality in psychotherapy. *Journal of Clinical Psychology, 64*(5), 589–600. doi:10.1002/jclp.20480

Zanarini, M. C., Frankenburg, F. R., Reich, D., & Fitzmaurice, G. (2010). Time to attainment of recovery from borderline personality disorder and stability of recovery: A 10-year prospective follow-up study. *The American Journal of Psychiatry, 167*(6), 663–667. doi:10.1176/appi .ajp.2009.09081130

Zarin, D. A., West, J. C., Pincus, H. A., & McIntyre, J. S. (1996). The American Psychiatric Association Practice Research Network. In L. I. Sederer & B. Dickey (Eds.), *Outcomes assessment in clinical practice* (pp. 146–155). Baltimore, MD: Williams & Wilkins.

Zimmerman, M., Martinez, J., Attiullah, N., Friedman, M., Toba, C., & Boerescu, D. A. (2012). Symptom differences between depressed outpatients who are in remission according to the Hamilton Depression Rating Scale who do and do not consider themselves to be in remission. *Journal of Affective Disorders, 142*(1–3), 77–81. doi:10.1016/j.jad.2012.03.044

Zlomke, K., & Davis, T. E., III. (2008). One-session treatment of specific phobias: A detailed description and review of treatment efficacy. *Behavior Therapy, 39*, 207–223.

Zuckerman, A., & Mitchell, G. L. (2004). Psychology interns' perspectives on the forced termination of psychotherapy. *The Clinical Supervisor, 23*(1), 55–70. doi:10.1300/J001v23n01_04

Index

CPSIA information can be obtained
at www.ICGtesting.com
Printed in the USA
LVOW05s2041260917
550143LV00008B/93/P

9 780826 199157